Autodesk Inventor 2027 Black Book Part II

By

Gaurav Verma

Matt Weber

(CADCAMCAE Works)

Edited by

Kristen

ISBN # 978-1-77459-216-8

DEDICATION

To teachers, who make it possible to disseminate knowledge
to enlighten the young and curious minds
of our future generations

To students, who are the future of the world

THANKS

To my friends and colleagues

To my family for their love and support

Training and Consultant Services

At CADCAMCAE Works, we provide effective and affordable one to one online training on various software packages in Computer Aided Design(CAD), Computer Aided Manufacturing(CAM), Computer Aided Engineering (CAE), Computer programming languages (C/C++, Java, .NET, Android, Javascript, HTML, and so on). The training is delivered through remote access to your system and voice chat via Internet at any time, any place, and at any pace to individuals, groups, students of colleges/ universities, and CAD/CAM/CAE training centers. The main features of this program are:

Training as per your need

Highly experienced Engineers and Technician conduct the classes on the software applications used in the industries. The methodology adopted to teach the software is totally practical based, so that the learner can adapt to the design and development industries in almost no time. The efforts are to make the training process cost effective and time saving while you have the comfort of your time and place, thereby relieving you from the hassles of traveling to training centers or rearranging your time table.

Software Packages on which we provide basic and advanced training are:

CAD/CAM/CAE: CATIA, Creo Parametric, Creo Direct, SolidWorks, Autodesk Inventor, Solid Edge, UG NX, AutoCAD, AutoCAD LT, EdgeCAM, MasterCAM, SolidCAM, DelCAM, BOBCAM, UG NX Manufacturing, UG Mold Wizard, UG Progressive Die, UG Die Design, SolidWorks Mold, Creo Manufacturing, Creo Expert Machinist, NX Nastran, Hypermesh, SolidWorks Simulation, Autodesk Simulation Mechanical, Creo Simulate, Gambit, ANSYS, and many others.

Computer Programming Languages: C++, VB.NET, HTML, Android, Javascript and so on.

Game Designing: Unity.

Civil Engineering: AutoCAD MEP, Revit Structure, Revit Architecture, AutoCAD Map 3D and so on.

We also provide consultant services for design and development on the above mentioned software packages

For more information you can mail us at:
cadcamcaeworks@gmail.com

Table of Contents

Chapter 12 : Sheetmetal Design

Chapter 16 : Analyses and Simulation

Chapter 17 :Model Based Annotations

Preface

Autodesk Inventor is a product of Autodesk Inc. Autodesk Inventor 2027 is a parametric, feature-based solid modeling tool that not only unites the three-dimensional (3D) parametric features with two-dimensional (2D) tools, but also addresses every design-through-manufacturing process. The continuous enhancements in the software has made it a complete PLM software. The software is capable of performing analysis with an ease. Its compatibility with CAM software is remarkable. Its seamless integration with Autodesk Assistant AI agent delivers on-the-go support. Based mainly on the user feedback, this solid modeling tool is remarkably user-friendly and it allows you to be productive from day one.

The **Autodesk Inventor 2027 Black Book** is the 7th edition of our series on Autodesk Inventor. The book is divided into two parts **Autodesk Inventor 2027 Black Book Part I** and **Autodesk Inventor 2027 Black Book Part II**. With lots of features and thorough review, we present a book to help professionals as well as beginners in creating some of the most complex solid models. The book follows a step by step methodology. In this book, we have tried to give real-world examples with real challenges in designing. We have tried to reduce the gap between university use of Autodesk Inventor and industrial use of Autodesk Inventor. The Part II of the book covers advanced topics of Autodesk Inventor like Advanced Assembly, Design Accelerator Components, Frame Design and Analysis, Sheet Metal Design, Weldment Design, Surface Design, Mold Design, Analysis and Simulation, Model Based Annotation, and so on. Some of the salient features of this book are :

In-Depth explanation of concepts

Every new topic of this book starts with the explanation of the basic concepts. In this way, the user becomes capable of relating the things with real world.

Topics Covered

Every chapter starts with a list of topics being covered in that chapter. In this way, the user can easy find the topic of his/her interest easily.

Instruction through illustration

The instructions to perform any action are provided by maximum number of illustrations so that the user can perform the actions discussed in the book easily and effectively. There are about 790 small and large illustrations that make the learning process effective.

Tutorial point of view

At the end of concept's explanation, the tutorial make the understanding of users firm and long lasting. Almost each chapter of the book has tutorials that are real world projects. Moreover most of the tools in this book are discussed in the form of tutorials.

Project

Projects and exercises are provided to students for practicing.

For Faculty

If you are a faculty member, then you can ask for video tutorials on any of the topic, exercise, tutorial, or concept. As faculty, you can register on our website to get electronic desk copies of our latest books, self-assessment, and solution of practical. Faculty resources are available in the **Faculty Member** page of our website (**cadcamcaeworks**) once you login. Note that faculty registration approval is manual and it may take two days for approval before you can access the faculty website.

Formatting Conventions Used in the Text

All the key terms like name of button, tool, drop-down, etc. are kept bold.

Free Resources

Link to the resources used in this book are provided to the users via email. To get the resources, mail us at ***cadcamcaeworks@gmail.com*** with your contact information. With your contact record with us, you will be provided latest updates and informations regarding various technologies. The format to write us mail for resources is as follows:

Subject of E-mail as ***Application for resources of ________book***.
Also, given your information like
Name:
Course pursuing/Profession:
E-mail ID:

Note: We respect your privacy and value it. If you do not want to give your personal informations then you can ask for resources without giving your information.

About Authors

Gaurav Verma is a Mechanical Design Engineer with deep knowledge of CAD, CAM and CAE field. He has an experience of more than 15 years on CAD/CAM/CAE packages. He has delivered presentations in Autodesk University Events on AutoCAD Electrical and Autodesk Inventor. He is an active member of Autodesk Knowledge Share Network. He has provided content for Autodesk Design Academy. He is also working as technical consultant for many Indian Government organizations for Skill Development sector. He has authored books on SolidWorks, Mastercam, Creo Parametric, Autodesk Inventor, Autodesk Fusion, and many other CAD-CAM-CAE packages. He has developed content for many modular skill courses like Automotive Service Technician, Welding Technician, Lathe Operator, CNC Operator, Telecom Tower Technician, TV Repair Technician, Casting Operator, Maintenance Technician and about 50 more courses. He has his books published in English, Russian and Hindi worldwide.

He has trained many students on mechanical, electrical, and civil streams of CAD-CAM-CAE. He has trained students online as well as offline. He also owns a small workshop of 20 CNC and VMC machines where he tests his CAM skills on different Automotive components. He is providing consultant services to more than 15 companies worldwide. You can contact the author directly at cadcamcaeworks@gmail.com

For Any query or suggestion

If you have any query or suggestion, please let us know by mailing us on ***cadcamcaeworks@gmail.com***. Your valuable constructive suggestions will be incorporated in our books and your name will be addressed in special thanks area of our books on your confirmation.

Chapter 10

Advanced Assembly and Design

Topics Covered

The major topics covered in this chapter are:

- ***Sub-Assembly***
- ***Pattern in Assembly***
- ***Mirror and Copy in Assembly***
- ***Bolted Connections***
- ***Pin Joints***
- ***Shaft Design***
- ***Gear Design***
- ***Belt Design***
- ***Bearing Design***
- ***Key Design***
- ***Cam Design***

INTRODUCTION

In previous chapter, we learnt to insert various components in an assembly and apply different type of constraints between them. In this chapter, we will do some advanced operations on the assemblies. We will learn to use sub-assemblies. We will perform tasks related to reusability of assembly/assembly's components. We will also learn about various design components that can be directly used in our assemblies.

SUB-ASSEMBLIES

As the name suggests, sub-assemblies are the small sections of big assemblies. When we are working on an assembly where a group of components are repeating then it is a good idea to make a sub-assembly of those components and use it in the main assembly. There is no special tool to create sub-assemblies. They are created in the same way as assemblies. An example of using sub-assembly is discussed next in the form of tutorial.

Use of Sub-Assembly

We need to create an assembly as shown in Figure-1. Note that the wheel assembly is repeating in the main assembly, so we can make a sub-assembly of wheel and use it in the main assembly. The steps to do so are given next.

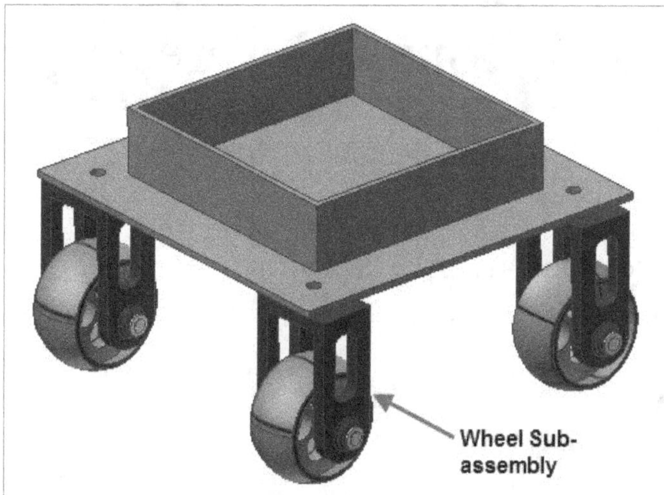

Figure-1. Trolley Assembly

- Create an assembly of the components used in the wheel and save it by the name Wheel sub-assembly; refer to Figure-2.

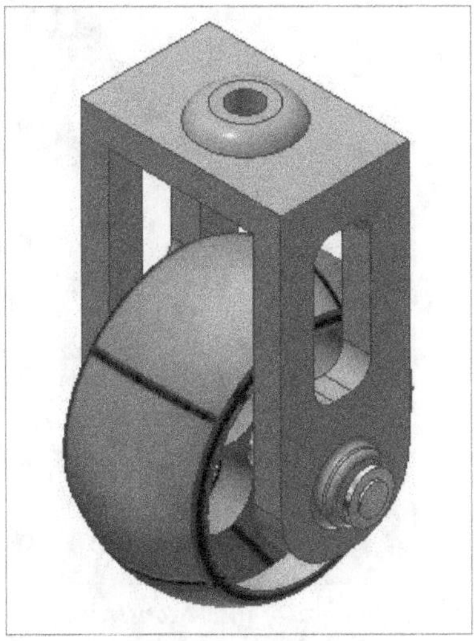

Figure-2. Wheel sub-assembly

- Start a new assembly and click on the **Place** button from the **Component** panel in the **Assemble** tab of the **Ribbon**. The **Place Component** dialog box will be displayed.
- Double-click on the Base component file from the downloaded resource folder using the **Place Component** dialog box and place it as grounded in the viewport.
- Double-click on the Wheel sub-assembly file from the dialog box. The component get attached to cursor.
- Click in the viewport to place the component.
- Move the cursor over the top round edge of the Wheel sub-assembly and click on it; refer to Figure-3. The sub-assembly get attached to the cursor.

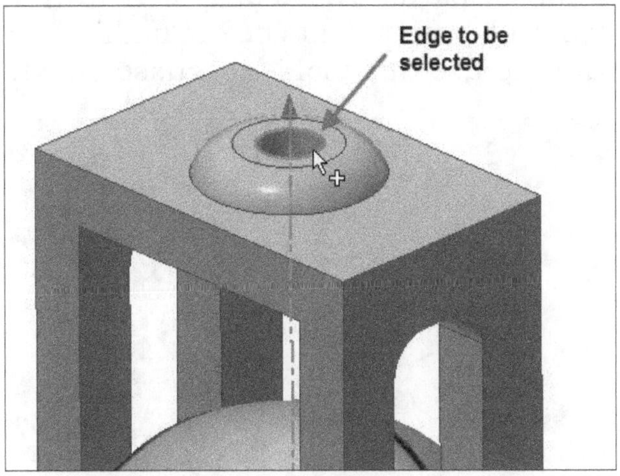

Figure-3. Edge of sub-assembly to be selected

- Move the cursor on the round edge of holes in the base. Preview of the **Insert** constraint will be displayed; refer to Figure-4. Click at this location to place the sub-assembly.

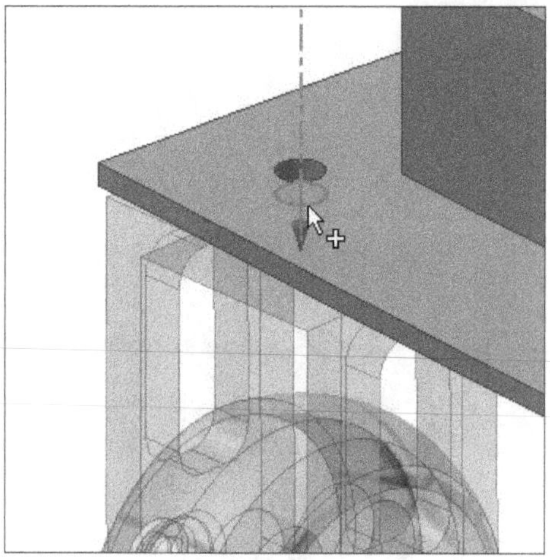

Figure-4. Preview of insert constrain

- Click on the **OK** button from the toolbar displayed. Repeat the procedure for rest of the wheel sub-assemblies.
- Press **ESC** when you have inserted all the wheel sub-assemblies.

From this small tutorial, you can understand the use of sub-assemblies in the main assembly.

MAKE LAYOUT

The **Make Layout** tool is used to create a layout component within an assembly to represent tentative motion of parts. The tool is generally used to create general guidelines for various assembly components before making design components; refer to Figure-5. The procedure to use this tool is discussed next.

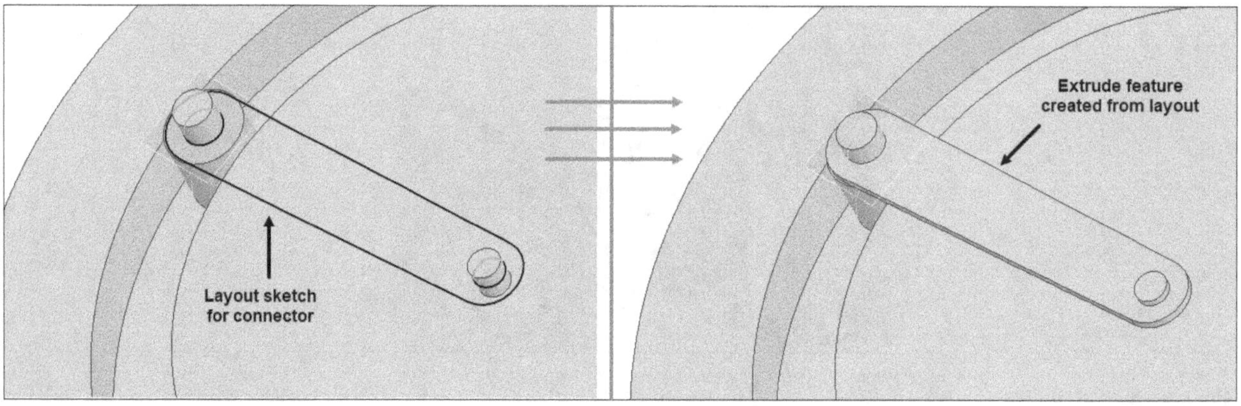

Figure-5. Example of layout

- Click on the **Make Layout** tool from the expanded **Component** panel of **Assemble** tab in the **Ribbon**. The **Make Layout** dialog box will be displayed; refer to Figure-6.

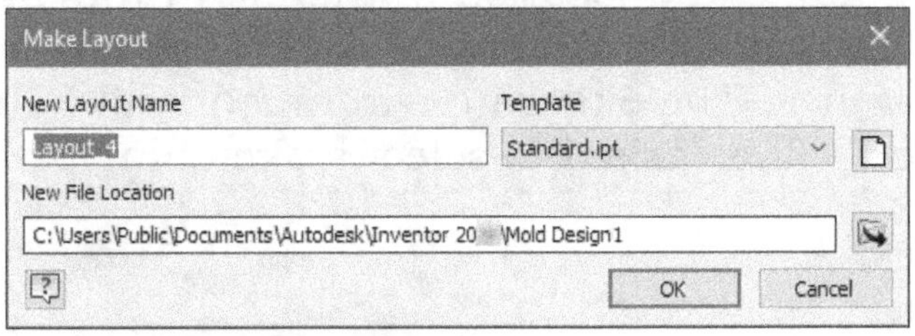

Figure-6. Make Layout dialog box

- Click in the **New Layout Name** edit box and specify desired name of the new layout part file.
- Select desired option from the **Template** drop-down to define template for the new file to be created. You can also use the Browse Templates button to access various templates. Click on the **Browse Templates** button. The **Open Template** dialog box will be displayed; refer to Figure-7.

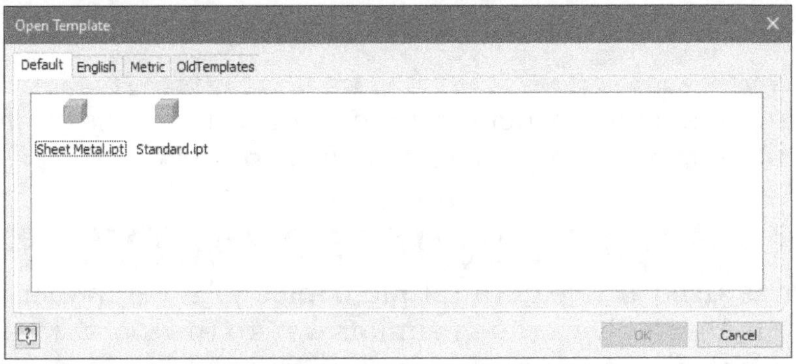

Figure-7. Open template dialog box

- Select desired template from the dialog box and click on the **OK** button.
- Click on the button from **New File Location** area to define directory location where layout part file will be saved. The **Save As** dialog box will be displayed; refer to Figure-8.

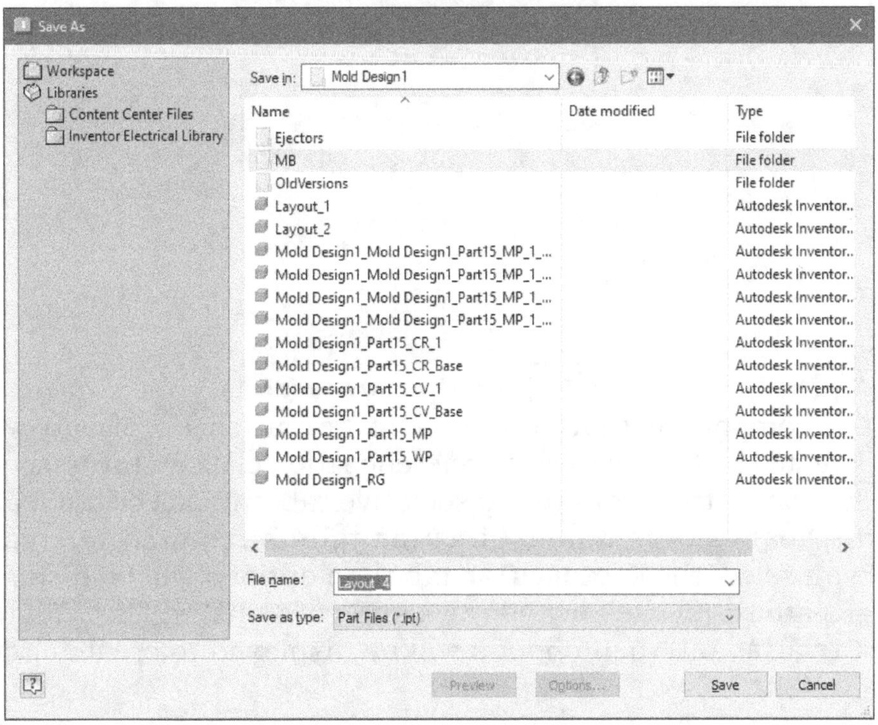

Figure-8. Save as dialog box

- Specify desired file name and location of the file in the dialog box and click on the **Save** button from the dialog box and then click on the **OK** button from the **Make Layout** dialog box. The **Sketch** environment will be displayed to create a new sketch and you will be asked to select a sketching plane; refer to Figure-9.

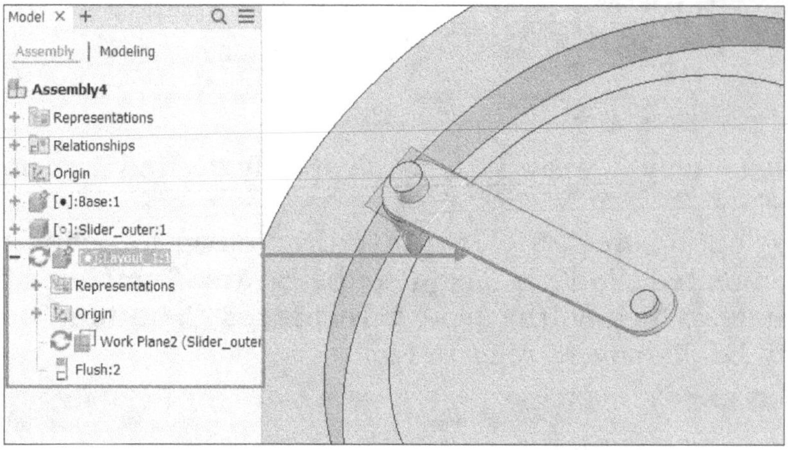

Figure-9. Layout example

- Create the outline sketch for defining motion layout of assembly and then click on the **Return** tool from **Ribbon** to exit the environment.

PATTERN IN ASSEMBLY

The **Pattern** tool is used to create multiple copies of a component/sub-assembly. The **Pattern** tool in Assembly works in similar way to the tool discussed in Modeling environment. The procedure to use this tool in Assembly environment is given next.

- Click on the **Pattern** tool from **Pattern** panel in the **Assemble** tab of the **Ribbon**. The **Pattern Component** dialog box will be displayed; refer to Figure-10. Also, you will be asked to select the components to be patterned.

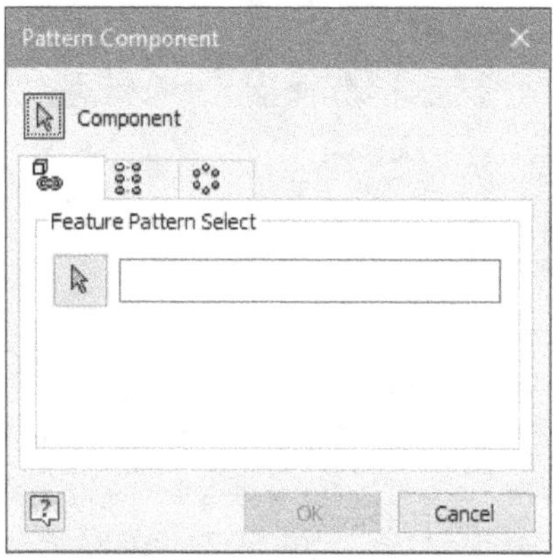

Figure-10. Pattern Component dialog box

- Click on the component that you want to be patterned. If you want to use a previously created feature pattern as reference then click on the Associated Feature Pattern selection button from the Associative tab and select the feature pattern.
- Click on the **Rectangular** tab or **Circular** tab as required to create respective pattern. If you select the **Rectangular** tab then options will be displayed to create rectangular pattern (in the form of rows and columns); refer to Figure-11. If you select the **Circular** tab then options will be displayed to create circular pattern; refer to Figure-12.

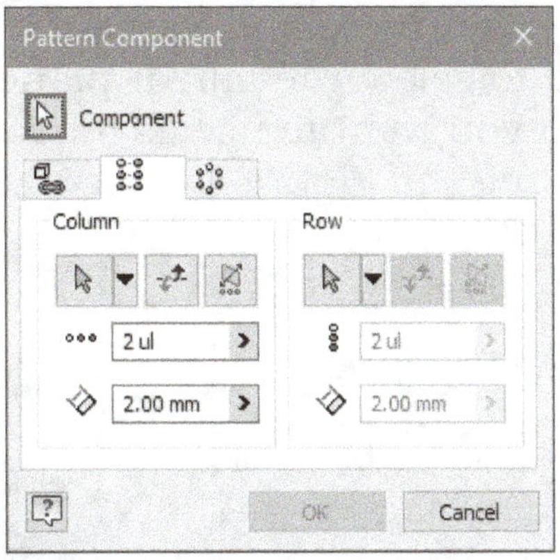

Figure-11. Pattern Component dialog box with Rectangular tab selected

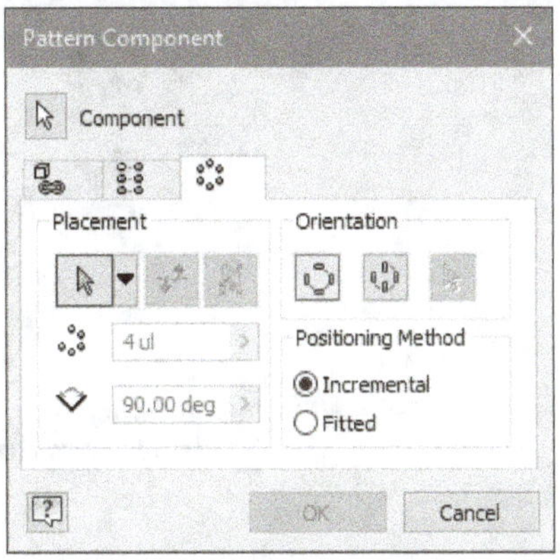

Figure-12. Pattern Component dialog box with Circular tab selected

- Rest of the procedure is same as discussed in chapter related to 3D Modeling.

MIRROR AND COPY

The **Mirror** tool and **Copy** tool in Assembly environment work in the same way as they do in 3D Modeling environment. We will discuss the procedure to use **Mirror** tool. You can use similar steps to use **Copy** tool.

- Click on the **Mirror** tool from **Pattern** panel in the **Assemble** tab of the **Ribbon**. The **Mirror Components** dialog box will be displayed; refer to Figure-13. Also, you will be asked to select the components to be mirrored.

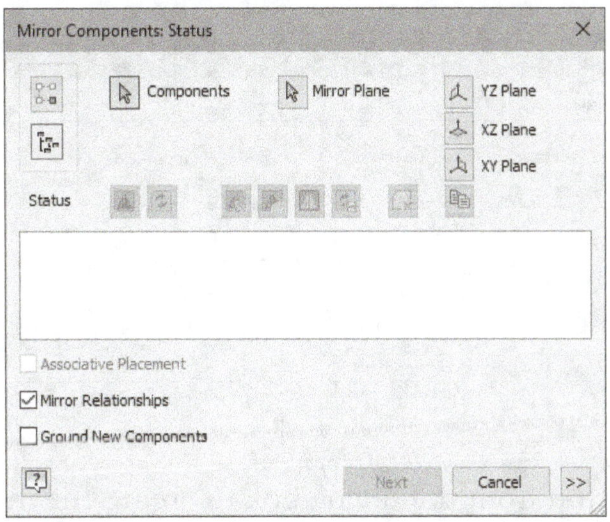

Figure-13. Mirror Components dialog box

- Select the components to be mirrored and then click on the **Mirror Plane** selection button. You will be asked to select the mirror plane.
- Click on a plane/face that you want to use as mirror plane. Preview of the mirror feature will be displayed; refer to Figure-14.

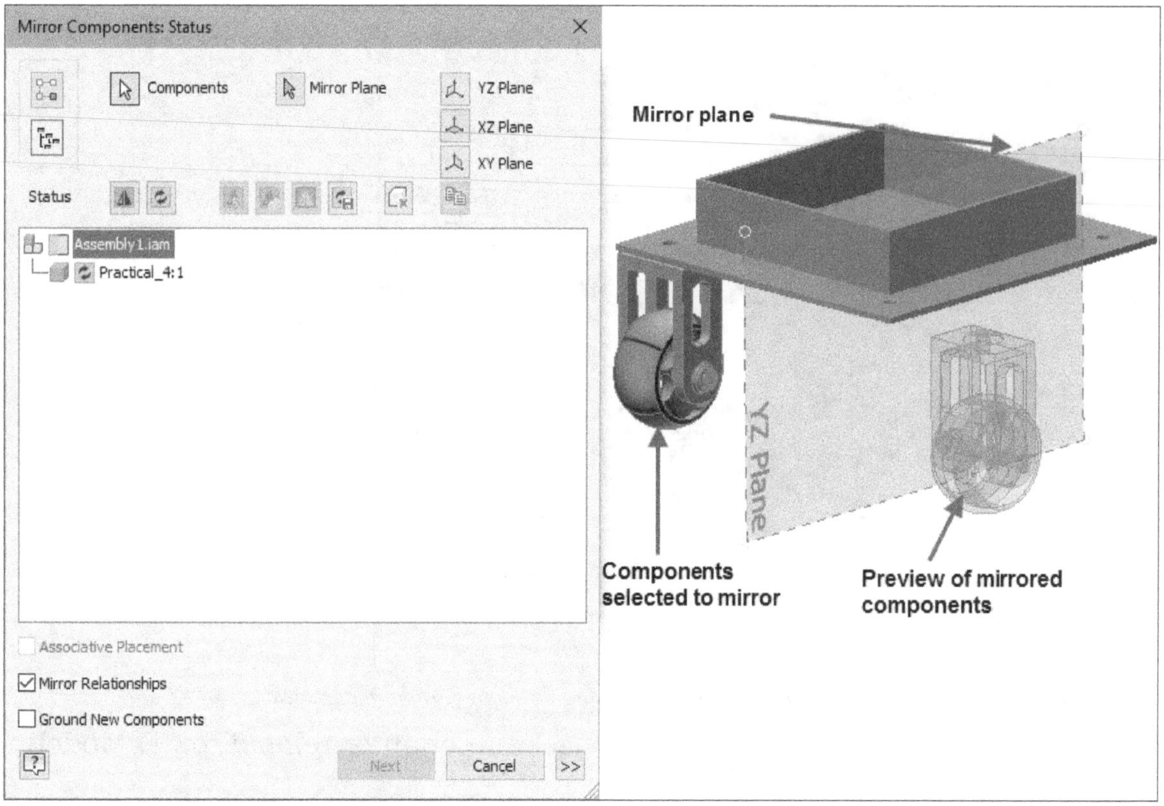

Figure-14. Preview of the mirror feature

- Exclude desired components by selecting them and then clicking on the **Exclude** button from the **Status** area of the dialog box. If you want to create a new file by copying selected components then select the **Mirror** button and if you want to just reuse the mirrored components but do not want a new file to be generated by mirroring then select the **Reuse** button.
- Click on the **Next** button after performing desired changes. The **Mirror Components** dialog box will be displayed with list of components to be mirrored; refer to Figure-15.

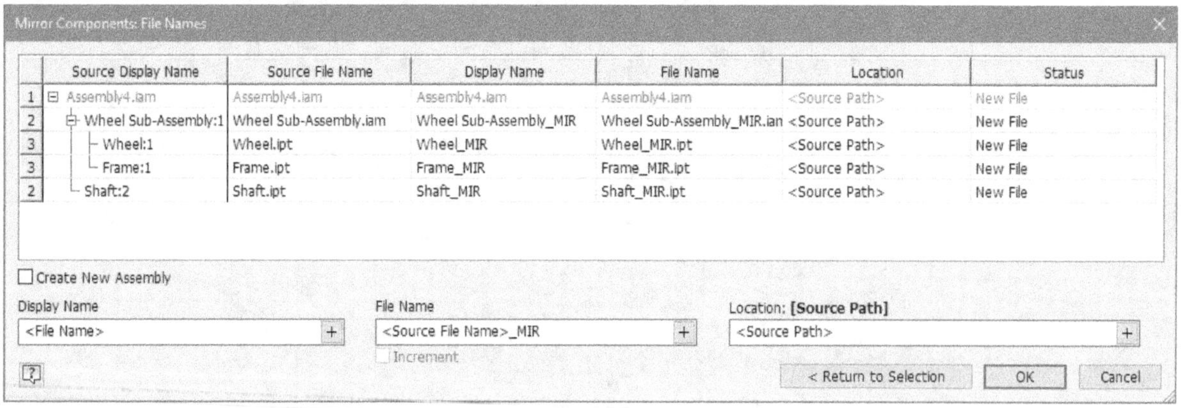

Figure-15. Mirror Components dialog box with list of components

- Click on the **OK** button from the dialog box to create the mirror copy.

iCopy

The **iCopy** tool is used to insert an iCopy-authored assembly that automatically adjusts its size based on its position within the parent assembly (procedure discussed in next topic). The procedure to use this tool is discussed next.

- Click on the **iCopy** tool from the expanded **Pattern** panel in **Assemble** tab of the **Ribbon**. The **Select Source Assembly** dialog box will be displayed; refer to Figure-16.

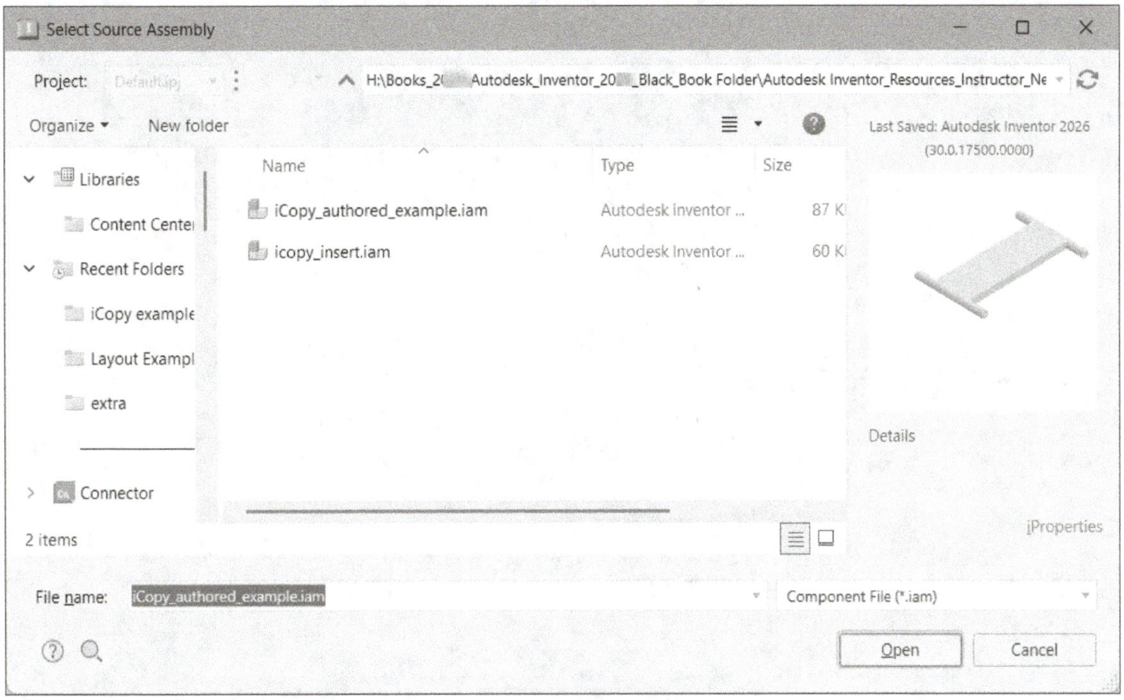

Figure-16. Select source assembly dialog box

- Select desired file which has iCopy authored assembly from the dialog box and click on the **Open** button. The **Constrain iCopy** dialog box will be displayed; refer to Figure-17.

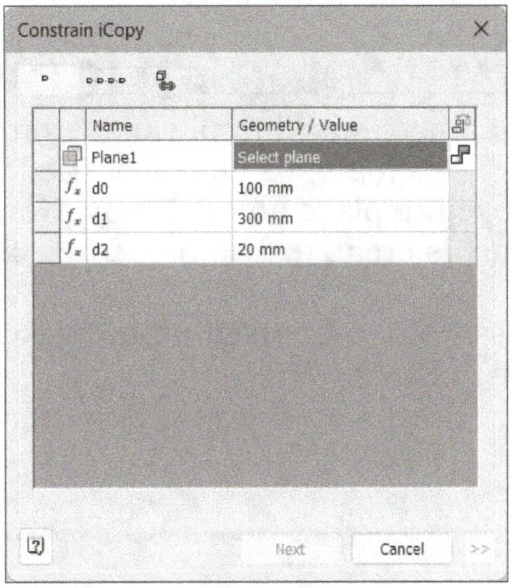

Figure-17. Constrain iCopy dialog box

- Select the reference plane/geometries to define placement of the inserted iCopy of assembly; refer to Figure-18. Change the parameters as desired in the dialog box and click on the **Next** button. The **Copy/Reuse iCopy Components** dialog box will be displayed; refer to Figure-19.

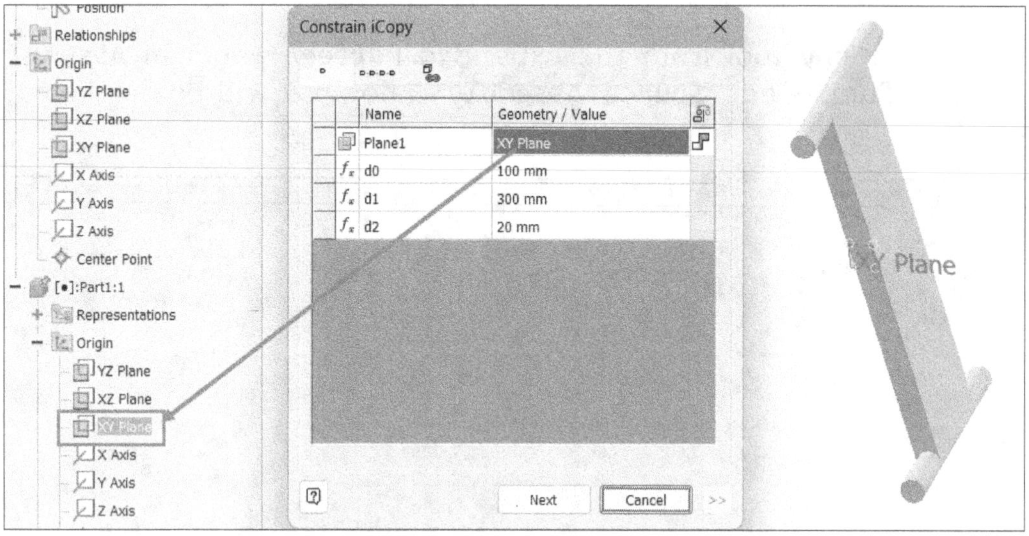

Figure-18. Preview of iCopy assembly

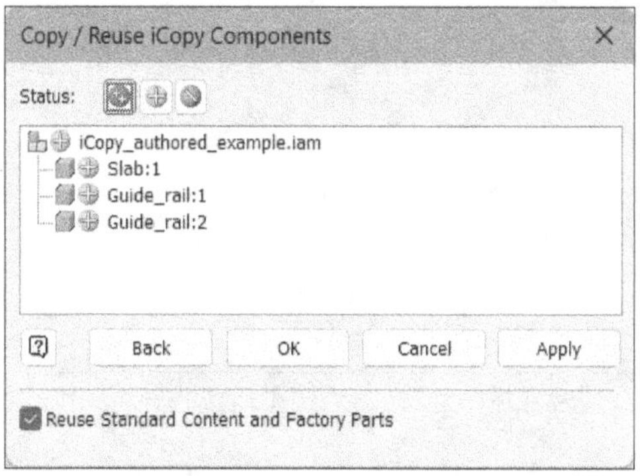

Figure-19. Copy Reuse iCopy Components dialog box

- Set the parameters as discussed earlier to show/hide various components of iCopy assembly and click on the **OK** button.

AUTHORING AN ICOPY

iCopy also called intelligent copy is used to place customized copies of an assembly or part in the design. In previous topic, you have learned to place an assembly icopy. Similar method can be applied to place a part iCopy. Now, you will learn about how an iCopy of assembly or part is created. The procedure is given next.

- Create the model or assembly to be used as iCopy with all the dimensions and reference features; refer to Figure-20.

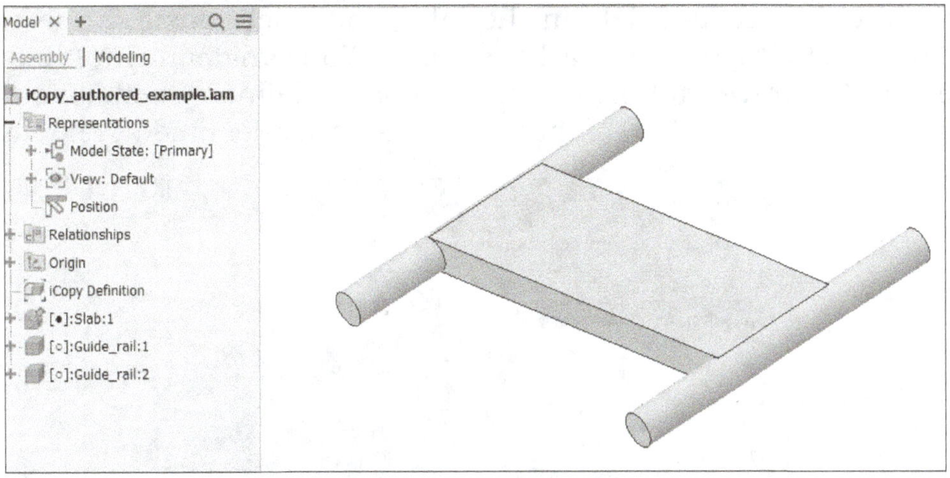

Figure-20. Model created for iCopy

- Click on the **iCopy Author** tool from the **Author** panel in the **Manage** tab of the **Ribbon**. The **iCopy Author** dialog box will be displayed and you will be asked to select the component to be iCopy authored; refer to Figure-21.

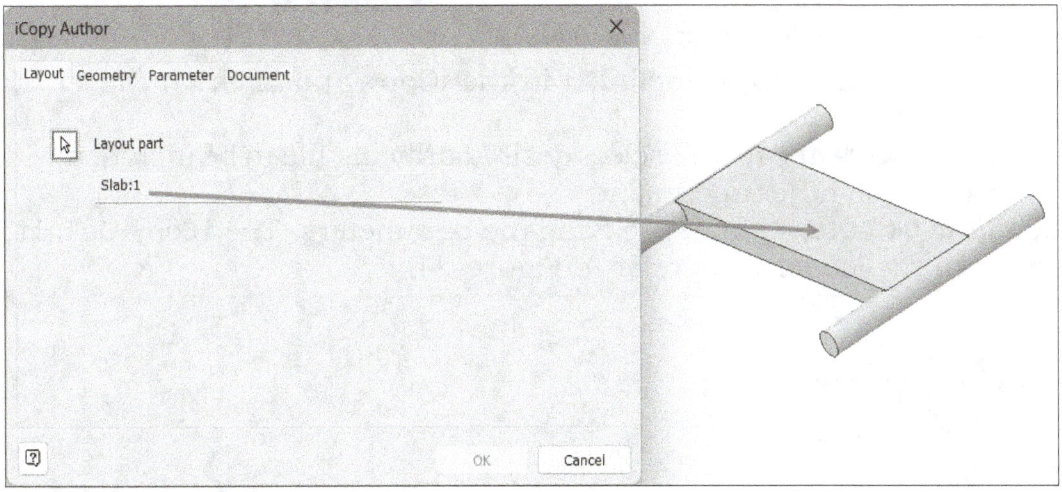

Figure-21. Selecting layout part

- Click on the **Geometry** tab to define the geometry reference to be used for defining placement of the iCopy. The options in dialog box will be displayed as shown in Figure-22.

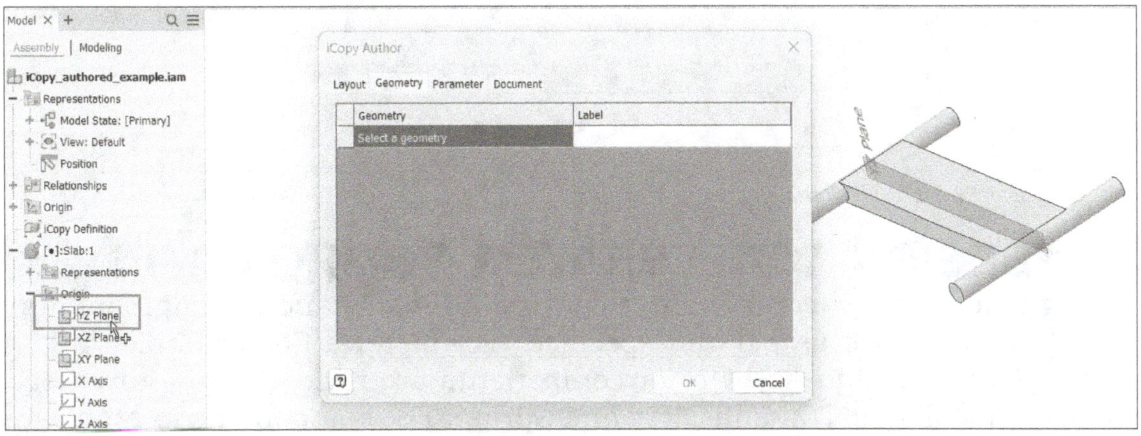

Figure-22. Geometry tab in iCopy Author dialog box

- Click in the **Click to add** field in the table and select desired reference plane/axis/point from the layout part earlier selected. You can define multiple references.
- Click on the **Parameter** tab in the dialog box to define dimensions that can be changed when inserting iCopy of the model in another document; refer to Figure-23.

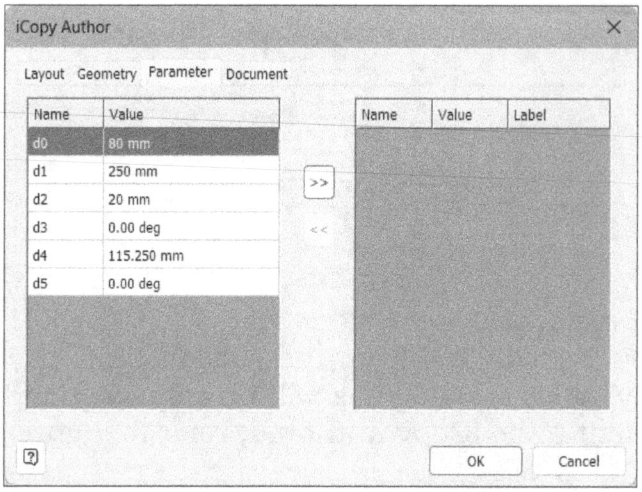

Figure-23. Parameter tab of iCopy Author dialog box

- Select the parameter to be included in the iCopy and click on the **>>** button to add it.
- Click on the **Document** tab and select desired drawing file to be included with iCopy when inserting in other document.
- Click on the **OK** button after specifying the parameters. The **iCopy Definition** will be added in the Model Tree; refer to Figure-24.

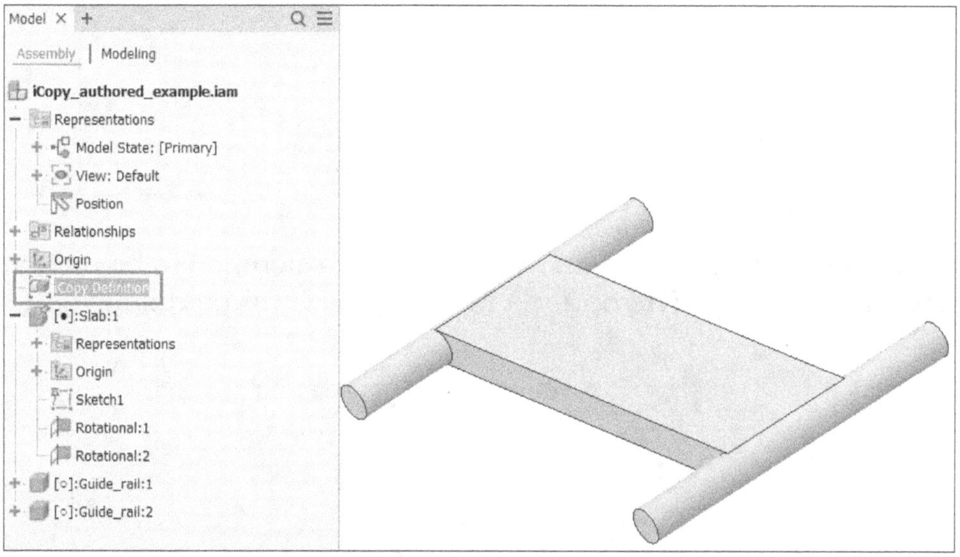

Figure-24. iCopy Definition added in Model Tree

DESIGN ACCELERATOR COMPONENTS

The Design Accelerator components are mechanical standard components that change shape and size as per the specified parameters. For example, bolt, cam, gears, etc. All the Design Accelerator components are divided into four categories; Fastener, Frame, Power Transmission, and Spring. The components in each category are discussed next.

COMPONENTS FOR FASTENING

There are two type of fastening components available as Design Accelerator components: Bolt and Pin. The procedure to use each of the component is given next.

Bolted Connection

The Bolted connection component is used to represent the bolted connection in assembly with real-world parameters. The procedure to apply bolted connection is given next.

- Click on the **Bolted Connection** tool from **Fasten** panel in the **Design** tab of the **Ribbon**. The **Bolted Connection Component Generator** dialog box will be displayed; refer to Figure-25.

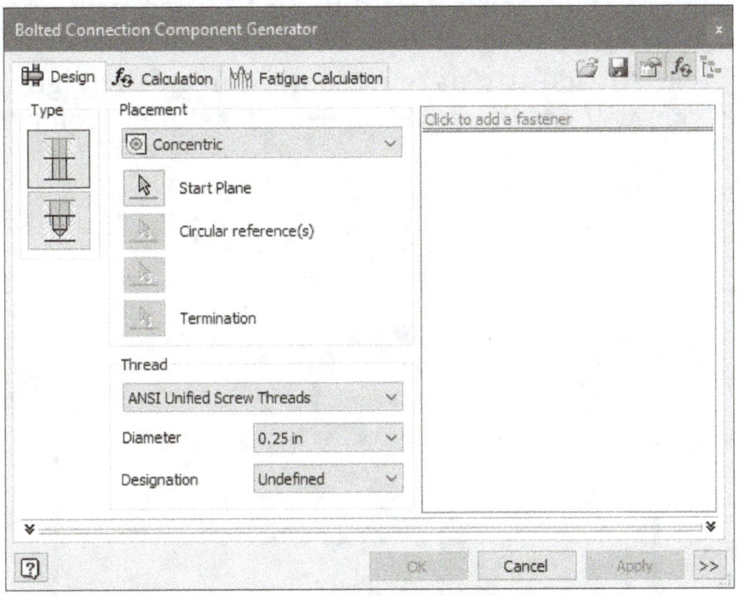

Figure-25. Bolted Connection Component Generator dialog box

- Select desired type of hole by selecting **Through All** or **Blind** connection type buttons from the left area in the dialog box. If you select the **Through All** button then the bolt created will be have nut on the other end. If you select the blind connection then bolt created will terminate with blind hole (Like a foundation bolt).
- Select the **Linear** option from the drop-down at top in the **Placement** area of dialog box to define linear (straight edges) references for placing the bolt. Select the **Concentric** option from the drop-down if you want to place bolt concentric to selected hole edge. Select the **On point** option from the drop-down to place bolts at selected points. Select the **By hole** option from the drop-down to place bolts using previously created holes as reference. We have selected **Concentric** option in our case.
- On selecting desired button, you will be asked to select a face/plane to specify starting point of the bolted connection.
- Click on desired face/plane. You will be asked to select circular reference to specify axis of the bolted connection.
- Select the circular face/edge of the hole for which you want to create bolted connection. You will be asked to select plane/face to specify termination or blind start plane depending on the connection type button selected.
- Select desired face/plane. Preview of connection will be displayed with dashed line; refer to Figure-26.

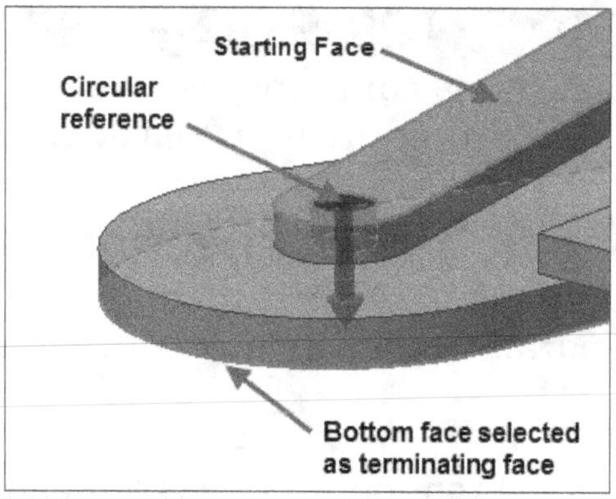

Figure-26. Preview of bolted connection

- Note that we have selected **Concentric** option from the drop-down in **Placement** area of the dialog box, you can select different option and specify references for bolted connection accordingly.
- Click on the **Click to add a fastener** option from the right area of the dialog box. A selection box will be displayed to select fastener; refer to Figure-27.

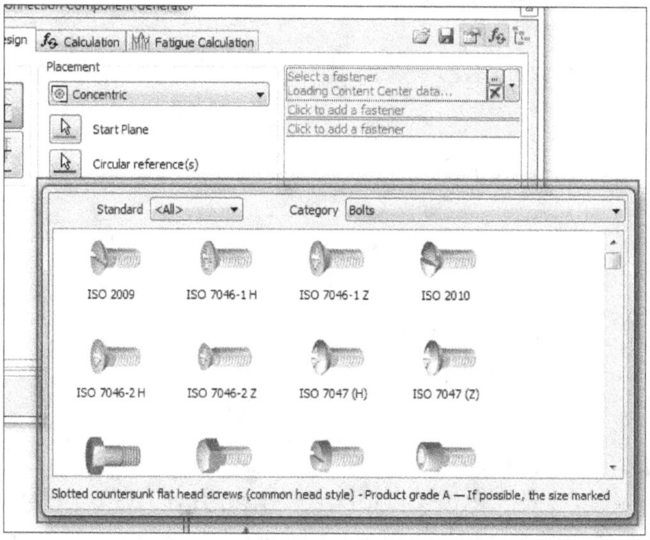

Figure-27. Selection box for fasteners

- Click in the **Category** drop-down in selection box and select desired category. The bolts in selected category will be displayed; refer to Figure-28.

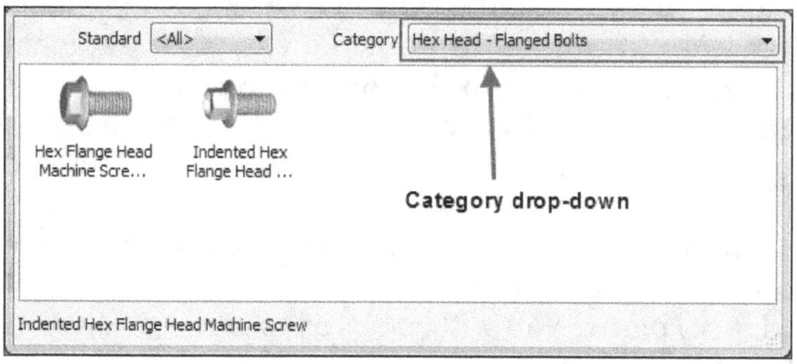

Figure-28. Category drop-down in selection box

- Click on desired fastencr. Preview of the fastener will be displayed in the viewport; refer to Figure-29.

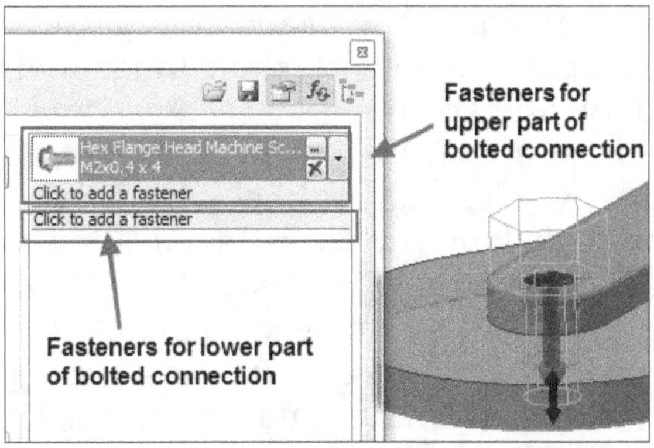

Figure-29. Preview of fastener

- Click again on the **Click to add a fastener** option in the dialog box to add more parts of the bolted connection and apply other fasteners of the bolted connection. Note that the options above dividing line are for upper part and options below dividing line are for lower part of bolted connection; refer to Figure-29. Figure-30 shows preview of a bolted connection after adding washers and nut.

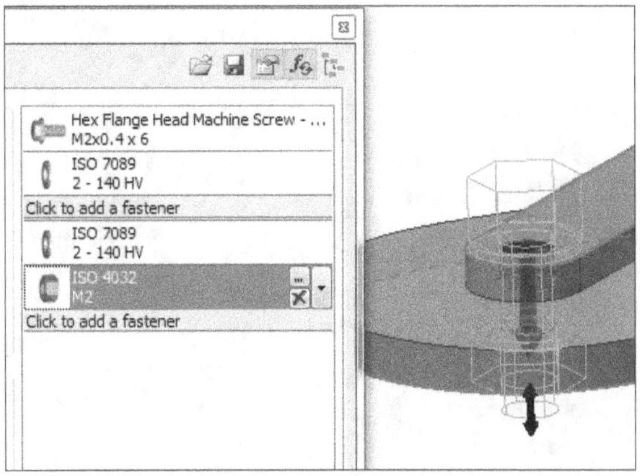

Figure-30. Preview of bolted connection with fasteners

- Click on the **Calculation** tab in the dialog box. The dialog box will be displayed as shown in Figure-31.

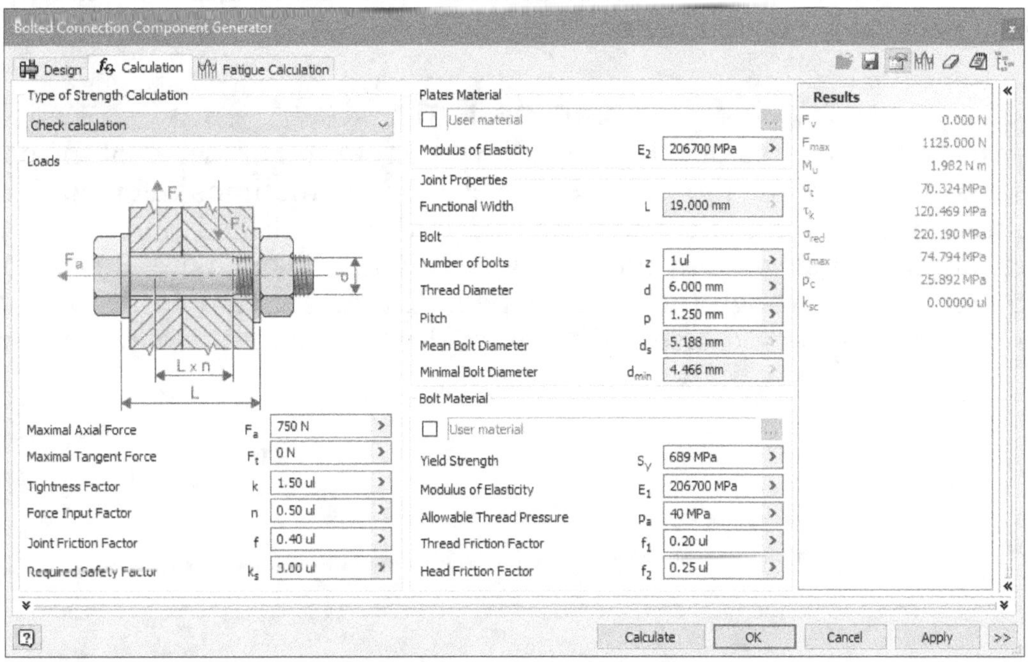

Figure-31. Calculation tab in Bolted Connection Component Generator dialog box

- Specify the design parameters in the **Loads** area of the dialog box like, maximal axial force that can be applied on bolt, maximal tangential force that can be applied on bolt, Factor of Safety, and so on.
- Specify the material properties for bolt and plate, or you can select the material available in the library by selecting the check box in the respective area.
- After specify the values, click on the **Calculate** button to check whether the use of current bolt is feasible; refer to Figure-32. Note that factor of safety is much lower than the standard value, so we need to modify the bolt parameters. There are many ways to change parameters of bolt to make it feasible like, change **Thread Diameter** from 2 to 4, change the material to more tough material, or increase the number of bolts from 1 to 5.

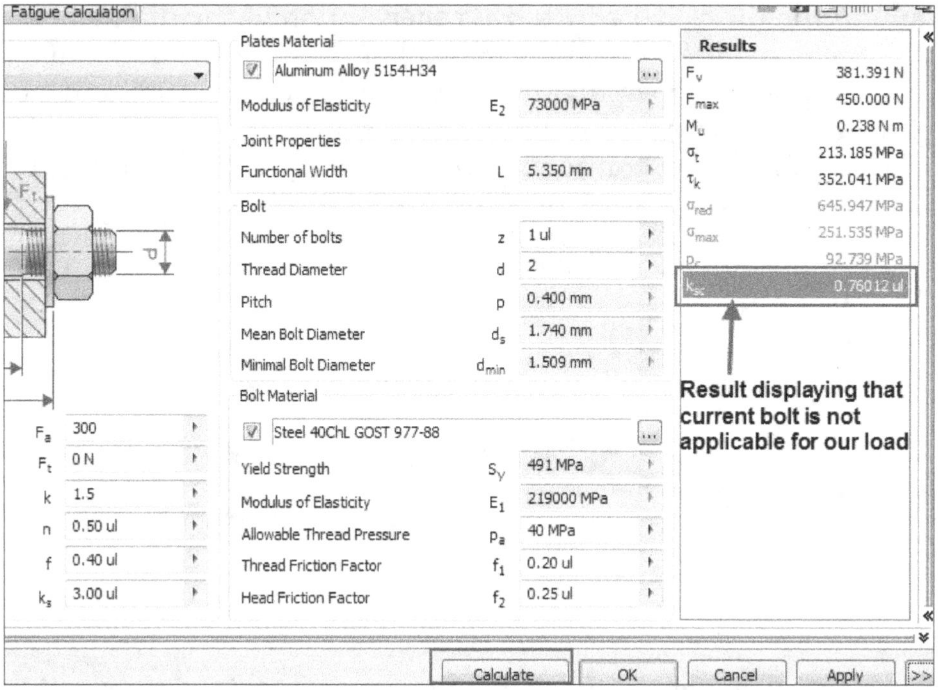

Figure-32. Result of bolt loading calculation

- Set the other parameters as discussed earlier and click on the **OK** button from the dialog box to create bolted connection.

Clevis Pin

Clevis Pin is a type of fastener that will allow the rotation or swivel of the connected parts about the axis of the pin linkage. A clevis pin, sometimes referred to as a link pin or hinge pin, consists of a head, shank, and cross drilled hole. When using a fastening, such as a clevis pin, the hole which is at the opposite end of the pin to the head is inserted through the items to be linked and then a cotter pin, R clip, or similar retaining fastener is inserted through the hole to fix the clevis pin in place.

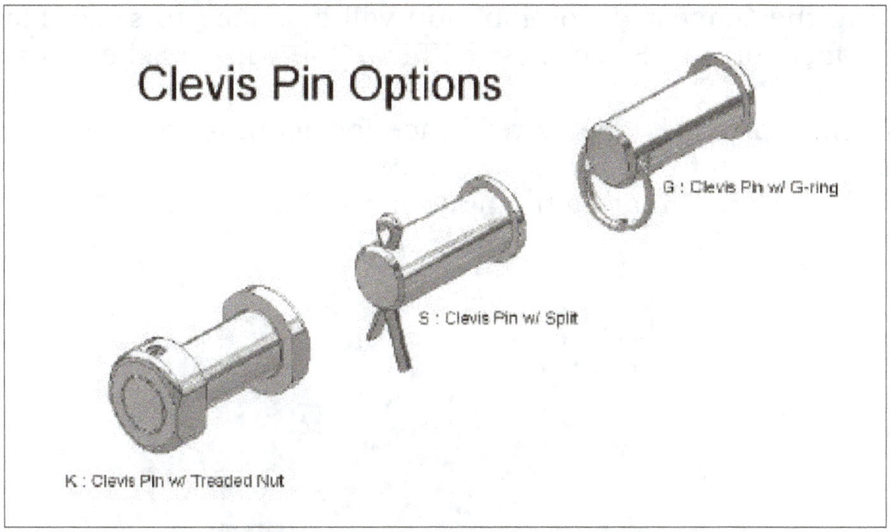

The procedure to create clevis pin component is given next.

- Click on the **Clevis Pin** tool from **Fasten** panel in the **Design** tab of the **Ribbon**. The **Clevis Pin Component Generator** dialog box will be displayed; refer to Figure-33.

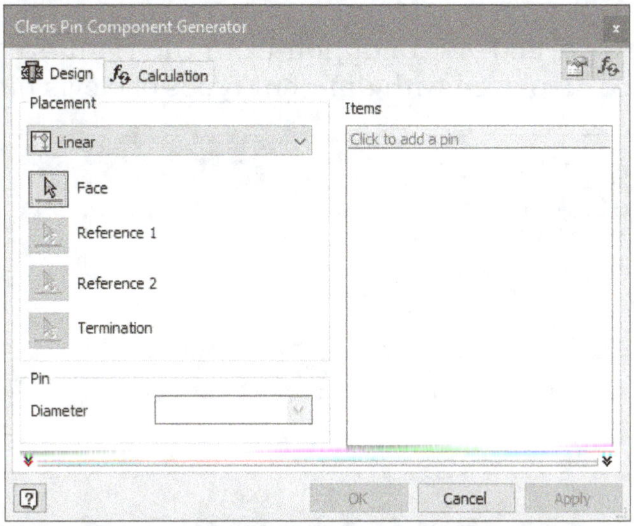

Figure-33. Clevis Pin Component Generator dialog box

- Click on the **Linear** option from **Placement** drop-down in the dialog box. Various placement options will be displayed in the drop-down; refer to Figure-34. Click on desired option for placement. (We have selected **Concentric** option because we want to make the pin placed concentric to hole.)

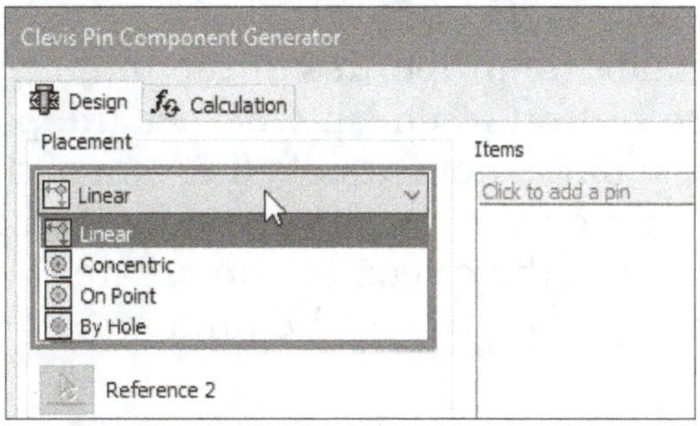

Figure-34. Drop-down for placement options

- On selecting the **Concentric** option, you will be asked to select face to be used as starting face for pin. Select desired face. You will be asked to select circular reference.
- Select the circular edge/face as reference for defining the diameter of pin. You will be asked to select the terminating face.
- Select the face for terminating the pin; refer to Figure-35.

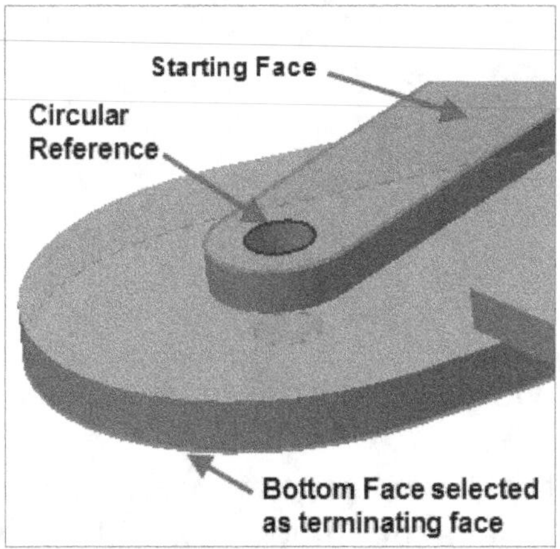

Figure-35. References selected for Clevis pin

- Click on the **Click to add a pin** option from the right area of the dialog box. A selection box will be displayed with different types of clevis pins; refer to Figure-36.

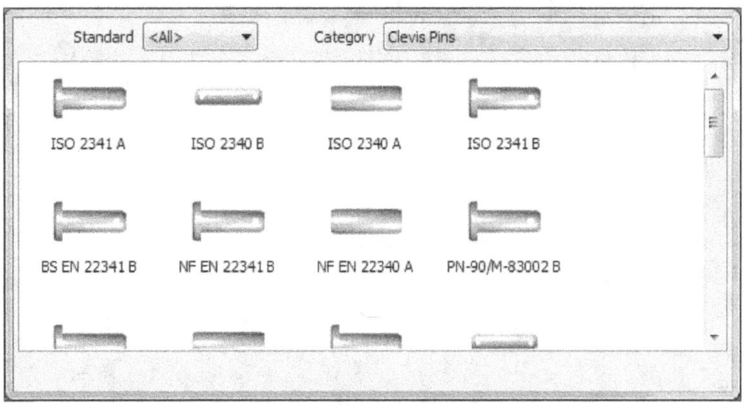

Figure-36. Selection box for clevis pin

- Select desired type of pin from the selection box. Preview will be displayed.
- Click on the **Calculation** tab from the dialog box. The dialog box will be displayed as shown in Figure-37.
- Specify the loads, dimensions, and joint properties in the respective edit boxes to input the actual parameters of your joint.
- Similarly, specify the material properties of the pin, clevis, and rod.
- Click on the **Calculate** button to check whether the pin is feasible for specified parameters or not. If the pin is not feasible (i.e. one of the parameter in results is displayed as red) then perform the necessary modifications.
- Click on the **OK** button from the dialog box to create the pin.
- Click on the **OK** button again to accept the name and location of component.

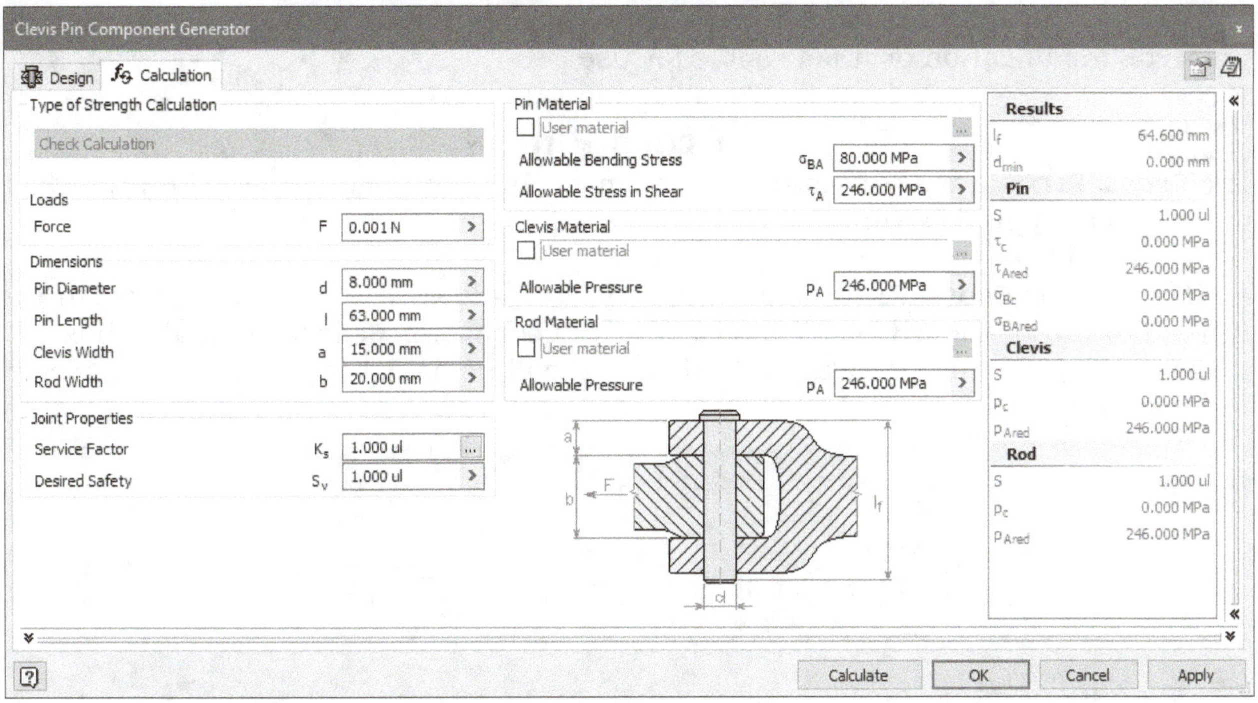

Figure-37. Calculation tab in Clevis Pin Component Generator dialog box

Secure Pin

The **Secure Pin** is fastener used to bind together two rotating parts along their common axis. The procedure to create secure pin is given next.

- Click on the **Secure Pin** tool from the **Pin** drop-down in the **Fasten** panel in the **Design** tab of the **Ribbon**. The **Secure Pin Component Generator** dialog box will be displayed; refer to Figure-38. Also, you will be asked to select face to specify location of pin.

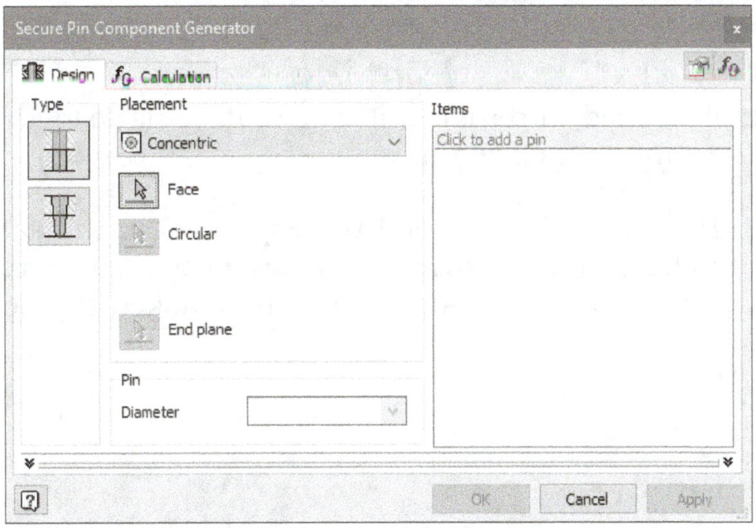

Figure-38. Secure Pin Component Generator dialog box

- Select the starting face. You will be asked to select a circular reference.
- Select the circular reference. You will be asked to select the end plane.
- Select the end plane. Preview of the pin will be displayed.
- Now, select desired pin type from the selection box as discussed for clevis pin.

- Click on the **Calculation** tab and check by using the options in tab whether pin needs modification or it is feasible for use.

Cross Pin

The **Cross Pin** is a type of pin used to connect draw rod and sleeve. The procedure to create cross pin is given next.

- Click on the **Cross Pin** tool from the **Pin** drop-down in the **Fasten** panel in the **Design** tab of the **Ribbon**. The **Cross Pin Component Generator** dialog box will be displayed; refer to Figure-39. Also, you will be asked to select face to specify location of pin.

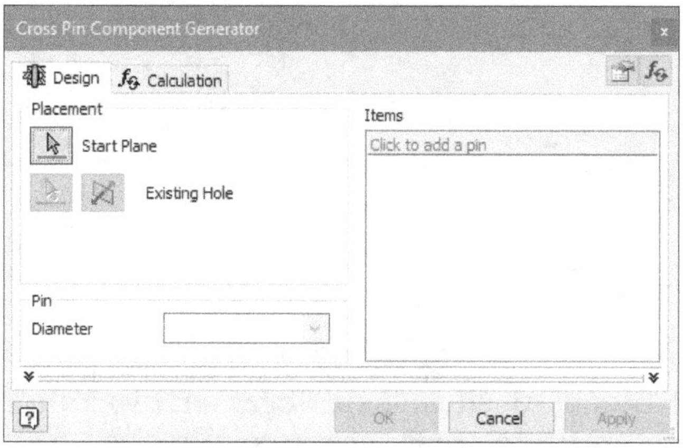

Figure-39. Cross Pin Component Generator dialog box

- Select the starting face. You will be asked to select a hole.
- Select the hole to be used as circular reference for pin.
- Now, select desired pin type from the selection box as discussed for clevis pin.
- Click on the **Calculation** tab and check by using the options in tab whether pin needs modification or it is feasible for use.

Joint Pin

The **Joint Pin** tool is used to design and calculate pins loaded with torque. The procedure to create joint pin is given next.

- Click on the **Joint Pin** tool from the **Pin** drop-down in the **Fasten** panel in the **Design** tab of the **Ribbon**. The **Joint Pin Component Generator** dialog box will be displayed; refer to Figure-40. Also, you will be asked to select face to specify location of pin.

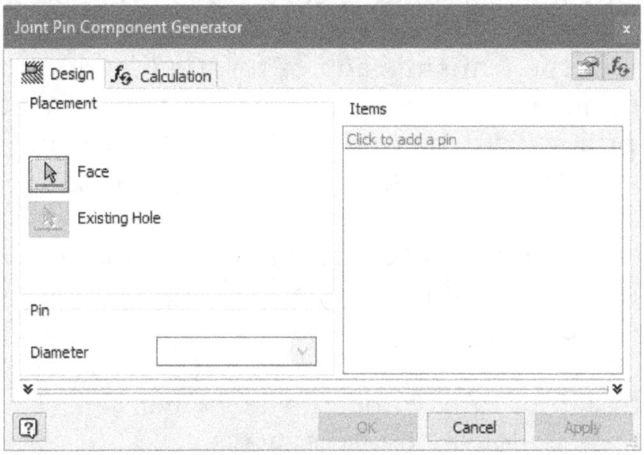

Figure-40. Joint Pin Component Generator dialog box

- Select the starting face. You will be asked to select a hole reference.
- Select the hole to be used as circular reference for pin.
- Now, select desired pin type from the selection box as discussed for cross pin.
- Click on the **Calculation** tab and check by using the options in tab whether pin needs modification or it is feasible for use.

Radial Pin

The procedure to create radial pin is same as discussed for cross pin.

- Click on the **Radial Pin** tool from the **Pin** drop-down in the **Fasten** panel in the **Design** tab of the **Ribbon**. The **Radial Pin Component Generator** dialog box will be displayed. Also, you will be asked to select face to specify location of pin.
- Do the same as discussed earlier for **Cross pin**.

The tools related to frame designing are discussed in next chapter.

COMPONENTS FOR POWER TRANSMISSION

There are various components for transmission like shaft, gears, bearing, belts, cams, and so on. The procedures to create various power transmission components are given next.

Shaft

A shaft is a rotating machine element used to transmit power from one location to other. Power is delivered to the shaft by some tangential force and resultant torque generated in the shaft makes the transfer of power to other linked elements. The standard size of transmission shafts are given as:

25 mm to 60 mm diameter with 5 mm steps
60 mm to 110 mm diameter with 10 mm steps
110 mm to 140 mm diameter with 15 mm steps
140 mm to 500 mm diameter with 20 mm steps

Standard lengths of shafts are 5 m, 6 m, and 7 m.

While designing a shaft, we need to take care of following stresses:

1. Shear stresses due to the transmission of torque (i.e. due to torsional load).
2. Bending stresses (tensile or compressive) due to the forces acting upon machine elements like gears, pulleys, etc. as well as due to the weight of the shaft itself.
3. Stresses due to combined torsional and bending loads.

According to American Society of Mechanical Engineers (ASME) code for the design of transmission shafts, the maximum permissible working stresses in tension or compression may be taken as,

(a) 112 MPa for shafts without allowance for keyways.
(b) 84 MPa for shafts with allowance for keyways.

The maximum permissible shear stress may be taken as
(a) 56 MPa for shafts without allowance for key ways.
(b) 42 MPa for shafts with allowance for keyways.

In Autodesk Inventor Assembly environment, the **Shaft** tool is used to create shaft in an assembly to transmit power. The procedure to create shaft is given next.

- Click on the **Shaft** tool from the **Power Transmission** panel in the **Design** tab of the **Ribbon**. The **Shaft Component Generator** dialog box will be displayed; refer to Figure-41. Also, preview of the shaft will be displayed attached to the cursor; refer to Figure-41.

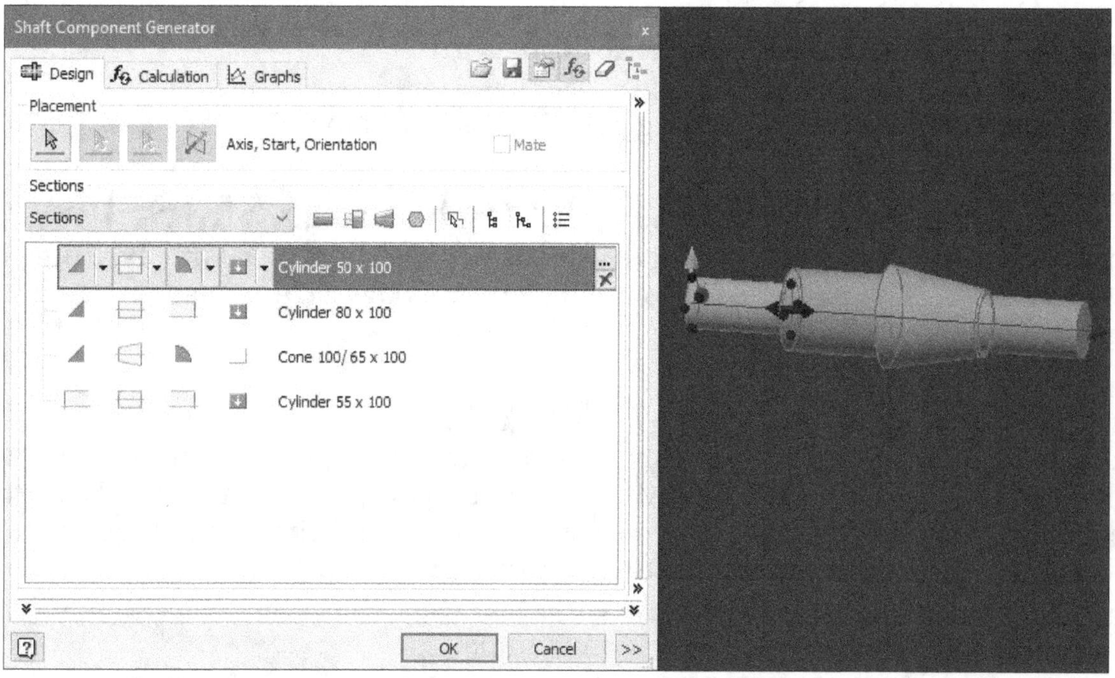

Figure-41. Shaft Component Generator dialog box

- Change the sections of the shaft as required. Each shaft section has four features to change; First edge feature, Section type, Second edge feature, and Section feature like keyways, etc. To change the shape of section, click on the drop-down for desired feature. Various options will be displayed; refer to Figure-42.

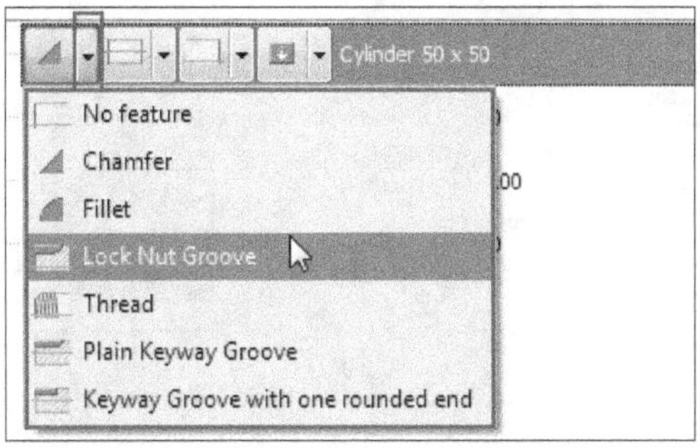

Figure-42. First Edge Feature drop-down

- Select desired option from the drop-down. The related dialog box will be displayed to specify parameter. Specify the parameter and click on the **OK** button.
- Similarly, you can change other features of selected section.
- To add a new section in the shaft, select the shaft section from the list or from the model preview after which you want to add the new section and select desired button from the dialog box; refer to Figure-43.

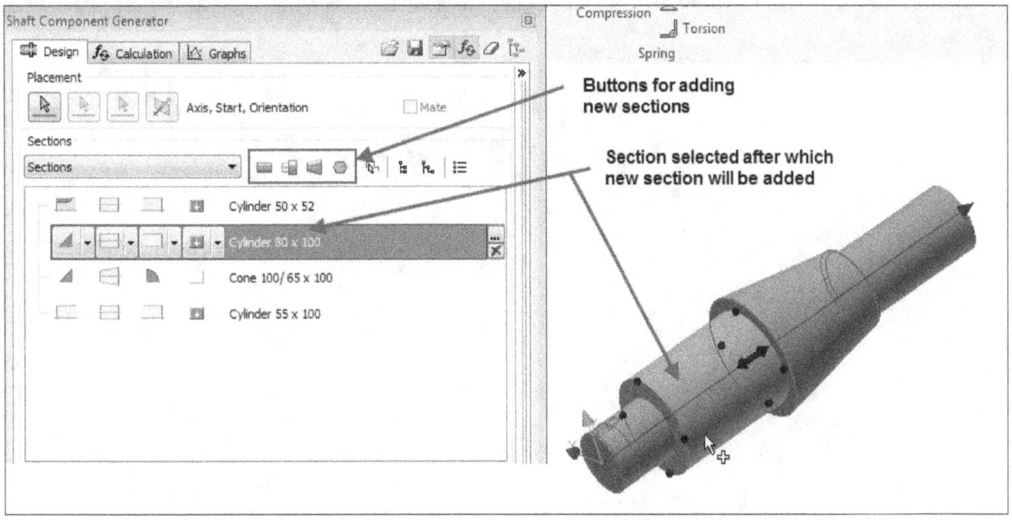

Figure-43. Adding new sections in shaft

- On selecting the button, a new section will be added in the shaft. To change the parameters of shaft section, click on the **Section Properties** button next to the selected section; refer to Figure-44. The related dialog box will be displayed; refer to Figure-45.

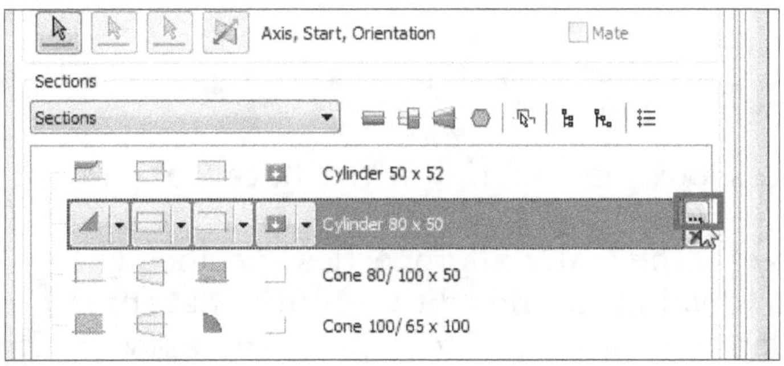

Figure-44. Section Properties button

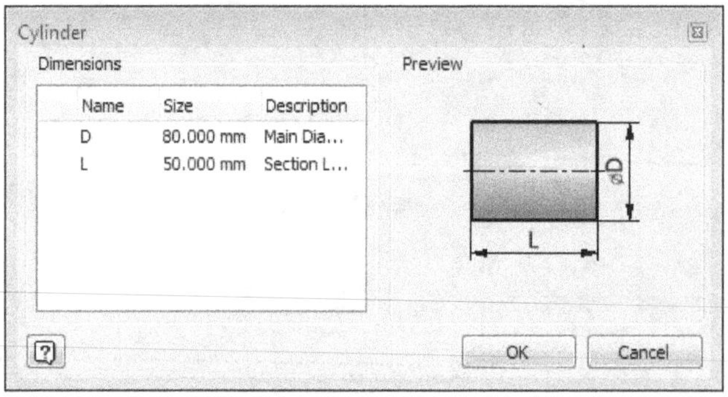

Figure-45. Cylinder dialog box

- Click on the dimension value in the dialog box that you want to change and specify desired value. Click on the **OK** button to exit.
- After making desired shape, click on the **Calculation** tab in the dialog box. The dialog box will be displayed as shown in Figure-46.

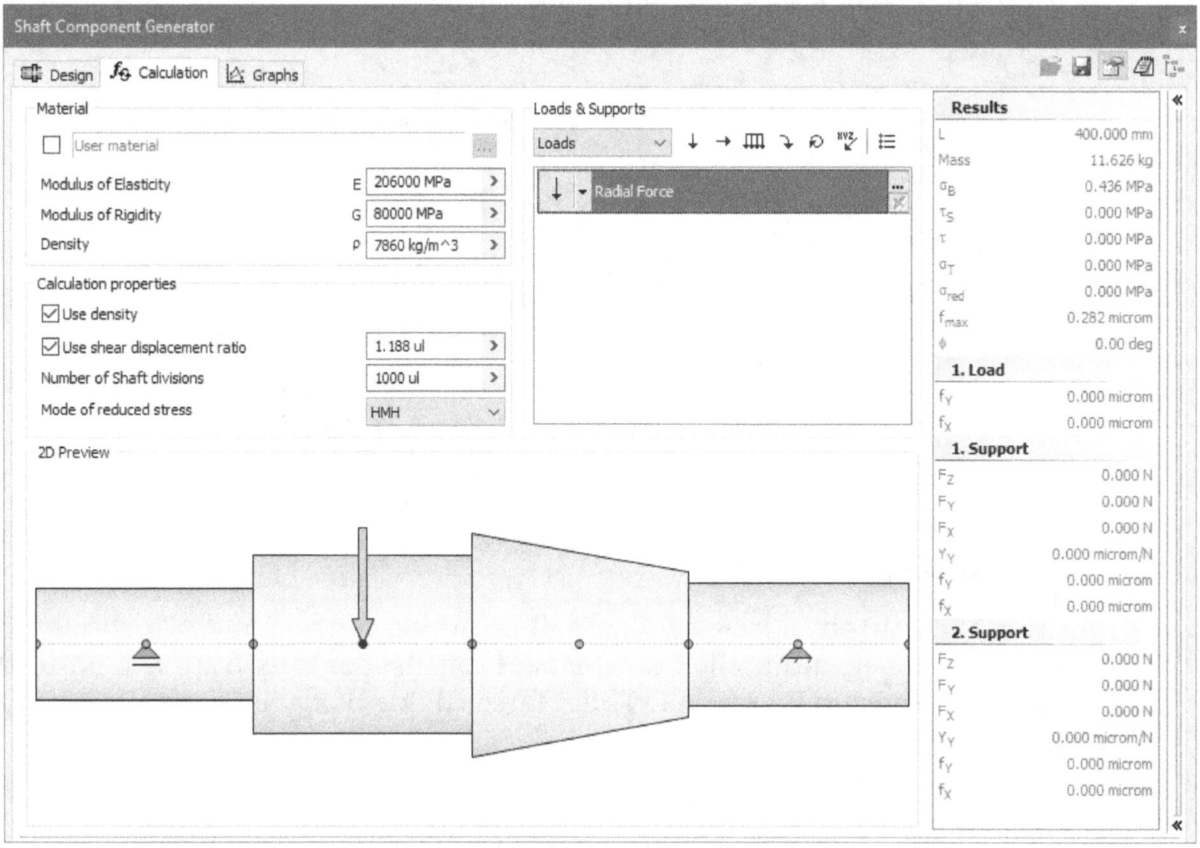

Figure-46. Shaft Component Generator dialog box with Calculation tab

- Click on the check box for material in the **Material** area of the dialog box and select desired material.
- If you want to specify the material properties specifically then clear the check box and specify desired values in the edit box of the **Material** area.
- Select the **Use Density** check box to include the mass in the calculation. If you clear the check box then Density is not included in the calculation.
- Select the **Use shear displacement ratio** check box if the shaft profile is thick/rigid. Default value of ratio for cylindrical profile is 1.18. Note that if the shaft has thin profile then effect of shear force is not counted.

- Specify the number of shaft divisions for calculations in the **Number of Shaft divisions** edit box.
- Click on the drop-down for **Mode of reduced stress** in the **Calculation Properties** area of the dialog box and select either **HMH** or **Tresca-Guest** mode of reduced stress calculation.

Formula for reduced stress is given by,
Reduced stress:

$$\sigma_{red} = \sqrt{(\sigma_B + \sigma_T)^2 + \alpha * (\tau^2 + {\tau_S}^2)}$$

where:

σ_B bending stress
σ_T tension stress
τ torsion stress
τ_S shear stress
α constant $\alpha = 3$ for HMH
$\alpha = 4$ for Tresca-Guest

- Now, we need to apply loads and supports for our calculations. To apply a load, select the **Loads** option from the drop-down in the **Loads & Supports** area of the dialog box; refer to Figure-47. The buttons in the **Loads & Supports** area are displayed as shown in Figure-48.

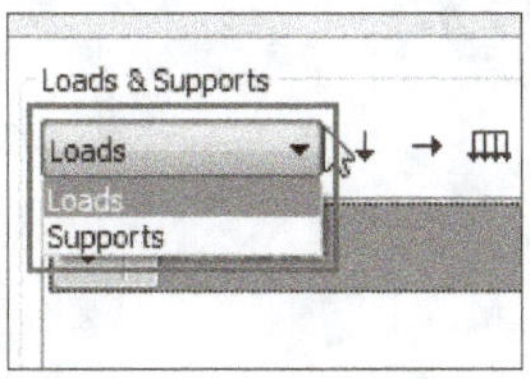

Figure-47. Drop-down in Loads & Supports area

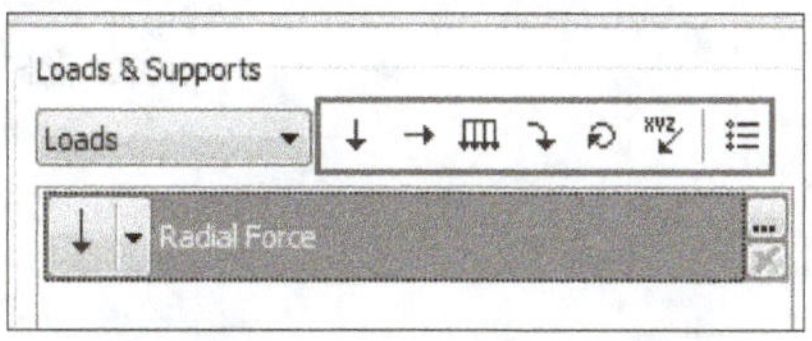

Figure-48. Buttons in the Loads & Supports area

- Click on desired point on which you want to apply load from the **2D Preview** area of the dialog box; refer to Figure-49.

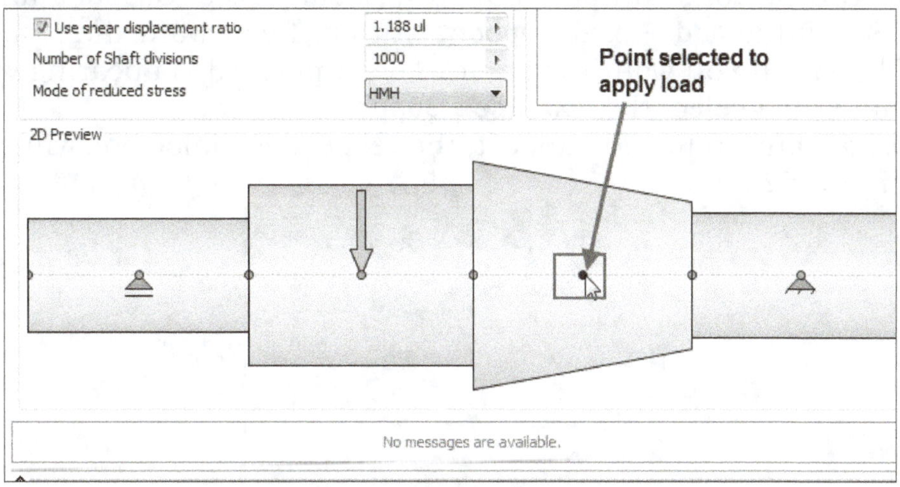

Figure-49. Selecting point to apply load

- Click on desired button to apply respective force. There are six types of loads that can be applied; Radial Force, Axial Force, Continuous Load, Bending Moment, Torque, and Common Load. On clicking at the button, respective dialog box will be displayed. Like, we have selected **Add Axial Force** button from the **Loads & Supports** area. The **Axial Force** dialog box will be displayed; refer to Figure-50.

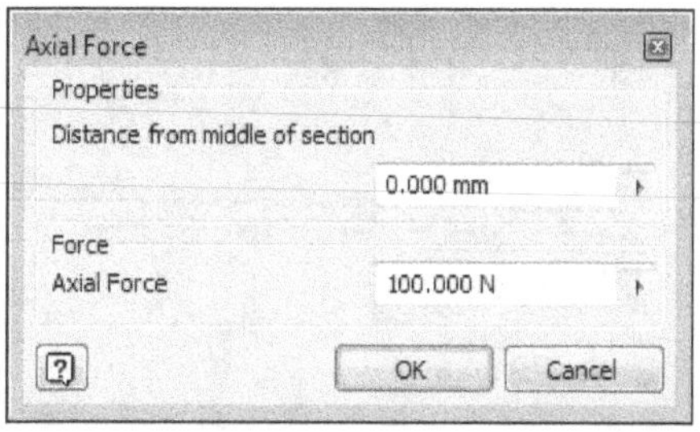

Figure-50. Axial Force dialog box

- Specify desired parameters in the dialog box and click on the **OK** button to exit. The load with specified parameters will be applied. Note that if you are applying Torque then you must apply equal and opposite torque at other point of shaft to form the equilibrium equation for stress calculations.
- To add support to the shaft, click on the drop-down in the **Loads & Supports** area and select the **Supports** option. The buttons in the area will be displayed as shown in Figure-51.

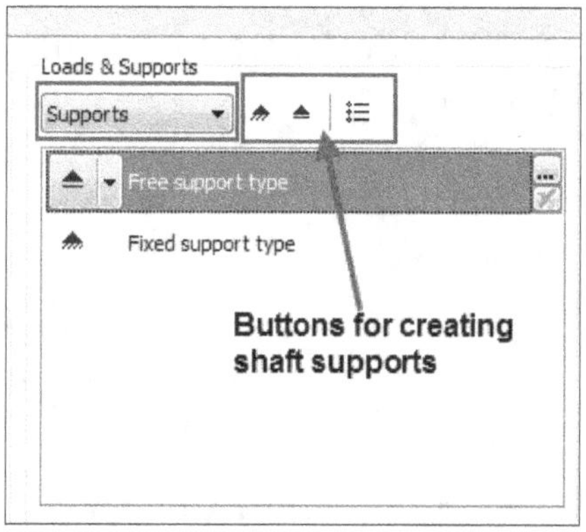

Figure-51. Creating shaft supports

- There are two buttons to apply supports; **Add Fixed Support** and **Add Free Support**. Select the **Add Fixed Support** button if you want the shaft to be fixed at desired point. If you want the shaft to be supported via bearing which means free to rotate then select the **Add Free Support** button.
- On selecting a button to add support, the respective dialog box will be displayed; refer to Figure-52.

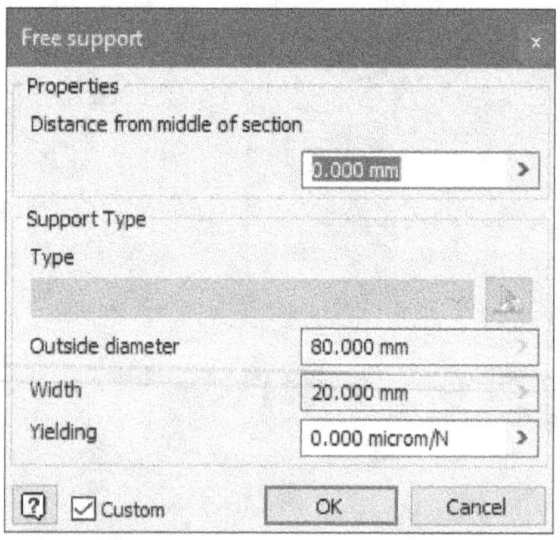

Figure-52. Free Support dialog box

- Specify desired parameters in the dialog box and click on the **OK** button. The support will be added to the shaft.
- Click on the **Calculate** button from the dialog box. The related results will be displayed in the right area of the dialog box. Note that you may need to double-click on the splitter to expand dialog box for checking results.
- Change the parameters if there is any error in the results then perform the related modification in shaft.
- Click on the **Graphs** tab to check the results graphically; refer to Figure-53.

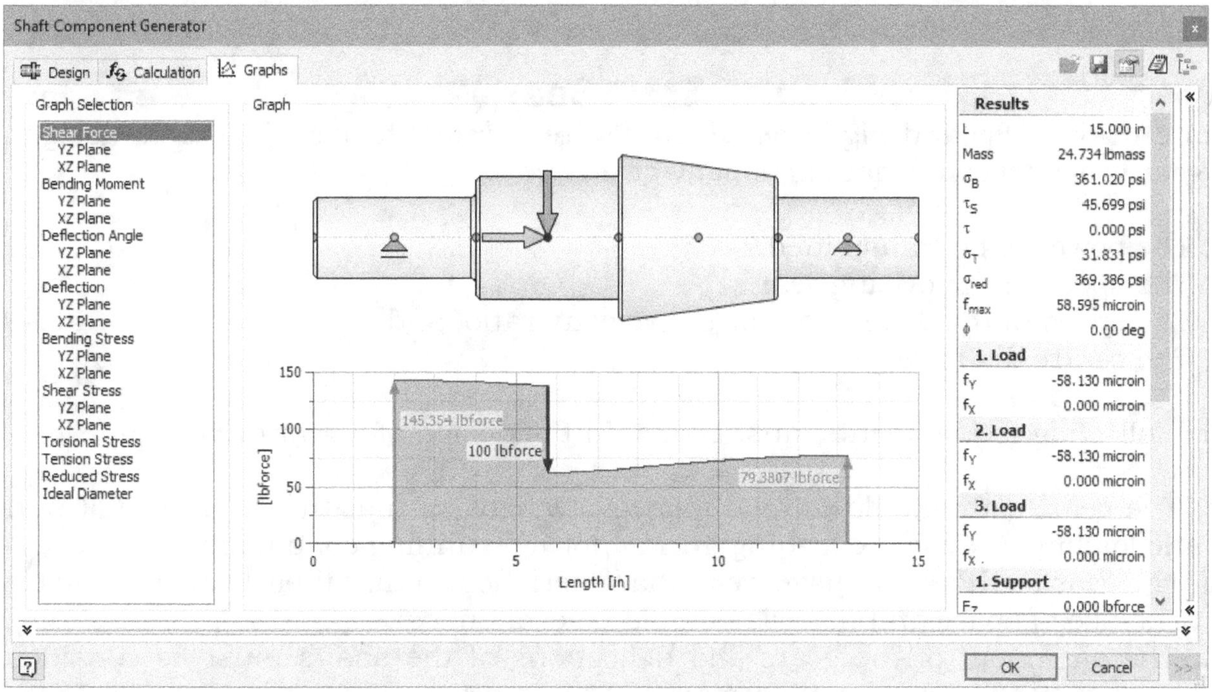

Figure-53. Graphs tab in the dialog box

- Click on the **OK** button from the dialog box to create the shaft.

Finding Torque

Most of the time in real world problems, you will get the load in Watt and RPM like, a shaft need to transfer 20KW load at 200 RPM. In such cases, you need to convert this value into torque. The formula is given next.

$$T = \frac{P \times 60}{2\pi N}$$

Here, T is torque, P is the power to be transferred, and N is the RPM.

After getting the torque value, you can apply it on the model to test the failure of shaft.

> Example, A line shaft rotating at 200 r.p.m. is to transmit 20 kW. The shaft may be assumed to be made of mild steel with an allowable shear stress of 42 MPa. Determine the diameter of the shaft, neglecting the bending moment on the shaft.

Finding Bending Moment

Sometimes, you will get the problems like a load of 50kN is working at a distance of 100 mm outside the wheelbase. In such cases, you need to find out the bending moment by using the formula,

$$M = W \times L$$

Here, M is the bending moment, W is the load, and L is the distance from wheelbase.

Example, A pair of wheels of a railway wagon carries a load of 50 kN on each axle box, acting at a distance of 100 mm outside the wheel base. The gauge of the rails is 1.4 m. Find the diameter of the axle between the wheels, if the stress is not to exceed 100 MPa.

Spur Gear

For any kind of gear design, there are a few requirements of designers. In designing a gear drive, following data is usually given :

1. The power to be transmitted,
2. The speed of the driving gear,
3. The speed of the driven gear or the velocity ratio, and
4. The centre distance.

The following requirements must be met in the design of a gear drive :

(a) The gear teeth should have sufficient strength so that they will not fail under static loading or dynamic loading during normal running conditions.
(b) The gear teeth should have wear characteristics so that their life is satisfactory.
(c) The use of space and material should be economical.
(d) The alignment of the gears and deflections of the shafts must be considered because they effect on the performance of the gears.
(e) The lubrication of the gears must be satisfactory.

The different modes of failure of gear teeth and their possible remedies to avoid the failure, are as follows :

1. **Bending failure**. Every gear tooth acts as a cantilever. If the total repetitive dynamic load acting on the gear tooth is greater than the beam strength of the gear tooth then the gear tooth will fail in bending, i.e. the gear tooth will break. In order to avoid such failure, the module and face width of the gear is adjusted so that the beam strength is greater than the dynamic load.

2. **Pitting**. It is the surface fatigue failure which occurs due to many repetition of Hertz contact stresses. The failure occurs when the surface contact stresses are higher than the endurance limit of the material. The failure starts with the formation of pits which continue to grow resulting in the rupture of the tooth surface. In order to avoid the pitting, the dynamic load between the gear tooth should be less than the wear strength of the gear tooth.

3. **Scoring**. The excessive heat is generated when there is an excessive surface pressure, high speed, or supply of lubricant fails. It is a stick-slip phenomenon in which alternate shearing and welding takes place rapidly at high spots. This type of failure can be avoided by properly designing the parameters such as speed, pressure, and proper flow of the lubricant, so that the temperature at the rubbing faces is within the permissible limits.

4. **Abrasive wear**. The foreign particles in the lubricants such as dirt, dust, or burr enter between the tooth and damage the form of tooth. This type of failure can be avoided by providing filters for the lubricating oil or by using high viscosity lubricant oil which enables the formation of thicker oil film and hence permits easy passage of such particles without damaging the gear surface.

5. **Corrosive wear**. The corrosion of the tooth surfaces is mainly caused due to the presence of corrosive elements such as additives present in the lubricating oils. In order to avoid this type of wear, proper anti-corrosive additives should be used.

Designing Spur Gear

In order to design spur gears, the following procedure may be followed :

The design tangential tooth load is obtained from the power transmitted and the pitch line velocity by using the following relation :

$$W_T = \frac{P}{v} \times C_S$$

where W_T = Permissible tangential tooth load in newtons,
P = Power transmitted in watts,
v = Pitch line velocity in m / s = (πDN)/60
D = Pitch circle diameter in metres,

We know that circular pitch,

$p_c = \pi D / T = \pi m$
D = m.T

Thus, the pitch line velocity may also be obtained by using the following relation, i.e.

$$v = \frac{\pi D.N}{60} = \frac{\pi m.T.N}{60} = \frac{p_c.T.N}{60}$$

where, m = Module in metres, and
T = Number of teeth.

Now, we will learn the procedure to create spur gears in Autodesk Inventor.

- Click on the **Spur Gear** tool from the **Gear** drop-down in the **Power Transmission** panel of **Design** tab in the **Ribbon**. The **Spur Gears Component Generator** dialog box will be displayed; refer to Figure-54.

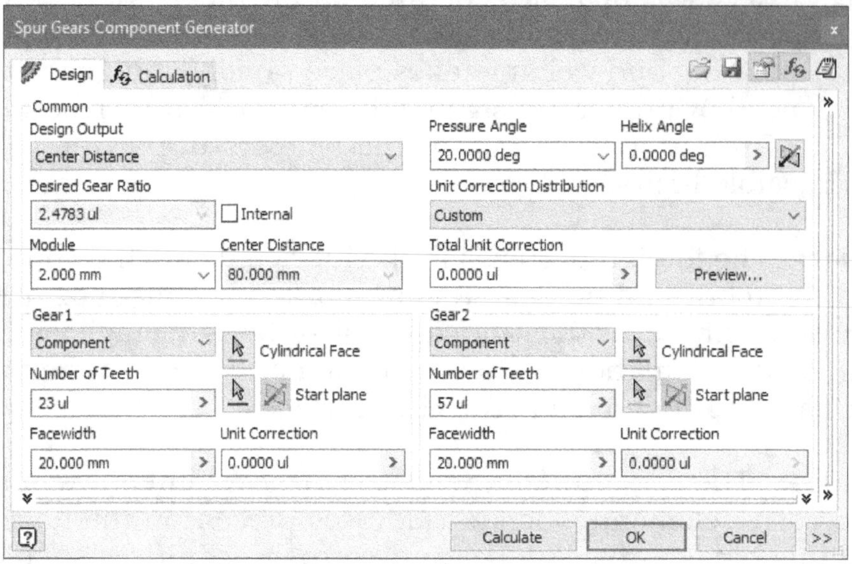

Figure-54. Spur Gear Component Generator dialog box

- Click in the **Design Output** drop-down in the **Common** area of **Design** tab in the dialog box. The options in the drop-down will be displayed as shown in Figure-55.

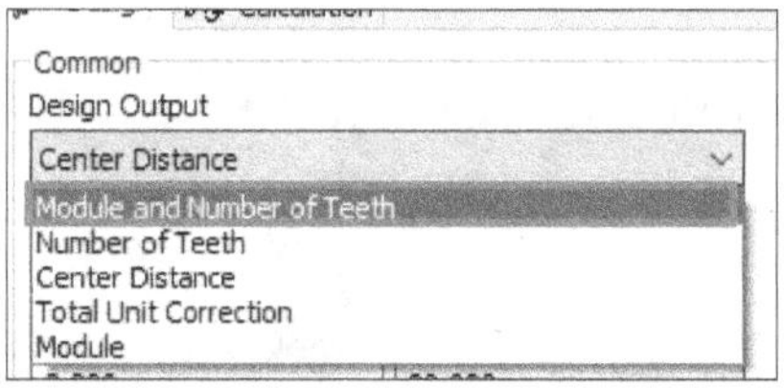

Figure-55. Design Output drop-down

- Select desired option from the drop-down. The parameters in the dialog box will be activated accordingly. Select only that option from the drop-down which you want to make variable. For example, if you select the **Module and Number of Teeth** option from drop-down then system will find out the module and number of teeth based on the parameters specified by you. If you know all the parameters of gear then you should select the **Total Unit Correction** option from the drop-down.
- Specify desired value of gear ratio, module, and center distance in the edit boxes. In engineering equations, gear ratio is given by $G = T_2/T_1$ where T_1 is number of teeth on first gear and T_2 is number of teeth on second gear. Module is given by m = (Pitch Circle Dia.)/ Number of teeth. The **Center Distance** is distance between centers of two mating gears.
- Click on the drop-down in **Gear 1** area of the dialog box and select desired option; refer to Figure-56. If you select the **Component** option from the drop-down then a new component for gear will be created. If you select the **Feature** option then gear will be created as featured on existing disc. If you selected **No Model** option then no model will be created.

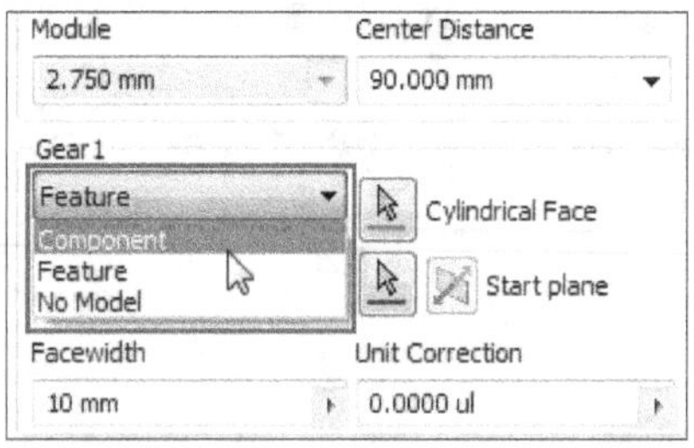

Figure-56. Drop-down in Gear 1 area

Creating Gear Component

- Select the **Component** option from the drop-down in the **Gear 1** area of the dialog box. The related options will be displayed in the area.
- Click in the **Facewidth** edit box and specify desired value. Note that facewidth is the thickness of gear from starting face to end face.
- Click on the **Cylindrical Face** selection button and select a face or axis to position the gear.
- Now, click on the **Start Plane** selection button and select the start face/plane for gear. Preview of the gear will be displayed; refer to Figure-57.

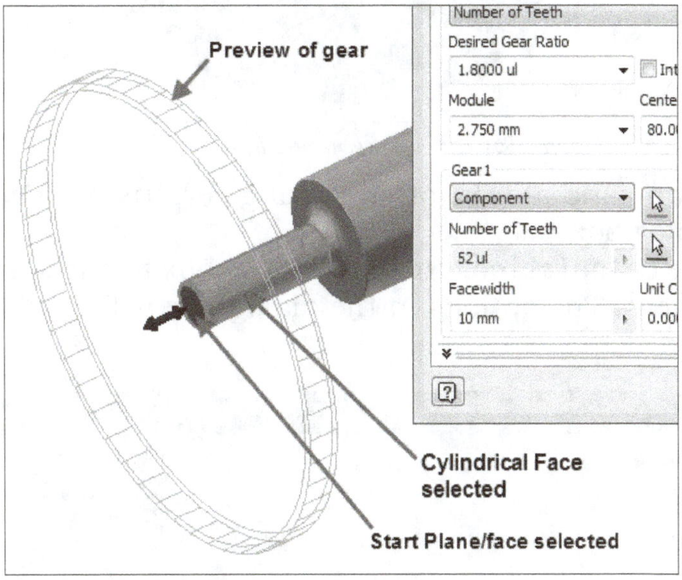

Figure-57. Preview of gear

- Specify the other parameters like number of teeth, center distance, module, etc. based on option selected in the **Design Guide** drop-down in the dialog box.

Creating Gear Feature

- Select the **Feature** option from the drop-down in the **Gear 1** area of the dialog box. The related options will be displayed in the area.
- Click in the **Facewidth** edit box and specify desired value.
- Click on the **Cylindrical Face** selection button and select a face or axis to position the gear.
- Now, click on the **Start Plane** selection button and select the start face/plane for gear. Preview of the gear will be displayed; refer to Figure-58.

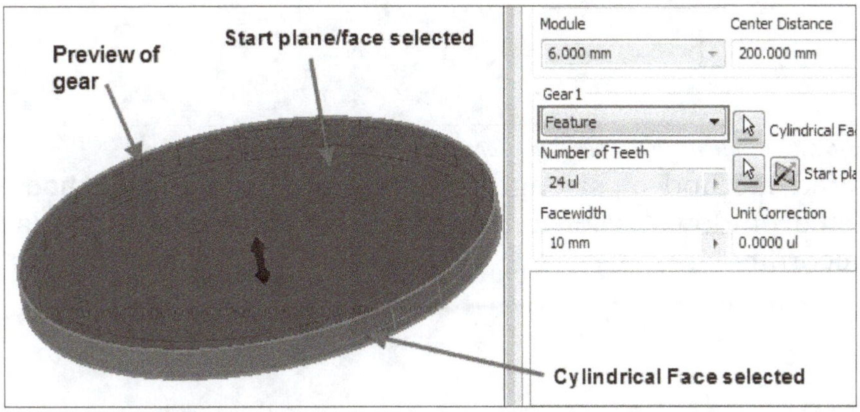

Figure-58. Creating gear feature

- Specify the other parameters like number of teeth, center distance, module, etc. based on option selected in the **Design Guide** drop-down in the dialog box.
- Note that you can also cut partial teeth on the disc by taking lesser facewidth in this method; refer to Figure-59.

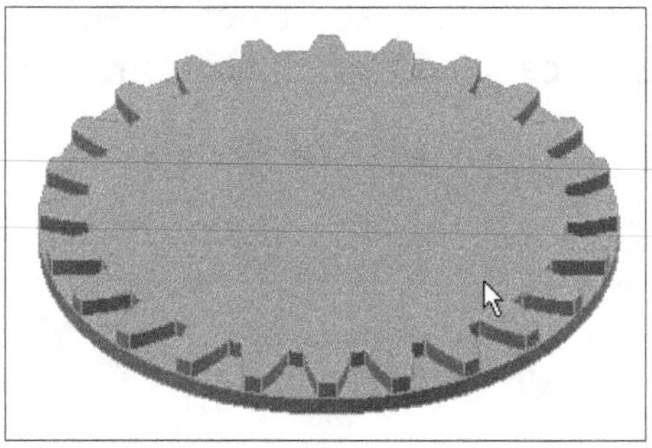

Figure-59. Gear feature generated by lesser face width

- Similarly, you can generate the other mating gear using the options in the **Gear 2** area of the dialog box.
- Now, click on the **Calculation** tab in the dialog box to check the feasibility of gear in real environment. The options in the dialog box will be displayed as shown in Figure-60.

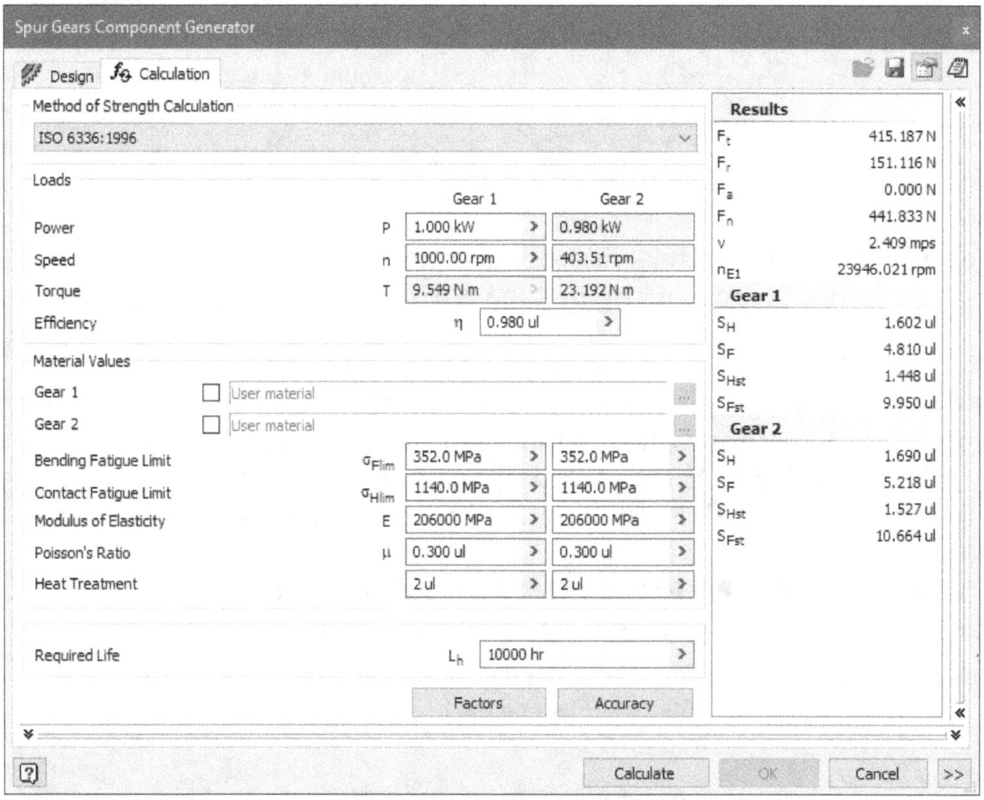

Figure-60. Calculation tab in Spur Gear Component Generator dialog box

- Select desired method of strength calculation from the **Method of Strength Calculation** drop-down; refer to Figure-61. The options in the dialog box will be modified accordingly.

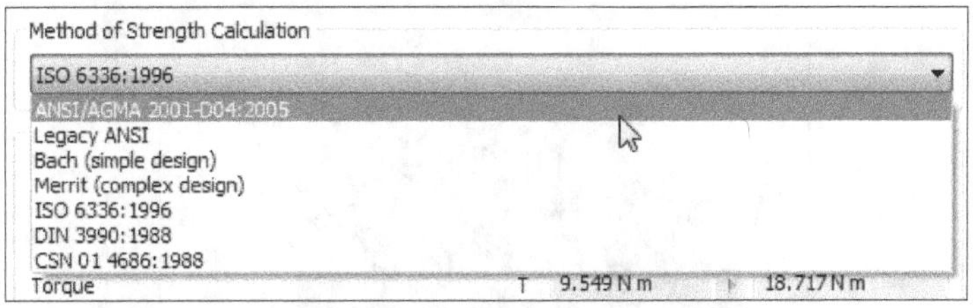

Figure-61. Method of Strength Calculation drop-down

- Specify the parameters related to load in the **Loads** area and parameters related to material in the **Material Values** area.
- Click on the **Calculate** button from the dialog box to check the feasibility of gear under specified load.
- Modify the gear if problems are displayed in the **Results** pane of dialog box and click on the **OK** button to create the gear.
- If you want to modify the minimum Factor of Safety and type of loading calculations then expand the dialog box by clicking on the **More options** button and specify desired values; refer to Figure-62.

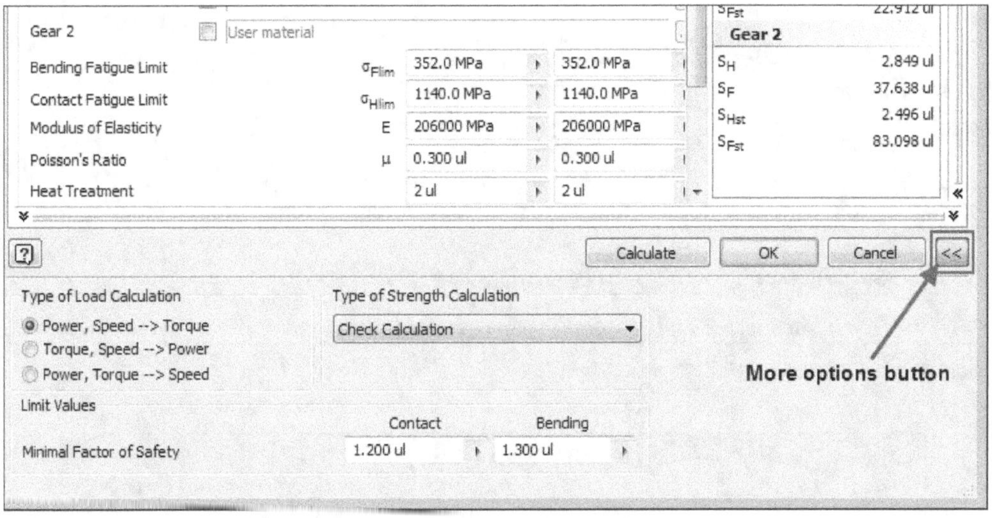

Figure-62. Expanded Spur Gear Component Generator dialog box

Designing Worm Gear

The Worm gear arrangement is used when large speed reduction is required. It is common for worm gears to have reductions of 20:1 and even up to 300:1 or greater. In a worm gear arrangement, there is one worm created on shaft and a worm gear. The axis of rotation of worm and worm gear is generally perpendicular to each other; refer to Figure-63.

The worm gearing is classified as non-interchangeable, because a worm wheel cut with a hob of one diameter will not operate satisfactorily with a worm of different diameter, even if the thread pitch is same. The following are two types of worms :

1. Cylindrical or straight worm and
2. Cone or double enveloping worm. Refer to Figure-64.

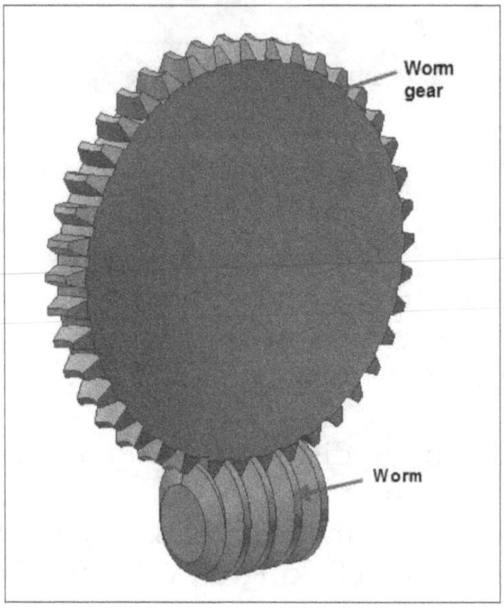

Figure-63. Worm gear arrangement

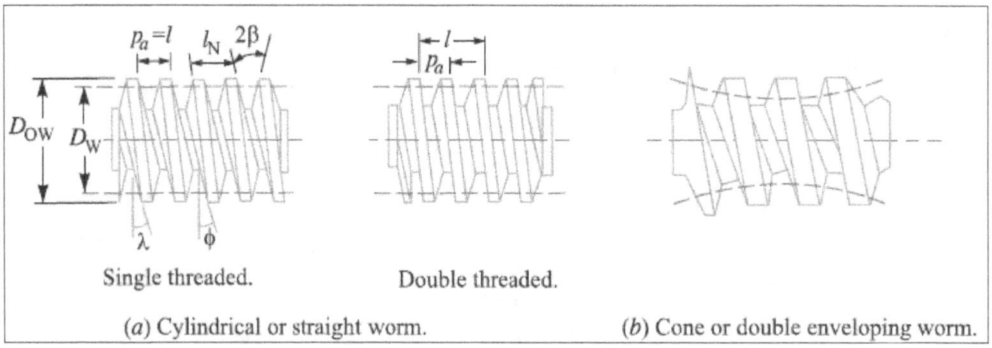

Figure-64. Type of worms

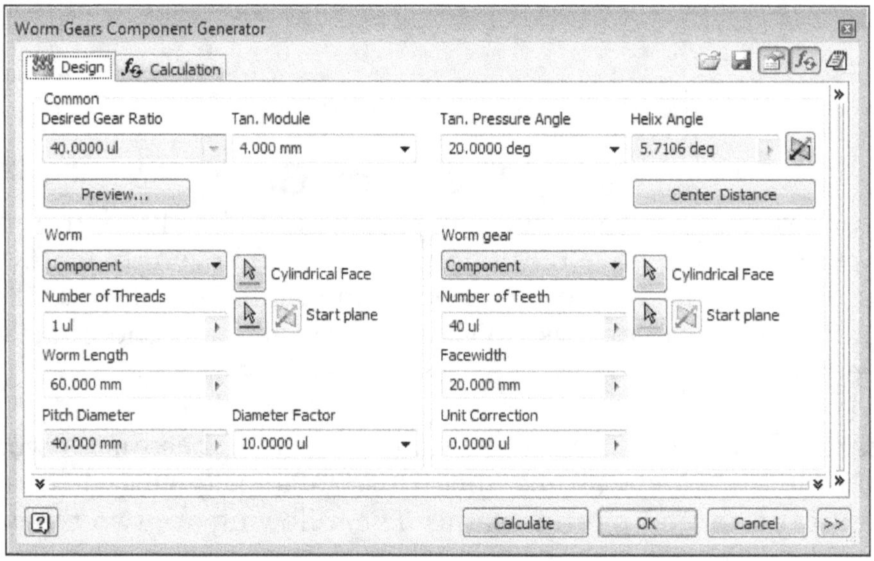

Figure-65. Worm Gears Component Generator dialog box

The procedure to create worm gear is given next.

- Click on the **Worm Gear** tool from the **Gear** drop-down in the **Power Transmission** panel of the **Design** tab in the **Ribbon**. The **Worm Gears Component Generator** dialog box will be displayed; refer to Figure-65.

- Specify the parameters as discussed earlier for spur gear. Note that you cannot specify the gear ratio directly for worm gear in the dialog box but you can change the value of number of teeth in worm gear or number of threads on worm to change the gear ratio.
- Click on the **Calculation** tab to modify the load parameters or material parameters.
- Click on the **Calculate** button from the dialog box. If errors are displayed then change the parameters accordingly.
- Click on the **OK** button to create the worm gear system.

Designing Bevel Gear

The Bevel gears are used for transmitting power at a constant velocity ratio between two shafts whose axes intersect at a certain angle. The pitch surfaces for the bevel gear are frustums of cones; refer to Figure-66.

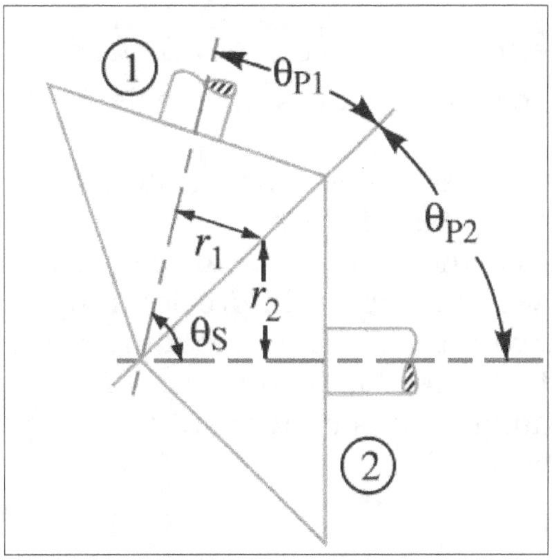

Figure-66. Bevel gear arrangement

Here, r_1 and r_2 are radii of gear 1 and gear 2, respectively.
Θ_{P1} and Θ_{P2} are cone angle for gears
and, Θ_S is shaft angle.

The procedure to create bevel gears is given next.

- Click on the **Bevel Gear** tool from the **Gear** drop-down in the **Power Transmission** panel of the **Design** tab in the **Ribbon**. The **Bevel Gears Component Generator** dialog box will be displayed; refer to Figure-67.

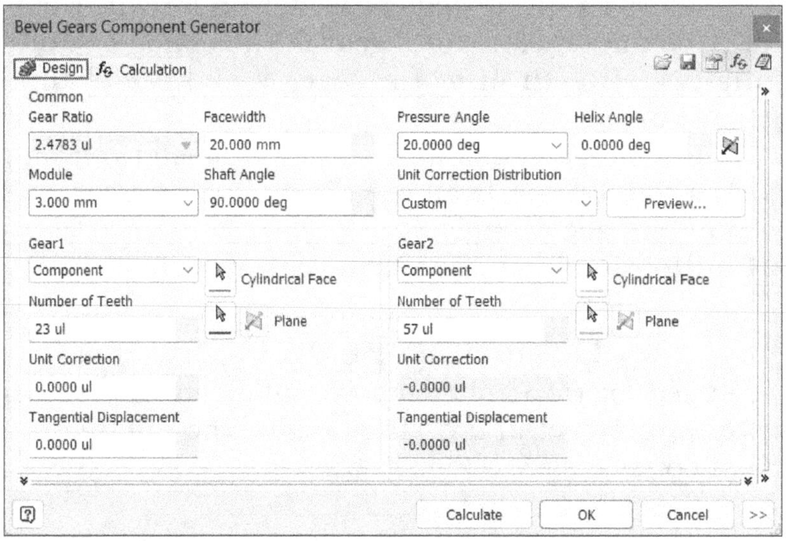

Figure-67. Bevel Gears Component Generator dialog box

- Specify the module, face width, and shaft angle in the respective edit boxes in the dialog box.
- Set the number of teeth for both the gears. Note that gear ratio will be calculated based on the specified number of teeth.
- Select the cylindrical face and start plane for gear 1 and gear 2 if required. These options have already been discussed in previous topics.
- Click on the **Calculation** tab and set the loading & material parameters.
- Click on the **Calculate** button. If results are fine then click on the **OK** button otherwise make the changes as per the results. The bevel gear arrangement will be created; refer to Figure-68.

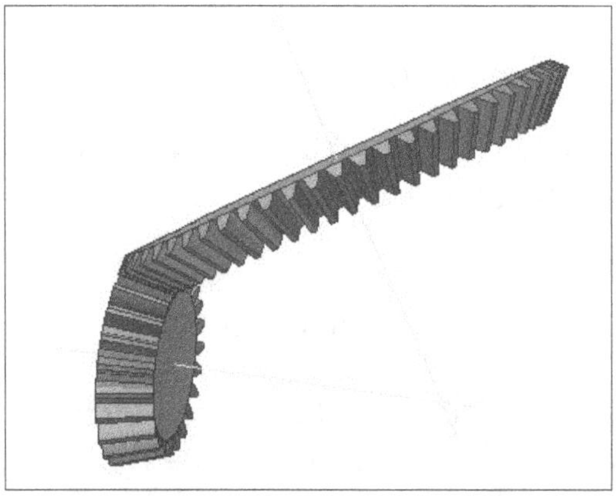

Figure-68. Bevel gear

Designing Bearing

A bearing is a machine element which support another moving machine element (known as journal). It permits a relative motion between the contact surfaces of the members, while carrying the load. A little consideration will show that due to the relative motion between the contact surfaces, a certain amount of power is wasted in overcoming frictional resistance and if the rubbing surfaces are in direct contact, there will be rapid wear. In order to reduce frictional resistance and wear and in some cases to carry away the heat generated, a layer of fluid (known as lubricant) may be provided. The lubricant used to separate the journal and bearing is usually a mineral oil refined from petroleum, but vegetable oils, silicon oils, greases, etc., may be used. Bearings are broadly classified in two ways:

Depending upon the direction of load to be supported. The bearings under this group are classified as:

(a) Radial bearings, and (b) Thrust bearings.

In radial bearings, the load acts perpendicular to the direction of motion of the moving element as shown in Figure-69.

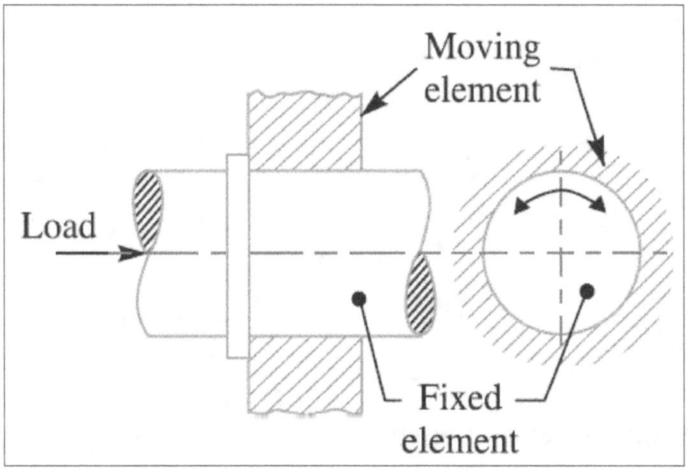

Figure-69. Radial Bearing

In thrust bearings, the load acts along the axis of rotation as shown in Figure-70.

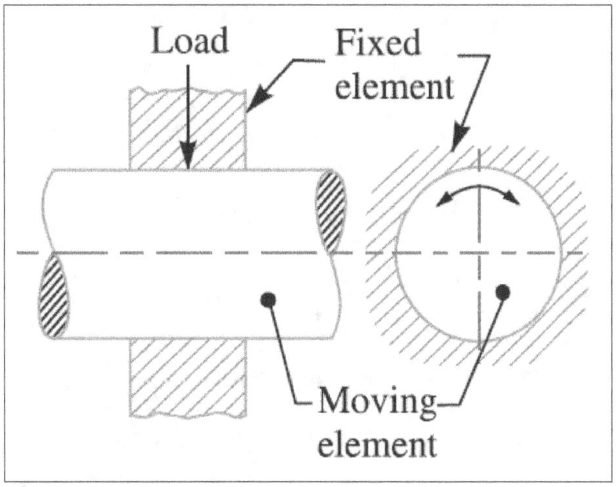

Figure-70. Thrust Bearing

Depending upon the nature of contact. The bearings under this group are classified as :
(a) Sliding contact bearings, and (b) Rolling contact bearings.

In sliding contact bearings, as shown in Figure-71, the sliding takes place along the surfaces of contact between the moving element and the fixed element. The sliding contact bearings are also known as plain bearings.

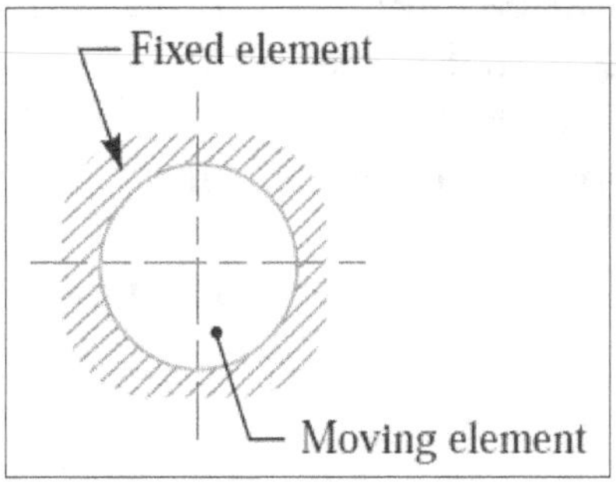

Figure-71. Sliding Contact Bearing

In rolling contact bearings, as shown in Figure-72, the steel balls or rollers, are interposed between the moving and fixed elements. The balls offer rolling friction at two points for each ball or roller.

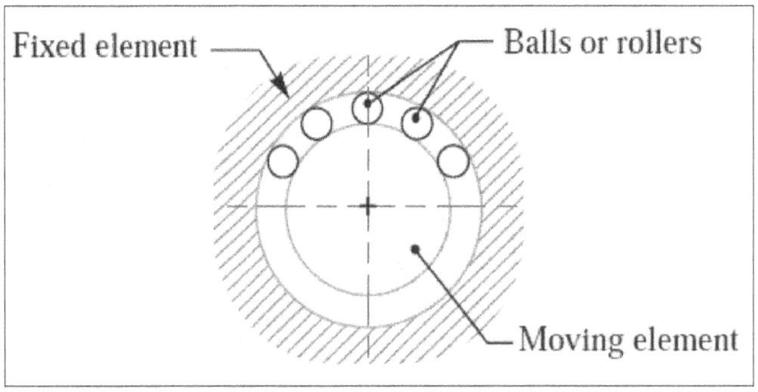

Figure-72. Rolling Contact Bearing

The procedure to design various bearings in Autodesk Inventor is given next.

- Click on the **Bearing** tool from the **Power Transmission** panel in the **Design** tab of the **Ribbon**. The **Bearing Generator** dialog box will be displayed; refer to Figure-73.

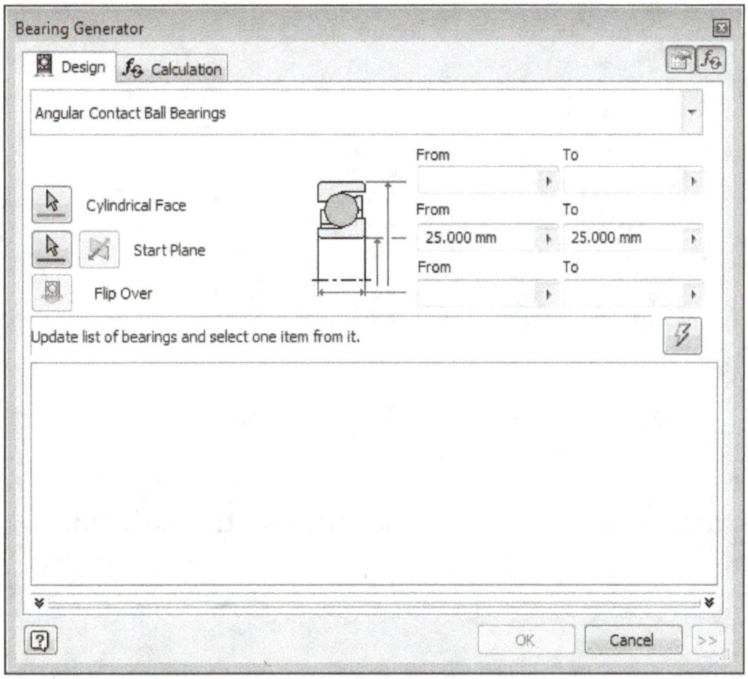

Figure-73. Bearing Generator dialog box

- Click on the **Angular Contact Ball Bearings (Browse for bearing)** drop-down at the top in the dialog box. The Content center for bearing will be displayed; refer to Figure-74.

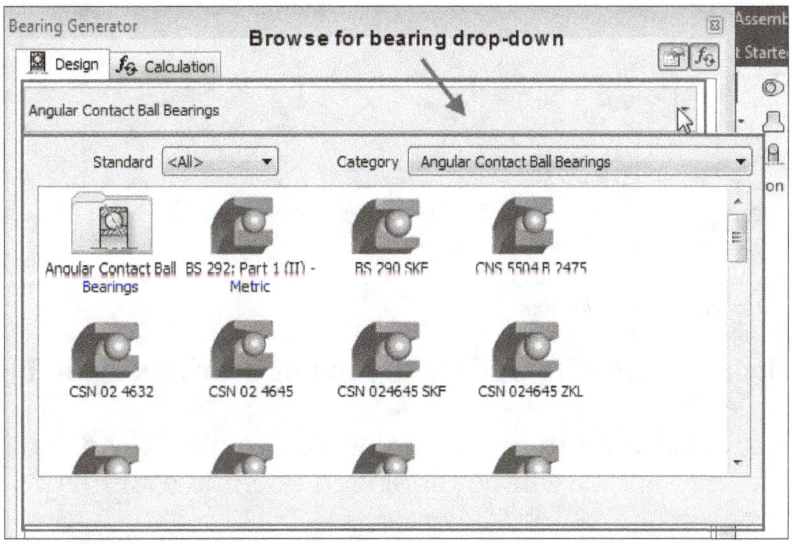

Figure-74. Content Center for Bearing

- Select desired standard and category of bearings from the **Standard** and **Category** drop-down in the Content center. List of short listed bearings will be displayed.
- Select the folder of bearing from the Content center; refer to Figure-75.

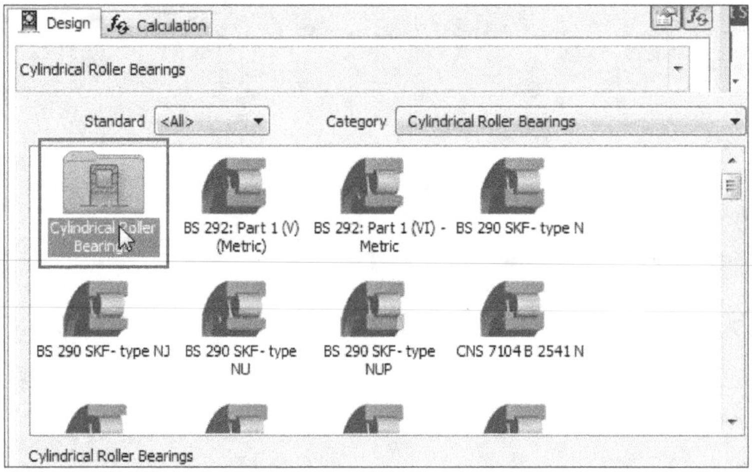

Figure-75. Folder for Bearings

- Specify the parameters for sizing of bearing in the edit boxes in the dialog box; refer to Figure-76.

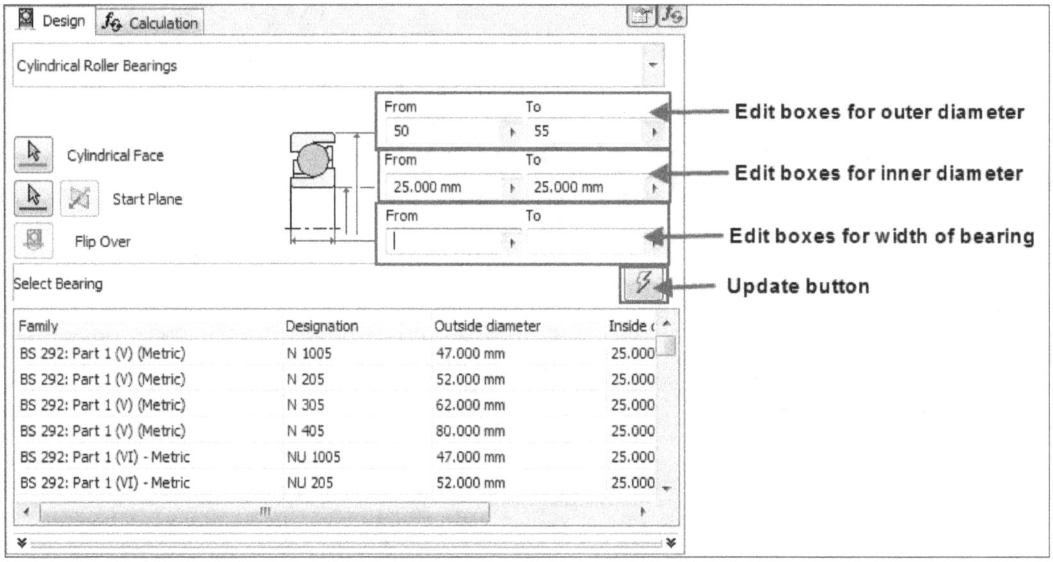

Figure-76. Parameters for sizing bearing

- Click on the **Update** button to update the list of bearings available in the Content center.
- Click on the **Calculation** tab in the dialog box to check the feasibility of bearing under load. The dialog box will be displayed as shown in Figure-77.

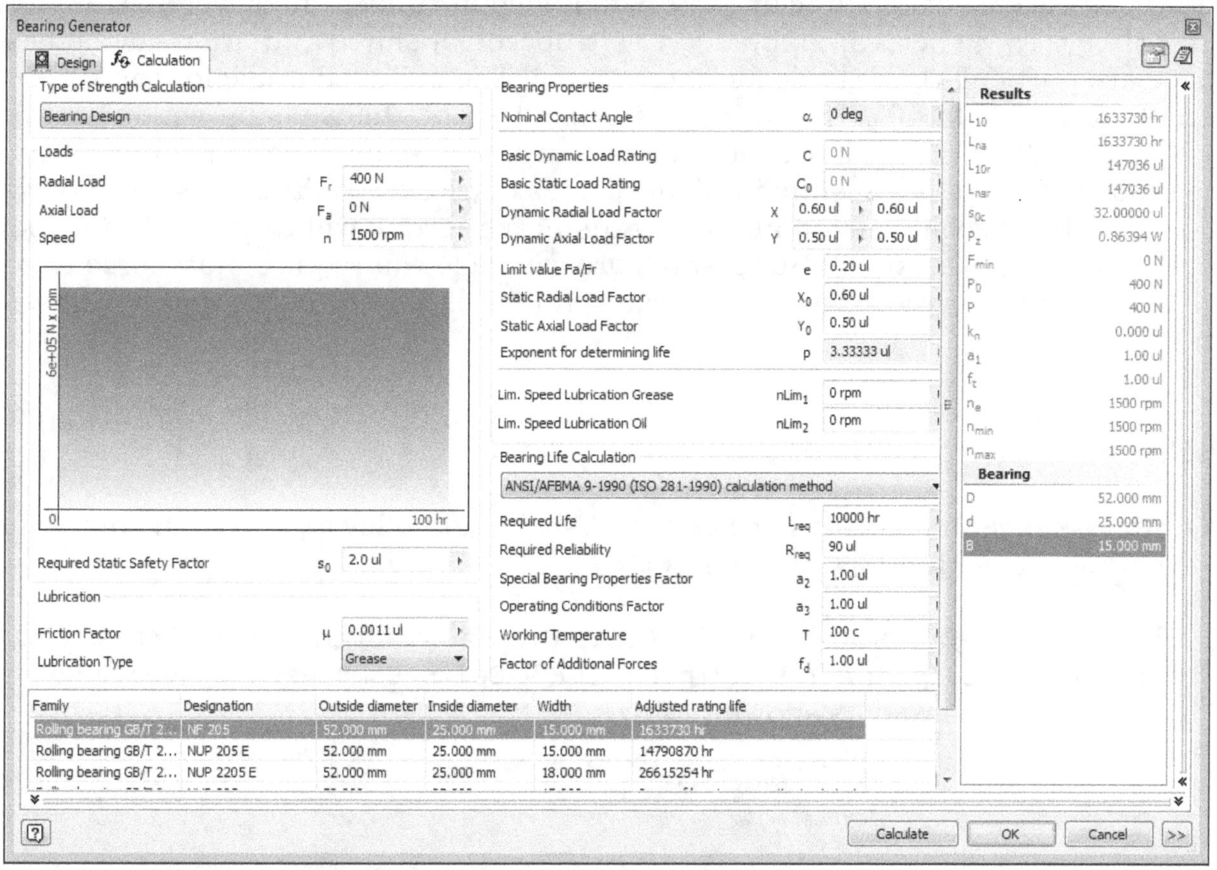

Figure-77. Calculation tab in Bearing Generator dialog box

- Specify the loading parameters and then click on the **Calculate** button. List of bearings qualifying the loading conditions will be displayed in the list at bottom in the dialog box.
- Select the suitable bearing and then click on the **OK** button. The bearing will get attached to the cursor. Click at desired location to place the bearing.

Designing V-Belts

The pulleys are used to transmit power from one shaft to another by means of flat belts, V-belts, or ropes. Since the velocity ratio is the inverse ratio of the diameters of driving and driven pulleys, therefore the pulley diameters should be carefully selected in order to have a desired velocity ratio. The pulleys must be in perfect alignment in order to allow the belt to travel in a line normal to the pulley faces. The pulleys may be made of cast iron, cast steel or pressed steel, wood, and paper. The cast materials should have good friction and wear characteristics. The pulleys made of pressed steel are lighter than cast pulleys, but in many cases they have lower friction and may produce excessive wear.

The V-belts are made of fabric and cords moulded in rubber and covered with fabric and rubber. These belts are moulded to a trapezoidal shape and are made endless. These are particularly suitable for short drives. The included angle for the V-belt is usually from 30° to 40°. The power is transmitted by the wedging action between the belt and the V-groove in the pulley or sheave. The wedging action of the V-belt in the groove of the pulley results in higher forces of friction. A little consideration will show that the wedging action and the transmitted torque will be more if the groove angle of the pulley is small. But a small groove angle will require more force to pull the belt out of the groove which will result in loss of power and excessive belt wear due to friction and heat.

Hence selecting groove angle is a compromise between the two. Usually, the groove angles of 32° to 38° are used.

In Autodesk Inventor, you can design both V-belt and pulley together. The procedure to create V-belt with pulley is given next.

- Click on the **V-Belts** tool from the **Belts** drop-down in the **Power Transmission** panel of the **Design** tab in the **Ribbon**. The **V-Belts Component Generator** dialog box will be displayed as shown in Figure-78.

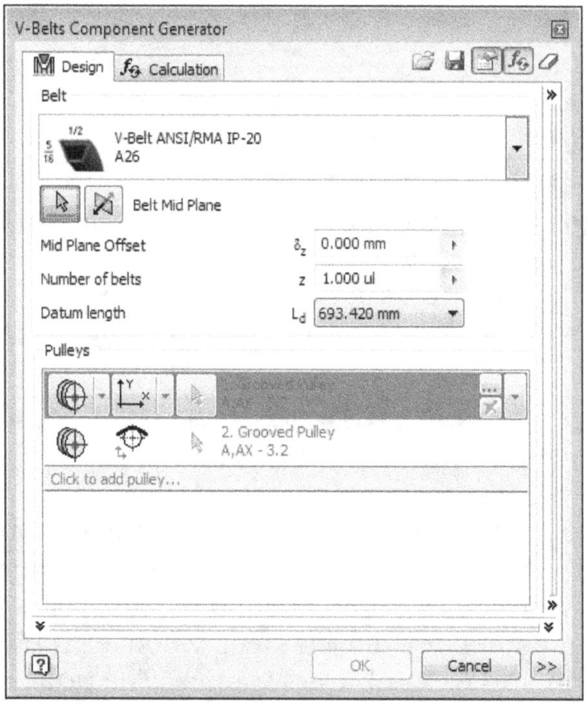

Figure-78. V-Belts Component Generator dialog box

- Click in the **Browse for belt type** drop-down at the top in the **Belt** area of dialog box and select desired belt type; refer to Figure-79.

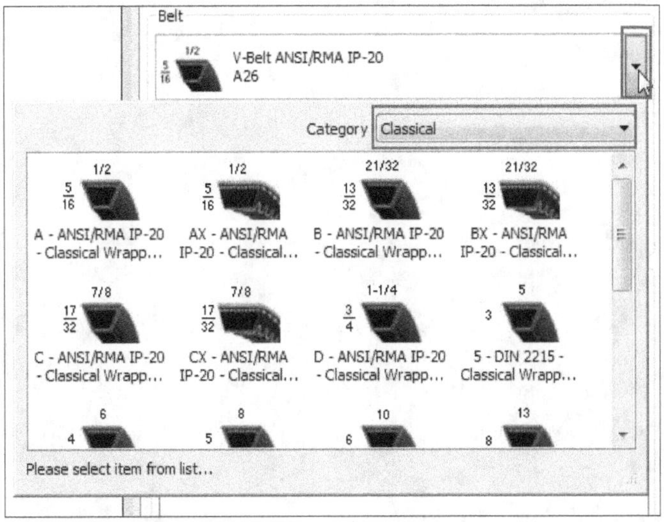

Figure-79. Browse for belt type drop-down

- Click on the selection button for **Belt Mid Plane** and select the middle plane/ face for belt and pulley creation. Preview of the belt and pulley will be displayed; refer to Figure-80.

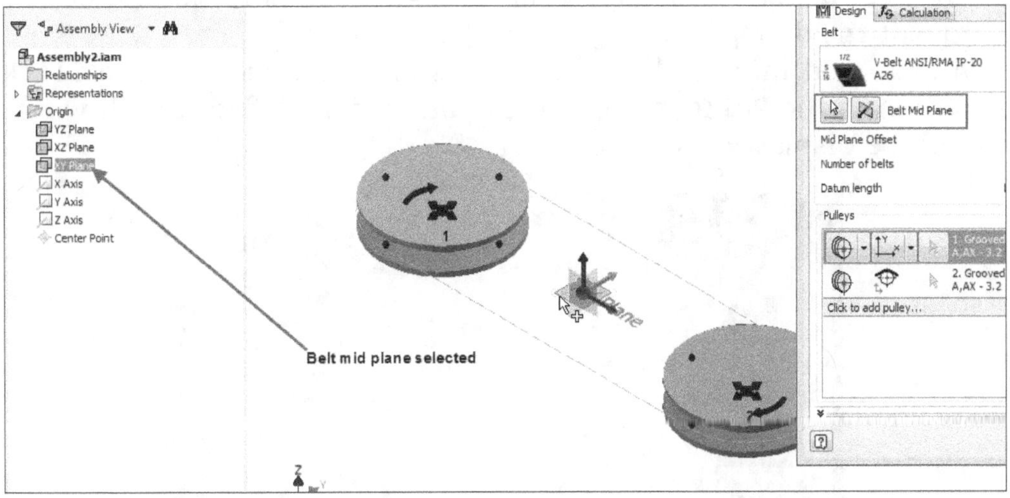

Figure-80. Mid plane selected for belt and pulley

- Specify the number of belts, datum length, and mid plane offset for the belt-pulley arrangement in the respective edit boxes.
- By default, two grooved pulleys are added in the system; refer to Figure-81. Double-click on the pulley from the **Pulleys** area to change its parameters using the **Groove pulley properties** dialog box; refer to Figure-82.

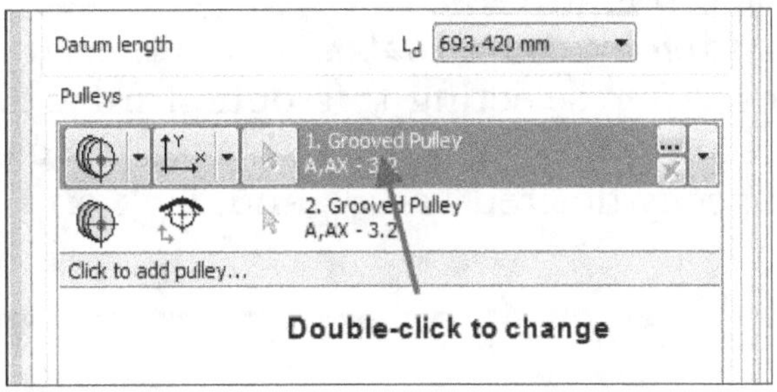

Figure-81. Pulleys

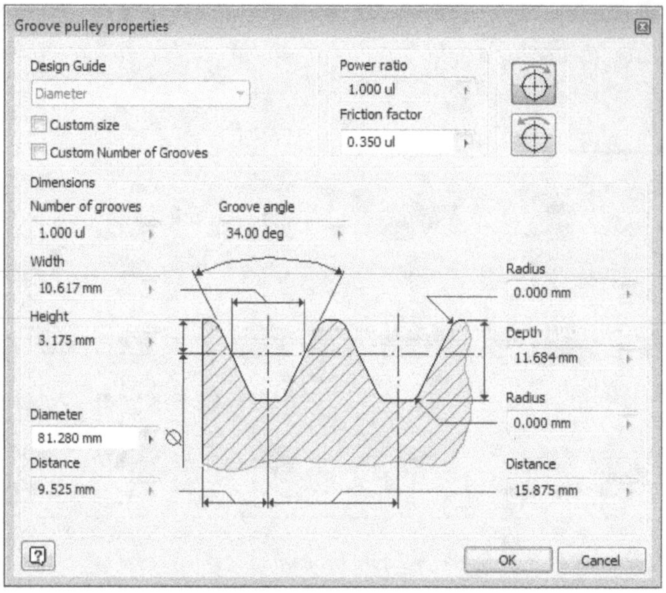

Figure-82. Groove pulley properties dialog box

- By default, you can change only the diameter of pulley and friction factor. If you want to change the other parameters then select the **Custom size** and **Custom Number of Grooves** check boxes. After changing the parameters, click on the **OK** button to exit the dialog box.
- If you want to add more pulleys in the system then click on the **Click to add pulley** option in the **Pulleys** area of the dialog box. A flyout with various pulley options will be displayed; refer to Figure-83.

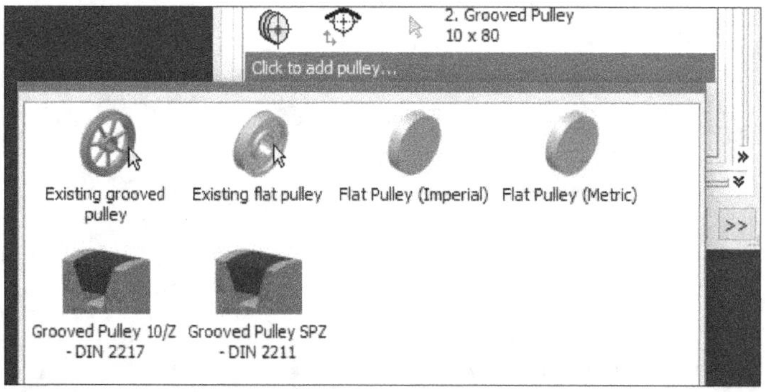

Figure-83. Flyout with various pulley options

- Select the **Grooved Pulley** option because we are creating pulley for V-belt. A new pulley will be added in the system. You can change the parameters of pulley as discussed earlier.
- To change the position of pulley, we have five options in the **Pulley placement guide** drop-down; refer to Figure-84.
- Select the **Fixed position by coordinates** option to change the position of pulley by giving coordinates. After selecting this option from drop-down, double-click on the move handles on pulley. The **Coordinates** dialog box will be displayed; refer to Figure-85. Specify desired values and click on the **OK** button to change the position of pulley.

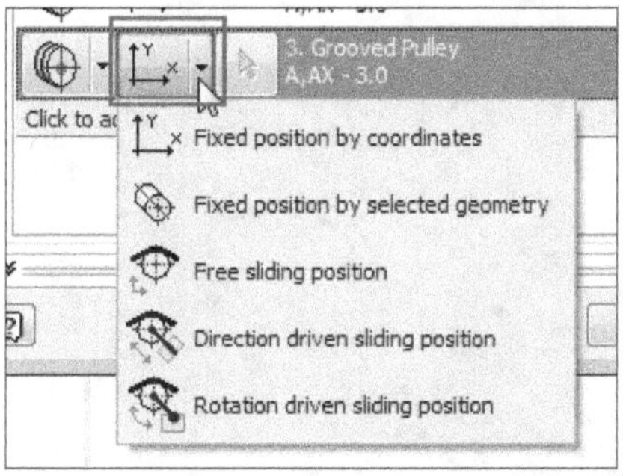

Figure-84. Pulley placement guide drop-down

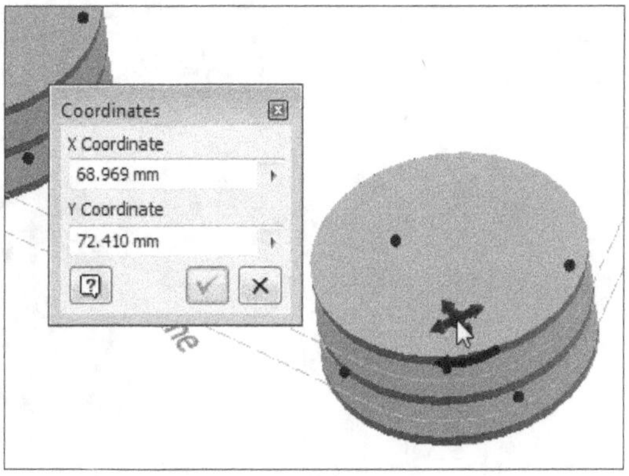

Figure-85. Coordinates dialog box

- Select the **Fixed position by selected geometry** option to place the pulley on selected geometry. You will be asked to select shaft axis, cylindrical or conical face, vertex, work point or work axis. Select desired geometry. The pulley will be placed accordingly.
- Select the **Free sliding position** option to freely move the pulley to desired location. On selecting this option, drag the pulley by using the move handles on the pulley; refer to Figure-86.

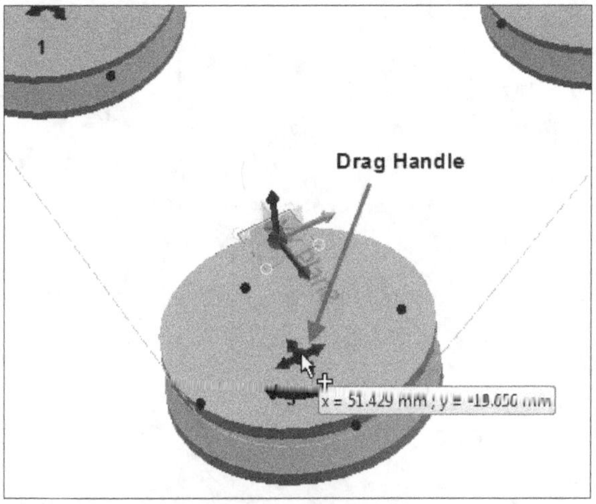

Figure-86. Drag handle on pulley

- Select the **Direction Driven Sliding Position** option to freely move the pulley along the selected plane or planar face. On selecting this option, you will be asked to select a sliding plane or planar face. Select a plane/planar face to be used as sliding plane. Drag handles will be displayed on the pulley. Move the pulley at desired location; refer to Figure-87. Note that pulley will automatically snap to the locations where belt lengths are available.

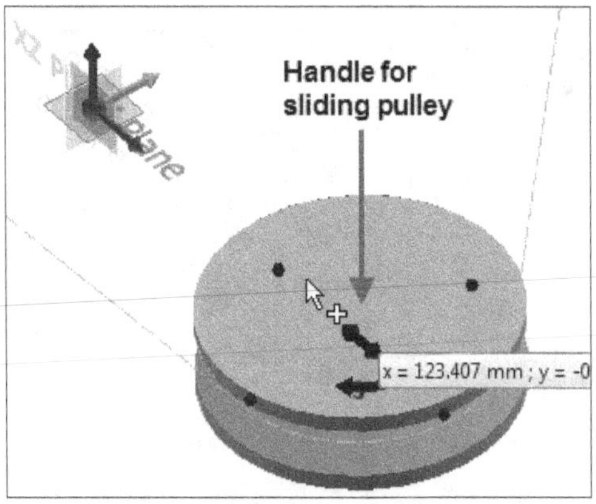

Figure-87. Handle for sliding along plane

- Similarly, select the **Rotation Driven Sliding Position** option to freely move the pulley around the selected axis.
- Click on the **Calculation** tab to check the feasibility of belt and pulley under specified load. The dialog box will be displayed; refer to Figure-88.

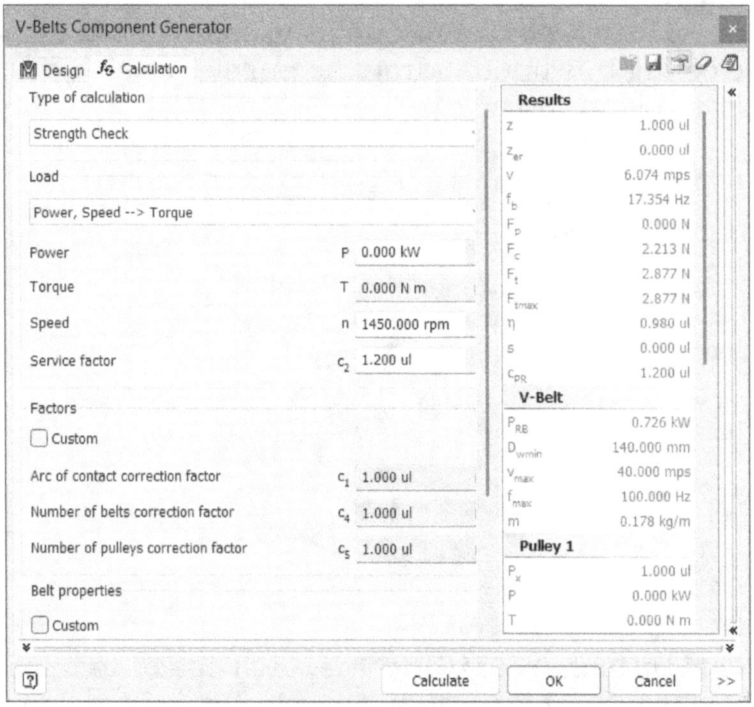

Figure-88. Calculation tab in V-Belts Component Generator dialog box

- Specify various parameters related to loading and belt properties.
- Click on the **Calculate** button. Modify the belt and pulley if error is displayed and then click on the **OK** button to create the V-belt system.

Designing Synchronous Belts

The synchronous belt, also called timing belt, toothed belt, cogged belt or cog belt is used as a non-slipping mechanical drive belt. It is made as a flexible belt with teeth moulded onto its inner surface. It runs over matching toothed pulleys or sprockets; refer to Figure-89. The procedure to create synchronous belt transmission system is same as discussed for V-Belt.

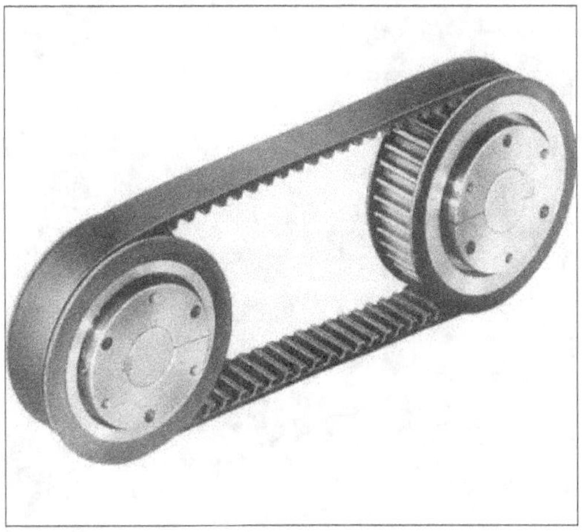

Figure-89. Synchoronous Belt

Designing Roller Chains

There is always some slippage in belt and rope transmission system. To avoid this slippage at shorter center distances, we use roller chain transmission system. In this system, the chains are made up of number of rigid links which are hinged together by pin joints in order to provide the necessary flexibility for wrapping around the driving and driven wheels.

These wheels have projecting teeth of special profile and fit into the corresponding recesses in the links of the chain as shown in Figure-90. The toothed wheels are known as sprocket wheels or simply sprockets. The sprockets and the chain are thus constrained to move together without slipping and ensures perfect velocity ratio.

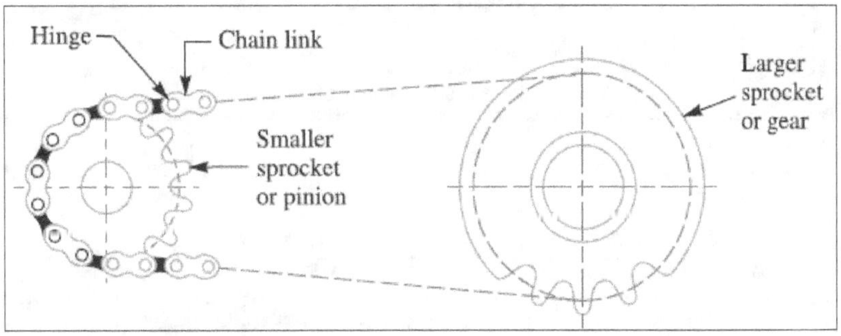

Figure-90. Roller Chain system

The chains are mostly used to transmit motion and power from one shaft to another, when the centre distance between their shafts is short such as in bicycles, motor cycles, agricultural machinery, conveyors, rolling mills, road rollers, etc. The chains may also be used for long centre distance of up to 8 metres. The chains are used for velocities up to 25 m/s and for power up to 110 kW. In some cases, higher power transmission is also possible.

The procedure to design roller chain system in Autodesk Inventor is given next.

- Click on the **Roller Chains** tool from the **Belts** drop-down in the **Power Transmission** panel of the **Design** tab in the **Ribbon**. The **Roller Chains Generator** dialog box will be displayed; refer to Figure-91.

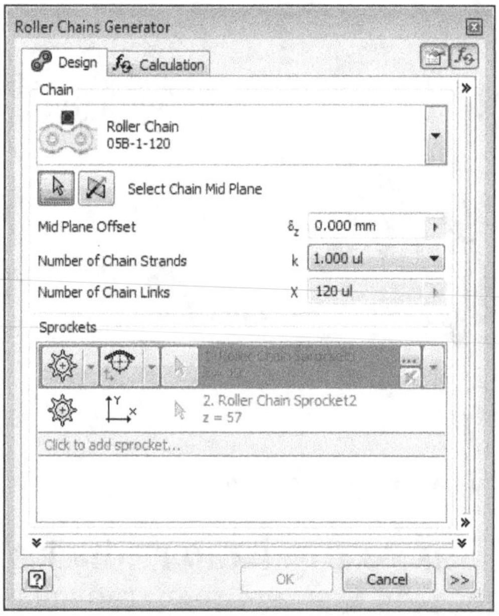

Figure-91. Roller Chains Generator dialog box

- Click on the **Browse for a chain** (**Roller Chain**) drop-down in the **Chain** area of the dialog box and select desired chain from the selection box displayed; refer to Figure-92.

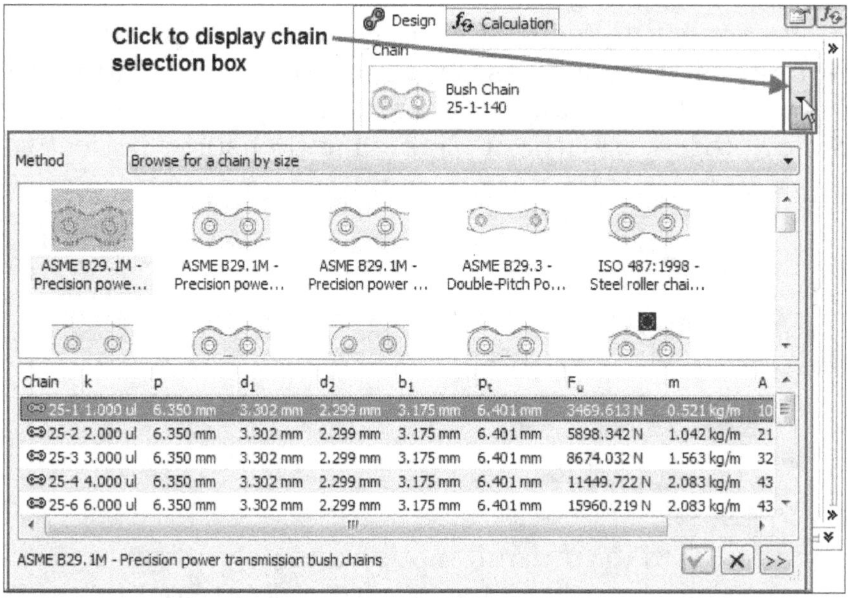

Figure-92. Chain selection box

- If you want to check the preview and maximum power transmission capacity of the selected chain then click on the **More options** button from the selection box and click on the related tab; refer to Figure-93.

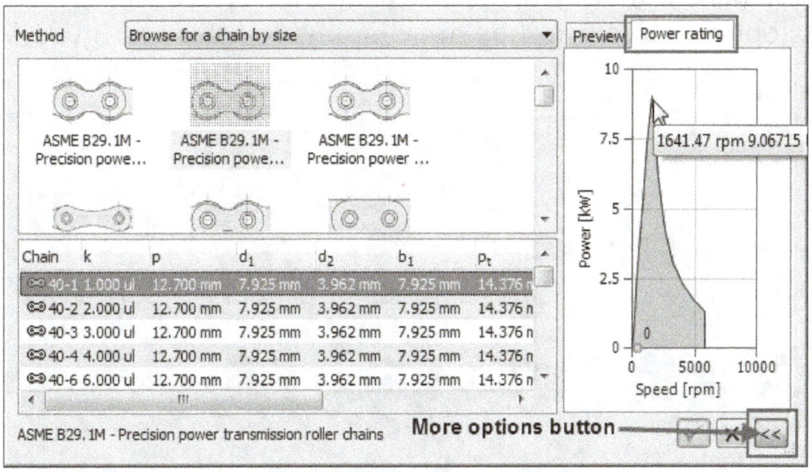

Figure-93. Power rating of selected chain

- Rest of the procedure to create chain system is same as discussed for V-Belt.

Designing Key

A key is a piece of mild steel inserted between the shaft and hub or boss of the pulley to connect these together in order to prevent relative motion between them. It is always inserted parallel to the axis of the shaft. Keys are used as temporary fastenings and are subjected to considerable crushing and shearing stresses. A keyway is a slot or recess in a shaft and hub of the pulley to accommodate a key.

The **Key** tool in Autodesk Inventor is used to generate both key and keyway based on the load requirements specified. The procedure to design key and keyway in Autodesk Inventor is given next.

- Click on the **Key** tool from the **Power Transmission** panel of the **Design** tab in the **Ribbon**. The **Parallel Key Connection Generator** dialog box will be displayed; refer to Figure-94.

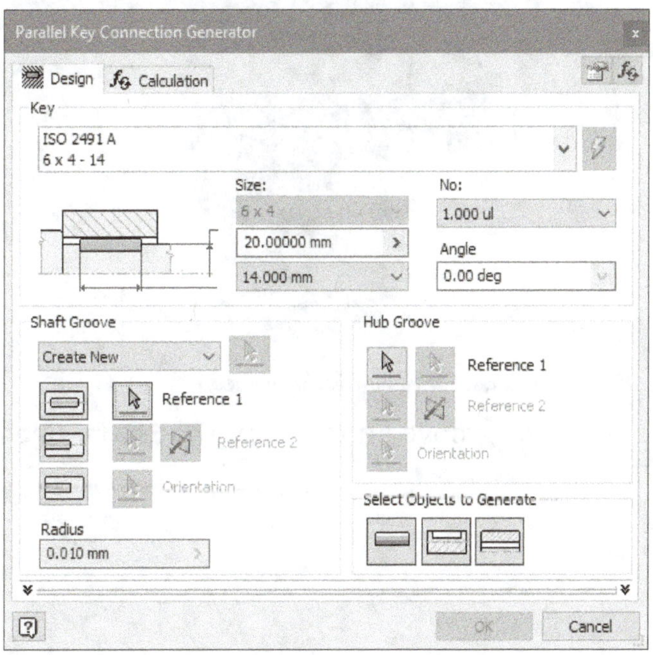

Figure-94. Parallel Key Connection Generator dialog box

- Click in the **Browse for key** drop-down at the top in the **Key** area of the dialog box. Various options to select key are displayed; refer to Figure-95.

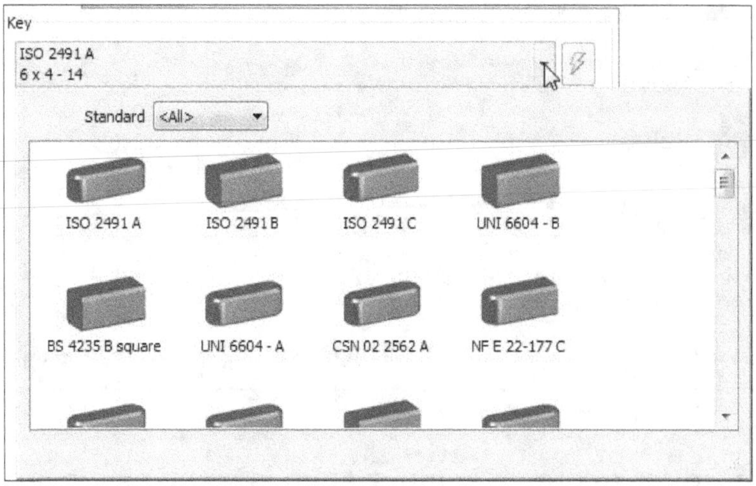

Figure-95. Browse for key drop-down

- Specify the size of key in the edit boxes available in the **Key** area of the dialog box.
- If you have a key groove in the shaft already then select the **Select Existing** option from the drop-down in the **Shaft Groove** area of the dialog box. You will be asked to select the existing groove. Select the groove.
- If you do not have groove created in the shaft then select the **Create New** option from the drop-down in the **Shaft Groove** area of the dialog box. You will be asked to select a cylindrical face for placing the groove (If not asked then click on the **Reference 1** selection button in the **Shaft Groove** area). Select the cylindrical face. You will be asked to select the starting face/plane for key groove. Select the face/plane; refer to Figure-96. Preview of the groove will be displayed.

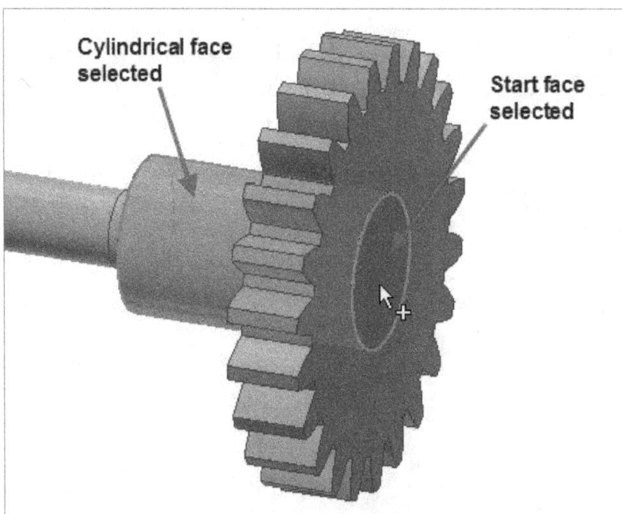

Figure-96. Faces selected for creating groove

- Click on desired button for groove shape from the **Shaft Groove** area of the dialog box; refer to Figure-97.

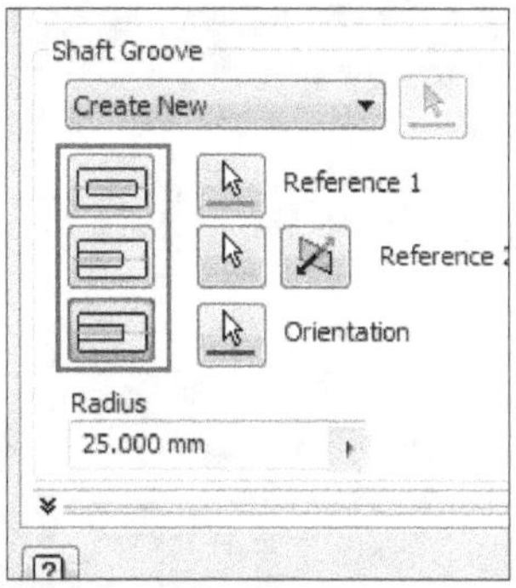

Figure-97. Buttons for shaping grooves

- Now, we need to create groove in the hub to place the key. Click on the selection button from **Reference 1** in the **Hub Groove** area of the dialog box. You will be asked to select a plane/face as starting reference.
- Select a face/plane from where the key in hub should start. The next selection button will become selected automatically and you will be asked to select a work point as center point for hub.
- Select circumferential edge of the hub or center point of the hub; refer to Figure-98. Preview of the groove will be displayed.

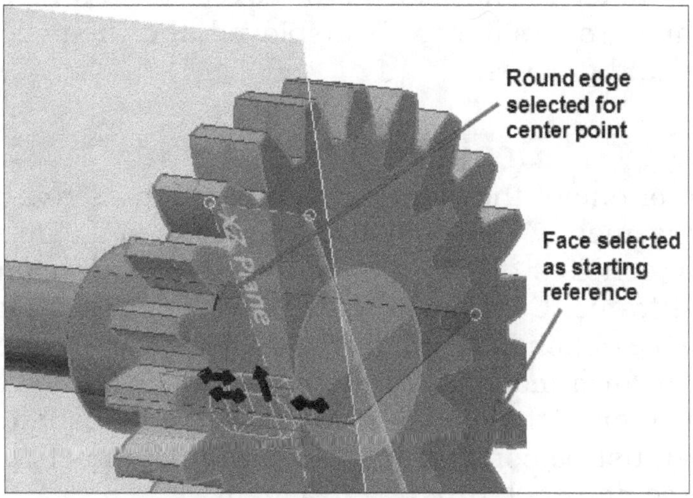

Figure-98. Selecting faces for groove in hub

- Select desired button from the **Select Objects to Generate** area of the dialog box.
- Click on the **Calculation** tab to check the feasibility of key under specified loads. The dialog box will be displayed as shown in Figure-99.

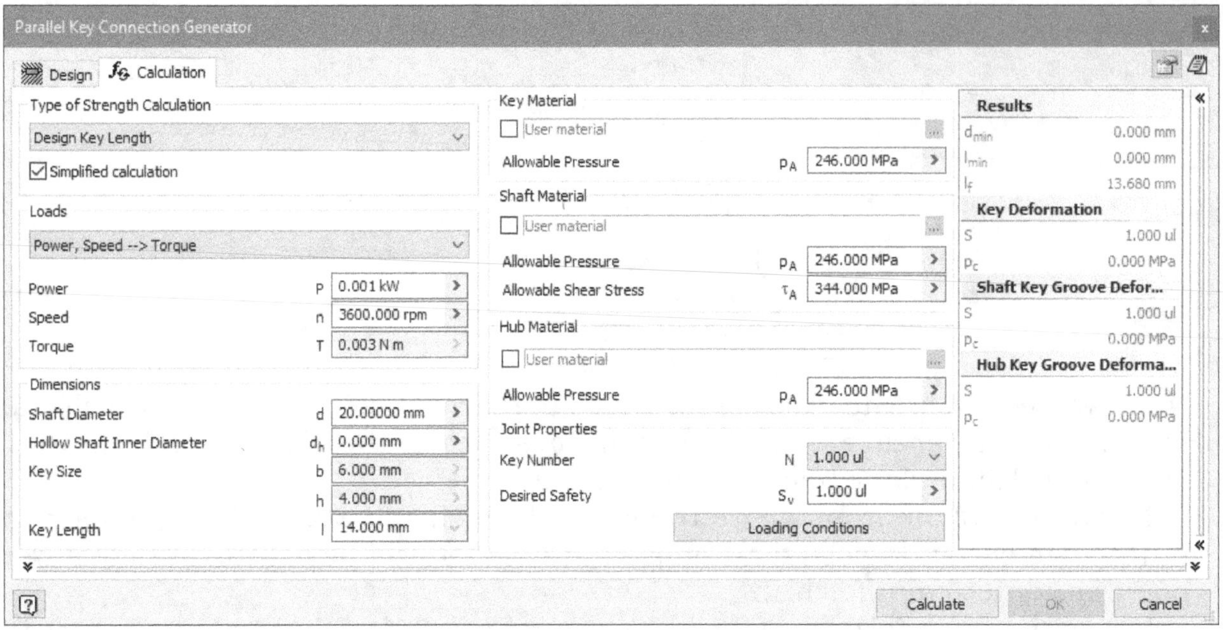

Figure-99. Calculation tab in Parallel Key Connection Generator dialog box

- Specify desired parameters and click on the **Calculate** button to check the results. Modify the key and grooves if error is displayed and then click on the **OK** button to create the key and grooves.

Designing Disc Cam

The transformation of one of the simple motions, such as rotation, into any other motions is often conveniently accomplished by means of a cam mechanism. A cam mechanism usually consists of two moving elements, the cam and the follower, mounted on a fixed frame. Cam devices are versatile, and almost any arbitrarily-specified motion can be obtained. In some instances, they offer the simplest and most compact way to transform motions. In Plate cam or disk cam, the follower moves in a plane perpendicular to the axis of rotation of the camshaft. A translating or a swing arm follower must be constrained to maintain contact with the cam profile. Figure-100 shows the nomenclature of a disc cam.

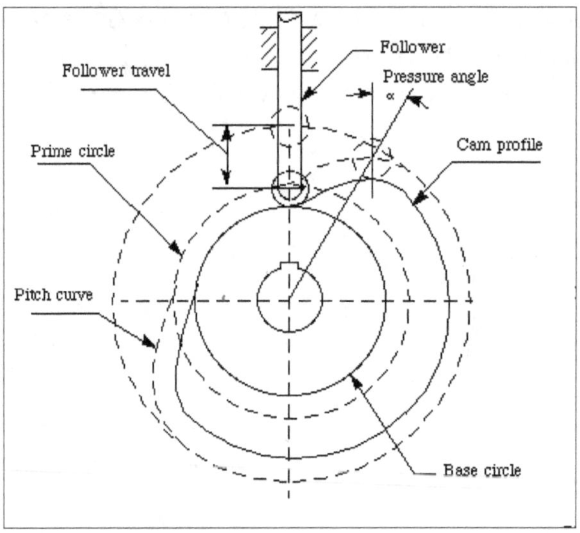

Figure-100. Disc cam nomenclature

The procedure to design disc cam in Autodesk Inventor is given next.

- Click on the **Disc Cam** tool from the **Cam** drop-down in the **Power Transmission** panel in the **Design** tab of the **Ribbon**. The **Disc Cam Component Generator** dialog box will be displayed; refer to Figure-101.

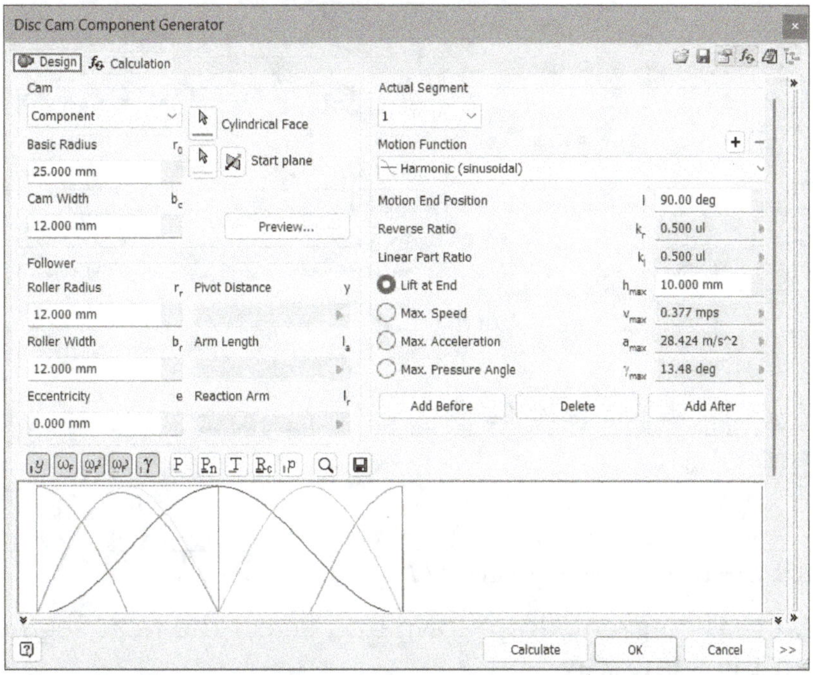

Figure-101. Disc Cam Component Generator dialog box

- Specify the base radius and width of cam in the **Basic Radius** and **Cam Width** edit boxes, respectively.
- Click on the **Preview** button if you want to check the preview of disc cam.
- Similarly, specify the roller radius, roller width, and eccentricity of roller in the edit boxes of the **Follower** area in the dialog box.
- Now, we will design profile of the cam. In Autodesk Inventor, cam profile is designed by segments like, for 0 to 120 degree, the total lift by cam will be 0 to 10 mm, after that the lift will move to 0 from 10 mm till 240 degree and then it will remain 0. To do so, click on the **Actual Segment** drop-down and select **1** in it, if not selected by default; refer to Figure-102.

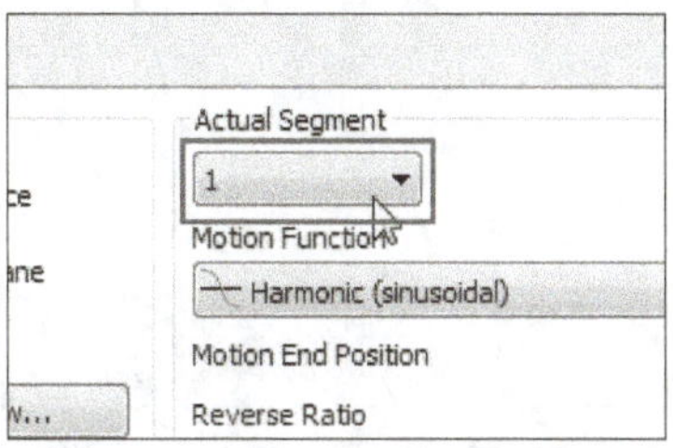

Figure-102. Actual Segment drop-down

- Click in the **Motion Function** drop-down and select desired motion type.
- Click in the **Motion End Position** edit box and specify the total angle span for current segment which is **120** for our current example.
- Select the **Lift at End** radio button to specify the lift in follower by the end of current segment which is **10** mm for current example. You can specify maximum speed, maximum acceleration, or maximum pressure angle in place of lift by using the respective radio button in the dialog box; refer to Figure-103.

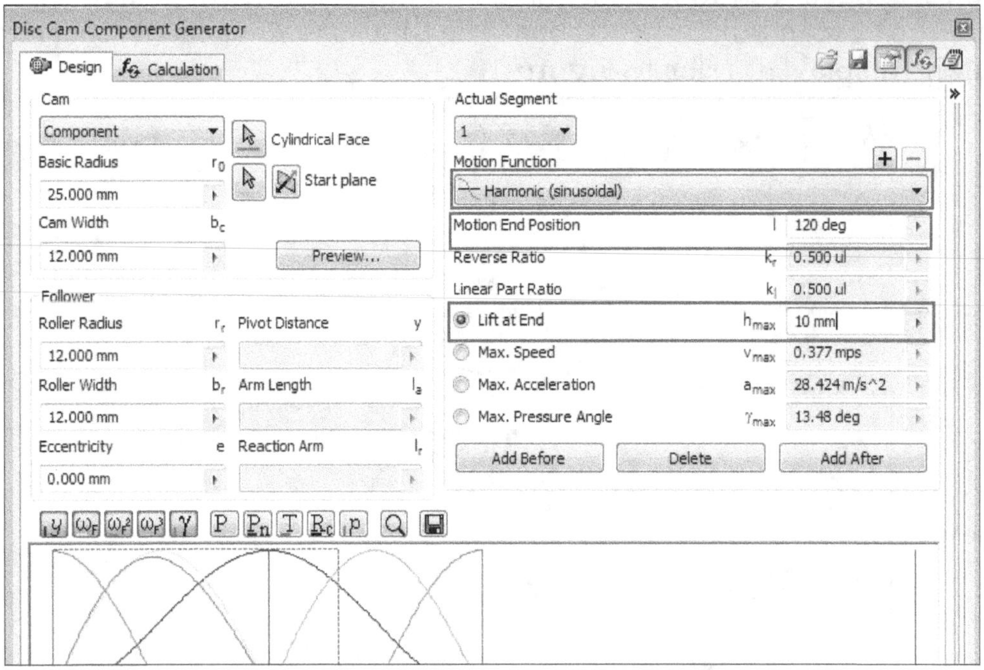

Figure-103. Cam profile parameters for segment 1

- Click in the **Actual Segment** drop-down and select the next segment. Specify the parameters in the same way.
- Note that the total motion of cam is **360** degree and you can make as many sections as you want in this total motion. To add a new motion segment, click on the **Add Before** or **Add After** button. A new segment will be added before or after the current segment as per the button selected.
- After performing the changes, click on the **Calculation** button to check the preview of cam profile in the preview area; refer to Figure-104.

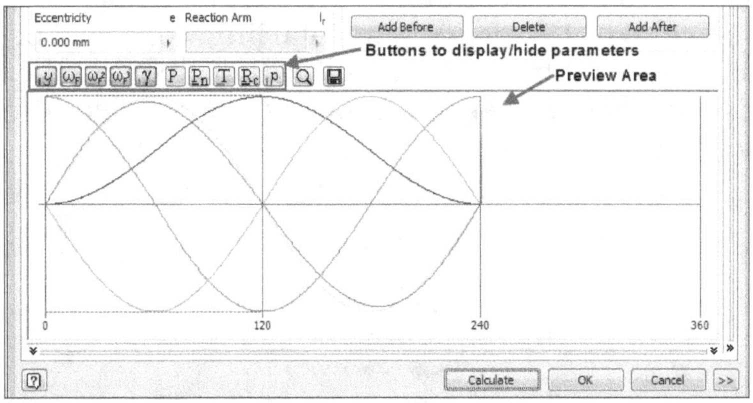

Figure-104. Preview of cam profile

- You can display or hide any parameter in the preview by using buttons overhead. You can save the graphical preview in the form of tab delimited text by using the **Save** button in the preview area.
- Click on the **Calculation** tab to check the feasibility of cam in real working environment. The dialog box will be displayed as shown in Figure-105.

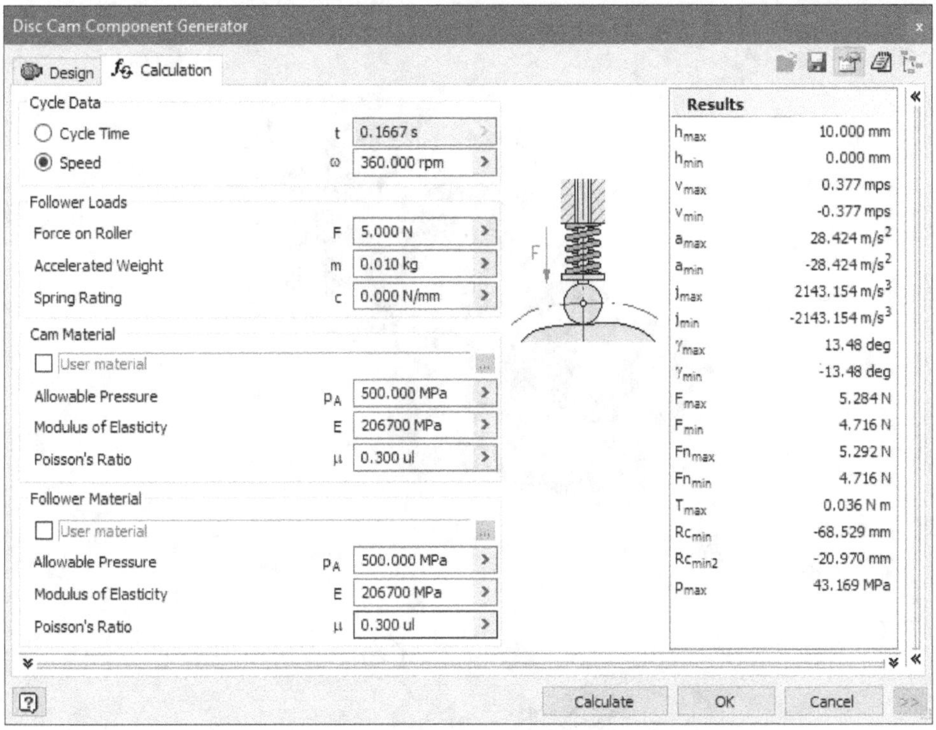

Figure-105. Calculation tab in Disc Cam Component Generator dialog box

- Specify the parameters like, speed of cam, loads on follower, material properties etc. and click on the **Calculate** button to check the report.
- Modify the cam and/or follower if error is displayed and then click on the **OK** button to create the disc cam; refer to Figure-106.

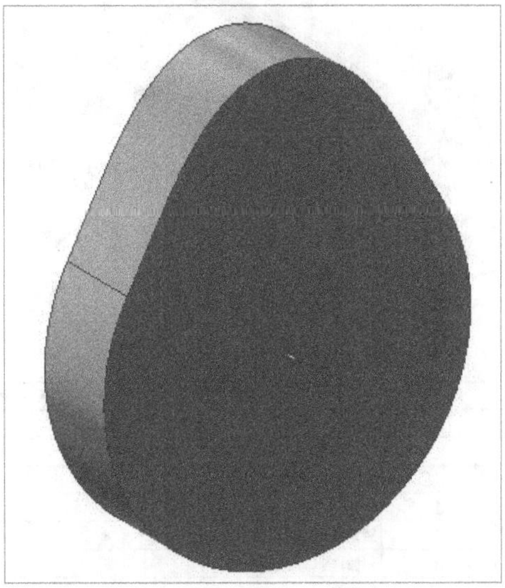

Figure-106. Disc cam created

Till this point, we have discussed various tools related to advanced assembly and design accelerator features/components. In the next chapter, we will learn more about the design accelerator features/components.

PRACTICE 1

In this practice problem, you need to create an assembly of vice as shown in Figure-107. The exploded view of the assembly is given in Figure-108. You can find the components of assembly in the resource kit of the book.

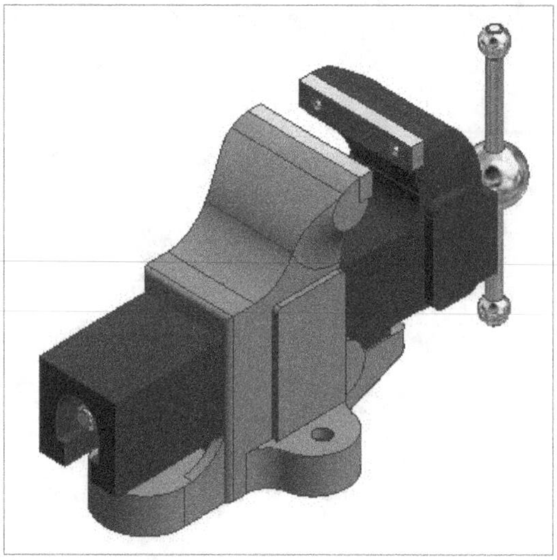

Figure-107. Vice

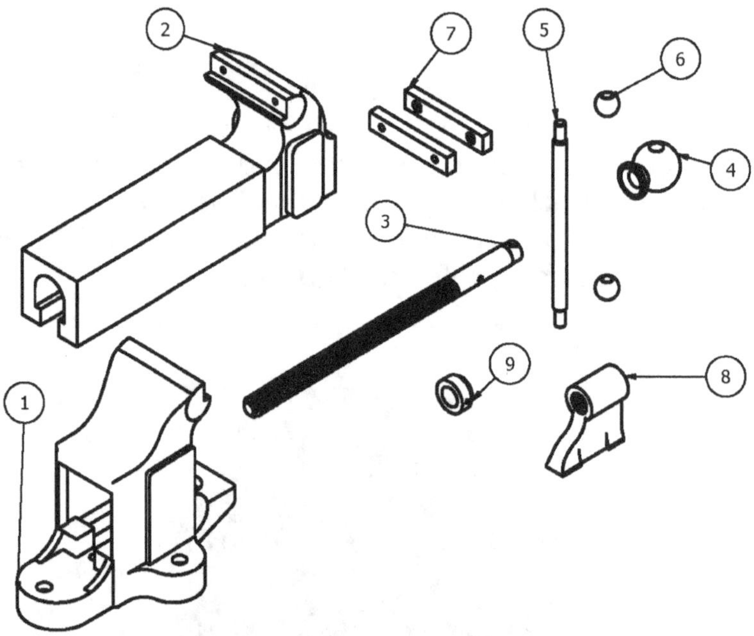

PARTS LIST			
ITEM	QTY	PART NUMBER	DESCRIPTION
1	1	Base	
2	1	Slider	
3	1	Slider Shaft	
4	1	Head Shaft	
5	1	Shaft handle	
6	2	Shaft Handle Head	
7	2	Block	
8	1	Shaft Housing	
9	1	Stopper	

Figure-108. Exploded view of vice

PRACTICE 2

In this practice problem, we will create an assembly of 3 Jaw Chuck as shown in Figure-109. Exploded view of the assembly is given in Figure-110. Note that you will find the assembly parts in resource kit for this book which can be asked at **cadcamcaeworks@gmail.com**.

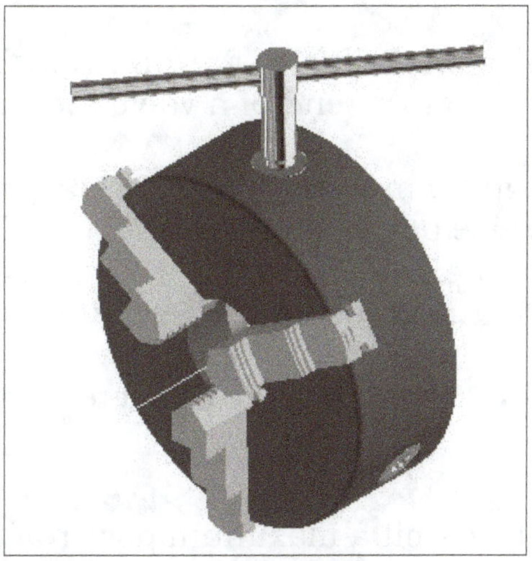

Figure-109. 3 Jaw Chuck Assembly

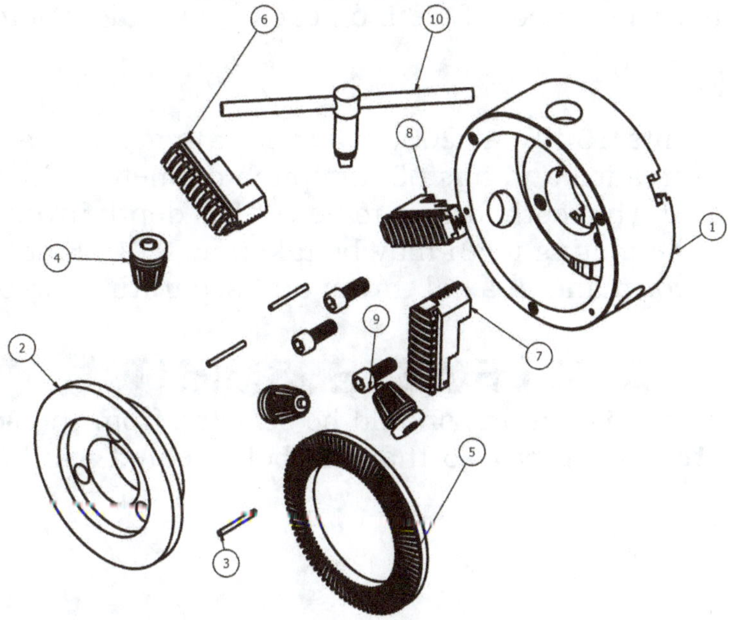

PARTS LIST			
ITEM	QTY	PART NUMBER	DESCRIPTION
1	1	Housing	
2	1	Flange	
3	3	pin	
4	3	Bevel Gear1	
5	1	Bevel Gear2	
6	1	jaws1	
7	1	jaws2	
8	1	jaws3	
9	3	screw flange	
10	1	key chuck	

Figure-110. Exploded view of 3 jaw chuck

PRACTICE 3

Design a cam, with a minimum radius of 25 mm, rotating clockwise at a uniform speed to give a roller follower, at the end of a valve rod, motion described below :

1. To raise the valve through 50 mm during 120° rotation of the cam ;
2. To keep the valve fully raised through next 30°;
3. To lower the valve during next 60°; and
4. To keep the valve closed during rest of the revolution i.e. 150°;

The diameter of the roller is 20 mm and the diameter of the cam shaft is 25 mm.

PRACTICE 4

A gear drive is required to transmit a maximum power of 22.5 kW. The velocity ratio is 1:2 and r.p.m. of the pinion is 200. The approximate centre distance between the shafts may be taken as 600 mm. The teeth has 20° stub involute profiles. Find the module, face width, and number of teeth on each gear. Take Factor of safety as 1.4.

PRACTICE 5

A worm drive transmits 15 kW at 2000 r.p.m. to a machine carriage at 75 r.p.m. The worm is triple threaded and has 65 mm pitch diameter. The worm gear has 90 teeth of 6 mm module. The tooth form is to be 20° full depth involute. The coefficient of friction between the mating teeth may be taken as 0.10. Find out : 1. tangential force acting on the worm and 2. axial thrust and separating force on worm.

SELF ASSESSMENT

Q1. Which of the following options should be selected from the **Bolted Connection Component Generator** dialog box so that the bolt created will be have nut on the other end?

a) Through All
b) Blind
c) Concentric
d) None of the Above

Q2. By selecting which of the following options, the **Clevis pin** can be placed in the assembly?

a) Concentric
b) By hole
c) Linear
d) All of the Above

Q3. Which type of pin is used to design and calculate pins loaded with torque?

a) Joint Pin
b) Cross Pin
c) Secure Pin
d) Radial Pin

Q4. What are the standard lengths of shafts?

a) 5m, 6m, and 7m
b) 3m, 5m, and 6m
c) 4m, 7m, and 8m
d) 6m, 7m, and 8m

Q5. What are the maximum permissible working stresses that can be taken for shafts in tension or compression?

a) 96 MPa without allowance and 86 MPa with allowance
b) 112 MPa without allowance and 84 MPa with allowance
c) 124 MPa without allowance and 96 MPa with allowance
d) 118 MPa without allowance and 88 MPa with allowance

Q6. What are the maximum permissible shear stresses that can be taken for shafts?

a) 66 MPa without allowance and 24 MPa with allowance
b) 72 MPa without allowance and 40 MPa with allowance
c) 56 MPa without allowance and 42 MPa with allowance
d) 48 MPa without allowance and 32 MPa with allowance

Q7. Which of the following loads cannot be applied in the **Shaft Component Generator** dialog box?

a) Radial Force
b) Tension Force
c) Axial Force
d) Bending Moment

Q8. Which of the following failures of gear teeth has a stick-slip phenomena in designing gear drive?

a) Bending Failure
b) Pitting
c) Scoring
d) Abrasive wear

Q9. Which of the following is the correct gear ratio in designing spur gears according to engineering equations?

a) T1 = G / T2
b) T2 = G / T1
c) G = T1 / T2
d) G = T2 / T1

Q10. The Synchronous Belt is also called as-

a) Timing Belt
b) Toothed Belt
c) Cogged Belt
d) All of the Above

Q11. Clevis Pin is a type of fastener that will allow the rotation or swivel of the connected parts about the axis of the pin linkage. (True/False)

Q12. Cross Pin is a type of fastener that will allow the rotation or swivel of the connected parts about the axis of the pin linkage. (True/False)

Q13. A .... is a rotating machine element used to transmit power from one location to other.

Q14. .... is the surface fatigue failure which occurs due to many repetition of Hertz contact stresses.

Q15. What is the primary purpose of creating sub-assemblies in an assembly model?

A. To reduce file size
B. To improve visual appearance
C. To reuse a group of components that repeat in the assembly
D. To improve animation quality

Q16. Which of the following steps is not part of placing a sub-assembly in a main assembly?

A. Use the Place button from the Component panel
B. Select the Base component file
C. Convert sub-assembly to a sketch
D. Click on the round edge of holes in the base

Q17. What does the Pattern tool in the Assembly environment allow you to do?

A. Apply textures to components
B. Create multiple copies of a component or sub-assembly
C. Add motion constraints
D. Combine two assemblies into one

Q18. What are the two pattern types available in the Pattern Component dialog box?

A. Horizontal and Vertical
B. Random and Linear
C. Rectangular and Circular
D. Internal and External

Q19. Which statement best describes the Mirror tool in the Assembly environment?

A. It only mirrors sketches
B. It works differently than in the Modeling environment
C. It mirrors components and allows reuse or creation of new files
D. It creates animations of mirrored parts

Q20. What is the main function of Design Accelerator components?

A. Import external parts
B. Simulate material behavior
C. Generate mechanical standard components with variable parameters
D. Export designs to different formats

Q21. Which two types of fastening components are part of the Design Accelerator components?

A. Rivet and Nail
B. Screw and Nut
C. Bolt and Pin
D. Spring and Shaft

Q22. What happens when the "Through All" connection type is selected in the Bolted Connection dialog?

A. Bolt will terminate with a foundation
B. Bolt has no thread
C. Nut is placed on the other end
D. Hole is created automatically

Q23. What type of force can be specified in the Calculation tab of Bolted Connection dialog?

A. Drag force
B. Axial and tangential force
C. Magnetic force
D. Thermal force

Q24. What distinguishes a Clevis Pin from other types of fasteners?

A. It can only be welded
B. It doesn't allow rotation
C. It allows rotation/swivel about the axis of the pin linkage
D. It's a temporary fastener only

Q25. What is the main difference between Clevis Pin and Secure Pin?

A. Secure Pin allows pivoting, Clevis Pin does not
B. Secure Pin is used for binding rotating parts, Clevis Pin allows swivel
C. Clevis Pin is threaded, Secure Pin is not
D. Secure Pin requires a washer, Clevis Pin does not

Q26. What is the purpose of the Joint Pin tool?

A. Design fasteners for plastic components
B. Design pins loaded with torque
C. Create exploded views
D. Add visual materials to pins

Q27. What tool is used to create a radial pin in Autodesk Inventor?

A. Shaft Tool
B. Spur Gear Tool
C. Radial Pin Tool
D. Worm Gear Tool

Q28. Which of the following is NOT a type of load that can be applied to a shaft in the dialog box?

A. Axial Force
B. Bending Moment
C. Radial Displacement
D. Torque

Q29. What formula is used to calculate the bending moment?

A. $T = (P \times 60) / (2\pi N)$
B. $M = W \times L$
C. $\sigma = F / A$
D. $P = V \times I$

Q30. What is a common cause of pitting failure in gears?

A. High static load
B. Lack of lubrication
C. Repetition of Hertz contact stresses
D. Shaft misalignment

Q31. Which gear failure is associated with excessive surface pressure and lubricant failure?

A. Pitting
B. Abrasive wear
C. Corrosive wear
D. Scoring

Q32. What type of worm gear is not interchangeable with others even if the pitch is the same?

A. Straight worm
B. Double enveloping worm
C. Cylindrical worm
D. Worm wheel cut with a different diameter hob

Q33. In designing bevel gears, what parameter is NOT specified directly in the dialog box?

A. Shaft angle
B. Gear ratio
C. Number of teeth
D. Module

Q34. What is the standard length of transmission shafts?

A. 2 m, 3 m, and 4 m
B. 5 m, 6 m, and 7 m
C. 6 m, 8 m, and 10 m
D. 4 m, 6 m, and 9 m

Q35. Which of the following stresses is not considered while designing a shaft?

A. Thermal stress
B. Shear stress due to torque
C. Bending stress
D. Combined torsional and bending load stress

Q36. In Autodesk Inventor, which tab contains the Spur Gear tool?
A. Assemble tab
B. Inspect tab
C. Design tab
D. View tab

Q37. Which failure in gear teeth is caused by high contact stress and forms pits on the tooth surface?

A. Bending failure
B. Scoring
C. Abrasive wear
D. Pitting

Q38. What is the default shear displacement ratio value for a cylindrical shaft profile?

A. 1.00
B. 1.10
C. 1.18
D. 1.25

Q39. Which type of support allows rotation and is usually applied via a bearing?

A. Fixed Support
B. Roller Support
C. Free Support
D. Hinge Support

Q40. In worm gear design, how is the gear ratio adjusted?

A. By changing the module only
B. By changing the diameter of the worm gear only
C. By changing number of teeth or number of threads
D. By changing the face width only

Chapter 11

Advanced Assembly and Design-II

Topics Covered

The major topics covered in this chapter are:

- ***Designing Linear and Cylindrical Cam***
- ***Designing Splines***
- ***Performing Design Related Calculations***
- ***Designing Frames***
- ***Measurement tools***

INTRODUCTION

In 1st part of the book, you have learnt about some advanced tools for assembly editing. We have also learned about various design accelerator components. In this chapter, we will continue discussing about various design accelerator components used in machineries.

POWER TRANSMISSION COMPONENTS

We have discussed about various power transmission components like shaft, gear, bearing, belts, keys, and so on. We will now continue discussing about rest of the power transmission components.

Designing Linear Cam

Linear Cam is also called flat plate cam. In this system, follower moves up and down as the linear cam moves left and right; refer to Figure-1. The procedure to design linear cam in Autodesk Inventor is given next.

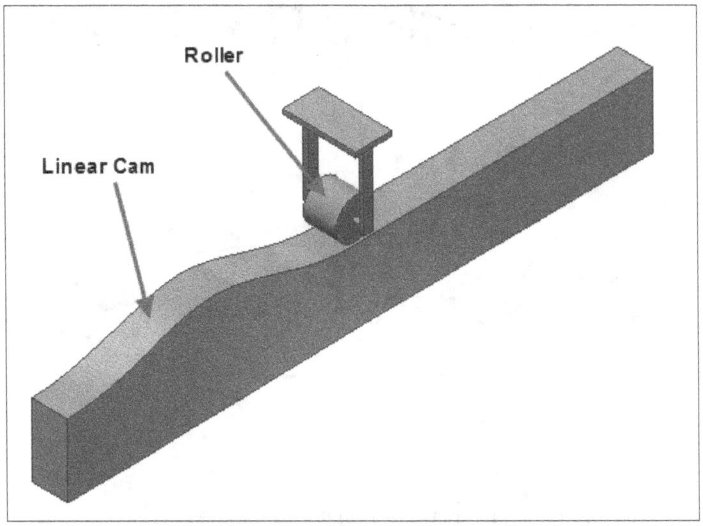

Figure-1. Linear cam

- Click on the **Linear Cam** tool from **Cam** drop-down in the **Power Transmission** panel of the **Design** tab in the **Ribbon**. The **Linear Cam Component Generator** dialog box will be displayed; refer to Figure-2.
- Specify the cam width and length in the **Cam Width** and **Motion Length** edit boxes, respectively.
- Similarly, specify the parameters for follower in the **Follower** area of the dialog box.
- Create the motion path of cam as created in previous chapter under **Disc Cam** topic.
- Click on the **More options** button at the bottom right corner of the dialog box to expand the dialog box; refer to Figure-3.

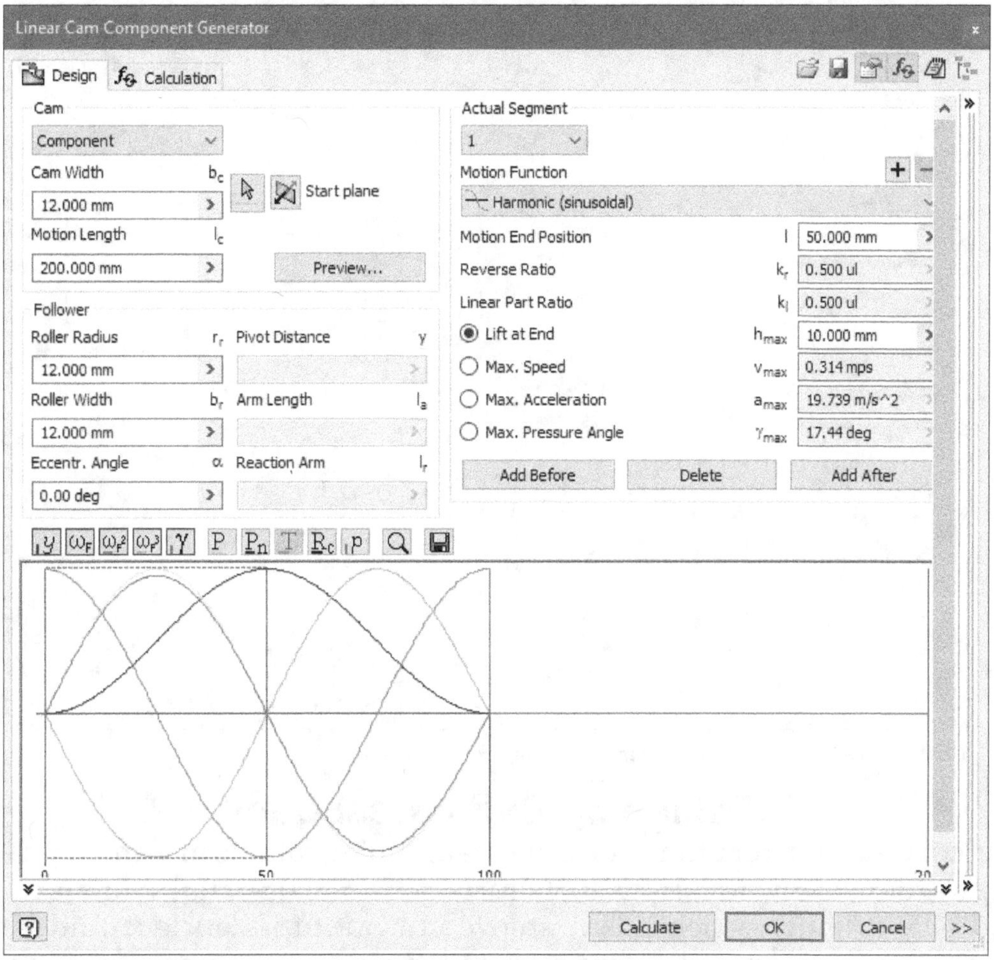

Figure-2. Linear Cam Component Generator dialog box

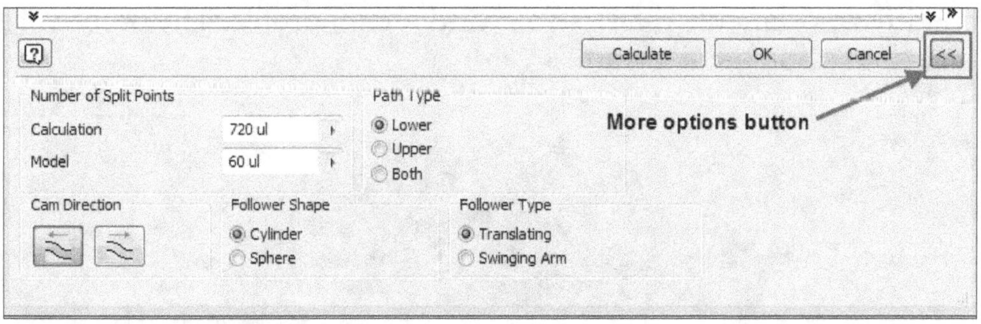

Figure-3. Expanded dialog box

- Set the advanced parameters for cam in the expanded dialog box and click on the **Calculation** tab. The dialog box will be displayed as shown in Figure-4.
- Set the parameters for calculation in the edit boxes of the dialog box and click on the **Calculate** button. Modify the cam and follower if error occurs otherwise click on the **OK** button to create the cam.

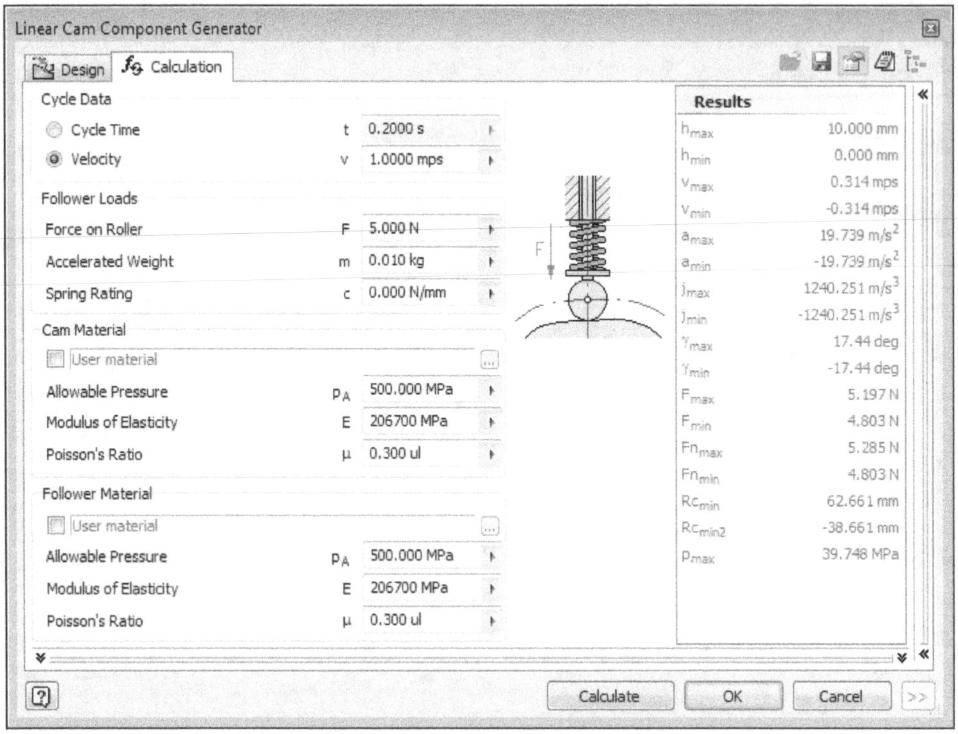

Figure-4. Calculation tab in Linear Cam Component Generator dialog box

Designing Cylindrical Cam

In Cylindrical Cam/Barrel Cam, a cylinder cam profile rotates and makes the follower moves upwards/downward; refer to Figure-5. These unusual cams are normally composed of a cylinder which has a groove cut out of its surface and it is in this that the follower runs up and down; refer to Figure-6. This type of cam can be seen in some old clock mechanisms and still in modern sewing machines. Machines that perform repetitive movements may use a cylinder cam profile. The procedure to design cylindrical cam is same as disc cam.

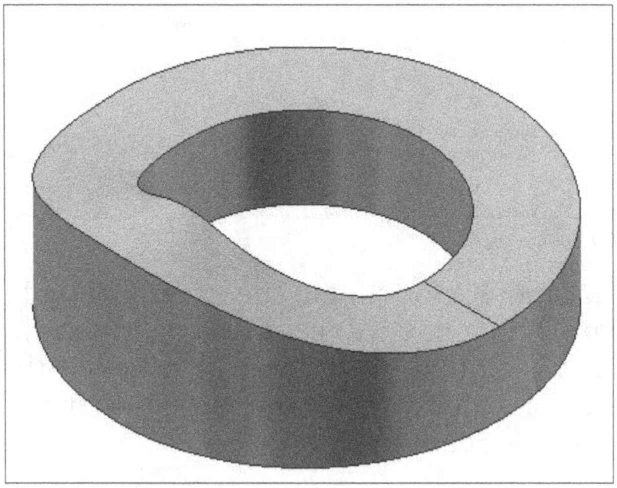

Figure-5. Cylindrical Cam

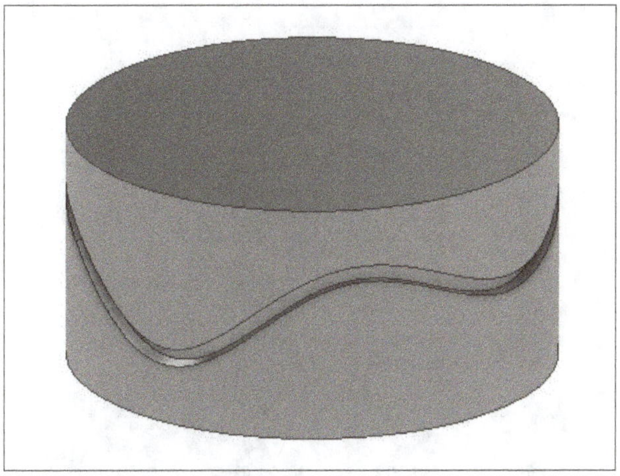

Figure-6. Cylindrical cam

Designing Parallel Spline

Splines are ridges or teeth on a drive shaft that mesh with grooves in a mating piece and transfer torque to it, maintaining the angular correspondence between them. The procedure to design parallel spline is given next. Note that to use this tool, you must have a shaft and a hub already in the drawing area.

- Click on the **Parallel Splines** tool from the **Parallel Spline** drop-down in the **Power Transmission** panel in the **Design** tab of the **Ribbon**. The **Parallel Splines Connection Generator** dialog box will be displayed as shown in Figure-7.

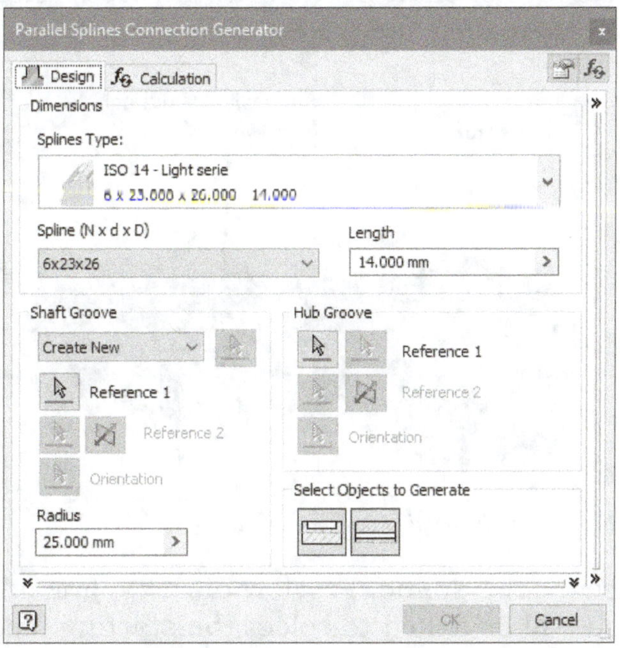

Figure-7. Parallel Splines Connection Generator dialog box

- Click in the **Splines Type** drop-down and select desired type of spline; refer to Figure-8.

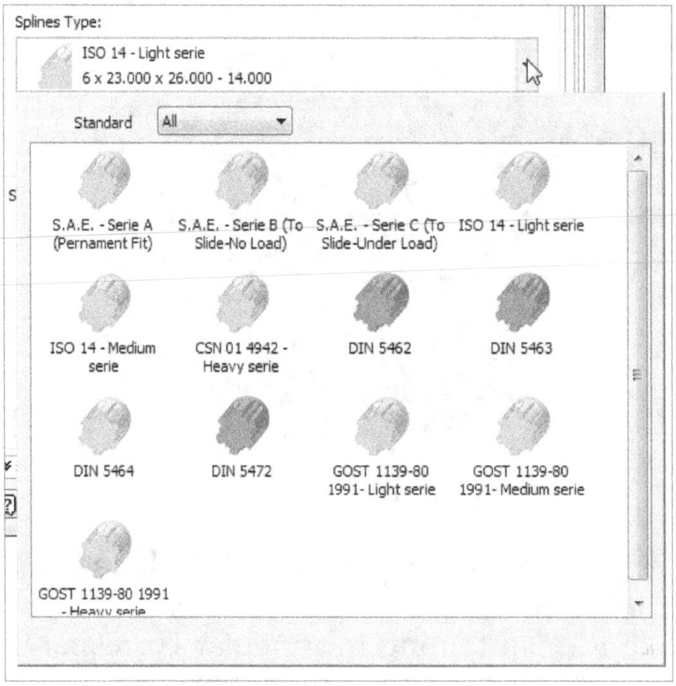

Figure-8. Splines Type drop-down

- Click in the **Spline (N x d x D)** drop-down and select desired size of spline.
- Select the **Create New** option from the drop-down in the **Shaft Groove** area of the dialog box to create spline grooves on the shaft. You will be asked to select the cylindrical face of the shaft.
- Select the cylindrical face of shaft in the drawing area; refer to Figure-9. You will be asked to select starting face for the spline.

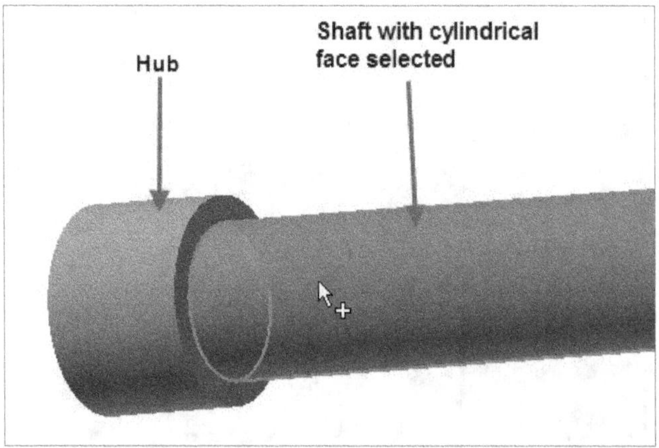

Figure-9. Cylindrical face of shaft selected

- Select the start face for the spline. Preview of the spline grooves on shaft will be displayed. Also, you will be asked to select the starting face of hub.
- Click on the starting face of hub. You will be asked to select center point for spline on hub.
- Select a work point or edge of a circular face to select its center. Preview of the spline connection will be displayed; refer to Figure-10.

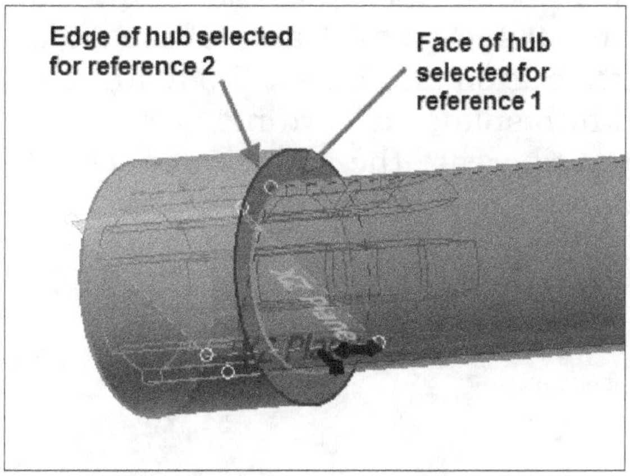

Figure-10. Preview of spline connection

- Specify desired value of runout radius in the **Radius** edit box of the dialog box. Run out radius should not be confused with the run out used in GD&T for deviation in geometric center and actual center of shaft, it is the radius provided at the ends of spline grooves for soft locking of hub and shaft.
- Specify the length of spline grooves on the shaft in **Length** edit box.
- Click on the **Calculation** tab to check the feasibility of the spline connection. The dialog box will be displayed as shown in Figure-11.

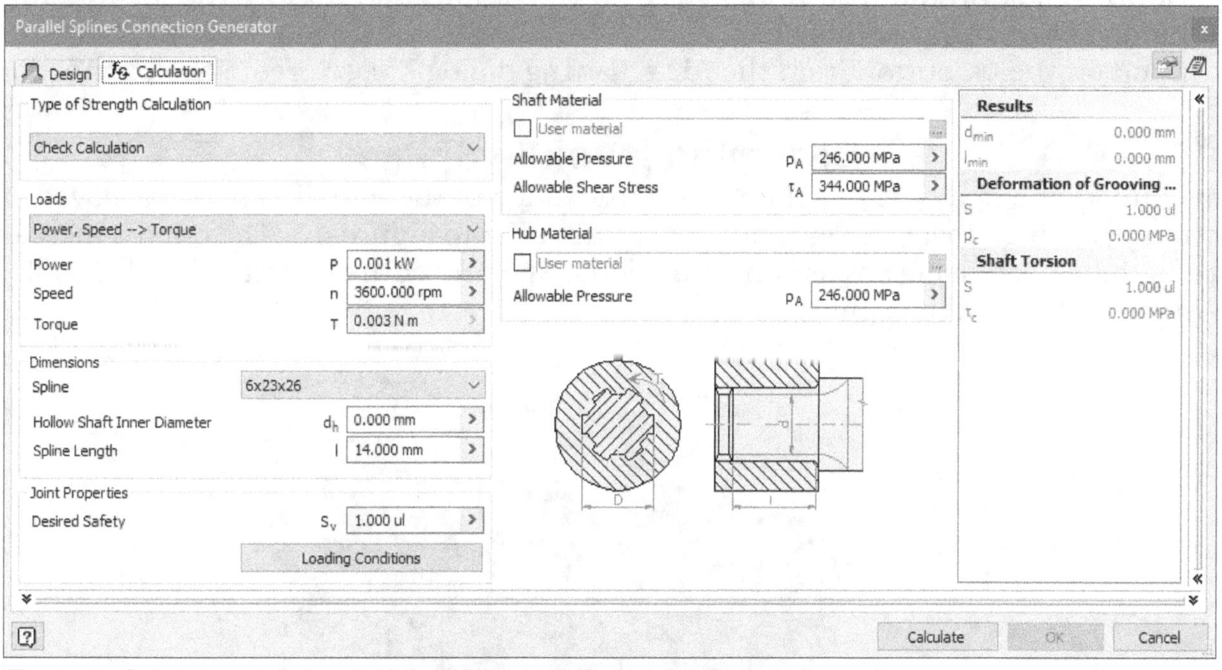

Figure-11. Calculation tab in Parallel Splines Connection Generator dialog box

- Select desired option from the **Type of Strength Calculation** drop-down. There are three options in the drop-down; **Check Calculation**, **Length Design**, and **Diameter Design**. Select the **Check Calculation** option if you know all the parameters of spline connection and just want to check whether the connection will do the job or not. Select the **Length Design** option if you want the length of spline to be decided by system based on the load calculations. Select the **Diameter Design** option if you want the diameter of spline to be decided by system based on the load calculations.
- Select desired option from the **Loads** drop-down and specify the parameters in the edit boxes of **Loads** area.

- Similarly, apply the material properties to shaft and hub by using the options in the **Shaft Material** and **Hub Material** area of the dialog box.
- Click on the **Calculate** button and check the results. If there is some error then modify the shaft and hub splines accordingly.
- Click on the **OK** button to create the spline connection. The **File Naming** dialog box will be displayed; refer to Figure-12.

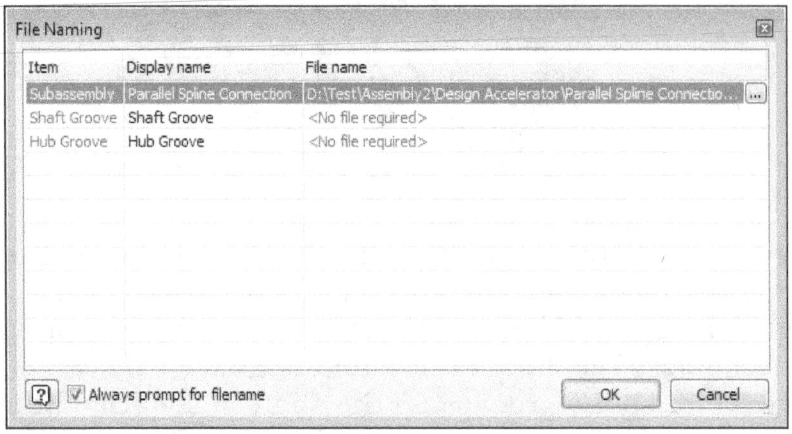

Figure-12. File Naming dialog box

- Double-click on the field under **File name** column and specify the location and name of the sub-assembly file.
- Click on the **OK** button from the **File Naming** dialog box to create the connection.

Designing Involute Spline

Involute spline is a type of spline where the sides of the equally spaced grooves are involute, as in an involute gear, but not as tall; refer to Figure-13. The curves increase strength by decreasing stress concentrations. The procedure to create involute spline is same as for Parallel spline.

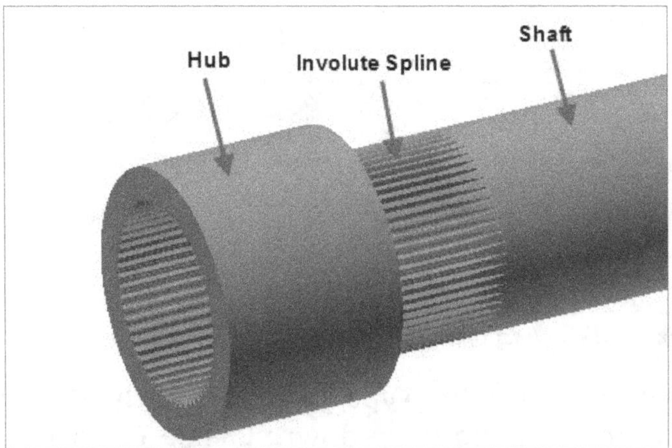

Figure-13. Involute spline created

Generating O-Ring

An O-ring, also known as a packing, or a toric joint, is a mechanical gasket in the shape of a torus; it is a loop of elastomer with a round cross-section, designed to be seated in a groove and compressed during assembly between two or more parts, creating a seal at the interface. The O-ring may be used in static applications or in dynamic applications where there is relative motion between the parts and the O-ring. Dynamic examples include rotating pump shafts and hydraulic cylinder pistons.

The procedure to generate O-ring in Inventor is given next.

- Click on the **O-Ring** tool from **Power Transmission** panel in the **Design** tab of the **Ribbon**. The **O-Ring Component Generator** dialog box will be displayed; refer to Figure-14. Also, you will be asked to select a cylindrical surface, planar face, or work plane.

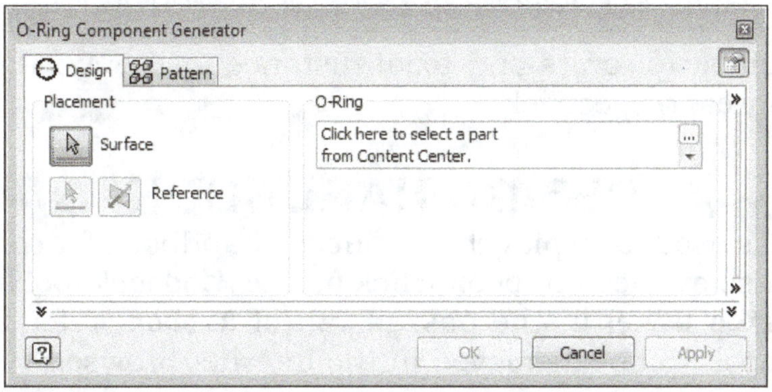

Figure-14. O-Ring Component Generator dialog box

- Select desired reference, you will be asked to specify positional reference for the O-ring.
- Select the positional reference. Note that if you have selected cylindrical surface earlier then you will be prompted to select planar face/work plane for positional reference and if you have selected planar face/work plane earlier then you will be prompted to select edge, point, or axis for positional reference.
- After selecting the references, click in the **Browse for o-ring** drop-down in the **O-Ring** area of the dialog box. The options in the drop-down will be displayed as shown in Figure-15.

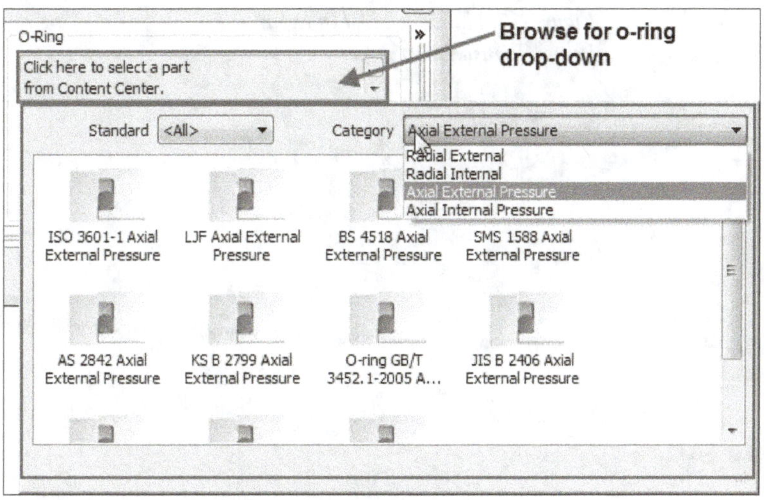

Figure-15. O-Ring drop-down

- Click in the **Category** drop-down and select desired category of rings and then select the o-ring from list displayed. Preview of the ring will be displayed.
- If you want to create more than one rings then click on the **Pattern** tab and select the **Axial** radio button from the dialog box; refer to Figure-16.

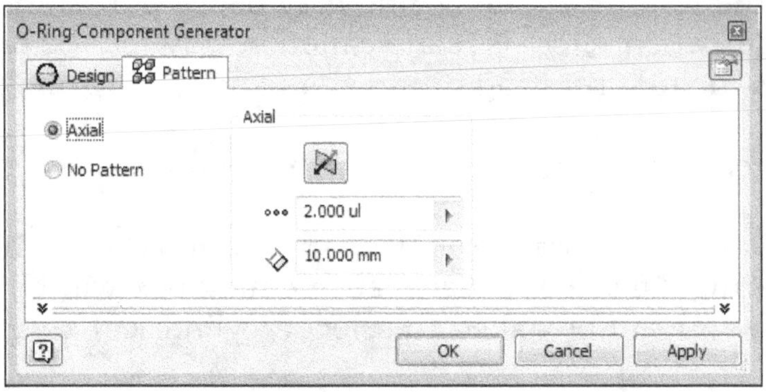

Figure-16. Pattern tab in O-Ring Component Generator dialog box

- Specify the number of units and axial distance in the **Axial count** and **Axial Spacing** edit boxes, respectively.

DESIGN HANDBOOK

The **Handbook** tool is used to display the engineer's handbook for common mechanical components. To display the handbook, click on the **Handbook** tool from the expanded **Power Transmission** panel in the **Design** tab of **Ribbon**; refer to Figure-17. The Engineer's Handbook will be displayed in the internet browser; refer to Figure-18.

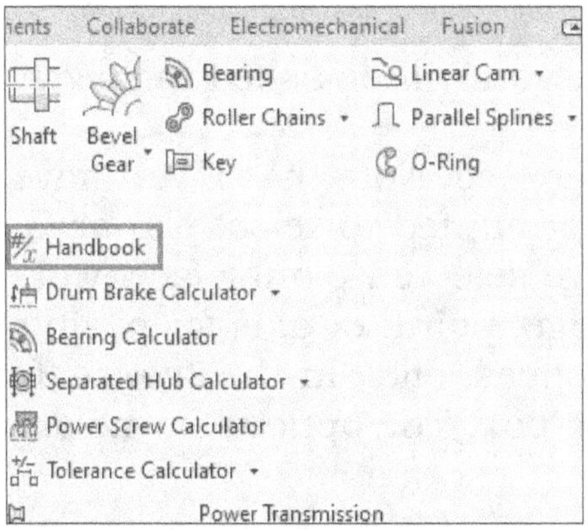

Figure-17. Handbook tool in expanded Power Transmission panel

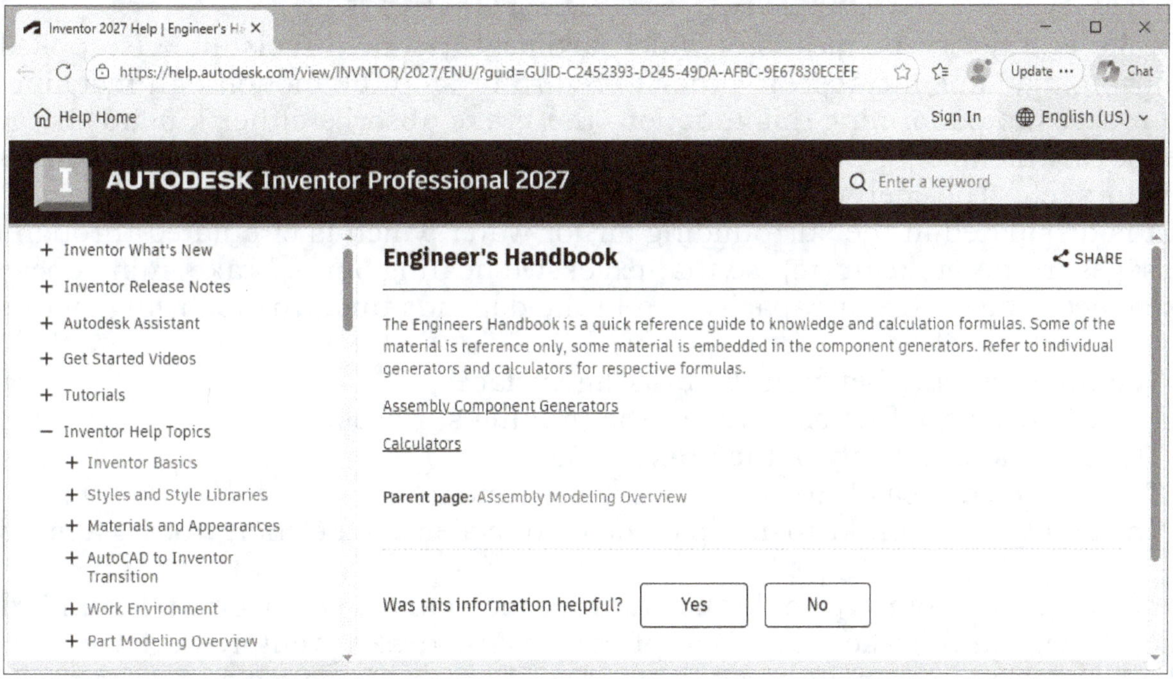

Figure-18. Engineer's Handbook in browser

- Click on desired topic in the browser. Related calculation formulae will be displayed; refer to Figure-19.

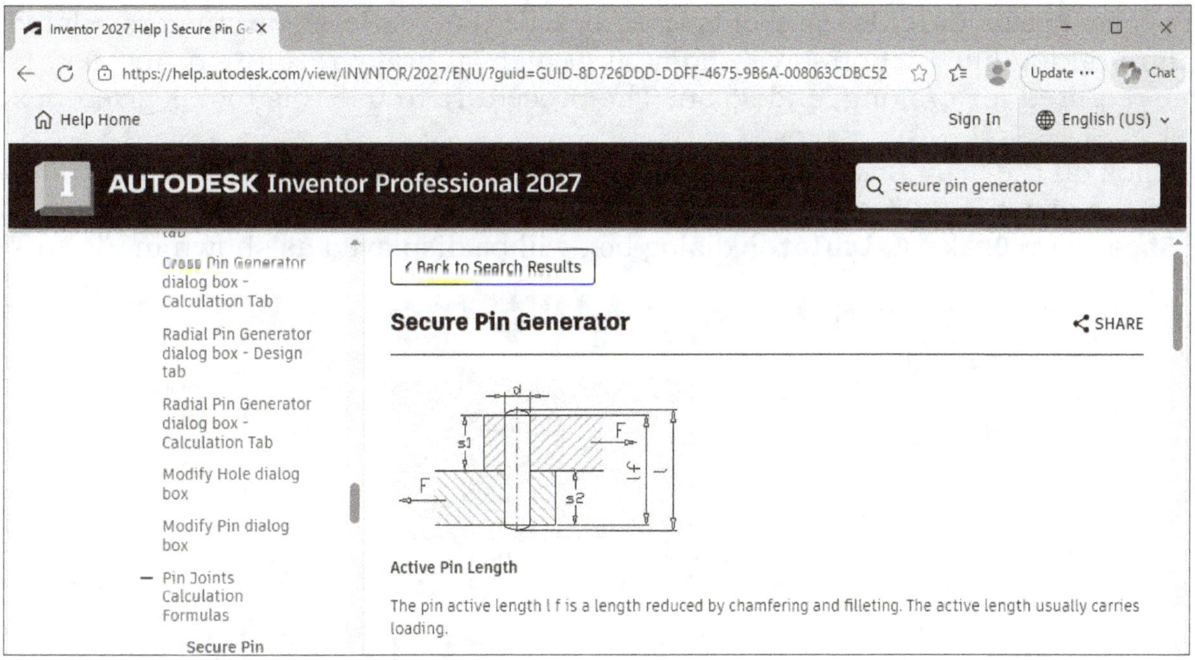

Figure-19. Secure Pin Generator calculations

BRAKE CALCULATORS

A brake is a device by means of which artificial frictional resistance is applied to a moving machine member, in order to retard or stop the motion of a machine. In the process of performing this function, the brake absorbs either kinetic energy of the moving member or potential energy given up by objects being lowered by hoists, elevators, etc. The energy absorbed by brakes is dissipated in the form of heat. This heat is dissipated in the surrounding air (or water which is circulated through the passages in the brake drum), so that excessive heating of the brake lining does not take place. The design or capacity of a brake depends upon the following factors :

1. The unit pressure between the braking surfaces,
2. The coefficient of friction between the braking surfaces,
3. The peripheral velocity of the brake drum,
4. The projected area of the friction surfaces, and
5. The ability of the brake to dissipate heat equivalent to the energy being absorbed.

There are mainly four type of brakes used in mechanical engineering; Drum brake, Disc brake, Band brake, and Cone brake. In Autodesk Inventor, we have tools to calculate various parameters related to these brakes. These tools and their related calculations are discussed next.

Drum Brake Calculator

The **Drum Brake Calculator** tool is used to calculate various parameters related to drum braking like friction force, moment of inertia, brake revolution number, total time required for braking, and so on. The procedure to use this tool is given next.

- Click on the **Drum Brake Calculator** tool from the **Brake Calculators** drop-down in the expanded **Power Transmission** panel in the **Design** tab of the **Ribbon**. The **Shoe Drum Brake Calculator** dialog box will be displayed as shown in Figure-20.

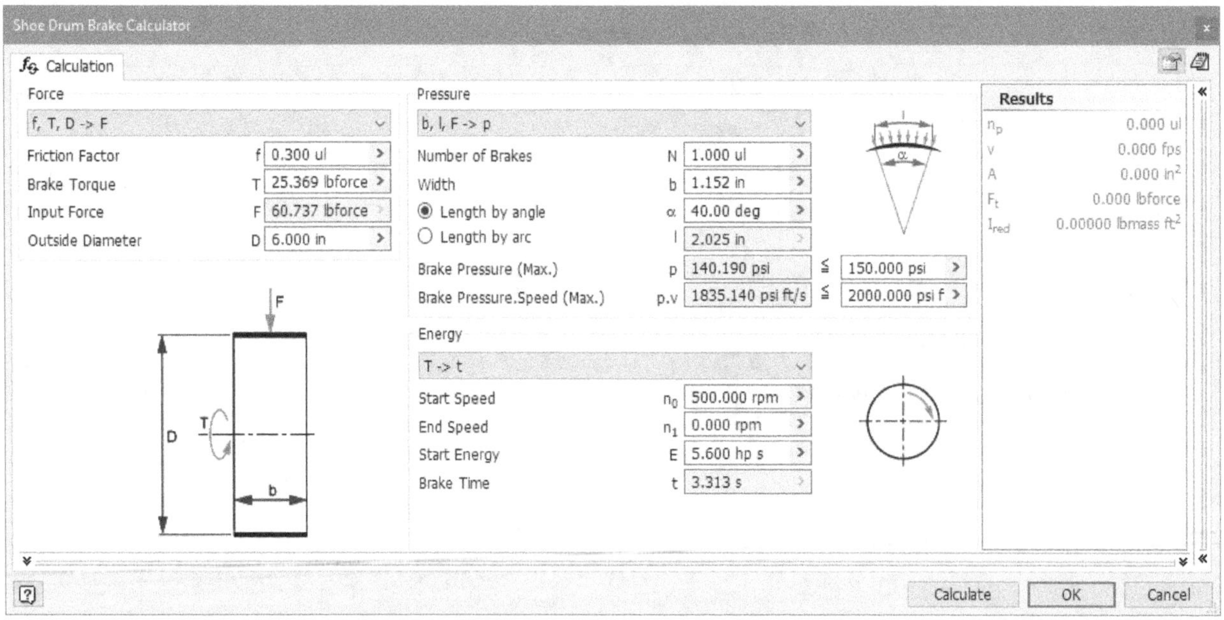

Figure-20. Shoe Drum Brake Calculator dialog box

- Click in the **Force** drop-down and select desired option. There are four options in the drop-down; **f,T,D->F**, **T,D,F->f**, **f,D,F->T**, and **f,T,F->D**. Note that the parameters which are on the left side of arrow in these options are specified by user and the parameter on the other side of arrow is calculated by system based on the inputs.
- Specify desired parameters in the **Force** area of the dialog box.
- Similarly, specify the parameters in **Pressure** and **Energy** areas of the dialog box.
- Click on the **Calculate** button and check the results in **Results** area and driven edit boxes; refer to Figure-21.

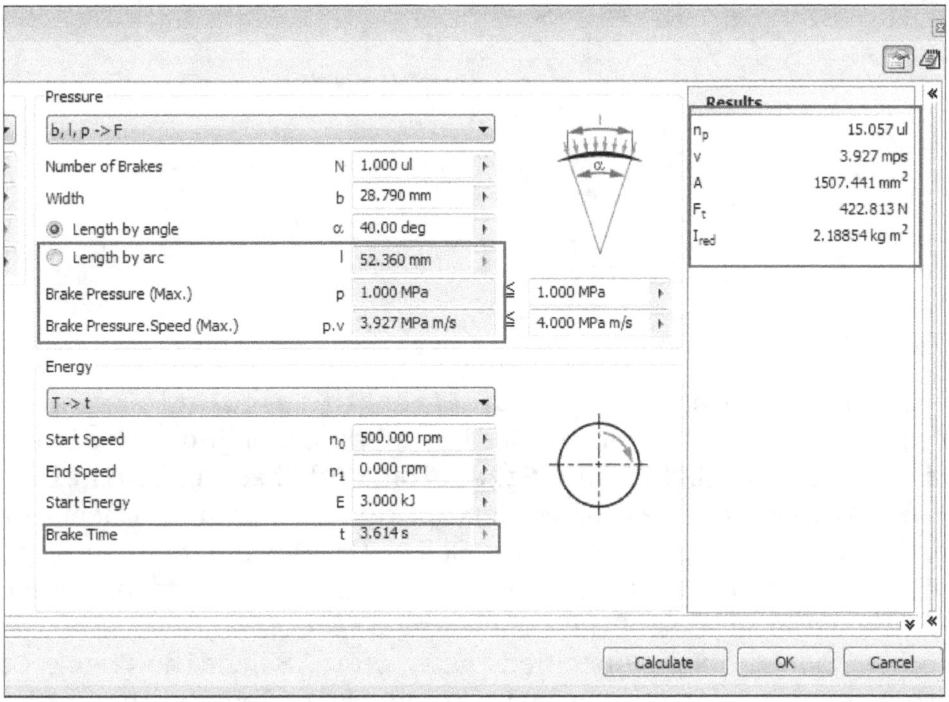

Figure-21. Results of shoe drum brake calculator

- Click on the **OK** button to add calculations of shoe drum brake in the **Model Browser Bar**.

Disc Brake, Band Brake, and Cone Brake Calculator

The **Disc Brake Calculator**, **Band Brake Calculator**, and **Cone Brake Calculator** tools are used to calculate parameter related to disc brake, band brake, and cone brake. The procedure to use these tools is similar to the procedure discussed in previous topic.

BEARING CALCULATOR

The **Bearing Calculator** tool is used to calculate parameters related to journal bearing like, minimum journal diameter, bearing clearance design, lubricant selection and so on. The procedure to use the **Bearing Calculator** tool is given next.

- Click on the **Bearing Calculator** tool from the expanded **Power Transmission** panel in the **Design** tab of the **Ribbon**. The **Plain Bearing Calculator (SI units)** dialog box will be displayed; refer to Figure-22.

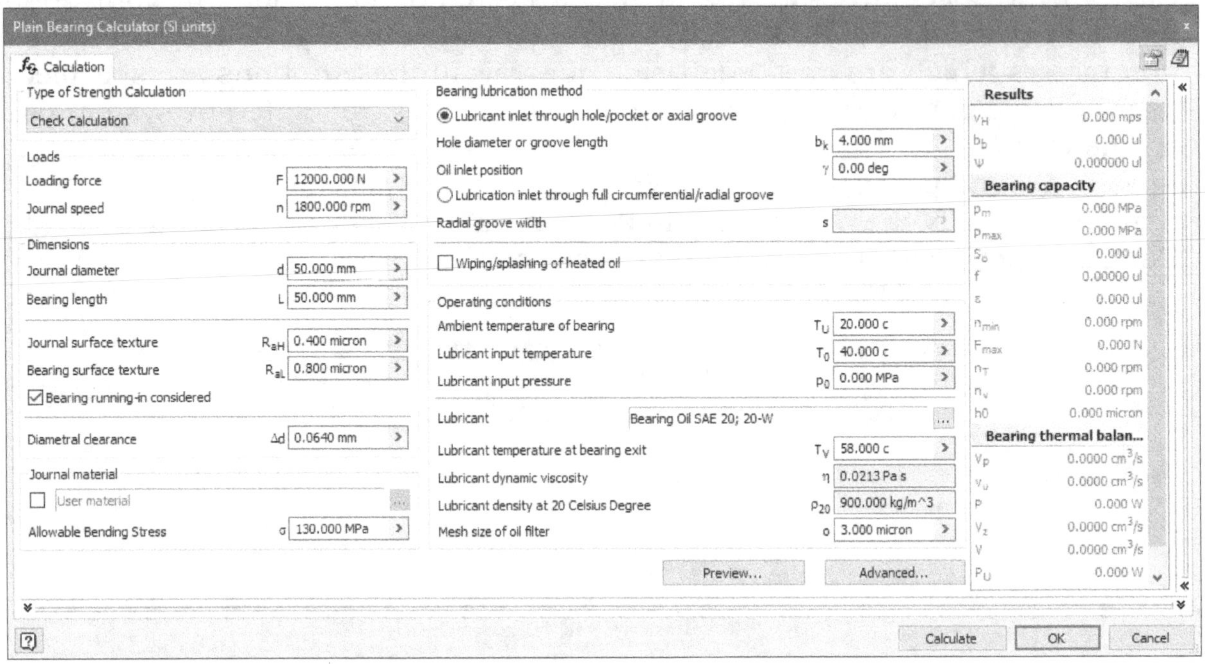

Figure-22. Plain Bearing Calculator dialog box

- Select desired option from the **Type of Strength Calculation** drop-down. There are four options in this drop-down; **Design of minimum journal diameter**, **Design of bearing clearance**, **Lubricant Selection**, and **Check Calculation**. Select the **Design of minimum journal diameter** option if you want to design the journal diameter based on the specified data. Select the **Design of bearing clearance** option if you want to design the bearing clearance based on the parameters specified in calculator. Select the **Lubricant Selection** option if lubricant type is to be selected based on the specified parameters. Select the **Check Calculation** option from the drop-down if you want to check the feasibility of journal bearing under current loading conditions.
- Click on the **Calculate** button and check the results. If there is some error then modify the parameters accordingly.
- Click on the **OK** button to add calculation in **Model Browser Bar**. The **File Naming** dialog box will be displayed. Specify the location for file and then click on the **OK** button.

SEPARATED HUB CALCULATOR

Hubs are used to transmit mechanical power from a drive motor by coupling it to an output device such as a wheel or an arm. A separated hub is made of two halves joined by bolts. The **Separated Hub Calculator** tool in Autodesk Inventor is used to check the feasibility of designed hub under specified loading conditions. The procedure to use this tool is given next.

- Click on the **Separated Hub Calculator** tool from the **Hub Calculator** drop-down in the expanded **Power Transmission** panel in the **Design** tab of the **Ribbon**. The **Separated Hub Joint Calculator** dialog box will be displayed; refer to Figure-23.

- Select desired option from the **Type of Strength Calculation** drop-down in the dialog box. There are three options in this drop-down; **Hub Length Design**, **Shaft Diameter Design**, and **Check Calculation**. Select the **Hub Length Design** option if you want to design the length of hub based on the loads specified. Select the **Shaft Diameter Design** if you want to modify the shaft diameter based specified loading conditions. If you want to check the feasibility of separated hub for the specified loading conditions and parameter then select the **Check Calculation** option.

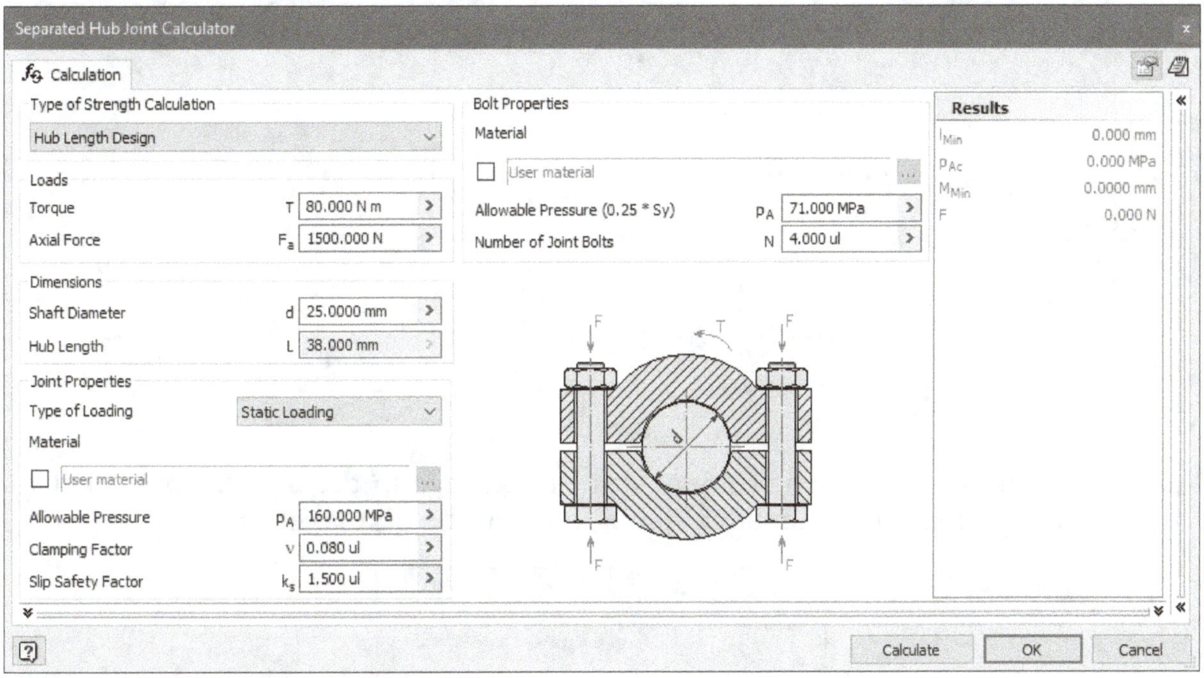

Figure-23. Separated Hub Joint Calculator dialog box

- Specify the load values and dimensions in the **Loads** and **Dimensions** areas, respectively.
- Select desired type of loading from the **Type of Loading** drop-down in the **Joint Properties** area of the dialog box. There are three options in this drop-down; **Static Loading**, **Repeated Loading**, and **Alternating Loading**. If the load to be applied is stable then select the **Static Loading** option. If the loading is repeated in small intervals then select the **Repeated Loading** option. If the loading inverse after small intervals then select the **Alternating Loading** option.
- Specify the other parameters and click on the **Calculate** button. Check the results if there is any error then modify the parameters accordingly.
- Click on the **OK** button to add the calculation to **Model Browser Bar**. Click **OK** in the **File Naming** dialog box displayed.

In the same way, you can use the **Slotted Hub Calculator** and **Cone Joint Calculator** tools available in the **Hub** drop-down and **Power Screw Calculator** tool in the expanded **Power Transmission** panel.

TOLERANCE CALCULATOR

The **Tolerance Calculator** tool is used to find out the tolerance of a dimension based on the other related dimensions. The procedure to use this tool is given next.

- Click on the **Tolerance Calculator** tool from the **Fit/Tolerance Calculator** drop-down in the expanded **Power Transmission** panel in the **Design** tab of the **Ribbon**. The **Tolerance Calculator** dialog box will be displayed as shown in Figure-24.

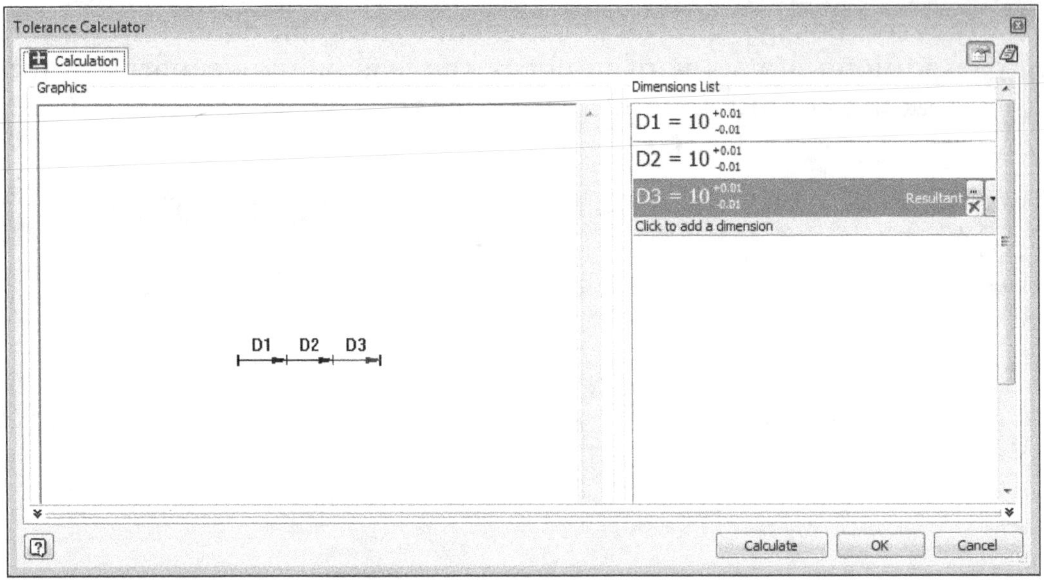

Figure-24. Tolerance Calculator dialog box

- Double-click on the dimension you want to change in the **Dimensions List** area of the dialog box. The **Tolerance** dialog box will be displayed; refer to Figure-25.

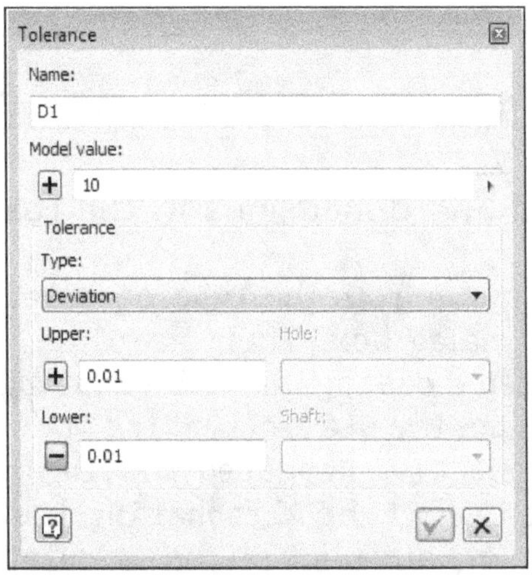

Figure-25. Tolerance dialog box

- Specify desired model value and tolerance values in the related edit boxes. Click on the **OK** button to apply the changes.
- Click on the **Click to add a dimension** option from the dialog box to add more dimensions. Note that the dimension value with cyan color background is the resultant dimension, so you need to drag all the dimensions above it to calculate their resultant.
- Now, click on the **Calculate** button to find out the resultant dimension with equal tolerance. The value of resultant dimension will be displayed in the **Dimensions List** area and graphical form of dimension will be displayed in the **Graphics** area of the dialog box.

LIMITS/FITS CALCULATOR

The **Limits/Fits Calculator** tool is used to check the appropriate limit/fit values for the shaft and hole. The procedure to use this tool is given next.

- Click on the **Limits/Fits Calculator** tool from the **Fit/Tolerance Calculator** drop-down in the expanded **Power Transmission** panel of the **Design** tab in the **Ribbon**. The **Limits and Fits Mechanical Calculator** dialog box will be displayed; refer to Figure-26.

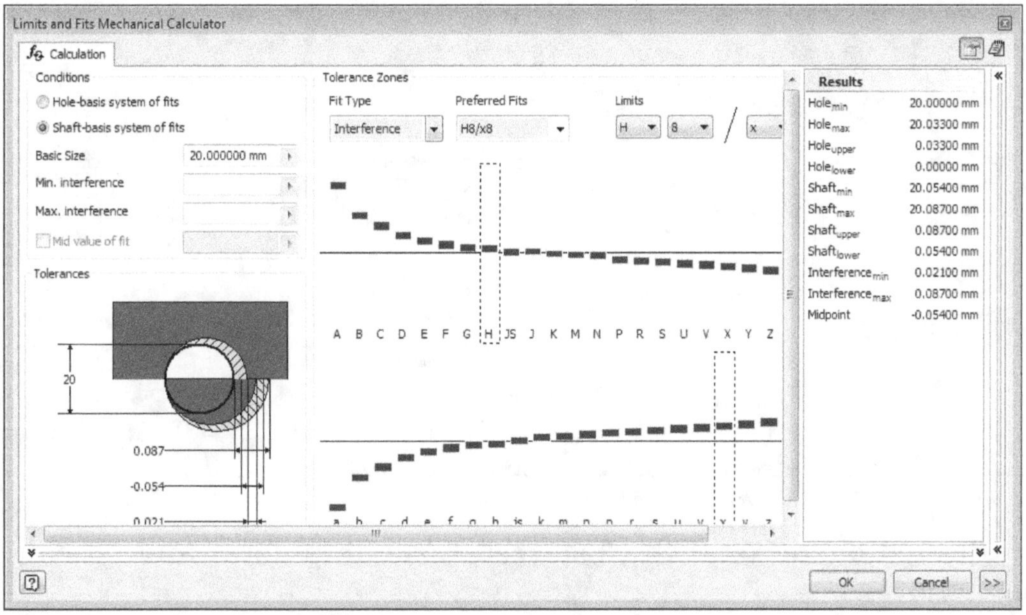

Figure-26. Limits and Fits Mechanical Calculator dialog box

- Select desired radio button from the **Conditions** area. There are two radio buttons; **Hole-basis system of fits** and **Shaft-basis system of fits**. Select the **Hole-basis system of fits** radio button if you want to design limits/fits based on hole. If you want to design limits/fits based on shaft then select the other radio button.
- Specify the diameter of shaft or hole, based on radio button selected, in the **Basic Size** edit box.
- Specify the minimum interference and maximum interference in the respective edit boxes or you can define the mid value of fit by selecting the **Mid value of fit** check box and specifying the value in related edit box.
- Select desired option from the **Fit Type** drop-down, the most relevant fits and limits will be selected automatically in the **Preferred Fits** and **Limits** drop-downs.
- Click on the **OK** button to add the Limits and Fits calculations in the **Model Browser Bar**. The **File Naming** dialog box will be displayed. Click on the **OK** button.

PRESS FIT CALCULATOR

The **Press Fit Calculator** tool is used to check the parameters related to press fitting of shaft in the hole. Press fitting of shaft is based on the thermal expansion of metals. When we heat up the hole and insert shaft in it then after gradual cooling, the hole contracts and tightly holds the shaft. The procedure to use this tool is given next.

- Click on the **Press Fit Calculator** tool from the **Fit/Tolerance** drop-down in the expanded **Power Transmission** panel of the **Design** tab in **Ribbon**. The **Press Fit Calculator** dialog box will be displayed; refer to Figure-27.

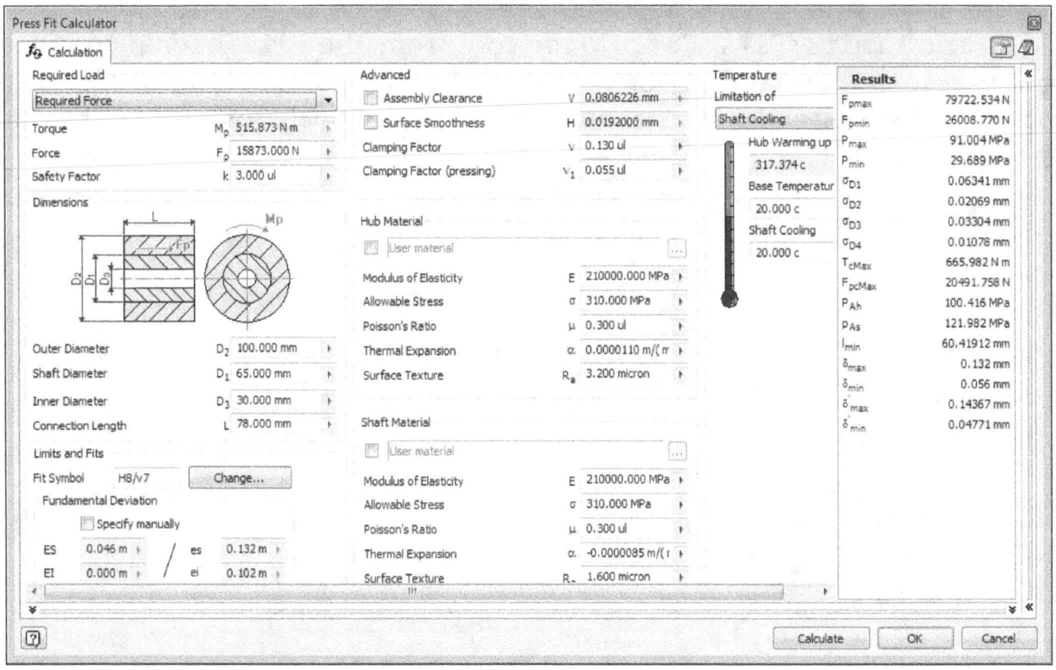

Figure-27. Press Fit Calculator dialog box

- Select desired option from the **Required Load** drop-down and specify the load parameters.
- Specify the basic diameters of shaft and hole, and the connection length in the **Dimensions** area of the dialog box.
- To change the limit/fit of shaft-hole connection, click on the **Change** button in the **Limits and Fits** area of the dialog box. The **Limits and Fits Mechanical Calculator** dialog box will be displayed as discussed earlier. Change the parameters as required and click on the **OK** button.
- Specify the other parameters related to material and temperature.
- Click on the **Calculate** button. If error is displayed then modify the parameters accordingly.
- Click on the **OK** button to add calculation in **Model Browser Bar**.

SPRINGS

A spring is defined as an elastic body, whose function is to distort when loaded and to recover its original shape when the load is removed. The various important applications of springs are as follows :

1. To cushion, absorb, or control energy due to either shock or vibration as in car springs, railway buffers, air-craft landing gears, shock absorbers, and vibration dampers.
2. To apply forces, as in brakes, clutches, and spring loaded valves.
3. To control motion by maintaining contact between two elements as in cams and followers.
4. To measure forces, as in spring balances and engine indicators.
5. To store energy, as in watches, toys, etc.

There are four tools in Autodesk Inventor to create springs viz. **Compression**, **Extension**, **Belleville**, and **Torsion**. The procedure to use these tools are discussed next.

Designing Compression Spring

The **Compression** tool in Autodesk Inventor is used to design compression springs. The procedure to do so is given next.

- Click on the **Compression** tool from the **Spring** panel in the **Design** tab of the **Ribbon**. The **Compression Spring Component Generator** dialog box will be displayed; refer to Figure-28.

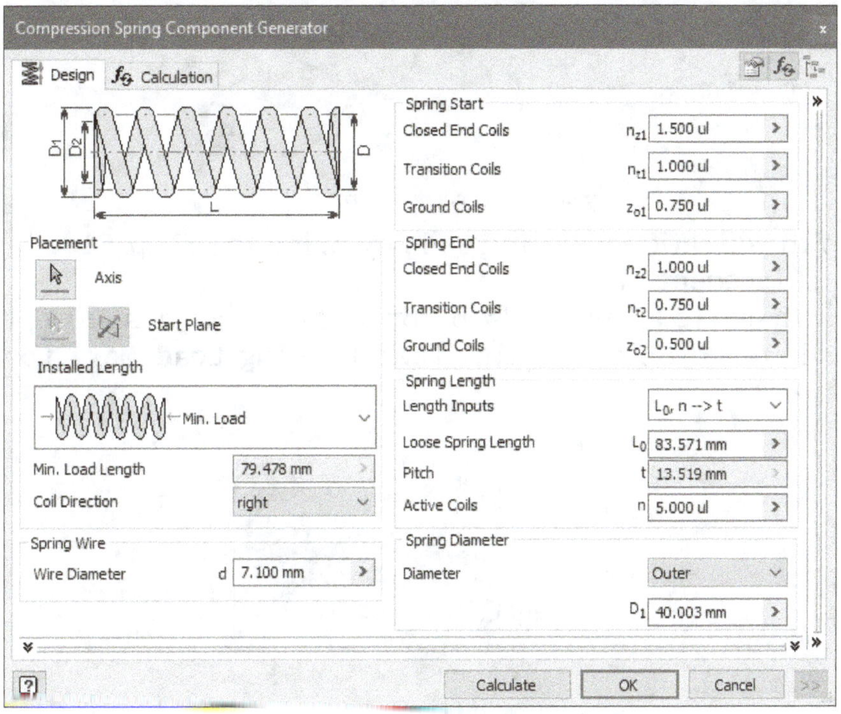

Figure-28. Compression Spring Component Generator dialog box

- Click on the **Axis** selection button from the **Placement** area of the dialog box. You will be asked to select the center axis for the spring.
- Select an axis. You will be asked to select the starting plane.
- Click on the plane/planar face you want to use as starting plane. Preview of the spring will be displayed in the drawing area; refer to Figure-29.

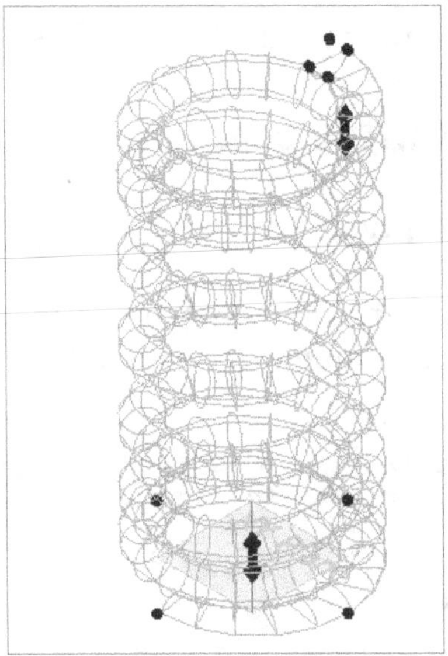

Figure-29. Preview of spring

- You can flip the direction of spring coils by using the **Flip Side** button for **Start Plane** in the **Placement** area.
- Click in the **Installed Length** drop-down and select desired option. There are four options in this drop-down; **Min. Load**, **Working Load**, **Max. Load**, and **Custom**; refer to Figure-30.

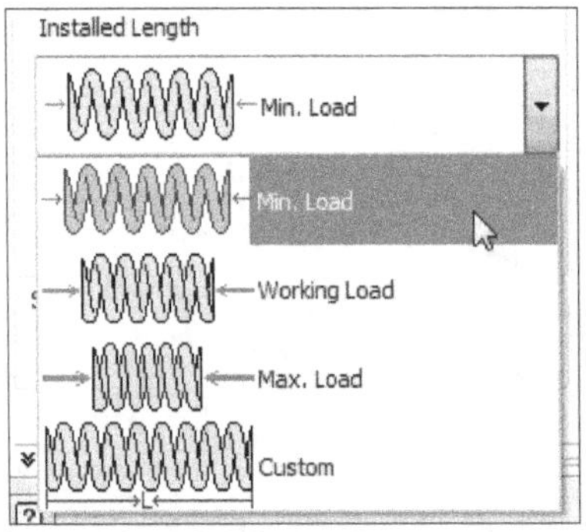

Figure-30. Installed Length drop-down

- Select the **Min. Load** option to define installed length of spring at minimum load. Select the **Working Load** option to define installed length of spring at working load. Select the **Max. Load** option to define installed length of spring at maximum load. Note that on selecting these options, the installed length is automatically calculated based on inputs given in **Spring Length** area of the dialog box. Select the **Custom** option to define the installed length manually. Note that the specified value must be less than loose spring length and greater than maximum load length.
- Specify the other parameters related to spring start coil, spring end coil, spring length, and spring diameter in the relative areas of the dialog box.
- Click in the **Spring Strength Calculation** drop-down and select desired option. There are three options in this drop-down viz. **Compression Spring Design**, **Spring Check Calculation**, and **Work Forces Calculation**. Select the **Compression Spring Design** option to design compression spring based on the specified parameters. Select the **Spring Check Calculation** option to check the feasibility of spring for specified loading conditions. Select the **Work Forces Calculation** option to find out the minimum, maximum, and working load of spring.

- Select desired option from the **Design Type** drop-down if you have selected the **Compression Spring Design** option from the **Spring Strength Calculation** drop-down. If you have selected the **F,D-->d,L0,n,Assembly Dimension** from the **Design Type** drop-down then you can select desired option from the **Design of Assembly Dimensions** drop-down to specify the assembly parameters.
- The options in the **Method of Stress Curvature Correction** drop-down are used to apply correction in stress curvature of the calculation.
- Specify the other parameters based on the options selected in the drop-downs.
- Click on the **Calculate** button. The driven parameters will be calculated automatically based on your inputs. If there is any error displayed then change the parameters accordingly.
- Click on the **OK** button to create the spring. The **File Naming** dialog box will be displayed.
- Set desired location and file names and then click on the **OK** button. The spring will get attached to the cursor.
- Click in the drawing area to place it.

Designing Extension Spring

Extension springs, also known as a tension spring, are helical wound coils, wrapped tightly together to create tension. Extension springs usually have hooks, loops, or end coils that are pulled out and formed from each end of the body. The function of an extension spring is to provide extended force when the spring is pulled apart from its original length. In Autodesk Inventor, the **Extension** tool is used to design extension springs. The procedure to do so is given next.

- Click on the **Extension** tool from the **Spring** panel in the **Design** tab of the **Ribbon**. The **Extension Spring Component Generator** dialog box will be displayed; refer to Figure-31.

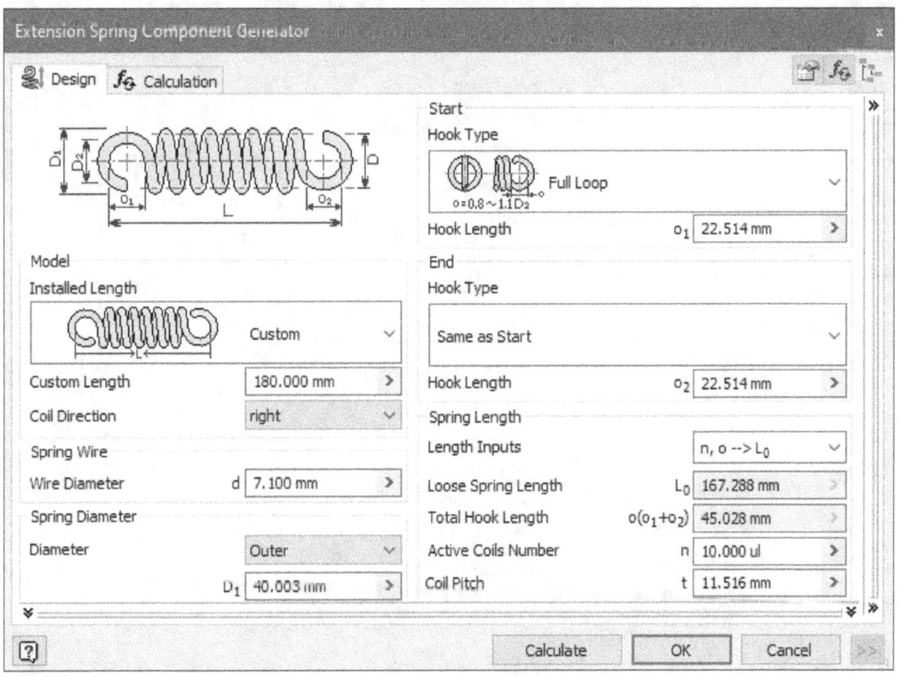

Figure-31. Extension Spring Component Generator dialog box

- Click in the **Installed Length** drop-down of **Model** area of the dialog box. Four options viz. **Min. Load**, **Working Load**, **Max. Load**, and **Custom** will be displayed. Select desired option. Use of each option has already been discussed in previous topic.
- Specify spring wire diameter and spring diameter in the respective edit boxes.
- Click in the **Hook Type** drop-down for both start and end, and select desired type of hook; refer to Figure-32.

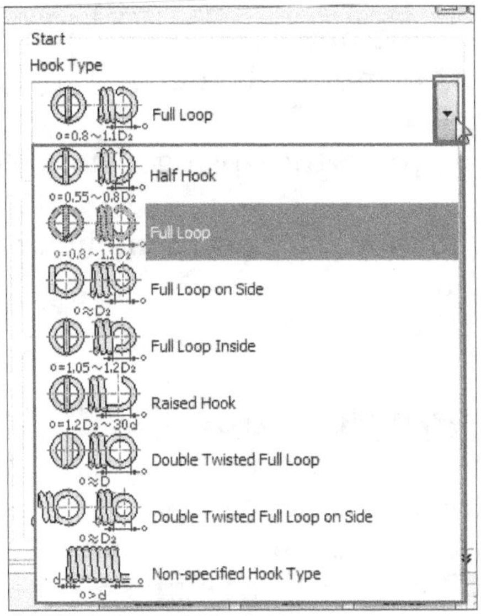

Figure-32. Hook Type drop-down

- Specify the other parameters related to spring length and hook length.
- Click on the **Calculate** button to check the validity of parameters specified so far.
- Click on the **Calculation** tab to check the feasibility of spring under specified load. The dialog box will be displayed as shown in Figure-33.

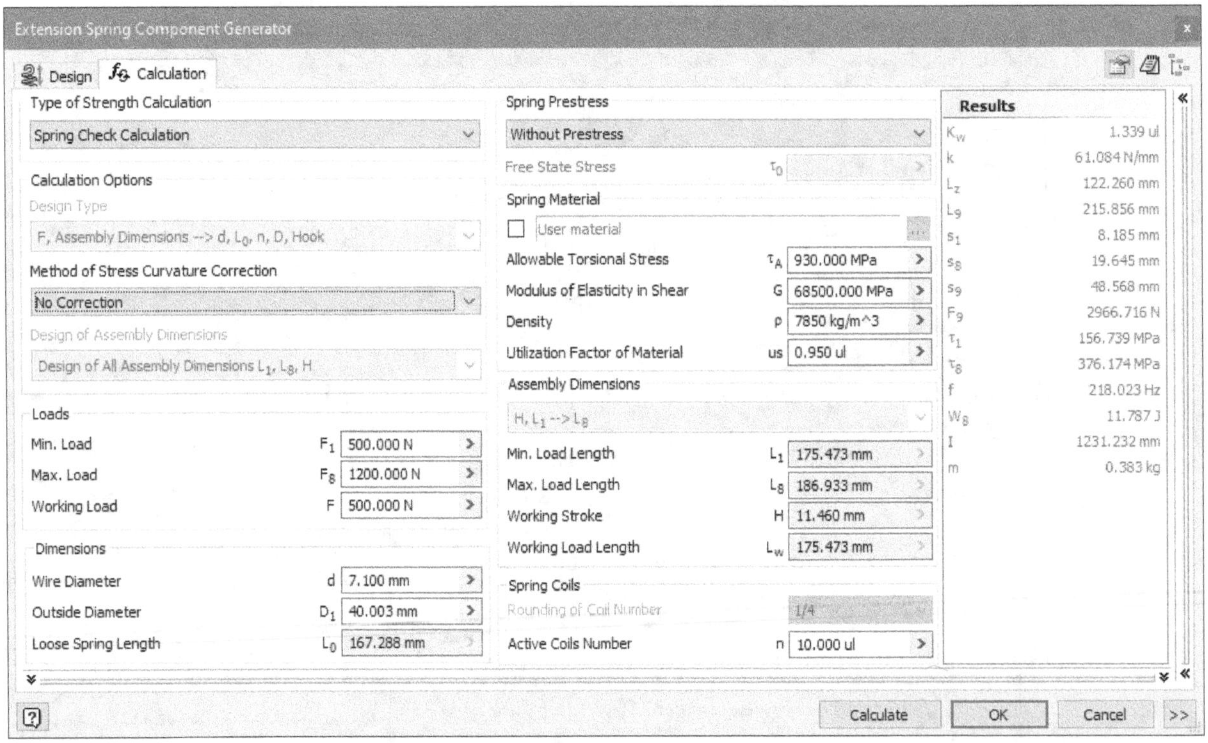

Figure-33. Calculation tab in Spring Component Generator dialog box

- Specify the parameters as discussed in previous topic and click on the **Calculate** button. If an error is displayed then modify the spring accordingly.
- Click on the **OK** button to create the spring. The **File Naming** dialog box will be displayed.
- Specify desired name and location and then click on the **OK** button to create the spring. The spring will get attached to the cursor.
- Click at desired location in the drawing area to place the spring; refer to Figure-34.

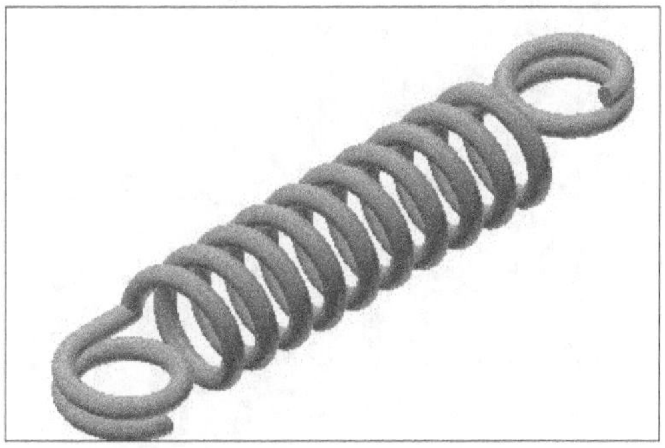

Figure-34. Spring created

Similarly, you can design Belleville and Torsion springs by using the **Belleville** and **Torsion** tools in the **Spring** panel of **Design** tab in **Ribbon**.

FRAME DESIGNING

In Autodesk Inventor, there is a set of tools specifically grouped to design frames in the **Frame** panel of **Design** tab in the **Ribbon**; refer to Figure-35.

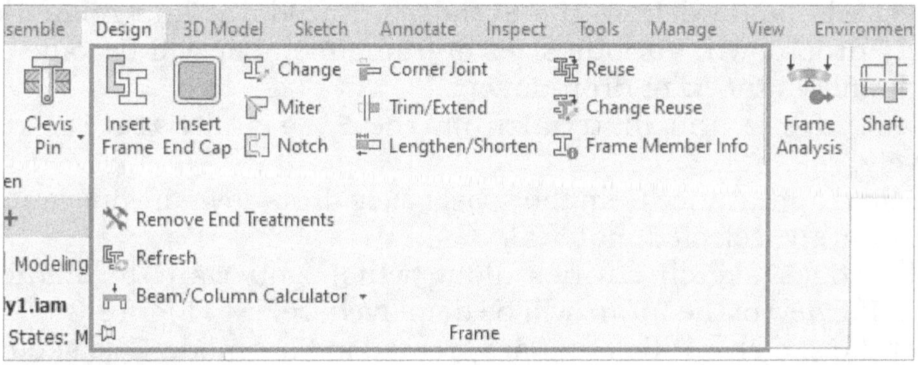

Figure-35. Frame panel

The **Insert Frame** tool in the **Frame** panel is used to insert the base members of frame and the other tools are used to perform various modifications in the frame. The procedures to use these tools are discussed next.

Inserting Frame

The **Insert Frame** tool is used to insert the frame members along the selected edges or point to point. The procedure to use this tool is given next.

- Click on the **Insert Frame** tool from the **Frame** panel in the **Design** tab of the **Ribbon**. The **Insert Frame** dialog box will be displayed; refer to Figure-36.

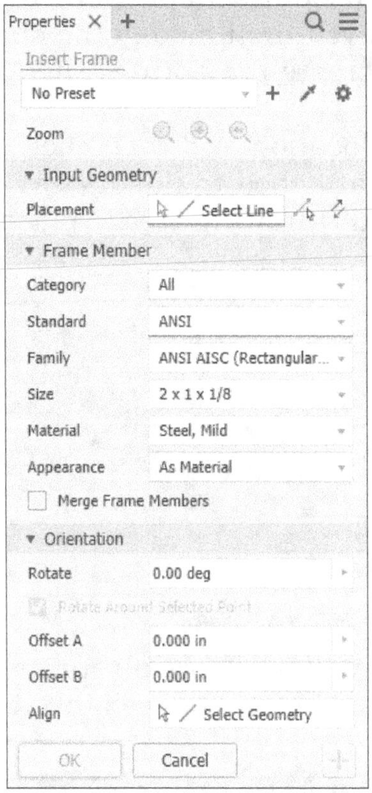

Figure-36. Insert Frame dialog box

- Select desired category type of frame member from the **Category** drop-down in the dialog box like Angles, Channels, I-Beams, and so on.
- Select desired standard from the **Standard** drop-down and related shape from the **Family** drop-down. Various sizes of frame member will become available for selected family in the **Size** drop-down.
- Select desired size and material from the **Size** and **Material** drop-downs, respectively.
- Select desired appearance from the **Appearance** drop-down if you want appearance different from the selected material.
- Select the edges/sketch entities along which you want to create the frame members. Preview of the frame will be displayed; refer to Figure-37. Note that you can select the sketch entities that are created in Part mode. The sketches created in the Assembly environment can not be used to create frame.
- If the frame members are intersecting at corner points then select the **Merge Frame Members** check box to merge them at intersections.

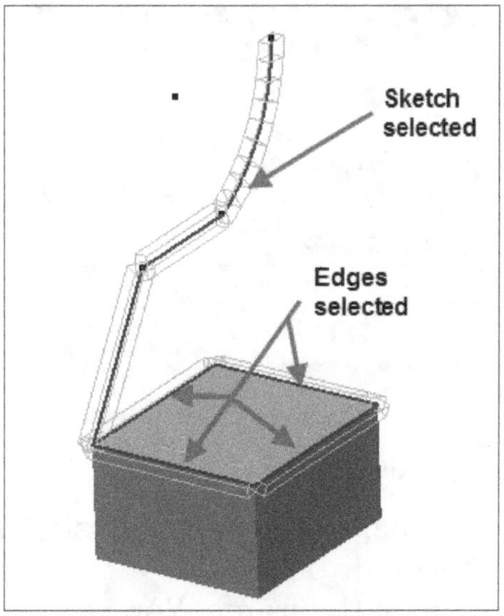

Figure-37. Preview of Frame members

- If you want to select start and end points in place of edges/lines then click on the **Insert Members between Points** button from the **Input Geometry** area of the dialog box.
- Click on the **Flip Direction** button in the **Input Geometry** area to reverse the direction of frame member along selected edge/line/points.
- Specify the offset values in the **Vertical Offset** and **Horizontal Offset** edit boxes if required.
- Click in the **Rotate** edit box and specify desired angle value if you want to rotate the frame member about its center line.
- If the frame members are not aligned as desired then click in the **Align** selection box of **Orientation** area. You will be asked to select a geometry to which the frame members are to be aligned. Select desired geometry, the frame members will be aligned to it; refer to Figure-38.

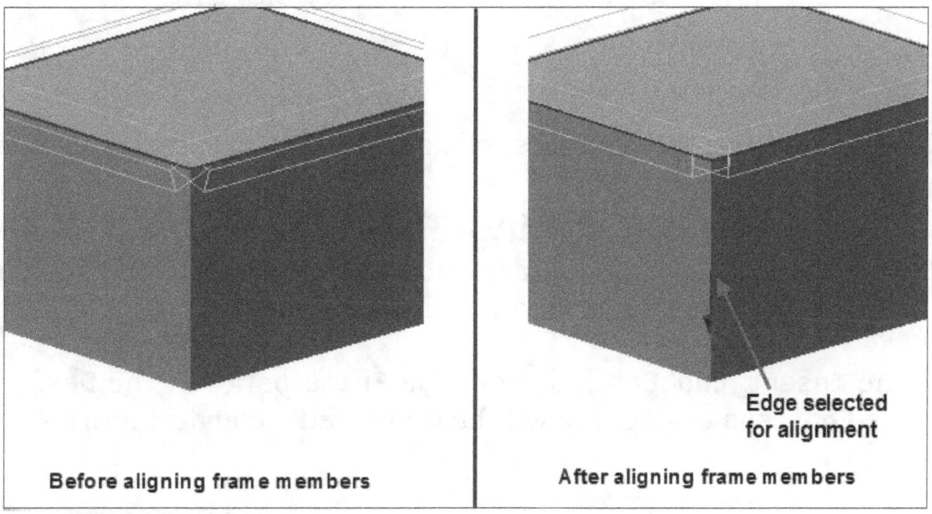

Figure-38. Aligning frame members

- Click on the **OK** button to create the frame members. The **Create New Frame** dialog box will be displayed; refer to Figure-39.

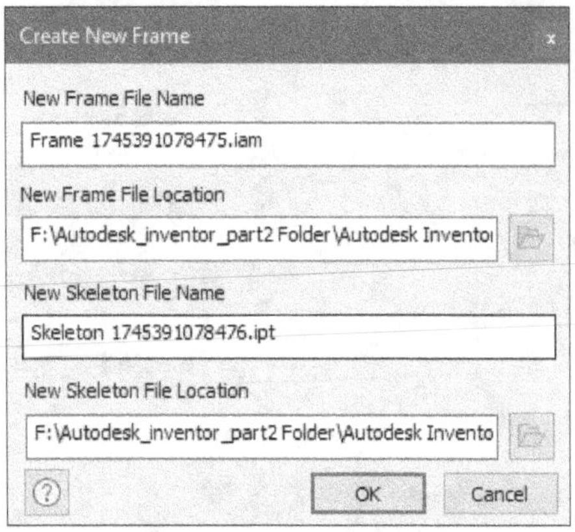

Figure-39. Create New Frame dialog box

- Specify desired frame file name, frame location, skeleton file name, and skeleton file location in the respective edit boxes.
- Click on the **OK** button to create the frame. You can hide the base object now. The **Frame Member Naming** dialog box will be displayed; refer to Figure-40.

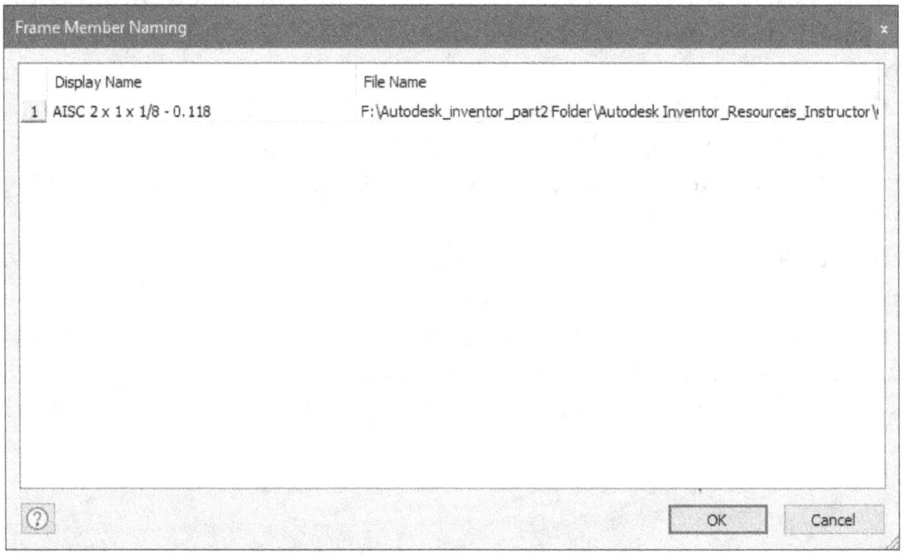

Figure-40. Frame member naming dialog box

- After specifying desired parameters, click on the **OK** button from the dialog box.

Inserting End Cap

The **Insert End Cap** tool is used to place end caps on selected frame members. The procedure to use this tool is discussed next.

- Click on the **Insert End Cap** tool from the **Frame** panel in the **Design** tab of the **Ribbon**. The **End Caps** dialog box will be displayed; refer to Figure-41.

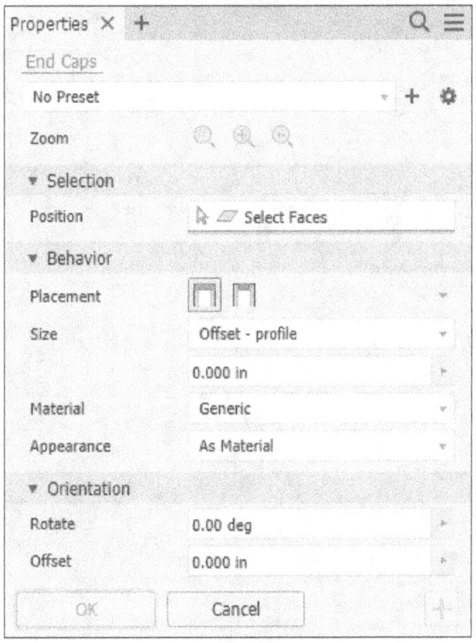

Figure-41. End Caps dialog box

- Select the frame member from the drawing area on which you want to place the end caps. Parameters of the selected member will be displayed in the dialog box.
- Select the frame member with desired parameters by using the options in the dialog box. The options in the dialog box are same as discussed in previous topic.
- Click on the **OK** button to apply the changes.

Changing Frame Members

The **Change** tool in the **Frame** panel in the **Design** tab of the **Ribbon** is used to change the parameters related to frames. The procedure to use this tool is discussed next.

- Click on the **Change** tool from the **Frame** panel in the **Design** tab of the **Ribbon**. The **Change Frame** dialog box will be displayed; refer to Figure-42.

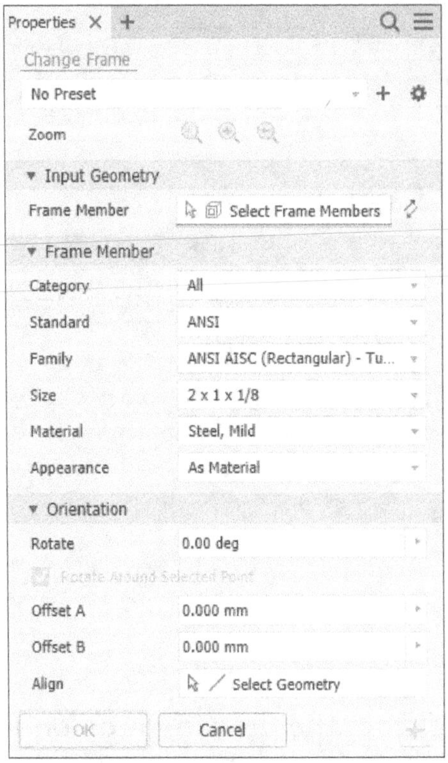

Figure-42. Change Frame dialog box

- Select the frame member that you want to change from the drawing area. Parameters of the selected member will be displayed in the dialog box.
- Select the frame member with desired parameters by using the options in the dialog box. The options in the dialog box are same as discussed in previous topic.
- Click on the **OK** button to apply the changes.

Mitering Corners

A miter joint (mitre in British English), sometimes shortened to miter, is a joint made by beveling each of two parts to be joined, usually at a 45° angle, to form a corner. The procedure to apply miter to a joint is discussed next.

- Click on the **Miter** tool from the **Frame** panel in the **Design** tab of the **Ribbon**. The **Miter** dialog box will be displayed; refer to Figure-43. Also, you will be asked to select the frame member to be cut.

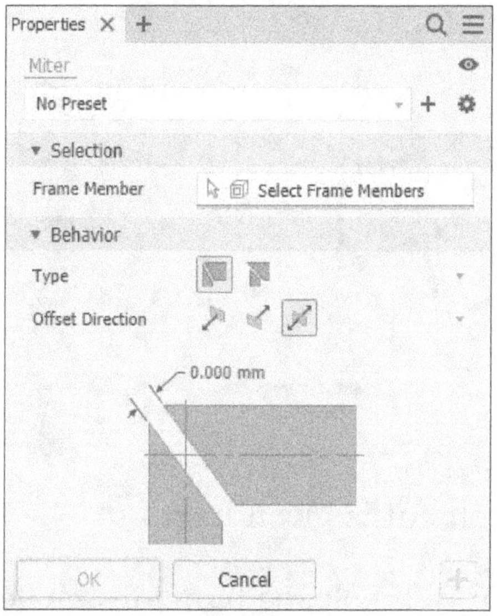

Figure-43. Miter dialog box

- Select a frame member you want to be cut. You will be asked to select the other member to be cut.
- Select the other intersecting frame member. Preview of the miter cut will be displayed.
- By default, the **Full Miter Cut** option is selected from **Type** drop-down in the **Behavior** area of the dialog box to match full edges of both the frame members after miter cut. If you want frame member to be joined at their bisector then select the **Bisect Miter Cut** option from **Type** drop-down.
- Select desired offset type from **Offset** drop-down in the dialog box and specify desired offset distance in the **Miter Offset** edit box.
- Click on the **Apply** button to create the current miter cut and continue to create the next or click on the **OK** button to create the miter cut and exit the tool. The miter cut will be created; refer to Figure-44.

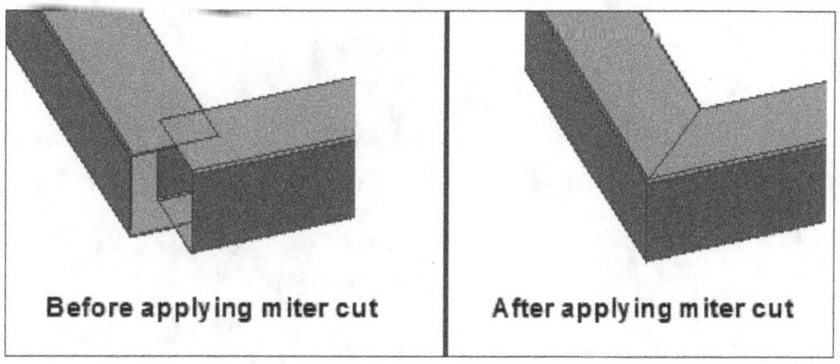

Figure-44. Applying Miter cut

Applying Notch Cut

The notch cutting is used to cut the ends of two frame members so that they can be joined. Sometimes notching is done to make other joints like miter joints; refer to Figure-45.

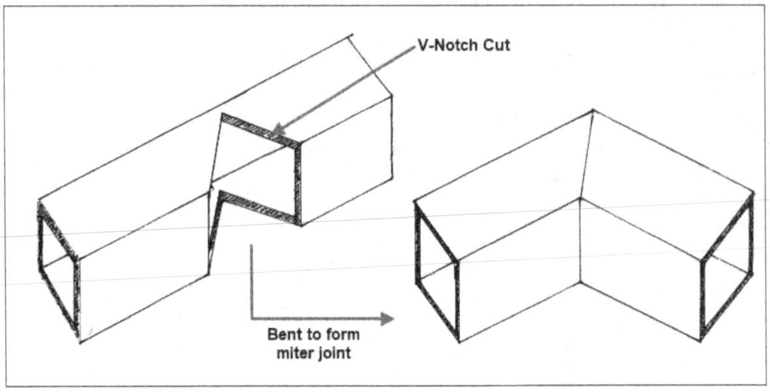

Figure-45. Notched tube

The procedure to apply notch cut is given next.

- Click on the **Notch** tool from the **Frame** panel in the **Design** tab of the **Ribbon**. The **Notch** dialog box will be displayed; refer to Figure-46. Also, you will be asked to select the frame member to be cut.

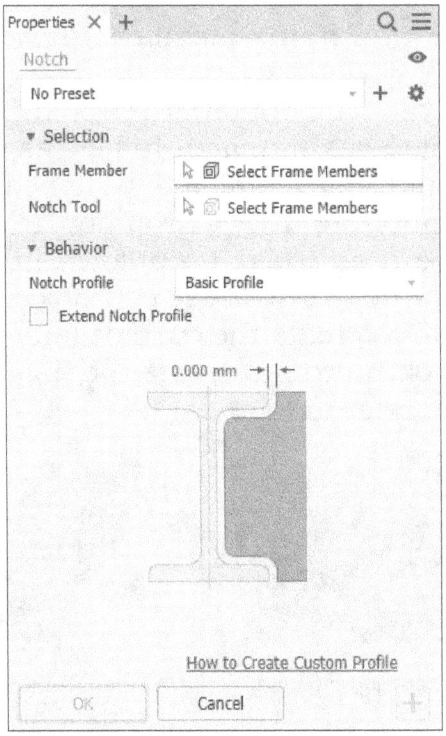

Figure-46. Notch dialog box

- Select the frame member that you want to be cut. You will be asked to select the notch tool.
- Select the notch tool to be used as cutting tool reference.
- Select desired option from **Notch Profile** drop-down in the **Behavior** area of the dialog box. There are three options in this drop-down, viz. **Basic Profile**, **Custom Profile**, and **Custom I template**. Select the **Basic Profile** option to set a single offset value for the notch. Select the **Custom Profile** option, if available, to use the custom notch profile in the Content Center family. Or select the **Custom I template** option, if available, to set multiple offset values.
- Select the **Extend Notch Profile** check box, if available, to extend the profile to an intersection.

- Select the **Perpendicular Cut** check box, if available, to create precise intersections such as a laser cut notch for a pipe.
- Specify desired value in the **Notch Offset** edit box in the dialog box.
- Click on the **OK** button, the notch cut will be applied; refer to Figure-47.

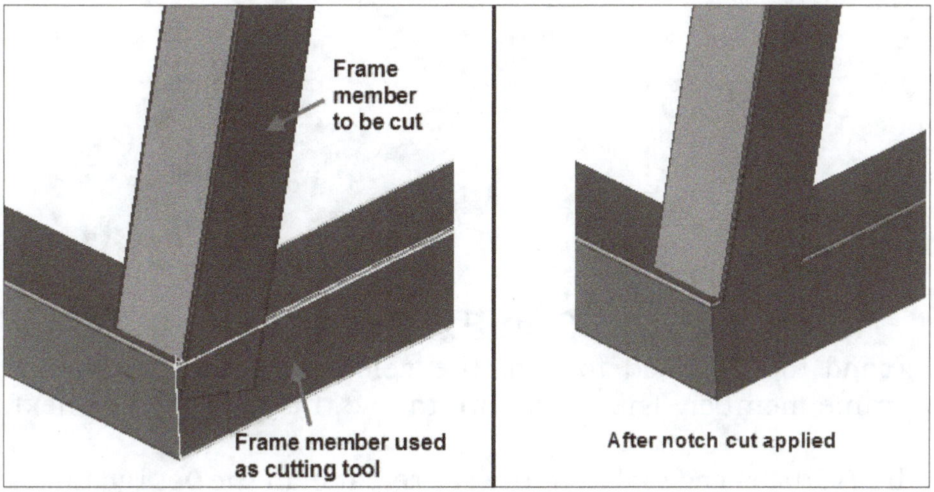

Figure-47. Applying notch cut

Corner Joint

The **Corner Joint** tool is used to join two intersecting frame members by trimming or extending the members. The procedure to use this tool is given next.

- Click on the **Corner Joint** tool from the **Frame** panel in the **Design** tab of **Ribbon**. The **Corner Joint** dialog box will be displayed; refer to Figure-48.

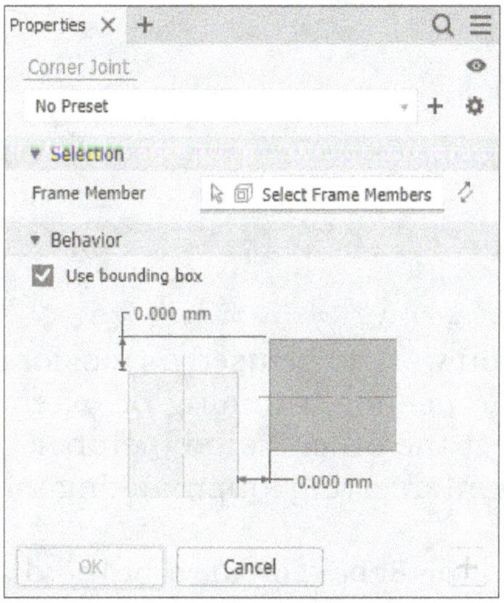

Figure-48. Corner Joint dialog box

- Select the two intersecting frame members where you want to create corner joint. Preview of corner joint will be displayed; refer to Figure-49.
- Specify desired distance values in the edit boxes of **Behavior** area in dialog box and click on the **OK** button to create the joint.

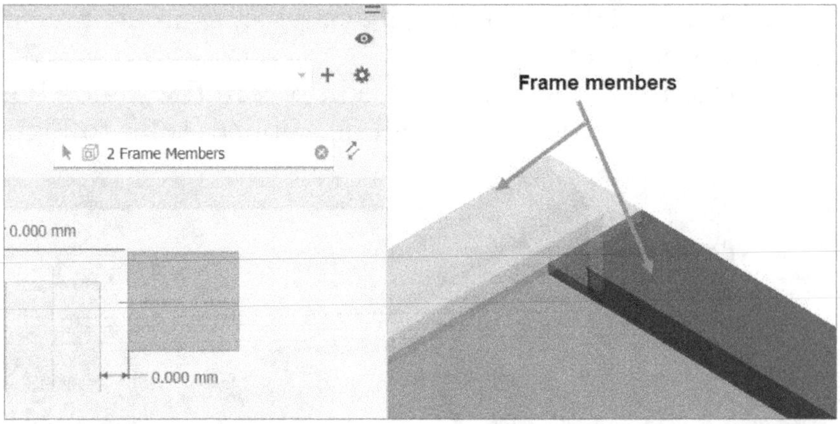

Figure-49. Corner joint preview

Trim/Extend

The **Trim/Extend** tool is used to trim the selected frame member at the other intersecting frame member. The procedure to use this tool is given next.

- Click on the **Trim/Extend** tool from the **Frame** panel in the **Design** tab of the **Ribbon**. The **Trim/Extend** dialog box will be displayed; refer to Figure-50.

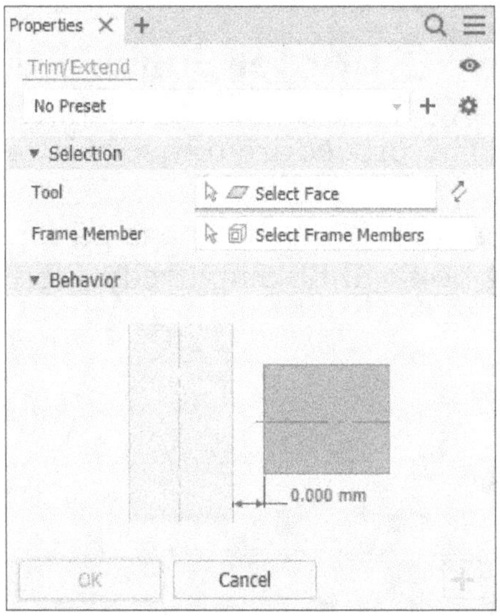

Figure-50. Trim Extend dialog box

- Select desired face that you want to be used as tool for trimming. Note that selected face will be used as reference for trimming or extension. On selecting the face, you will be asked to select the other frame member to be trimmed or extended.
- Select the frame member intersecting/approaching the first one. Preview of feature will be displayed.
- Specify the gap values in the **Behavior** area of the dialog box, if required.
- Click on the **Apply** button to create the current trimming and continue to create the next or click on the **OK** button to create the trimmed parts and exit the tool. The trimmed frame members will be created; refer to Figure-51.

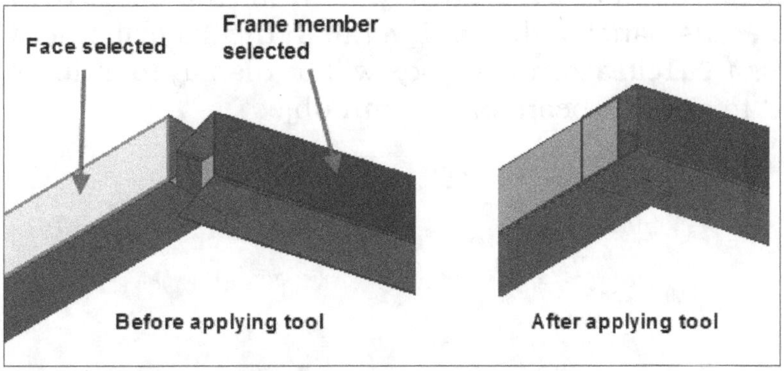

Figure-51. Trimming-Extending frame member

Lengthen/Shorten Frame Member

The **Lengthen/Shorten** tool is used to lengthen/shorten the frame member by specified value. The procedure to use this tool is given next.

- Click on the **Lengthen/Shorten** tool from the **Frame** panel in the **Design** tab of the **Ribbon**. The **Lengthen/Shorten** dialog box will be displayed; refer to Figure-52.

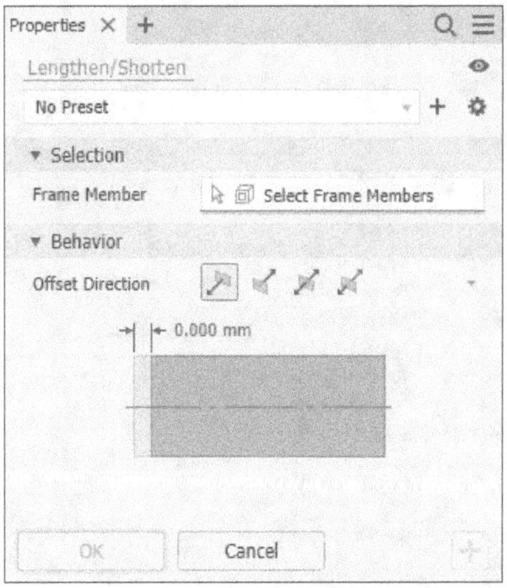

Figure-52. Lengthen Shorten dialog box

- Select the frame member(s) you want to shorten/lengthen.
- Select desired option from the **Offset Direction** drop-down in the **Behavior** area of the dialog box.
- Specify desired value in the **Lengthen/Shorten** edit box of the dialog box.
- Click on the **OK** button to apply the changes and exit the tool.

Similarly, you can use the other editing tools like **Reuse** tool, **Change Reuse** tool, **Remove End Treatments** (in expanded **Frame** panel) etc. available in the **Frame** panel.

Beam/Column Calculations

After creating the frame, next step is to check whether it will sustain the specified load or not. The procedure to perform these calculations is given next.

- Click on the **Beam/Column Calculator** tool from the **Calculators** drop-down in the expanded **Frame** panel of the **Design** tab in the **Ribbon**; refer to Figure-53. The **Beam and Column Calculator** dialog box will be displayed; refer to Figure-54. Also, you are asked to select a beam or column object.

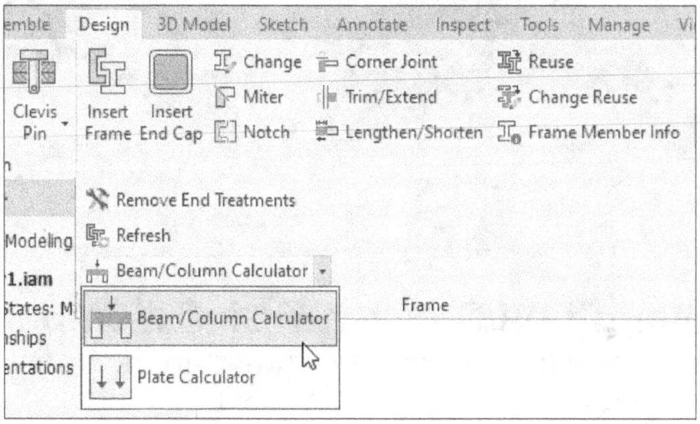

Figure-53. Beam-Column Calculator tool

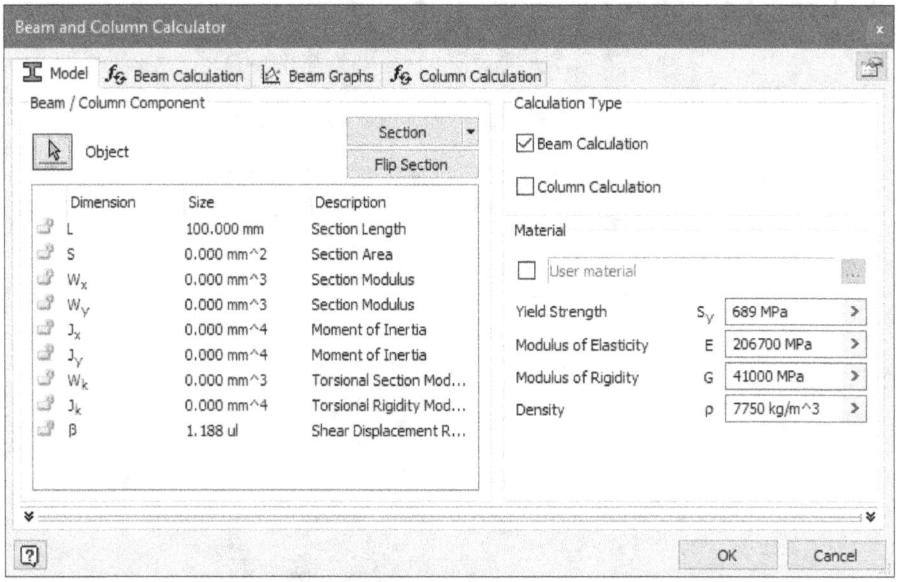

Figure-54. Beam and Column Calculator dialog box

- Select a frame member on which you want to perform the loading test.
- Click on the **Section** button and select the shape that closely match to your frame member; refer to Figure-55. Specify the dimensions of section in the dialog box displayed and click **OK** button.

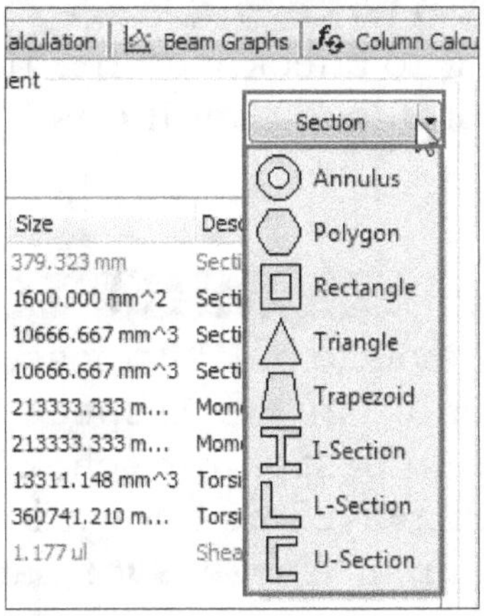

Figure-55. Section drop-down

- Select desired check box from the **Calculation Type** area to mark it as beam or column. If you want to perform both type of calculations then select both the check boxes in the area.
- Specify the material properties in the **Material** area of the dialog box.
- Click on the **Beam Calculation** tab to check the effect of load on the selected frame member. The dialog box will be displayed as shown in Figure-56. Make sure that you have selected the **Beam Calculation** check box from the **Calculation Type** area of the **Model** tab in the dialog box.

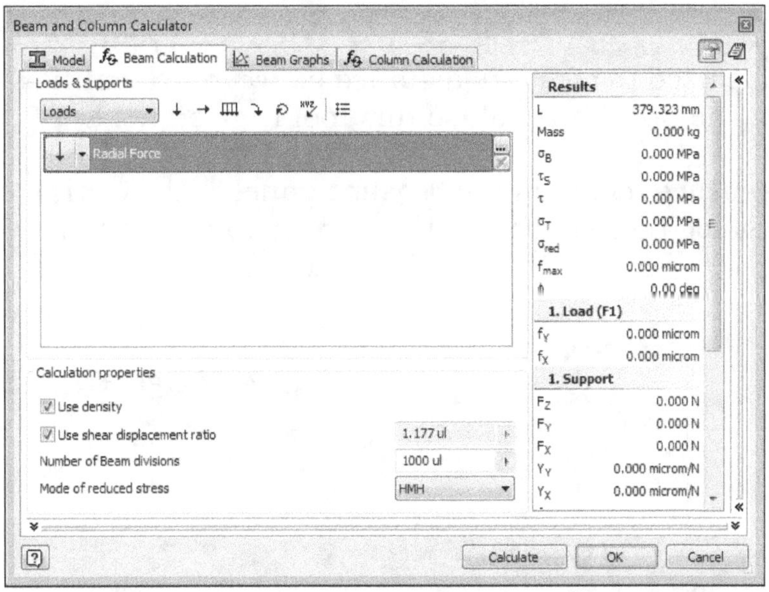

Figure-56. Beam Calculation tab in Beam and Column Calculator dialog box

- Specify desired loads as discussed in previous chapter and click on the **Calculate** button. The results will be displayed in the **Results** area of dialog box. Modify the frame member, if error occurs.
- Similarly, you can perform the column calculations and check the beam graph.
- After performing calculations, click on the **OK** button to exit the dialog box.

FRAME ANALYSIS

The **Frame Analysis** tool is used to check whether the created frame will be able to sustain under specified real-world load conditions. You will learn about this tool in Chapter 16.

MEASUREMENT TOOLS

There are various measurement tools to quickly measure the components in Autodesk Inventor. These tools are available in the **Inspect** tab as well as **Design** tab. To display the measurement tools in **Design** tab, click on the down button in **Design** tab. A shortcut menu will be displayed as shown in Figure-57. Select the **Measure** check box and click in drawing area. The **Measure** panel will be added in the **Ribbon**.

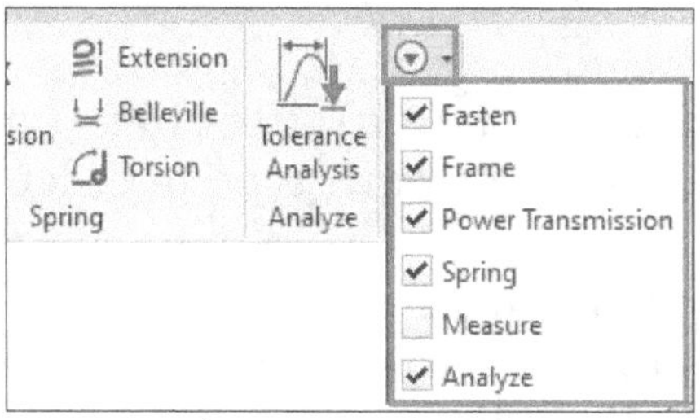

Figure-57. Option to add measurement tool

The tools in the **Measure** panel are discussed next.

Measure Tool

The **Measure** tool is used to measure distance between two entities like points, lines, edges, faces, etc. The procedure to use this tool is given next.

- Click on the **Measure** tool from the **Measure** panel in the **Design** tab of the **Ribbon**. The **Measure** dialog box will be displayed; refer to Figure-58.

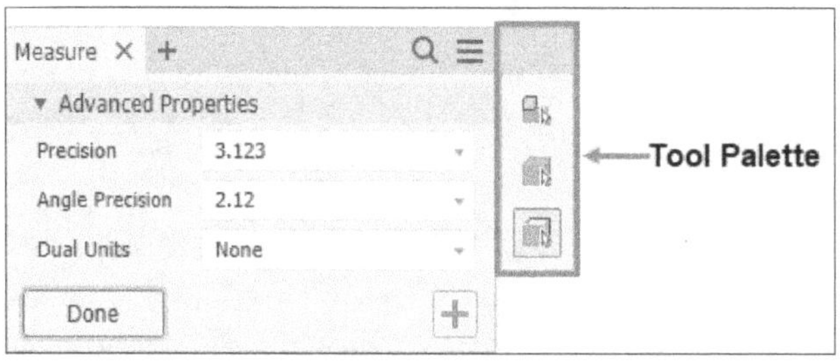

Figure-58. Measure dialog box

- The tool palette displays the selection priority options; refer to Figure-58. Select desired selection priority option from the **Component Priority**, **Part Priority**, or **Select Faces and Edges**.
- Select an edge or line to measure its length. Select an arc to measure its radius. Select a circle to measure its diameter. Select a face to measure its perimeter and area.
- Click on the **Restart Measure** button from the dialog box before measuring next entity; refer to Figure-59.

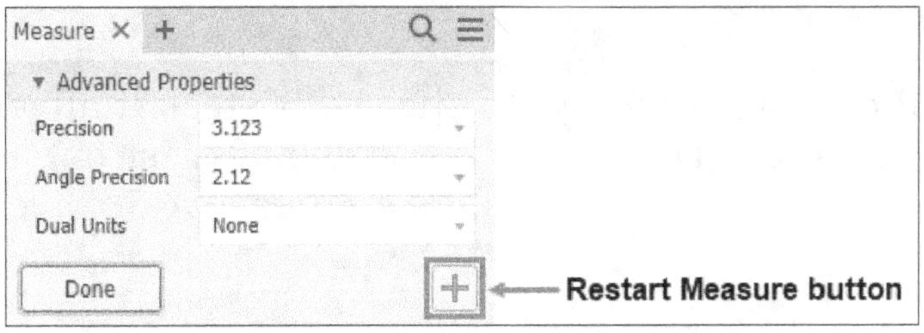

Figure-59. Restart Measure button in Measure dialog box

- To measure distance between two lines, edges, or faces, select the first entity and then hold the **CTRL** key while selecting the next entity; refer to Figure-60.

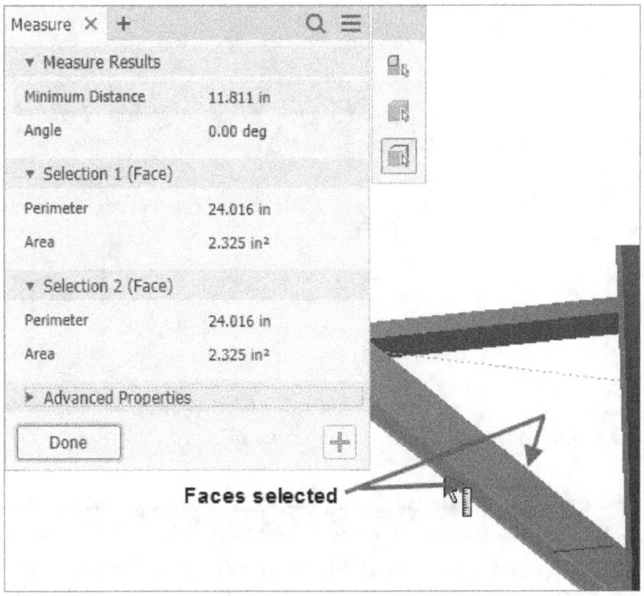

Figure-60. Faces selected for measurement

- Similarly, you can use the other options in **Measure** dialog box to measure various parameters.

PROBLEM 1

A compression coil spring made of an alloy steel is having the following specifications :

Mean diameter of coil = 50 mm ; Wire diameter = 5 mm ; Number of active coils = 20.

If this spring is subjected to an axial load of 500 N; Design the spring.

PROBLEM 2

Design and draw a valve spring of a petrol engine for the following operating conditions:

Spring load when the valve is open = 400 N
Spring load when the valve is closed = 250 N
Maximum inside diameter of spring = 25 mm
Length of the spring when the valve is open = 40 mm
Length of the spring when the valve is closed = 50 mm
Maximum permissible shear stress = 400 MPa

PROBLEM 3

The splined ends and gears attached to the A-36 steel shaft are subjected to the torques shown in Figure-61. Determine the angle of twist of end B with respect to end A. The shaft has a diameter of 40 mm. Properties of A-36 steel should be checked online.

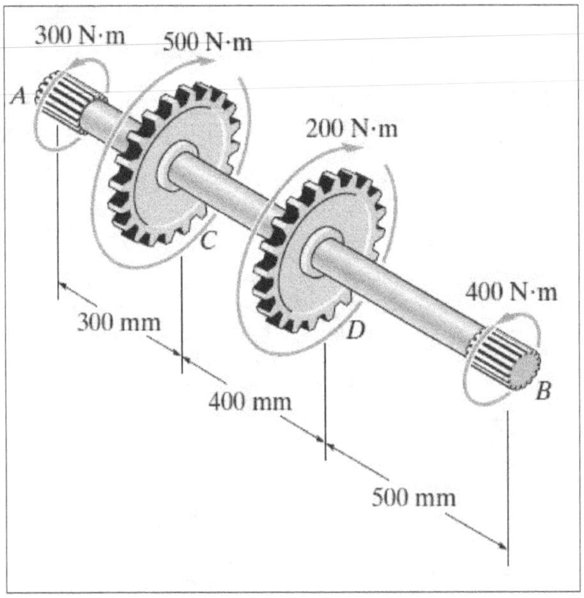

Figure-61. Gear spline system under load

SELF ASSESSMENT

Q1. Which of the following options is also known as **Toric Joint** which is a power transmission component?

a) O-Ring
b) Involute Spline
c) Parallel Spline
d) Linear Cam

Q2. Which of the following factors are responsible for design or capacity of a **Brake Calculator**?

a) The unit pressure between the braking surfaces
b) The projected area of the friction surfaces
c) Both a and b
d) None of the Above

Q3. Which of the following types of **Brake Calculator** is not used in Mechanical Engineering?

a) Drum Brake Calculator
b) Disc Brake Calculator
c) Dynamic Brake Calculator
d) Cone Brake Calculator

Q4. Which of the following options should be selected in the **Bearing Calculator** dialog box to check the feasibility of journal bearing under current loading conditions?

a) Lubricant Selection
b) Check Calculation
c) Design of minimum Journal Diameter
d) None of the Above

Q5. Which of the following statements is incorrect?

a) Springs are used to control or absorb energy due to either shock or vibration as in car springs, railway buffers, etc.

b) Springs are used to apply forces as in brakes, clutches, etc.

c) Springs are used to control motion by maintaining contact between two elements as in cams and followers.

d) Springs are used to measure distance as in spring balances and engine indicators.

Q6. Which of the following tools is not used in creating springs?

a) Centrifugal
b) Compression
c) Extension
d) Belleville

Q7. Splines are ridges or teeth on a drive shaft that mesh with grooves in mating piece. (True/False)

Q8. A brake is a device by means of which artificial speed is applied to a static machine member. (True/False)

Q9. Extension springs, also known as a tension spring, are helical wound coils, wrapped tightly together to create tension. (True/False)

Q10. .... also known as .... are helical wound coils, wrapped tightly together to create tension.

Q11. The dimension value with .... color background is the resultant dimension in the **Tolerance Calculator** dialog box.

Q12. .... are used to transmit mechanical power from a drive motor by coupling it to an output device such as a wheel or an arm.

Q13. What is another name for a Linear Cam?

A. Plate Cam
B. Disc Cam
C. Shaft Cam
D. Cylindrical Cam

Q14. In Autodesk Inventor, which tab contains the Linear Cam tool?

A. Insert tab
B. Design tab
C. View tab
D. Tools tab

Q15. What must be done before using the Parallel Spline tool?

A. Create a motion path
B. Select a bearing
C. Have a shaft and hub in the drawing area
D. Activate simulation mode

Q16. What shape is typically associated with the cross-section of an O-ring?

A. Square
B. Oval
C. Hexagonal
D. Round

Q17. Which type of cam is used in machines performing repetitive movement and seen in old clocks and sewing machines?

A. Linear cam
B. Cylindrical cam
C. Disc cam
D. Plate cam

Q18. What is the purpose of the Runout Radius in spline connections?

A. For oil clearance
B. For smooth rotation
C. For soft locking of hub and shaft
D. For increasing strength of grooves

Q19. What kind of calculator is used to design and evaluate journal bearings in Autodesk Inventor?

A. Shaft Calculator
B. Hub Calculator
C. Bearing Calculator
D. Motion Calculator

Q20. Which parameter is not listed as a factor influencing brake design?

A. Unit pressure between braking surfaces
B. Brake pad thickness
C. Peripheral velocity of the drum
D. Coefficient of friction

Q21. What does the Check Calculation option in spline design do?

A. Designs groove dimensions automatically
B. Adjusts diameter based on load
C. Validates all input parameters to check feasibility
D. Optimizes the material
Q22. What is a common use case of the Separated Hub in mechanical systems?

A. Absorbing vibrations
B. Connecting hydraulic lines
C. Transmitting mechanical power
D. Cooling of shafts

Q23. Which calculator in Autodesk Inventor is used to calculate parameters like friction force and braking time?

A. Band Brake Calculator
B. Disc Brake Calculator
C. Drum Brake Calculator
D. Cone Brake Calculator

Q24. How many options are available in the Type of Strength Calculation drop-down in the Bearing Calculator?

A. Two
B. Three
C. Four
D. Five

Q25. Which Autodesk Inventor feature launches the engineer's handbook for mechanical components?

A. Reference Tool
B. Calculator Tool
C. Design Guide
D. Handbook Tool

Q26. Which tool is used to find the tolerance of a dimension based on other related dimensions?

A. Limits Calculator
B. Press Fit Calculator
C. Tolerance Calculator
D. Spring Strength Calculator

Q27. Where is the Tolerance Calculator located in Autodesk Inventor?
A. Design tab → Spring panel
B. Tools tab → Calculators
C. Design tab → Power Transmission panel
D. View tab → Dimension Tools

Q28. In the Tolerance Calculator, what color indicates the resultant dimension?

A. Green
B. Red
C. Cyan
D. Yellow

Q29. Which button must be clicked to get the final calculated dimension in the Tolerance Calculator?

A. Apply
B. Add
C. Calculate
D. Generate

Q30. What does the Limits/Fits Calculator help determine?

A. Frame joint tolerance
B. Hole and shaft fits
C. Wire size for springs
D. Chamfer angles

Q31. In the Limits/Fits Calculator, which system is selected when designing fits based on the hole?

A. Shaft-basis
B. Assembly-basis
C. Hole-basis
D. Manual system

Q32. What must be specified in the Limits/Fits Calculator for shaft/hole fitting?

A. Length of assembly
B. Temperature coefficient
C. Basic size and interference
D. Load type

Q33. What is press fitting based on?

A. Gravity compression
B. Electrical expansion
C. Thermal expansion
D. Magnetic contraction

Q34. Where can you change shaft-hole connection limits/fits in Press Fit Calculator?

A. Edit Geometry
B. Material Properties
C. Limits and Fits area
D. Orientation tab

Q35. What should you do if the Press Fit Calculator shows an error during calculation?

A. Restart Inventor
B. Modify parameters
C. Click "Force Calculate"
D. Switch to Manual Mode

Q36. What does the Compression tool in the Spring panel help you create?

A. Helical springs
B. Compression springs
C. Hooked springs
D. Torsional bars

Q37. Which of the following is NOT an option in the Installed Length drop-down for springs?

A. Max. Load
B. Loose Length
C. Working Load
D. Custom

Q38. What does the "Flip Side" button do in the Compression Spring design dialog?

A. Flips hook types
B. Changes spring coil direction
C. Switches spring material
D. Inverts pressure axis

Q39. Which option is used to check spring feasibility for specific loading?

A. Spring Feasibility Calculator
B. Spring Load Calculator
C. Spring Check Calculation
D. Spring Design Type

Q40. What does the "Work Forces Calculation" option calculate?

A. Hook angles
B. Installed length
C. Min, max, and working load
D. Coil thickness

Q41. What kind of spring is created using the Extension tool in the Spring panel?

A. Compression spring
B. Torsion spring
C. Tension spring
D. Constant force spring

Q42. What feature distinguishes an extension spring from a compression spring?

A. Color
B. Diameter
C. Hooks or loops at ends
D. Spiral direction

Q43. Which of the following is a spring hook type selection option?

A. Coiled Hook
B. Solid Hook
C. Hook Type Drop-down
D. Hook Placement Panel

Q44. Where do you check the feasibility of an extension spring under load?

A. Model tab
B. Load dialog
C. Spring panel
D. Calculation tab

Q45. What tool in the Frame panel is used to insert base members of a frame?

A. Insert Beam
B. Insert Frame
C. Create Frame
D. Frame Generator

Q46. What check box should be selected to merge intersecting frame members at corners?

A. Snap Corners
B. Merge Frame Ends
C. Merge Frame Members
D. Combine Geometry

Q47. What kind of joint is created by the Miter tool?

A. 90° corner joint
B. 30° butt joint
C. 45° bevel joint
D. U-shaped corner joint

Q48. What is the purpose of the Notch tool in frame design?

A. Join flat panels
B. Create spacing gaps
C. Cut ends of frames for joining
D. Round edges for safety

Chapter 12

Sheetmetal Design

Topics Covered

The major topics covered in this chapter are:

- ***Creating Sheet Metal part files***
- ***Setting Sheet Metal Defaults***
- ***Industrial Terms related to Sheet Metal Design***
- ***Sheet Metal Creation and Modification Tools***
- ***Creating Flat Patterns***
- ***Practical on Sheet Metal Design***
- ***Practice and Problems***

INTRODUCTION

Sheet metal work is an important aspect of Mechanical engineering. Many parts around us are manufactured via sheetmetal processes. For example, car body, vents in houses, Air-conditioner ducts, spoon, metal bowls, and so on. The sheetmetal parts generally have thickness ranging from fraction of millimeter to 12.5 millimeters i.e. up to half inch. Like welding and machining, sheetmetal also has its own processes like, bending, punching, stamping, spinning, rolling, and so on. In this chapter, we will discuss about the tools available in Autodesk Inventor related to sheetmetal designing.

STARTING SHEETMETAL ENVIRONMENT

In Autodesk Inventor, there are two ways to start sheetmetal environment:

1. Make a part in the Standard Part environment and then convert it to Sheetmetal.
2. Start a new file in the Sheetmetal environment by using Sheetmetal template.

You will learn about converting the part in to sheetmetal later in this chapter. We will now start a new file in sheetmetal environment.

Starting A New File in Sheetmetal Environment

The procedure to start a new file in sheetmetal environment is given next.

- Start Autodesk Inventor and click on the **New** button from **New** cascading menu in the **File** menu of the **Ribbon**. The **Create New File** dialog box will be displayed; refer to Figure-1.

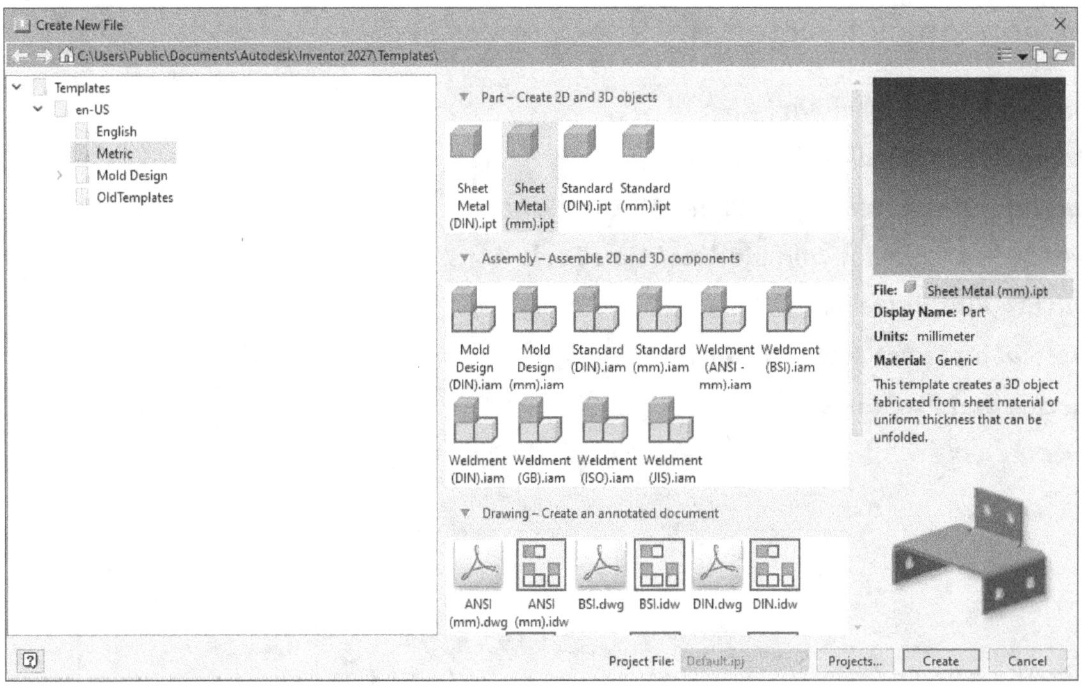

Figure-1. Create New File dialog box

- Select the **Sheet Metal(mm).ipt** template or **SheetMetal(DIN).ipt** template to start a new file in sheetmetal environment using metric units. Click on the **Create** button from the dialog box. A new file will be created in sheetmetal environment; refer to Figure-2.

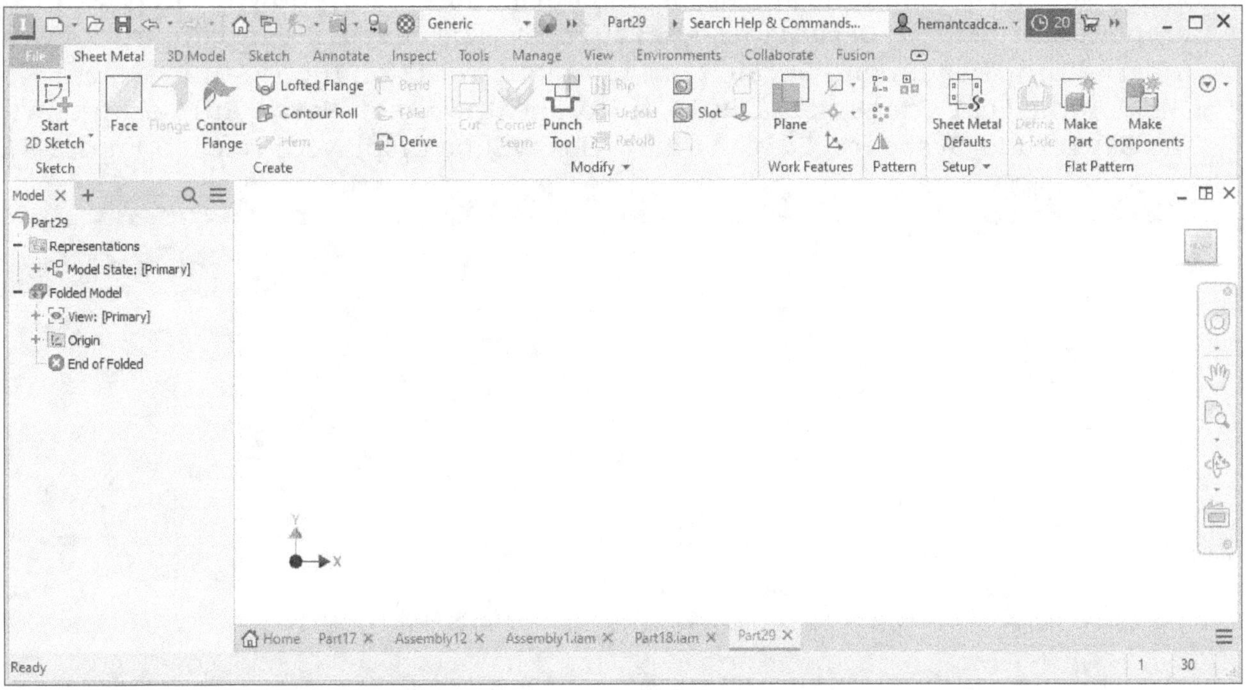

Figure-2. Sheetmetal Environment

Now, we have entered in the Sheetmetal environment; the next step is to set sheetmetal parameters.

SHEET METAL DEFAULTS SETTING

The sheetmetal defaults are the default values of various parameters related to sheetmetal designing. Once you have set the default values then they will be applied on the sheetmetal project automatically. The procedure to change the sheetmetal defaults is given next.

- Click on the **Sheet Metal Defaults** tool from the **Setup** panel in the **Sheet Metal** tab of the **Ribbon**. The **Sheet Metal Defaults** dialog box will be displayed; refer to Figure-3.

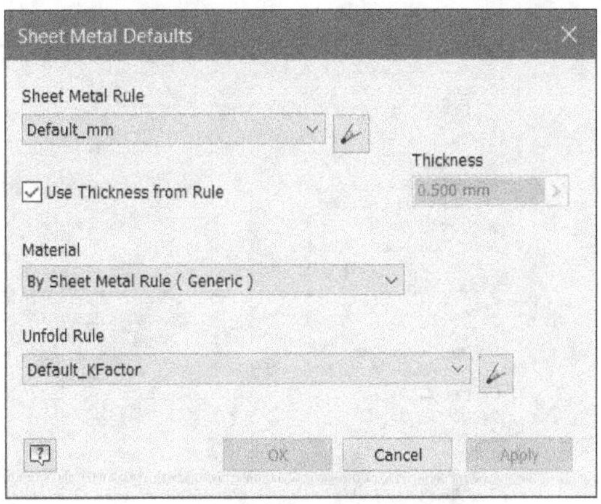

Figure-3. Sheet Metal Defaults dialog box

- Select desired template from the **Sheet Metal Rule** drop-down. There are two templates by default; **Default** and **Default mm**. The **Default** template works with imperial unit system and **Default mm** template works on metric unit system.
- Click on the **Edit Sheet Metal Rule** button next to **Sheet Metal Rule** drop-down. The **Style and Standard Editor** dialog box will be displayed; refer to Figure-4.

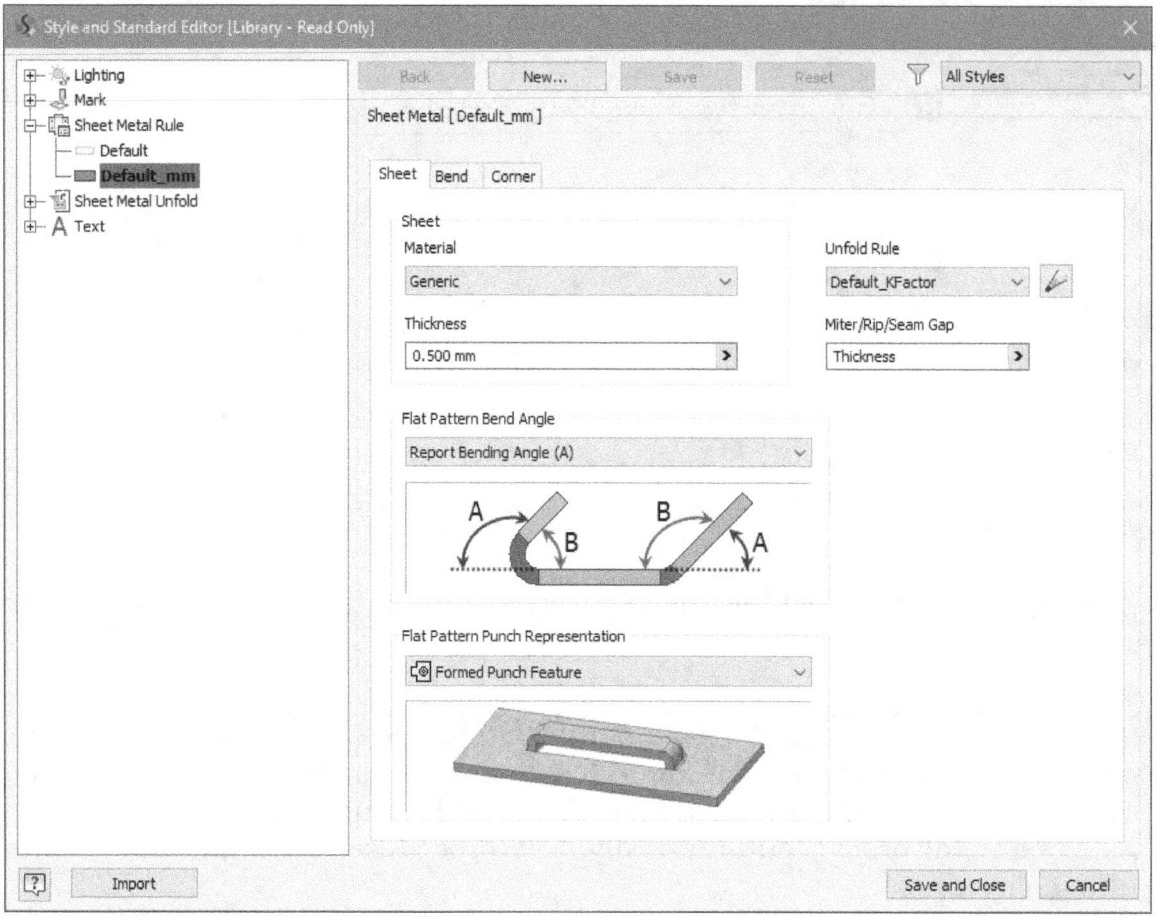

Figure-4. Style and Standard Editor dialog box for sheetmetal

- Click in the **Material** drop-down of **Sheet** area in **Sheet** tab of the dialog box. A list of materials stored in library will be displayed; refer to Figure-5.

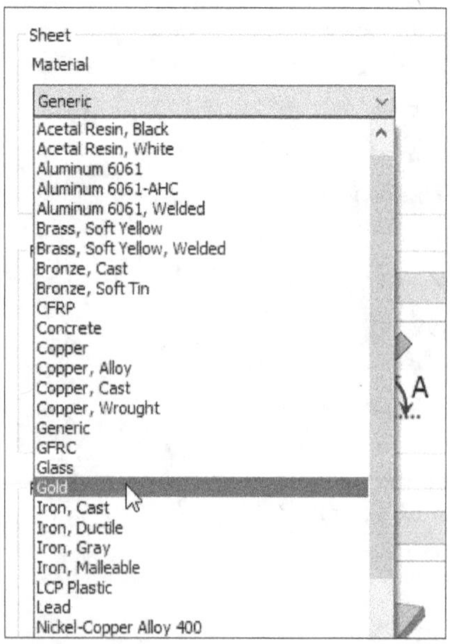

Figure-5. Material drop down

- Select desired material from the drop-down.
- Click in the **Thickness** edit box and specify desired value of the thickness.
- Click in the **Miter/Rip/Seam Gap** edit box and specify desired value of gap. By default, the **Thickness** value is specified in the edit box which means the gap will be equal to thickness of sheetmetal.
- Click in the **Unfold Rule** drop-down and select desired rule for unfolding of sheetmetal object. There are two options in this drop-down; **BendCompensation** and **Default KFactor**. Select the **BendCompensation** option if you want to compensate for the length of sheet required in creating bend by using the custom formulas based on bending angle and thickness of sheet. Select the **Default KFactor** option if you want to compensate for bend length by using the K factor.
- Similarly, you can set the other parameters in the **Sheet** tab like punch representation in flat pattern and flat pattern bending angle.
- Click on the **Bend** tab from the dialog box. The dialog box will be displayed; refer to Figure-6.

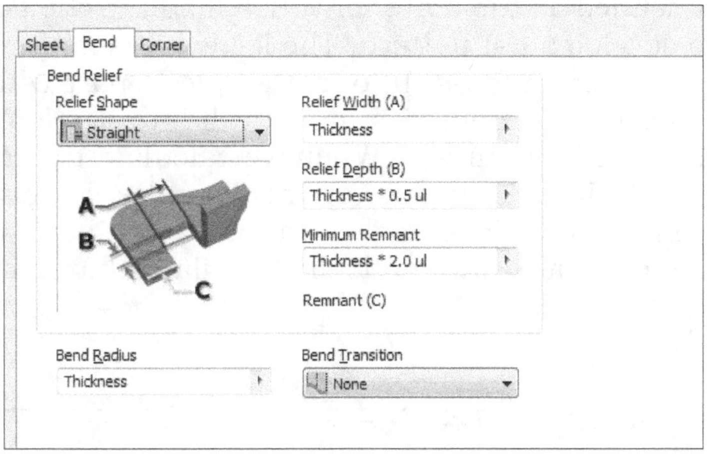

Figure-6. Bend tab in the Style and Standard Editor dialog box

- Select desired shape of bend relief from the **Relief Shape** drop-down in the **Bend Relief** area of the dialog box.
- Similarly, select desired option from the **Bend Transition** drop-down.
- Click in the **Bend Radius**, **Relief Width**, **Relief Depth**, and **Minimum Remnant** edit boxes and specify desired values.
- Similarly, click on the **Corner** tab in the dialog box and specify the relief parameters for corners in sheetmetal parts.
- Click on the **Save and Close** button to save and apply the parameters specified.

SHEET METAL DESIGN TERMS

While going forward in the chapter, you will come across some technical terms which are used in sheet metal industry. Here, we will discuss about these technical terms and their effects on production.

Sheet Metal Definition

Metal that has been rolled into a sheet having a thickness between foil and plate. The thickness of metal can vary from fraction of millimeters to 12.5 mm, in general.

Gauge

Gauge is a traditional measurement unit of sheet thickness commonly used in USA, India, and many other parts of world. It is a non-linear unit. Higher the gauge number, the thinner is the sheet metal. Like gauge 0000000 means 12.7 mm thickness and gauge 38 means 0.16 mm thickness. You can find a table on gauge to mm conversion easily in local stores. Use of Gauge to designate sheet metal thickness is discouraged by numerous international standards organizations. For Example, ASTM states in specification ASTM A480-10a "The use of gauge number is discouraged as being an archaic term of limited usefulness not having general agreement on meaning."

Bend Allowance

When the sheet metal is put through the process of bending, the metal around the bend is deformed and stretched. As this happens, you gain a small amount of total length in your part. Likewise, when you are trying to develop a flat pattern, you will have to make a deduction from your desired part size to get the correct flat size. The **Bend Allowance** is defined as the material you will add to the actual leg lengths of the part in order to develop a flat pattern. The leg lengths are the part of the flange which is outside of the bend radius. In our example, a part with flange lengths of 2" and 3" with an inside radius of .250" at 90° will have leg lengths of 1.625" and 2.625", respectively; refer to Figure-7. When we calculate the Bend Allowance, we find that it equals .457". In order to develop the flat pattern, we add .457" to 1.625" and 2.625" to arrive at 4.707". In Autodesk Inventor, you don't need to specify the value of bend allowance as it is automatically calculated based on K factor.

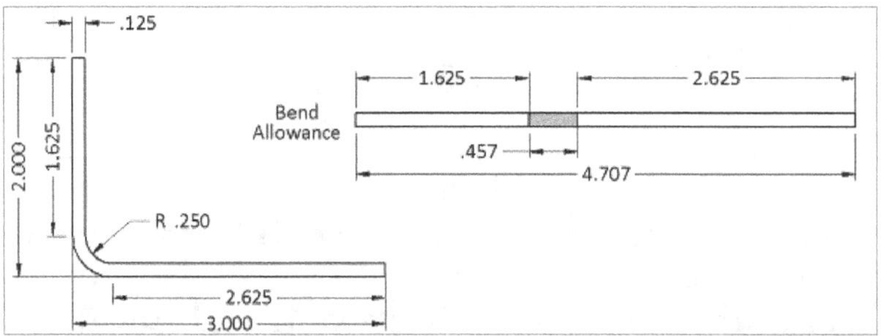

Figure-7. Bend Allowance example

K-Factor

The K-Factor in sheet metal designing is the ratio of the neutral axis to the material thickness. When metal is bent, the upper section is going to compress and the lower section is going to stretch. The line where the transition from compression to stretching occurs is called the neutral axis. The location of the neutral axis varies and is based on the material's physical properties and its thickness. The K-Factor is the ratio of the Neutral Axis' Offset (t) and the Material Thickness (MT). Figure-8 shows how the top of the bend is compressed and the bottom is stretched.

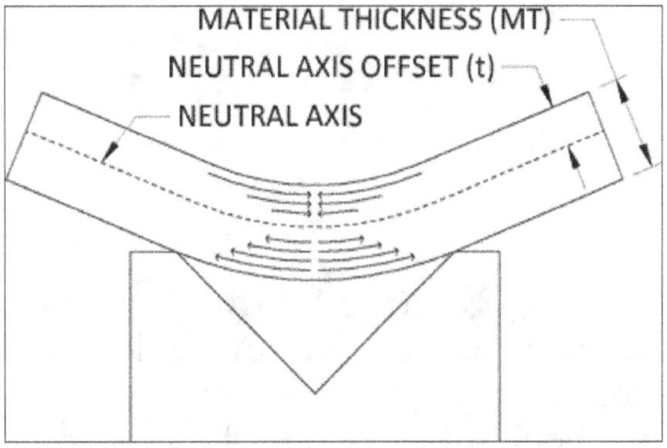

$$K = t/MT$$

Generally, K is taken as 0.33 for soft materials and 0.4 for hard materials as a thumb rule. Since, K factor is not just mathematical term, you need experiments to find exact value of K for your material situations. We have given the general steps to find out K-factor by experiment.

Calculating the K-Factor

Since, the K-Factor is based on the property of the metal and its thickness, there is no simple way to calculate it ahead of the first bend. Typically, the K-Factor is going to be between 0 and .5. In order to find the K-Factor, you will need to bend a sample piece and deduce the Bend Allowance. The Bend Allowance is then plugged into the equation to find the K-Factor.

- Begin by preparing sample blanks which are of equal and known sizes. The blanks should be at least a foot long to ensure an even bend, and a few inches deep to make sure you can sit them against the back stops. For our example, let's take a piece that is 14 Gauge, .075", 4" Wide and 12" Long. The length of the piece won't be used in our calculations. Preparing at least 3 samples and taking the average measurements from each will help.
- Set up your press brake with desired tooling, you'll be using to fabricate this metal thickness and place a 90° bend in the center of the piece. For our example, this means a bend at the 2" mark.
- Once you've bent your sample pieces carefully, measure the flange lengths of each piece. Record each length and take the average of lengths. The length should be something over half the original length. For our example, the average flange length is 2.073".
- Second, measure the inside radius formed during the bending. A set of radius gauges will get you fairly close to finding the correct measurement. However to get an exact measurement, an optical comparator will give you the most accurate reading. For our example, the inside radius is measured at .105".
- Now that you have your measurements, we'll determine the Bend Allowance. To do this, first determine your leg length by subtracting the material thickness and inside radius from the flange length. (Note this equation only works for 90° bends because the leg length is from the tangent point.) For our example, the leg length will be 2.073 – .105 – .075 = 1.893.
- Subtract twice the leg length from the initial length to determine the Bend Allowance. 4 – 1.893 * 2 = .214.
- Plug the Bend Allowance (BA), the Bend Angle (A), Inside Radius (R), and Material Thickness (T) into the below equation to determine the K-Factor (K).

$$K = \frac{-R + \frac{BA}{\pi A/180}}{T}$$

Spline Factor

The **Spline factor** is a special term used in Autodesk Inventor for sheet metal work. Since, we can create Contour Flanges, Contour Rolls, or Lofted Flanges with elliptical or spline segments within the feature profile, there is some extra length created in flat pattern of these features. To compensate for this extra length in these special cases, you specify the value of Spline factor in Sheet Metal Defaults. By default, the value is 0.5.

CREATION TOOLS

The tools to create components in sheetmetal are available in the **Create** panel of the **Sheet Metal** tab of the **Ribbon**; refer to Figure-8.

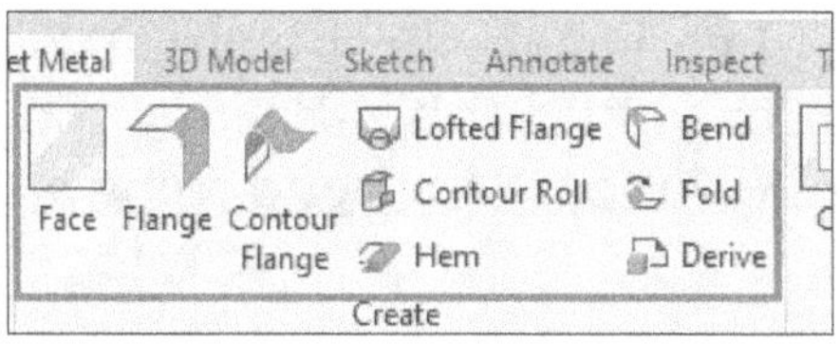

Figure-8. Create panel in Sheet Metal tab

The procedures of using the tools in this panel are discussed next.

Using Face Tool

The **Face** tool is used to create a sheet metal body by extruding closed sketch profile. The procedure to use this tool is given next.

- Create the closed sketch profile and click on the **Face** tool from **Create** panel in the **Sheet Metal** tab of the **Ribbon**. The **Face** dialog box will be displayed; refer to Figure-9.

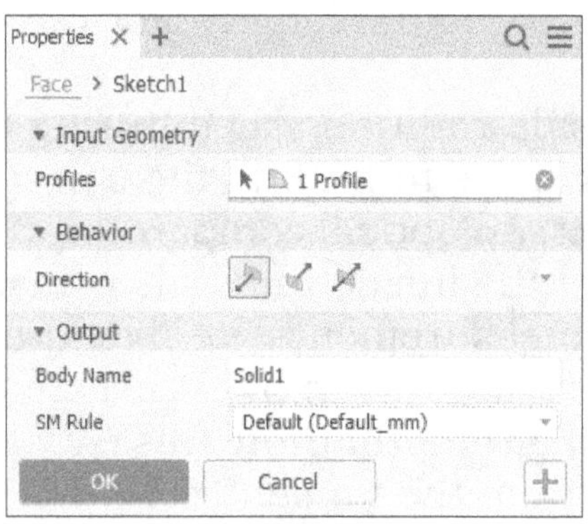

Figure-9. Face dialog box

- If there is single sketch in the drawing area then it will get automatically selected otherwise you will be asked to select a sketch using which you want to create a face feature; refer to Figure-10.

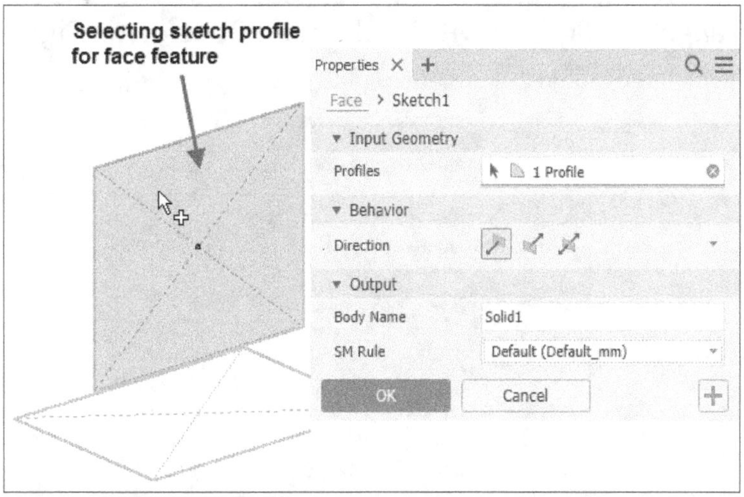

Figure-10. Sketch profile selected for face feature

- On selecting the profile, preview of the sheetmetal face feature will be displayed. Note that the default thickness will be added to the profile.
- Select desired button from the **Direction** area in the **Behavior** rollout of the dialog box to define the side of thickness with respect to selected profile.
- By default, the Sheet Metal Default values are applied for unfolding and bending but you can change the values by using the options in the **Bend Properties** rollout. The options in these tabs are same as discussed earlier.
- Click on the **Apply** button and select the other profile to create face feature or click on the **OK** button to create the current face feature and exit the tool.

Using Flange Tool

The **Flange** tool is used to create a face of sheet metal at specified angle to the selected edge; refer to Figure-11.

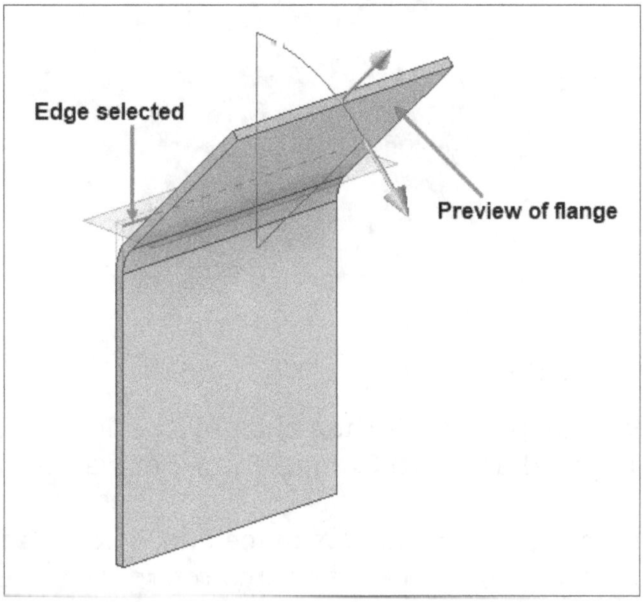

Figure-11. Preview of flange

The procedure to use this tool is given next.

- Click on the **Flange** tool from the **Create** panel in the **Sheet Metal** tab of the **Ribbon**. The **Flange** dialog box will be displayed; refer to Figure-12 and you will be asked to select an edge.

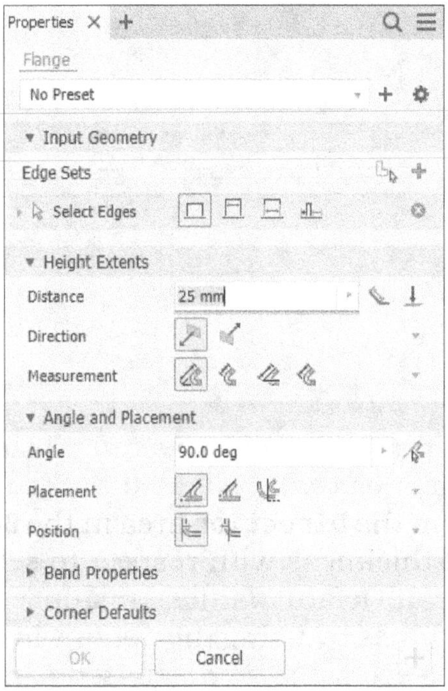

Figure-12. Flange dialog box

- Select the edge/edges on which you want to create the flange. Preview of the flange/flanges will be displayed; refer to Figure-13.

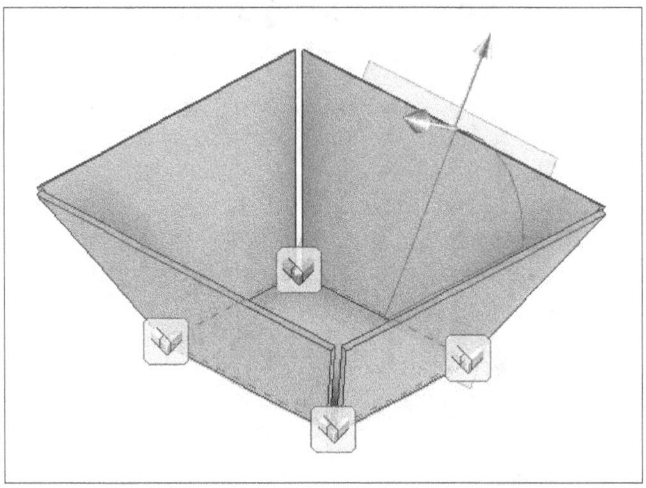

Figure-13. Preview of flanges

- If you want to select a loop of edges then click on the **Sets selection priority to edge loops** button adjacent to **Flange Edge Sets** area in the **Input Geometry** rollout.
- Apply desired value of height in the **Distance** edit box of **Height Extents** rollout.
- If you want to extend the flanges up to selected reference vertex or point then select the **To** option from the **Height Extents** rollout and select the reference point. You can also specify the offset value in the **Offset** edit box displayed.
- Click in the **Angle** edit box of **Angle and Placement** rollout and specify desired value of flange angle.

- Click in the **Bend Radius** edit box from **Bend Properties** rollout and specify desired value of bend radius at the selected edges. By default, the value set in **Sheet Metal Defaults** is applied.
- Change the reference for measuring height of flange by selecting desired button from the **Measurement** area of **Height Extents** rollout.
- You can change the bend position by selecting desired button from the **Position** area of **Angle and Placement** rollout.
- If you want to flip the direction of flanges then click on the **Flipped** button from **Direction** area of **Height Extents** rollout.

Mitered Flange

Mitered Flanges are created in similar way to creating edge flange in Autodesk Inventor with the only difference that the **Auto-Mitering (Symmetric Gap)** check box is selected in the **Corner Defaults** rollout of the dialog box; refer to Figure-14. In mitered flanges, you can define the gap between two consecutive flanges as miter gap. Figure-15 shows mitered flanges and edge flanges.

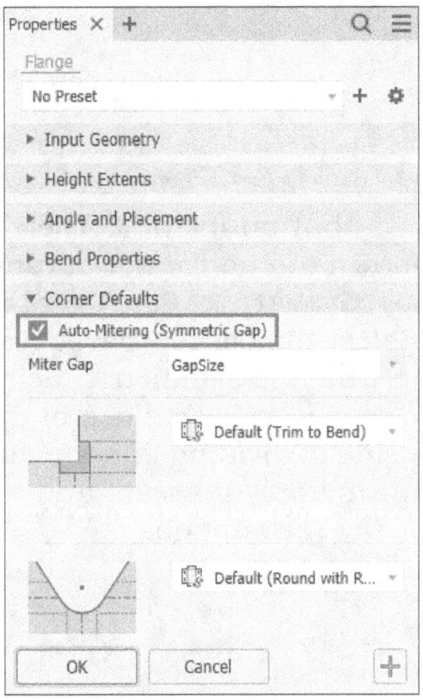

Figure-14. Auto Mitering check box

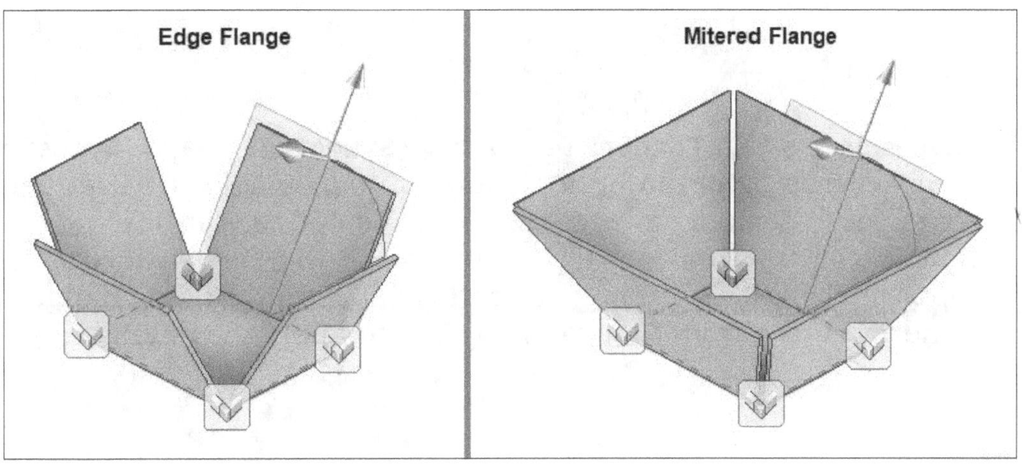

Figure-15. Edge Flange and Mitered Flange

Dynamic Editing of Flange (not showing this button)

If you look at the preview of flange in drawing area then **Corner Edit** buttons are displayed on corners. These buttons are used to dynamically modify flanges at corners individually. The procedure to use the buttons is given next.

- Click on the **Corner Edit** button to edit the parameters related to respective corner. The **Corner Overrides** section will be displayed in the **Flange** dialog box with corner parameters for selected corner; refer to Figure-16.

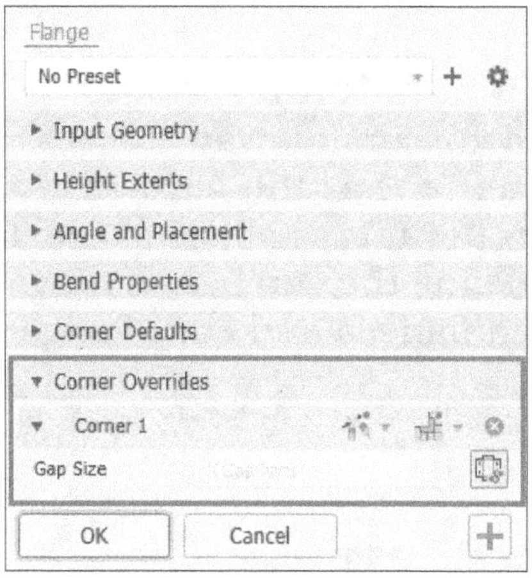

Figure-16. Corner parameters in Flange dialog box

- Click on the drop-down button in the **Corner** rollout. The five options will be displayed in the drop-down to change the parameters related to gap; **Corner Defaults (Symmetric Gap)**, **Symmetric Gap**, **Overlap**, **Reverse Overlap**, and **No Seam**; refer to Figure-17. Select the **Corner Defaults (Symmetric Gap)** option to use the default type of gap which is symmetric. Select the **Symmetric Gap** option if you want the gap to be equal on both sides of dividing line at corner. If you want the gap to be on one side of dividing line then select the **Overlap** or **Reverse Overlap** option. If you want to apply no seam and want the flanges created with default gap then select the **No Seam** option.

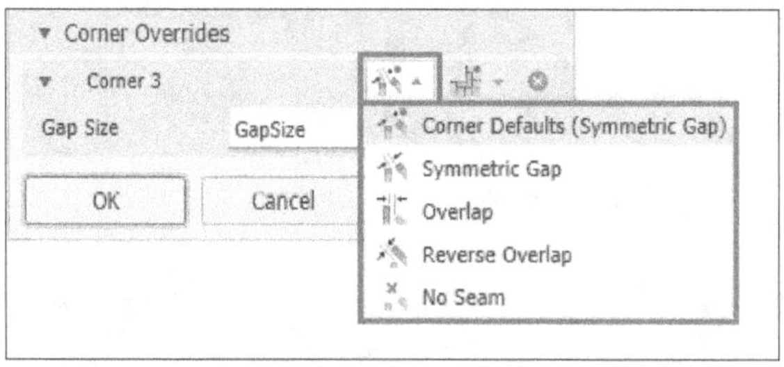

Figure-17. Gap drop-down

- If you have selected the **Corner Defaults (Symmetric Gap)**, **Symmetric Gap**, **Overlap**, or **Reverse Overlap** option then you can toggle the **Use Default** button and specify desired value of gap in the **Gap Size** edit box.
- Similarly, click on the drop-down button in the **Corner** rollout and select desired option related to trimming at bends of sheet for making flange.
- Click on the **OK** button from **Flange** dialog box to apply the changes.

Using Contour Flange

The **Contour Flange** tool is used to create flange with specified shape (contour). The procedure to use this tool is given next.

- Click on the **Contour Flange** tool from the **Create** panel in the **Sheet Metal** tab of the **Ribbon**. The **Contour Flange** dialog box will be displayed; refer to Figure-18. Make sure that you have an open sketch in the drawing area; refer to Figure-19.

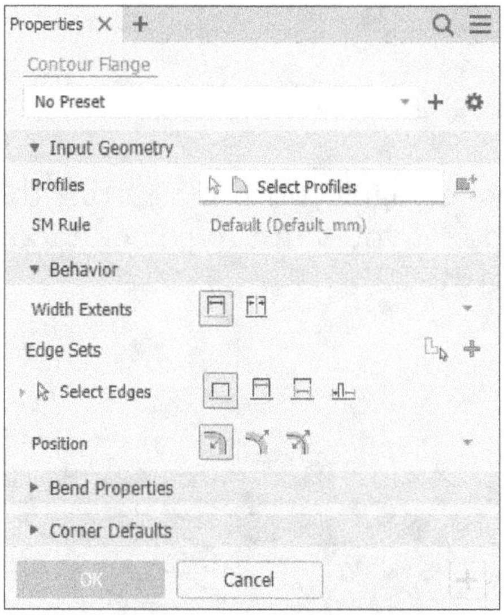

Figure-18. Contour Flange dialog box

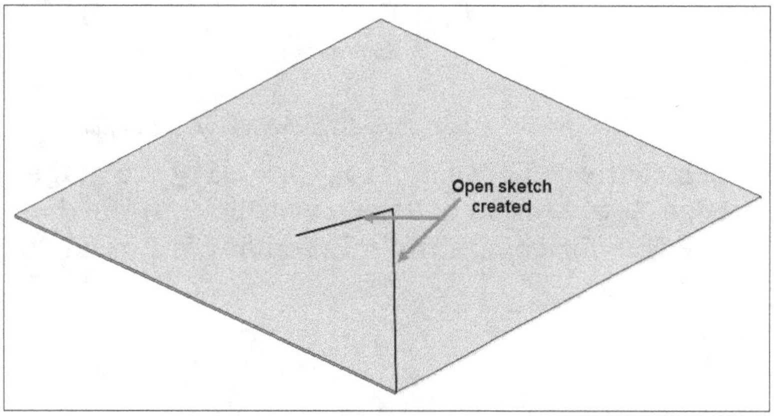

Figure-19. Open sketch created for Contour flange

- If there is only one profile sketch then it will be selected automatically. If there are two or more profile sketches then first created profile will be selected. To select a different profile, click in the **Profile** selection box and select desired profile sketch; refer to Figure-20.

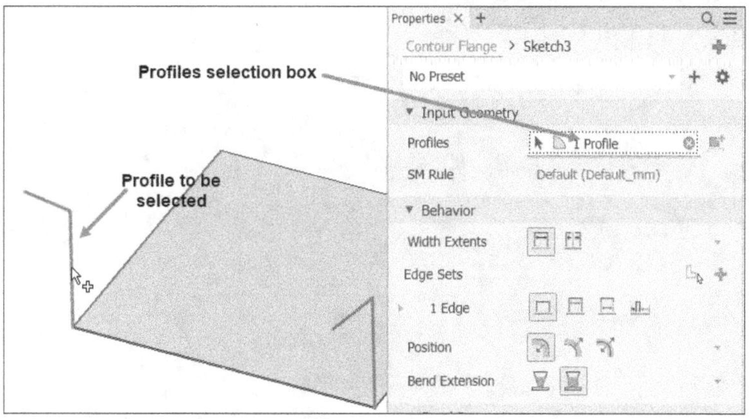

Figure-20. Profile to be selected

- On selecting the profile, you will be asked to select the connected edge. Select an edge and preview of the contour flange will be displayed; refer to Figure-21. Select more edges if required, preview will be displayed accordingly.

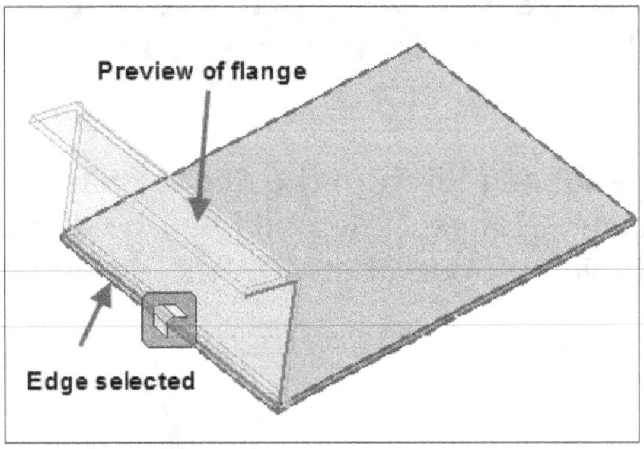

Figure-21. Preview of contour flange

- Select the **Sets selection priority to edge loops** toggle button from the **Edge Sets** section of **Behavior** rollout in the dialog box if you want to select a loop of edges for generating mitered flanges; refer to Figure-22.

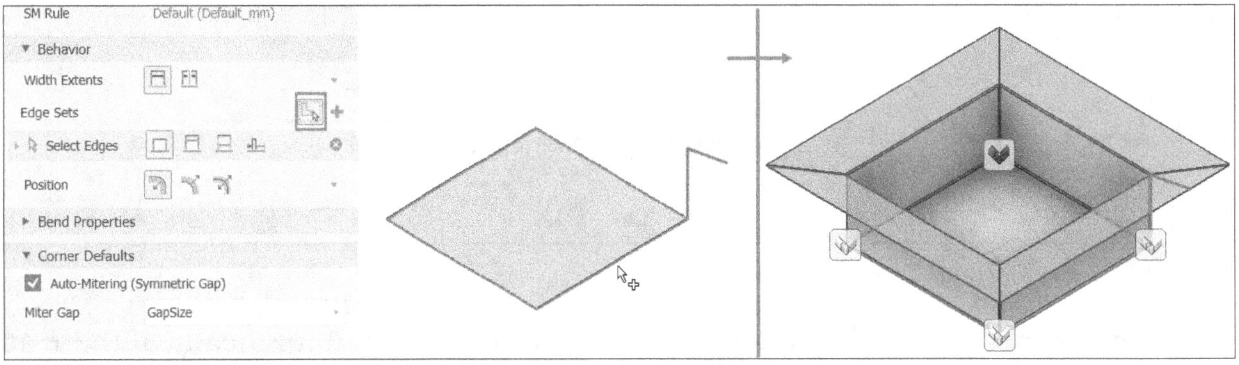

Figure-22. Flange using loop

- Most of the options in this dialog box are same as discussed for **Flange** tool except options in the **Width Extends** drop-down of the **Behavior** area in the **Contour Flange** dialog box; refer to Figure-23.

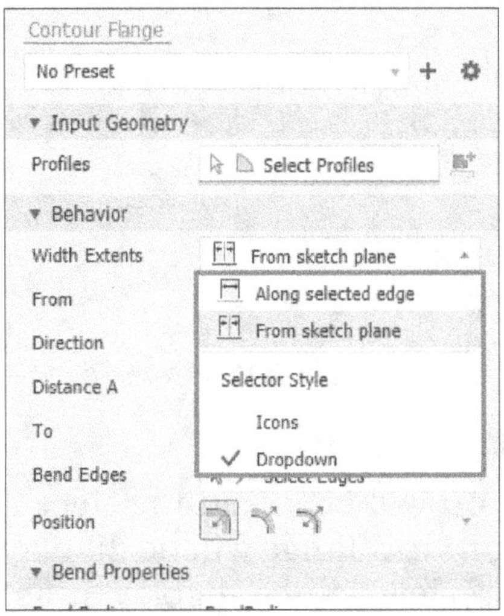

Figure-23. Width Extents drop-down

- If you do not have edges as path reference and want to create a contour flange at straight path of specified distance then select the **From sketch plane** option from the **Width Extend** drop-down in the **Behavior** rollout of the dialog box. The options to specify distance and direction will be displayed in the dialog box; refer to Figure-24.

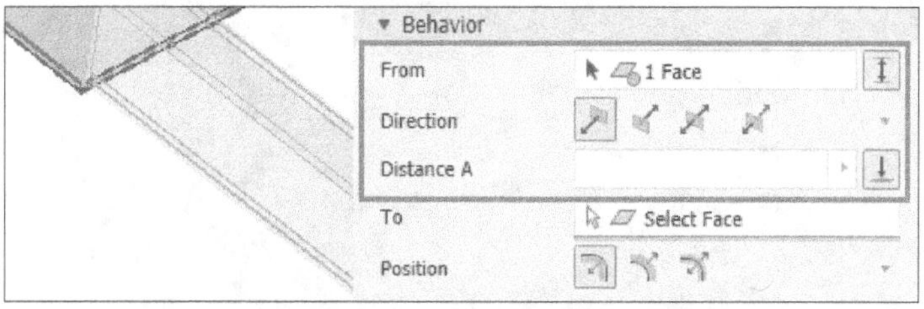

Figure-24. Options to specify distance and direction

- Specify desired value of distance and select desired direction.
- Click on the **OK** button to create the flange.

Using Lofted Flange Tool

The **Lofted Flange** tool is used to create flange between two selected profile sketches. Note that the edges of the created flange will be shaped as selected profiles. The procedure to create lofted flange is given next.

- Create the two sketches of profiles for lofted flanges; refer to Figure-25.

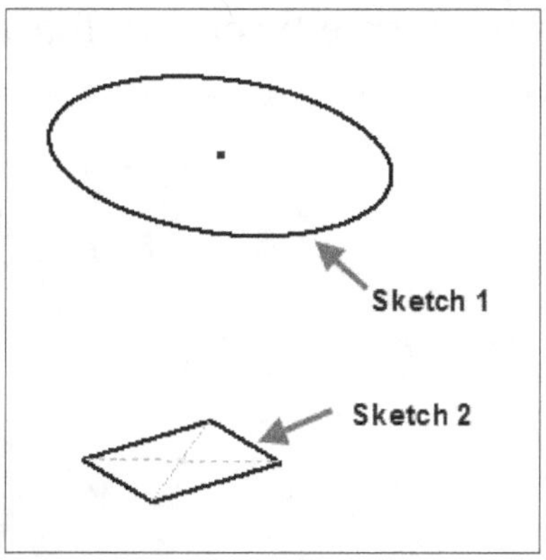

Figure-25. Profile sketches for lofted flange

- Click on the **Lofted Flange** tool from the **Create** panel in the **Sheet Metal** tab of the **Ribbon**. The **Lofted Flange** dialog box will be displayed; refer to Figure-26.

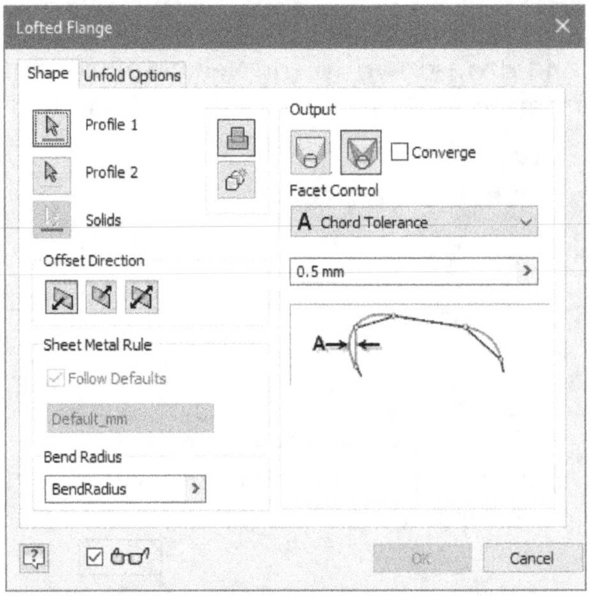

Figure-26. Lofted Flange dialog box

- Select the first profile from the drawing area. You will be asked to select the second profile.
- Click on the second profile from the drawing area. Preview of the lofted flange will be displayed; refer to Figure-27.
- Click on the **Die Formed** button from the **Output** area of the dialog box if you want the flange created as die formed; refer to Figure-28.

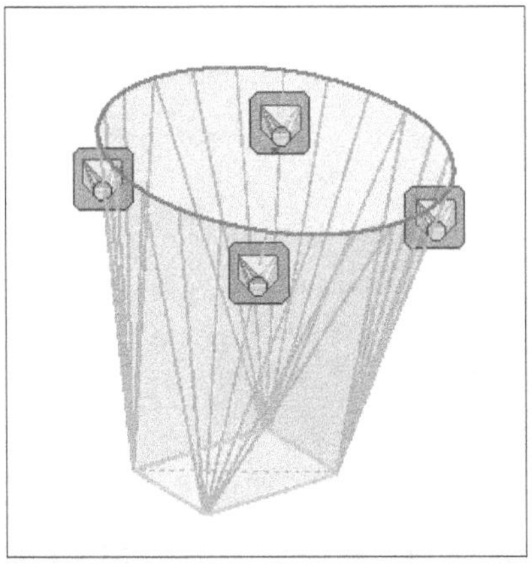

Figure-27. Preview of the lofted flange

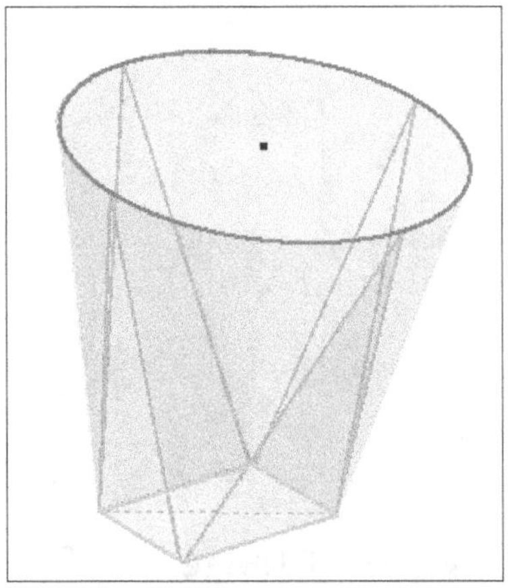

Figure-28. Preview of die formed lofted flange

- Click on the **Press Brake** button from the **Output** area of the dialog box if you want to create the flange formed by Press-Brake bending machine; refer to Figure-27.
- If you have selected the **Press Brake** button then you can set the chord tolerance, facet angle, and facet distance of the lofted flange. All the three parameters are used to modify the surface shape of lofted flange.
- Select the **Converge** check box to converge all the break lines at one point; refer to Figure-29.

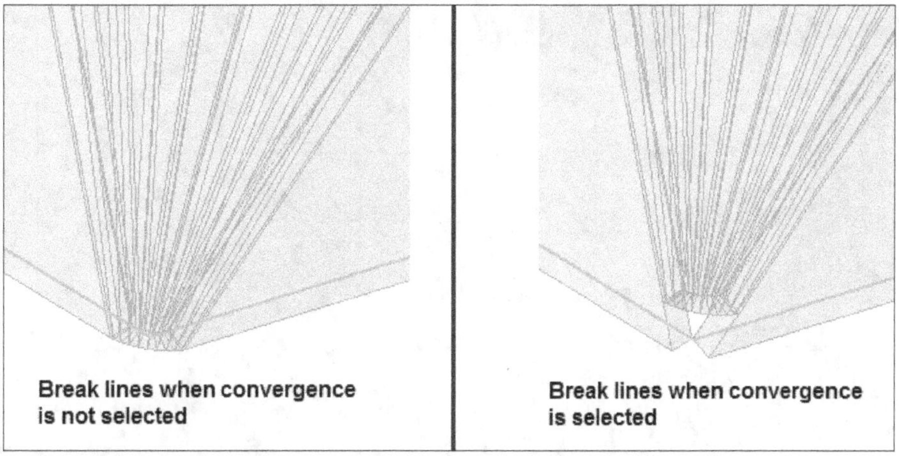

Figure-29. Effect of Convergence check box

- The options in the **Unfold Options** tab of the dialog box have already been discussed.
- Note that if **Enable/Disable feature preview** check box  is not selected in the dialog box then you will not be able to see the preview while creating the feature.
- Click on the **OK** button to create the feature.

Using Contour Roll Tool

The **Contour Roll** tool is used to create sheet metal flange by rolling the selected profile about an axis. The procedure to use this tool is given next.

- Create a sketch with an axis similar to shown in Figure-30.

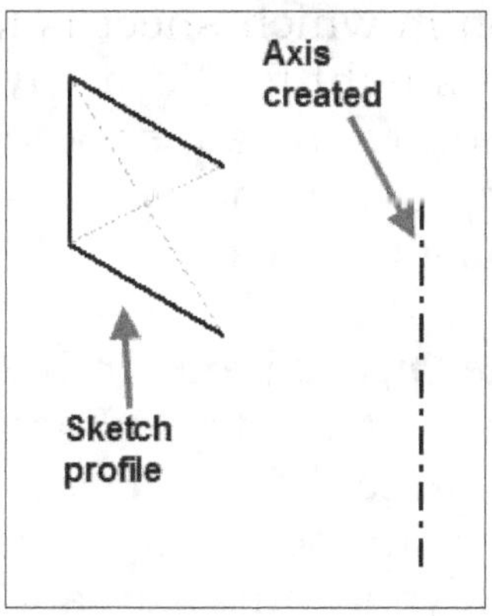

Figure-30. Sketch created for contour roll feature

- Click on the **Contour Roll** tool from the **Create** panel in the **Sheet Metal** tab of the **Ribbon**. The **Contour Roll** dialog box will be displayed; refer to Figure-31. If you have only a profile sketch and axis then preview will be displayed with profile sketch and axis selected automatically; refer to Figure-32.

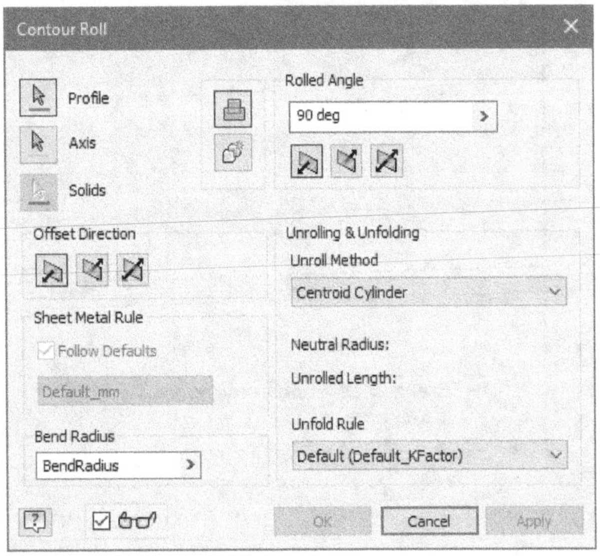

Figure-31. Contour Roll dialog box

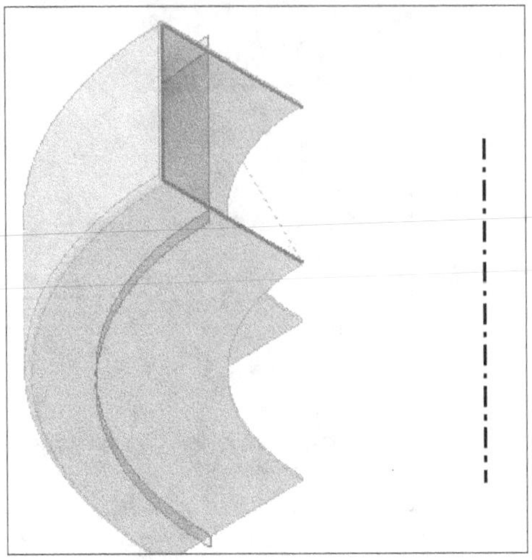

Figure-32. Preview of the contour rolled flange

- Set desired angle value of roll in the **Rolled Angle** edit box.
- The three buttons in the **Offset Direction** area of the dialog box are used to flip the thicken side of flange with respect to profile sketch.
- The three buttons in the **Rolled Angle** area of the dialog box are used to flip the direction of rolling.
- Set desired unfolding and unrolling options and then click on the **OK** button from the dialog box to create the feature.

Using Hem Tool

Hemming is a forming operation in which sheet is folded on its edge or folded over another part in order to achieve a tight fit. Normally, hemming operations are used to connect parts together, to improve the appearance of a part and to reinforce part edges. In Autodesk Inventor, we use **Hem** tool to create hemming in sheet metal part. The procedure to use this tool is given next.

- Click on the **Hem** tool from the **Create** panel in the **Sheet Metal** tab of the **Ribbon**. The **Hem** dialog box will be displayed; refer to Figure-33. Also, you will be asked to select an edge to create hem. Note that the **Hem** tool will be active in **Create** panel only when you have a sheet metal base part created in the drawing area.
- Select an edge through which you want to create hem. Preview of the hem will be displayed; refer to Figure-34.

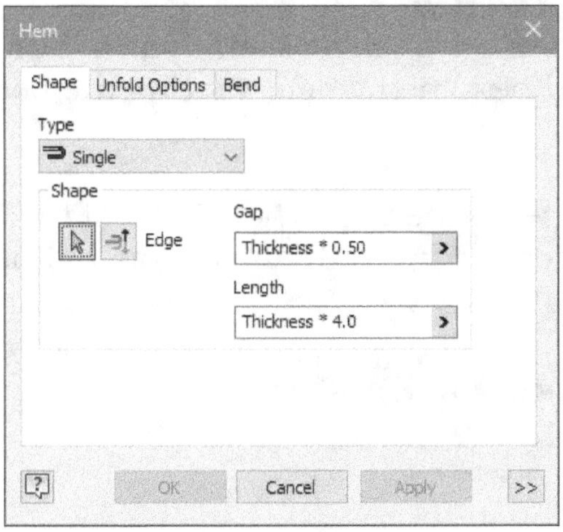

Figure-33. Hem dialog box

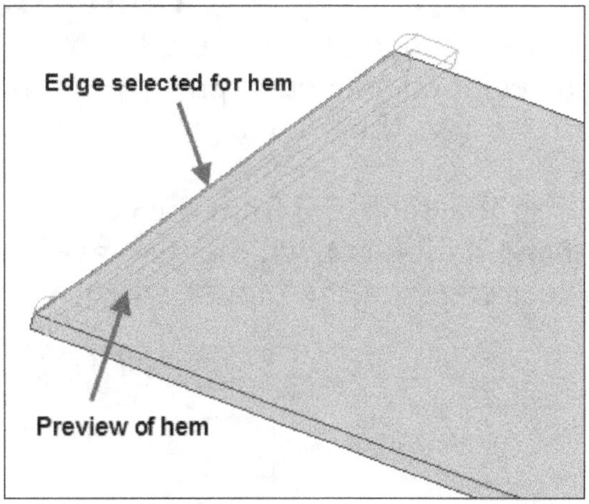

Figure-34. Preview of hem

- Specify desired value of **Gap** and **Length** in the respective edit boxes in the dialog box.
- If you want to create **Teardrop**, **Rolled**, or **Double** hem then select the respective option from the **Type** drop-down. Specify desired parameters based on your selection.
- Expand the dialog box to modify the options related to **Width Extents**; refer to Figure-35.

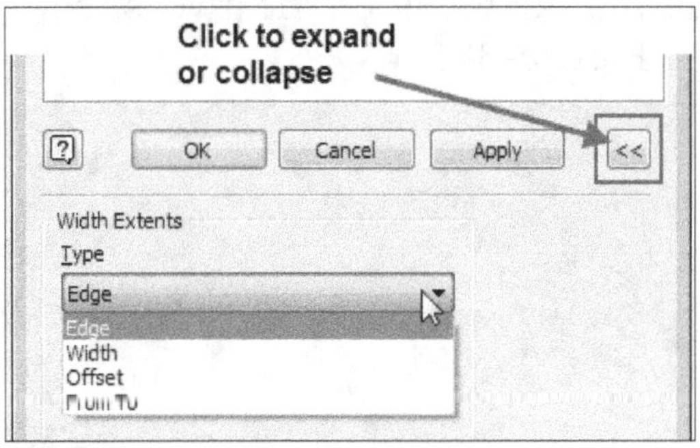

Figure-35. Expanded Hem dialog box

- Specify the other required parameters as discussed earlier in the chapter. Click on the **OK** button to create the feature; refer to Figure-36.

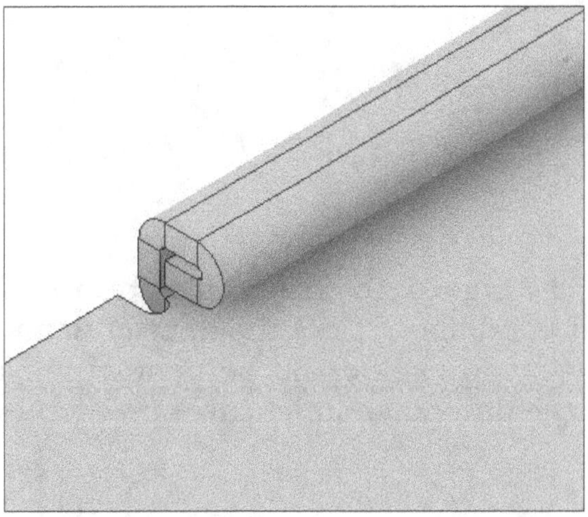

Figure-36. Double hem with width specified and round relief

Using Bend Tool

The **Bend** tool is used to create a bend by joining two sheet metal parts. You will be asked to select edge of each part that should be joined while creating the bend. The procedure to use this tool is given next.

- Click on the **Bend** tool from the **Create** panel in the **Sheet Metal** tab of the **Ribbon**. The **Bend** dialog box will be displayed; refer to Figure-37. Also, you will be asked to select edges of the planar sheet metal faces.

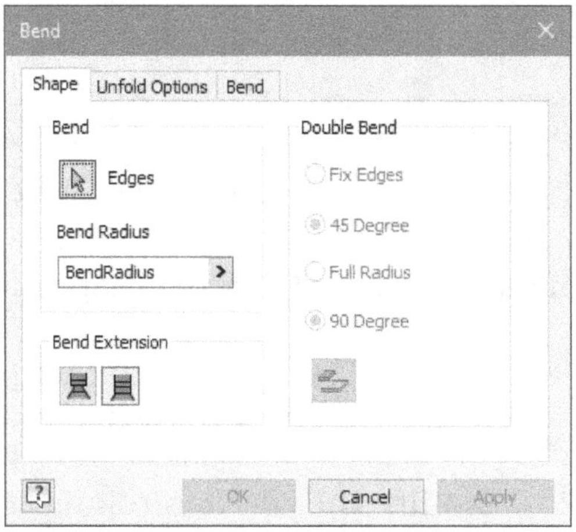

Figure-37. Bend dialog box

- Select the edges of the planar faces of the two sheetmetal parts that are to be joined by bend; refer to Figure-38.

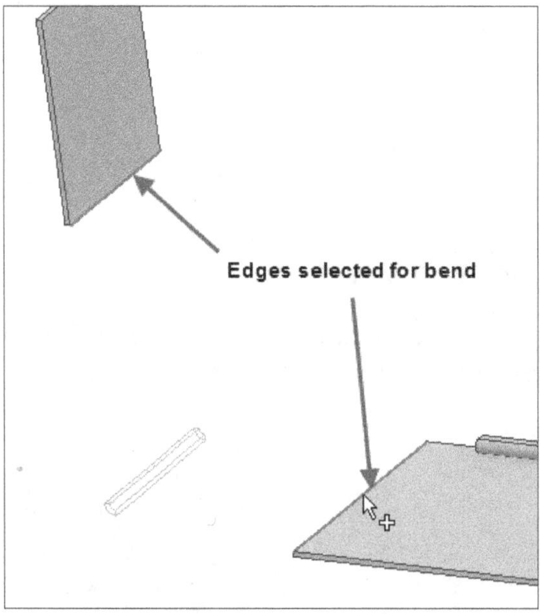

Figure-38. Edges selected for bend

- Select the **Extend Bend Aligned to Side Faces** button if you want to extend the side faces to match at bend line. Select the **Extend Bend Perpendicular to Side Faces** button if you want to extend the perpendicular face up to the side face. Figure-39 illustrates the difference in features created by selecting two button.

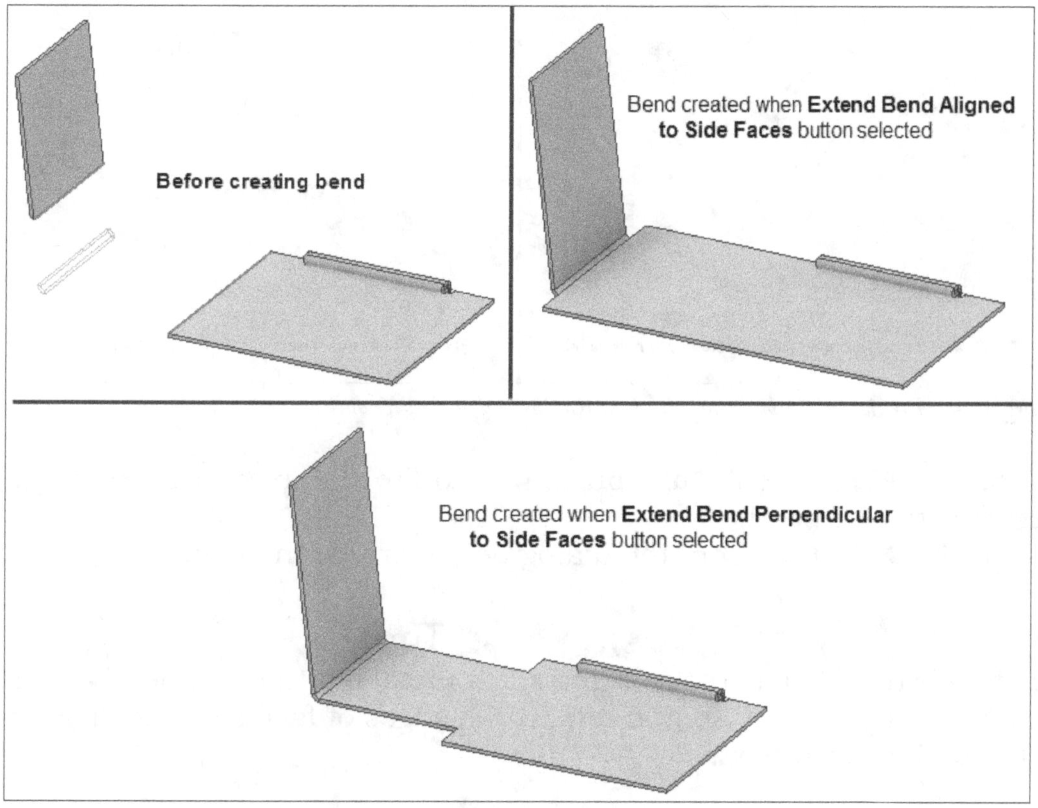

Figure-39. Bend created using different Bend Extension options selected

- Specify desired value of bend radius in the **Bend Radius** edit box.
- If you have two parallel sheet metal planar faces not in the same plane to join by bend then options in the **Double Bend** area of the dialog box will become active on selecting the edges. Figure-40 shows the preview of bend using **Fix Edges** and **45 Degree** radio buttons. Figure-41 shows the preview of bend using the **Full Radius** and **90 Degree** radio buttons.

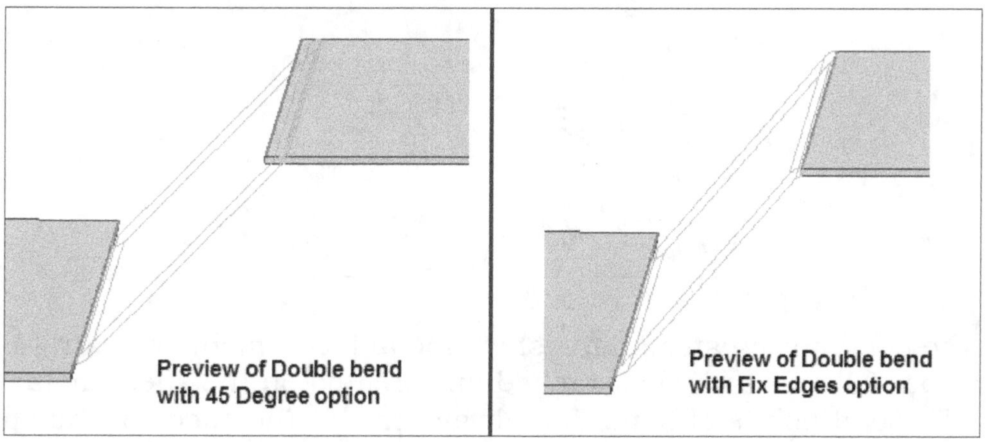

Figure-40. Preview of double bend with 45 Degree and Fix Edges options

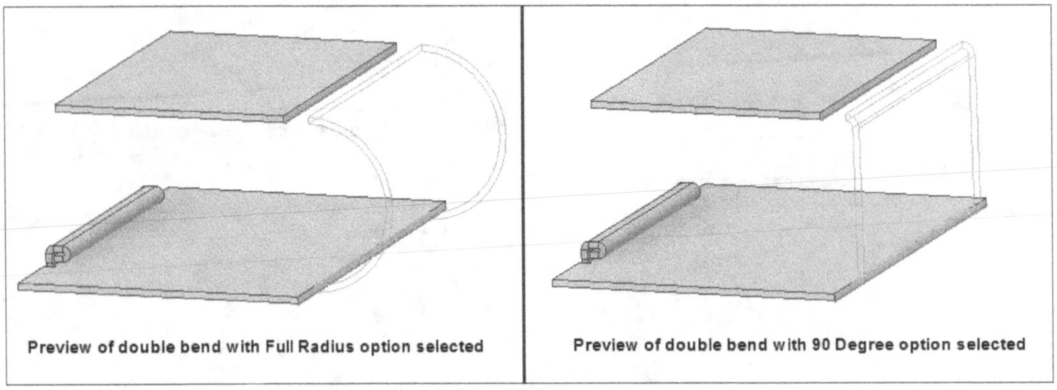

Figure-41. Preview of double bend with Full Radius and 90 Degree options

- Click on the **Flip Fixed Edge** button to flip the fixed edge between the two edges selected for bend.
- Click on the **OK** button from the dialog box to create the bend.

Using Fold Tool

The **Fold** tool is used to fold the selected sheet metal face using a bend line. Note that the end points of bend line should end at the edges of face selected. The procedure to use this tool is given next.

- Click on the **Fold** tool from the **Create** panel in the **Sheet Metal** tab of the **Ribbon**. The **Fold** dialog box will be displayed as shown in Figure-42. Also, you will be asked to select the bend line.

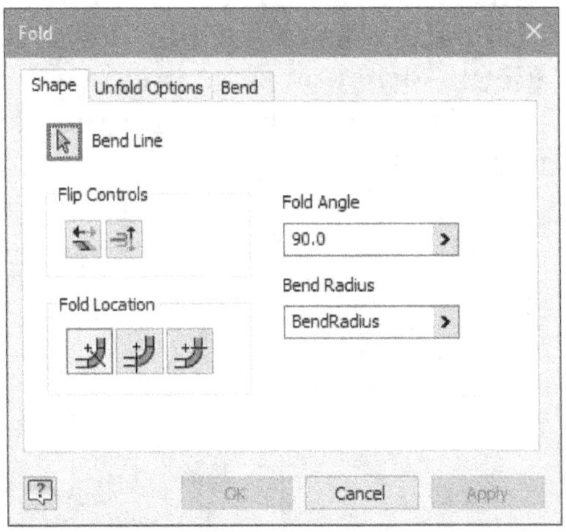

Figure-42. Fold dialog box

- Select the bend line created on the sheet metal face which you want to fold. Note that the bend line is a single sketched line created on the sheet metal face to be folded. The end points of bend line always end at the edges of the sheet metal face to be folded.
- On selecting the bend line, two arrows are displayed on the bend line which denote the direction of fold. The horizontal arrow directs towards the side that will be folded (the side opposite to horizontal arrow direction will remain fixed). The vertical arrow directs toward the direction in which the face will be folded, it can be upward or downward. To change the direction of fold, click on the buttons in the **Fold Controls** area of the dialog box.

- Select desired button from the **Fold Location** area of the dialog box to change the start location of fold.
- The other options in the **Fold** dialog box are same as discussed earlier. Click on the **OK** button to create the fold feature; refer to Figure-43.

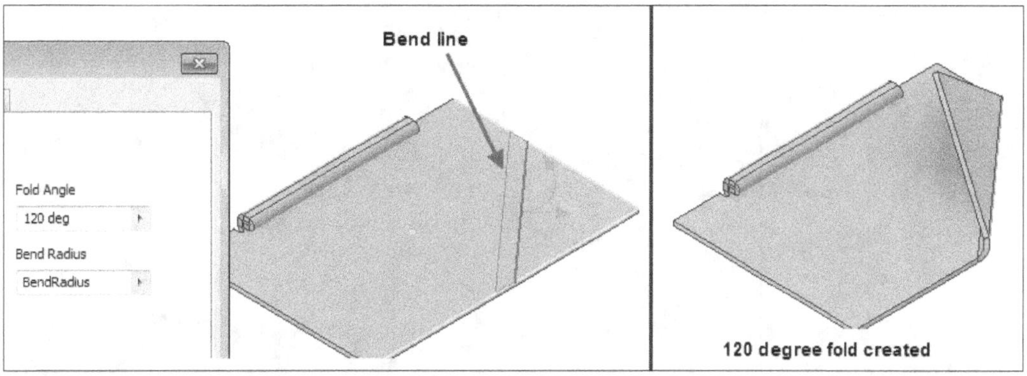

Figure-43. Fold feature creation

Using Derive Tool

The **Derive** tool is used to derive solid parts or assemblies into the current environment. The procedure to use this tool is given next.

- Click on the **Derive** tool from the **Create** panel in the **Sheet Metal** tab of the **Ribbon**. The **Open** dialog box will be displayed as shown in Figure-44.

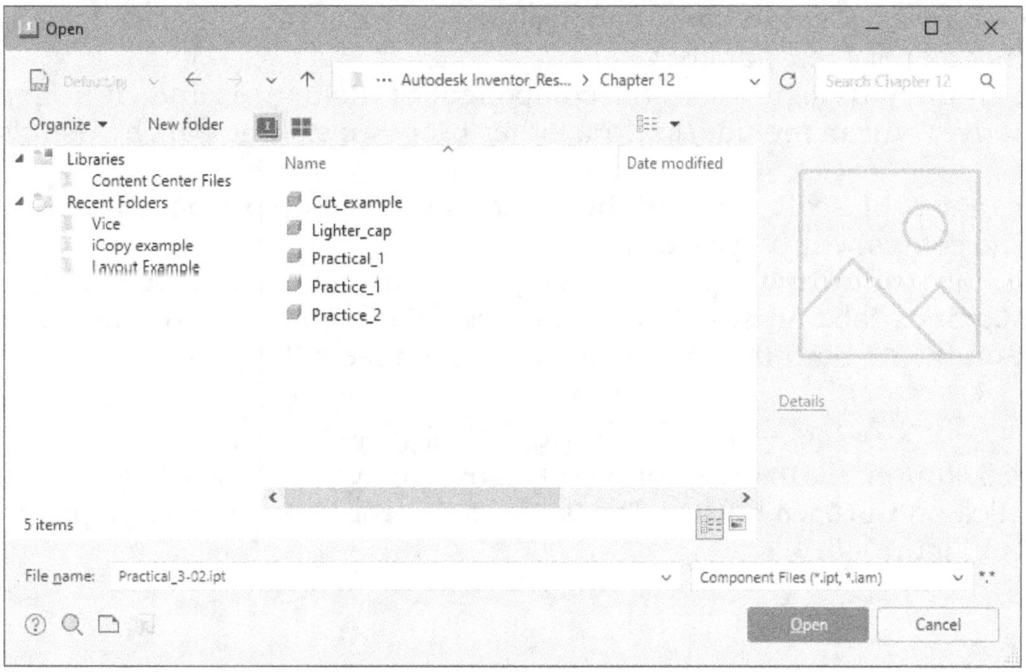

Figure-44. Open dialog box for deriving parts or assemblies

Deriving part

- Select a part file from the dialog box and click on the **Open** button. The **Derived Part** dialog box will be displayed as shown in Figure-45.

Figure-45. Derived Part dialog box

- Select desired derive style from the **Derive Style** options. There are four buttons to change derive style in the dialog box; **Single solid body merging out seams between planar faces**, **Solid body keep seams between planar faces**, **Maintain each solid as a solid body**, and **Body as Work Surface**. These buttons perform the task as per their names.
- Click on the plus sign before the component to include/exclude it from deriving. Similarly, you can include/exclude other properties of the part by using the plus sign.
- You can set the scale factor in the **Scale factor** edit box from **Options** tab to re-size the component by proportion.
- If you want the mirror copy of derived part then select the **Mirror part** check box from **Options** tab and select desired mirror plane from the drop-down below it.
- Click on the **OK** button from the dialog box to insert the part.

Deriving Assembly

- After clicking on the **Derive** tool, select an assembly in the **Open** dialog box displayed and click on the **Open** button. The **Derived Assembly** dialog box will be displayed; refer to Figure-46.

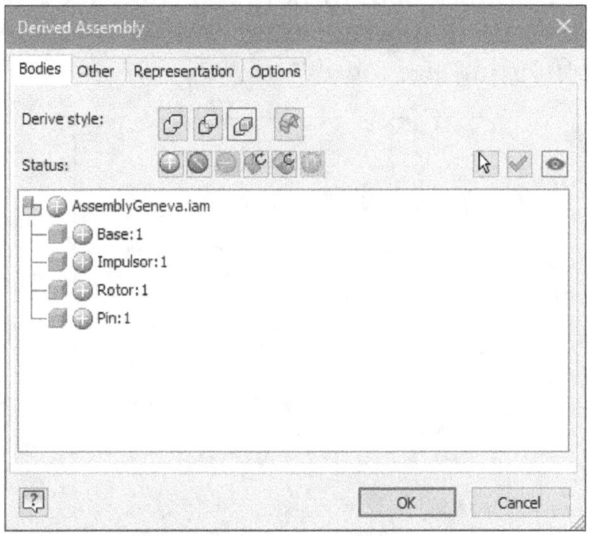

Figure-46. Derived Assembly dialog box

- The options for derive style are same as discussed earlier.
- Click on the plus sign before the component to switch between different modes of deriving like includes the selected components, excludes the selected components, subtracts the selected components, includes bounding boxes of the selected component, or intersects the selected components with the derived result.
- Click on the **Other** tab in the dialog box and select the component to be included/excluded in deriving. The options in this tab have already been discussed.
- The options in the **Representation** tab are used to change the orientation, presentation, and level of detail for deriving assembly components.
- The options in the **Options** tab are used to modify miscellaneous details of deriving assembly components like scale factor, hole patching, mirroring assembly, and so on.
- After setting desired values, click on the **OK** button to derive the selected components.

Till this point, we have discussed about the sheet metal feature creation tool. Now, we will discuss about the tools used for modification in sheet metal parts.

MODIFICATION TOOLS

The modification tools are available in the **Modify** panel of the **Sheet Metal** tab in the **Ribbon**; refer to Figure-47. The procedures to use these tools are discussed next.

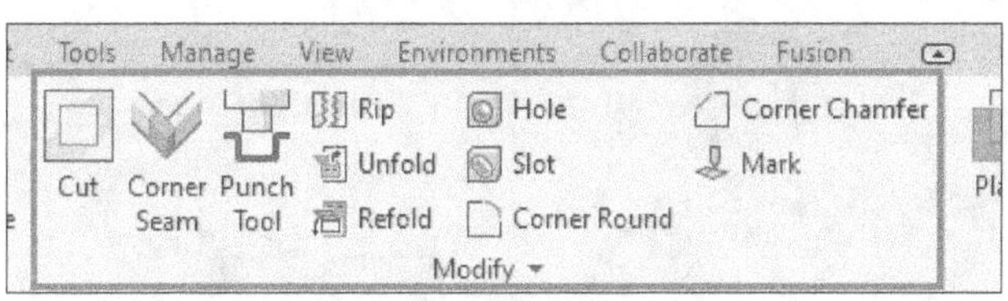

Figure-47. Modify panel in Sheet Metal tab

Using Cut Tool

The **Cut** tool, as the name suggests is used to cut material from the sheet metal face. The procedure to use this tool is given next.

- Click on the **Cut** tool from the **Modify** panel in the **Sheet Metal** tab of the **Ribbon**. The **Cut** dialog box will be displayed; refer to Figure-48. Also, you will be asked to select a close profile to make a cut.

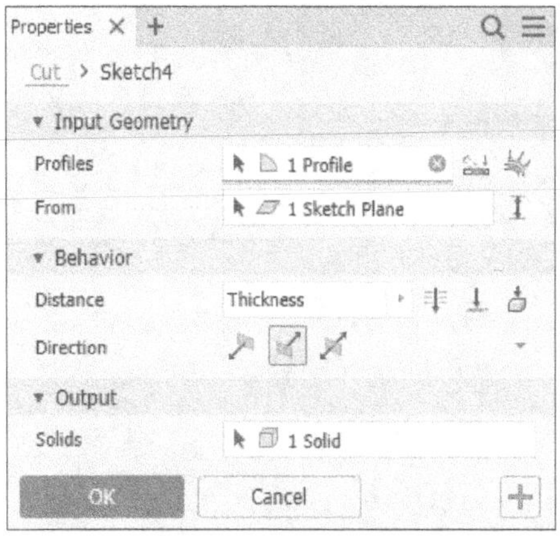

Figure-48. Cut dialog box

- Select the profile sketch from the drawing area. Preview of the cut will be displayed; refer to Figure-49.

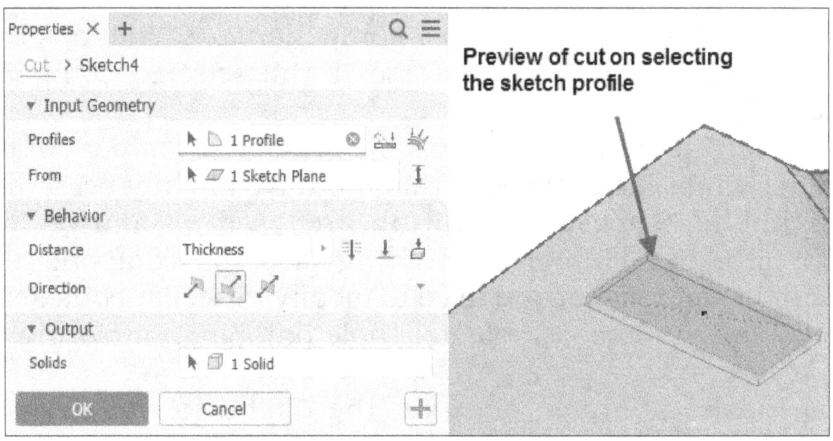

Figure-49. Preview of cut

- Select desired extent option from the drop-down in the **Behavior** rollout and specify the related parameters. Most of the time, we select the **To Next** option from the **Distance** area because generally we are cutting one layer of sheet metal at a time.
- If you are cutting a sheet metal at bend then you have two options to select:- **Cut Across Bend** and **Cut Normal**. Select the **Cut Across Bend** toggle button if you want the complete selected profile to be cut from base material; refer to Figure-50.

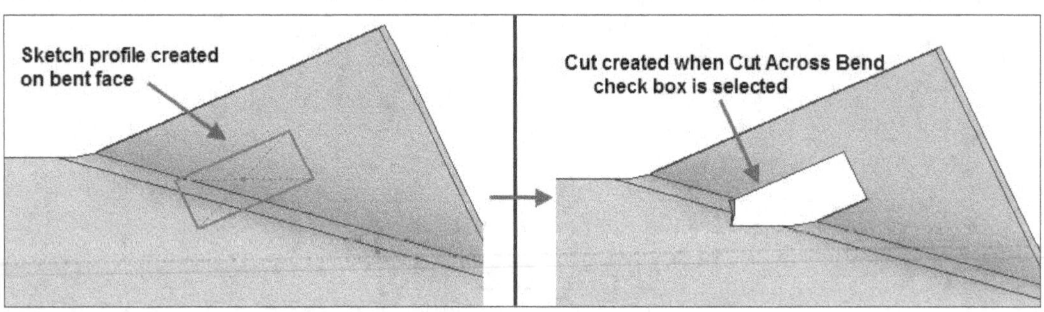

Figure-50. Cut created using Cut Across Bend check box

- If you have selected the **Cut Normal** toggle button in place of **Cut Across Bend** in the same example then the cut would be created as shown in Figure-51.

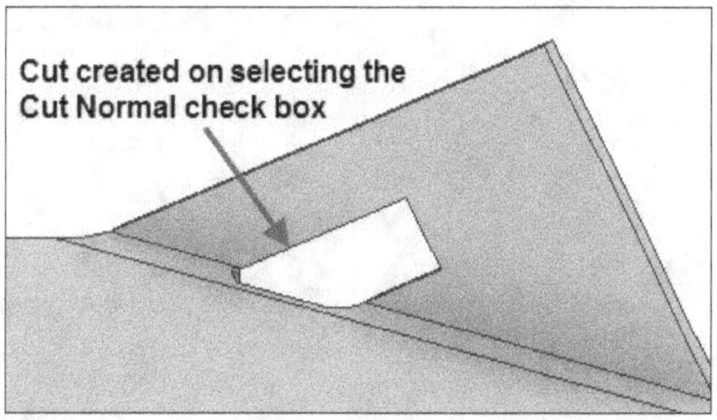

Figure-51. Cut created using Cut Normal check box

Using Corner Seam Tool

The **Corner Seam** tool is used to define or create gap between the adjoining faces of flange walls. The procedure to use this tool is given next.

- Click on the **Corner Seam** tool from the **Modify** panel in the **Sheet Metal** tab of the **Ribbon**. The **Corner Seam** dialog box will be displayed; refer to Figure-52.

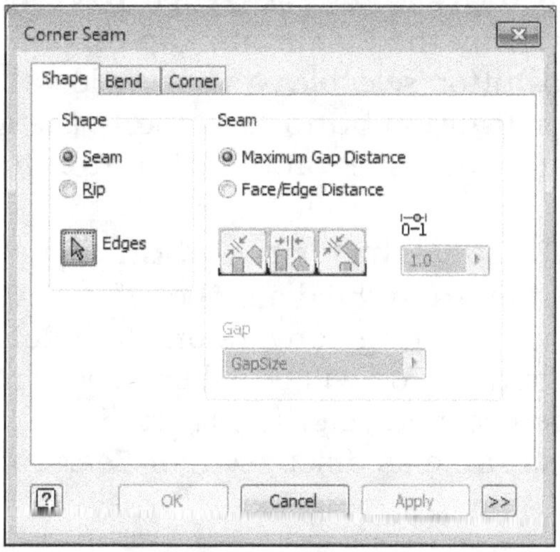

Figure-52. Corner Seam dialog box

Using Seam Option

- Select the **Seam** radio button to modify bend/corner already created. You will be asked to select the edges to be seamed.
- Select two adjacent edges of bend faces. Preview of the seam will be displayed; refer to Figure-53.

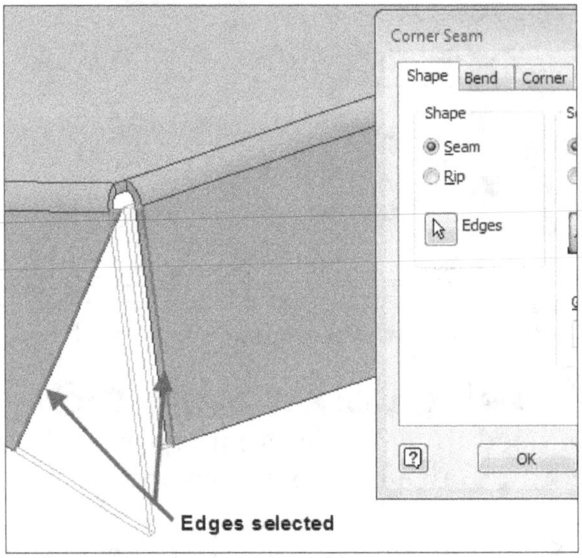

Figure-53. Edges selected for corner seam

- Select the **Maximum Gap Distance** or **Face/Edge Distance** radio button to specify whether you want to specify the maximum gap distance or face/edge distance.
- Depending on the radio button selected, you can select the **Symmetric Gap**, **Overlap**, **No Overlap**, or **Reverse Overlap** button to modify the gap between two faces.
- Specify desired gap value and click on the **OK** button to create the seam.

Using Rip Option

- Select the **Rip** radio button from the dialog box if you want to control gap created by **Rip** tool or gap created during conversion from solid to sheetmetal part. On selecting the **Rip** radio button, you will be asked to select the edge of ripped section.
- Select the edge of ripped corner; refer to Figure-54.
- Rest of the procedure is same as discussed for **Seam** radio button.

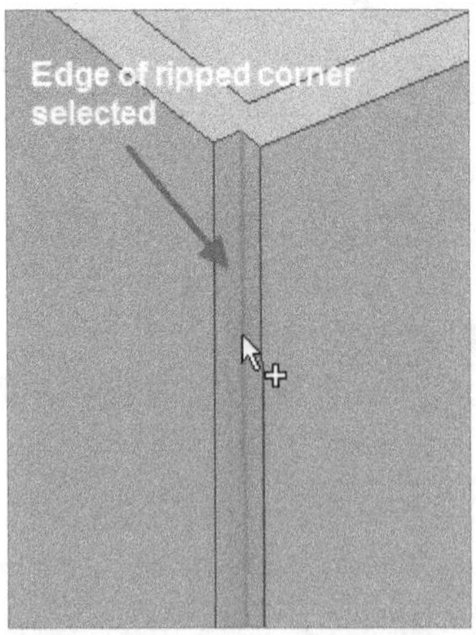

Figure-54. Edge of ripped corner selected

Using Punch Tool

The **Punch Tool** is used to make indent mark of the shape carved on punch on to the sheet metal face. The procedure to use this tool is given next.

- Click on the **Punch Tool** from the **Modify** panel in the **Sheet Metal** tab of the **Ribbon**. The **PunchTool** dialog box will be displayed; refer to Figure-55. Note that before using this tool on sheet metal face, you must have a sketch point on the face of sheet metal part to be punched; refer to Figure-56.

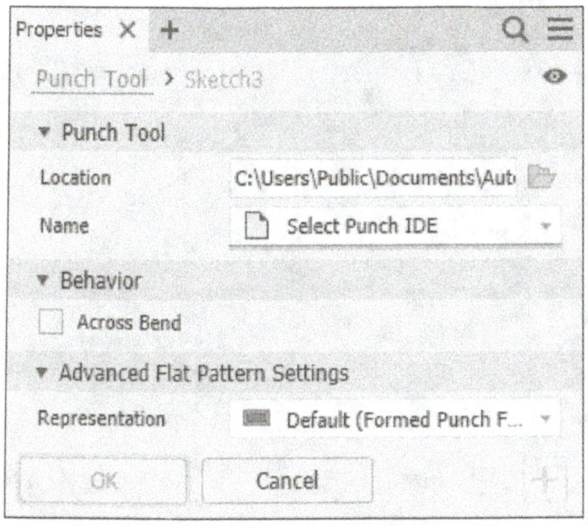

Figure-55. PunchTool dialog box

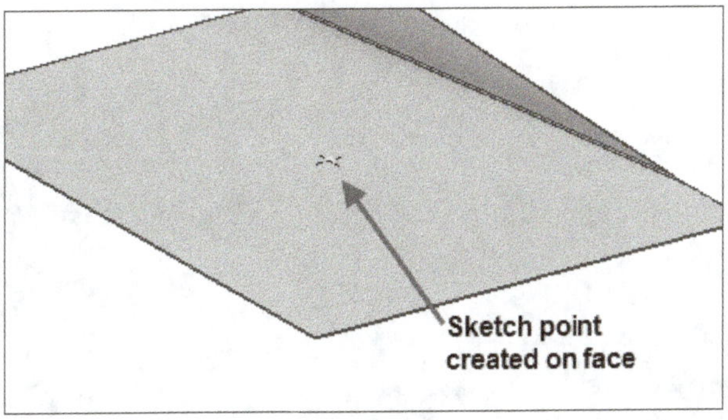

Figure-56. Sketch point created on face

- Click on the **Browse to another Punch Tool location** button from the dialog box. The **Select Punch Tool** dialog box will be displayed; refer to Figure-57.

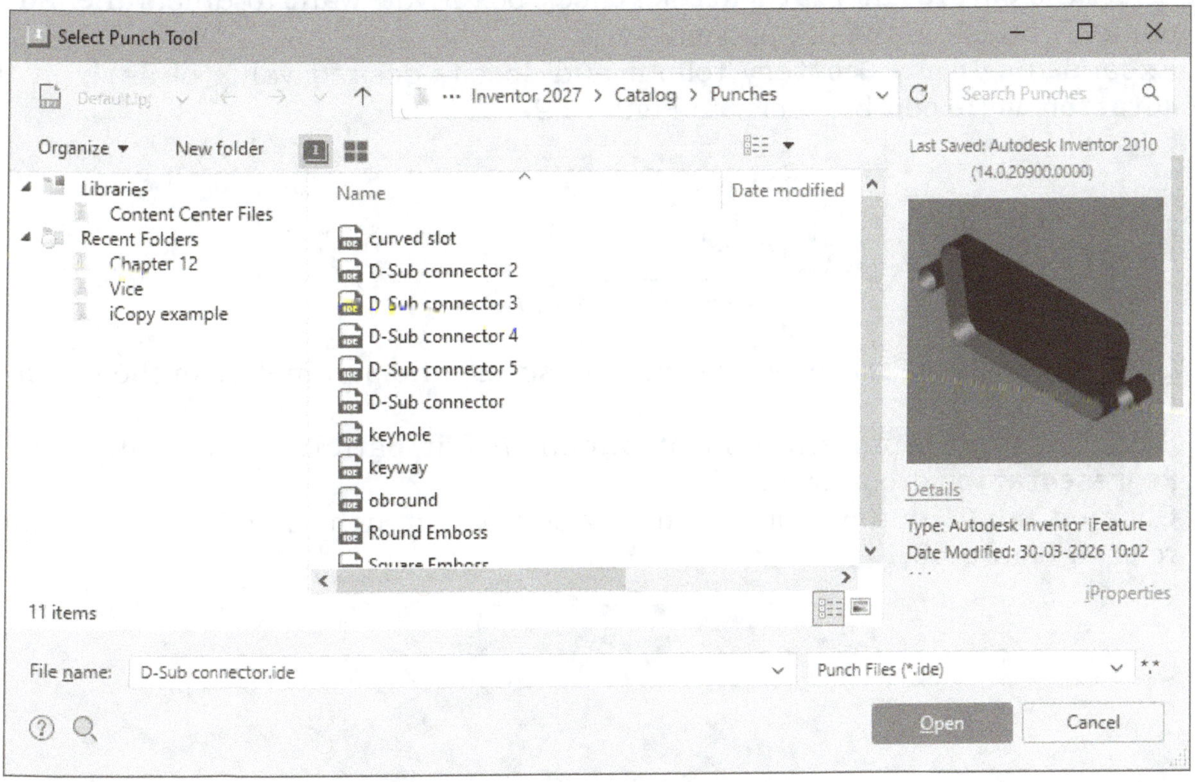

Figure-57. PunchTool Directory dialog box

- Select desired punch file from the dialog box and click on the **Open** button. The **PunchTool** dialog box will be displayed along with preview sketch of punch; refer to Figure-58.

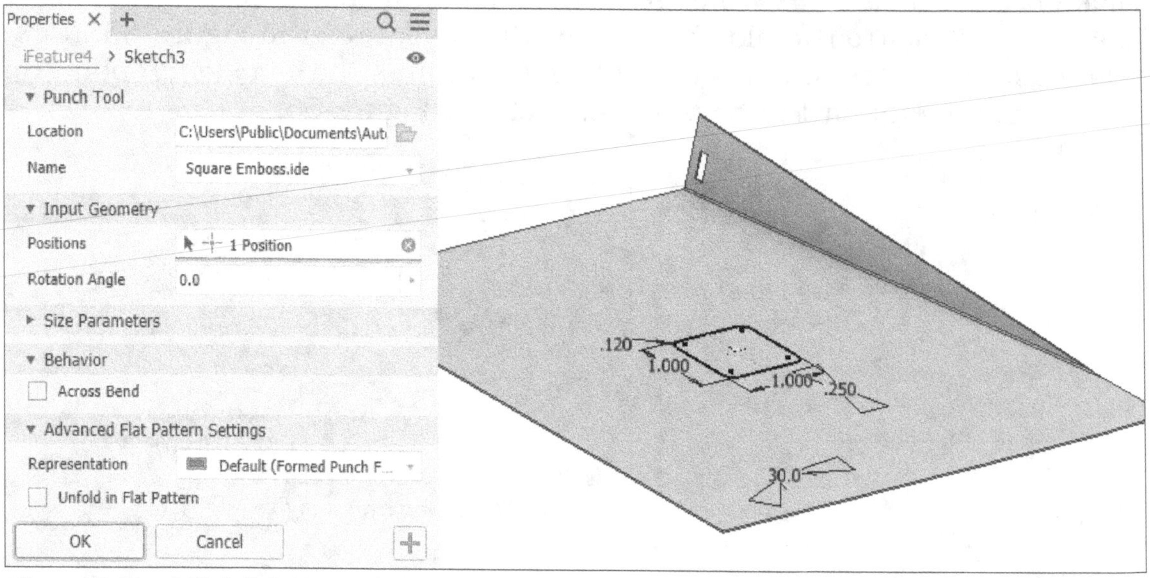

Figure-58. Punch Tool dialog box with sketch preview

- Select the **Across Bend** check box if you want the imprint of punch across the bends. If this check box is not selected then punch will stop at bends.
- Select the **Unfold in Flat Pattern** check box if you want to unfold the indent made by punch in the flat pattern.
- Expand the **Input Geomtery** rollout and specify desired value of angle in the **Rotation Angle** edit box; refer to Figure-59.

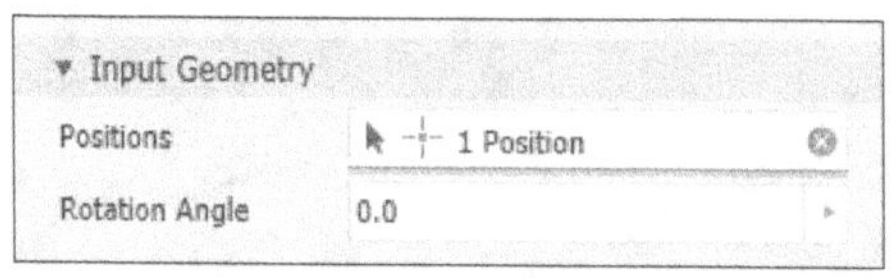

Figure-59. Angle edit box in PunchTool dialog box

- Click on the **Size Parameters** rollout and specify the parameters of the punch in the table.
- Select desired representation of punch in flat pattern by clicking on the **Representation** drop-down.
- Click on the **OK** button from the dialog box. The punch indent will be created; refer to Figure-60.

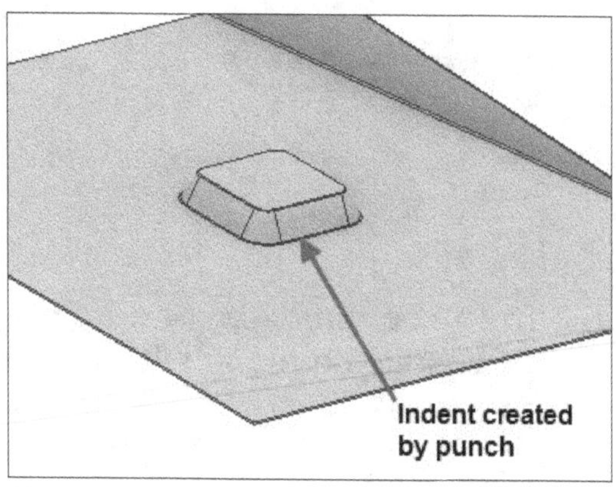

Figure-60. Indent created by punch

Using Rip Tool

The **Rip** tool is used to provide relief at the corners and edges for folding/unfolding of sheet metal components. This tool is most commonly used after creating lofted sheet metal feature. The procedure of using this tool is given next.

- Click on the **Rip** tool from the **Modify** panel in the **Sheet Metal** tab of the **Ribbon**. The **Rip** dialog box will be displayed as shown in Figure-61.

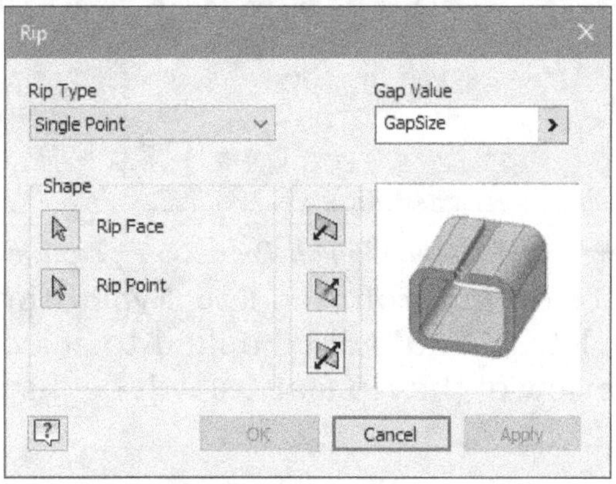

Figure-61. Rip dialog box

- There are three option in the **Rip Type** drop-down to rip the face(s). Select the **Single Point** option if you want to rip the face by the straight line passing through the selected point. You will be asked to select rip face and then rip point. Select the entities, preview of the rip feature will be displayed; refer to Figure-62.

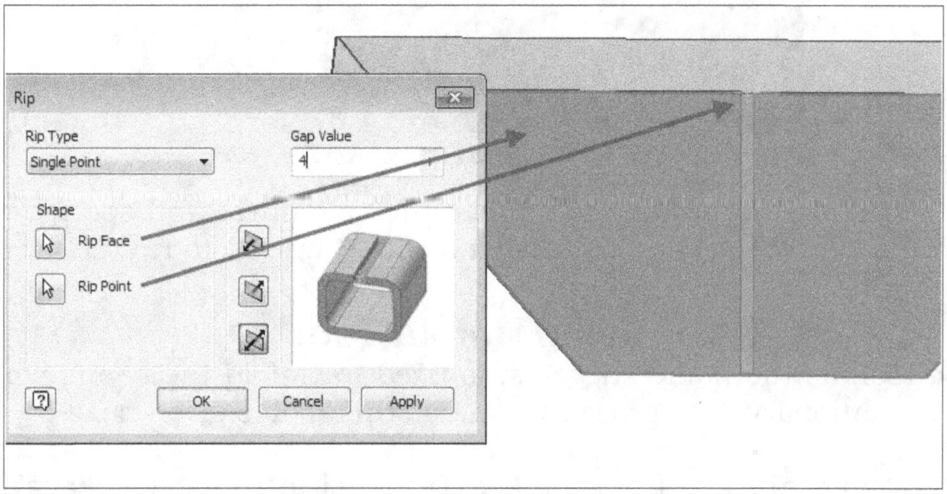

Figure-62. Preview of Rip with Single Point Rip Type option selected

- Select the **Point to Point** option from the **Rip Type** drop-down if you want to rip face between the two selected points. You will be asked to select rip face, start point, and then end point of rip feature. Select the entities accordingly. Preview of the rip feature will be displayed; refer to Figure-63.

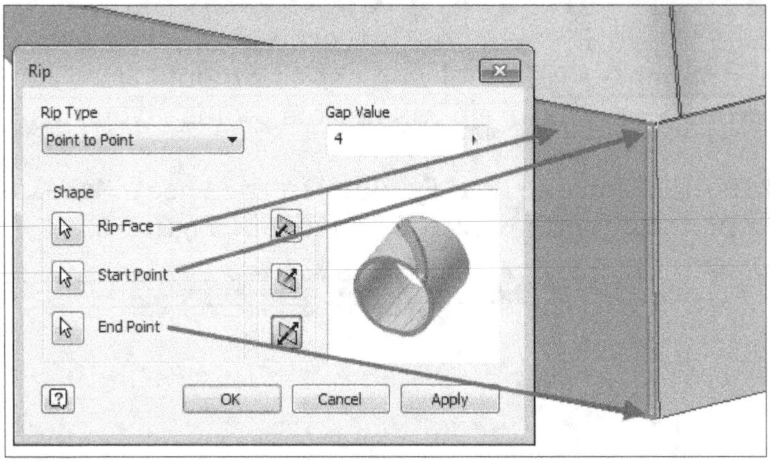

Figure-63. Preview of Rip with Point to Point Rip Type option selected

- Select the **Face Extents** option from the **Rip Type** drop-down if you want to rip the selected face completely. You will be asked to select rip face. Select the face you want to rip off. Preview of the rip feature will be displayed; refer to Figure-64.

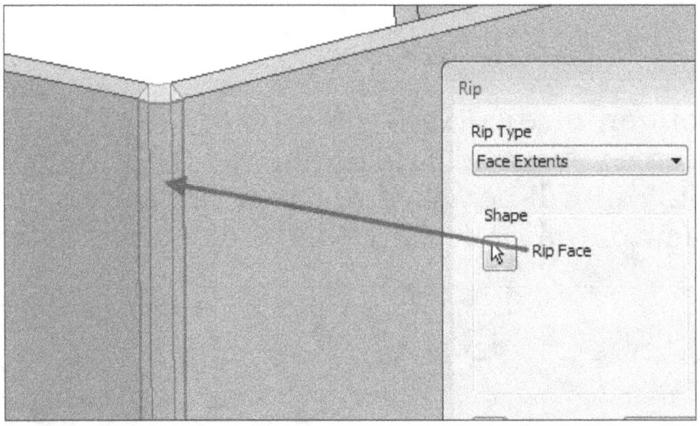

Figure-64. Preview of Rip with Face Extents Rip Type option selected

- Select the **Flip Side** buttons to change the side of rip and specify desired gap value in the **Gap Value** edit box. Click on the **OK** button to rip the face.

Using Unfold Tool

The **Unfold** tool, as the name suggests, is used to unfold the bends while making selected face stationary. The procedure to use this tool is given next.

- Click on the **Unfold** tool from the **Modify** panel in the **Sheet Metal** tab of the **Ribbon**. The **Unfold** dialog box will be displayed; refer to Figure-65. Also, you will be asked to select a stationary face.

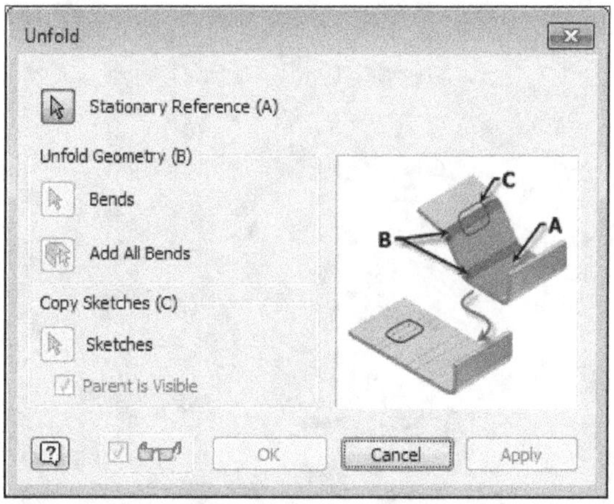

Figure-65. Unfold dialog box

- Select a stationary face of the sheet metal part to be unfolded. You will be asked to select bends to be unfolded.
- Select desired bend/bends. Preview of the unfold feature will be displayed; refer to Figure-66.

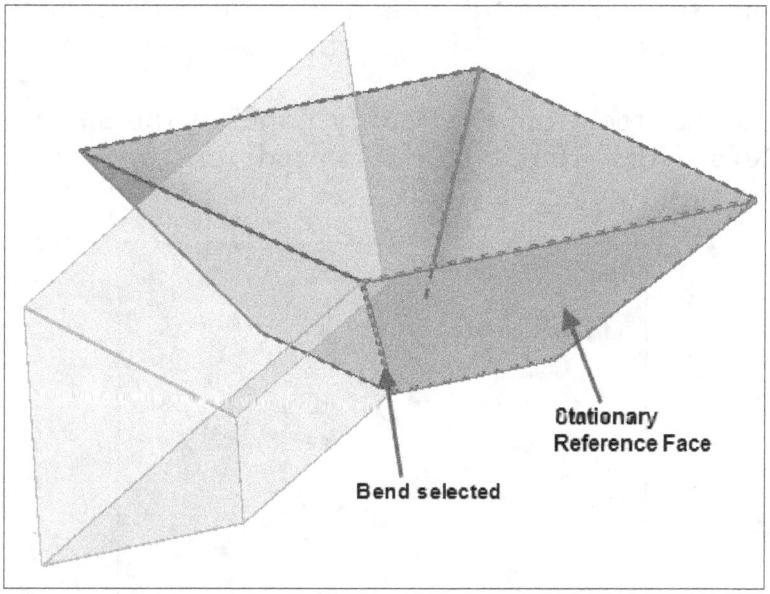

Figure-66. Preview of unfold feature

- If you want to unfold all the bends in the part then click on the **Add All Bends** button from the **Unfold Geometry** area of the dialog box.
- If you have a sketch on the face to be unfolded then you can select it after clicking on the **Sketches** selection button in the **Copy Sketches** area of the dialog box. The preview of unfolded feature with copied sketch will be displayed; refer to Figure-67.

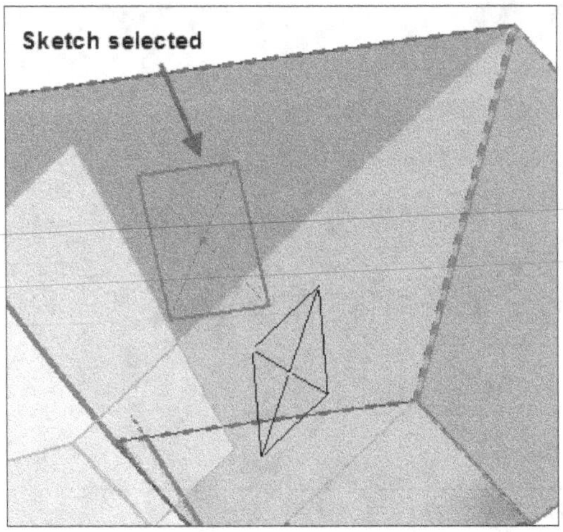

Figure-67. Preview of unfold feature with copied sketch

- Click on the **OK** button from the dialog box to create the unfold feature.

Using Refold Tool

The **Refold** tool is used to refold the unfolded bends. In simple words, it does the reverse of **Unfold** tool. The procedure to use this tool is given next.

- Click on the **Refold** tool from the **Modify** panel in the **Sheet Metal** tab of the **Ribbon**. The **Refold** dialog box will be displayed; refer to Figure-68. Also, you will be asked to select stationary reference.

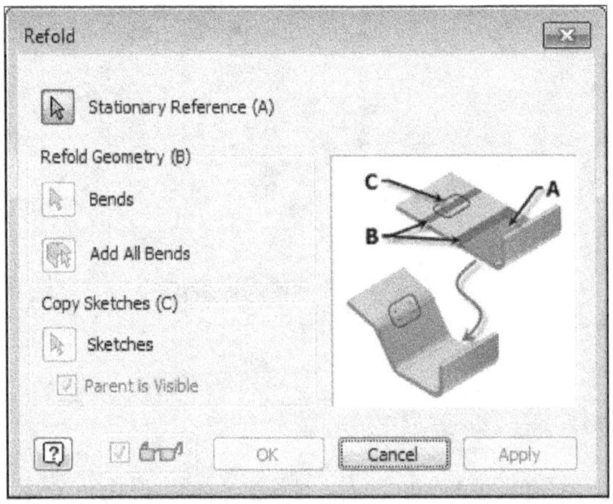

Figure-68. Refold dialog box

- Select the face of unfolded part that you want to be stationary. You will be asked to select the bends.
- Select the unfolded bend. Preview of the refold feature will be displayed; refer to Figure-69. Rest of the procedure is same as discussed for **Unfold** tool.

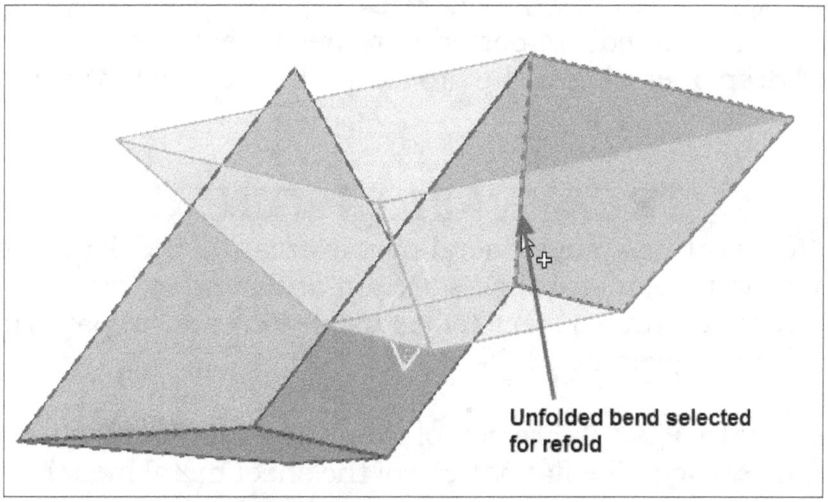

Figure-69. Preview of refold feature

The **Hole** tool and **Slot** tool in **Sheet Metal** tab works in the same way as **Hole** tool in **3D Model** tab which has been discussed already. The **Corner Chamfer** and **Corner Round** tools work in the same way as **Chamfer** tool in **3D Model** tab but in case of sheet metal, you can select only corner edges on choosing these tools; refer to Figure-70 and Figure-71.

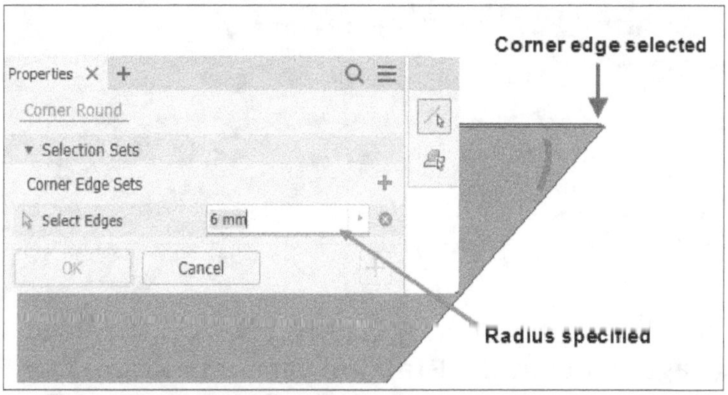

Figure-70. Corner Round preview

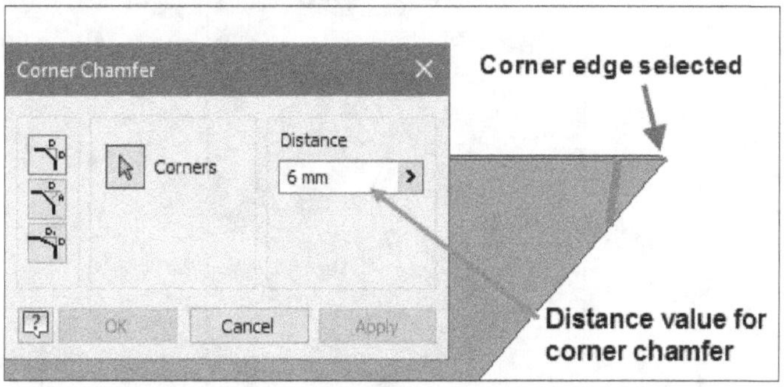

Figure-71. Preview of corner chamfer

Mark

The **Mark** tool is used to prepare the text for machining via processes like laser marking, etching, and engraving. The procedure to use this tool has been discussed in **Part 1** of the book.

Direct

The **Direct** tool is used to edit imported parametric features of the model by using simple drag and drop operations. The procedure to use this tool has been discussed in **Part 1** of the book.

CREATE FLAT PATTERN

The last step after creating a sheet metal part is creating the flat pattern of the part. Based on this flat pattern, metal sheets are cut and bend to form the required sheet metal part. The **Create Flat Pattern** tool is used to create flat pattern of sheet metal part. The procedure is given next.

- Click on the **Create Flat Pattern** tool from the **Flat Pattern** panel in the **Sheet Metal** tab of the **Ribbon**. The flat pattern of the sheet metal model will be displayed; refer to Figure-72.

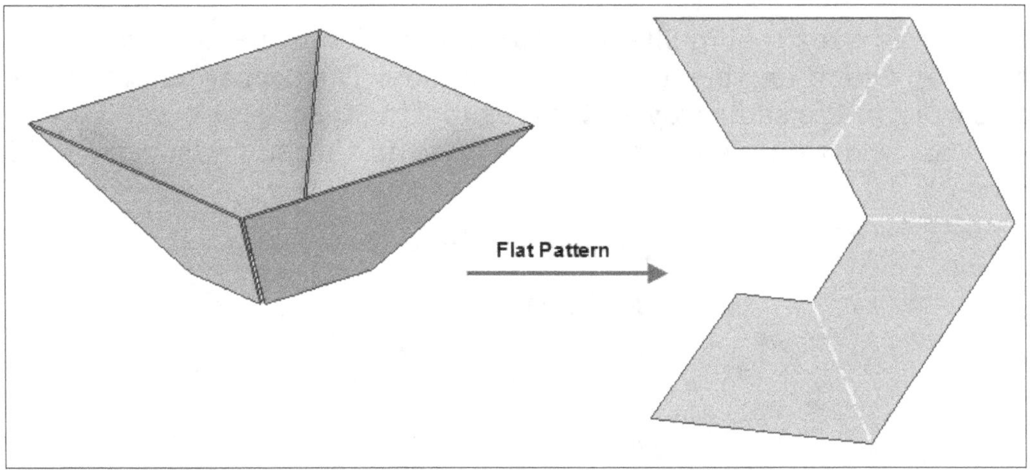

Figure-72. Flat pattern created

- To display the bending order of flat pattern, click on the **Bend Order Annotation** tool from the **Manage** panel in the **Flat Pattern** tab after using **Flat Pattern** tool. The bending order will be annotated on the flat pattern; refer to Figure-73.

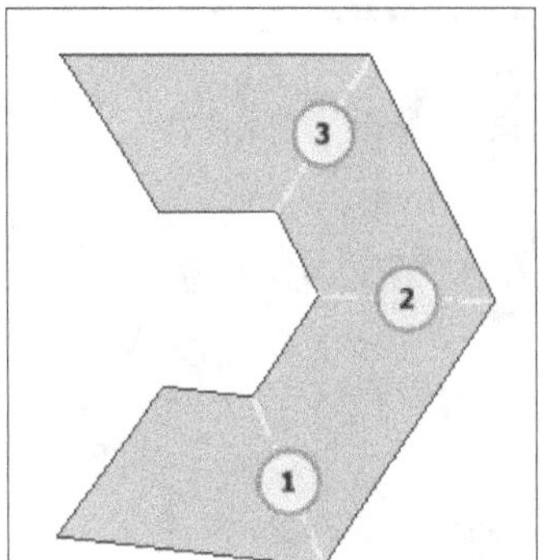

Figure-73. Bending order annotated on flat pattern

- To revert back to folded part, click on the **Go to Folded Part** tool from the **Folded Part** panel in the **Flat Pattern** tab of the **Ribbon**.

PRACTICAL 1

Create the sheet metal model as shown in Figure-74. The drawing is given in Figure-75.

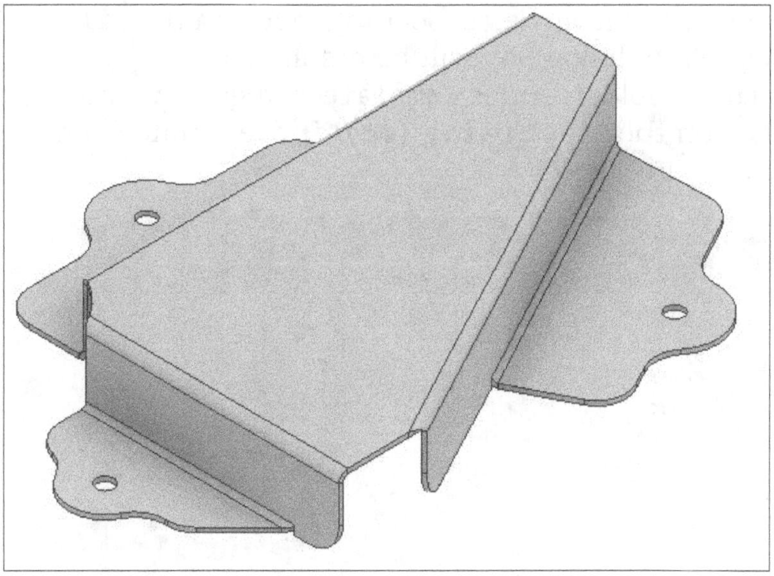

Figure-74. Model for Practical 1

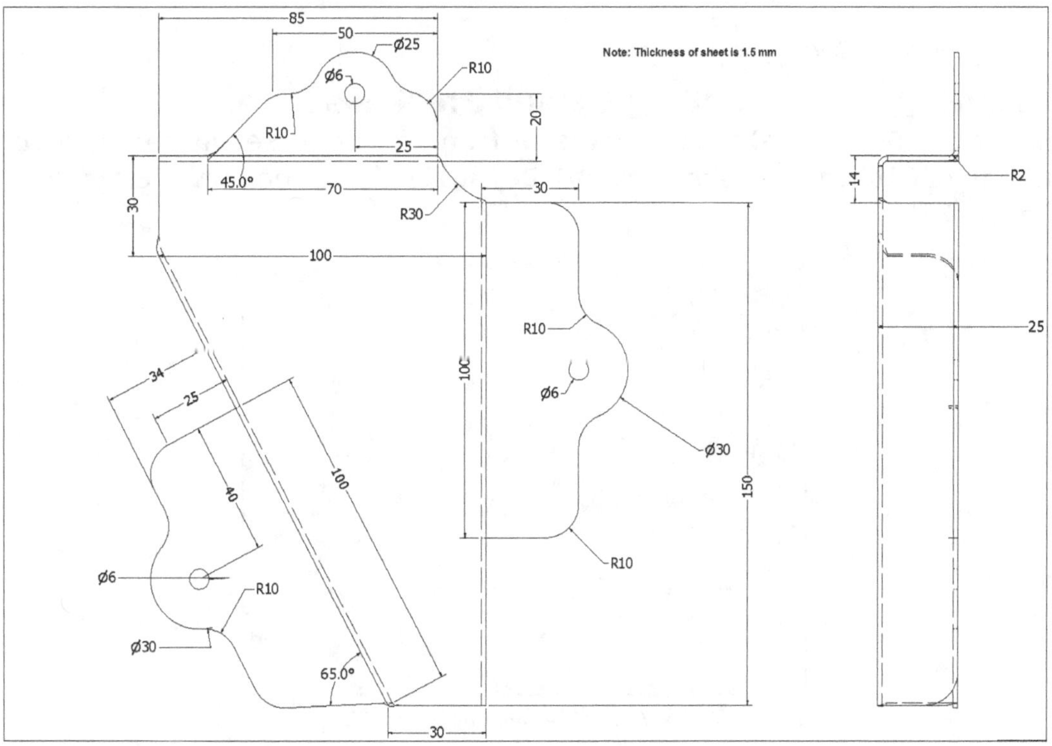

Figure-75. Drawing for Practical 1

Although, the drawing may look terrible at first look but if you read the drawing in pieces then you will find that there is a base of triangular shape with very clear dimensions then there are flanges on the edges and then there are flat faces on each flange with clear dimensions. We will create this sheet metal part in steps as given next.

Start a New Sheet Metal Part

- Start **Autodesk Inventor** by using **Start** menu or icon on the Desktop of your computer (If not started yet).
- Click on the **New** button from **New** cascading menu in the **File** menu of the **Ribbon**. The **Create New File** dialog box will be displayed.
- Click on the **Metric** folder under **Template** category in the left of the dialog box and double click on the **Sheet Metal (mm).ipt** template from the **Part** area of the dialog box; refer to Figure-76.

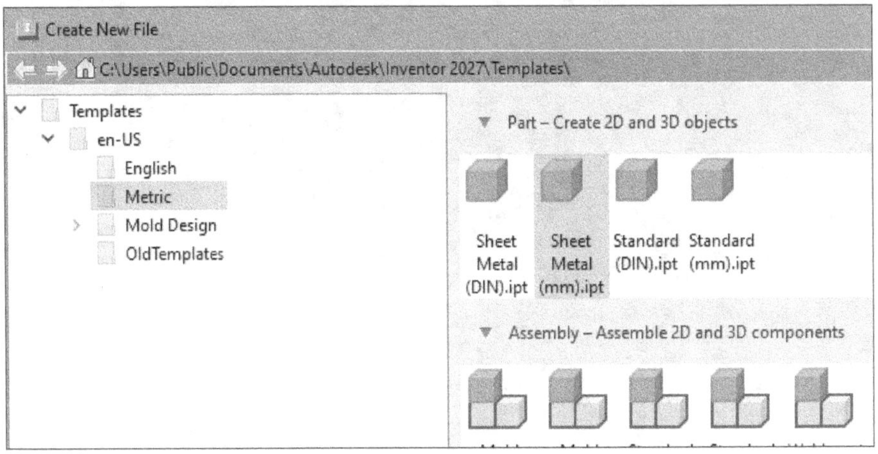

Figure-76. Starting new sheet metal part

Setting Default Thickness

- Click on the **Sheet Metal Defaults** button from the **Setup** panel in the **Sheet Metal** tab of **Ribbon**. The **Sheet Metal Defaults** dialog box will be displayed; refer to Figure-77.

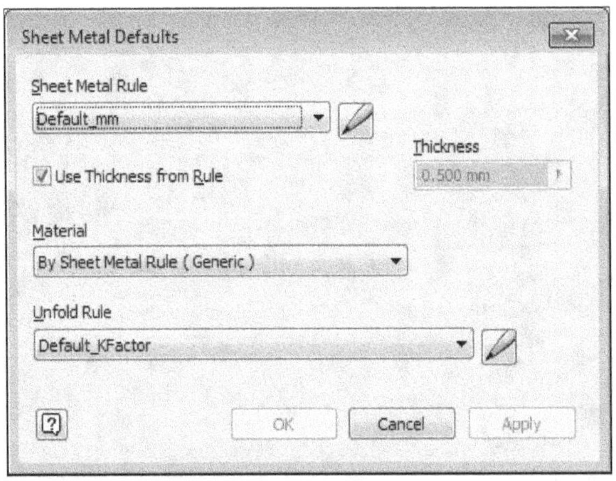

Figure-77. Sheet Metal Defaults dialog box

- Clear the **Use Thickness from Rule** check box and specify the sheet thickness as **1.5** mm in the **Thickness** edit box.
- Click on the **OK** button to apply the settings.

Creating Base

- Click on the **Start 2D Sketch** button from the **Sketch** panel in the **Sheet Metal** tab of the **Ribbon**. You will be asked to select a sketching plane.
- Select the **XZ** Plane as sketching plane. The **Sketch** tab in **Ribbon** will become active and tools related to sketching will be displayed.

- Create the sketch as shown in Figure-78.

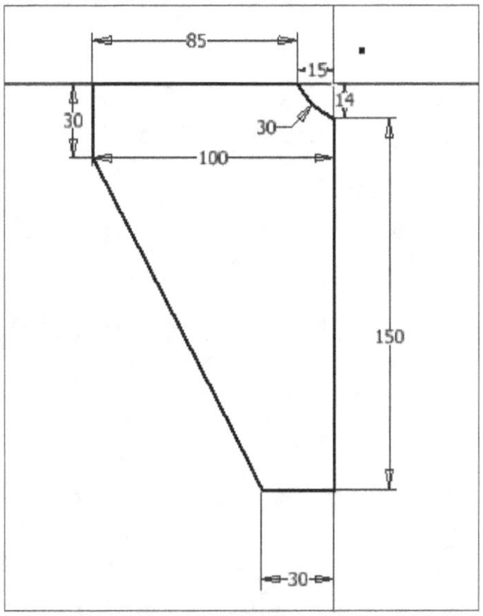

Figure-78. Sketch for base

- After creating the sketch, click on the **Finish Sketch** button from the **Finish** drop-down in the **Exit** panel of the **Sketch** tab in the **Ribbon**.
- Click on the **Face** tool from the **Create** panel in the **Sheet Metal** tab of the **Ribbon**. The **Face** dialog box will be displayed. Also, the sketch will be selected automatically.
- Specify the parameters as per the drawing and click on the **OK** button from the dialog box. The face will be created.

Creating Flanges

As per the model and drawing displayed in Figure-74 and Figure-75, there are three flanges created on the edges of the base with depth of **25** mm. The steps to create flanges are given next.

- Click on the **Flange** tool from the **Create** panel in the **Sheet Metal** tab of the **Ribbon**. The **Flange** dialog box will be displayed and you will be asked to select edges.
- Select the lower edges of the side faces as shown in Figure-79. The preview of the flanges will be displayed.

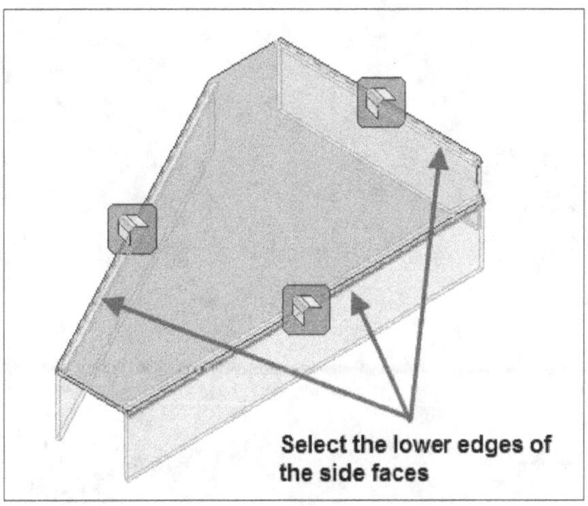

Figure-79. Edges selected for flange creation

- Click in the **Distance** edit box of **Height Extents** rollout of the **Flange** dialog box and specify the value as **25** mm. Make sure the other parameters is same as given in Figure-80.

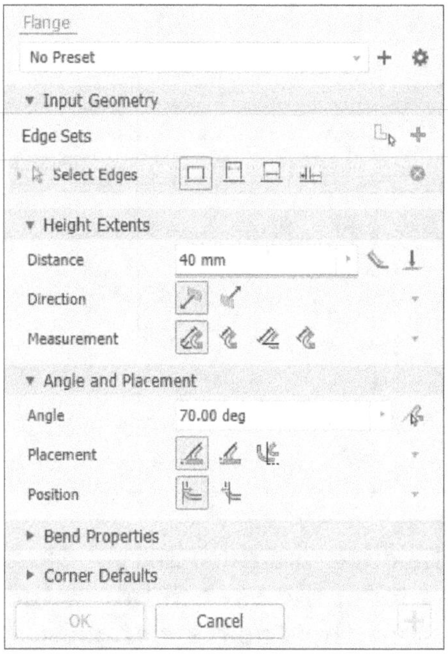

Figure-80. Flange dialog box with values specified

- Click on the **OK** button from the dialog box. The flanges will be created.

Creating First Face Feature on Flange

As per the model, there are three faces created on three flanges. We will create the face feature on first flange near round cut. The procedure is given next.

- Click on the **Start 2D Sketch** button from the **Sketch** panel in the **Sheet Metal** tab of the **Ribbon**. You will be asked to select the sketching plane.
- Select the planar face of flange near round cut as shown in Figure-81. The sketching environment will be activated.

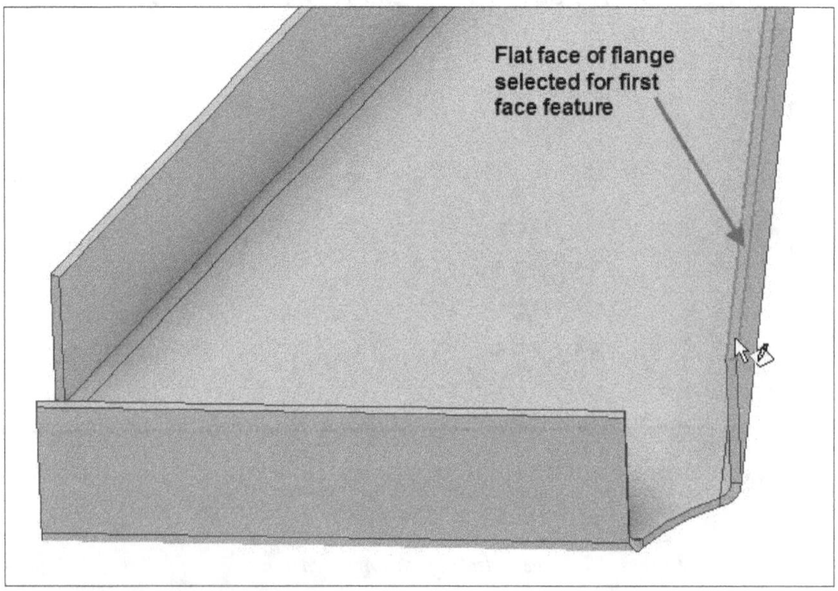

Figure-81. Face of flange selected for first face feature

- Create the sketch as shown in Figure-82.

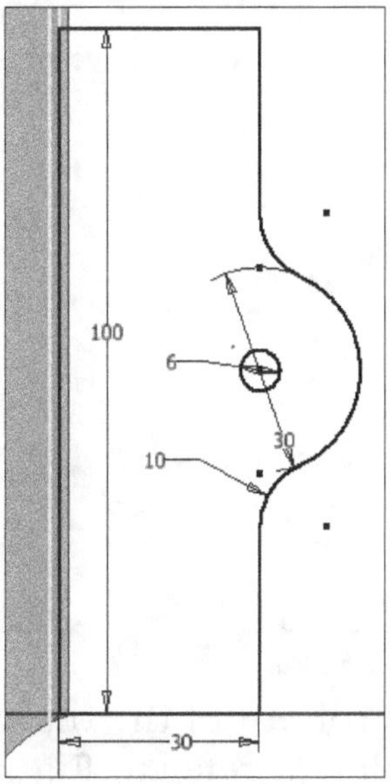

Figure-82. Sketch created for first face feature

- Click on the **Finish Sketch** button and then click on the **Face** tool from the **Create** panel in the **Ribbon**. You will be asked to select a profile.
- Select the newly created sketch by clicking inside the sketch; refer to Figure-83. Preview of the face feature will be displayed.

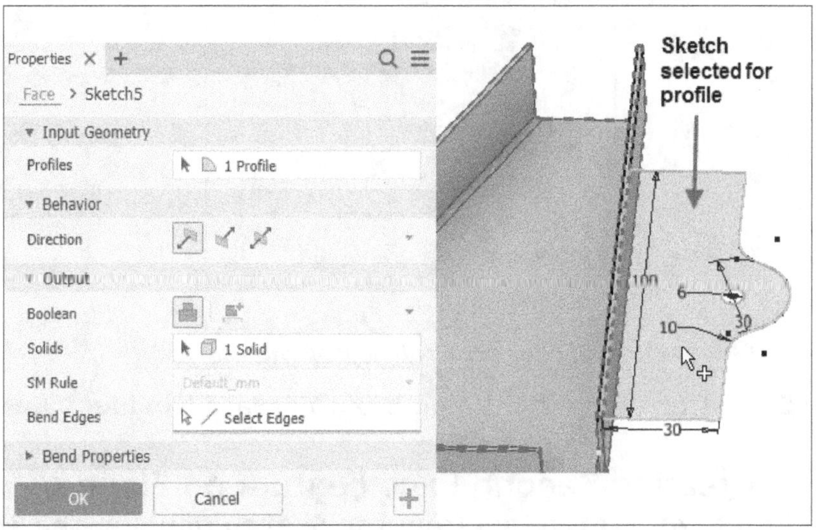

Figure-83. Selecting sketch for face profile

- Click on the **Edges** selection button in the **Bend Edges** area of the dialog box. You will be asked to select reference edge for creating bend.
- Select the edge of the flange wall as shown in Figure-84. Preview of the bend will be displayed.

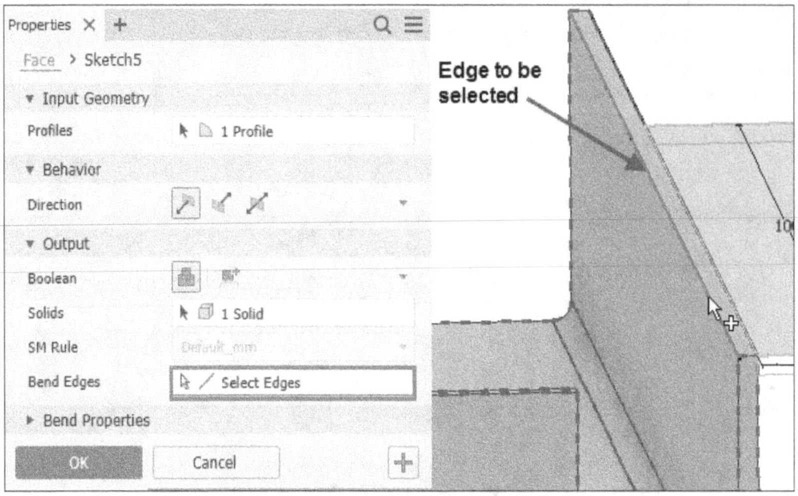

Figure-84. Edge selected for bending

- Click on the **Bend Properties** rollout of the dialog box and select the **Tear** option from the **Relief Shape** drop-down; refer to Figure-85.

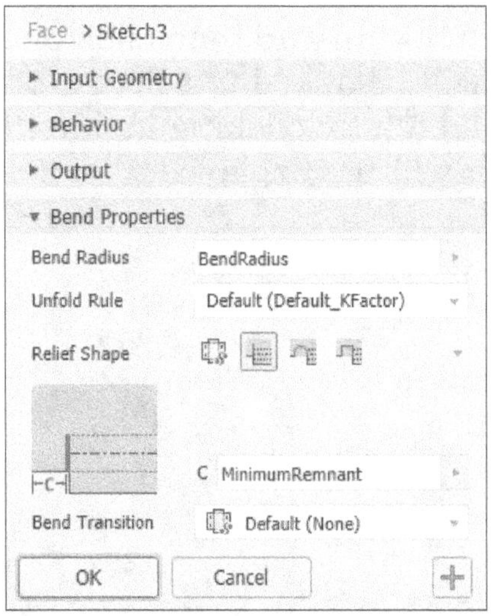

Figure-85. Tear option in Bend Properties rollout

- Click on the **OK** button from the dialog box to create the face.

Creating Second Face Feature on Flange

- Click on the **Start 2D Sketch** tool from the **Sketch** panel in the **Sheet Metal** tab of the **Ribbon**. You will be asked to select a sketching face/plane.
- Select the flat face of the smaller flange as shown in Figure-86. The sketching environment will be displayed.

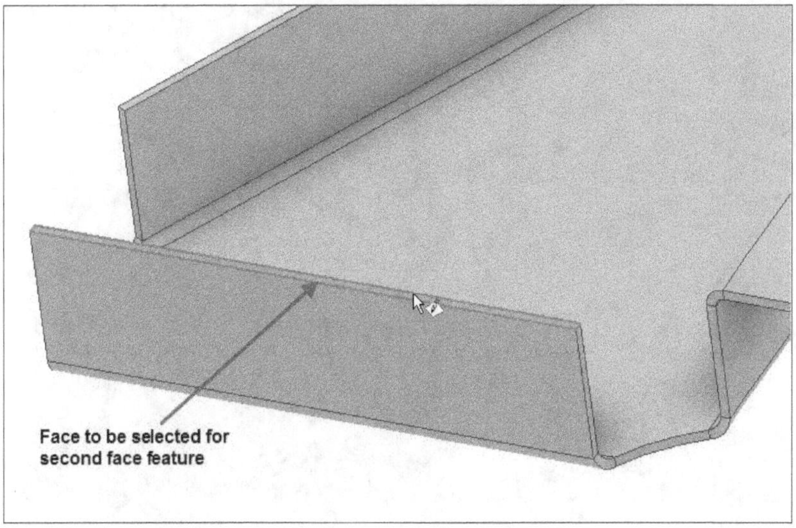

Figure-86. Face of flange selected for second face feature

- Create the sketch on face as shown in Figure-87.

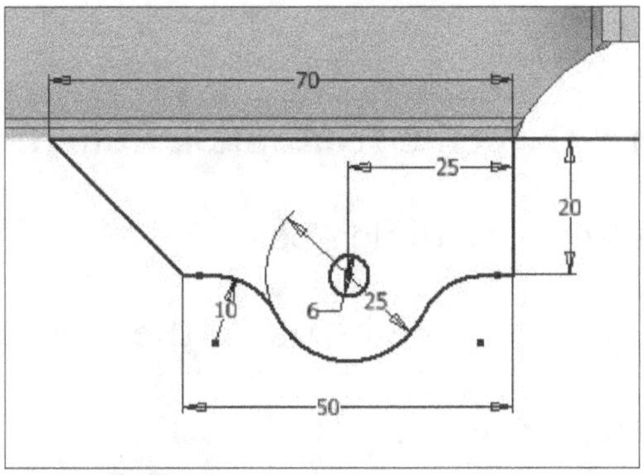

Figure-87. Sketch created for second face feature

- Click on the **Finish Sketch** button from the **Ribbon** and then click on the **Face** tool from the **Create** panel in the **Sheet Metal** tab of the **Ribbon**. The **Face** dialog box will be displayed.
- Select the newly created sketch by clicking inside it. Preview of the face feature will be displayed.
- Click on the **Edges** selection button and select the bend edge as shown in Figure-88.

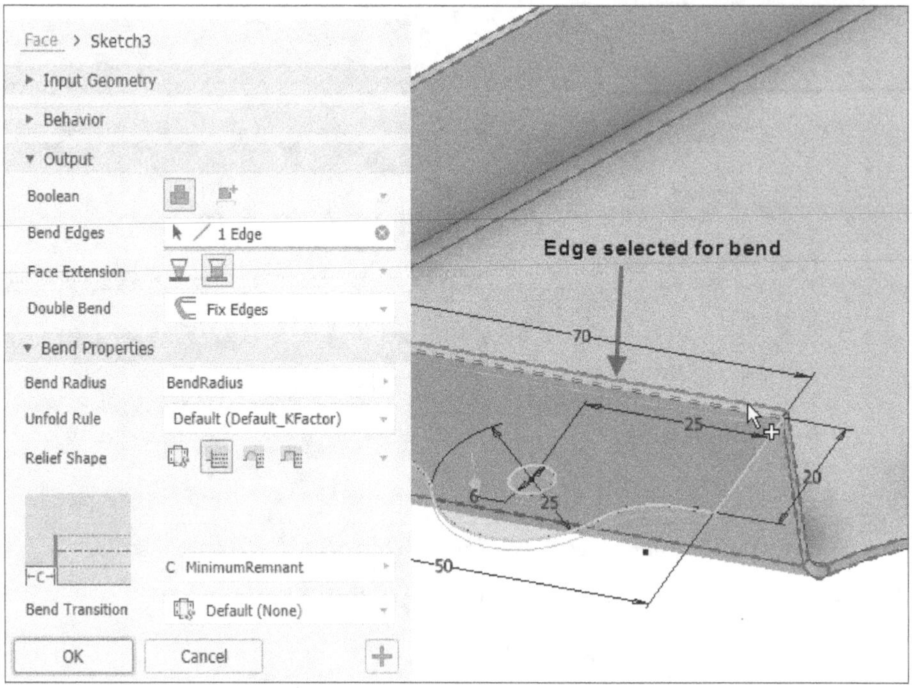

Figure-88. Bend edge selected for second feature

- Click on the **Bend** tab and select the **Tear** option from the **Relief Shape** drop-down as discussed earlier.
- Click on the **OK** button from the dialog box.

Similarly, create the third face feature by using the sketch as shown in Figure-89.

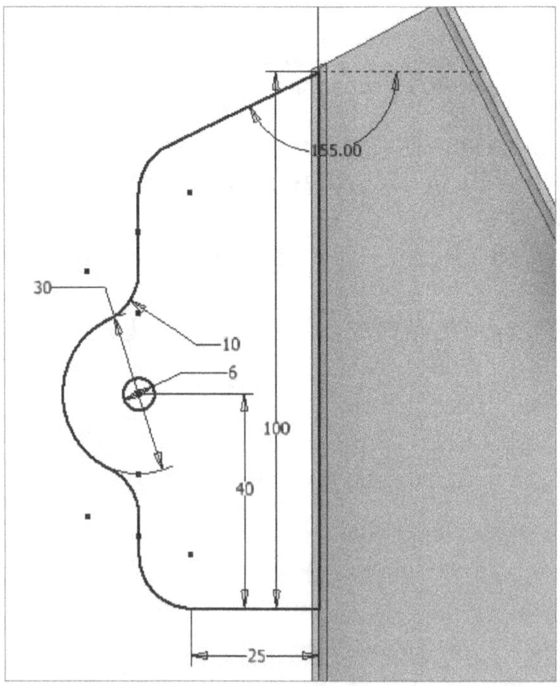

Figure-89. Sketch for third face feature

Applying Corner Rounds

- Click on the **Corner Round** tool from the **Modify** panel in the **Sheet Metal** tab of the **Ribbon**. The **Corner Round** dialog box will be displayed; refer to Figure-90.

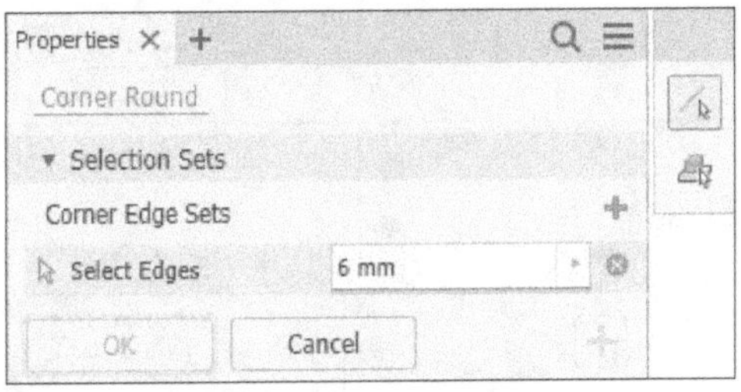

Figure-90. Corner Round dialog box

- Click on the **Radius** value and specify it as **10** mm.
- Click on the **Feature** radio button from the **Select Mode** area of the dialog box. You will be asked to select the feature.
- Click on the flange wall and then click on the **OK** button from the dialog box. Rounds will be applied to corners.

PRACTICAL 2

Create the sheet metal model of lighter cap as shown in Figure-91. The drawing is given in Figure-92.

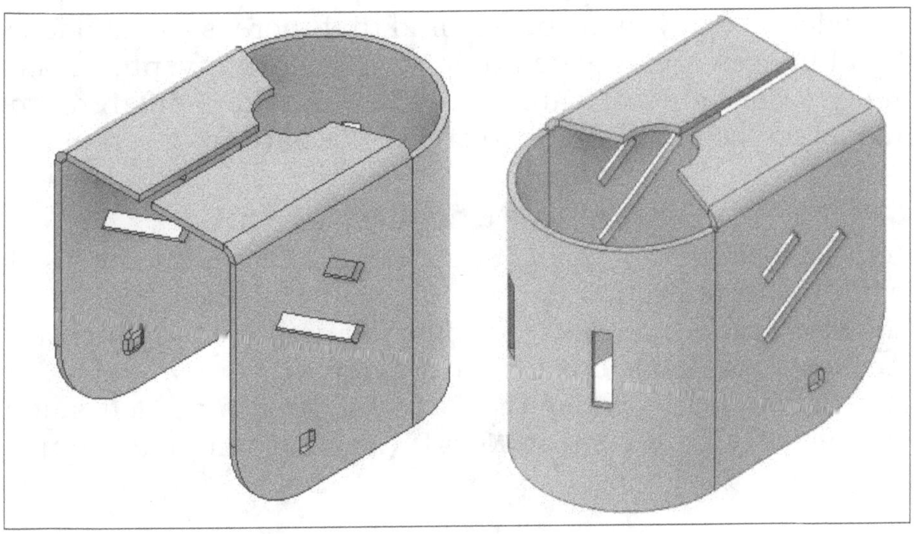

Figure-91. Model of Lighter cap

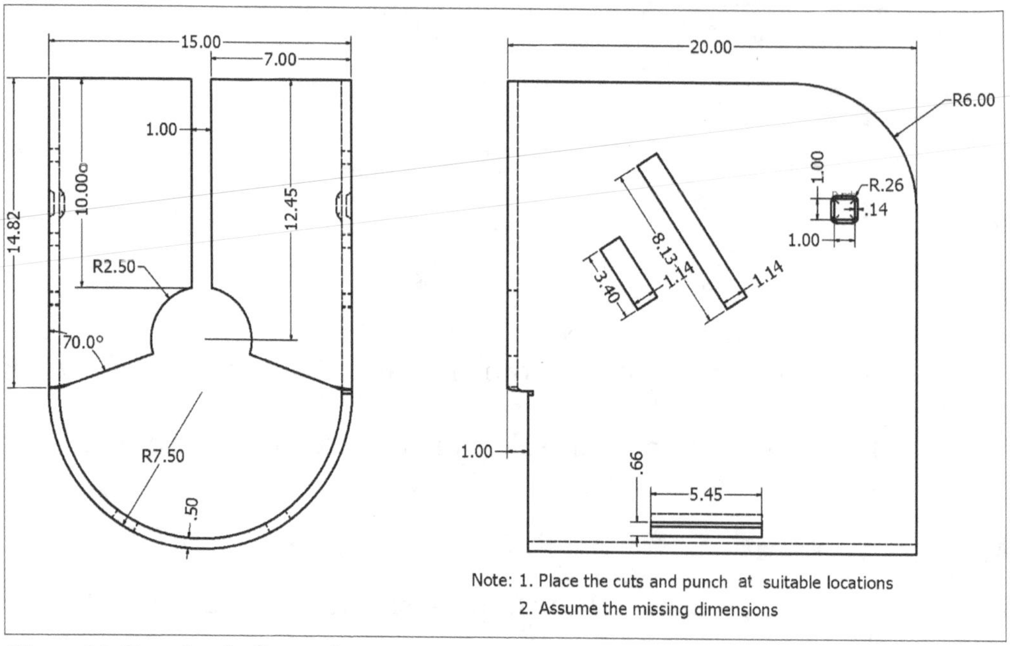

Figure-92. Drawing for Practical 2

If you see the model carefully then you will find that there is a round face in the sheet metal model and flanges are attached to it. In Autodesk Inventor, it is not possible to create flange on Contour roll feature. So, we will take a different approach here using Solid modeling tools. The steps to create the part are given next.

Start a New Sheet Metal Part

- Start Autodesk Inventor by using Start menu or icon on the Desktop of your computer (If not started yet).
- Click on the **New** button from **New** cascading menu in the **File** menu of the **Ribbon**. The **Create New File** dialog box will be displayed.
- Click on the **Metric** folder under **Template** category in the left side of the dialog box and double click on the **Sheet Metal (mm).ipt** template from the **Part** area of the dialog box.

Setting Default Thickness

- Click on the **Sheet Metal Defaults** button from the **Setup** panel in the **Sheet Metal** tab of **Ribbon**. The **Sheet Metal Defaults** dialog box will be displayed.
- Clear the **Use Thickness from Rule** check box and specify the sheet thickness as **0.5 mm** in the **Thickness** edit box.
- Click on the **OK** button to apply the settings.

Creating Extrusion

- Click on the **Start 2D Sketch** button from the **Sketch** panel in the **Sheet Metal** tab of the **Ribbon**. You will be asked to select a sketching plane.
- Select the **XZ** plane from the Model Tree. The sketching tools will become active.
- Create the sketch as shown in Figure-93. Click on the **Finish Sketch** button from the **Finish** drop-down in the **Ribbon** to exit.

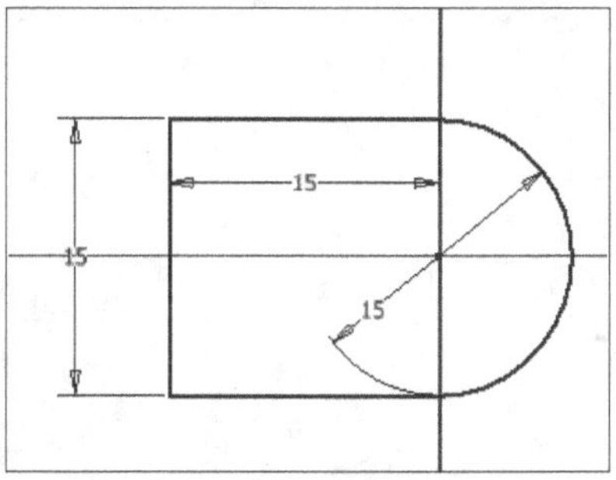

Figure-93. Sketch for extrusion

- Click on the **Extrude** tool from the **Create** panel in the **3D Model** tab of the **Ribbon**. The **Extrude** dialog box will be displayed along with preview of extrusion.
- Specify the distance value as **20** mm in the **Distance** edit box; refer to Figure-94.

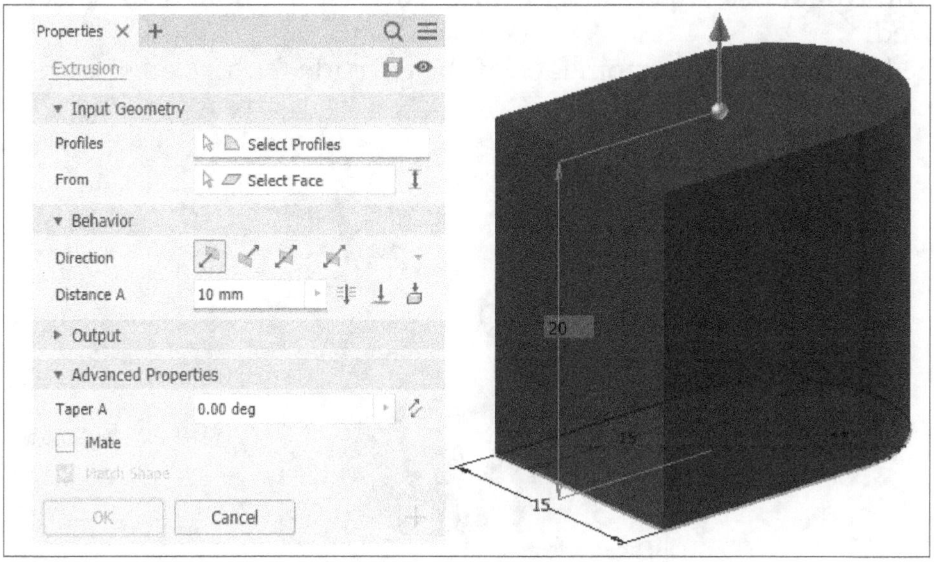

Figure-94. Distance edit box

- Click on the **OK** button from the dialog box.

Applying Shell Feature

We have the outer shape of the sheet metal model but we have the solid model not suitable for sheet metal operations. We will scoop out the extra material to form the part as sheet metal part. The steps are given next.

- Click on the **Shell** tool from the **Modify** panel in the **3D Model** tab of the **Ribbon**. The **Shell** dialog box will be displayed along with the preview of shell; refer to Figure-95.

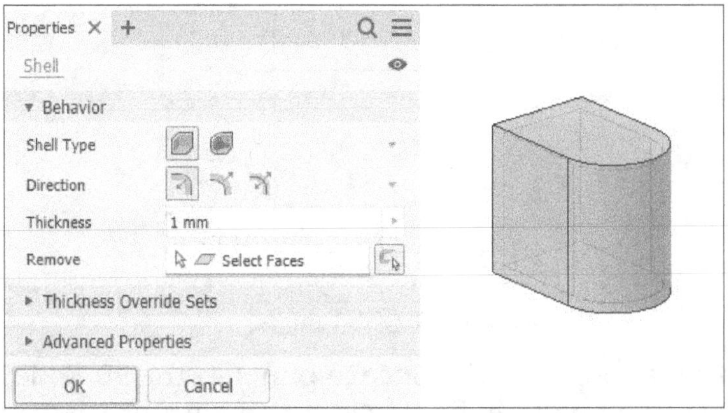

Figure-95. Shell dialog box

- Specify the thickness value as **0.5** mm. You will be asked to select the faces to be removed.
- Select the back face and bottom face of the extrude feature as shown in Figure-96.

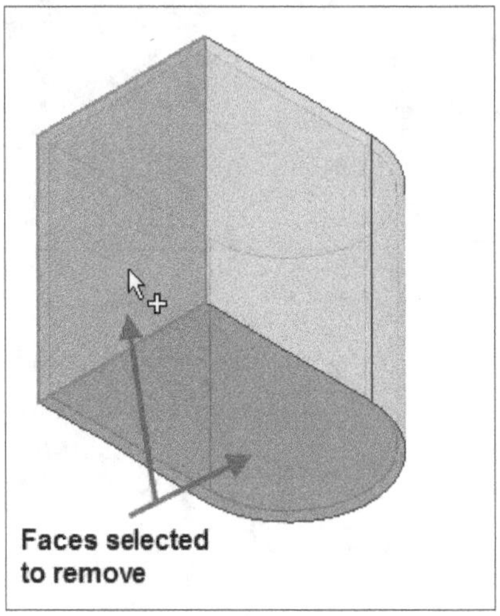

Figure-96. Faces to be selected for removing

- Click on the **OK** button from the dialog box to create the feature. The model will be displayed as shown in Figure-97.

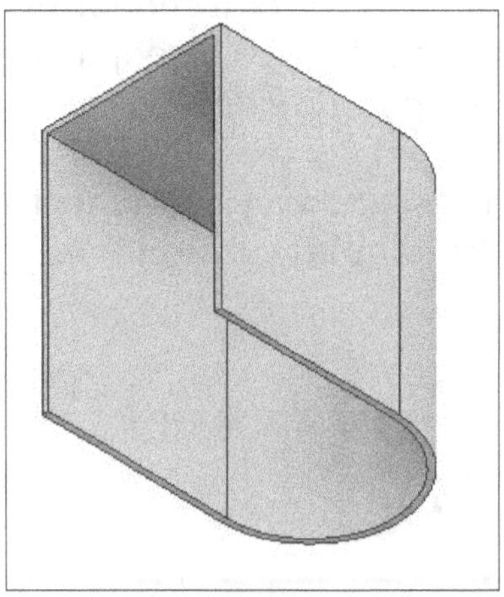

Figure-97. Model after applying shell tool

Creating Cut Feature on Top Face

- Click on the **Start 2D Sketch** tool from the **Sketch** panel in the **Ribbon** and select the top face of the model as sketching plane; refer to Figure-98.

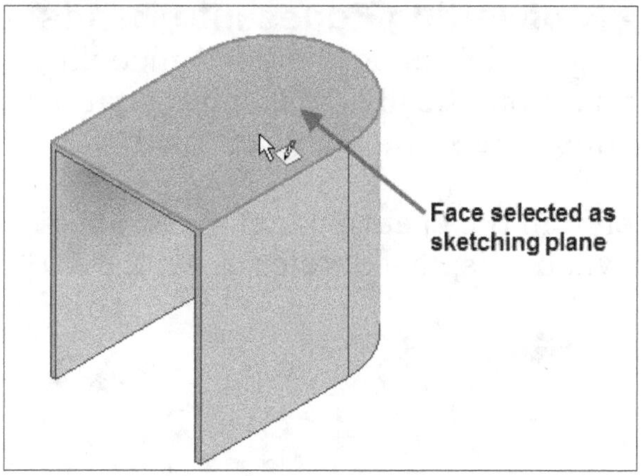

Figure-98. Face selected as sketching plane

- Create the sketch as shown in Figure-99. Click on the **Finish Sketch** button from the **Ribbon** to exit.

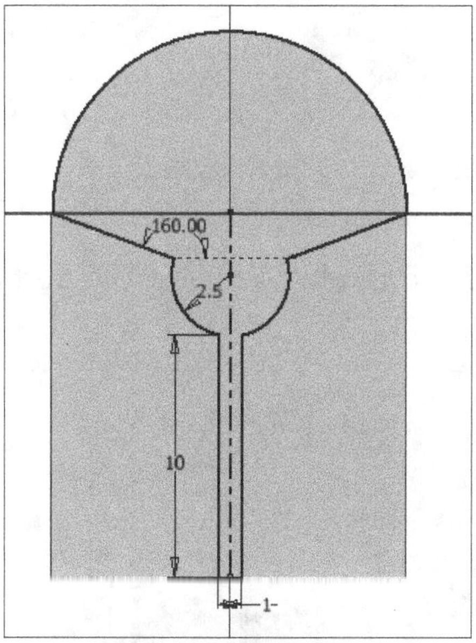

Figure-99. Sketch for cut feature

- Click on the **Cut** tool from the **Modify** panel in the **Sheet Metal** tab of the **Ribbon**. The **Cut** dialog box will be displayed along with the preview of cut feature; refer to Figure-100.

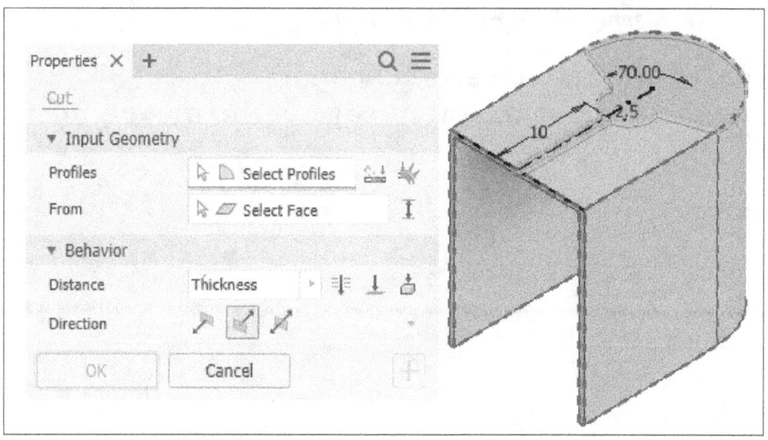

Figure-100. Cut dialog box with cut feature

Converting Edges into Bends

Since, we started creating model using the solid modeling tools, so we will not be able to create flat pattern automatically. To facilitate flat pattern, we need to convert the sharp edges into bends. The steps are given next.

- Click on the **Bend** tool from the **Create** panel in the **Sheet Metal** tab of the **Ribbon**. The **Bend** dialog box will be displayed; refer to Figure-101. Also, you will be asked to select edges.

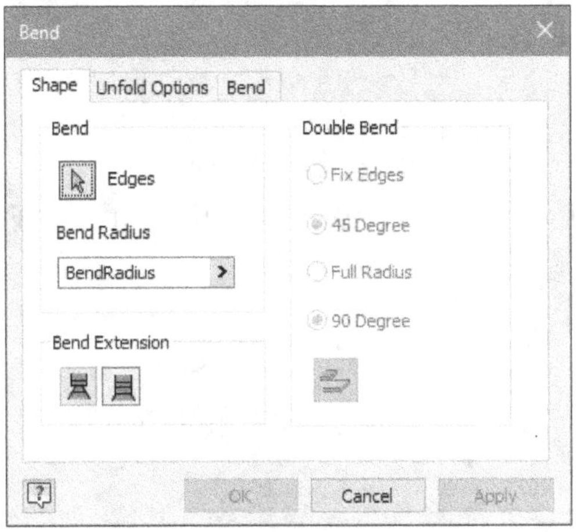

Figure-101. Bend dialog box

- Select the sharp edge of the model. Preview of the bend will be displayed; refer to Figure-102.

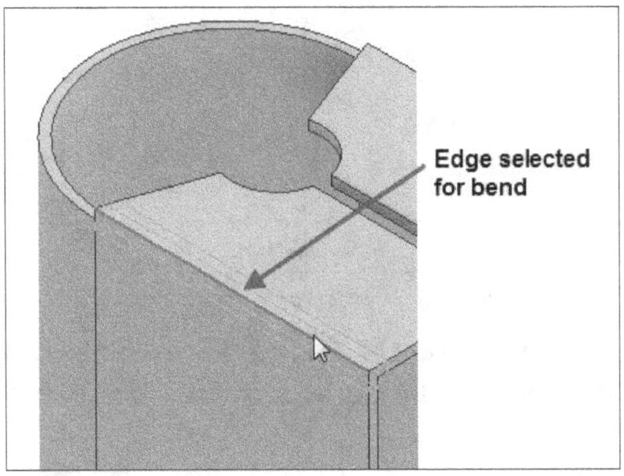

Figure-102. Edge selected for bend

- Click on the **Apply** button to create the bend.
- Similarly, create the bend at the other edge of the model; refer to Figure-103.

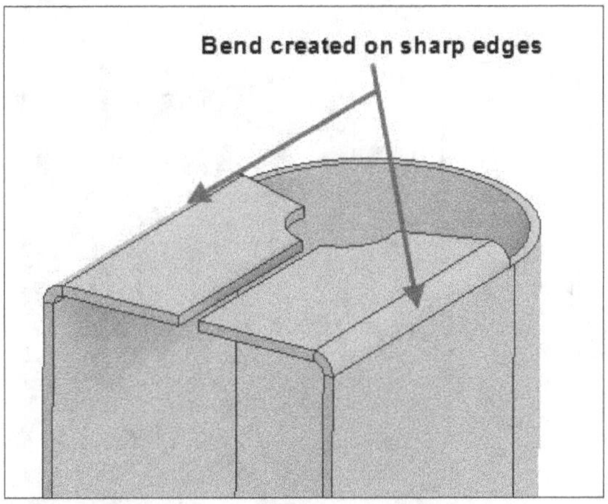

Figure-103. Bend created on sharp edges

Applying Corner Rounds

- Click on the **Corner Round** tool from the **Modify** panel in the **Sheet Metal** tab of the **Ribbon**. The **Corner Round** dialog box will be displayed.
- Select the **Feature** radio button from the **Select Mode** area of the dialog box and select the model. Preview of the corner round will be displayed.
- Make sure the radius value is specified as **6** mm and then click on the **OK** button to create corner round; refer to Figure-104.

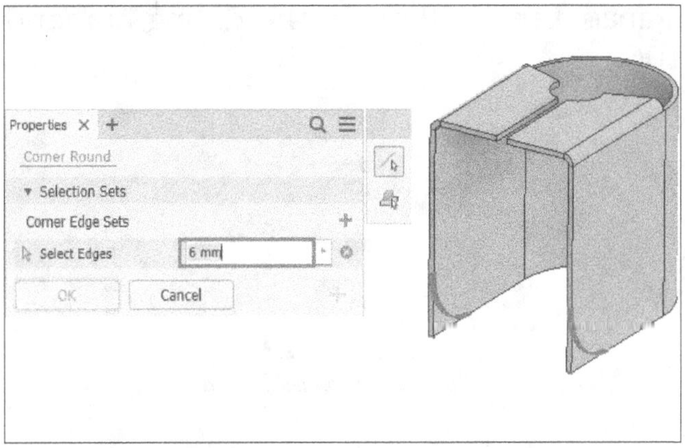

Figure-104. Preview of corner round

Creating Punch Marks

- Click on the **Start 2D Sketch** tool from the **Sketch** panel in the **Ribbon** and create a point on the inner face of model as shown in Figure-105.

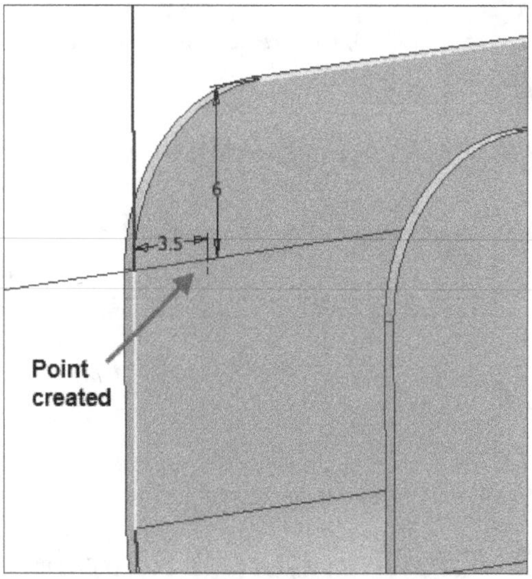

Figure-105. Point created on inner face

- Click on the **Finish Sketch** button from the **Finish** drop-down in the **Ribbon** to exit.
- Click on the **Punch Tool** from the **Modify** panel in the **Sheet Metal** tab of the **Ribbon**. The **Select Punch Tool** dialog box will be displayed.
- Double-click on **Square Emboss.ide** file from the dialog box. Preview of punch with **PunchTool** dialog box will be displayed.
- Expand the **Size Parameters** rollout in the dialog box and specify the value as shown in Figure-106.

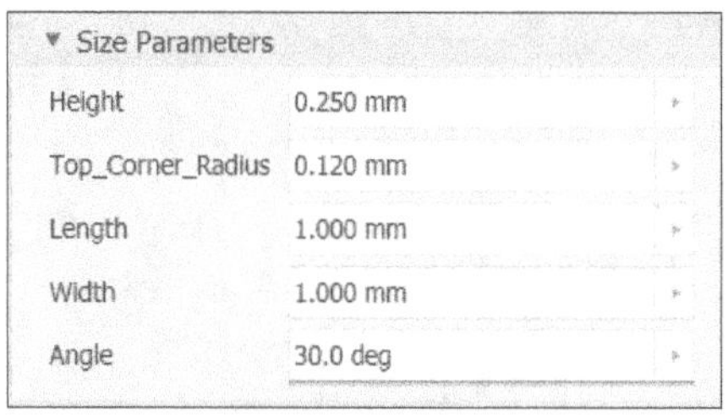

Figure-106. Values specified in mm

- Click on the **OK** button from the dialog box to create the feature.
- Click on the **Mirror** tool from the **Pattern** panel in the **Sheet Metal** tab of the **Ribbon**. The **Mirror** dialog box will be displayed. Also, you will be asked to select the feature to be mirrored.
- Select the punch mark created and then click on the **Mirror Plane** selection button from the dialog box; refer to Figure-107. You will be asked to select the mirror plane.

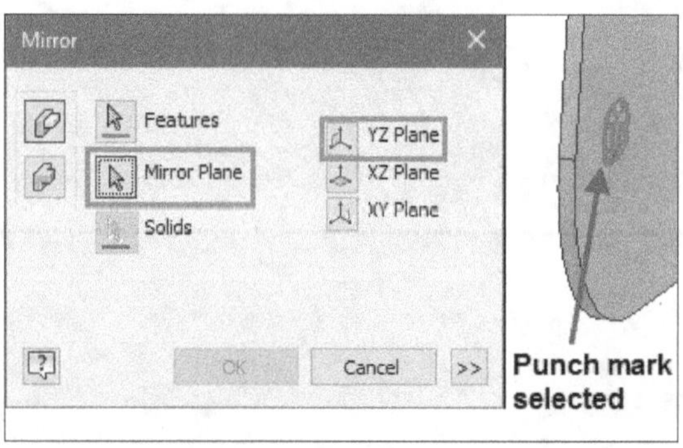

Figure-107. Punch mark selected and Mirror Plane selection button

- Select the **YZ** Plane as mirror plane from the dialog box and then click on the **OK** button from the dialog box.

Creating Cuts

There are some cuts to be made on the lighter cap to facilitate heat escape. We can not create cuts on round faces directly. To do so, we will flatten the sheet metal part and then perform the operation.

- Click on the **Unfold** tool from the **Modify** panel in the **Sheet Metal** tab of **Ribbon**. The **Unfold** dialog box will be displayed and you will be asked to select a stationary reference.
- Select the face as shown in Figure-108. You will be asked to select the bends.

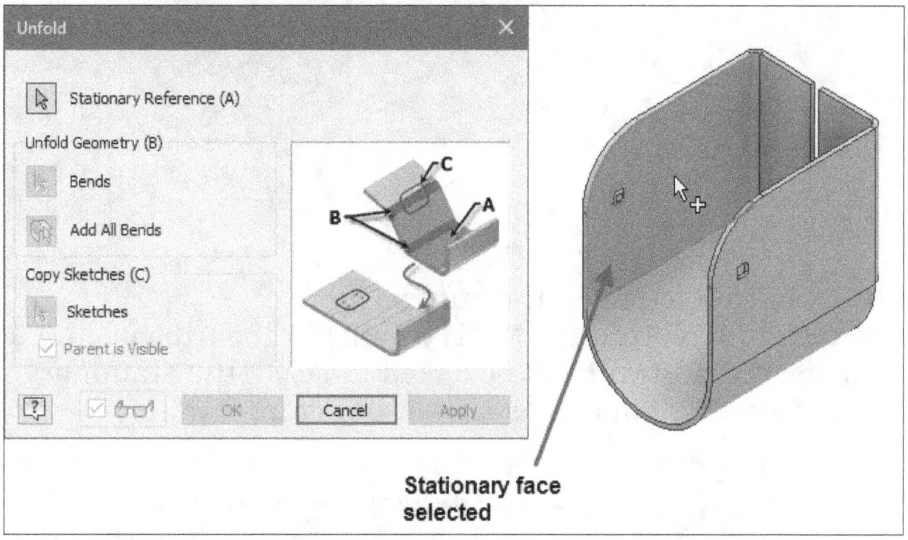

Figure-108. Stationary reference to be selected

- Click on the **Add All Bends** button from the dialog box and then click on the **OK** button. The unfold feature will be created.
- Create 2D sketch on the flattened face as shown in Figure-109. Dimensions are as per the drawing given in Figure-92.

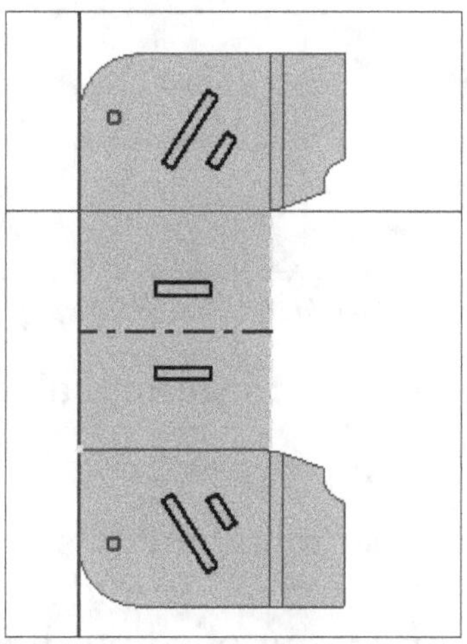

Figure-109. Sketch created on flattened face

- Click on the **Cut** tool from the **Modify** panel in the **Sheet Metal** tab of the **Ribbon**. You will be asked to select the profile sketch.

- Select all the close loops in the sketch and also select the **Cut Across Bend** check box from the dialog box; refer to Figure-110.

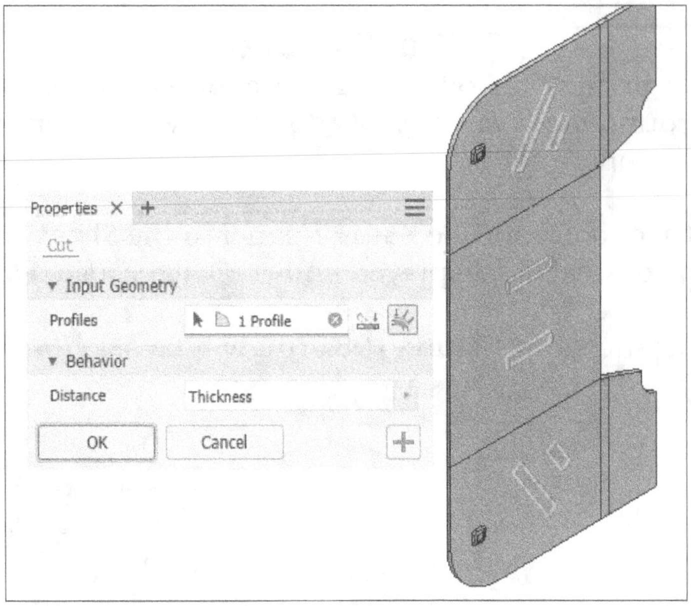

Figure-110. Profile selected for cut feature

- Click on the **OK** button to create the cut feature.
- Click on the **Refold** tool from the **Modify** panel in the **Ribbon**. The **Refold** dialog box will be displayed and you will be asked to select the stationary reference.
- Select the side face of the model as shown in Figure-111.

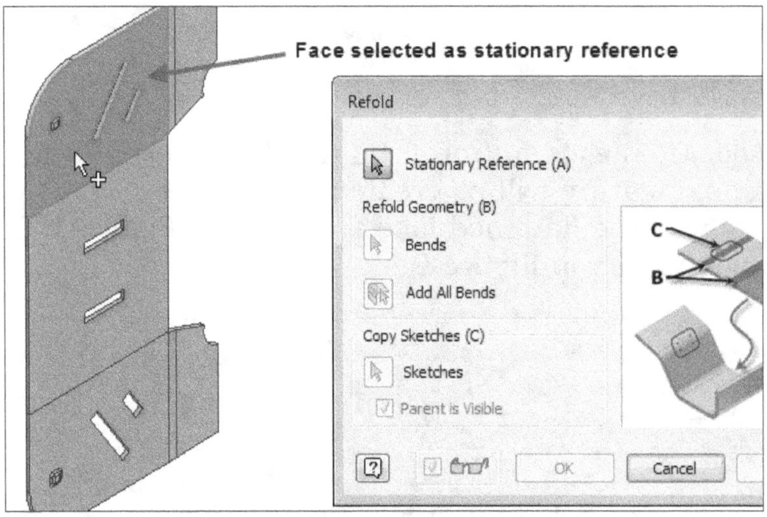

Figure-111. Face selected for refold stationary reference

- Click on the **Add All Bends** button from the dialog box and then click on the **OK** button. The part will be created.

In this chapter, we have created sheet metal models but things are not manufactured barely on the basis of sheet metal models. In industry, we need flat patterns with all the dimensions and bending orders applied on them. In the next chapter, we will learn about creating drawings for shop floor prints. In next chapter, we will also work on creating flat patterns of sheet metal models with necessary dimensions.

PROBLEM 1

Create the sheet metal model of door hand as shown in Figure-112. Drawing of the model is given in Figure-113.

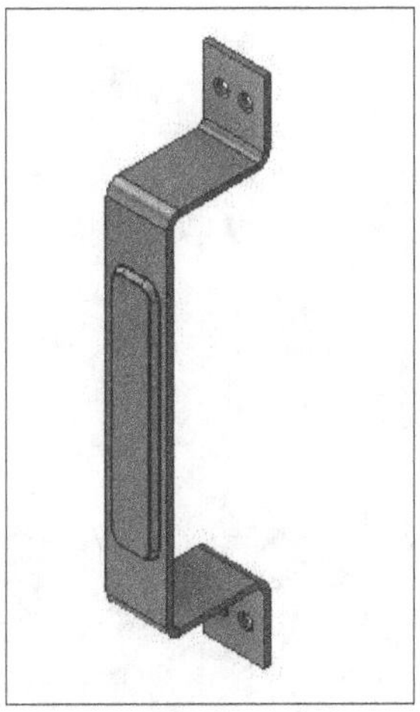

Figure-112. Practice 1 Model

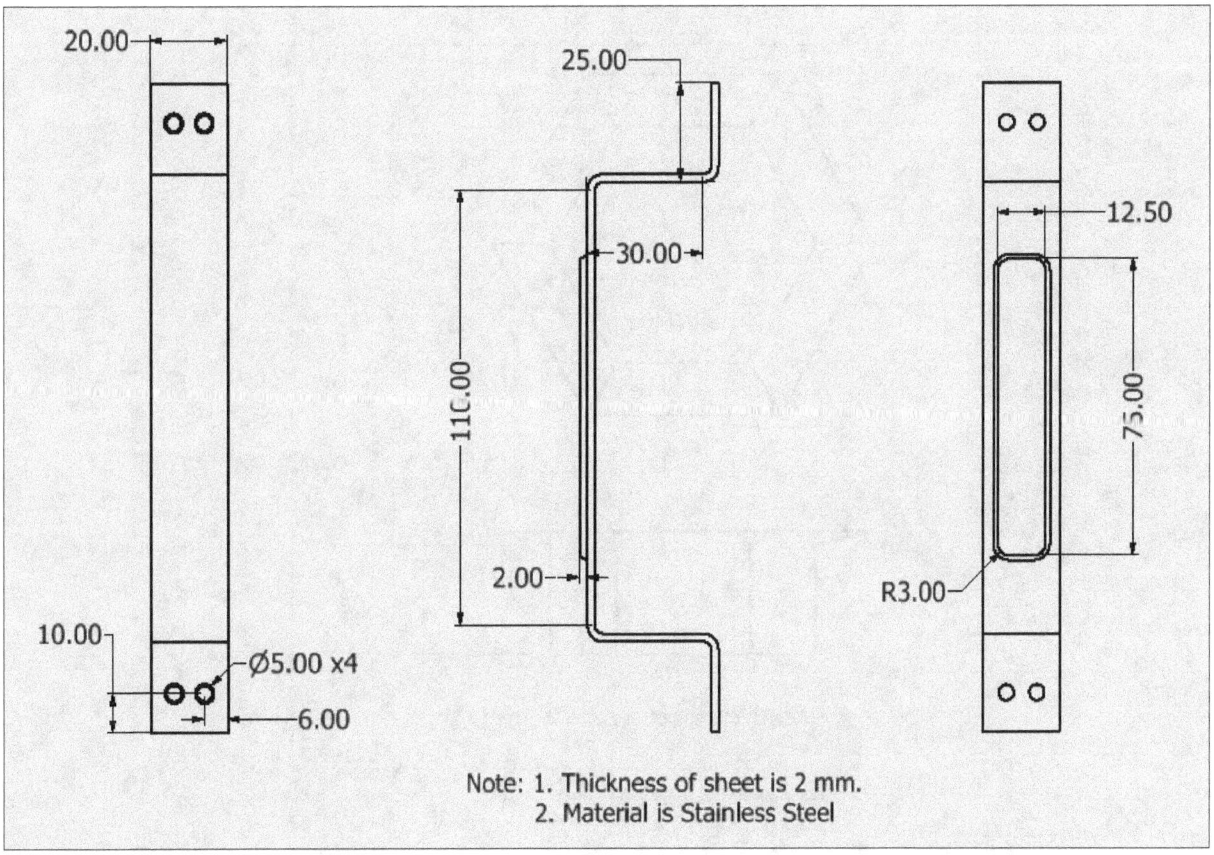

Figure-113. Practice 1 Drawing

PROBLEM 2

Create the sheet metal model of hexagonal cover as shown in Figure-114. The dimensions of the model are given in Figure-115.

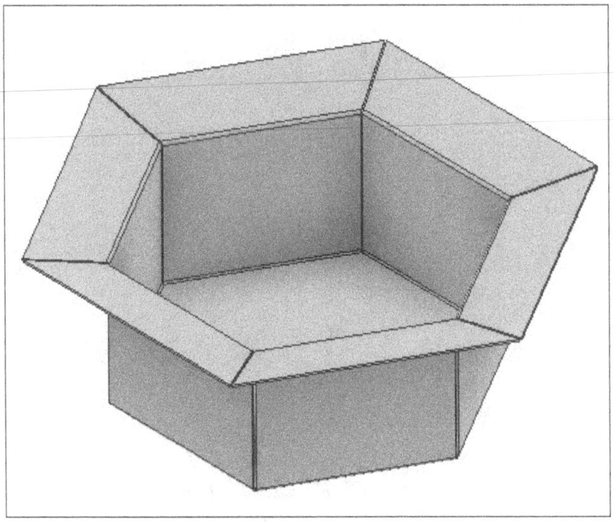

Figure-114. Model for Practice 2

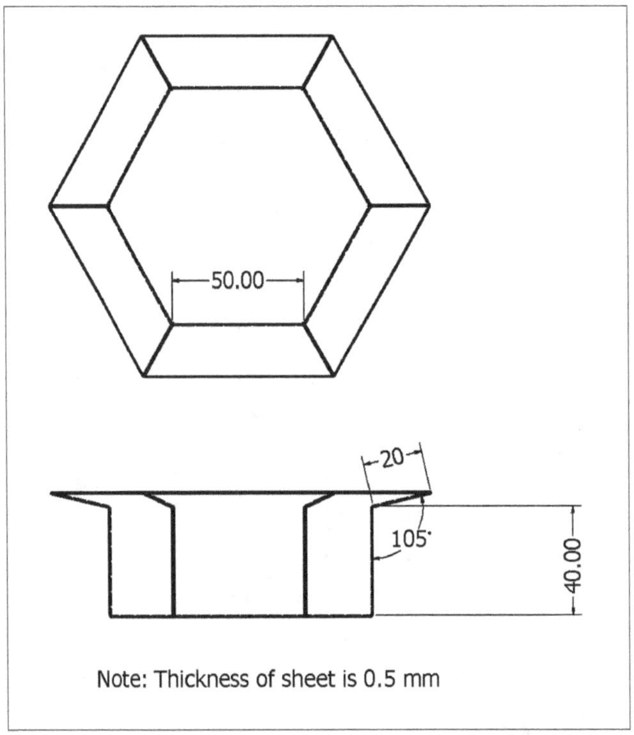

Figure-115. Drawing for Practice 2

SELF ASSESSMENT

Q1. Which of the following templates should be selected to start a new file in sheetmetal environment?

a) SheetMetal(mm).igt
b) SheetMetal(DIM).ipt
c) Both a and b
d) None of the Above

Q2. Which of the following statement is incorrect about the term 'Gauge' in sheetmetal?

a) Gauge is a traditional measurement unit of sheet thickness
b) Gauge is a non-linear unit
c) Higher the gauge number, the thicker is the sheetmetal
d) None of the Above

Q3. Which of the following tools is used to create a face of sheetmetal at specified angle to the selected edge?

a) Face
b) Flange
c) Contour Flange
d) Lofted Flange

Q4. By selecting which of the following options in the **Bend** dialog box, the bend will not be create in the sheetmetal parts?

a) Half Radius
b) 45 Degree
c) Full Radius
d) 90 Degree

Q5. Which of the following equation shows the correct ratio of K-Factor in sheet metal designing which is the ratio of the Neutral Axis' Offset (t) to the Material Thickness (MT)?

a) MT = t / K
b) t = K / MT
c) K = t / MT
d) K = MT / t

Q6. The **Fold** tool is used to fold the selected sheet metal face using a straight line. (True/False)

Q7. The **Corner Seam** tool is used to define or create gap between the adjoining faces of flange walls. (True/False)

Q8. The **Refold** tool is used to refold the folded bends. (True/False)

Q9. The .... tool is used to provide relief at the corners and edges for folding or unfolding of sheetmetal components.

Q10. The value of **Spline Factor** in **Sheet Metal Defaults** is ....

Q11. When metal is bent, the upper section is going to compress and the lower section is going to stretch. The line where the transition from compression to stretching occurs is called the ....

Q12. .... is a forming operation in which sheet is folded on its edge or folded over another part in order to achieve a tight fit.

Q13. Which of the following is NOT a method to start a sheet metal environment in Autodesk Inventor?

A. Converting a part from the Standard Part environment
B. Starting a new file using Sheetmetal template
C. Importing a STEP file into Sheetmetal environment
D. Using Sheet Metal Defaults directly from the Ribbon

Q14. What does the 'Default mm' sheet metal rule template use as a unit system?

A. Imperial
B. Metric
C. Gauge
D. Inches

Q15. What happens when you click on the 'Edit Sheet Metal Rule' button?

A. It exits the Sheet Metal environment
B. The default gauge table opens
C. The Style and Standard Editor dialog box opens
D. The drawing gets exported

Q16. Which drop-down menu in the Sheet Metal Defaults dialog allows the selection between BendCompensation and Default KFactor?
A. Material
B. Thickness
C. Unfold Rule
D. Bend Radius

Q17. What is the primary purpose of the Bend Allowance in sheet metal design?

A. To increase thickness
B. To calculate correct flat pattern size
C. To remove material at corners
D. To adjust spline factors

Q18. What is the value of K-Factor commonly used for soft materials as a rule of thumb?

A. 0.1
B. 0.2
C. 0.33
D. 0.5

Q19. What does the Spline Factor compensate for in Autodesk Inventor?

A. Bend angle
B. Tooling tolerance
C. Extra length in flat pattern due to spline or elliptical shapes
D. Sheet thickness

Q20. What tool is used to create a sheet metal body from a closed sketch profile?

A. Flange Tool
B. Face Tool
C. Lofted Flange Tool
D. Contour Tool

Q21. Which feature allows the creation of a flange at a specific angle to an existing edge?

A. Lofted Flange
B. Contour Flange
C. Flange Tool
D. Corner Edit

Q22. What is enabled when you check the 'Auto-Mitering' checkbox in the Mitered Flange dialog?

A. Auto thickness adjustment
B. Creation of symmetric gaps between flanges
C. Flattening of flanges
D. Seam removal

Q23. What option should be selected to use the default type of corner gap in dynamic flange editing?

A. Symmetric Gap
B. Overlap
C. Reverse Overlap
D. Corner Defaults (Symmetric Gap)

Q24. What is the minimum number of profiles required to use the Lofted Flange tool?

A. One
B. Two
C. Three
D. None

Q25. What does selecting the 'Press Brake' option in the Lofted Flange dialog enable?

A. Sheet smoothing
B. Radius editing
C. Parameters like chord tolerance, facet angle, and facet distance
D. K-Factor override

Q26. What is the primary function of the Contour Roll tool in sheet metal design?

A. To create a hem on the edge of a sheet
B. To cut profiles across bends
C. To create flange by rolling a profile about an axis
D. To create corner seams in sheet metal parts

Q27. Which area in the Contour Roll dialog box is used to flip the direction of the rolling?

A. Offset Direction area
B. Rolling Control area
C. Angle Direction area
D. Rolled Angle area

Q28. What must be created before the Hem tool becomes active in the Create panel?

A. A contour sketch
B. A base solid body
C. A flange profile
D. A sheet metal base part

Q29. Which of the following is NOT a type of hem you can create using the Hem tool?

A. Teardrop
B. Rolled
C. Circular
D. Double

Q30. What does the Bend tool require for operation?

A. A base flange
B. Edges of planar sheet metal faces
C. An axis and a sketch
D. A face and a bend line

Q31. In the Bend tool, what option allows the side faces to extend to the bend line?

A. Extend Bend Perpendicular to Side Faces
B. Extend Bend Aligned to Side Faces
C. Align to Bend Line
D. Match Sides to Bend

Q32. What must be selected to apply the Fold tool?

A. A closed profile sketch
B. A flange face
C. A sketched bend line ending at face edges
D. Two planar edges

Q33. What does the Derive tool primarily do in a sheet metal environment?

A. Converts solid parts to sheet metal
B. Derives parts or assemblies into the current environment
C. Adds 3D sketches to existing parts
D. Cuts faces of assemblies

Q34. Which of the following is a Derive Style option?
A. Sheet Form Mode
B. Maintain as Separate Parts
C. Solid body keep seams between planar faces
D. Merge Faces by Angle

Q35. Which tab in the Derive dialog box allows setting of scale factor and mirror options?

A. Representation
B. Options
C. Geometry
D. Parameters

Q36. What is the main use of the Cut tool?

A. Create corner reliefs
B. Cut material from sheet metal face
C. Create hems
D. Fold face along bend line

Q37. Which option ensures the profile is completely cut through the base at a bend?

A. Cut Normal
B. Cut Direction
C. Cut Straight
D. Cut Across Bend
Q38. What is the function of the Corner Seam tool's Seam option?

A. To punch a hole at seam
B. To define or modify existing bend/corner
C. To unfold seams for flat pattern
D. To roll edges

Q39. What does selecting the Rip radio button in Corner Seam tool allow?

A. Create an automatic hem
B. Seam the opposite face
C. Control rip or conversion gaps
D. Select a punching profile

Q40. Which tool is used to create an indent shape on a sheet metal face?

A. Hem Tool
B. Bend Tool
C. Punch Tool
D. Rip Tool

Q41. What is a requirement before using the Punch Tool on a sheet face?
A. A closed profile sketch
B. A bend line
C. A sketch point on face
D. A fixed edge

Q42. What does the Rip tool allow you to do?

A. Create flange with a profile
B. Add holes to sheet face
C. Provide relief at corners/edges
D. Align seams

Q43. Which Rip Type allows ripping completely through the face?

A. Single Point
B. Face Extents
C. Point to Point
D. Full Face Line

Q44. What does the Unfold tool require you to select first?

A. A bend line
B. A closed profile
C. A corner seam
D. A stationary face

Q45. What is the function of the Add All Bends button in the Unfold tool?

A. Automatically flip all bends
B. Add bends to punch preview
C. Select all bends for unfolding
D. Reset bend values

Chapter 13

Weldment Assembly

Topics Covered

The major topics covered in this chapter are:

- ***Welding Symbols and Representations***
- ***Dimensioning of Weld Bead***
- ***Starting Weldment Assembly***
- ***Creating Fillet Weld and Fillet Weld Dimension***
- ***Creating Groove/Plug Weld and Weld Dimension***
- ***Creating Cosmetic Welds***
- ***Calculating Weld Bead size by Weld Calculators***
- ***Practical on Weldment Assembly***
- ***Practice and Problems***

INTRODUCTION

Welding is known to almost every engineer and designer. Like every other dimension, welding symbols are also included in the engineering drawings. In Autodesk Inventor, we have a separate environment to apply weldment representations and symbols to the assembly which later can be derived in engineering drawing. In this chapter, we will discuss the tools related to weldments. But, before we start using Autodesk Inventor for weldments, it's important to revise some basics of welding.

WELDING SYMBOLS AND REPRESENTATION IN DRAWING

The symbols to represent various type of welds are given next.

Butt/Groove Weld Symbols

Various symbols that come under this category are given next. Refer to Figure-1 and Figure-2.

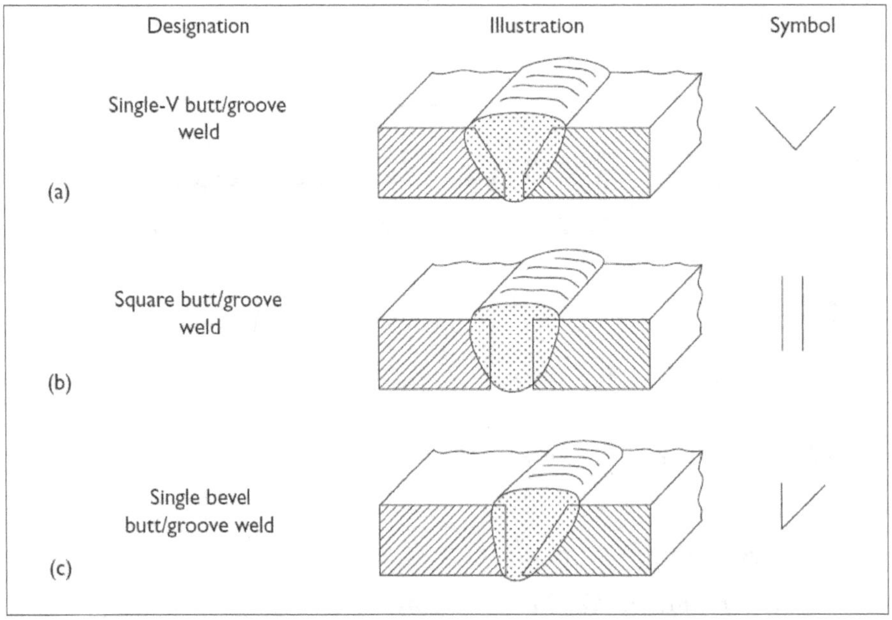

Figure-1. Welding symbols list 1

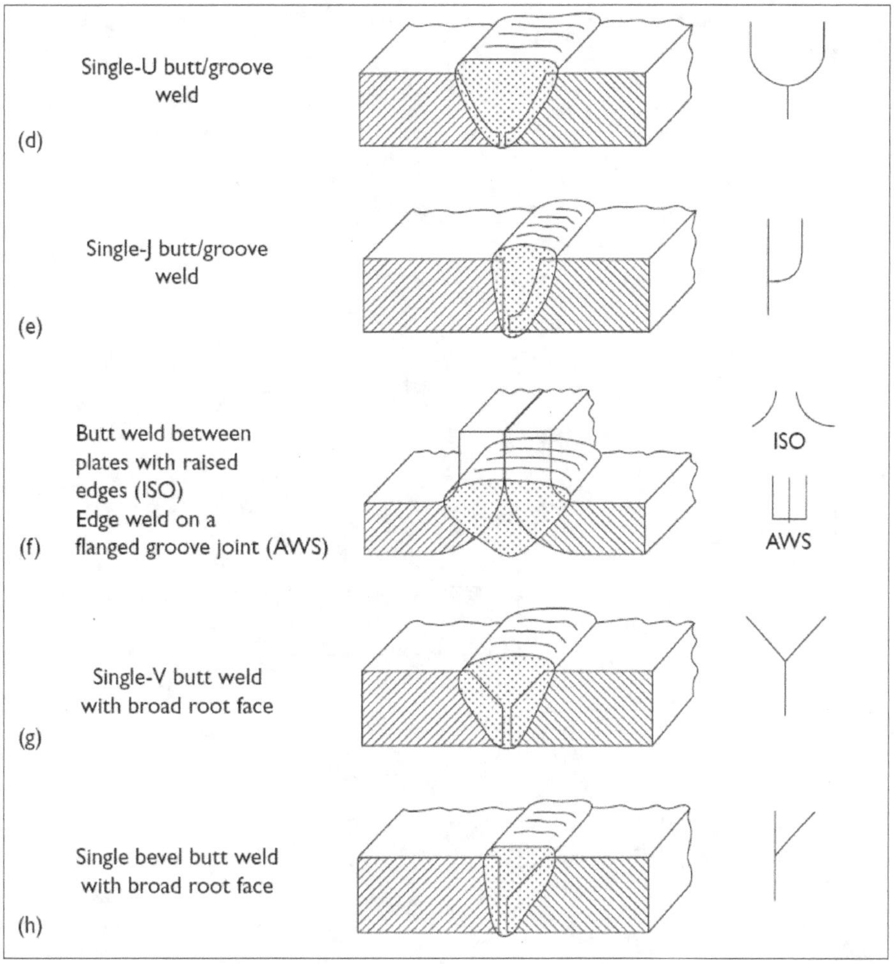

Figure-2. Welding symbols list 2

Fillet and Edge Weld Symbols

Various symbols that come under this category are given next. Refer to Figure-3.

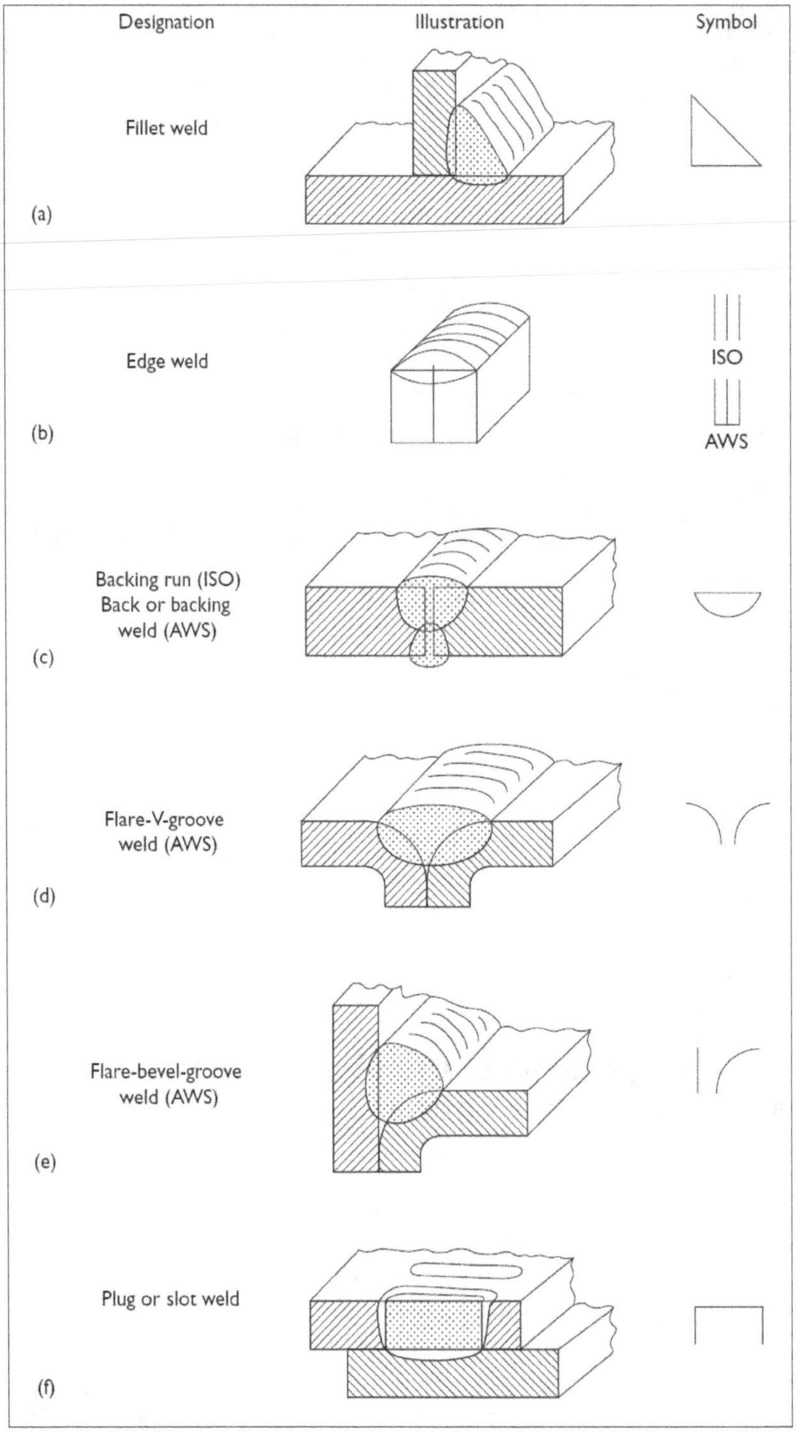

Figure-3. Welding symbols list 3

Miscellaneous Weld Symbols

Various symbols that come under this category are given next. Refer to Figure-4.

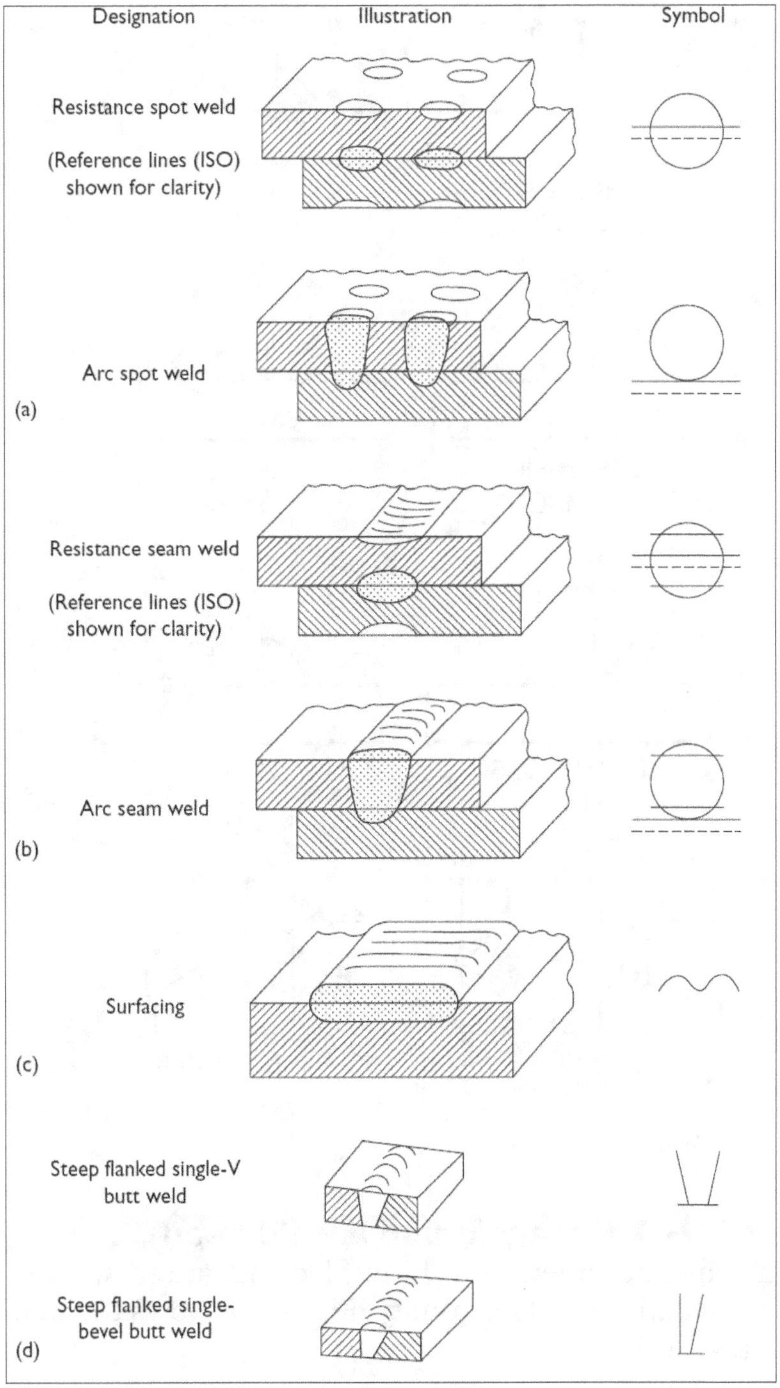

Figure-4. Welding symbols list 4

Now, we know various symbols used in welding drawings but keep a note that placement of welding symbol along the arrow decides the side on which the welding will be done on the object; refer to Figure-5.

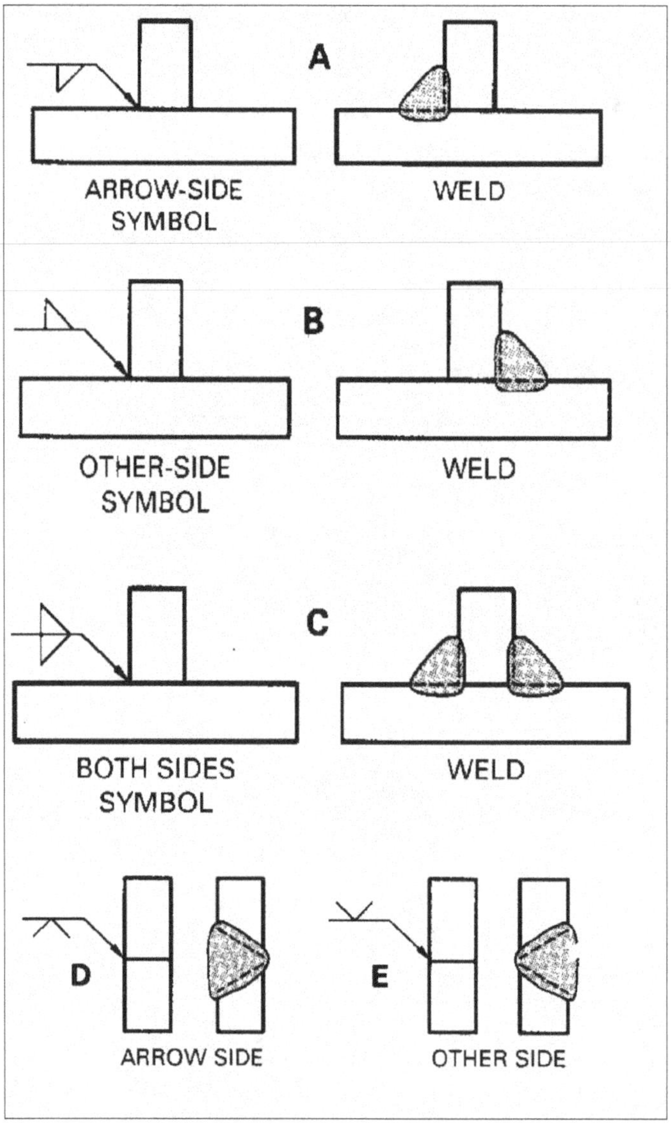

Figure-5. Deciding weld bead side

Dimensioning a weld bead

Just like the other measurements, weld is also measured with respect to various references, so that we can control its quality. Figure-6 shows the information required for dimensioning a weld bead.

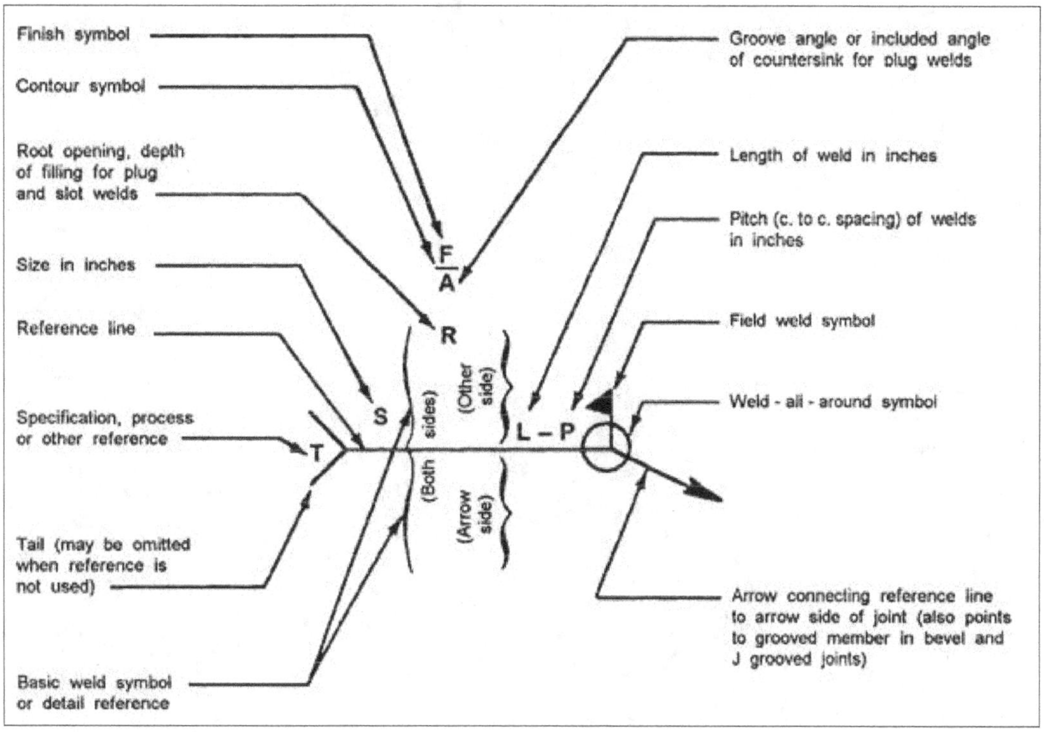

Figure-6. Welding dimension

Till this point, we have learned the basics of weld symbol representations in drawings. So, we are ready to dive into Autodesk Inventor for creating welding representations.

STARTING WELDMENT ASSEMBLY

- Start Autodesk Inventor if not started yet. Click on the **New** button from **New** cascading menu in the **File** menu of the **Ribbon**. The **Create New File** dialog box will be displayed.
- Double-click on the **Weldment (ANSI-mm).iam** template or any other required template of weldment in the **Assembly** area of the dialog box; refer to Figure-7. The assembly environment will be displayed with **Weld** tab selected; refer to Figure-8.

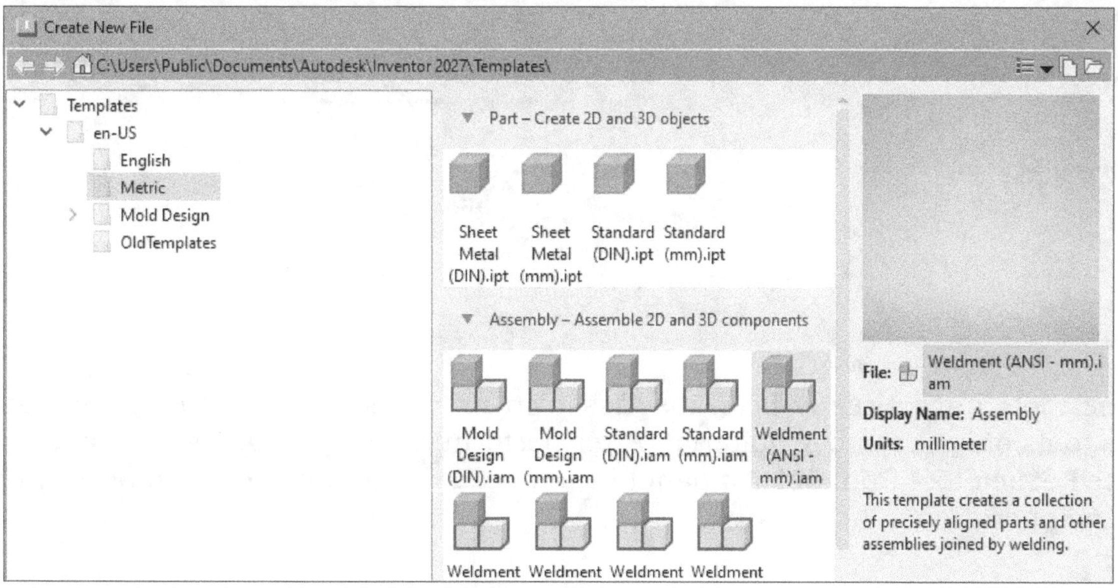

Figure-7. Weldment template in Create New File dialog box

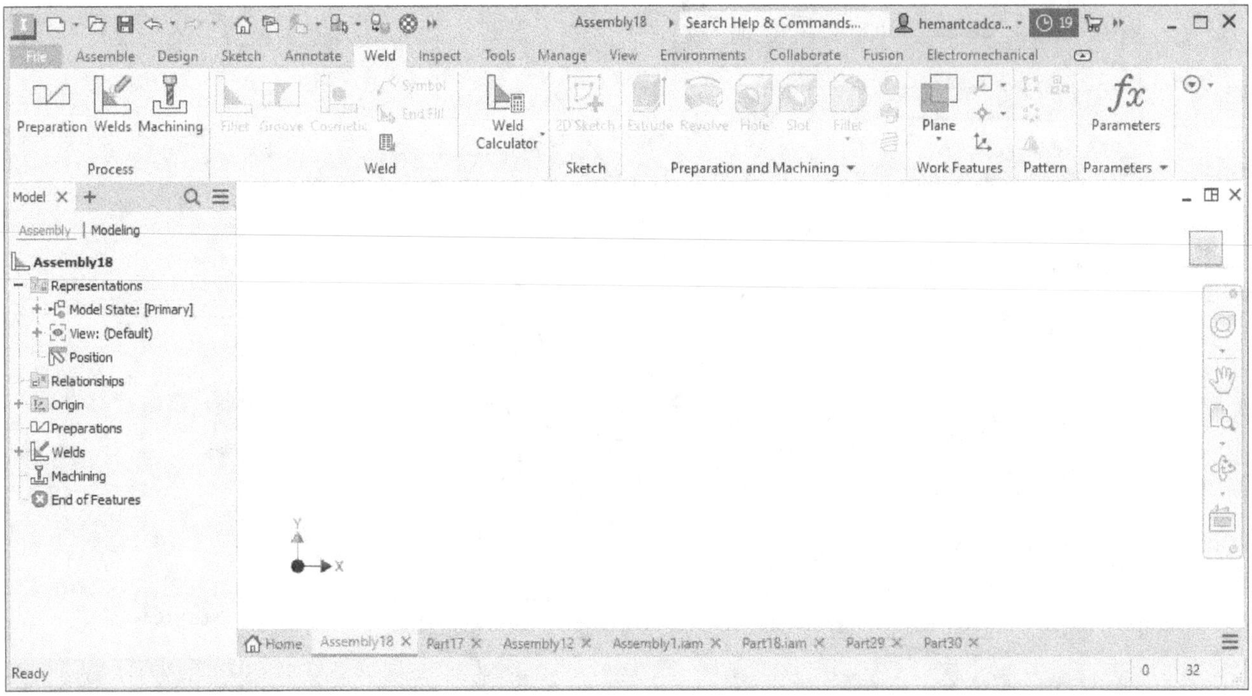

Figure-8. Assembly environment with Weld tab selected

In Autodesk Inventor, the weldment parts are prepared in three processes; Part Preparation, Machining, and Welding. The tools related to these processes discussed next.

PREPARATION

Before we apply welding representations to the model, it is necessary to prepare the part for welding. The tools to perform preparation of model are activated on clicking **Preparation** tool from the **Process** panel in the **Weld** tab of the **Ribbon**; refer to Figure-9.

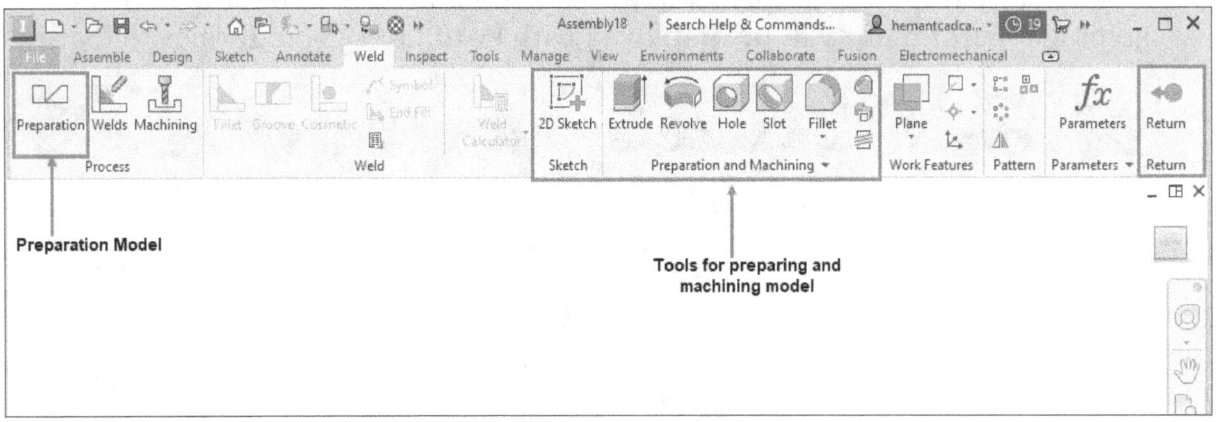

Figure-9. Tools for preparing model

All the tools have already been discussed in previous chapter. Here, you can use these tools only to remove material. After performing the preparation of model, click on the **Return** tool from **Return** panel in the **Weld** tab of the **Ribbon** to perform other welding operation.

WELDING

The **Welds** tool in **Process** panel of **Weld** tab is used to activate the tools related to welding; refer to Figure-10. The procedures of using these tools are discussed next.

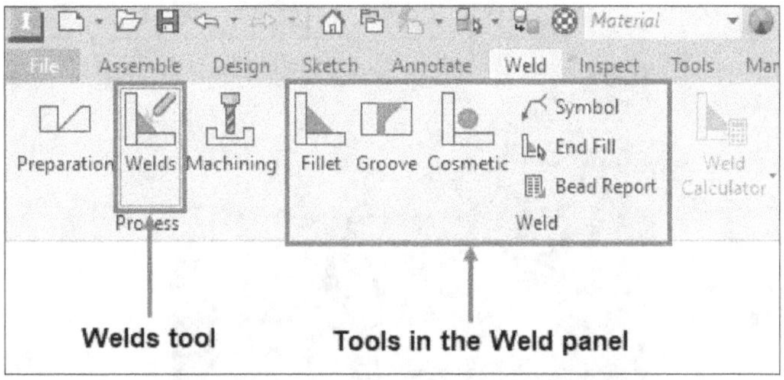

Figure-10. Welding tools

Using Fillet Weld Tool

 The **Fillet Weld** tool is used to create fillet shaped weld. Various types of fillet welds have been shown in Figure-3. The procedure to apply fillet weld is given next.

- Click on the **Fillet Weld** tool from the **Weld** panel in the **Weld** tab of the **Ribbon**. The **Fillet Weld** dialog box will be displayed; refer to Figure-11. Also, you will be asked to select the faces to be welded by fillet weld.

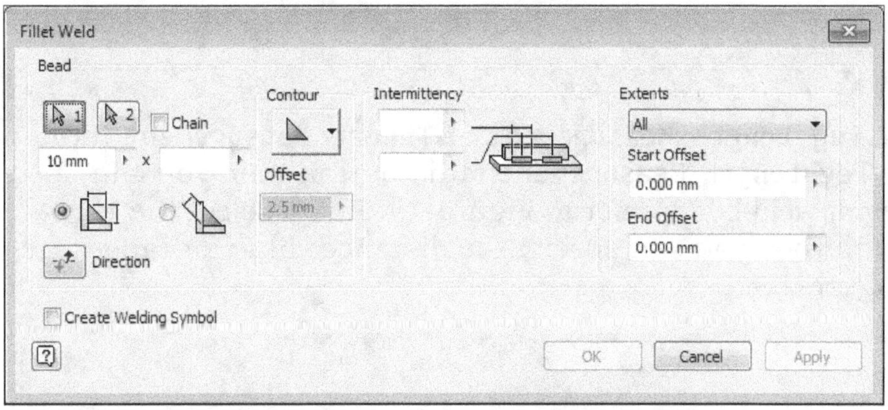

Figure-11. Fillet Weld dialog box

- Select the face/faces of the first face group. Refer to Figure-12.

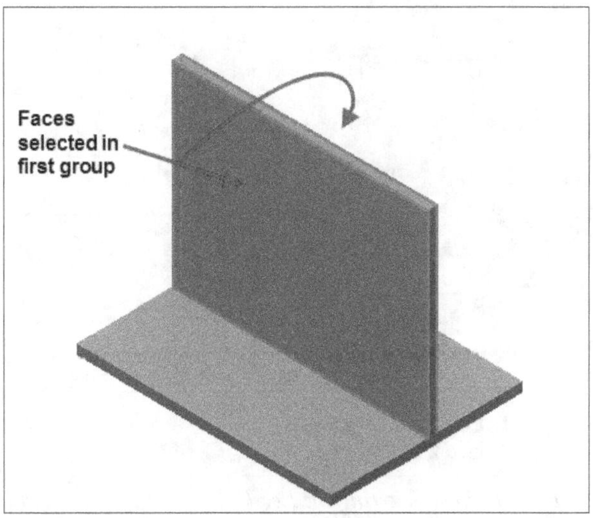

Figure-12. Faces selected in first group for weld

- Click on the **2** selection button from the **Bead** area of the dialog box. You will be asked to select the second face.
- Select the second set of faces. Preview of the fillet weld will be displayed; refer to Figure-13.

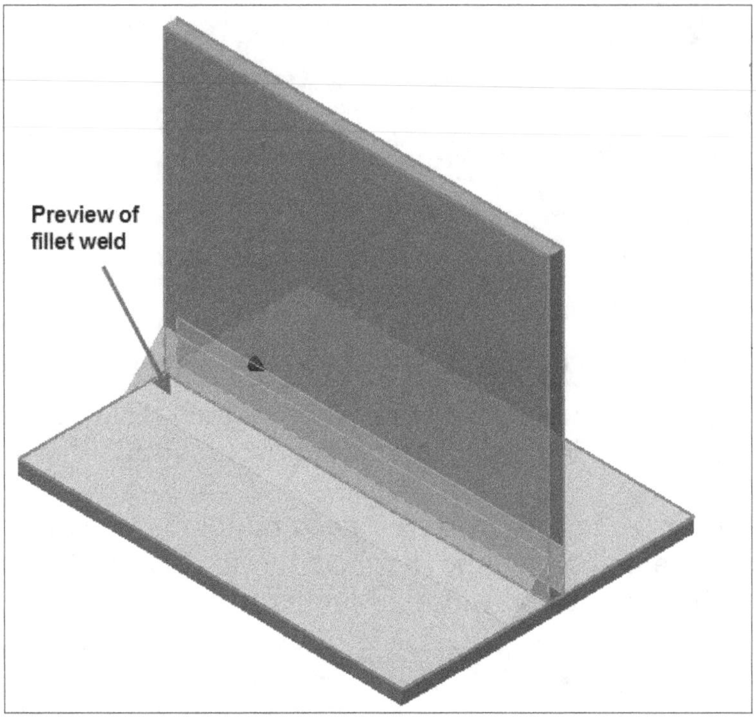

Figure-13. Preview of fillet weld

- Select the **Leg Length Measurement** or **Throat Measurement** radio button. If you select the **Leg Length Measurement** radio button then you can specify the length of each leg of weld bead; refer to Figure-14. If you select the **Throat Measurement** radio button then you can specify the distance value for taper face of weld bead; refer to Figure-15.

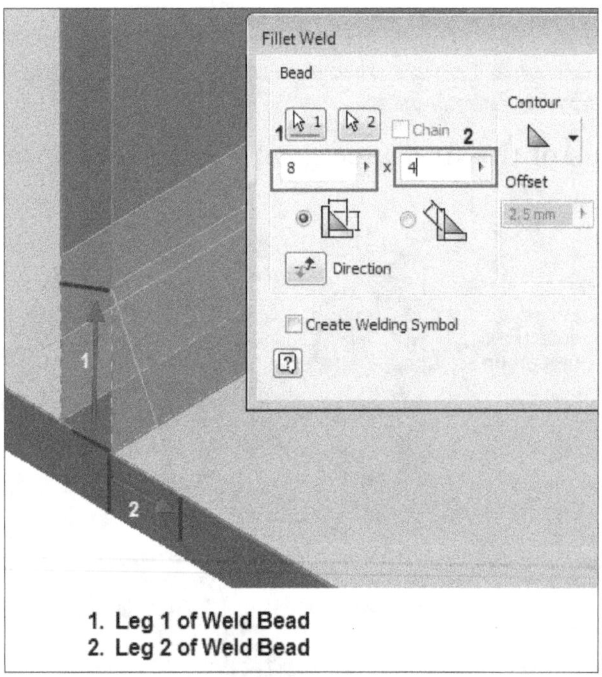

Figure-14. Fillet Bead on selecting the Leg Length Measurement radio button

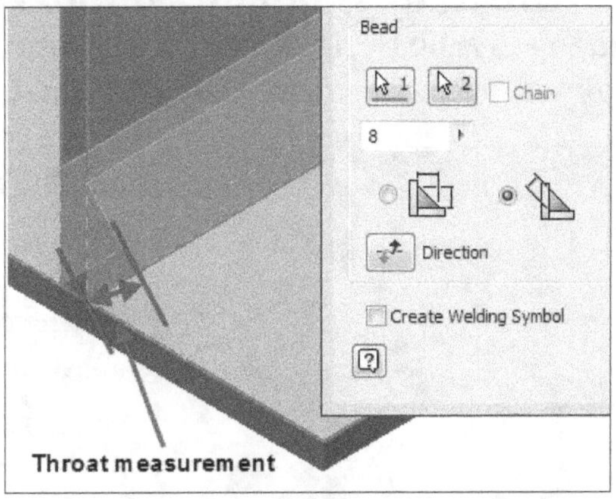

Figure-15. Preview of fillet weld with Throat Measurement radio button selected

- Select desired contour of weld bead from the **Contour** drop-down in the **Contour** area of the dialog box; refer to Figure-16.

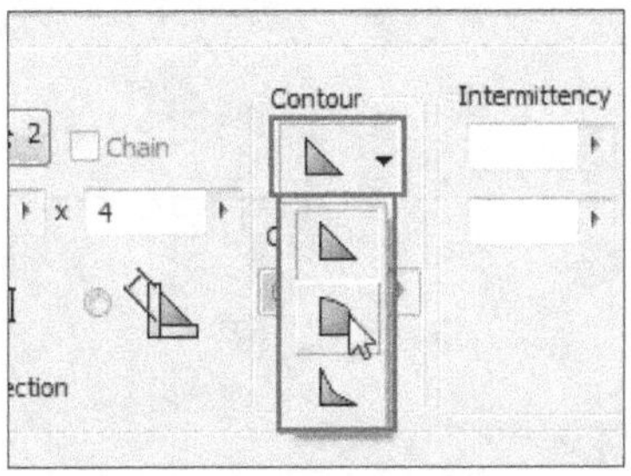

Figure-16. Contour drop-down

- If you have selected the **Convex** or **Concave** contour button then you can specify the contour offset value in the **Offset** edit box to change the shape of contour.
- If you want to create intermittent weld then specify the intermittent length and pitch in the respective edit boxes in the **Intermittency** area of the dialog box.
- Similarly, you can set the starting or end offset value in the **Extents** area of the dialog box to modify starting and end position of the welding bead; refer to Figure-17.

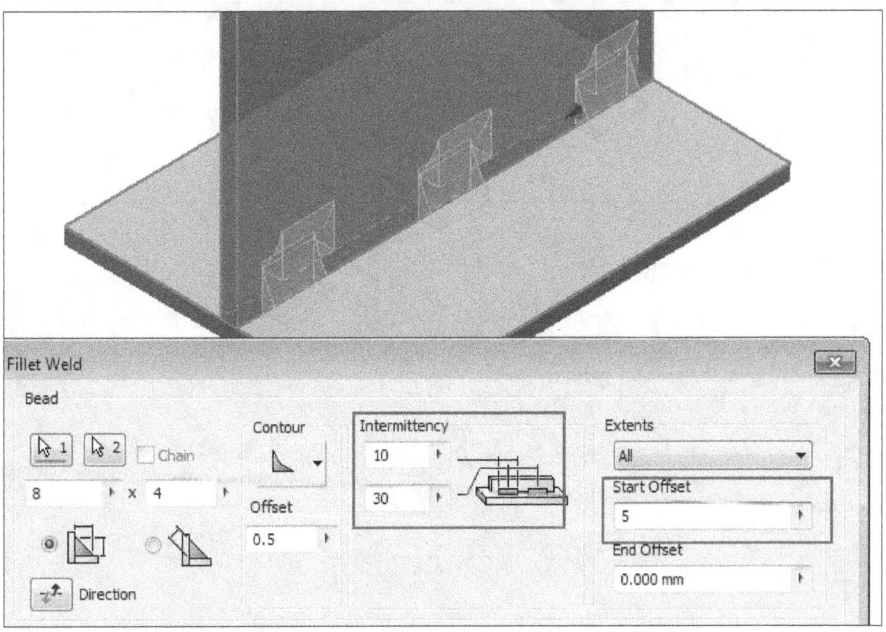

Figure-17. Intermittent welding bead with start offset

Creating Welding Symbol

- Select the **Create Welding Symbol** check box at the bottom of the dialog box. The **Fillet Weld** dialog box will expand as shown in Figure-18.

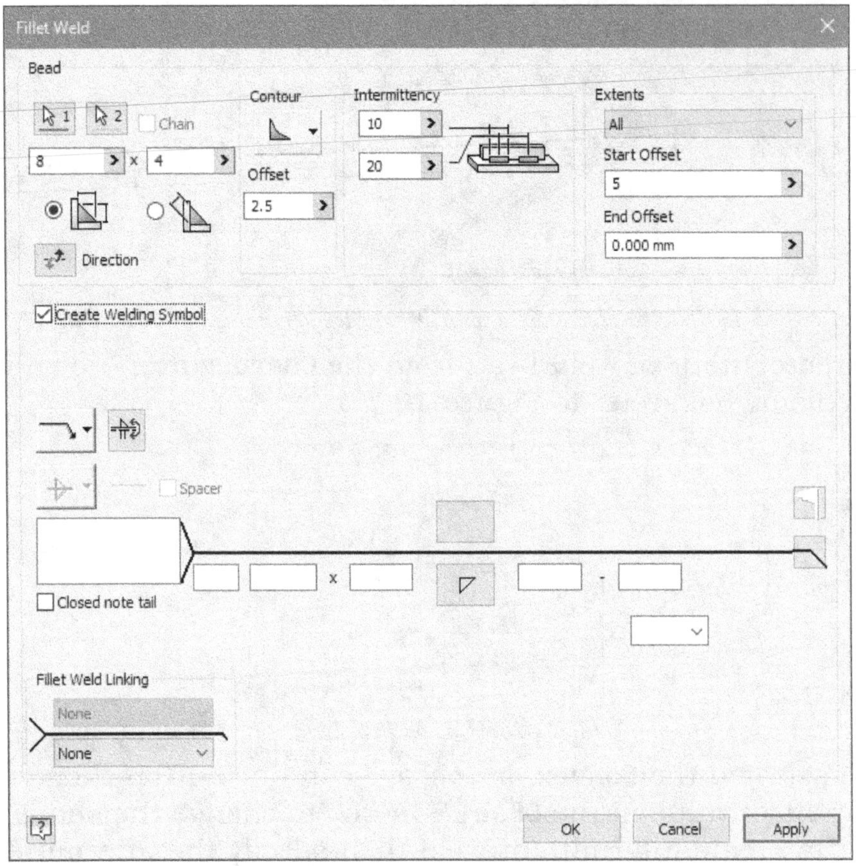

Figure-18. Expanded Filled Weld dialog box

- The edit boxes and drop-downs linked to the weld symbol are used to specify various parameters of weld. We have numbered each option of weld symbol in Figure-19 and use of each option is discussed in table next.

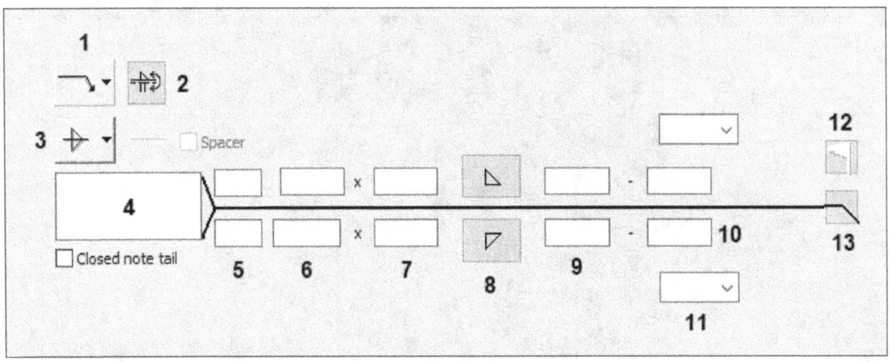

Figure-19. Welding symbol options numbered

Option Number in figure	Option Name	Use in symbol
1	Identification Line drop-down	In welding symbol, identification line is used to denote that weld is to be done at a position far from this symbol location. If the welds are symmetrical on both sides of the plate then identification line is omitted. If the identification line is above the full line then the symbol for the nearside weld is drawn below the reference line and the symbol for the far side weld is above the dashed line.
2	Swap Arrow/ Other Symbols button	The **Swap Arrow/Other Symbols** button is used to swap the parameters above the symbol line with parameters below the symbol line.
3	Stagger drop-down	The options in this drop-down are active only when you are creating weld symbol for both weld of model face. There are four options to create staggered weld.
4	Tail Note Box	This is an edit box used to specify notes on weld like welding class or standard used. Select the **abc** check box to enclose note in a box.
5	Prefix edit box	The **Prefix** edit box is used to specify prefix for value specified in **Leg 1** edit box.
6	Leg 1	This edit box is used to specify the dimension for first leg of weld bead.
7	Leg 2	This edit box is used to specify the dimension for second leg of weld bead.
8	Weld Symbol	This button is used to select the desired symbol for weld.
9	Length	This edit box is used to specify the length of weld bead.
10	Pitch	This edit box is used to specify the gap distance between intermittent weld.

11	Contour drop-down	The options in this drop-down are used to specify the contour of weld bead. On selecting the contour type, the Method drop-down gets displayed next to it. Select the desired option from the drop-down to specify the method of contouring. C means Chipping, G means Grinding, R means Rolling, H means Hammering, M means Machining, and U means Unspecified Mechanical means.
12	Field Welding Symbol	Select this button if you want to tell manufacturer that welding will be done on the assembly line.
13	All Around Symbol	Select this button if you want the weld to be done all around the joint.

- Set desired parameters and click on the **OK** button to create the weld symbol and representation; refer to Figure-20.

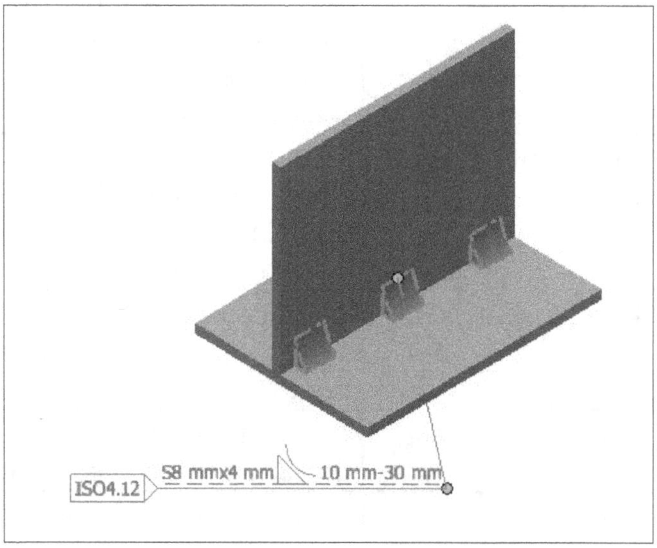

Figure-20. Fillet weld with respective drawing symbol

Using Groove Weld Tool

The **Groove Weld** tool is used to create weld bead to fill groove between two components. With the help of groove, more metal is filled and hence a stronger bond is created. The procedure of using this tool is given next.

- Click on the **Groove Weld** tool from the **Weld** panel in the **Weld** tab of the **Ribbon**. The **Groove Weld** dialog box will be displayed; refer to Figure-21. Also, you will be asked to select the first set of faces.

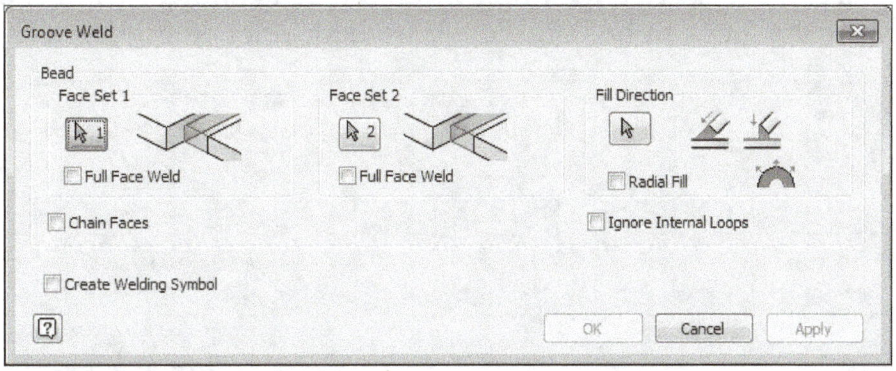

Figure-21. Groove Weld dialog box

- Click on the first face/set of faces.
- Click on the **2** selection button in the **Face Set 2** area of the dialog box. You will be asked to select the second face/set of faces.
- Select the second set of faces; refer to Figure-22.

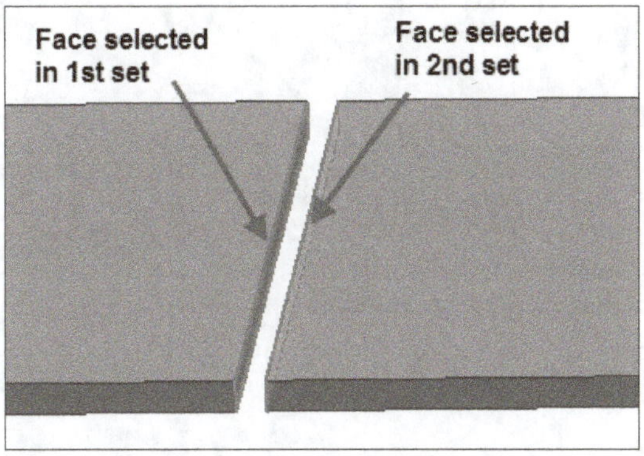

Figure-22. Faces selected for groove weld

- Click on the **Select Fill Direction** selection button in the **Fill Direction** area of the dialog box. You will be asked to select the direction reference for fill direction.
- Select desired face/plane/edge/axis to specify direction of weld filling. Preview of the weld bead will be displayed; refer to Figure-23.

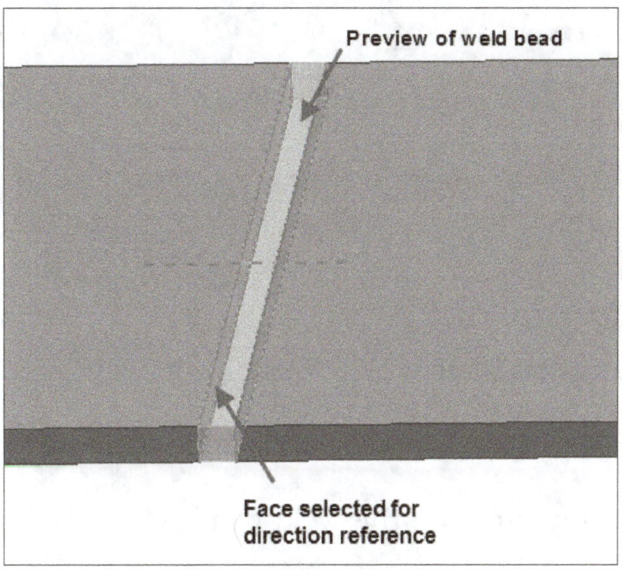

Figure-23. Preview of groove weld bead

- Select the **Full Face Weld** check box when a face is shorter than the joining face but you want the faces to be completely welded; refer to Figure-24.

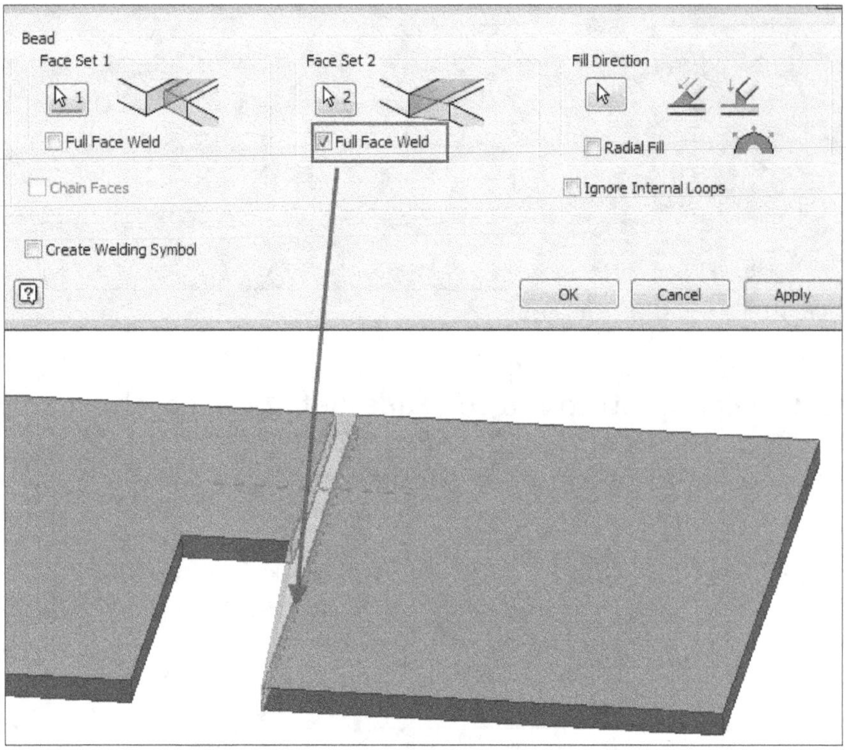

Figure-24. Preview of full face groove weld

- Select the **Radial Fill** check box if you have round faces to be welded; refer to Figure-25.

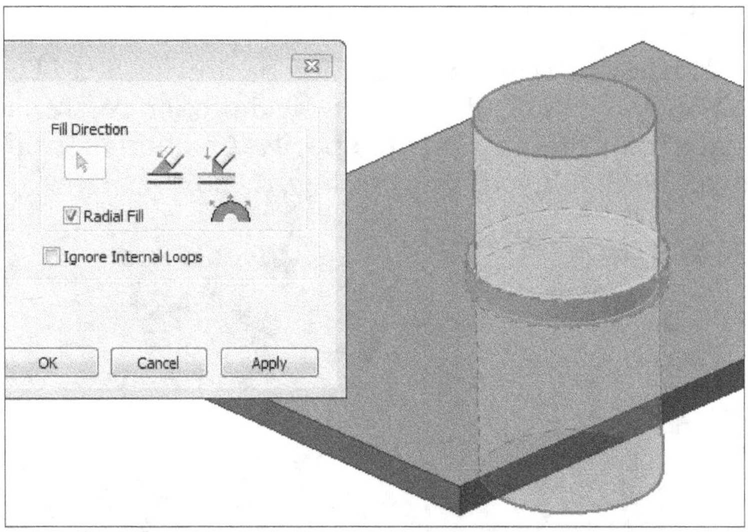

Figure-25. Preview of groove weld with radial fill

- Select the **Ignore Internal Loops** check box if you want to make sure that internal faces are not getting welded automatically.
- Select the **Create Welding Symbol** check box to create the welding symbol as discussed earlier.
- Click on the **OK** button to create the weld bead.

Using Cosmetic Weld Tool

The **Cosmetic Weld** tool is used to assign welding symbol to desired edge(s)/loop. If you apply cosmetic weld then graphical weld will not be displayed. The procedure of using this tool is given next.

- Click on the **Cosmetic Weld** tool from the **Weld** panel in the **Weld** tab of the **Ribbon**. The **Cosmetic Weld** dialog box will be displayed; refer to Figure-26.

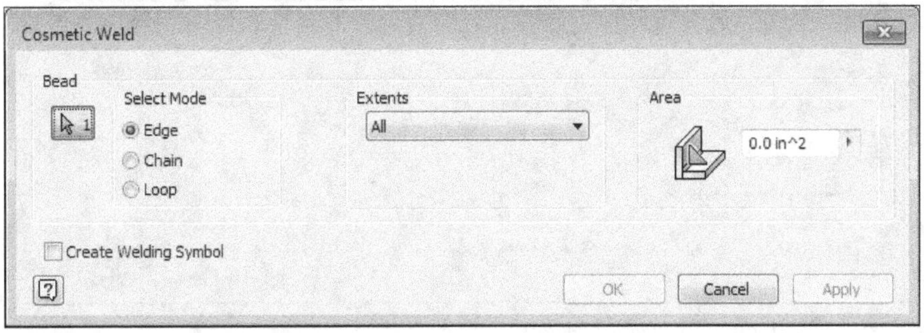

Figure-26. Cosmetic Weld dialog box

- Select desired radio button from the **Select Mode** area of the dialog box. There are three options; **Edge**, **Chain**, and **Loop**.
- Select the entities based on the radio button selected.
- Click in the edit box of **Area** area and specify desired value of cross-section area of weld bead.
- Select the **Create Welding Symbol** check box and specify the values for welding symbol as discussed earlier.
- Click on the **OK** button to create the cosmetic weld.

Using Welding Symbol Tool

The **Welding Symbol** tool is used to assign welding symbol to welding beads for which welding symbols have not been created. Before using this tool, make sure that welding beads without welding symbol are available in the drawing area. The procedure of using this tool is given next.

- Click on the **Welding Symbol** tool from the **Weld** panel in the **Weld** tab of the **Ribbon**. The **Welding Symbol** dialog box will be displayed; refer to Figure-27. Also, you will be asked to select the welding bead.

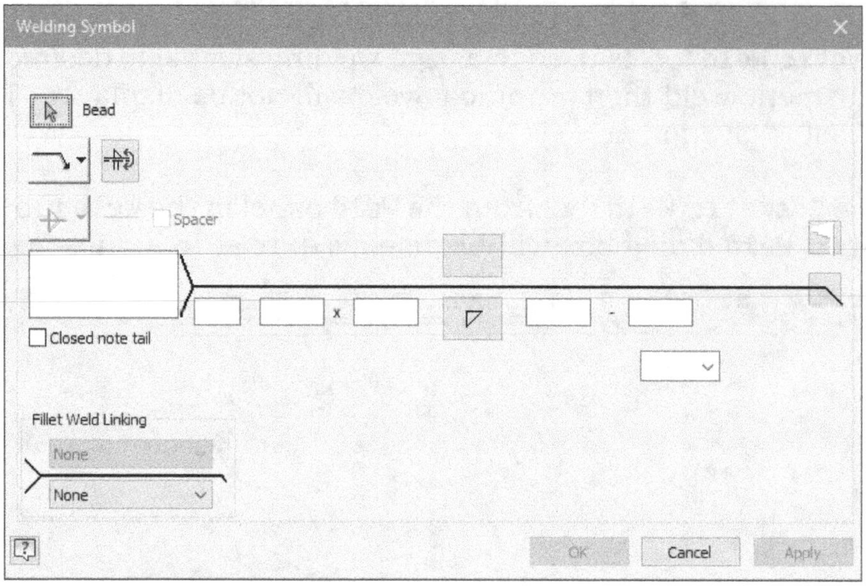

Figure-27. Welding Symbol dialog box

- Select the welding bead to which the welding symbol will be attached.
- Specify the parameters of welding symbol as discussed earlier.
- Click on the **OK** button to create the weld symbol.

Using End Fill

The **End Fill** tool is used to assign end to the weld bead. Fillet welds get end fill automatically assigned but groove welds are not assigned end fills and hence, we need to assign end fills to the faces of groove weld beads. The procedure of using this tool is given next.

- Click on the **End Fill** tool from the **Weld** panel in the **Weld** tab of the **Ribbon**. You will be asked to select the faces to be recognized as end fills.
- Select the faces of the weld bead to be recognized as end fills; refer to Figure-28.
- Right-click in the drawing area and select the **OK** button to create the feature; refer to Figure-29.

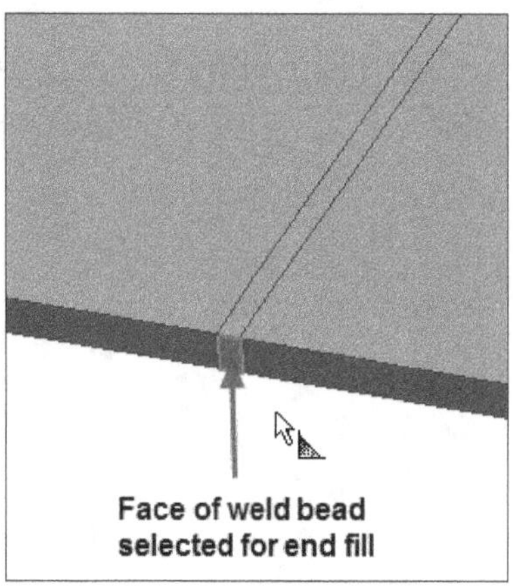

Figure-28. Face selected for end fill

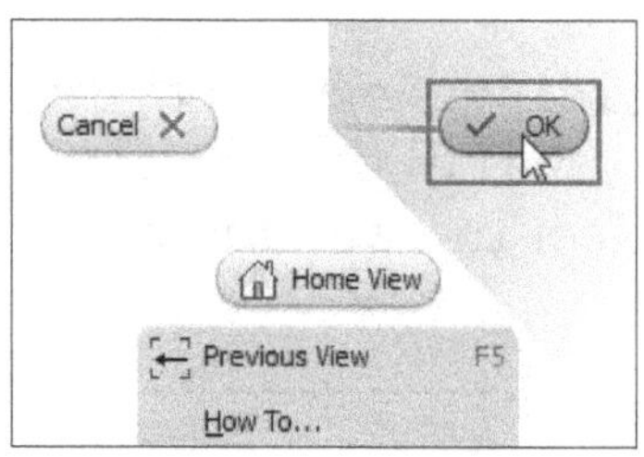

Figure-29. Right-click menu

Using Bead Report

The **Bead Report** tool is used to create weld bead report in Microsoft Excel format or other tabulated data formats. The procedure of using this tool is given next.

- Click on the **Bead Report** tool from the **Weld** panel in the **Weld** tab of the **Ribbon**. The **Weld Bead Report** dialog box will be displayed; refer to Figure-30.

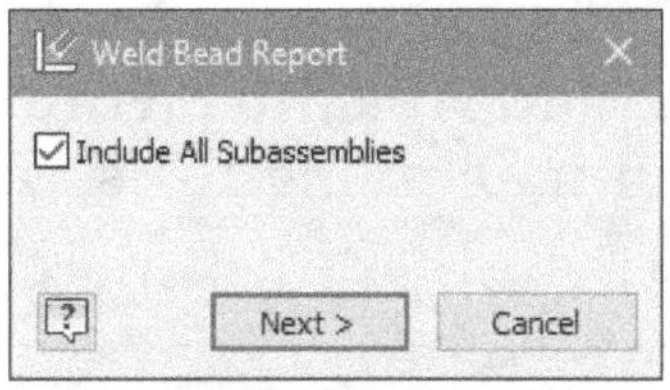

Figure-30. Weld Bead Report dialog box

- Select the **Include All Subassemblies** check box if you want to include weld beads from all the sub-assemblies otherwise the weld beads of current assembly file will only be included.
- Click on the **Next** button from the dialog box. The **Report Location** dialog box will be displayed; refer to Figure-31.

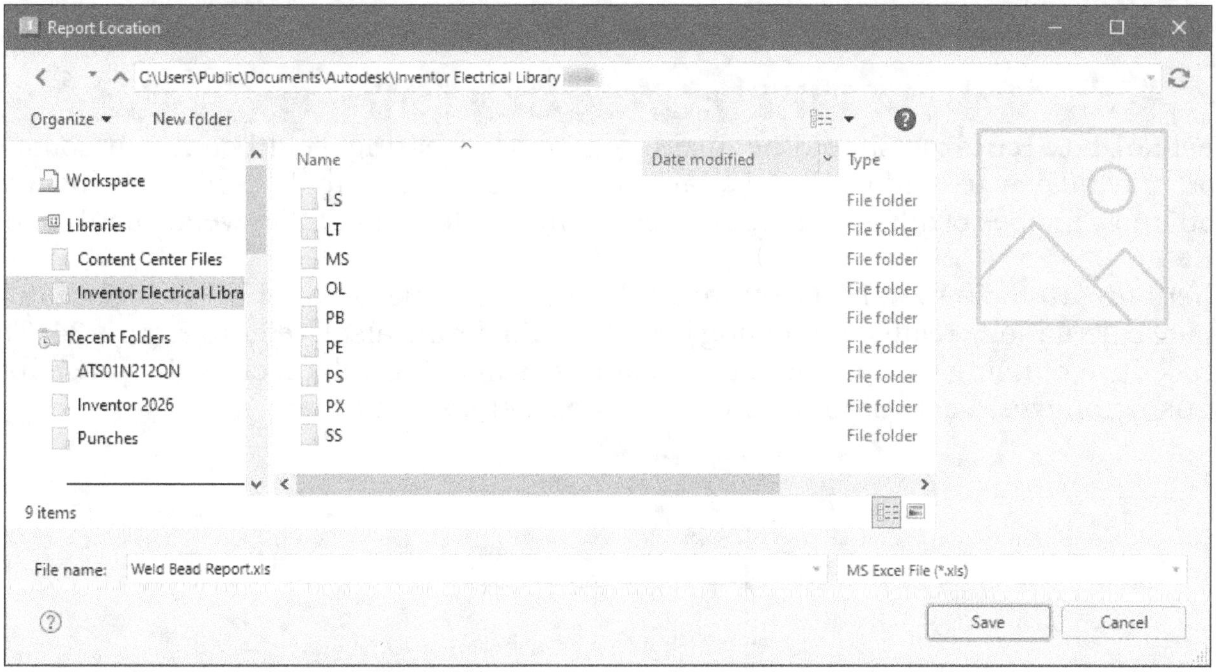

Figure-31. Report Location dialog box

- Specify the name of file and desired location in the dialog box. Click on the **Save** button to save the report. The report file will be created; refer to Figure-32.

Document	ID	Type	Length	UoM	Mass	UoM	Area	UoM	Volume	UoM
Weld_assembly.iam	Groove Weld 1	Groove	N/A		0.001	kg	812	mm^2	480	mm^3
	Fillet Weld 2	Fillet	320	mm	0.022	kg	7.93E+03	mm^2	8.00E+03	mm^3
	Fillet Weld 3	Fillet	56.549	mm	0.002	kg	955.644	mm^2	588.91	mm^3
	Fillet Weld 4	Fillet	56.549	mm	0.002	kg	955.644	mm^2	588.91	mm^3

Figure-32. Weld Bead Report

MACHINING

The tools for the machining process are active when you click on the **Machining** tool from the **Process** panel in the **Weld** tab of the **Ribbon**. Note that the tools for preparation and machining are same; refer to Figure-33. There is only one difference between use of preparation and machining tools, you cannot use the preparation tools after creating weld beads.

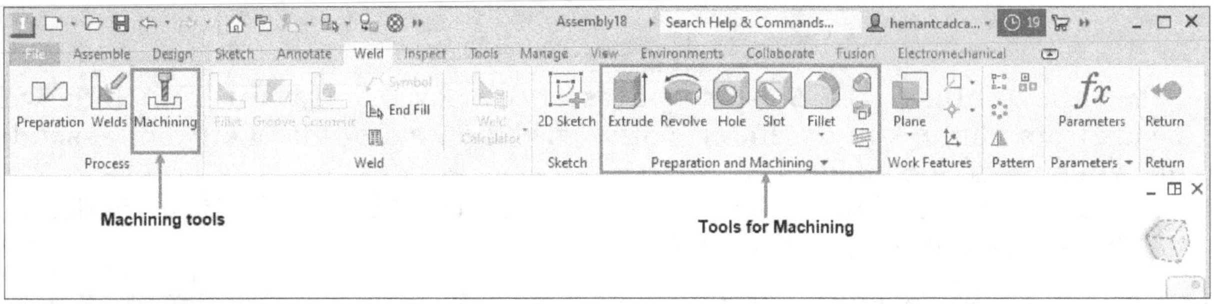

Figure-33. Tools for machining

WELD CALCULATOR

Yes! **Weld Calculator** should be discussed before creating weld beads but some of you may be new to welding, so I explained the weld creation tools earlier. In this way, you know shapes of different types of welds which will be helpful in weld calculations.

There are **10** tools in **Weld Calculator** drop-down in **Weld** panel of the **Weld** tab to make calculations related to welding bead (and Soldering also); refer to Figure-34. The procedure of using all the calculator is almost same. We will discuss the procedure of using one weld calculator and you can apply the same other.

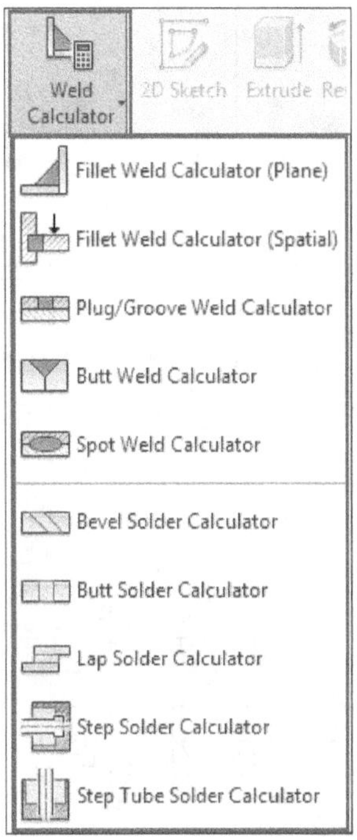

Figure-34. Weld Calculator dialog box

Fillet Weld Calculator (Plane)

The **Fillet Weld Calculator (Plane)** tool in the **Weld Calculator** drop-down is used to calculate whether the fillet weld bead will be able to sustain the given load conditions or not. The procedure of using this tool is given next.

- Click on the **Fillet Weld Calculator (Plane)** tool from the **Weld Calculator** drop-down in the **Weld** panel of the **Weld** tab in the **Ribbon**. The **Fillet Weld (Connection Plane Load) Calculator** dialog box will be displayed; refer to Figure-35.

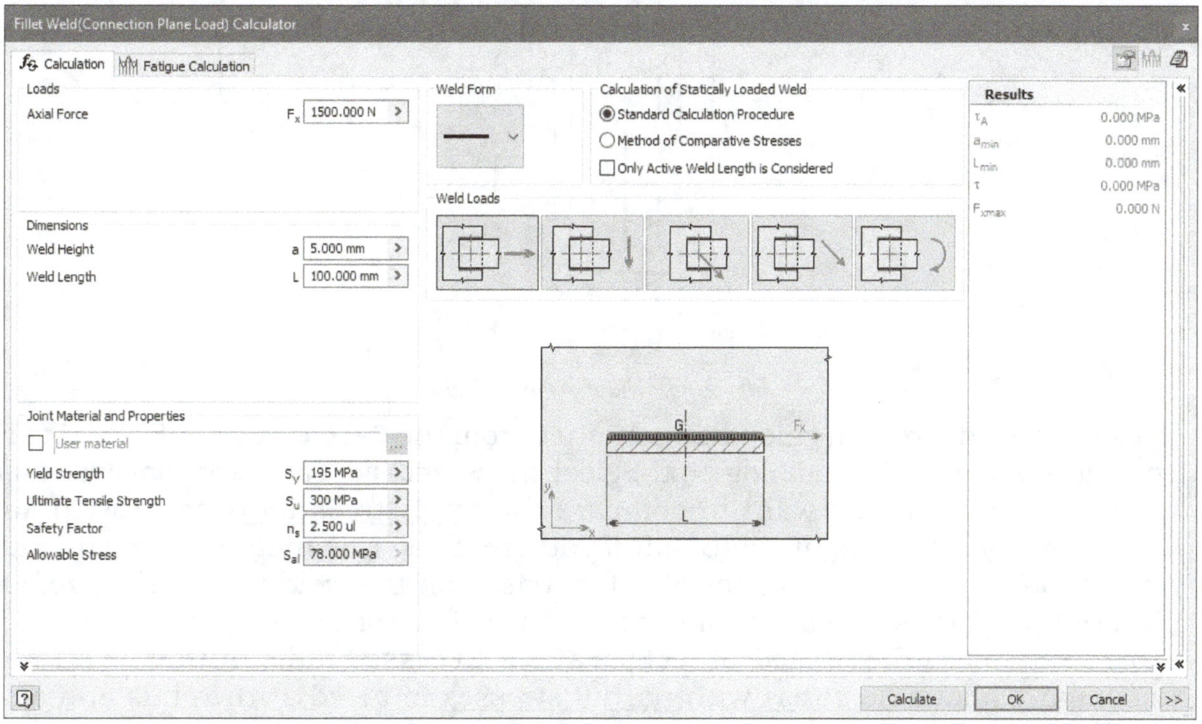

Figure-35. Fillet Weld (Connection Plane Load) Calculator dialog box

- Select desired weld form from the **Weld Form** drop-down; refer to Figure-36. The options in the **Weld Form** drop-down represent the shape of welding bead around the welded objects.

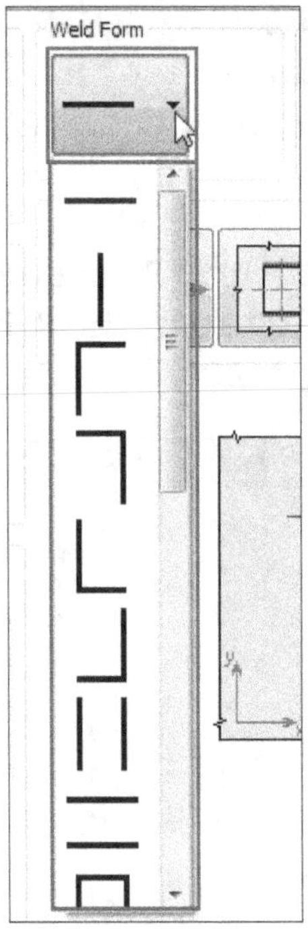

Figure-36. Weld Form drop-down

- Select the weld strength calculation method from the **Calculation of Statically Loaded Weld** area of the dialog box. Select the **Standard Calculation Procedure** radio button when you want to compare the total stress induced in weld joint with allowable stress limit. Note that if you are using this method then you must have appropriate value of factor of safety based on the weld type, weld size, and material properties. The recommended values of factor of safety are given in the table next. Select the **Method of Comparative Stresses** radio button if you want to compare allowable stress with partial stresses induced at the ends and sides of weld bead. The recommended range of factor of safety is less than or equal to 1.25 and above 2.

Weld type, loading	n_S
Butt welds loaded with traction	1.6 to 2.2
Butt welds loaded with bend	1.5 to 2.0
Butt welds loaded with shear	2.0 to 3.0
Butt welds loaded with loading	1.4 to 2.7
Fillet welds loaded in the plane of joining the part	2.0 to 3.0
Fillet welds loaded spatially	1.4 to 2.7
Plug and groove welds	2.0 to 3.0
Plug (resistant) welds loaded with shear	1.6 to 2.2
Plug (resistant) welds loaded with tearing	2.5 to 3.3

- Select the **Only Active Weld Length is Considered** check box to make sure that the active weld length is considered in calculations.

- Select desired load from the **Weld Loads** area of the dialog box based on the selected weld form. There are five buttons in the **Weld Loads** area named **Axial force**, **Bending Force parallel with the neutral axis of the weld group**, **Common force acting in the center of gravity of the weld group**, **Common force acting outside the center of gravity of the weld group**, and **Bending Moment**. On selecting the load, the graphical preview of load action will be displayed in the **Weld Loads** area; refer to Figure-37.

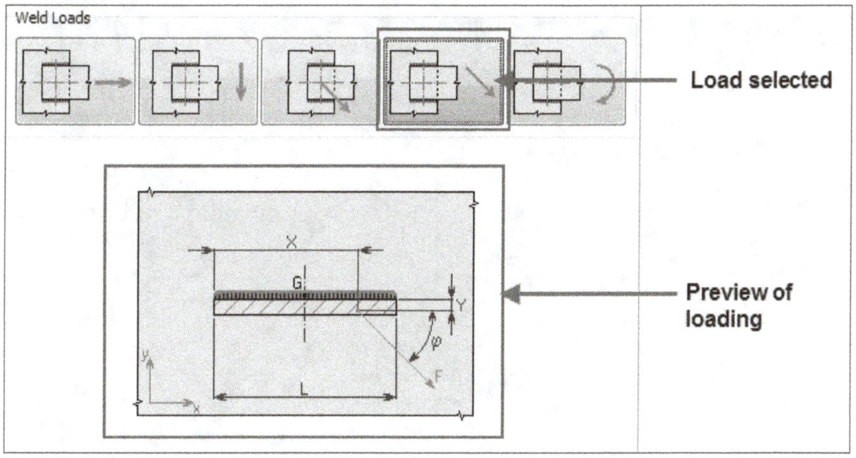

Figure-37. Preview of load on weld bead

- Specify the parameters related to load in the edit boxes of **Loads** area of the dialog box.
- Similarly, set the weld bead size in the **Dimensions** area of the dialog box.
- Set the material properties in the **Joint Material and Properties** area of the dialog box. Specify the Safety Factor value carefully as it can make huge impact on calculation and usability of component made using the design.
- Click on the **More options** button at the bottom right corner of the dialog box to expand the dialog box; refer to Figure-38.

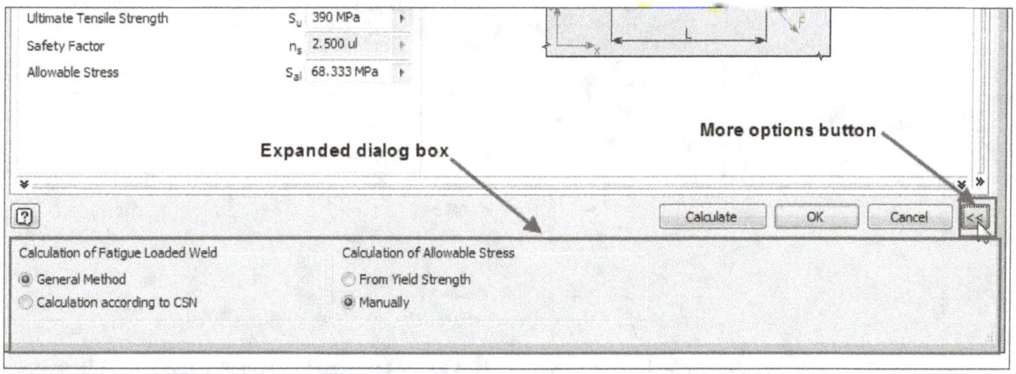

Figure-38. Expanded Fillet Weld (Connection Plane Load) Calculator dialog box

- Select the **Manually** radio button from the **Calculation of Allowable Stress** area of the expanded dialog box to manually specify the allowable stress.
- Select the **Calculation according to CSN** radio button from the **Calculation of Fatigue Loaded Weld** area in the expanded dialog box to change the method of fatigue stress calculations.

Fatigue Calculation

- Click on the **Enable/disables fatigue calculation** button from the top-right corner of the dialog box. The **Fatigue Calculation** tab in the dialog box will become active. Note that the **Enable/disables fatigue calculation** button will not be available for single straight weld bead weld form.
- Click on the **Fatigue Calculation** tab from the dialog box. The dialog box will be displayed as shown in Figure-39.

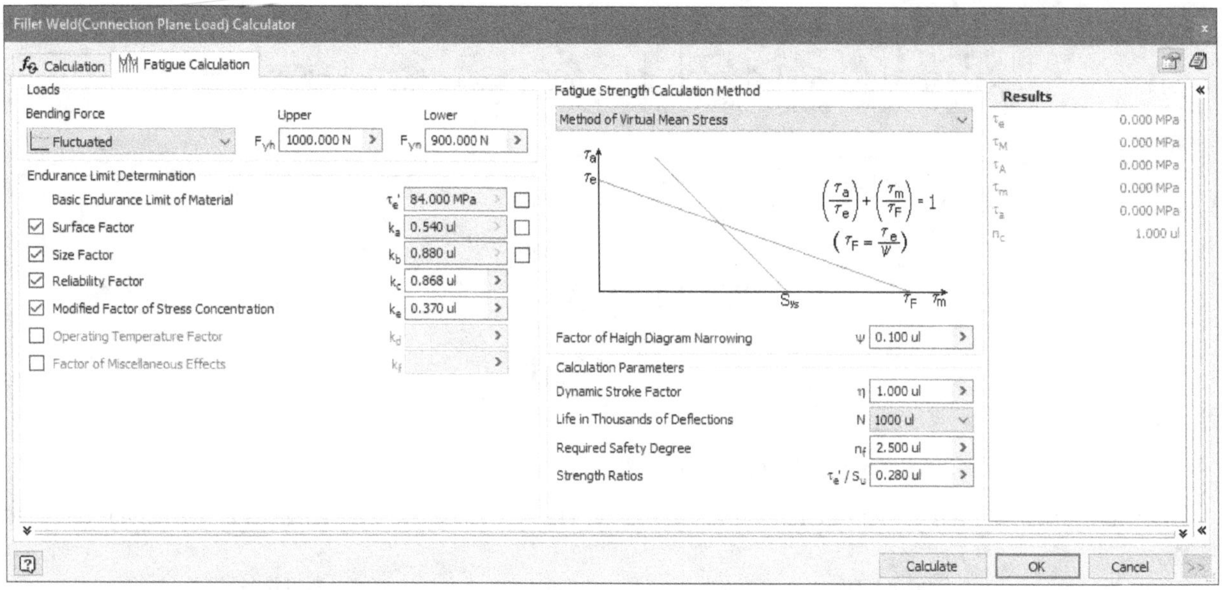

Figure-39. Fatigue Calculation tab in Fillet Weld (Connection Plane Load) Calculator dialog box

- Select the method of load repetition from the drop-down in the **Loads** area of the dialog box; refer to Figure-40.

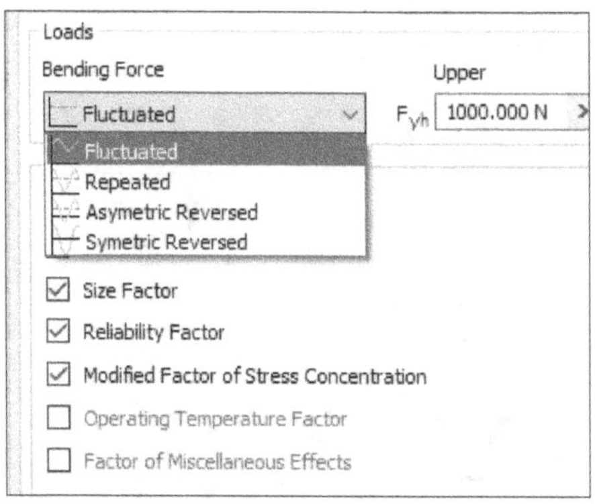

Figure-40. Drop-down in Loads area

- Specify the upper and lower load value in the **Upper** and **Lower** edit boxes.
- Set the other parameters for calculations and endurance limit.
- Click on the **Calculate** button. The result will be calculated and displayed in right pane of the dialog box; refer to Figure-41.

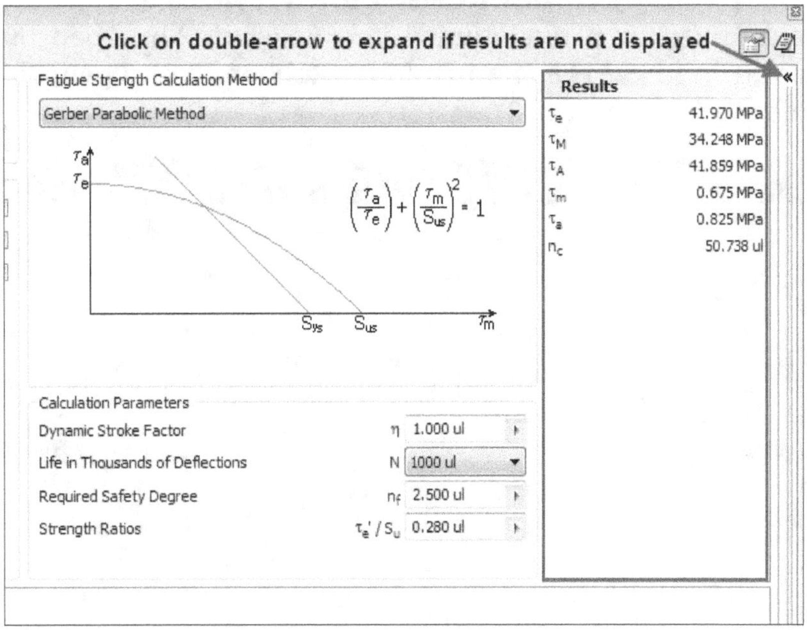

Figure-41. Results of fatigue calculation for fillet weld

- If the factor of safety is above required value then the weld bead can sustain the specified load. Based on the results, you can create weld bead in the model as discussed earlier in the chapter.

In the same way, you can use the calculators in the **Weld Calculator** drop-down.

PRACTICAL 1

In this practical, we will apply plug weld on the assembly model as shown in Figure-42.

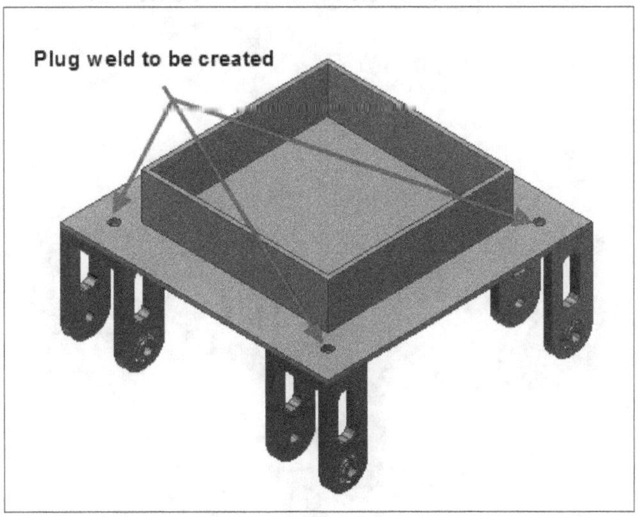

Figure-42. Plug weld in model for Practical 1

When we create a weldment assembly in Autodesk Inventor, the first step is to find out appropriate size of weld for desired load conditions. Once, we get the right size of weld, we can use welding tools to model the weld and apply welding symbols. The steps to create weldment model for Practical 1 are given next.

Opening Assembly File

- Start Autodesk Inventor if not started yet. Click on the **Open** button from **Open** cascading menu in the **File** menu of the **Ribbon**. The **Open** dialog box will be displayed; refer to Figure-43.

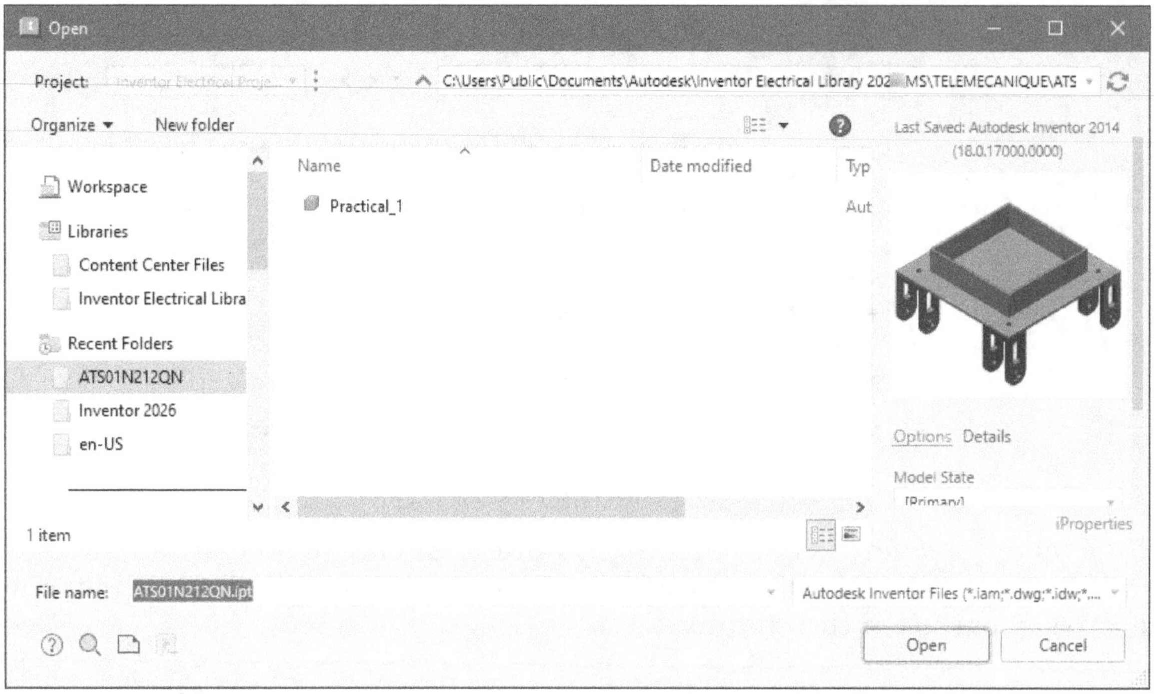

Figure-43. Open dialog box

- Double-click on the **Practical 1** file in **Chapter 13** folder of resource kit. The model will be displayed as shown in Figure-44. (Note that you need to write us an e-mail at cadcamcaeworks@gmail.com to get resource kit of the book.)

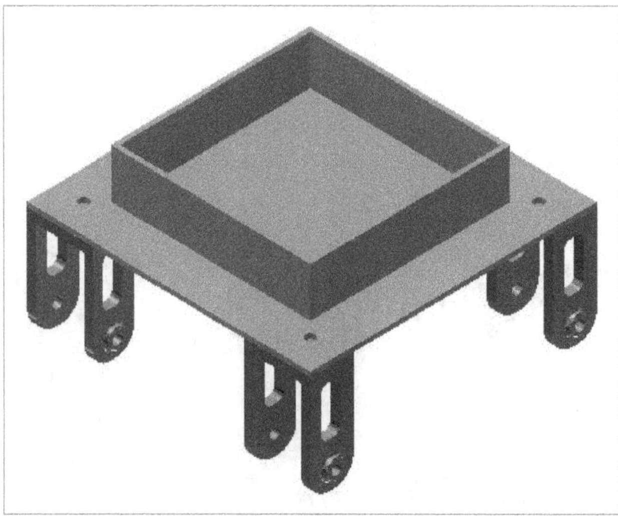

Figure-44. Model for Practical 1

Calculating Plug Weld Size

- Click on the **Plug/Groove Weld Calculator** tool from the **Weld Calculator** drop-down in the **Weld** panel of the **Weld** tab in the **Ribbon**. The **Plug and Groove Weld Calculator** dialog box will be displayed; refer to Figure-45.

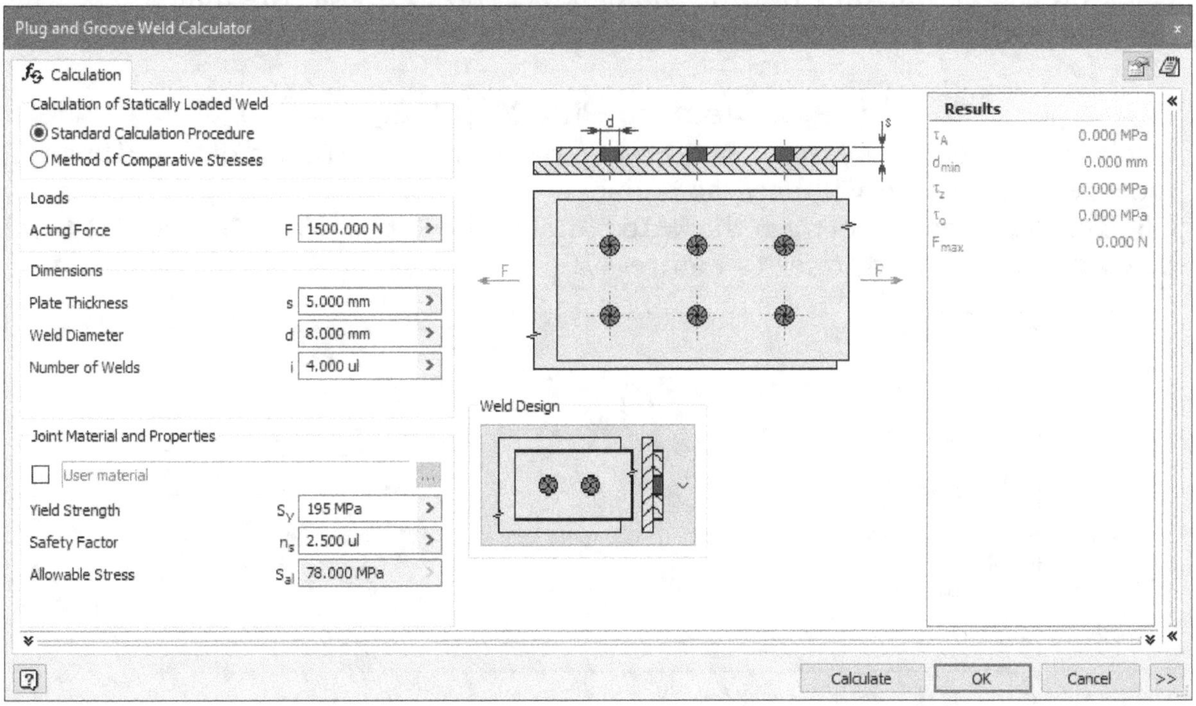

Figure-45. Plug and Groove Weld Calculator dialog box

- Specify the value of force as **15000 N** in the **Acting Force** edit box in the **Loads** area of the dialog box.
- Specify the plate thickness as **5** mm, Weld diameter as **11** mm, and number of welds as **1**. These values are taken after measuring the plate thickness and diameter of hole.
- Click on the **User material** edit box in the **Joint Material and Properties** area of the dialog box. The **Joint Material** dialog box will be displayed; refer to Figure-46.

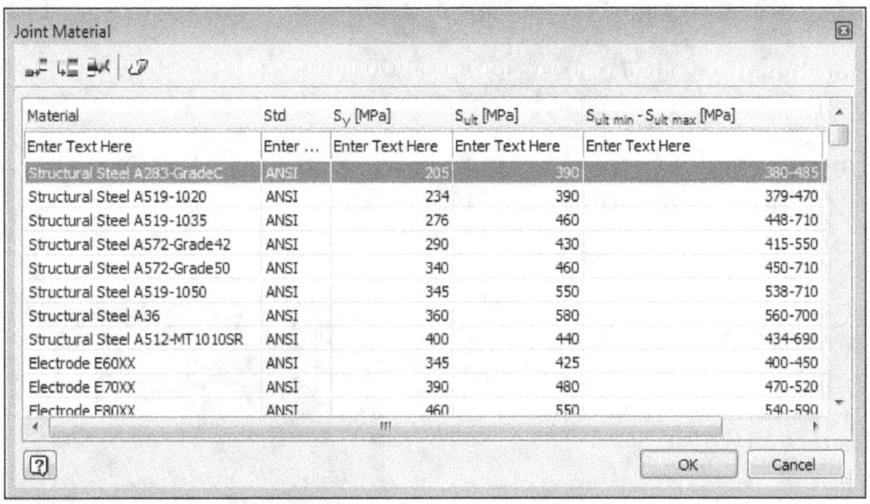

Figure-46. Joint Material dialog box

- Select the **Electrode E120XX** material from the dialog box and click on the **OK** button.
- Click on the **Calculate** button from the **Plug and Groove Weld Calculator** dialog box to test the strength of weld. We get the message "Calculation indicates design compliance!" which means we can create the plug weld of size specified in the **Dimensions** area of the dialog box. If you get any error in calculation results then you need to increase the plug diameter, increase number of welds or weld material.

- Click on the **OK** button from the dialog box. The **File Naming** dialog box will be displayed. Click on the **OK** button to create the calculation feature.

Creating Plug Weld

- Click on the **Welds** tool from the **Process** panel in the **Weld** tab of the **Ribbon**. The tools related to weld will become active.
- Click on the **Groove** tool from the **Weld** panel in the **Ribbon**. The **Groove Weld** dialog box will be displayed; refer to Figure-47.

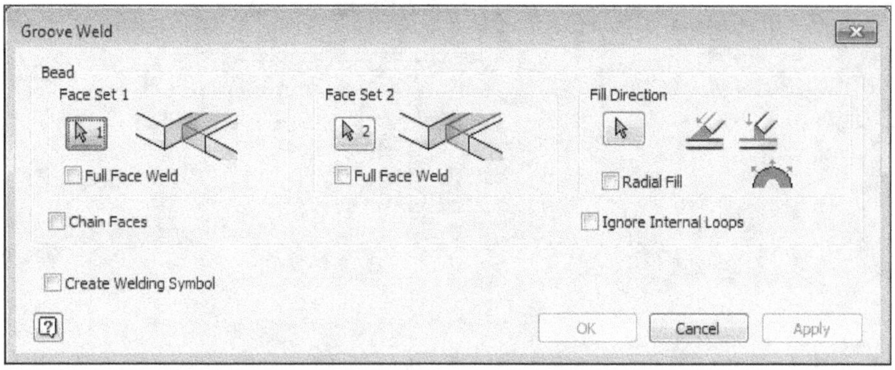

Figure-47. Groove Weld dialog box

- Select the round face of the hole as shown in Figure-48.

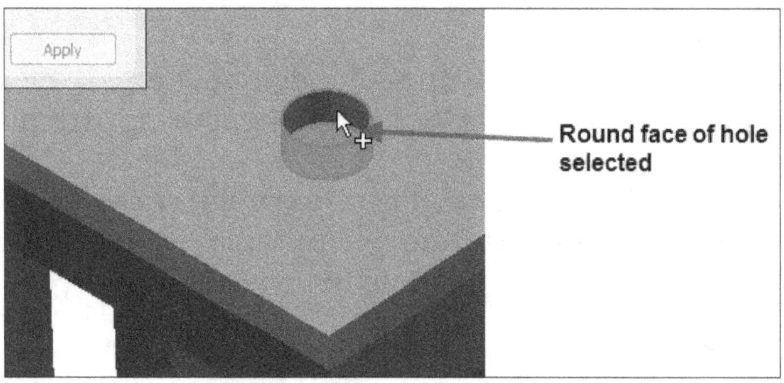

Figure-48. Round face of hole selected

- Click on the selection button in the **Face Set 2** area of dialog box and select the face below the hole; refer to Figure-49.

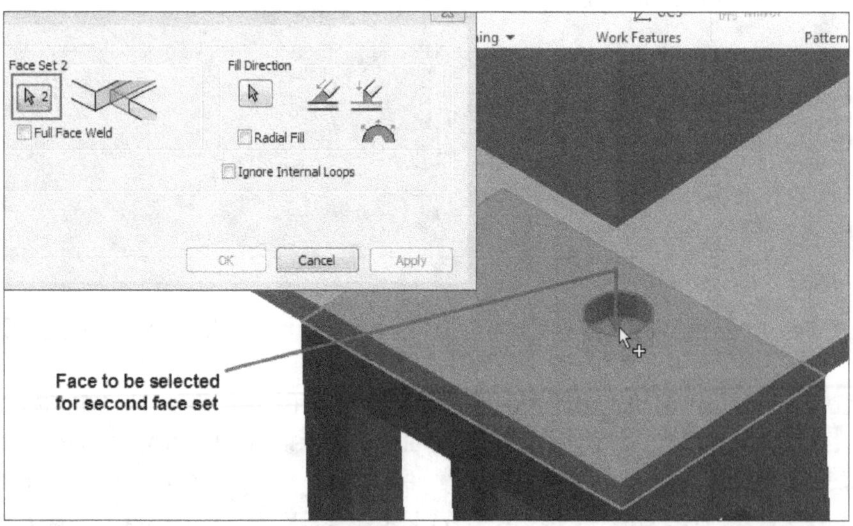

Figure-49. Face selected for Face Set 2

- Select the **Radial Fill** check box. Preview of the plug weld will be displayed.
- Select the **Create Welding Symbol** check box. The dialog box will get expanded.
- Set the parameters of welding symbol as shown in Figure-50.

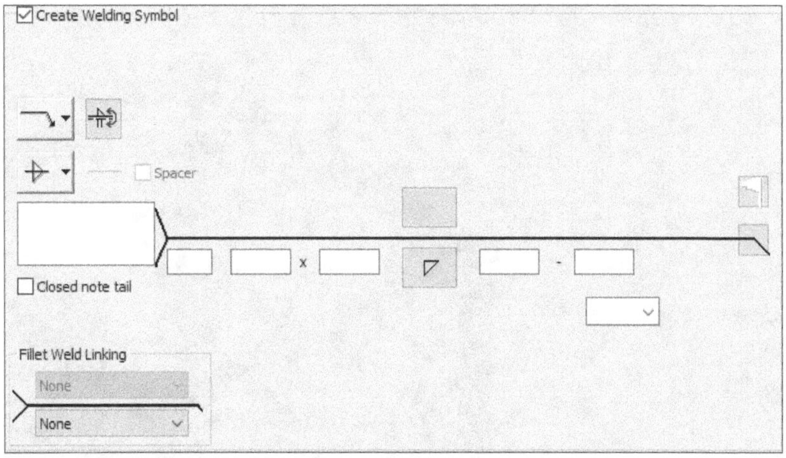

Figure-50. Parameters for welding symbol

- Click on the **OK** button to create the weld bead and symbol. Repeat the same procedure for other holes.

CONVERTING FRAME ASSEMBLY TO WELDMENT ASSEMBLY

In chapter 11, you have learned to create a frame design assembly using Design Accelerator components. In this chapter, you have earlier learned to create weldment assemblies. Most of the time in real-world scenario, you will be combining the two to get your product. A frame design is generally welded at joints to create a stable frame product. Now, you will learn how to convert the completed Frame design assembly into a weldment assembly so that welding report can be generated along with material cut list. The procedure to do so is given next.

- Open/create the frame design assembly as discussed earlier in the book; refer to Figure-51.
- Click on the **Convert to Weldment** tool from the **Convert** panel in the **Environments** tab of the **Ribbon**. A message box will be displayed telling you that if you convert the frame assembly to weldment assembly then Bill of Materials structure will not be editable. Bill of Materials (BOM) structure define the stage at which bill of materials is created. It can be Normal, Inseparable, Purchased, Phantom, or Reference. These options have been discussed earlier in the book. Click on the **Yes** button from the dialog box to perform conversion. The **Convert to Weldment** dialog box will be displayed; refer to Figure-52.

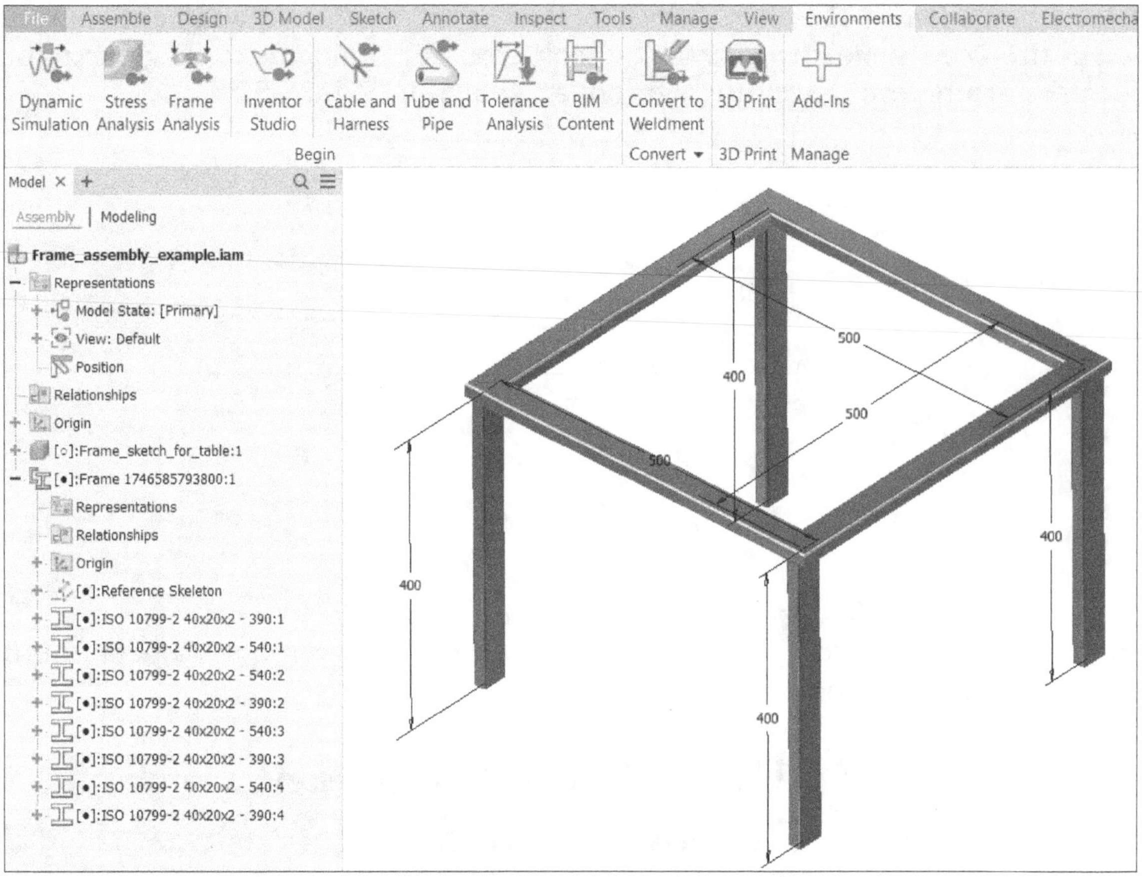

Figure-51. Frame assembly

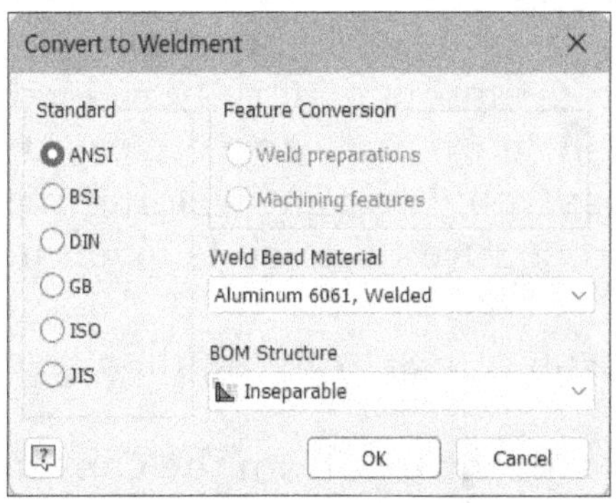

Figure-52. Convert to Weldment dialog box

- Select desired radio button from the **Standard** area in the dialog box to define dimension standard for the converted assembly.
- Select desired option from the **Weld Bead Material** drop-down to define the material for welding bead to be used for the assembly.
- Set the other parameters as discussed earlier and click on the **OK** button. The weldment tools will become active in the **Ribbon**. Perform the weld design operations as discussed earlier in this chapter.

Till this chapter, you have learned about modeling and assembly tools as well as weldment assembly. Now, I want you to open up your imaginations and make the components around you in CAD. Grab a ruler and measuring tape, and start making assemblies (for this reason we have not given any exercise for this chapter!). Use the Student Notes area next to note down the drawings of component you have found around you.

SELF ASSESSMENT

Q1. Which of the following Butt/Groove Weld Symbols represent the Single-U butt/groove weld symbol?

a) 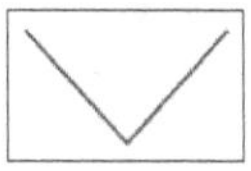

b) 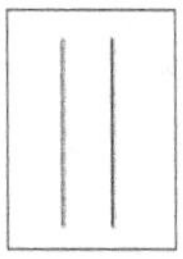

c) 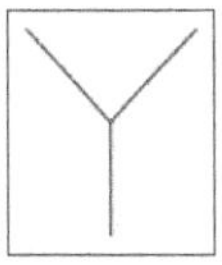

d) 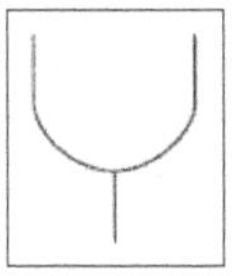

Q2. Which of the following weld symbols represent the Arc Seam Weld symbol?

a) 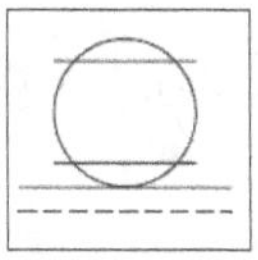

b) 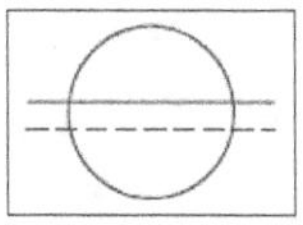

c) 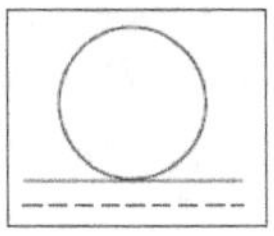

d) 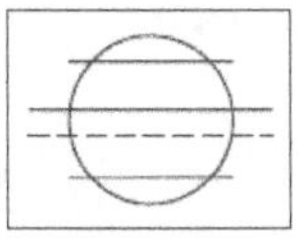

Q3. By which of the following processes, the weldment parts are prepared?

a) Machining
b) Welding
c) Both a and b
d) None of the Above

Q4. Which of the following options is incorrect definition of contour type for fillet weld symbol?

a) C means Chipping
b) G means Grooming
c) R means Rendering
d) H means Hammering

Q5. By using which of the following weld tools, more metal is filled and hence a stronger bond is created?

a) Groove Weld
b) Fillet Weld
c) Cosmetic Weld
d) Both a and c

Q6. Which of the following welds required End Fill to be assigned to the faces of weld beads?

a) Fillet Weld
b) Cosmetic Weld
c) Groove Weld
d) Both a and c

Q7. Which of the following weld loads is not present in the **Fillet Weld Calculator** dialog box?

a) Axial Force
b) Bending Moment
c) Common force acting inside the CoG of weld group
d) Common force acting beside the CoG of weld group

Q8. Which of the following values is a result value of analysis rather than properties of material?

a) Yield Strength
b) Ultimate Tensile Strength
c) Safety Factor
d) Allowable Stress

Q9. The **Bead Report** tool is used to create weld bead report in Microsoft Excel format. (True/False)

Q10. With the help of Groove weld, less metal is filled and hence a weaker bond is created. (True/False)

Q11. In the **Groove Weld** dialog box, select the .... check box when a face is shorter than the joining face but you want the faces to be completely welded.

Q12. In the **Fillet Weld Calculator** dialog box, select the .... radio button when you want to compare total stress induced in weld joint with allowable stress limit.

Q13. What is the first step to start a weldment assembly in Autodesk Inventor?
A. Open the Groove Weld tool
B. Click on the End Fill tool
C. Click on the New button in the File menu
D. Select the Bead Report tool

Q14. How many processes are involved in creating weldment parts in Autodesk Inventor?
A. One
B. Two
C. Three
D. Four

Q15. What does the Preparation tool allow you to do in the weldment process?
A. Add material to the model
B. Remove material from the model
C. Measure the dimensions
D. Rotate the model

Q16. Which tab in Autodesk Inventor provides access to welding tools?
A. Home
B. View
C. Weld
D. Assemble

Q17. What does the Fillet Weld tool create?
A. Square welds
B. Threaded joints
C. Fillet-shaped welds
D. Grooved beads

Q18. What does the 'Throat Measurement' in the Fillet Weld dialog box specify?
A. Length of leg of weld bead
B. Total length of weld
C. Distance of taper face
D. Number of weld passes

Q19. What does selecting the 'Convex' or 'Concave' contour option allow?
A. Rotate the weld preview
B. Specify contour offset
C. Create field welds
D. Swap welding symbols

Q20. Which edit box lets you specify distance between intermittent welds?
A. Length
B. Offset
C. Pitch
D. Area

Q21. What is the function of the 'Identification Line' in a welding symbol?
A. Denotes direction of weld
B. Denotes remote weld location
C. Indicates groove size
D. Defines weld thickness

Q22. Which option in welding symbol is used to write notes such as standards?
A. Tail Note Box
B. Prefix edit box
C. Leg 1
D. Swap Arrow

Q23. What does the 'All Around Symbol' indicate?
A. Weld to be done later
B. Weld at remote location
C. Weld to be done around entire joint
D. Weld to be ignored

Q24. What is the Groove Weld tool used for?
A. Create cosmetic welds
B. Assign welding symbols
C. Fill grooves between components
D. Add material to faces

Q25. Which check box ensures complete welding when one face is shorter?
A. Radial Fill
B. Create Welding Symbol
C. Ignore Internal Loops
D. Full Face Weld

Q26. Which mode does the Cosmetic Weld tool NOT support?
A. Edge
B. Loop
C. Surface
D. Chain

Q27. What is the main difference between cosmetic weld and regular weld?
A. Cosmetic weld shows graphical welds
B. Cosmetic weld is invisible
C. Cosmetic weld includes material properties
D. Cosmetic weld can only be applied on grooves

Q28. What must exist in the drawing area to use the Welding Symbol tool?
A. At least one weld bead without a symbol
B. At least one cosmetic weld
C. A completed machining process
D. Only edge selection

Q29. What is the purpose of the End Fill tool?
A. Add cosmetic symbols
B. Assign end to groove welds
C. Cut the welds
D. Adjust pitch value

Q30. Which weld type automatically gets end fills?
A. Groove welds
B. Cosmetic welds
C. Fillet welds
D. Edge welds

Q31. What does the Bead Report tool do?
A. Applies welding material
B. Creates 3D fillet shapes
C. Generates Excel report of weld beads
D. Assigns symbols to weld beads

Q32. What should you select in the Weld Bead Report dialog to include all subassemblies?
A. Pitch edit box
B. Identification Line
C. Include All Subassemblies
D. Full Face Weld

Q33. What is the only difference between preparation and machining tools?
A. Machining tools are in a separate tab
B. Preparation tools can be used after welding
C. Machining tools can be used after welding
D. Preparation removes material while machining adds

Q34. What is the primary purpose of the Weld Calculator tools in Autodesk Inventor?
A. To create welding beads directly on the model
B. To perform simulations of welded assemblies
C. To calculate whether the weld bead can sustain given load conditions
D. To convert cosmetic welds to actual welds

Q35. Which tool from the Weld Calculator drop-down helps in calculating fillet weld strength under planar load conditions?
A. Groove Weld Calculator
B. Cosmetic Weld Calculator
C. End Fill Calculator
D. Fillet Weld Calculator (Plane)

Q36. What does the "Standard Calculation Procedure" in the weld calculator compare?
A. Partial stress with bending moment
B. Induced stress with the safety factor
C. Total stress induced in weld joint with allowable stress
D. Load area with fatigue life

Q37. Which checkbox should be selected to consider only the active weld length in the calculation?
A. Weld Stress Active
B. Weld Length Considered
C. Only Active Weld Length is Considered
D. Consider Active Bead

Q38. Which area of the dialog box is used to define weld bead size?
A. Loads area
B. Dimensions area
C. Joint Material area
D. Safety Factor area

Q39. What does selecting the "Manually" radio button in Calculation of Allowable Stress allow you to do?
A. Automatically calculate fatigue resistance
B. Assign material grade
C. Manually enter the allowable stress
D. Select weld contour

Q40. What is activated when you click on the "Enable/disables fatigue calculation" button?
A. The Weld Symbol tab
B. The Groove Weld tab
C. The Fatigue Calculation tab
D. The Bead Report tab

Chapter 14

Mold Design

Topics Covered

The major topics covered in this chapter are:

- ***Guidelines for preparing plastic part for molding***
- ***Plastic Part Preparation Tools***
- ***Starting Mold Assembly***
- ***Importing Plastic Part***
- ***Setting gate location***
- ***Practical issues with pressure and temperature settings***
- ***Workpiece, Patch surface, and Runoff surface creation***
- ***Designing Runner, Cooling Channel, Gate, and Secondary Sprue***
- ***Mold Base assembly and component insertion***
- ***2D Drawing creation***

INTRODUCTION TO MOLD DESIGN

Mold Designing is the engineering of creating mold dies for manufacturing plastic parts. There are two major parts of mold; core and cavity. Both core and cavity are combined together and molten plastic is filled to create the component. The most important part of mold designing is preparing part and checking mold-ability. Below are some guidelines for preparing part for mold designing.

Designing Wall Thickness

Wall thickness strongly influences many key part characteristics, including mechanical performance and feel, cosmetic appearance, mold-ability, and economy. The optimum thickness is often a balance between opposing tendencies, such as strength versus weight reduction or durability versus cost. Give wall thickness careful consideration in the design stage to avoid expensive mold modifications and molding problems in production.

In simple, flat-wall sections, each 10% increase in wall thickness provides approximately a 33% increase in stiffness. Increasing wall thickness also adds to part weight, cycle times, and material cost. Consider using geometric features—such as ribs, curves, and corrugations — to stiffen parts. These features can add sufficient strength, with very little increase in weight, cycle time, or cost. Some materials, polycarbonate for example, lose impact strength if the thickness exceeds a limit known as the critical thickness. Above the critical thickness parts made of polycarbonate can show a marked decrease in impact performance. Walls with thickness greater than the critical thickness may undergo brittle, rather than ductile, failure during impact. The critical thickness reduces with lowering temperature and molecular weight. The critical thickness for medium-viscosity polycarbonate at room temperature is approximately 3/16 inch.

- Avoid designs with thin areas surrounded by thick perimeter sections as they are prone to gas entrapment problems,
- Maintain uniform nominal wall thickness; and
- Avoid wall thickness variations that result in filling from thin to thick sections; refer to Figure-1.

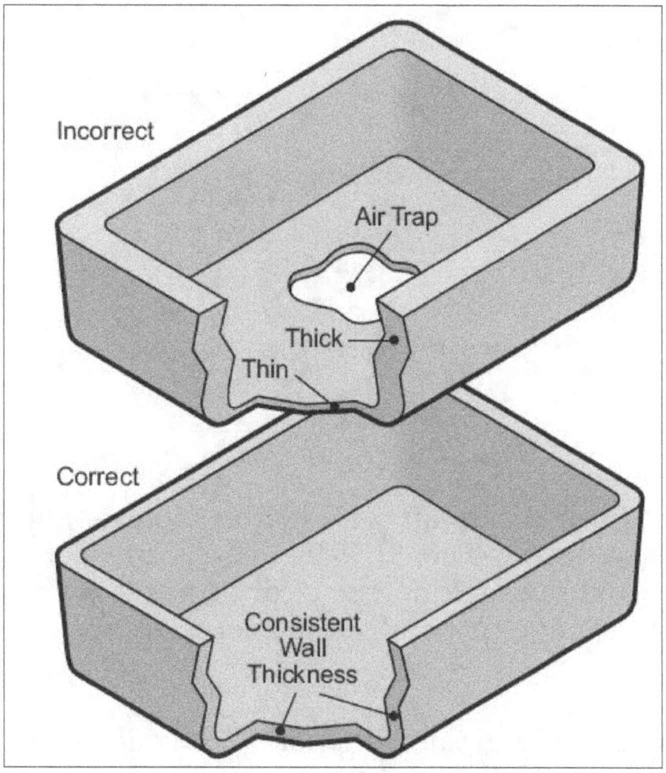

Figure-1. Problem with non uniform thickness of basic wall

Thin-walled parts — those with main walls that are less than 1.5 mm thick or those with wall thicknesses greater than 2 mm can also be considered as thin-walled parts if their flow-length to thickness ratios are too high for conventional molding.

Designing Ribs

Ribs provide a means to economically augment stiffness and strength in molded parts without increasing overall wall thickness. Other uses for ribs include:

- Locating and captivating components of an assembly;
- Providing alignment in mating parts; and
- Acting as stops or guides for mechanisms.

Proper rib design involves five main issues: thickness, height, location, quantity, and mold-ability. Consider these issues carefully when designing ribs.

Rib Thickness and Size

Many factors go into determining the appropriate rib thickness. Thick ribs often cause sink and cosmetic problems on the opposite surface of the wall to which they are attached; refer to Figure-2. On parts with wall thicknesses that are 1.0 mm or less, the rib thickness should be equal to the wall thickness. Rib thickness also directly affects mold-ability. Very thin ribs can be difficult to fill. Because of flow restrictions, thin ribs near the gate can sometimes be more difficult to fill than those farther away.

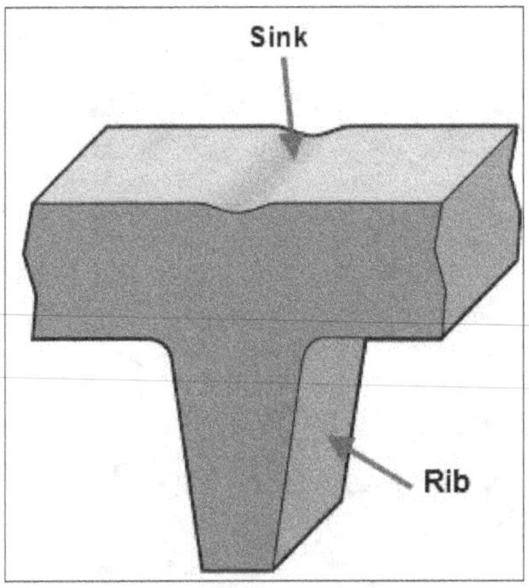

Figure-2. Sink opposite to rib

Ribs usually project from the main wall in the mold-opening direction and are formed in blind holes in the mold steel. To facilitate part ejection from the mold, ribs generally require at least one-half degree of draft per side; refer to Figure-3. More than one degree of draft per side can lead to excessive rib thickness reduction and filling problems in tall ribs.

Generally, taller ribs provide greater support. To avoid mold filling, venting, and ejection problems, standard rules of thumb limit rib height to approximately three times the rib-base thickness. Because of the required draft for ejection, the tops of tall ribs may become too thin to fill easily.

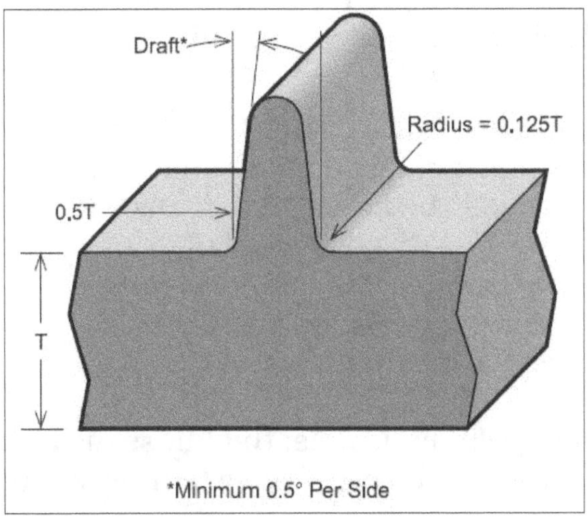

Figure-3. Rib thickness design

Rib Location and Numbers

Carefully, consider the location and quantity of ribs to avoid worsening problems the ribs were intended to correct. For example, ribs added to increase part strength and prevent breakage might actually reduce the ability of the part to absorb impacts without failure. Likewise, a grid of ribs added to ensure part flatness may lead to mold-cooling difficulties and warpage. Typically much easier to add than remove, ribs should be applied sparingly in the original design and added as needed to fine tune performance. Maintain enough space between ribs for adequate mold cooling: for short ribs allow at least two times the wall thickness. Replace the large problematic ribs with multiple shorter ribs; refer to Figure-4.

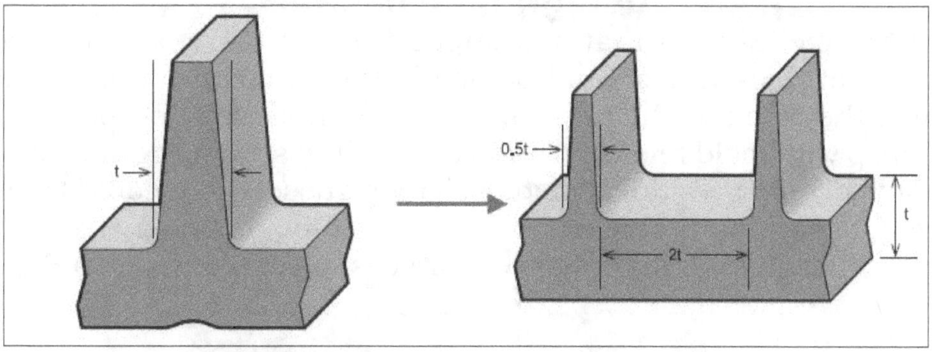

Figure-4. Replacing large rib with shorter ribs

Designing Bosses

Boss features find use in many part designs as points for attachment and assembly. The most common variety consists of cylindrical projections with holes designed to receive screws, threaded inserts, or other types of fastening hardware. As a rule of thumb, the outside diameter of bosses should remain within 2.0 to 2.4 times the outside diameter of the screw or insert; refer to Figure-5. Long core in bosses should be replaced as shown in Figure-6.

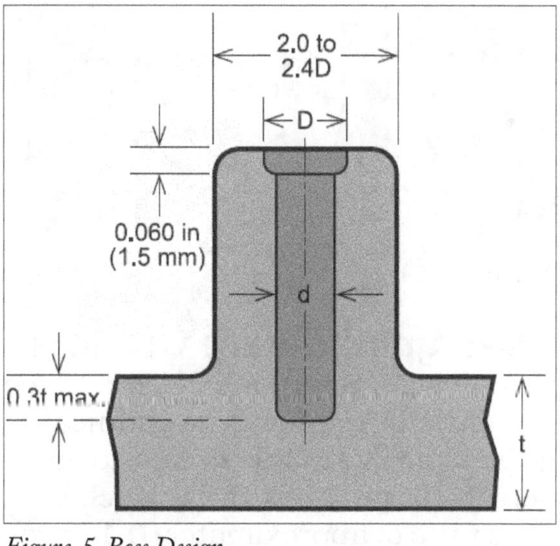

Figure-5. Boss Design

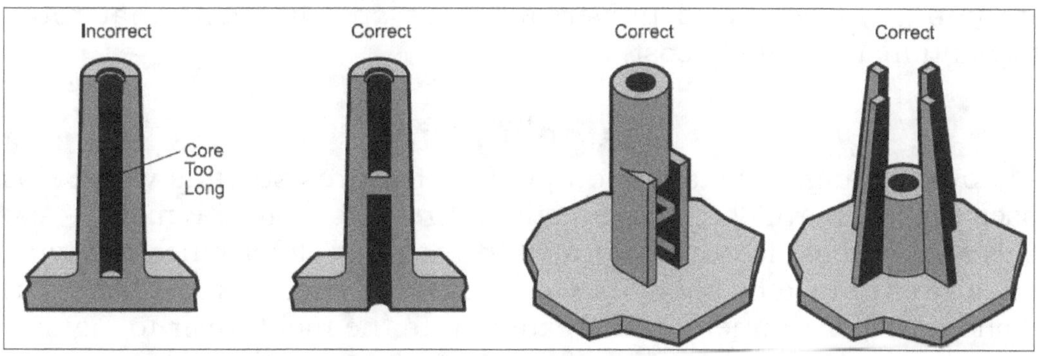

Figure-6. Long core replacement in boss

Designing Gussets

Gussets are rib-like features that add support to structures such as bosses, ribs, and walls. Gusset thickness should be one-half to two-thirds the thickness of the walls to which they are attached if sink is a concern. Specify proper draft and draw polishing to help with mold release. The location of gussets in the mold steel generally prevents practical direct venting. Avoid designing gussets that could trap gasses and cause filling and packing problems. Adjust the shape or thickness to push gasses out of the gussets and to areas that are more easily vented; refer to Figure-7.

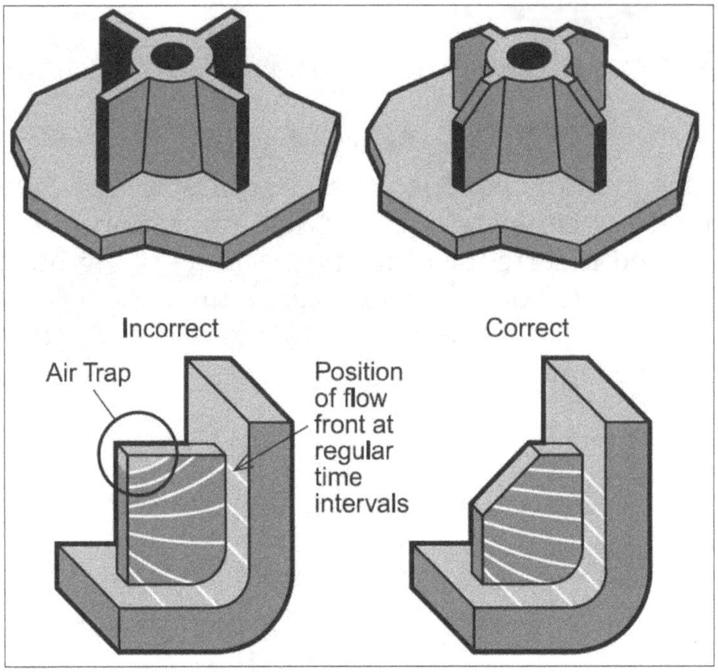

Figure-7. Gusset Designing

Designing Sharp Corners

Avoid sharp corners in your design. Sharp inside corners concentrate stresses from mechanical loading, substantially reducing mechanical performance. The stress concentration factor climbs sharply as the radius-to-thickness ratio drops below approximately 0.2. Conversely, large ratios cause thick sections, leading to sinks or voids. A radius-to-thickness ratio of approximately 0.15 provides a good compromise between performance and appearance for most applications subjected to light to moderate impact loads. Avoid universal radius specifications that round edges needlessly and increase mold cost.

Designing Draft

Draft — providing angles or tapers on product features such as walls, ribs, posts, and bosses that lie parallel to the direction of release from the mold — eases part ejection. How a specific feature is formed in the mold determines the type of draft needed. Features formed by blind holes or pockets — such as most bosses, ribs, and posts — should taper thinner as they extend into the mold; refer to Figure-8.

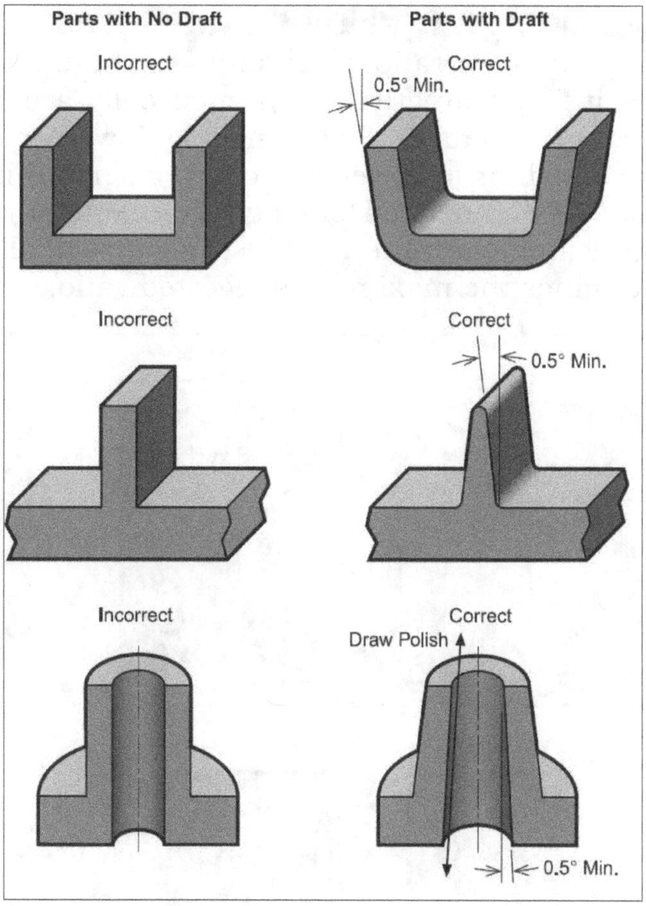

Figure-8. Draft Design

Surfaces formed by slides may not need draft if the steel separates from the surface before ejection. Other rules of thumb for designing draft include:

- Draft all surfaces parallel to the direction of steel separation;
- Angle walls and other features that are formed in both mold halves to facilitate ejection and maintain uniform wall thickness;
- Use the standard one degree of draft plus one additional degree of draft for every 0.001 inch of texture depth as a rule of thumb; and
- Use a draft angle of at least one-half degree for most materials. Design permitting, use one degree of draft for easy part ejection. SAN resins typically require one to two degrees of draft.

The mold finish, resin, part geometry, and mold ejection system determine the amount of draft needed. Generally, polished mold surfaces require less draft than surfaces with machined finishes. An exception is thermoplastic polyurethane resin, which tends to eject easier from frosted mold surfaces. Parts with many cores may need a higher amount of draft.

Designing Holes and Cores

Generally, the depth-to-diameter ratio for blind holes should not exceed 3:1. Ratios up to 5:1 are feasible if filling progresses symmetrically around the unsupported hole core or if the core is in an area of slow-moving flow. Consider alternative part designs that avoid the need for long delicate cores; refer to Figure-9. If the core is supported on both ends, the guidelines for length-to-diameter ratio double: typically 6:1 but up to 10:1 if the filling around the core is symmetrical. The level of support on the core ends determines the maximum suggested ratio.

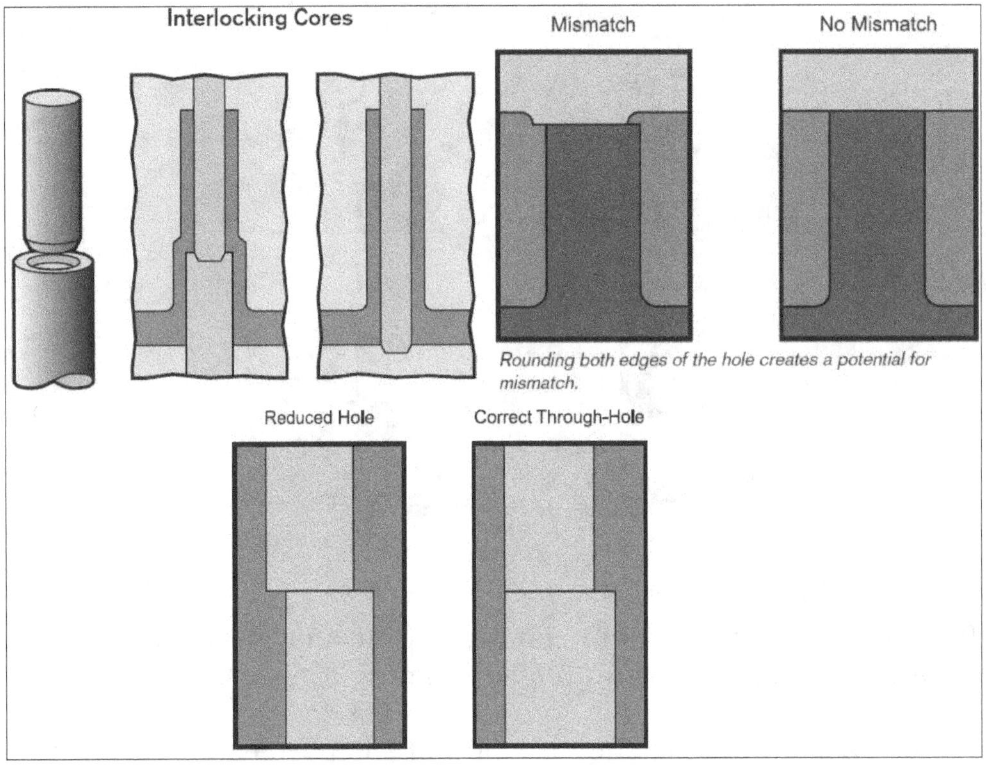

Figure-9. Designing Holes and cores

Designing Undercuts

Some design features, because of their orientation, place portions of the mold in the way of the ejecting plastic part.

Called "undercuts," these elements can be difficult to redesign. Sometimes, the part can flex enough to strip from the mold during ejection, depending upon the undercut's depth and shape and the resin's flexibility; refer to Figure-10. Undercuts can only be stripped if they are located away from stiffening features such as corners and ribs. Generally, avoid stripping undercuts in parts made of stiff resins such as polycarbonate, polycarbonate blends, and reinforced grades of polyamide 6. Undercuts up to 2% are possible in parts made of these resins, if the walls are flexible and the leading edges are rounded or angled for easy ejection. Typically, parts made of flexible resins, such as unfilled polyamide 6 or thermoplastic polyurethane elastomer, can tolerate 5% undercuts. Under ideal conditions, they may tolerate up to 10% undercuts. Most undercuts cannot strip from the mold, needing an additional mechanism in the mold to move certain components prior to ejection.

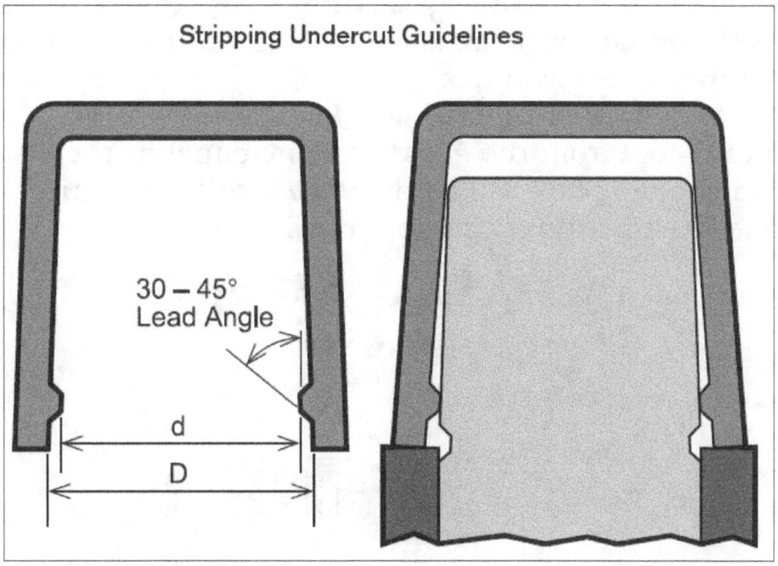

Figure-10. Undercut design

Till now in this chapter, we have discussed some basic rules for preparing part for mold design. Now, we will discuss the tools in Autodesk Inventor for making plastic part.

PLASTIC PART PREPARATION TOOLS

The tools to prepare plastic part are available in the Part environment which has been discussed next. To display tools for plastic part preparation, follow the steps given next.

- Start Autodesk Inventor and create a new part file with **Standard (mm).ipt** template.
- Click on the **Show Panels** button at the right corner in the **Ribbon**. The list of panels will be displayed; refer to Figure-11.
- Select the **Plastic Part** check box from the list. The **Plastic Part** panel will be added in the **Ribbon**; refer to Figure-12.

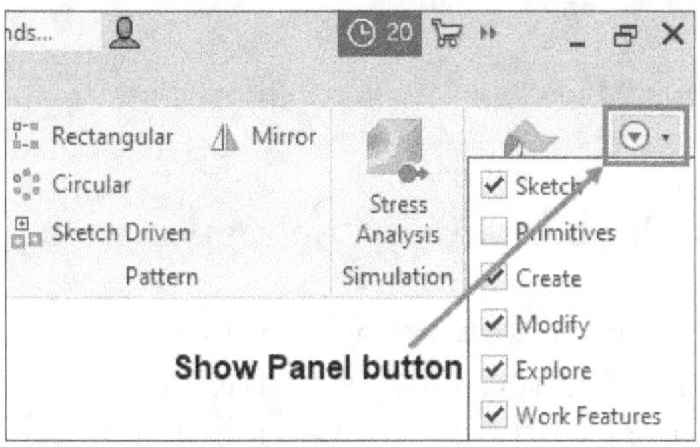

Figure-11. List of Panels

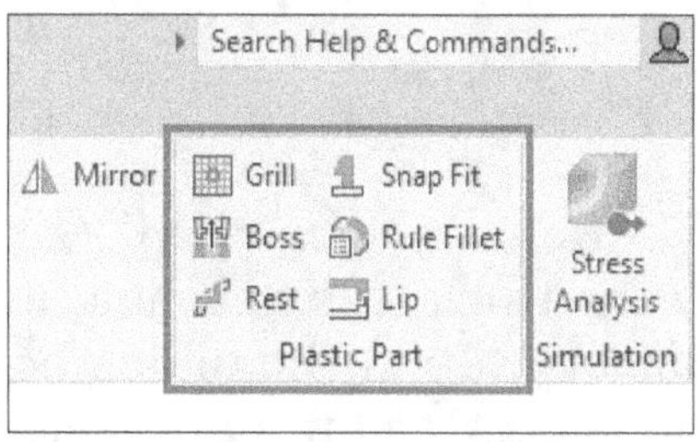

Figure-12. Plastic Part panel

In previous chapters, you have learned the use of 3D modeling tools, so we will not repeat the use of those tools here. Now, we will discuss the use of tools in **Plastic Part** panel.

Using Grill Tool

The **Grill** tool, as the name suggests, is used to create grill on the selected part. The procedure to use this tool is given next.

- Click on the **Grill** tool from the **Plastic Part** panel in the **3D Model** tab of the **Ribbon**. The **Grill** dialog box will be displayed; refer to Figure-13. Also, you will be asked to select the boundary curve for grill.

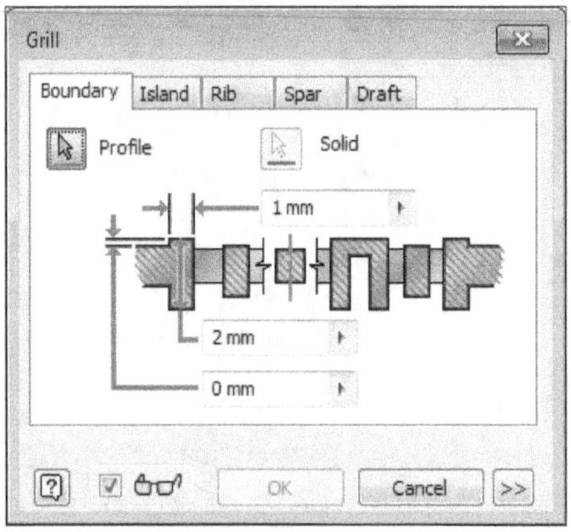

Figure-13. Grill dialog box

- Select the boundary lines of the sketch created for grill; refer to Figure-14.

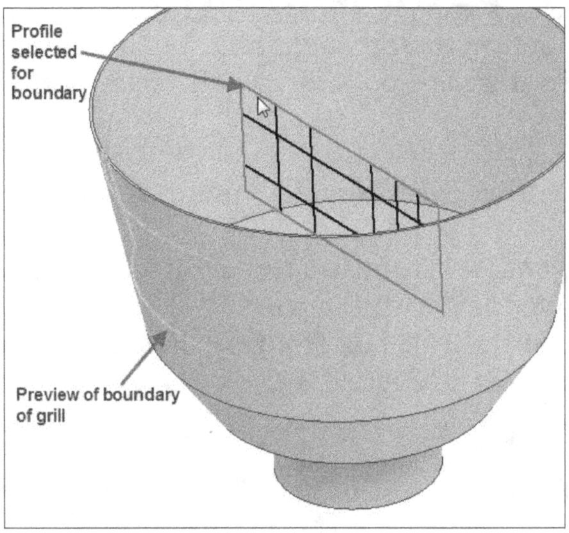

Figure-14. Profile selected for boundary of grill

- Specify the thickness and height of grill boundary in the respective edit boxes of the **Boundary** tab in the dialog box.
- Click on the **Island** tab and select the profile created for island feature. Preview of the feature will be displayed. Specify desired values in the edit boxes.
- Similarly, select the rib and spar profiles and specify values in the edit boxes to create the grill; refer to Figure-15.

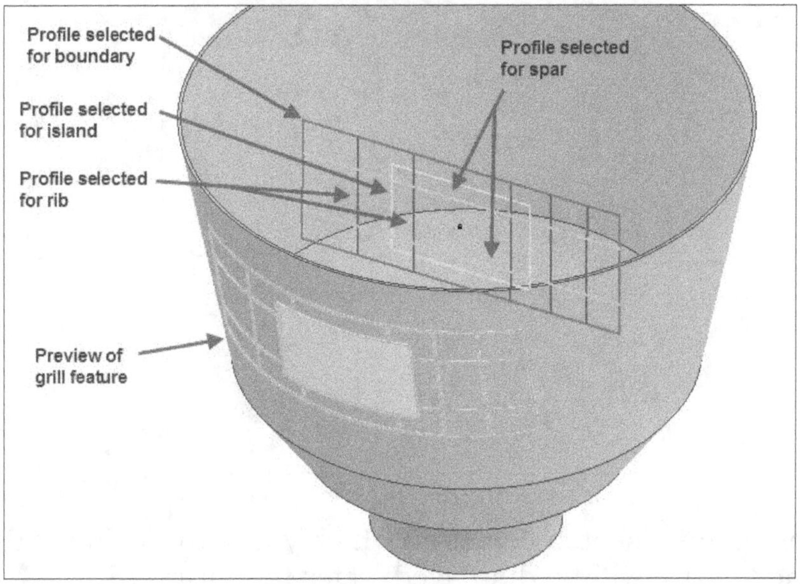

Figure-15. Profiles selected for grill feature

- Click on the **Draft** tab and specify desired value of draft angle in the edit box. If the grill fall on parting line then select the **Parting Element** check box and specify the offset distance.
- Click on the **OK** button to create the grill; refer to Figure-16.

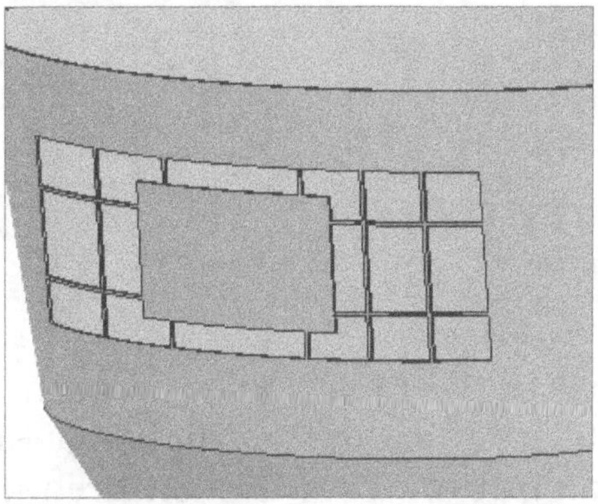

Figure-16. Grill created on the round face

Using Boss Tool

The **Boss** tool in **Plastic Part** panel is used to create boss feature at the specified location with parameters set in dialog box. The procedure of using this tool is given next.

- Click on the **Boss** tool from the **Plastic Part** panel in the **3D Model** tab of the **Ribbon**. The **Boss** dialog box will be displayed; refer to Figure-17.

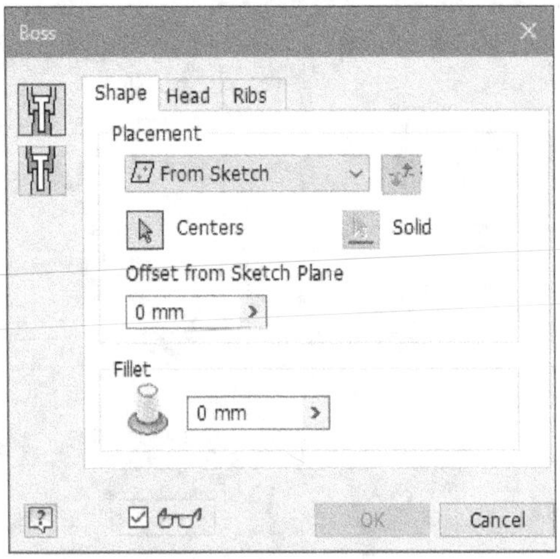

Figure-17. Boss dialog box

- Select the work points/sketch points on which you want to create the boss features. Preview of the feature will be displayed; refer to Figure-18.

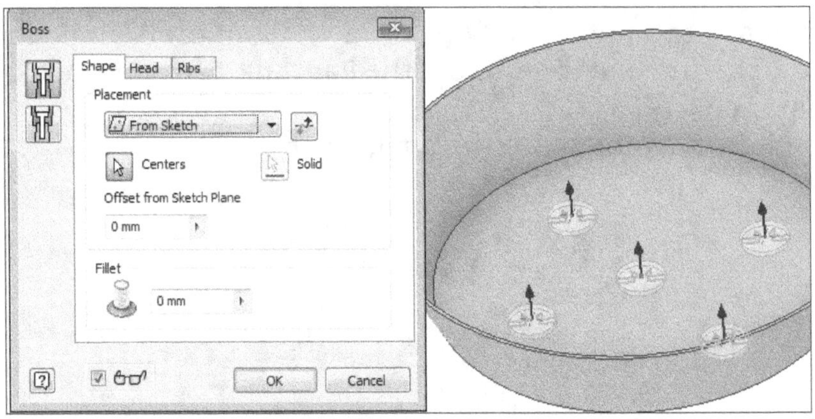

Figure-18. Preview of boss feature

- Set desired value of offset in the **Offset from Sketch Plane** edit box.
- Specify desired value of fillet radius in the edit box of **Fillet** area in the dialog box.
- Select the **Head** or **Thread** button from the left area in the dialog box. Select the **Head** button if you want to create the female part of the boss fastener. Select the **Thread** button from the dialog box if you want to create male part of the boss fastener.
- Click on the **Head** or **Thread** tab depending on the button selected. The dialog box will be displayed as shown in Figure-19.

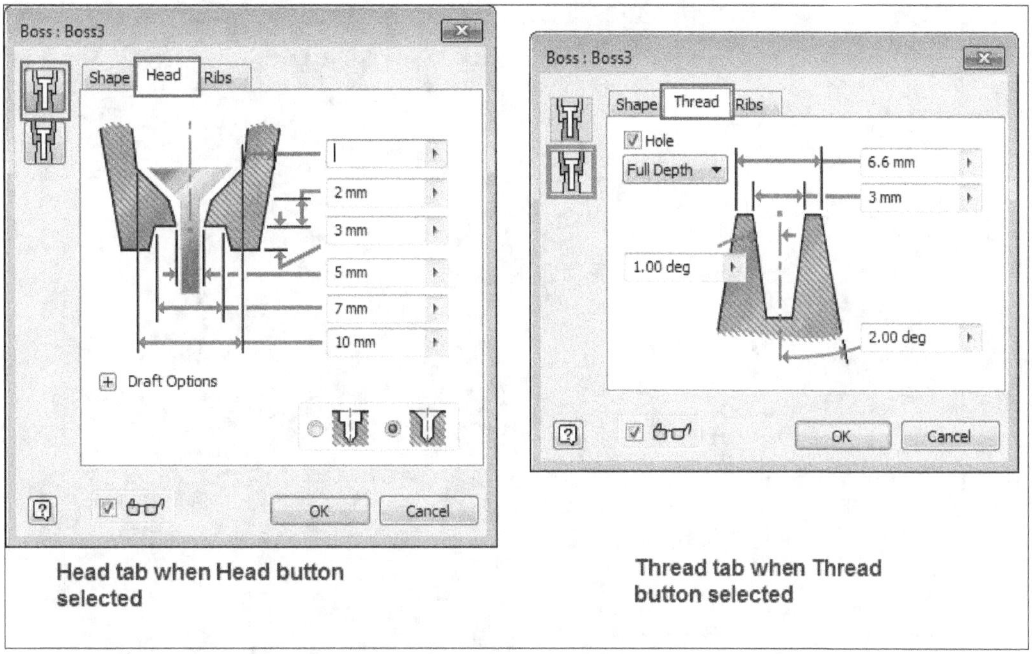

Figure-19. Head tab and Thread tab in Boss dialog box

- Specify desired parameters in the dialog box and then click on the **Ribs** tab. The **Boss** dialog box will be displayed as shown in Figure-20.
- Select the **Stiffening Ribs** check box to add ribs to the boss feature. Preview of ribs will be displayed; refer to Figure-21.

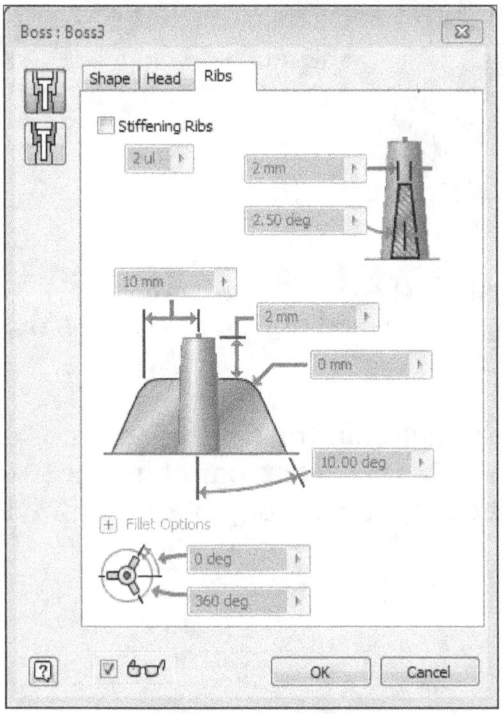

Figure-20. Boss dialog box with Rib tab selected

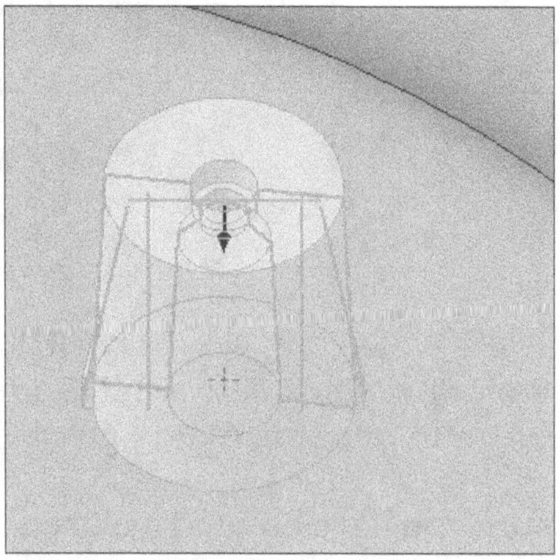

Figure-21. Preview of rib in head feature

- Set desired parameters for the rib in the dialog box; refer to Figure-22. Click on the **OK** button to create the boss feature; refer to Figure-23.

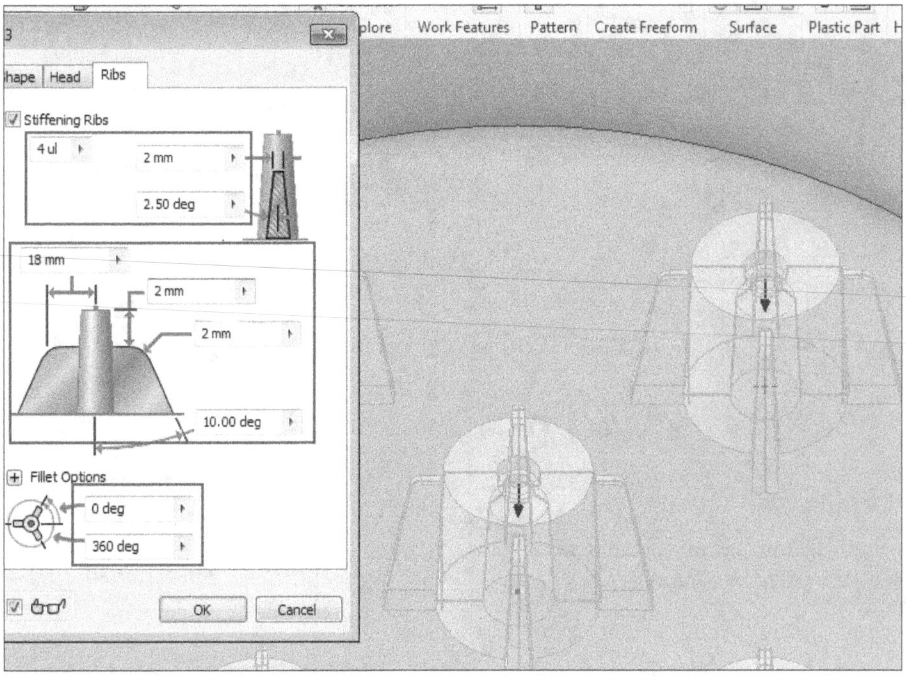

Figure-22. Parameters specified for rib

Figure-23. Boss feature created

Using Rest Tool

The **Rest** tool is used to create a flat landing area based on the provided closed sketch. The procedure to use this tool is given next.

- Make sure you have created a closed loop sketch in the drawing area prior to using this tool. Click on the **Rest** tool from the **Plastic Part** panel in the **3D Model** tab of the **Ribbon**. The **Rest** dialog box will be displayed along with the preview of rest feature; refer to Figure-24.

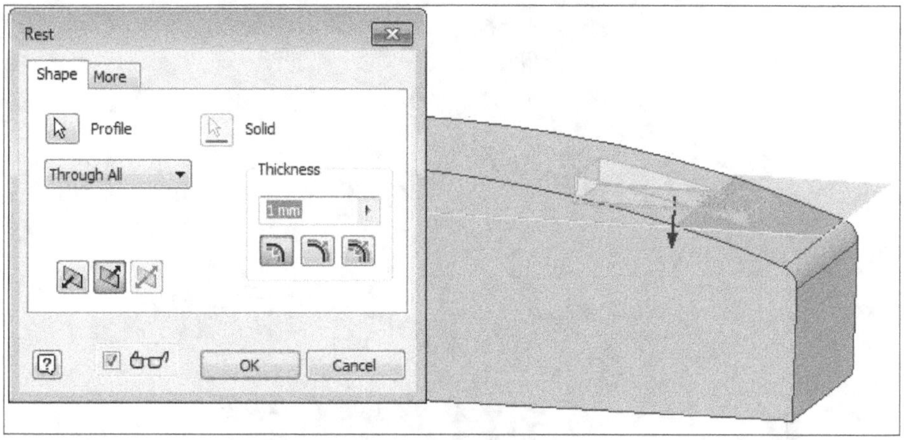

Figure-24. Rest dialog box with preview of rest feature

- Select desired option from the drop-down to specify depth of the rest feature; refer to Figure-25.

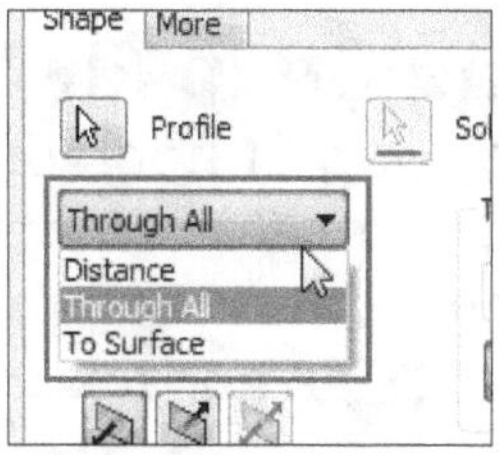

Figure-25. Drop-down for depth options

- Set desired depth and direction. Similarly, specify the thickness of rest feature in the **Thickness** edit box and set the direction of thickness.
- Click on the **More** tab to specify advanced options for rest feature. The dialog box will be displayed as shown in Figure-26.

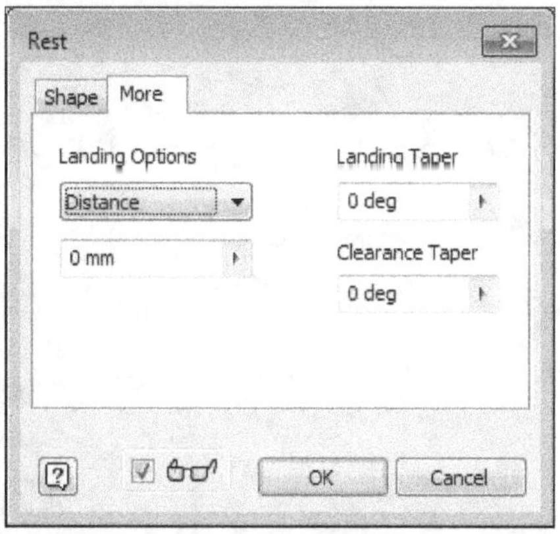

Figure-26. More tab in the Rest dialog box

- Set the landing distance value in the **Distance** edit box or select the **To surface** option from the **Landing Options** drop-down and select desired limiting surface.
- Specify landing taper and clearance taper angle values in the **Landing Taper** and **Clearance Taper** edit boxes, respectively.
- Click on the **OK** button to create the feature; refer to Figure-27.

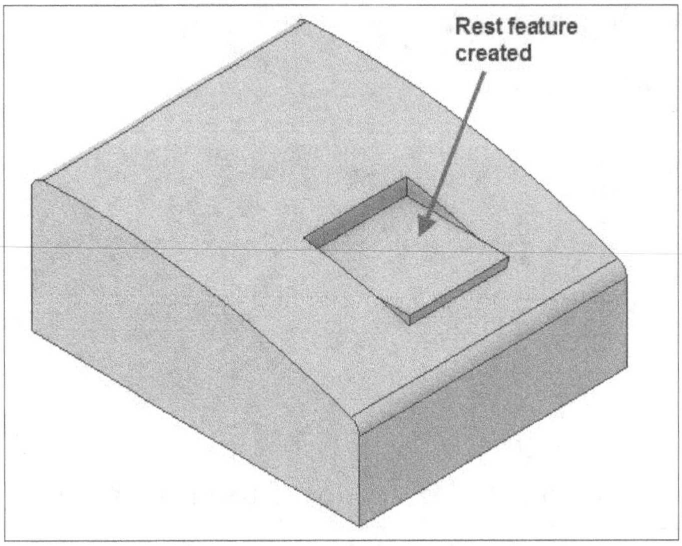

Figure-27. Rest feature created

Using Snap Fit Tool

The **Snap Fit** tool is used to create snap fit hook or loop, so that the two components can be joined without the use of screws, glues, clips, or other joining elements. Make sure you have created points at the locations required for snap fits before using this tool. The procedure to use this tool is given next.

- Click on the **Snap Fit** tool from the **Plastic Part** panel in the **3D Model** tab of the **Ribbon**. The **Snap Fit** dialog box will be displayed. Also, you will be asked to select the sketch or points to create the snap fit.
- Select the sketch or points on the part on which you want to create the snap fit. The preview of snap fit will be displayed as shown in Figure-28.

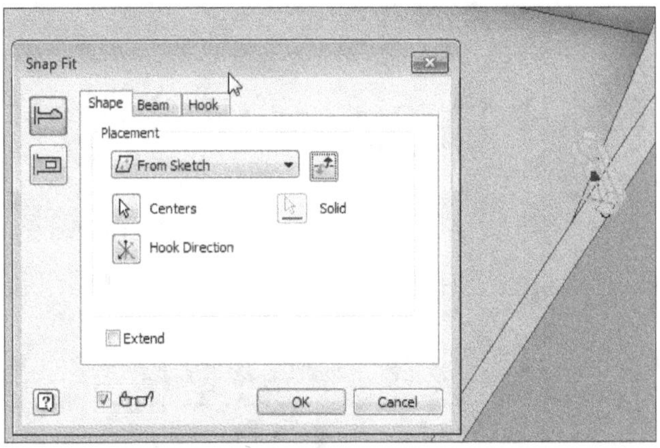

Figure-28. Snap Fit dialog box

- Click on the **Hook Direction** button to set the direction of hook. On clicking the button, you will be asked to select a yellow arrow of desired direction displayed with the preview. Select desired arrow to set hook direction.
- Click on the **Cantilever Snap Fit Hook** or **Cantilever Snap Fit Loop** button from the left area of the dialog box to create snap fit hook or loop.
- Specify the parameters in **Beam** and **Hook** tabs of the dialog box if you have selected the **Cantilever Snap Fit Hook** button. Similarly, specify the parameters in **Clip** and **Catch** tabs of the dialog box if you have selected the **Cantilever Snap Fit Loop** button.
- Click on the **OK** button to create the snap fit feature; refer to Figure-29.

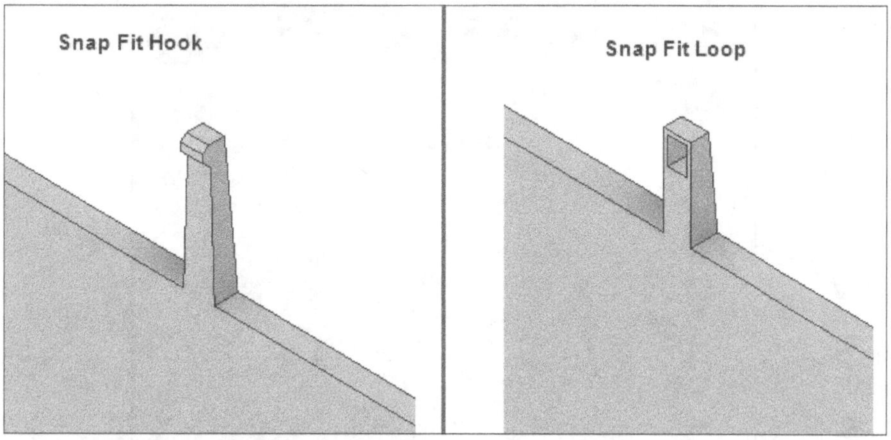

Figure-29. Snap Fit Hook and Loop created

Using Rule Fillet Tool

The **Rule Fillet** tool is used to fillet the edges based on specified rules. The steps to use this tool are given next.

- Click on the **Rule Fillet** tool from the **Plastic Part** panel in the **3D Model** tab of the **Ribbon**. The **Rule Fillet** dialog box will be displayed as shown in Figure-30.
- Click on the field under **Source** column and select **Feature** or **Face** option as required from the drop-down displayed; refer to Figure-31.

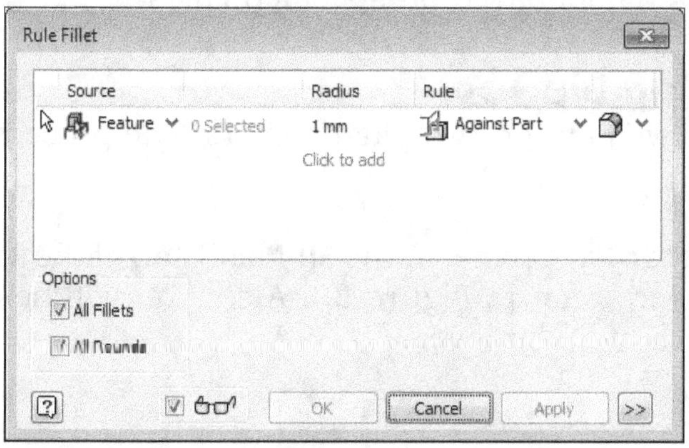

Figure-30. Rule Fillet dialog box

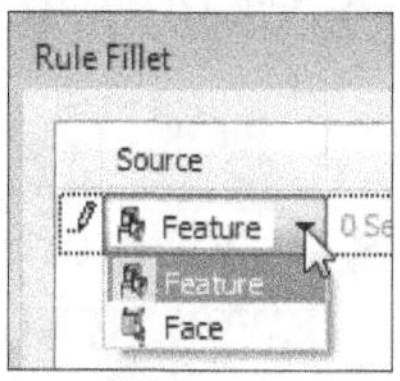

Figure-31. Drop-down in Source column

- Click in the field under **Radius** column and specify desired value of radius for fillet.
- Click in the field under **Rule** column and select desired rule from the drop-down. If you have selected the **Against Part** option then only the edges formed by the faces of the features and the faces of the part body are filleted. If you have selected the **Against Features** option then only the edges that are generated by intersection of selected features will be filleted. If you have selected the **Free Edges** option from the drop-down then all the edges formed by faces of the selected feature will be filleted. If you have selected the **All Edges** option then all the edges of the selected features will be filleted.
- To change the advanced parameters of the fillet, click on the **More** button at the bottom-right in the dialog box. The dialog box will expand as shown in Figure-32.

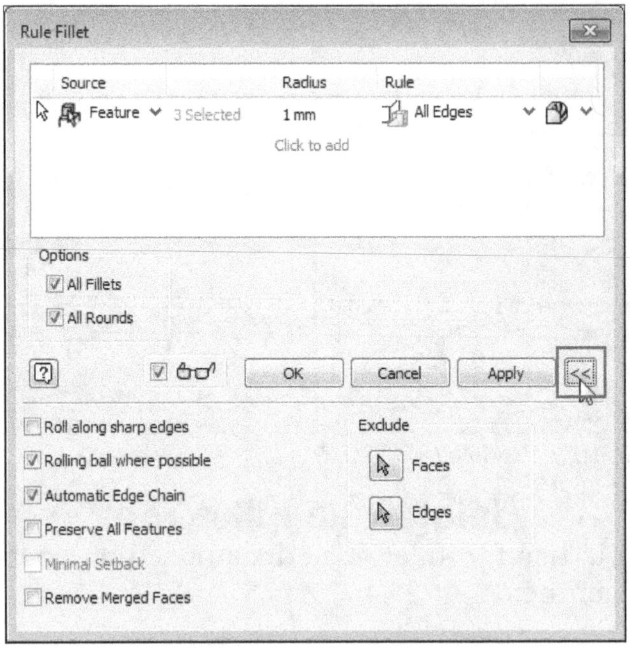

Figure-32. Expanded Rule Fillet dialog box

- Select desired check boxes from the expanded dialog box to modify fillet. Click on the **Faces** or **Edges** selection button from the **Exclude** area and select the entities that you do not want to be filleted.
- Click on the **OK** button to fillet the model based on specified rules.

Using Lip Tool

The **Lip** tool is used to create lip-groove joint on two plastic parts. The procedure to use this tool is given next.

- Click on the **Lip** tool from the **Plastic Part** panel in the **3D Model** tab of the **Ribbon**. The **Lip** dialog box will be displayed; refer to Figure-33. Also, you will be asked to select an edge to define the path of lip/groove.

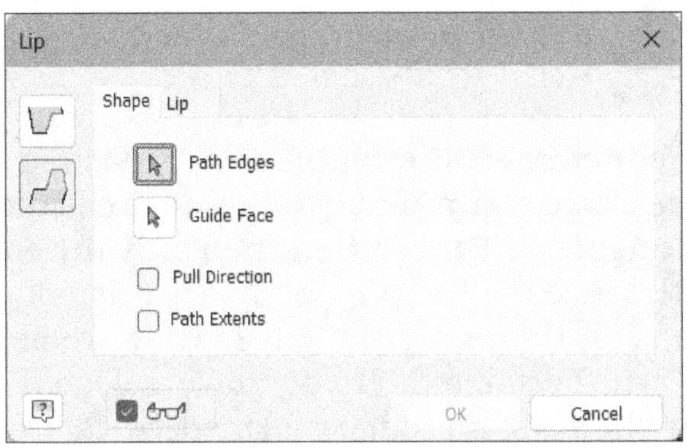

Figure-33. Lip dialog box

- Select the edge of plastic part on which you want to create the lip/groove.
- Click on the **Guide Face** selection button and select the face connected to earlier selected edge. Preview of the lip/groove will be displayed; refer to Figure-34.

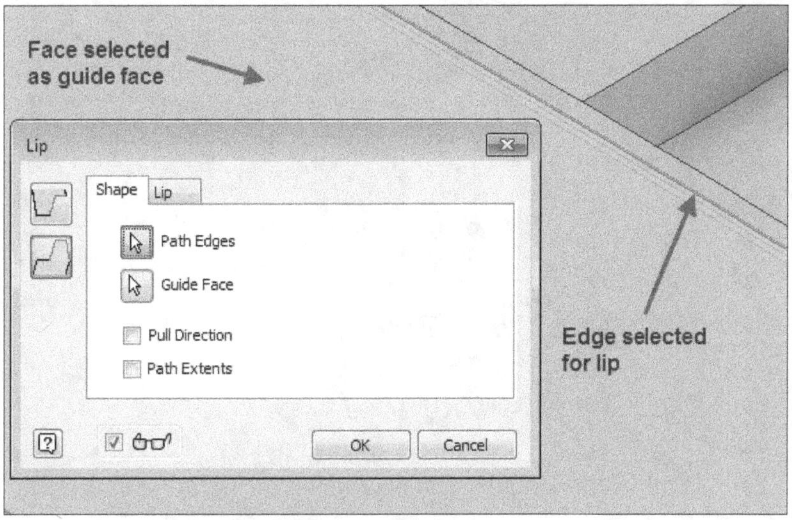

Figure-34. Lip preview at side face of model

- Click on the **Groove** or **Lip** button from the left area of the dialog box to create groove or lip, respectively. The **Groove** tab will be added in the dialog box if you have selected the **Groove** button and the **Lip** tab will be added in the dialog box if you have selected the **Lip** button from the left area.
- Click on the tab and specify desired dimensions for lip/groove; refer to Figure-35.

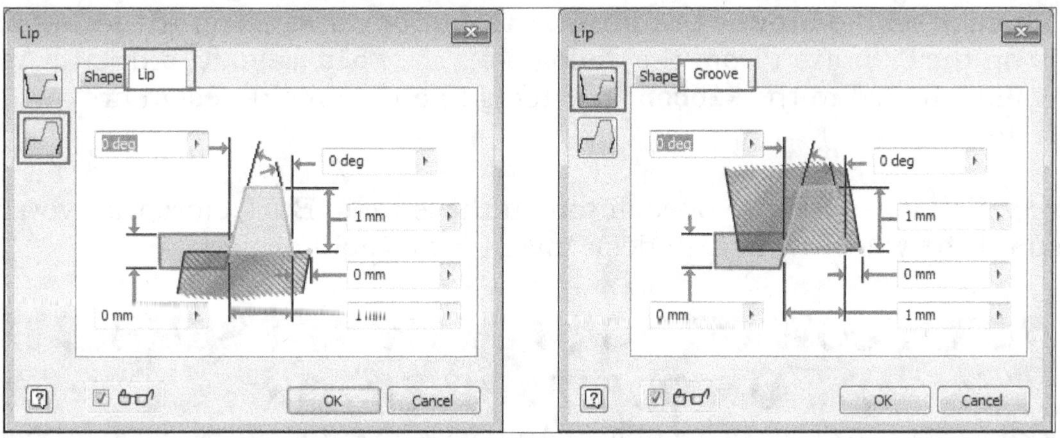

Figure-35. Lip and Groove tabs in the Lip dialog box

- After specifying the dimensions, click on the **OK** button to create the feature.

Till now in this chapter, we have learned about the tools specific to plastic part making. Now, we will discuss the tools in assembly environment which are used in mold making.

STARTING MOLD DESIGN ASSEMBLY

- Start Autodesk Inventor (if not started yet). If you have a file opened in Autodesk Inventor then save the file and close it. Next, click on the **New** button from **New** cascading menu in the **File** menu of the **Ribbon**. The **Create New File** dialog box will be displayed.
- Double-click on the **Mold Design (mm).iam** in the **Assembly** area of **Metric** folder in the dialog box. The **Create Mold Design** dialog box will be displayed with Assembly environment opened; refer to Figure-36.

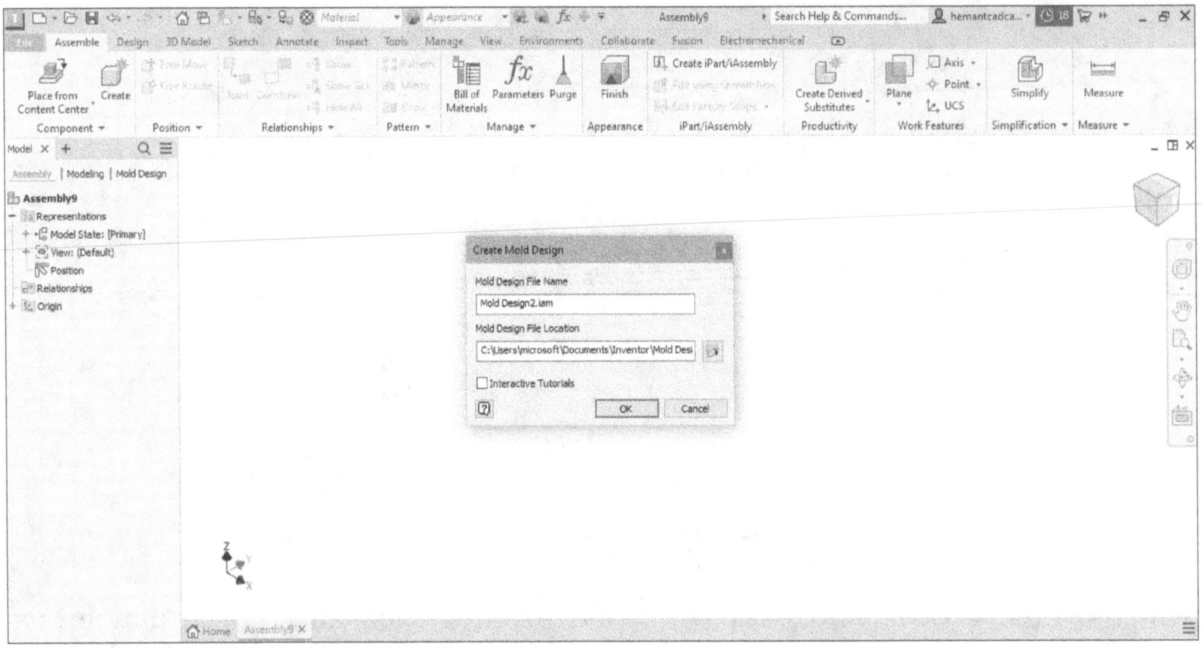

Figure-36. Create Mold Design dialog box

- Specify the name of mold design file in the **Mold Design File Name** edit box of the dialog box.
- Specify the location of mold design files in the **Mold Design File Location** edit box or click on the browse button next to edit box and select the location.
- Click on the **OK** button from the dialog box. The **Mold Layout** and **Mold Assembly** tab will be added to the **Ribbon**. The tools to create mold design are available in these tabs.

Now, we will discuss the use of each tool in these tabs. But before that you need to understand the workflow in Autodesk Inventor for mold design.

WORKFLOW OF MOLD DESIGN ASSEMBLY IN AUTODESK INVENTOR

The workflow of mold design assembly in Autodesk Inventor can be given by Figure-37.

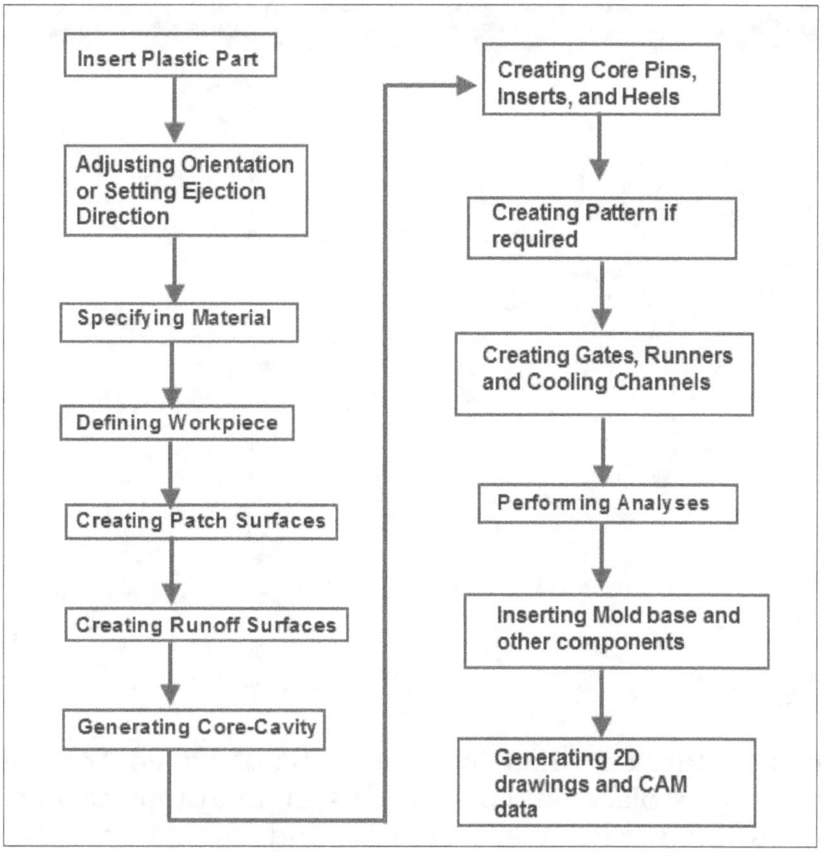

Figure-37. Workflow in Mold design

Now, we will discuss the tools involved in each step of the work flow in detail.

INSERTING PLASTIC PART

The very first step in mold designing is to insert the plastic part for which we are creating the mold. The procedure to insert plastic part is given next.

- Click on the **Plastic Part** tool from the **Mold Layout** panel in the **Mold Layout** tab of the **Ribbon**. The **Plastic Part** dialog box will be displayed as shown in Figure-38.

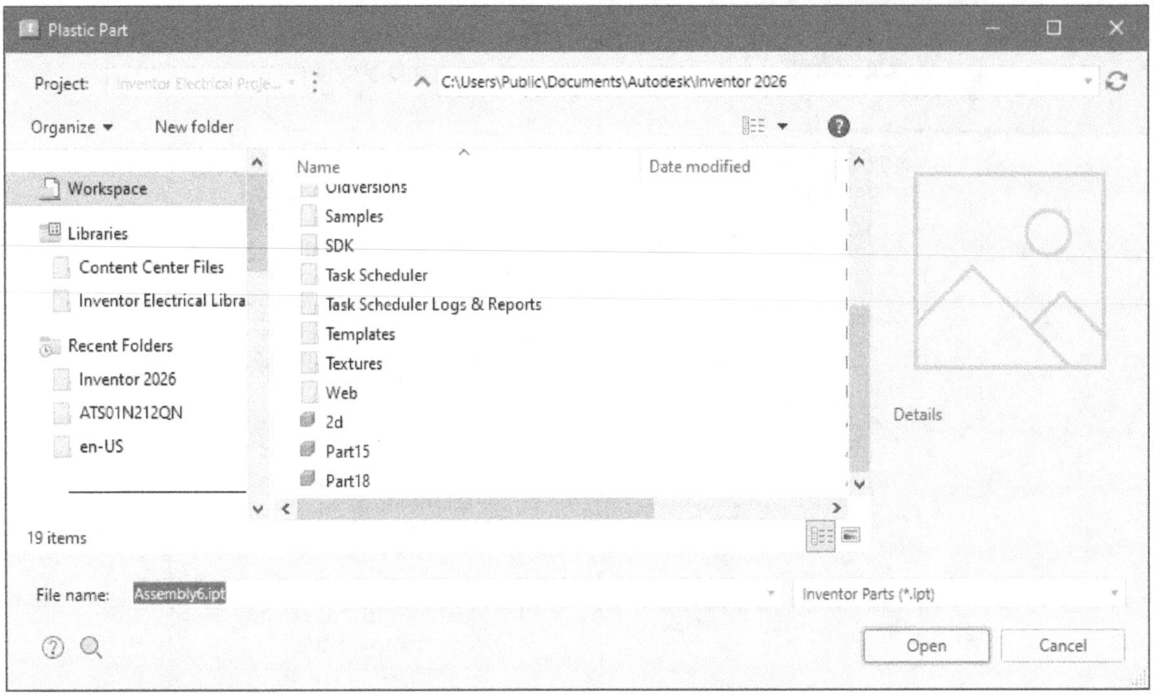

Figure-38. Plastic Part dialog box

- Select the plastic part for which mold is to be designed and click on the **Open** button. The part gets placed at coordinate system automatically.
- Click in the drawing area to place the part and exit the tool. The other tools in the panel will get activated.

PLACE CORE AND CAVITY

The **Place Core and Cavity** tool is used to place the core and cavity components in the assembly which were created earlier. The procedure to use this tool is discussed next.

- Click on the **Place Core and Cavity** tool from the **Mold Layout** panel in the **Mold Layout** tab of the **Ribbon**. The **Place Core and Cavity** dialog box will be displayed; refer to Figure-39.

Figure-39. Place core and cavity dialog box

- Click in the **Product Name** edit box and specify desired name of the product.
- Click on the button from the **Core File** area. The **Place Component** dialog box will be displayed to import the component; refer to Figure-40.
- Similarly, you can import the component for **Cavity File** area.

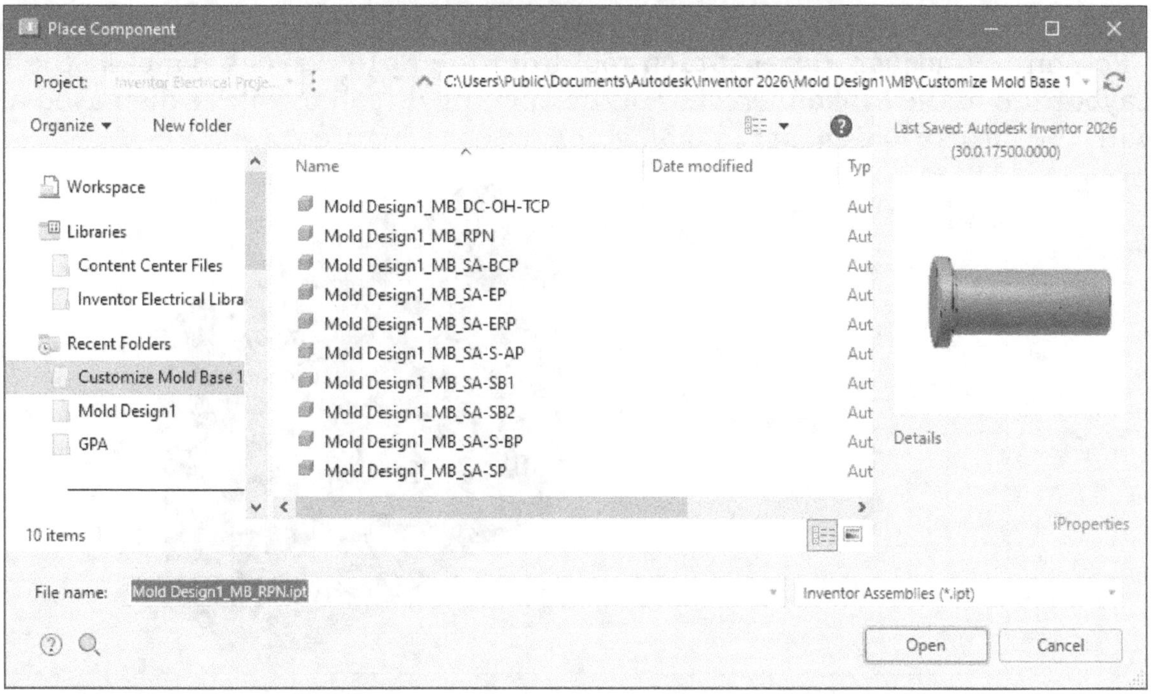

Figure-40. Place Component dialog box

- Select desired file from the dialog box and click on the **Open** button. The core and cavity files will be placed; refer to Figure-41.

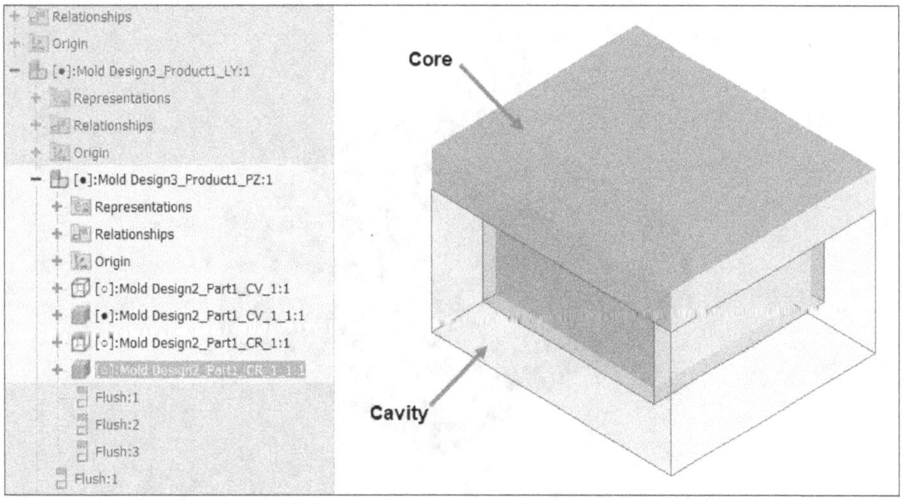

Figure-41. Core and cavity model

- Select **Activate Assembly Edit immediately** check box to edit the assembly after importing the core and cavity.
- After specifying desired parameters, click on the **OK** button from the dialog box.

ADJUSTING ORIENTATION/POSITION OF PART

The direction of mold ejection is based on the orientation of the part in mold. We will now learn how to orient the part or say decide the ejection direction of mold. The steps are given next.

Adjusting Orientation of Part

- Click on the **Adjust Orientation** tool from the **Mold Layout** panel in the **Mold Layout** tab of the **Ribbon**. Preview of the opening direction will be displayed along with the **Adjust Orientation** dialog box; refer to Figure-42.

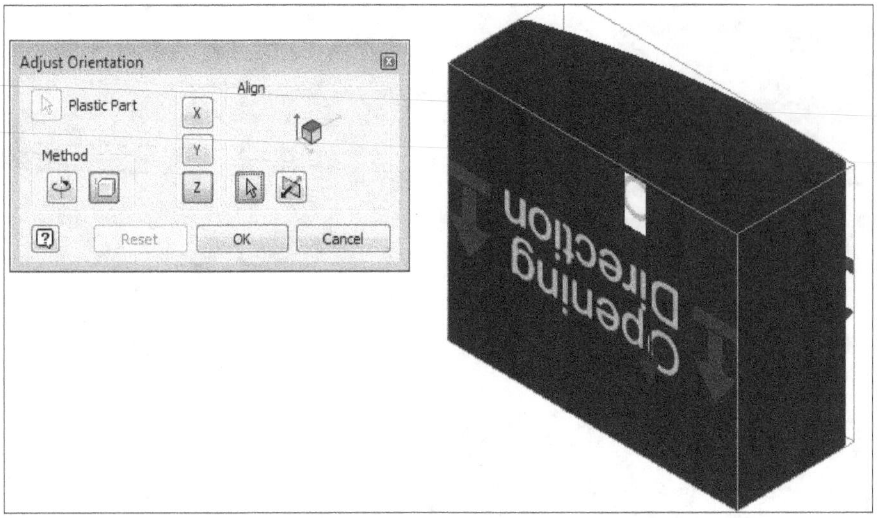

Figure-42. Adjust Orientation dialog box with preview of opening direction

- Make sure **Align with Axis** and **Z** buttons are selected in the dialog box. Select the flat face perpendicular to which you want the opening direction. The orientation of the model will change accordingly; refer to Figure-43.

Figure-43. Part after changing direction

- Flip the part if required by using the **Flip moldable part** button. Click on the **OK** button to set the orientation.

Adjusting Position of Part

- Click on **Adjust Position** tool from the **Adjust Orientation** drop-down in the **Mold Layout** panel of the **Ribbon**; refer to Figure-44. The **Adjust Position** dialog box will be displayed; refer to Figure-45. Also, you will be asked to select a flat face in the direction of opening to specify reference for positioning.

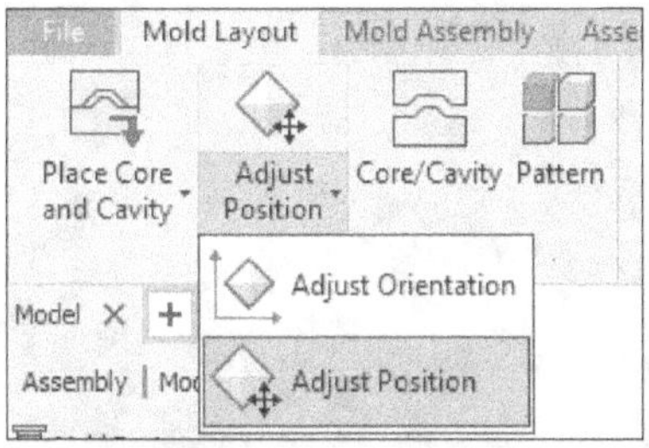

Figure-44. Adjust Position tool

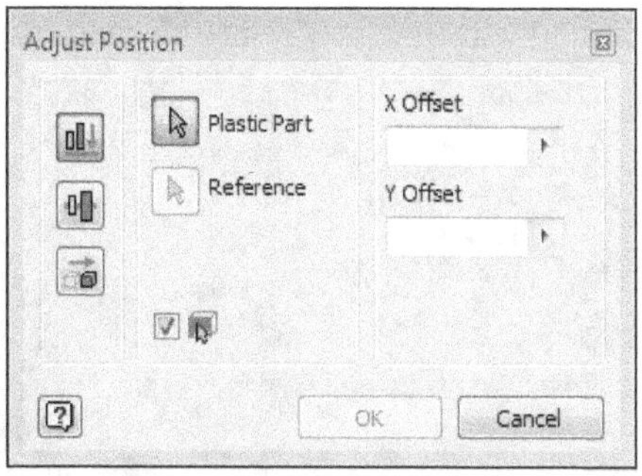

Figure-45. Adjust Position dialog box

- Select desired button from the left area of the dialog box. Select the **Align XY Plane with Reference** button if you want to position the part according to the **XY** plane of coordinate system; refer to Figure-46. Select the **Align Center with X/Y Direction** button if you want to position the plastic part along the X and Y directions of coordinate system selected; refer to Figure-47. Select the **Free Transform** button to position the plastic part freely in X, Y, and Z directions by specifying offset values; refer to Figure-48.

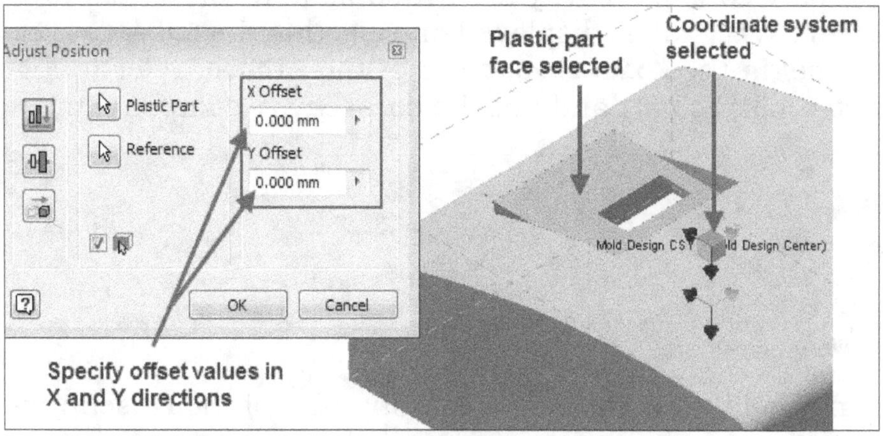

Figure-46. Adjusting position of part in XY plane

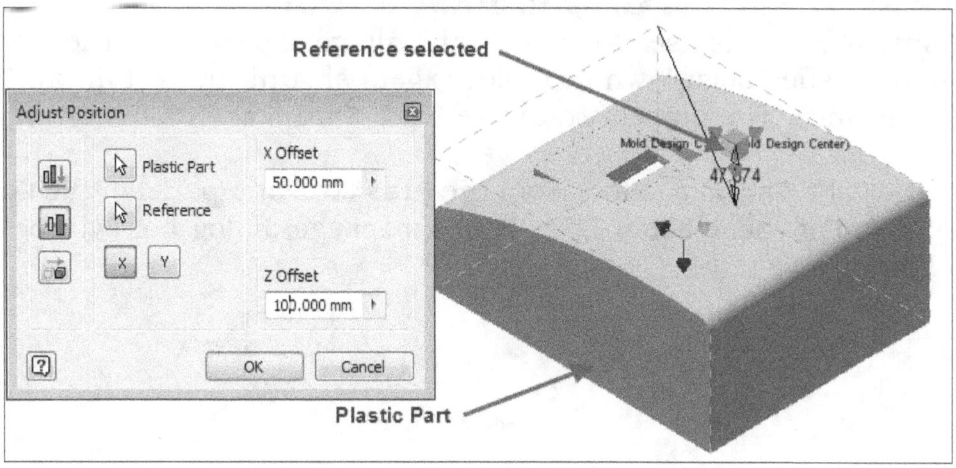

Figure-47. Adjusting position of part in X and Y directions

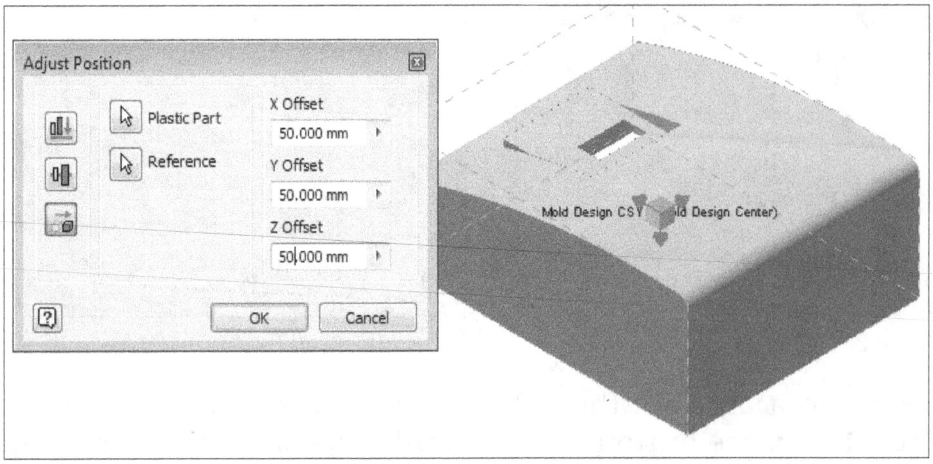

Figure-48. Adjusting position of part freely in X Y and Z directions

- After setting desired position, click on the **OK** button from the dialog box.

PREPARING CORE AND CAVITY

The tools to prepare core and cavity are available in a contextual tab named Core/ Cavity. The **Core/Cavity** tab is displayed on selecting the **Core/Cavity** tool from the **Mold Layout** panel in the **Mold Layout** tab of the **Ribbon**; refer to Figure-49 (when you have inserted plastic part and not the core/cavity components).

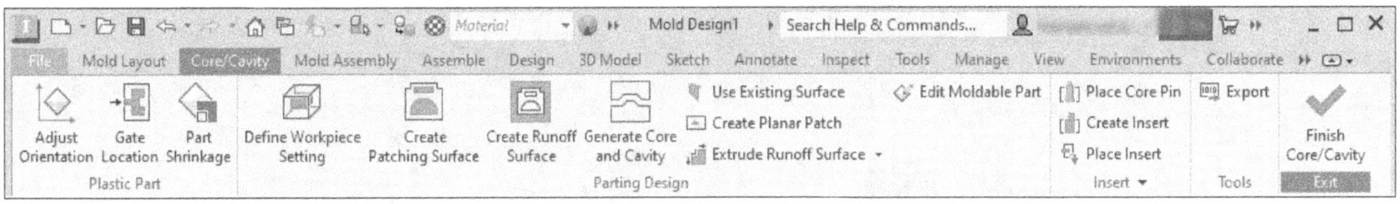

Figure-49. Core-Cavity contextual tab

Various tools in this tab are discussed next in order of their use in mold design.

Part Shrinkage Tool

The **Part Shrinkage** tool is used to provide shrinkage allowance in the plastic model. As the molten plastic cools down in mold, it gets shrunk by certain amount called shrinkage allowance. The procedure to use **Part Shrinkage** tool is given next.

- Click on the **Part Shrinkage** tool from the **Plastic Part** panel in the **Core/Cavity** contextual tab of the **Ribbon**. The **Part Shrinkage** dialog box will be displayed; refer to Figure-50.

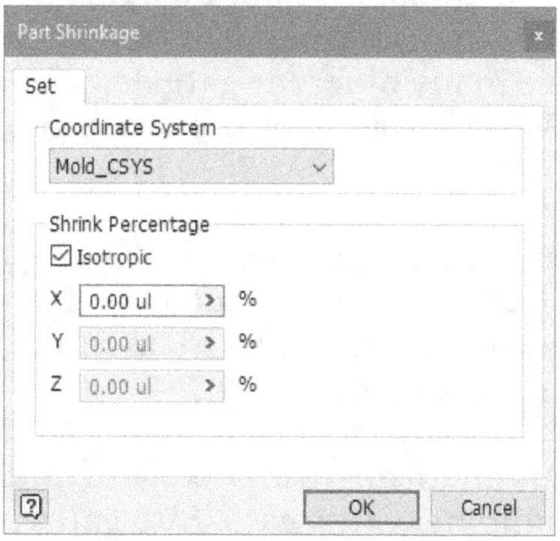

Figure-50. Part Shrinkage dialog box

- Select desired coordinate system from the drop-down in the **Coordinate System** area of the dialog box.
- Select the **Isotropic** check box from **Shrink Percentage** area if the shrinkage is equal in all three directions; X,Y, and Z. If shrinkage is not equal then clear the check box.
- Specify the percentage of shrinkage in the edit boxes of **Shrink Percentage** area.
- Click on the **OK** button to apply the changes.

Gate Location Tool

The **Gate Location** tool is used to specify the location of orifice to be used for filling the molten plastic in the mold. The procedure to use this tool is given next.

- Click on the **Gate Location** tool from the **Plastic Part** panel in the **Core/Cavity** contextual tab in the **Ribbon**. The **Gate Location** dialog box will be displayed; refer to Figure-51.
- Click at desired location on the plastic model to specify gate location.
- Click on the **Apply** button to create the gate location.
- Click on the **Done** button to finish the process.

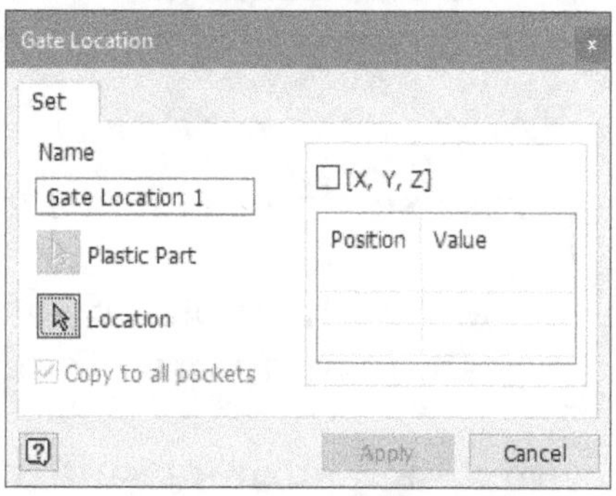

Figure-51. Gate Location dialog box

Gate Design

Although, Autodesk Inventor has a tool to suggest location of gates but there are a few guidelines which will be helpful to reduce rework losses in molding due to gate problems. Here is a short note on gate design:

Common Gate Designs

The largest factor to consider when choosing the proper gate type for your application is the gate design. There are many different gate designs available based on the size and shape of your part. Below are four of the most popular gate designs used by mold makers:

The **Edge Gate** is the most common gate design. As the name indicates, this gate is located on the edge of the part and is best suited for flat parts. Edge gates are ideal for medium and thick sections and can be used on multi-cavity two plate tools. This gate will leave a scar at the parting line.

The **Sub Gate** is the only automatically trimmed gate on the list. Ejector pins will be necessary for automatic trimming of this gate. Sub gates are quite common and have several variations such as banana gate, tunnel gate, and smiley gate to name a few. The sub gate allows you to gate away from the parting line, giving more flexibility to place the gate at an optimum location on the part. This gate leaves a pin sized scar on the part.

The **Hot Tip Gate** is the most common of all hot runner gates. Hot tip gates are typically located at the top of the part rather than on the parting line and are ideal for round or conical shapes where uniform flow is necessary. This gate leaves a small raised nub on the surface of the part. Hot tip gates are only used with hot runner molding systems. This means that, unlike cold runner systems, the plastic is ejected into the mold through a heated nozzle and then cooled to the proper thickness and shape in the mold.

The **Direct or Sprue Gate** is a manually trimmed gate that is used for single cavity molds of large cylindrical parts that require symmetrical filling. Direct gates are the easiest to design and have low cost and maintenance requirements. Direct gated parts are typically lower stressed and provide high strength. This gate leaves a large scar on the part at the point of contact.

Gate Locations

To avoid problems from your gate location, below are some guidelines for choosing the proper gate location(s):

- Place gates at the heaviest cross section to allow for part packing and minimize voids & sink.
- Minimize obstructions in the flow path by placing gates away from cores & pins.
- Be sure that stress from the gate is in an area that will not affect part function or aesthetics.
- If you are using a plastic with a high shrink grade, the part may shrink near the gate causing “gate pucker” if there is high molded-in stress at the gate.
- Be sure to allow for easy manual or automatic de-gating.
- Gate should minimize flow path length to avoid cosmetic flow marks.
- In some cases, it may be necessary to add a second gate to properly fill the parts.
- If filling problems occur with thin walled parts, add flow channels or make wall thickness adjustments to correct the flow.

- Sometimes, two gates are not better than one. When we fill melt through two gates then a weld line is formed at the middle of the gates. If this weld lines falls on highly stresses area of the part then your product will fail in its applications.
- If a part is round and needs to be absolutely round then you need to gate it in the center.
- If a part is long and narrow and needs to be absolutely straight then you need to gate it on the end.
- Try to gate into the thickest area and avoid gating into a thin area. Failure to do so can result in voids (air bubbles).

Practical Issues with Pressure and Temperature Parameters

There are a few issues that can cause problem in mold which are discussed next.

Excessive Injection Fill Speed

The speed and pressure of the melt as it enters the mold determine both density and consistency of melt in packing the mold. If the fill is too fast, the material tends to "slip" over the surface and will "skin" over before the rest of the material solidifies. The slipped skin area does not faithfully reproduce the mold steel surface, as does the material in other areas, because it has not been packed tightly against the steel.

Solution: One solution is to adjust the fill speed rate until the optimum has been achieved. This will help eliminate blushing.

Melt Temperature Too High Or Too Low

Although this may sound contradictory, either condition might cause blushing. If the injection barrel heat is too high, the material will flow too quickly, resulting in slippage of the surface skin, as mentioned above. If the barrel heat is too low, the material may solidify before full packing occurs and the plastic will not be pushed against the mold steel, especially in the gate area because that is the last area to pack.

Solution: Melt temperature must be adjusted to the optimum for a specific material and specific product design.

Low Injection Pressure

The plastic material must be injected into the mold in such a way as to cause proper filling and packing while maintaining consistent solidification of the melt. Injection pressure is one of the main control variables of the machine and must be high enough to pack the plastic molecules against the steel of the mold while the plastic cools. Low pressure will not achieve this packing and the material will appear dull in local areas that do not have enough pressure.

Solution: Increasing the injection pressure forces the material against the mold surface, producing a truer finish that replicates the steel finish.

Low Mold Temperature

A low mold temperature may cause the molten material to slow down and solidify before the mold is packed out. This will cause dull areas where the plastic was not forced against the steel finish.

Solution: Increasing the mold temperature allows the material to flow farther and pack properly. The material temperature could also be raised to accomplish the same effect.

Define Workpiece Setting Tool

The **Define Workpiece Setting** tool is used to create a block of steel from which the core and cavity is to be cut. The procedure to use this tool is given next.

- Click on the **Define Workpiece Setting** tool from the **Parting Design** panel in the **Core/Cavity** contextual tab of the **Ribbon**. The **Define Workpiece Setting** dialog box will be displayed; refer to Figure-52.

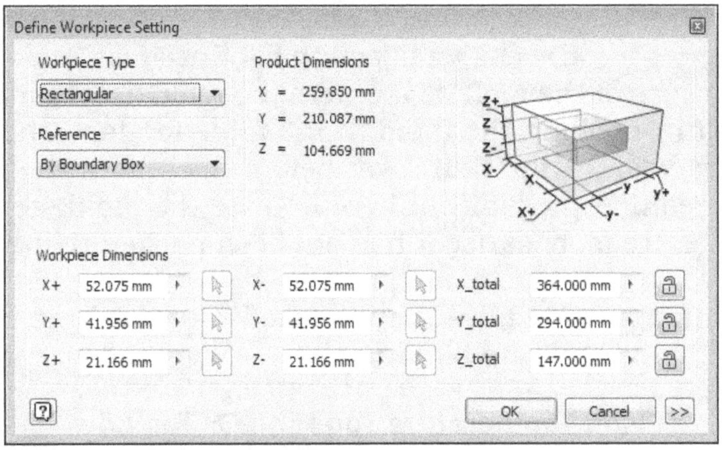

Figure-52. Define Workpiece Setting dialog box

- Select the shape of work piece from the **Workpiece Type** drop-down in the dialog box suitable for your mold base. There are two options in the drop-down; **Rectangular** and **Cylinder** to create rectangular and cylindrical workpiece, respectively.
- Specify the dimensions as per your requirement in the **Workpiece Dimensions** area of the dialog box.
- Click on the **OK** button. A transparent workpiece will be created around your plastic part; refer

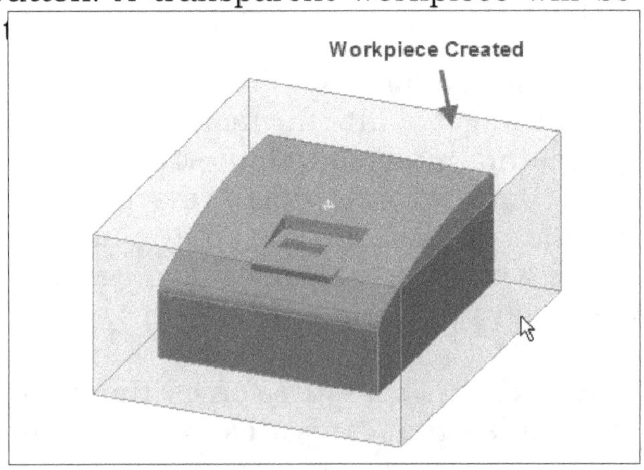

Figure-53. Workpiece created around plastic part

Create Patching Surface Tool

The **Create Patching Surface** tool is used to patch the cuts and holes in the model so that the core and cavity can be separated. The procedure to use this tool is given next.

- Click on the **Create Patching Surface** tool from the **Parting Design** panel in the **Core/Cavity** contextual tab of the **Ribbon**. The **Create Patching Surface** dialog box will be displayed; refer to Figure-54.

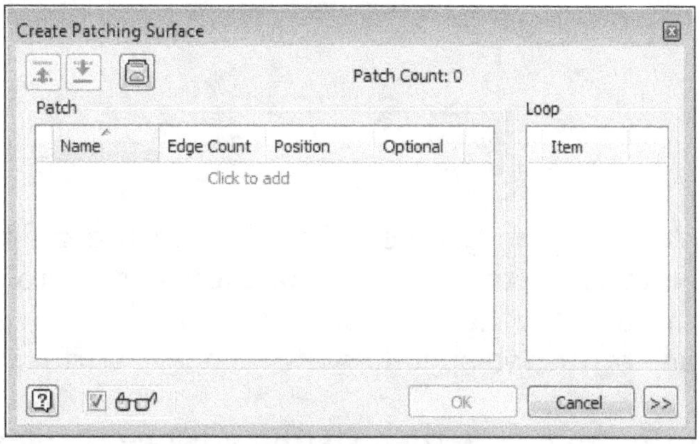

Figure-54. Create Patching Surface dialog box

- Click on the **Auto Detect** button from the dialog box. Preview of the patches will be displayed; refer to Figure-55.

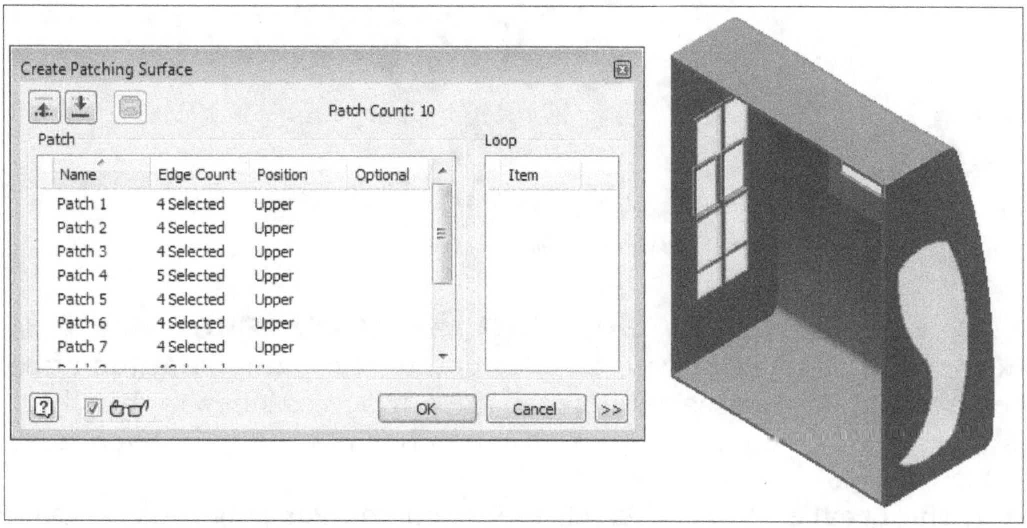

Figure-55. Preview of patches

- If you want to switch between upper and lower position of the patches then click on the **All Upper** or **All Lower** button from the dialog box.
- Click on the **OK** button from the dialog box to create the patch surface.

Use Existing Surface

The **Use Existing Surface** tool is used to designate an existing surface as either a patching surface or a runoff surface. The procedure to use this tool is discussed next.

- Click on the **Use Existing Surface** tool from the **Parting Design** panel in the **Core/Cavity** contextual tab of the **Ribbon**. The **Use Existing Surface** dialog box will be displayed; refer to Figure-56.

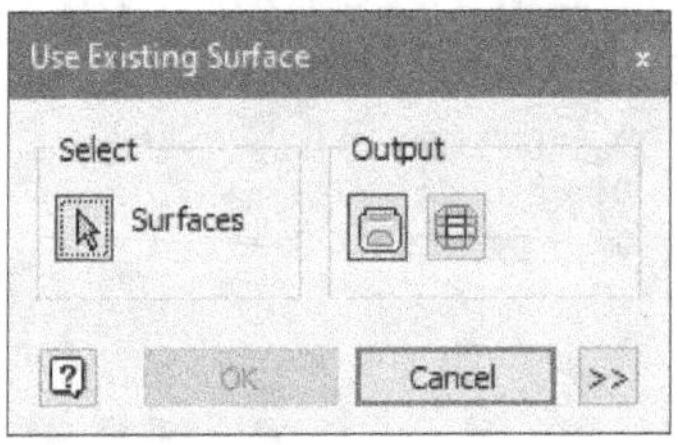

Figure-56. Use existing surface dialog box

- Select desired surface to specify a set of surface in the graphic window.
- Select **Patching Surface** button from the **Output** section to specifies the selected surface to convert to a patching surface.
- Select **Runoff Surface** button to specifies the selected surface to convert to a runoff surface.
- Click on the **OK** button to create the existing surface. The **Existing Surface** will be created; refer to Figure-57.

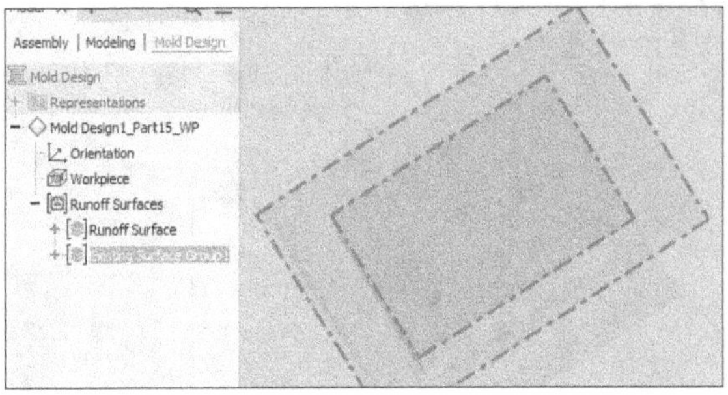

Figure-57. Existing surface created

Manually Creating Patch Surface

Using the previous tool, you were able to create the patches automatically. But, sometimes it becomes necessary to create the surface patches manually to achieve desired shape. The procedure to create the patches manually is given next.

- Click on the **Create Planar Patch** tool from the **Parting Design** panel in the **Core/Cavity** contextual tab of the **Ribbon**. The **Create Planar Patch** dialog box will be displayed; refer to Figure-58. Also, you will be asked to select connective edges to create surface patch.

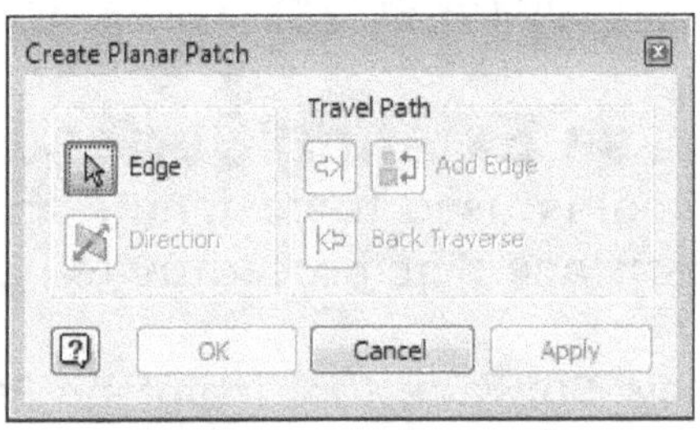

Figure-58. Create Planar Patch dialog box

- Select an edge of cut to be patched. The tools in the dialog box will become active and preview will be displayed; refer to Figure-59.

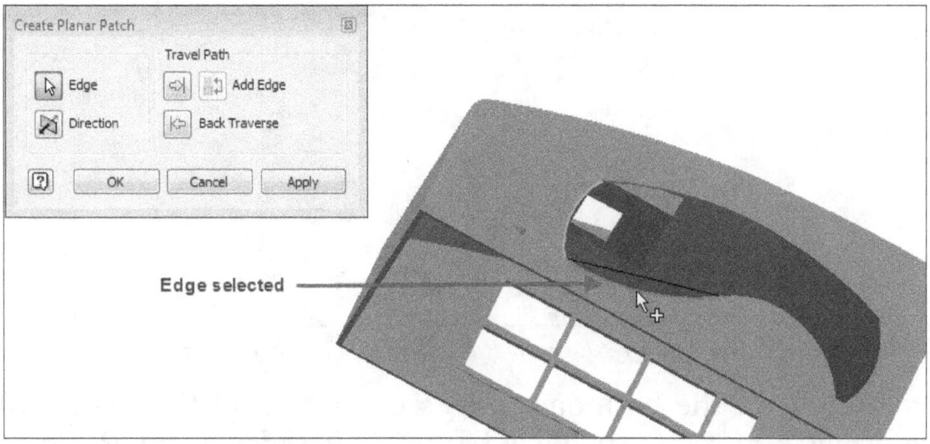

Figure-59. Preview of patch surface

- The orange colored edge in preview is next suggested edge to be selected. The black line in preview closing the selected edge into a loop is generated automatically and if we click on the **Apply** button now then this loop will become surface patch.
- Click on the **Add Edge** button in the **Travel Path** area of the dialog box to select the next suggested edge. Repeat this step until you get desired loop to create surface patch.
- To revert back in edge selection, click on the **Back Traverse** button in the **Travel Path** area of the dialog box.
- Click on the **OK** button to create the surface patch; refer to Figure-60.

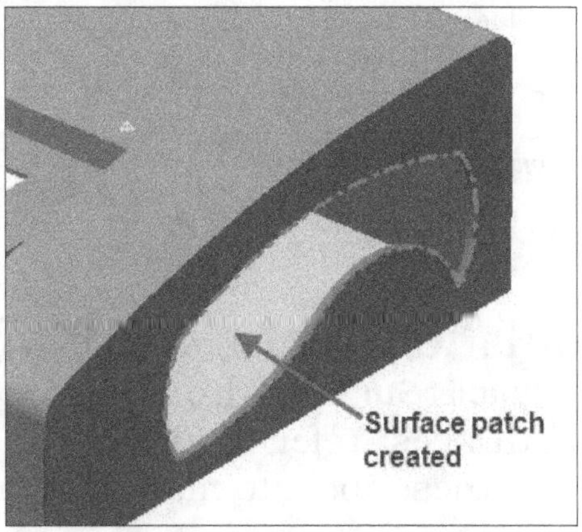

Figure-60. Planar surface patch created

Create Runoff Surface Tool

The **Create Runoff Surface** tool is used to create surface using the outer boundary edges of the model. This surface acts as a splitting tool to split core and cavity steel. The procedure to use this tool is given next.

- Click on the **Create Runoff Surface** tool from the **Parting Design** panel of the **Core/Cavity** contextual tab in the **Ribbon**. The **Create Runoff Surface** dialog box will be displayed; refer to Figure-61.

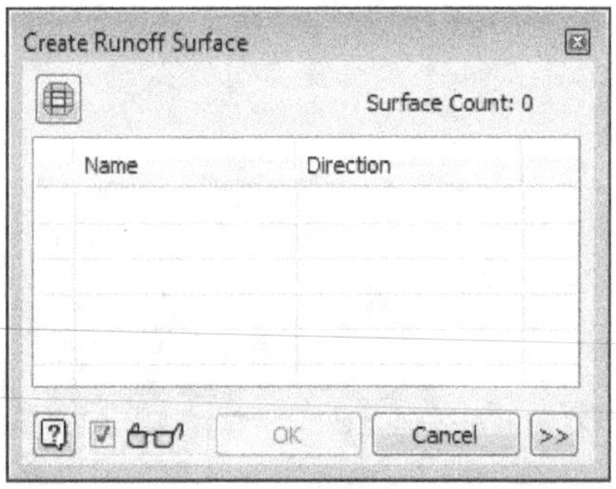

Figure-61. Create Runoff Surface dialog box

- One by one click on the boundary edges of the model to create runoff surface manually or click on the **Auto Detect** button. Preview of the Runoff surface will be displayed; refer to Figure-62.

Figure-62. Preview of runoff surface

- Click on the **OK** button to create the surface.

Other Tools to Create Runoff Surfaces

There are four tools in the **Runoff Surface** drop-down in **Parting Design** panel of the **Ribbon** to create runoff surfaces; refer to Figure-63. Besides the **Create Runoff Surface** tool, you can also use these tools to manually create runoff surfaces.

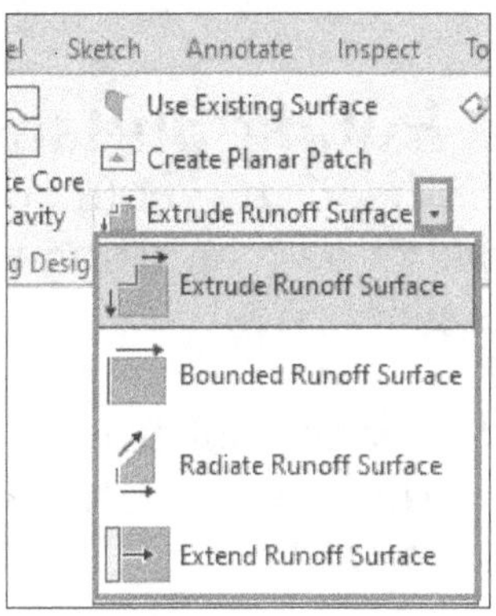

Figure-63. Runoff Surface drop-down

The application of each tool is discussed next.

Extrude Runoff Surface Tool

The **Extrude Runoff Surface** tool is used to create a runoff surface by extruding the selected curve/edge. The procedure to use this tool is given next.

- Click on the **Extrude Runoff Surface** tool from the **Runoff Surface** drop-down in the **Parting Design** panel of **Ribbon**. The **Extrude Runoff Surface** dialog box will be displayed; refer to Figure-64. Also, you will be asked to select the edges for creating extruded runoff surface.

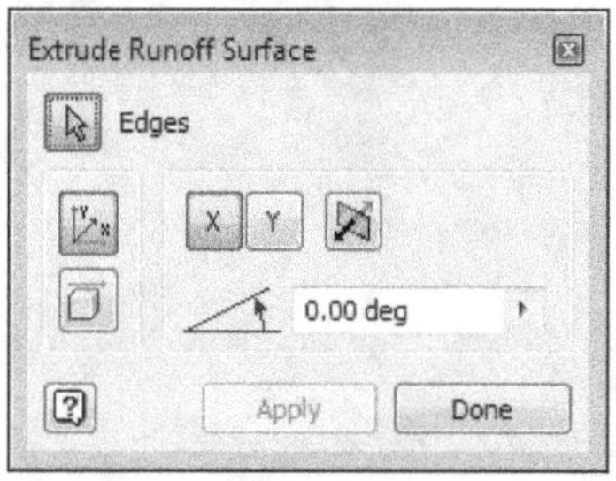

Figure-64. Extrude Runoff Surface dialog box

- Select an edge and then select the **X** or **Y** button to specify the direction of extrusion. Preview of the extruded surface will be displayed; refer to Figure-65. Click on the **Flip** button to change the side of extrusion if required.

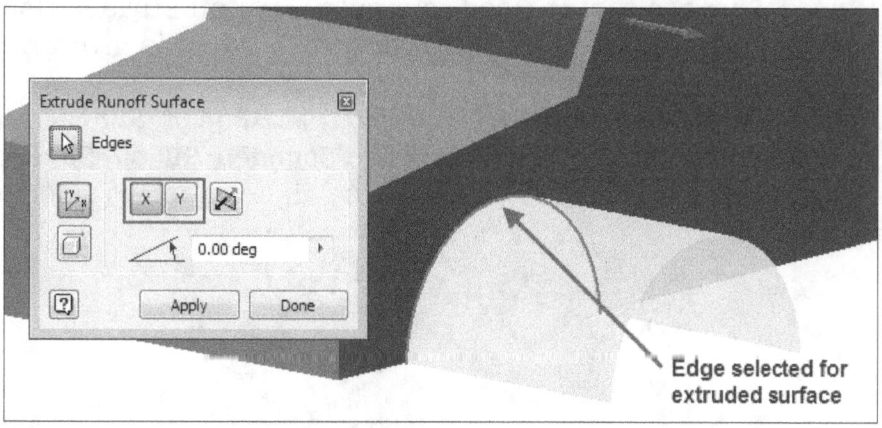

Figure-65. Preview of extruded runoff surface

- If you want to use any axis or edge to specify direction of extrusion then click on the **Align Axis** button from the dialog box and select the reference edge/axis to specify direction; refer to Figure-66.

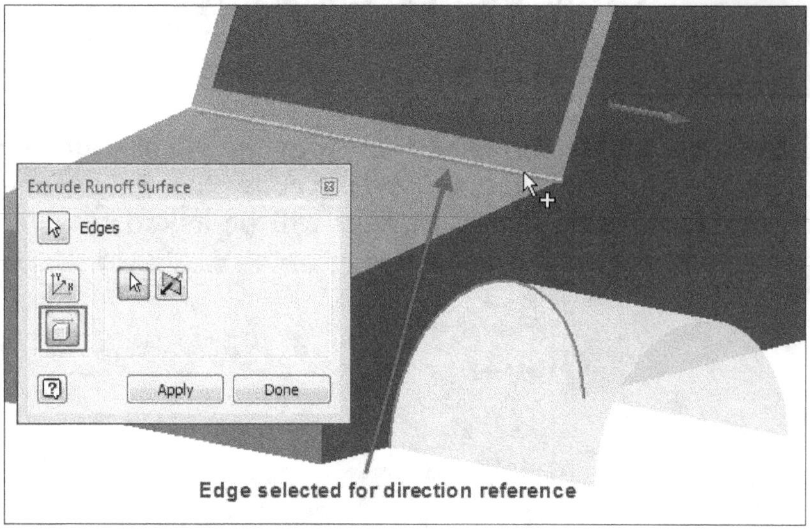

Figure-66. Edge selected for direction reference

- Click on the **Apply** button to create the surface and then click on the **Done** button to exit the dialog box.

Bounded Runoff Surface Tool

The **Bounded Runoff Surface** tool is used to create a runoff surface using the region bounded by selected curves. The procedure to use this tool is given next.

- Click on the **Bounded Runoff Surface** tool from the **Runoff Surface** drop-down in the **Parting Design** panel of the **Ribbon**. The **Bounded Runoff Surface** dialog box will be displayed; refer to Figure-67. Also, you will be asked to select the geometry for creating surface.

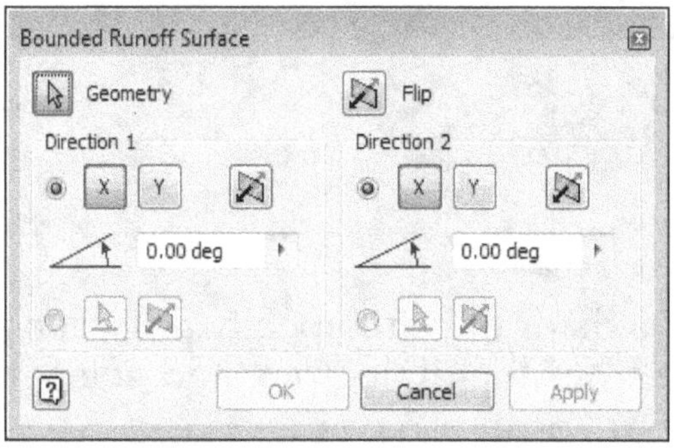

Figure-67. Bounded Runoff Surface dialog box

- Select the curve/edge of the plastic model to be used for creating bounded runoff surface. Preview of the surface will be displayed; refer to Figure-68.

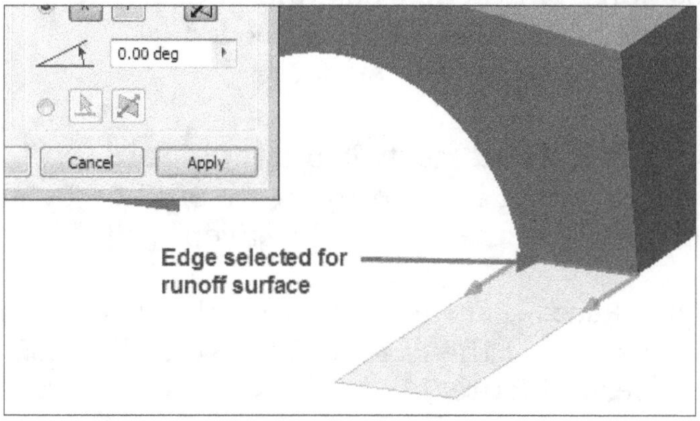

Figure-68. Preview of bounded runoff surface

- Set the other parameters as required and then click on the **OK** button to create the surface.

Radiate Runoff Surface Tool

The **Radiate Runoff Surface** tool is used to create non-planar runoff surfaces based on the selected curves. The procedure to use this tool is given next.

- Click on the **Radiate Runoff Surface** tool from the **Runoff Surface** drop-down in the **Parting Design** panel of the **Ribbon**. The **Radiate Runoff Surface** dialog box will be displayed; refer to Figure-69.

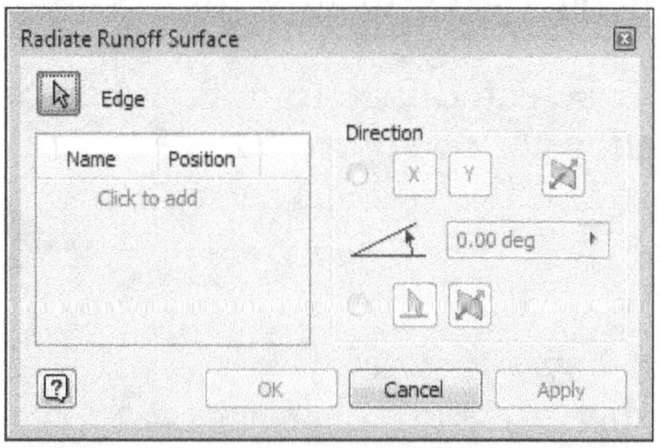

Figure-69. Radiate Runoff Surface dialog box

- Select the curve to create the surface. Preview of the surface will be displayed; refer to Figure-70.

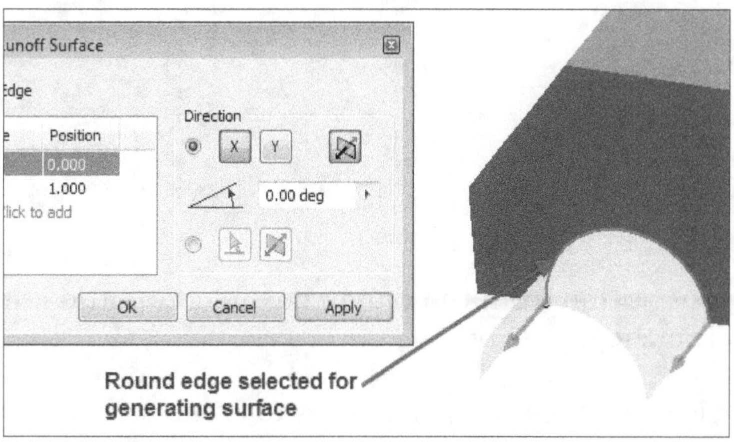

Figure-70. Preview of the radiate runoff surface

- Select desired position from the list box and change the direction using options in the **Direction** area of the dialog box, if needed.
- Click on the **OK** button to create the surface.

Extend Runoff Surface Tool

The **Extend Runoff Surface** tool is used to create surface by extending an edge of selected face. The procedure to use this tool is given next.

- Click on the **Extend Runoff Surface** tool from the **Runoff Surface** drop-down in the **Parting Design** panel of the **Ribbon**. The **Extend Runoff Surface** dialog box will be displayed; refer to Figure-71.

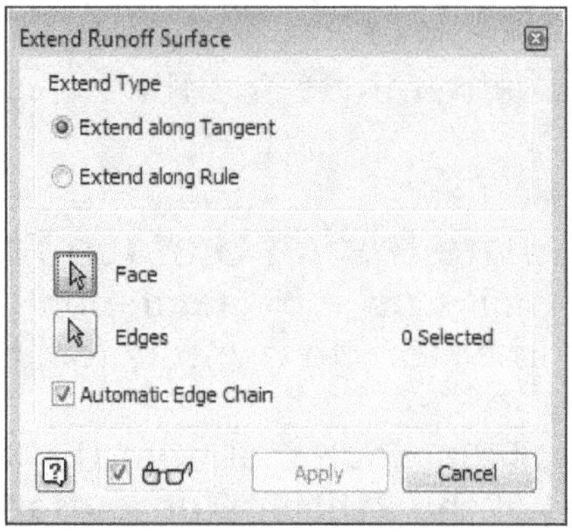

Figure-71. Extend Runoff Surface dialog box

- Select the face of plastic part which you want to extend to create runoff surface. You will be asked to select an edge.
- Select the edge of earlier selected face to define side of extension. Preview of the surface will be displayed; refer to Figure-72.

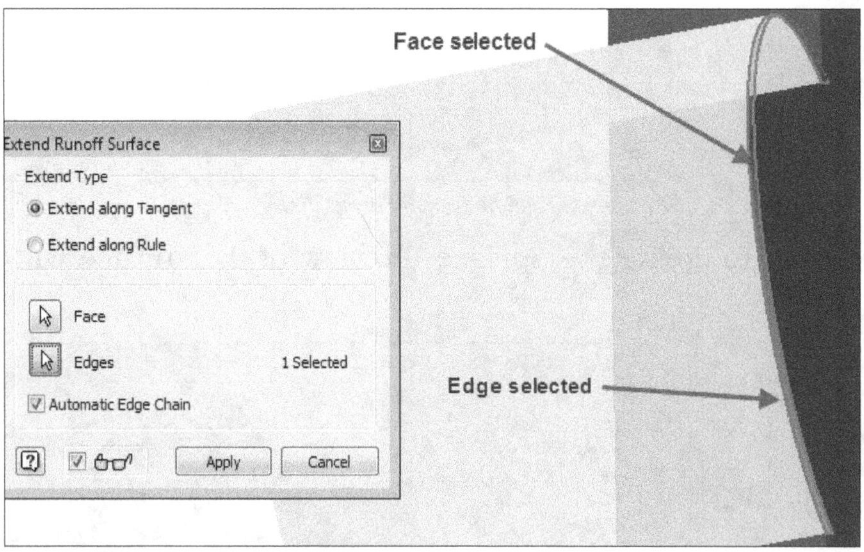

Figure-72. Preview of extend runoff surface

- Click on the **Apply** button from the dialog box to create the surface. Click on the **Done** button to exit the dialog box.

Although, we have learned the necessary steps to create core and cavity but there is one more tool which is important to discuss so that you can create core and cavity with sliders (inserts).

Edit Moldable Part

The **Edit Moldable Part** tool is used to activate the moldable part file while hiding the visibility of all other components. The procedure to use this tool is discussed next.

- Click on the **Edit Moldable Part** tool from the **Parting Design** panel of the **Ribbon**. The **3D** model environment will be displayed along with the moldable part to edit; refer to Figure-73.

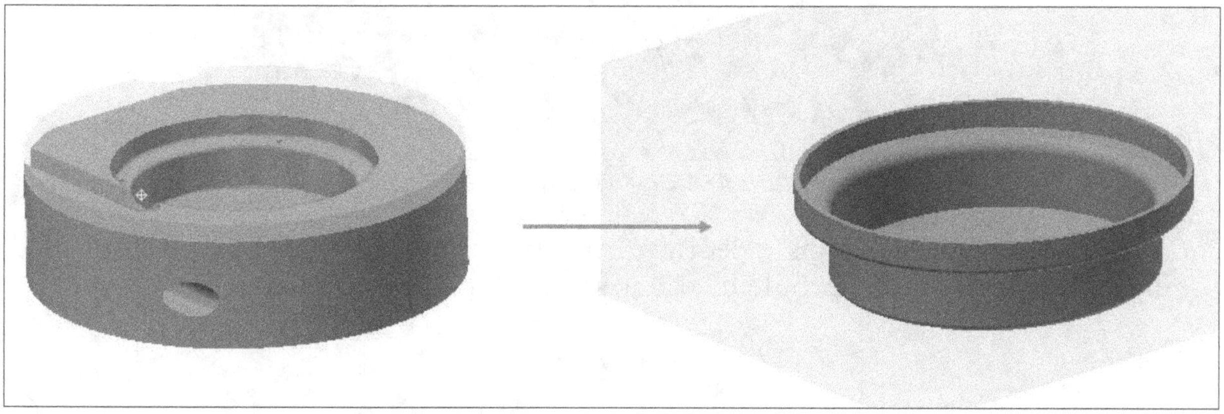

Figure-73. Edit moldable part displayed

Create Insert Tool

The **Create Insert** tool is used to create sliders or say inserts so that features with undercuts can be created in the plastic part. The procedure to use this tool is given next.

- Click on the **Create Insert** tool from the **Insert** panel in the **Core/Cavity** contextual tab of the **Ribbon**. The **Create Insert** dialog box will be displayed; refer to Figure-74. Also, you will be asked to specify the starting face of the insert.

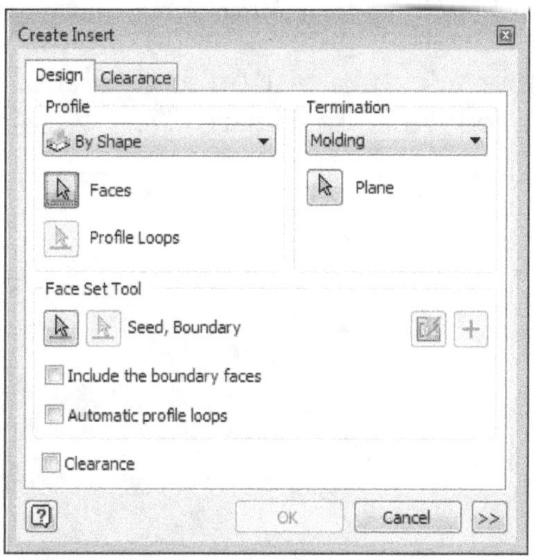

Figure-74. Create Insert dialog box

- Select the face/faces that you want to be head of the insert; refer to Figure-75.

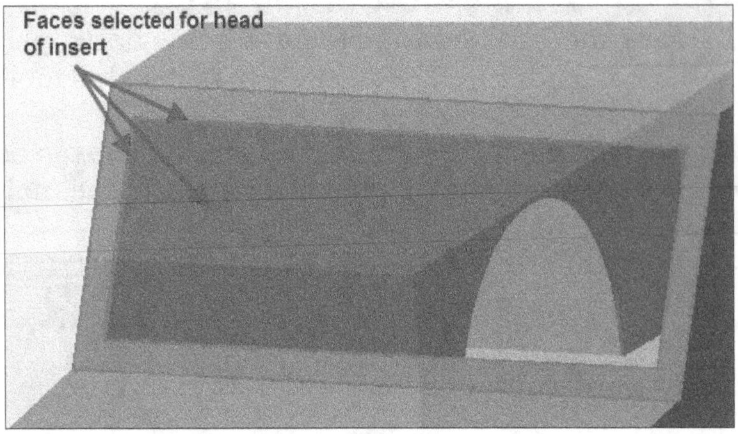

Figure-75. Faces selected for head of insert

- Click on the **Profile Loops** selection button from the dialog box and select the curves to specify outer profile of the insert; refer to Figure-76.

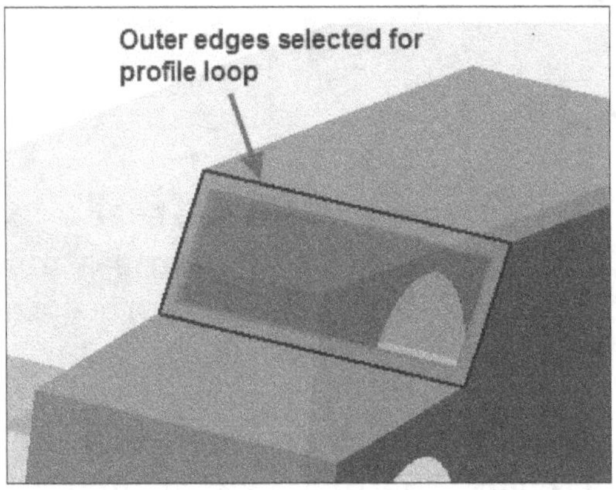

Figure-76. Edges selected for profile loop

- Select the **Molding** option from the drop-down in **Termination** area of the dialog box if you want the terminating face to be on mold. After selecting the **Molding** option, click on the **Plane** selection button and select the face of mold. Preview of the insert will be displayed; refer to Figure-77.

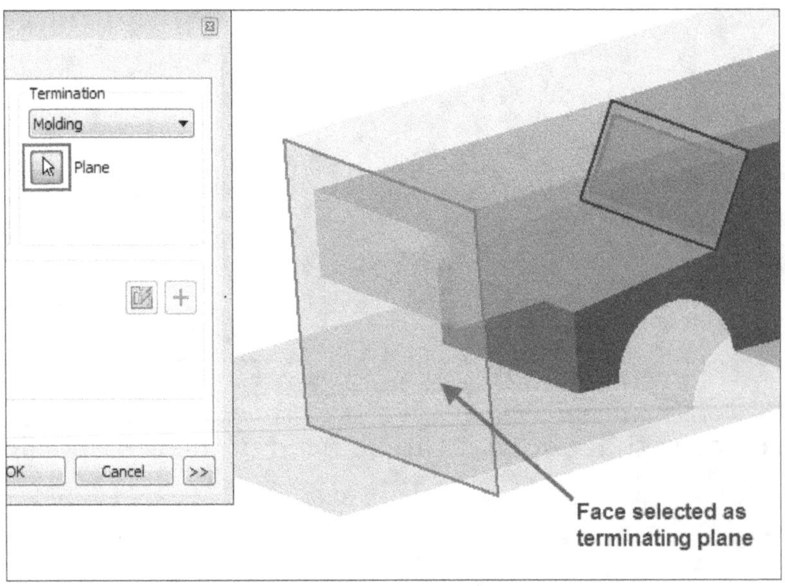

Figure-77. Preview of insert with molding termination

Or

- Select the **Distance** option from the drop-down in the **Termination** area of the dialog box if you want to specify the direction and length of the insert. On selecting the **Distance** option, you will be asked to select a direction reference. Select the face perpendicular to which you want to create the insert and specify desired length in the edit box displayed in **Termination** area of the dialog box. Preview of the insert will be displayed; refer to Figure-78.

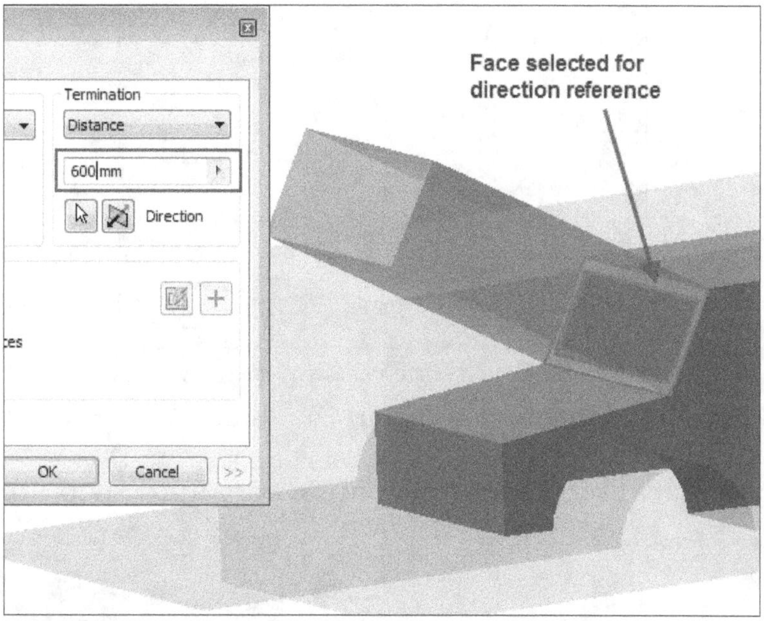

Figure-78. Preview of insert with distance termination

- Using the tools in the **Face Set Tool** area, you can define the shape of side faces of the insert.
- Select the **Clearance** check box and specify the required value of clearance for easy extraction of insert. Expand the dialog box by clicking on the **More** button and specify the clearance value in the edit box displayed; refer to Figure-79.

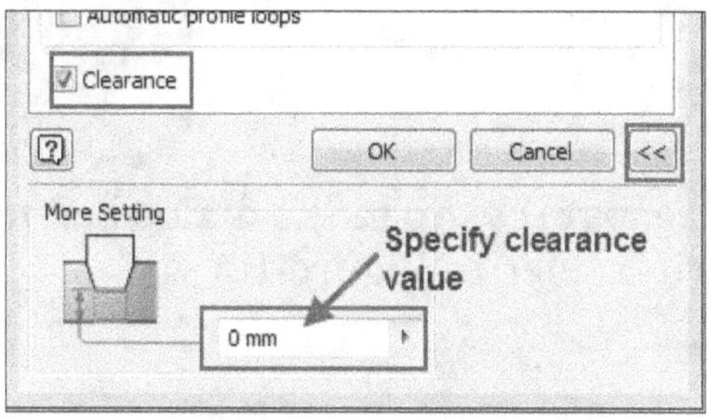

Figure-79. Specifying clearance value for insert

- Click on the **OK** button from the dialog box to create the insert.

Now, we are ready to generate the core and cavity. The tool is discussed next.

Generate Core and Cavity

The **Generate Core and Cavity** tool is used to generate the core and cavity based on specified parameters. The procedure to use this tool is given next.

- Click on the **Generate Core and Cavity** tool from the **Parting Design** panel of the **Core/Cavity** contextual tab in the **Ribbon**. The **Generate Core and Cavity** dialog box will be displayed; refer to Figure-80.

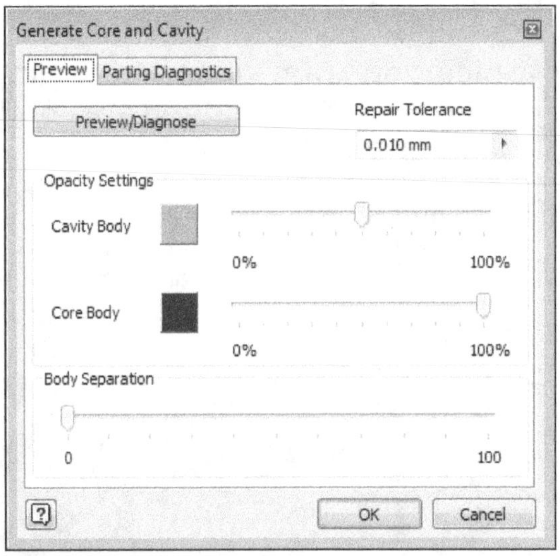

Figure-80. Generate Core and Cavity dialog box

- Click on the **Preview/Diagnose** button in the dialog box. Preview of the core and cavity will be displayed.
- Move the **Body Separation** slider to separate core and cavity; refer to Figure-81.

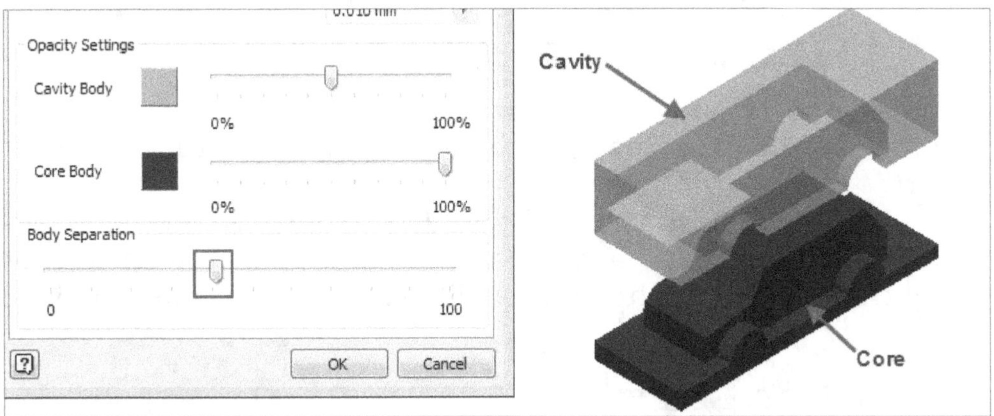

Figure-81. Separated core and cavity preview

- Click on the **Parting Diagnostics** tab in the dialog box to check the list of problems in current core and cavity; refer to Figure-82.

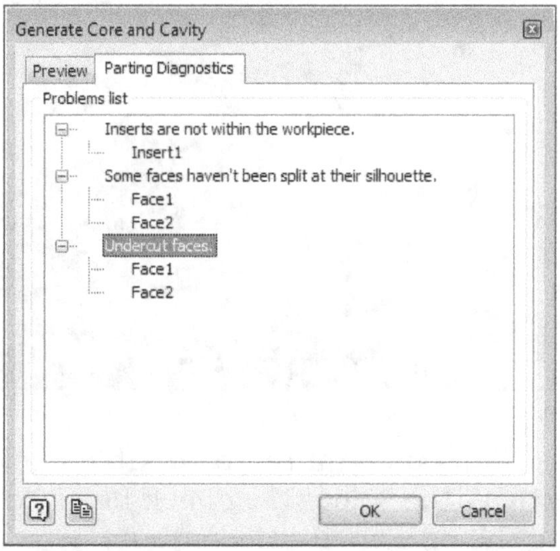

Figure-82. Parting Diagnostics tab in Generate Core and Cavity dialog box

- Click on the **Cancel** button and perform the changes in model as necessary to eradicate the problems.
- If you find that the problems displayed in the dialog box do not affect the molding quality then click on the **OK** button from the dialog box to create core and cavity.

Placing Core Pin

The **Place Core Pin** tool is used to place core pins in the core to create hole or cavity in the plastic part. The procedure to use this tool is given next.

- Click on the **Place Core Pin** tool from the **Insert** panel in the **Core/Cavity** contextual tab of the **Ribbon**. The **Place Core Pin** dialog box will be displayed; refer to Figure-83. Also, you will be asked to select a face to specify position of the core pin.

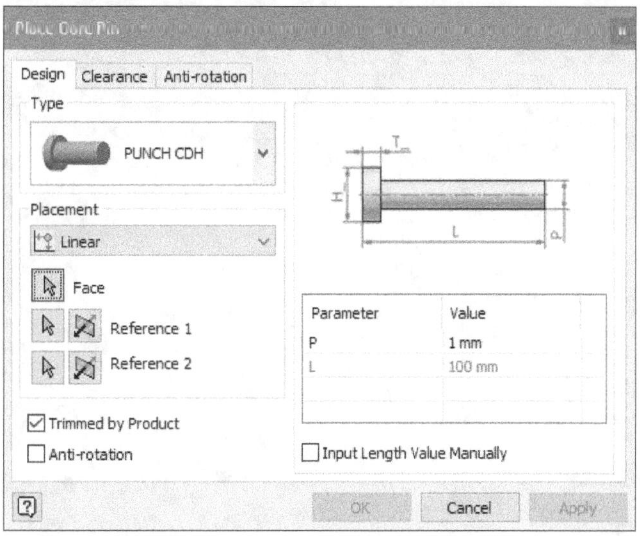

Figure-83. Place Core Pin dialog box

- Select the face on mold. You will be asked to specify first reference. Select an edge of the mold or plastic model in first direction. You will be asked to select second reference.
- Select the other edge of mold/plastic model in second direction. Preview of the core pin will be displayed; refer to Figure-84.

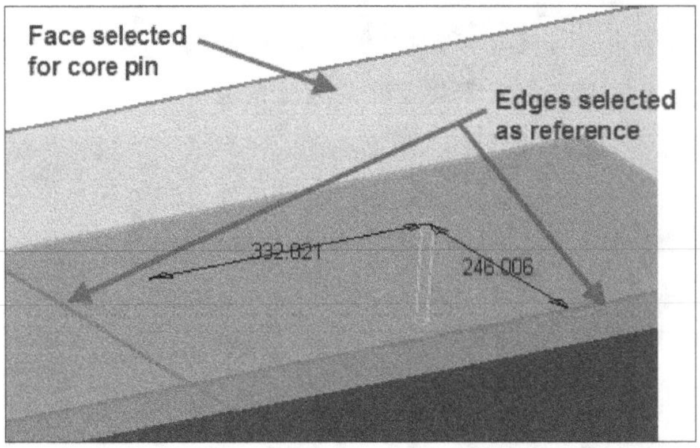

Figure-84. Preview of core pin

- Set the values of dimensions as required by double-clicking on them.
- Select the **Input Length Value Manually** check box and specify the diameters & length of the pin using the options in the list box.
- Set the other options as required and then click on the **OK** button. The core pin will be created.

Placing Insert

The **Place Insert** tool is used to add a previously created insert into the mold assembly. The procedure to use this tool is discussed next.

- Click on the **Place Insert** tool from the **Insert** panel in the **Core/Cavity** contextual tab of the **Ribbon**. The **Place Insert** dialog box will be displayed; refer to Figure-85.

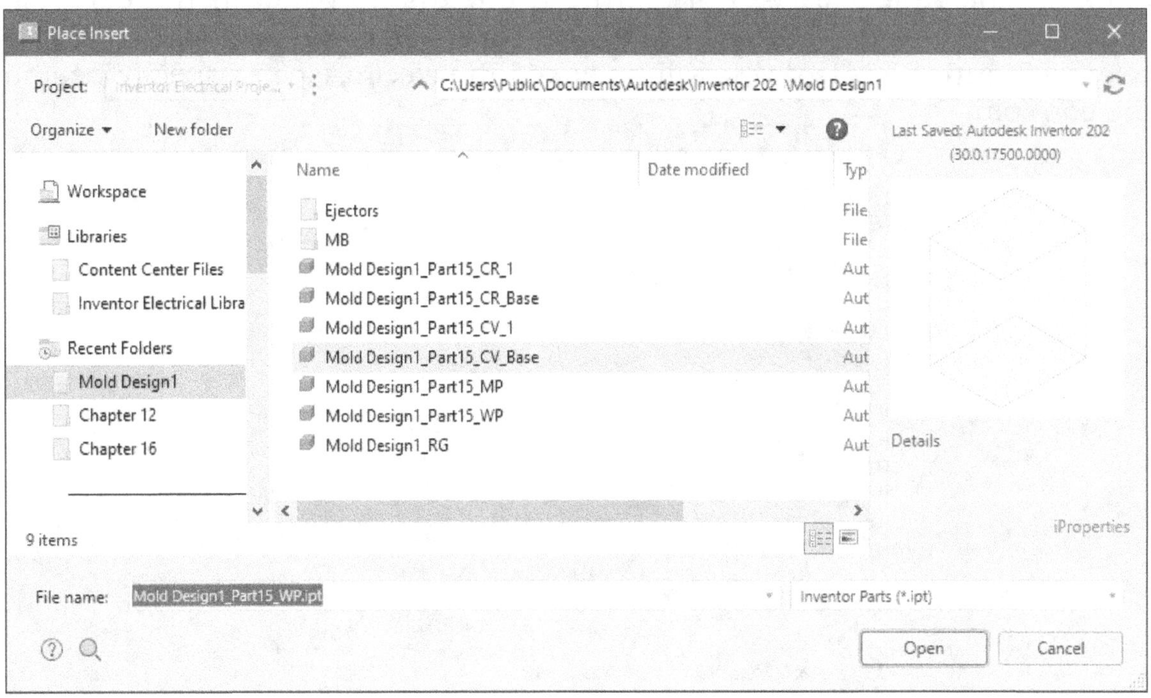

Figure-85. Place Insert dialog box

- Select desired file from the dialog box and click on the **Open** button. The inserted will be attached to cursor you will be asked to place the part.
- Click at desired location to place the part. The part will be inserted; refer to Figure-86 and the **Assemble** contextual tab will be displayed.

- Apply assembly constraints as needed and click on the **Return** button to exit the assembly environment.

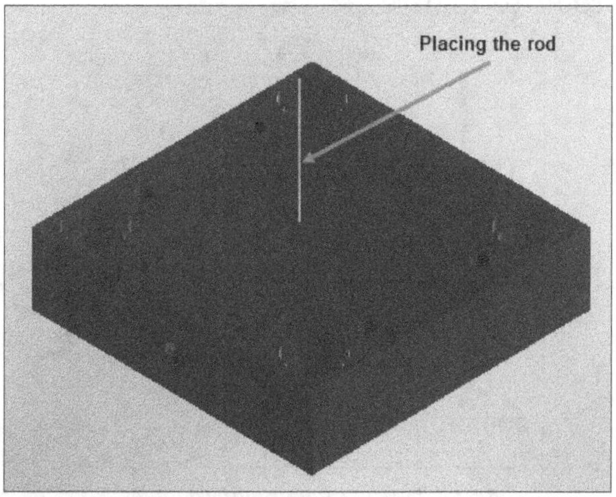

Figure-86. Inserting to place

Once you have performed the operations related to core and cavity generation then click on the **Finish Core/Cavity** button from the **Exit** panel in the **Core/Cavity** contextual tab of the **Ribbon** to exit the contextual tab.

CREATING PATTERN OF CORE AND CAVITY

For smaller parts, we create multiple core and cavities in the same mold to get many molded parts at a time. To facilitate this process, we create pattern of core and cavity in Autodesk Inventor. The procedure to do so is given next.

- Click on the **Pattern** tool from the **Mold Layout** panel in the **Mold Layout** tab of the **Ribbon**. The **Pattern** dialog box will be displayed; refer to Figure-87.

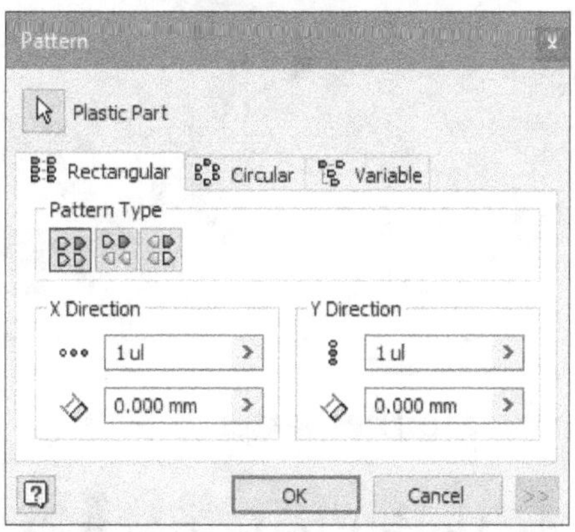

Figure-87. Pattern dialog box

Rectangular Pattern

- By default, the **Rectangular** tab is selected in the dialog box and hence you can create rectangular pattern of the molds.
- Specify desired number of instances and distance between them in the edit boxes of **X Direction** and **Y Direction** areas of the dialog box.
- Select the **Base Pattern**, **X Balance**, or **Y Balance** button from the **Pattern Type** area of the dialog box to specify the pattern type.
- Click on the **OK** button to create the pattern.

Circular Pattern

- Click on the **Circular** tab of the **Pattern** dialog box to display the options related to circular pattern; refer to Figure-88.

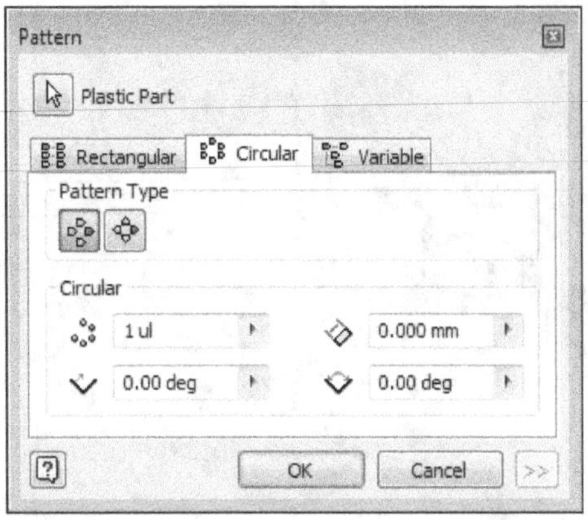

Figure-88. Circular tab in Pattern dialog box

- Specify the number of instances in the **Count** edit box. Specify the radius of circle in the **Radius** edit box. Specify the rotational angle of instance around its center points in the **Rotational Angle** edit box. Specify the space angle between the instances in the **Pattern Angle** edit box.
- Select the **Base Pattern** or **Radial Pattern** button from the **Pattern Type** area to specify the type of pattern. Preview of the pattern will be displayed; refer to Figure-89.

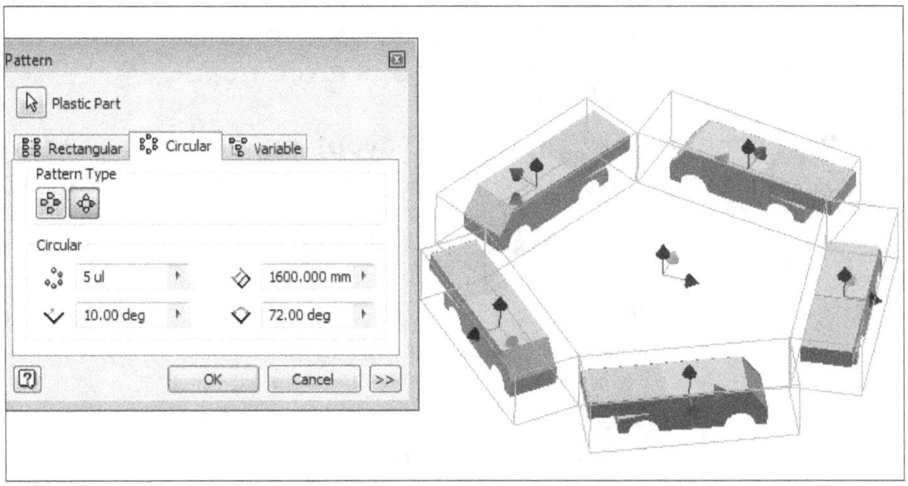

Figure-89. Preview of pattern

- Click on the **OK** button to create the pattern.

Variable Pattern

- Click on the **Variable** tab in the **Pattern** dialog box. The dialog box will be displayed as shown in Figure-90.

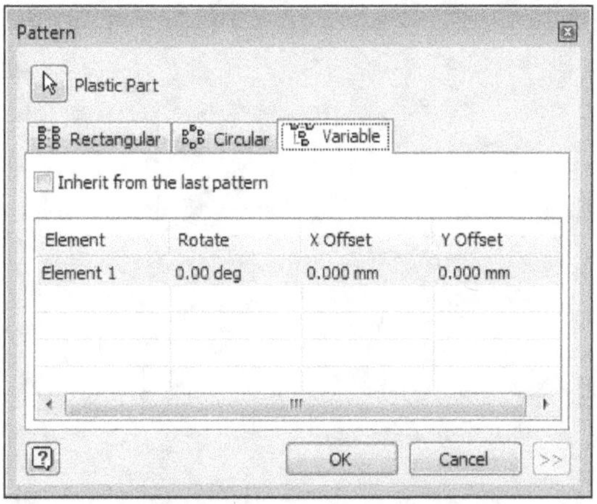

Figure-90. Variable tab in Pattern dialog box

- Right-click in the list box and select the **Add** option from the shortcut menu displayed; refer to Figure-91. A new instance will be added.
- Specify the rotation, x offset, and y offset as required by using the table in the list box.
- Repeat the procedure until you get required number of instances.

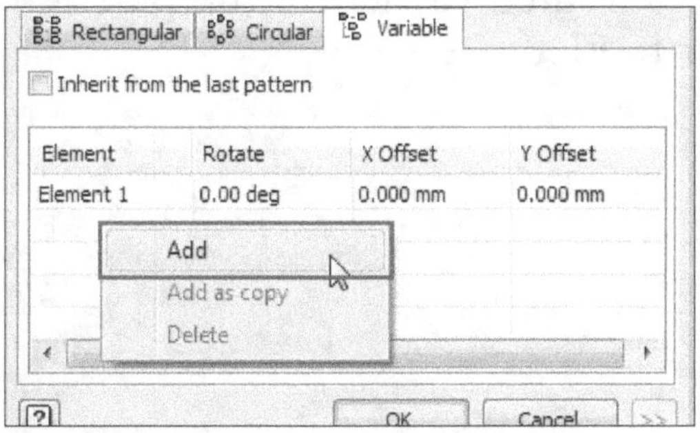

Figure-91. Add option for variable pattern

- Click on the **OK** button to create the pattern.

CREATING GATE

Earlier, we have learned to specify the location of gate. Now, we will learn to define the shape of gate. The procedure to do so is given next.

- Click on the **Gate** tool from the **Runners and Channels** panel of the **Mold Layout** tab in the **Ribbon**. The **Create Gate** dialog box will be displayed; refer to Figure-92.

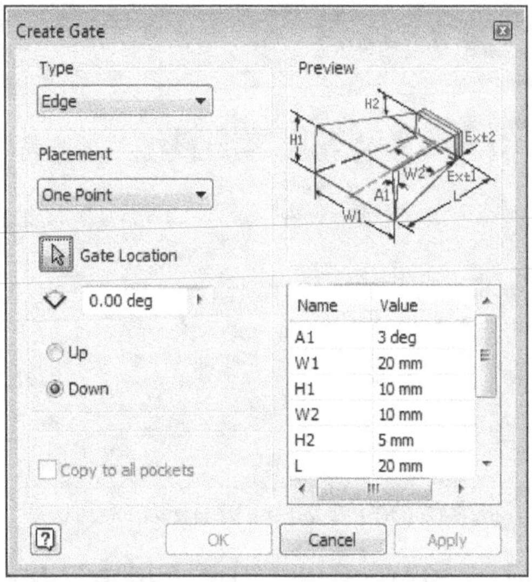

Figure-92. Create Gate dialog box

- Select the type of gate from the **Type** drop-down in the dialog box. You will be asked to select a gate location to place gate. (If you are not prompted to select gate location then click on the **Gate Location** selection button in the dialog box.)
- Click on a gate location created earlier on the plastic model. Preview of the gate will be displayed; refer to Figure-93.

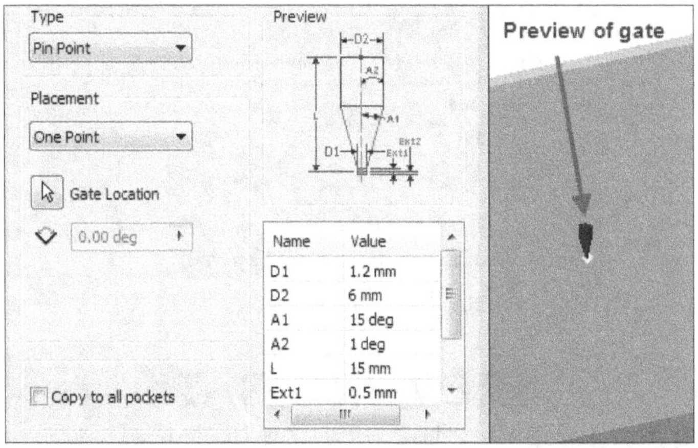

Figure-93. Preview of gate

- If you are using gate other than **Pin**, **Pin Point**, or **Sprue** type then you can select the **Up** or **Down** radio button from the dialog box to specify the orientation of the gate.
- Set the dimensions of the gate in the table at the bottom right in the dialog box.
- If you have multiple gate locations and want the same gate to be created on all the gate locations then select the **Copy to all pockets** check box from the dialog box.
- Click on the **OK** button to create the gate.

Types of Gates and Their Practical Applications

A gate is the connection between the runner system and the molded part. It must permit enough flow to fill the mold cavity, plus additional material to allow for part shrinkage and cooling. The gate type, location, and size has a great effect on the molding process. It affects physical properties, appearance, and size of the part.
Here, we will discuss the advantages and disadvantages of using different type of gates in mold design.

Edge Gate

An edge gate is located on the parting line of the mold and typically fills the part from the side, top, or bottom.

Sizing

The typical gate size is 6% to 75% of the part thickness (or 0.4 to 6.4 mm thick) and 1.6 to 12.7 mm wide. The gate land should be no more than 1.0 mm in length, with 0.5 mm being the optimum.

Advantages

An edge gate is primarily used for molding parts with large surfaces and thin walls. Some of the advantages of this gate are:

- Parallel orientation across the whole width (important for optical parts).
- In each case, uniform shrinkage in the direction of flow and transverse (important for crystalline materials).
- No inconvenient gate mark on the surface.

Disadvantages

This style gate is a problem with low viscosity, long fiber, or bead filled resins.

Fan Gate

A fan gate is a wide edge gate with variable thickness. It permits rapid filling of large parts or fragile mold sections through a large entry area. It is used to create a uniform flow front into wide parts, where warpage and dimensional stability are main concerns. The gate should taper in both width and thickness, to maintain a constant cross sectional area. This will ensure that:

- The melt velocity will be constant
- The entire width is being used for the flow
- The pressure is the same across the entire width.

Sizing

As with other manually trimmed gates, the maximum thickness should be no more than 75% of the part thickness. Typical gate sizes are from 0.25 to 1.6 mm thick. The gate width is typically from 6.4 mm to 25% of the cavity length.

Advantages

Fan gate is mainly applied to the tablet-shaped, shallow shell-shaped, and box-shaped article. Some of the advantages are:

- The injection speed is uniform which can reduce internal stress in the article and the possibility of air entrapment.
- Easy removal of the gate.
- Melt plastic flow from gate into the big cross-sectional area(cavity), so melt flow is good.
- Avoid deformation and maintain dimensional stability.

Disadvantages

The gate is best removed by using a trim fixture, especially on a thick section part. Since it makes a rather large scar, it is advisable to locate the gate at a non-cosmetic/ non-functional area, if possible.

Pin Gate

This type of gate relies on a three-plate mold design, where the runner system is on one mold parting line and the part cavity is in the primary parting line. Reverse taper runners drop through the middle (third) plate, parallel to the dircction of the mold opening. As the mold cavity parting line is opened, the small-diameter pin gate is torn from the part. A secondary opening of the runner parting line ejects the runners. Alternatively, the runner parting line opens first. An auxiliary, top-half ejector system extracts the runners from the reverse taper drops, tearing the runners from the parts.

Sizing

The gate diameter like that of all other gates depends on the section thickness of the part and the processed plastic material and is independent of the system. One can generally state that smaller cross-sections facilitate the break-off. Therefore, as high a melt temperature as possible is used in order to keep the gate as small as possible.

Advantages

The design is particularly useful when multiple gates per part are needed to assure symmetric filling or where long flow paths must be reduced to assure packing to all areas of the part.

Disadvantages

This gate type has disadvantage of too much scraps rates as the runner is big.

Pin Point Gate

The Pin Point gate or simply called point gate is similar to Pin gate in shape. But the size of gate is smaller in this case.

Sizing

Typical gate sizes are 0.25 to 1.6 mm in diameter.

Advantages

Since the size of gate is very small so smaller scar is generated on the plastic part. Some designs allow gating into a very small concave dish on the part surface to ensure that the scar break is below a flat surface. In such cases, we can use this type of gate.

Disadvantages

The small cross-sectional opening of the point gate becomes a problem with respect to resin filled plastic. This type of gate can cause a problem with low viscosity, long fiber, or bead filled resins. The small gate restriction could raise the melt temperature and affect heat sensitive resins. Ignoring these factors could result in high mold maintenance.

Submarine Gate

A submarine gate is used in two-plate mold construction. An angled, tapered tunnel is machined from the end of the runner to the cavity, just below the parting line. As the parts and runners are ejected, the gate is sheared at the part. If a large diameter pin is added to a non-functional area of the part, the submarine gate can be built into the pin, avoiding the need of a vertical surface for the gate. If the pin is on a surface that is hidden, it does not have to be removed.

Multiple submarine gates into the interior walls of cylindrical parts can replace a diaphragm gate and allow automatic de-gating. The out-of-round characteristics are not as good as those from a diaphragm gate, but are often acceptable.

Sizing

The typical size is 0.25 to 2.0 mm in diameter. It is tapered to the spherical side of the runner.

Advantages

- Submarine gate can be machined to the exact size, without the fitting problem as to shape.
- During the injection part stripping, it could be automatically removed from the product for full-automation production.
- This type of gate is widely employed for automatically plastic products production.

Disadvantages

The small cross-sectional opening of the submarine gate becomes a problem with respect to resin filled plastic. This style gate could be a problem with low viscosity, long fiber, or bead filled resins. The small gate restriction could raise the melt temperature and affect heat sensitive resins. Ignoring these factors could result in high mold maintenance.

The Tunnel, Flat Bottom Submarine, and Sprue gates share the same properties as of Submarine gate. These gates are used based on the requirement of runner.

CREATING RUNNER

Runner is a channel machined in the mold to supply molten plastic to the gates through which the melt goes into cavity. In Autodesk Inventor, runner creation process can be divided into two sections; runner sketch creation and runner model creation. These sections are discussed next.

Creating Runner Sketch

There are two tools in Autodesk Inventor to create runner; **Auto Runner Sketch** and **Manual Sketch**. If you select the **Auto Runner Sketch** tool then you will find some predefined shapes of runners. The procedure to use both the tools are discussed next.

Using Auto Runner Sketch Tool

- Click on the **Auto Runner Sketch** tool from the **Runner Sketch** drop-down in the **Runners and Channels** panel of the **Mold Layout** tab in the **Ribbon**. The **Auto Runner Sketch** dialog box will be displayed; refer to Figure-94.

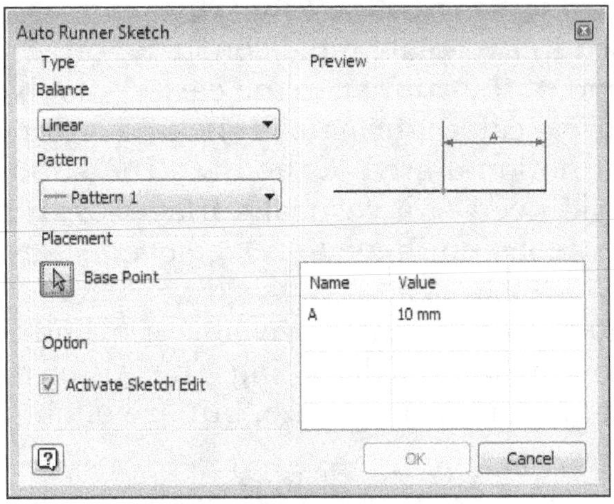

Figure-94. Auto Runner Sketch dialog box

- Select the type of runner from the **Balance** drop-down in the **Type** area of the dialog box and select desired pattern (shape) from the **Pattern** drop-down. You will be asked to specify the base point of the runner.
- Click on the mold at desired location to specify the base point. Preview of the runner sketch will be displayed.
- Set the dimensions for runner in the table given in dialog box. The preview of runner will change accordingly; refer to Figure-95.

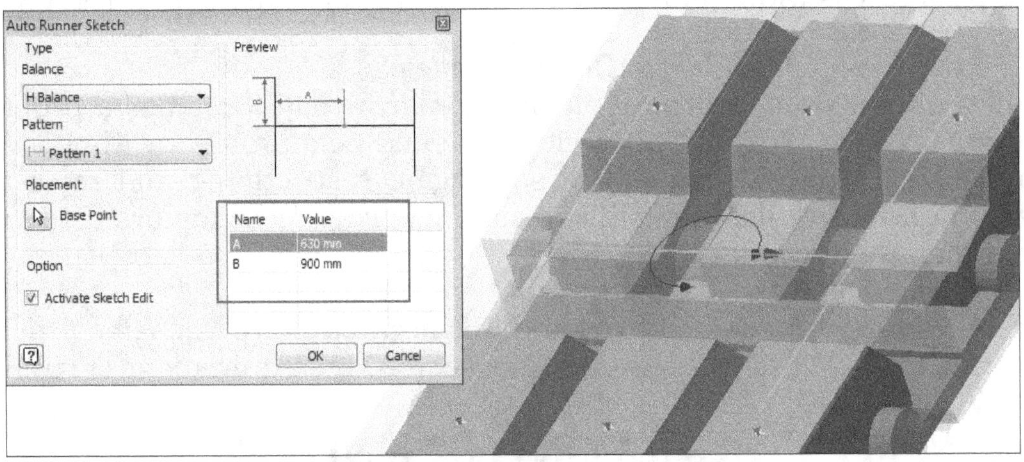

Figure-95. Preview of auto runner sketch

- Move and rotate the sketch as required by using the handles displayed on the preview.
- Clear the **Activate Sketch Edit** check box if you do not want to edit the sketch otherwise keep it selected.
- Click on the **OK** button from the dialog box. The sketch will be created. If the **Activate Sketch Edit** check box is selected then sketching environment will be displayed. Edit the runner sketch as required and then click on the **Finish Sketch** button from the **Exit** panel in the **Sketch** tab of the **Ribbon**. Click on the **Return** button from the **Return** panel in the **3D Model** tab of the **Ribbon** to return back to mold design environment.

Using Manual Sketch Tool

- Click on the **Manual Sketch** tool from the **Runner Sketch** drop-down in the **Runners and Channels** panel of the **Mold Layout** tab in the **Ribbon**. The **Manual Sketch** dialog box will be displayed; refer to Figure-96. Also, you will be asked to select a sketching plane.

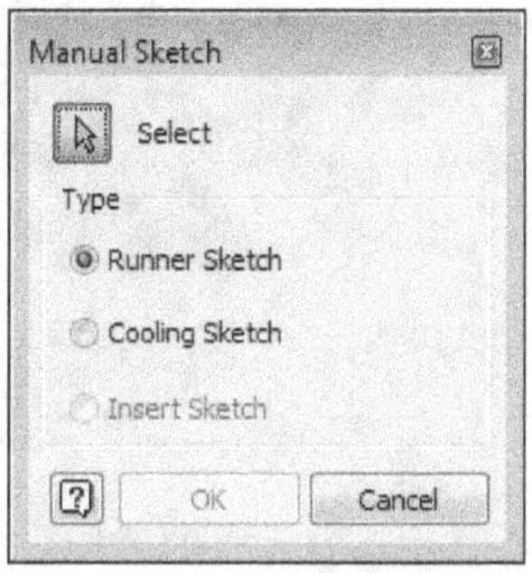

Figure-96. Manual Sketch dialog box

- Make sure the **Runner Sketch** radio button is selected in the dialog box and then click on the flat face of the mold to define sketching plane and click on the **OK** button from the dialog box. The sketching environment will be activated.
- Create the sketch of runner using the lines. Once the sketch is completed, click on the **Finish Sketch** button from the **Exit** panel in the **Ribbon** and then click on the **Return** button from **Return** panel in the **Ribbon**.

Creating Runner Model

The **Runner** tool is used to create 3D representation of the runner. The procedure to create runner is given next.

- Click on the **Runner** tool from the **Runner** drop-down in the **Runners and Channels** panel in the **Mold Layout** tab of the **Ribbon**. The **Create Runner** dialog box will be displayed; refer to Figure-97.

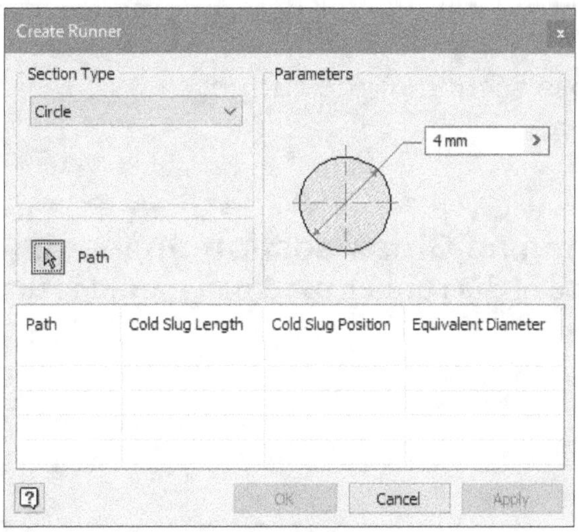

Figure-97. Create Runner dialog box

- Select desired section type from the **Section Type** drop-down in the dialog box. The preview of runner cross-section and related parameters will be displayed in the **Parameters** area of the dialog box.
- Set desired dimensions in the edit boxes of **Parameters** area of the dialog box.
- Select the runner sketch earlier created to draw the runner. Preview of the runner will be displayed; refer to Figure-98.

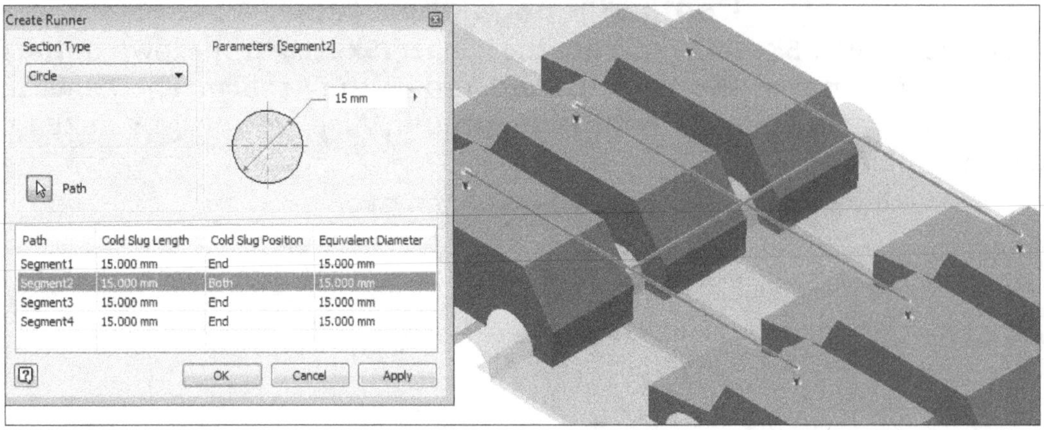

Figure-98. Preview of runner

- Select desired positions of cold slug from the field under **Cold Slug Position** column in the table of dialog box.
- Click on the **OK** button from the dialog box to create the runner.

Runner Design Guidelines

The runner is a channel machined into the mould plate to connect the sprue with the entrance or gate to the impression. In the basic two-plate mould, the runner is positioned on the parting surface while on more complex designs, the runner is positioned below the parting surface. Below are some points to be taken care of while making runner for mold.

- The wall of the runner channel must be smooth to prevent any restriction to flow.
- There must be no machine marks which would tend to retain. In the runner in the mould plate, to ensure this it is desirable for the mould design to specify that the runner is polished "in line of draw".

There are some other considerations for determining the runner.

- The shape of the cross section of the runner
- The size of the runner
- The runner layout

Determining Cross-section Shape of Runner

The cross sectional shape of the runner used in a mould is usually one of the following forms:

1. Fully round
2. Semi Round
3. U Shaped
4. Trapezoidal
5. Modified trapezoidal
6. Hexagonal

1. Full Round Runner: The full-round runner is the best in terms of a maximum volume-to-surface ratio, which minimizes pressure drop and heat loss. However, the tooling cost is generally higher because both halves of the mold must be machined so that the two semi-circular sections are aligned when the mold is closed.

2. Semi Round Runner: The use of semi round shaped runner is generally not recommended because of lower cross-section size of the runner. But when it is not possible to use trapezoidal, hexagonal, or u shaped runner then it is a cheaper option as compared to full round runner. For some plastics materials like Eastman polymers, the semi-round shape is recommended as it cause lesser flow restriction as compared to other runner shapes.

3. U Shaped Runner: The U shaped runner is second most efficient runner shape. The width of U-shape runner is smaller than that of circular runner. With the same efficiency and length (unit length), the volume of U-shape is minimal among the semicircular, ladder, and U-shape runners and next to that of circular runner. Therefore, U-shape is most suitable in the cool-runner mould.

4. Trapezoidal Runner: The trapezoidal runner permits the runner to be designed and cut on one side of the mold. It is commonly used in three-plate molds, where the full-round runner may not be released properly, and at the parting line in molds, where the full-round runner interferes with mold sliding action.

5. Modified Trapezoidal Runner: The modified trapezoidal runner is a combination of both trapezoidal runner and round runner. The bottom of runner is round and upper part is trapezoidal. This type of runner can be used in both hot and cold runners. But the material wastage in case of trapezoidal and modified trapezoidal is higher as compared to the first three runners discussed. Note that the material left in runner is wastage after molding.

6. Hexagonal Runner: The hexagonal runner is basically a double trapezoidal runner, where the two halves of the trapezium meet at parting surface. It is easier to match the two halves of the hexagonal runner compared to that of a round runner. This point applies particularly to runners, which are less than 3 mm in width. The hexagonal runner has minimum flow resistance after full round runner.

Hydraulic Diameter and Flow Resistance

To compare runners of different shapes, you can use the hydraulic diameter, which is an index of flow resistance. The higher the hydraulic diameter, the lower the flow resistance. Hydraulic diameter can be defined as:

$$D_h = \frac{4A}{P}$$

where D_h = hydraulic diameter
A = cross section area
P = perimeter

Based on this formula, the hydraulic diameters of different cross-sections are given next.

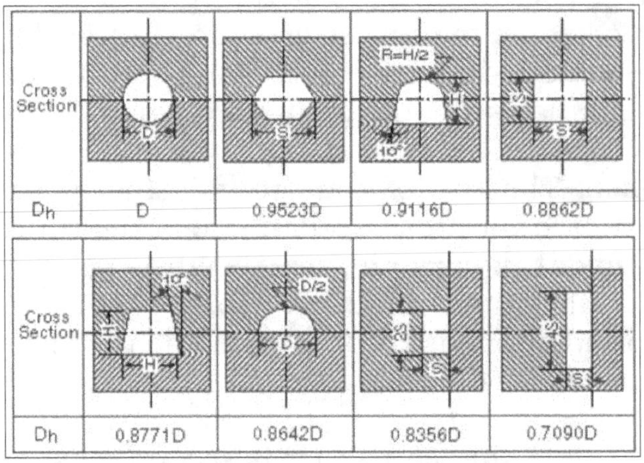

Determining Size of Runner

Ideally, the size of the runner diameter will take many factors into account — part volume, part flow length, runner length, machine capacity gate size, and cycle time. Generally, runners should have diameters equal to the maximum part thickness, but within the 4 mm to 10 mm diameter range to avoid early freeze-off or excessive cycle time. The runner should be large enough to minimize pressure loss, yet small enough to maintain satisfactory cycle time. Smaller runner diameters have been successfully used as a result of computer flow analysis where the smaller runner diameter increases material shear heat, thereby assisting in maintaining melt temperature and enhancing the polymer flow. Large runners are not economical because of the amount of energy that goes into forming, and then regrinding the material that solidifies within them.

By an empirical formula, calculation of main runner size can be given as:

$$D = (W^{1/2} X L^{1/4})/3.7$$

Where,
D=runner diameter (mm)
W=weight of moulding (g)
L=height/length of runner (mm)
Theoretically, the cross-sectional area of main runner should be equal to/in excess of the combined cross-sectional areas of the branch runners that is feeding the material.

Determining Runner Layout

The purpose of different type of runner layouts is to balance the flow of melt, so that all the cavities in mold are filled properly without pressure loss. In a balanced layout, the length of runner from sprue to gate is equal for all the mold cavities. Proper runner layout also makes it possible to produce family molds. In family molds, the flow of plastic is maintained by size and length of runner, so that cavities are filled in same time. There are hardly any guidelines for runner layout as it all depends on flow of plastic. Only way to find out best runner layout is to perform plastic flow analysis on the mold.

CREATING SECONDARY SPRUE

The secondary sprue, also called the sprue runner, is used to supply molten melt from one runner to the other runner. It is generally included in 3 plate molds. The procedure to create secondary sprue is given next.

- Click on the **Secondary Sprue** tool from the **Runner** drop-down in the **Runners and Channels** panel in the **Mold Layout** tab of the **Ribbon**. The **Create Secondary Sprue** dialog box will be displayed; refer to Figure-99. Also, you will be asked to select a sketch point to locate secondary sprue.

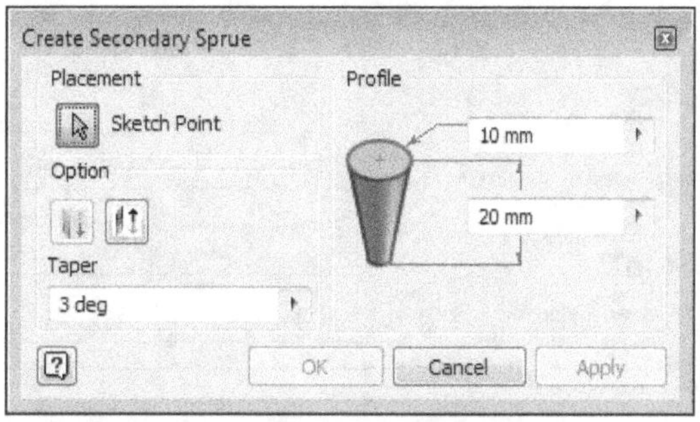

Figure-99. Create Secondary Sprue dialog box

- Select a sketch point created (by using the **Start 2D Sketch** tool) on the runner line. Preview of the secondary sprue will be displayed; refer to Figure-100.

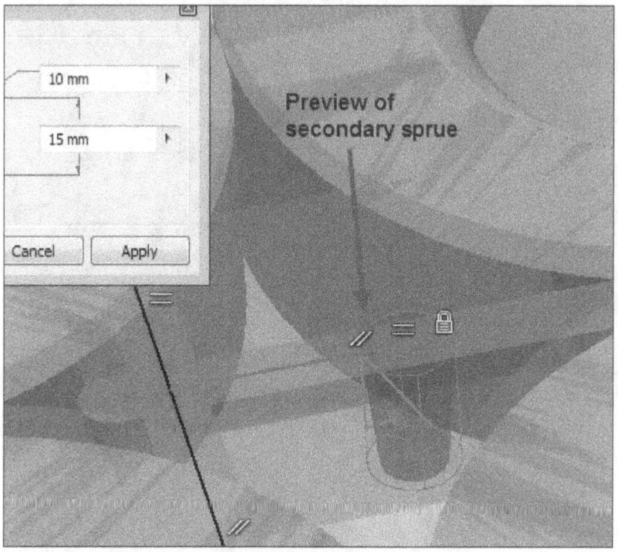

Figure-100. Preview of secondary sprue

- Specify desired parameters and click on the **OK** button to create the sprue.

Most of the designing work has been done till this point. Now, we will learn to add a mold base to the core and cavity so that we can check the practical fitting of core and cavity in mold plates.

ADDING MOLD BASE TO ASSEMBLY

The tools to add and manage mold base are available in the **Mold Assembly** tab of the **Ribbon**; refer to Figure-101.

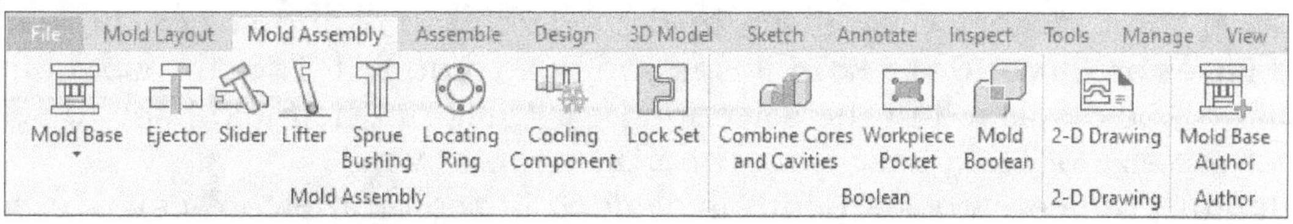

Figure-101. Mold Assembly tab in the Ribbon

The procedure to add mold base to the assembly is given next.

- Click on the **Mold Base** tool from the **Mold Base** drop-down in the **Mold Assembly** panel of **Mold Assembly** tab in the **Ribbon**. The **Mold Base** dialog box will be displayed; refer to Figure-102.

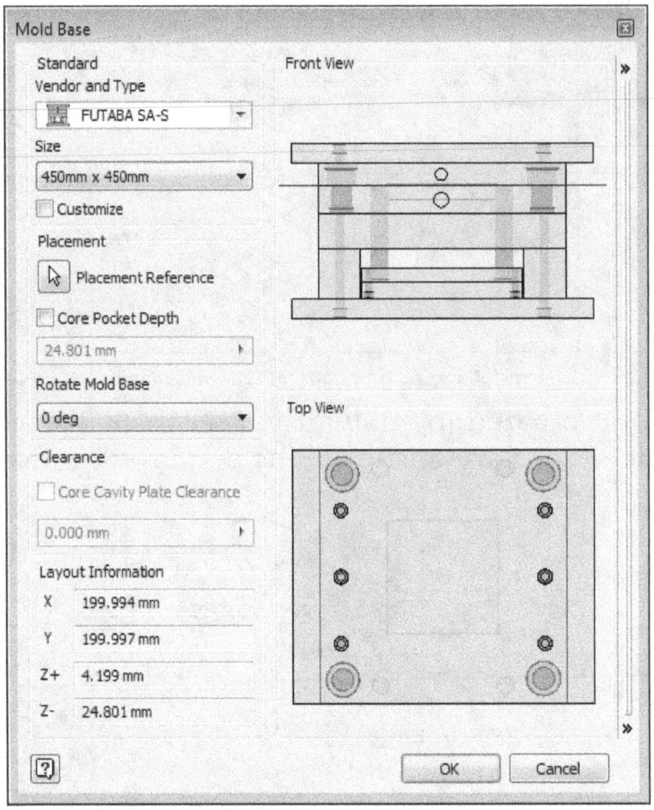

Figure-102. Mold Base dialog box

- Click in the **Vendor and Type** box of **Standard** area of the dialog box. The list of mold base vendor will be displayed in the selection box for selected categories; refer to Figure-103.

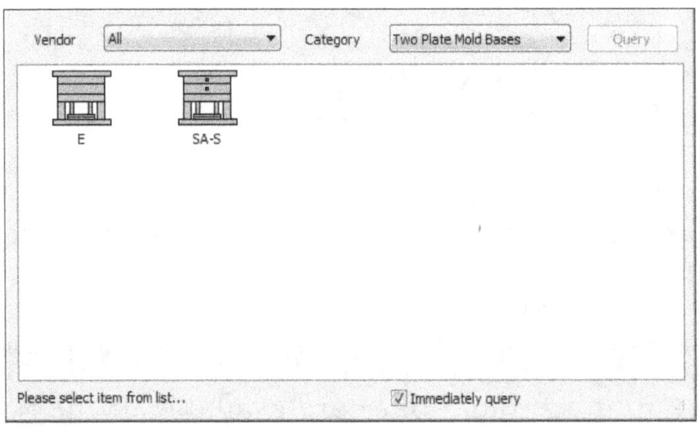

Figure-103. List of mold base vendors

- Click on the **Category** drop-down in the selection box and select the **Two Plate Mold Bases** or **Three Plate Mold Bases** option as required. The corresponding mold bases will be displayed in the selection box. Click on the mold base to select it.
- Select the size of mold base from the **Size** drop-down.
- By default, the core pocket depth is decided based on the core-cavity created by you but if you want to specify different core pocket depth then select the **Core Pocket Depth** check box and specify desired value in the edit box below it. Preview in the dialog box will be modified accordingly.

Customizing Mold Base Components

- If you want to customize the size of any of the component in the mold base then select the **Customize** check box in the **Standard** area of the dialog box. The dialog box will get expanded as shown in Figure-104.

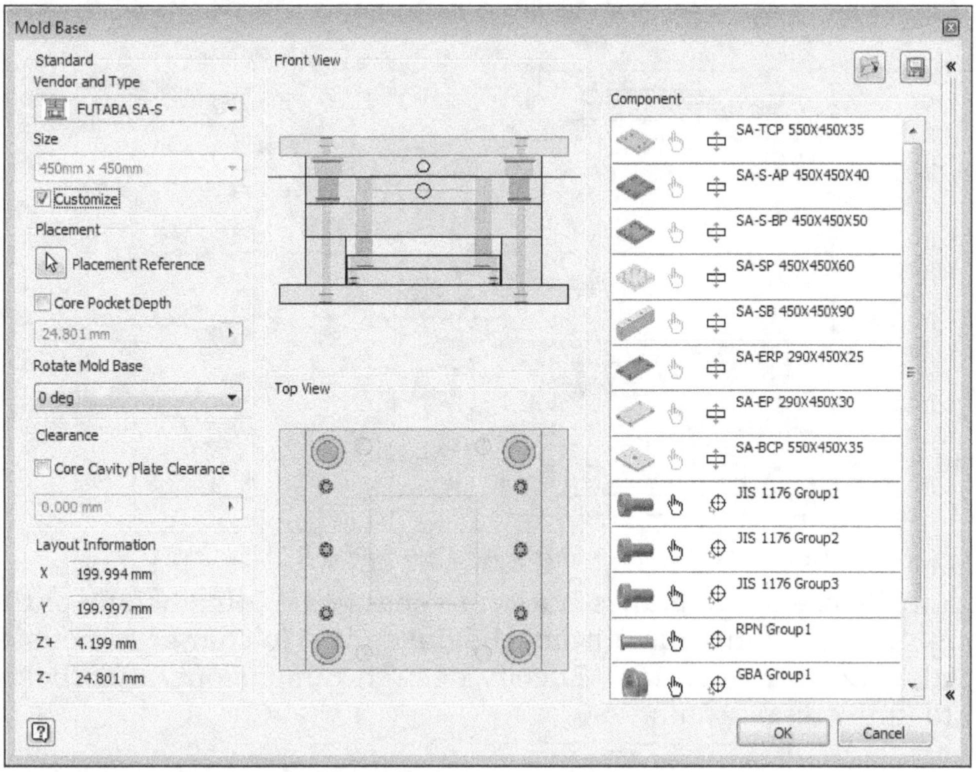

Figure-104. Expanded Mold Base dialog box

- There are four options to modify each component of the mold base; **Position Settings**, **Property Settings**, **Delete**, and **Type Settings**. These options are displayed on selecting the component from the **Component** area of the dialog box; refer to Figure-105.

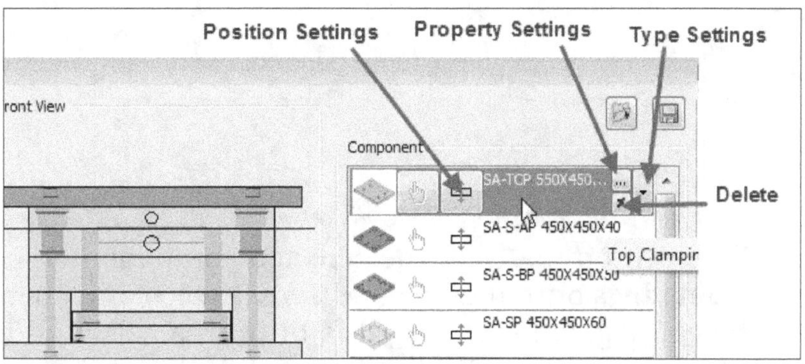

Figure-105. Options for mold base components

- Click on the **Position Settings** button of the component once and then click at desired location in the preview to place the component; refer to Figure-106.

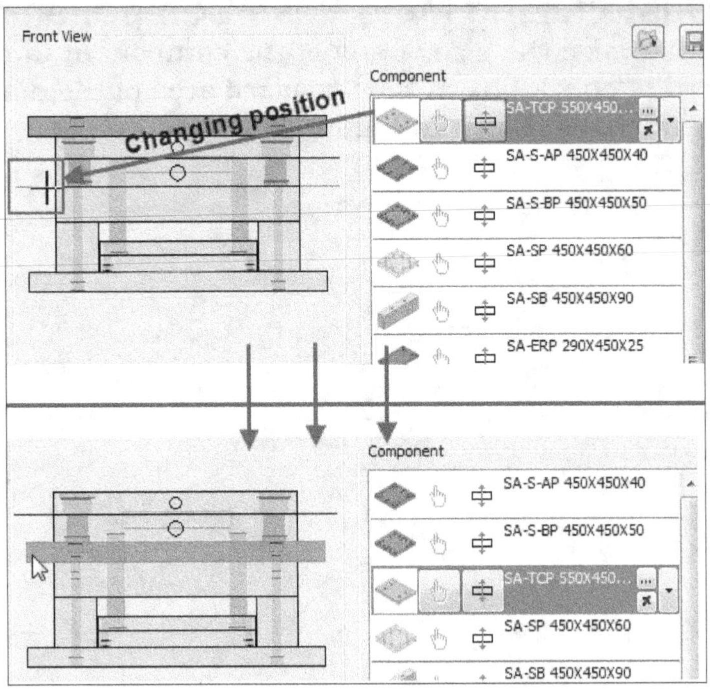

Figure-106. Changing position of mold base component

- Click on the **Property Settings** button to change the dimensions of the selected component. On clicking this button, the dialog box to change dimensions will be displayed; refer to Figure-107. Specify desired dimensions and click on the **OK** button to apply dimensions.

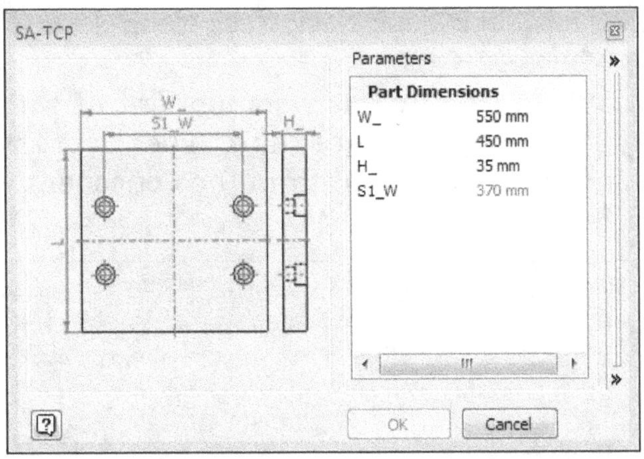

Figure-107. Dialog box to change dimensions

- Click on the **Delete** button to delete the selected component.
- Click on the **Type Settings** button to replace the selected component from the other component in the catalog. On selecting this button, a selection box is displayed with replacement components; refer to Figure-108. Select desired component to replace the current.

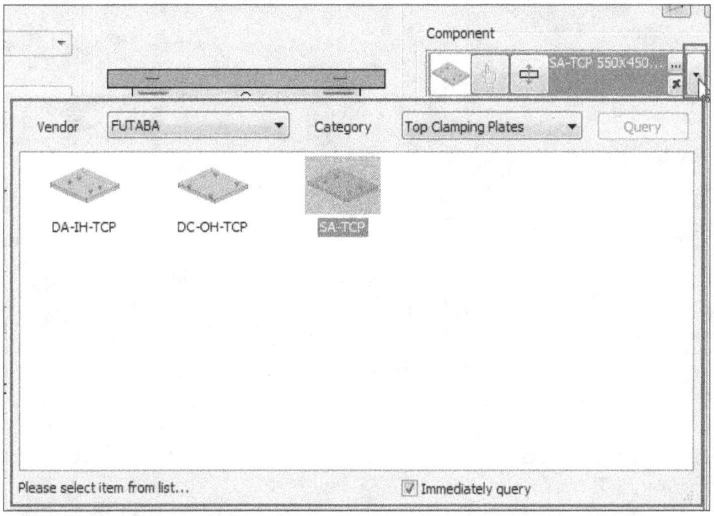

Figure-108. Changing component type

- After customizing the mold base, click on the **OK** button from the dialog box to add mold base to the assembly. The mold assembly will be placed in the mold base automatically based on the specified parameters; refer to Figure-109.

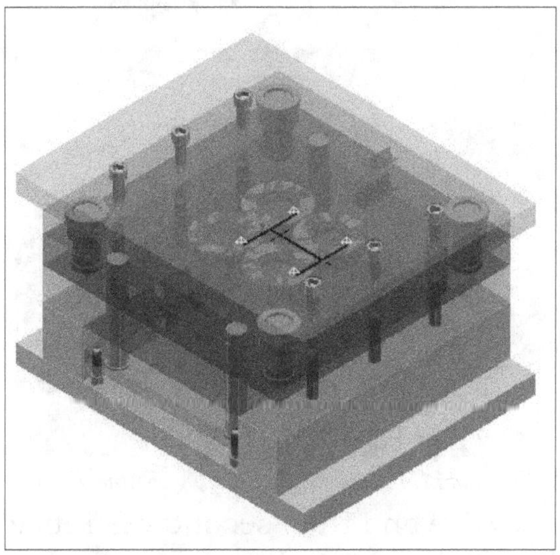

Figure-109. Mold assembly with mold base

COOLING CHANNEL

As runner is important for transportation of plastic melt to the cavity, in the same way cooling channel is important to maintain right temperature in the mold. Most of the people think that the work of cooling channel is to cool down molds but this is half correct. A cooling channel may raise the temperature of mold at some points if necessary. In this way, it gives equal time to all areas of the plastic component to cool down. The procedure to create cooling channel is discussed next.

Creating Cooling Channel

- Click on the **Cooling Channel** tool from the **Runners and Channels** panel in the **Mold Layout** tab of the **Ribbon**. The **Cooling Channel** dialog box will be displayed; refer to Figure-110. Also, you will be asked to select a face to place cooling line.

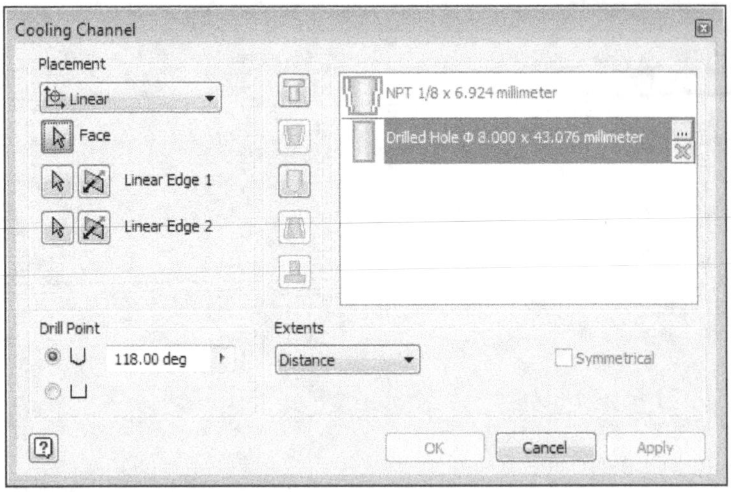

Figure-110. Cooling Channel dialog box

- Select the face of mold base to place the cooling channel line. Preview of the cooling line will be displayed; refer to Figure-111. Also, you will be asked to select linear edge for dimension reference.

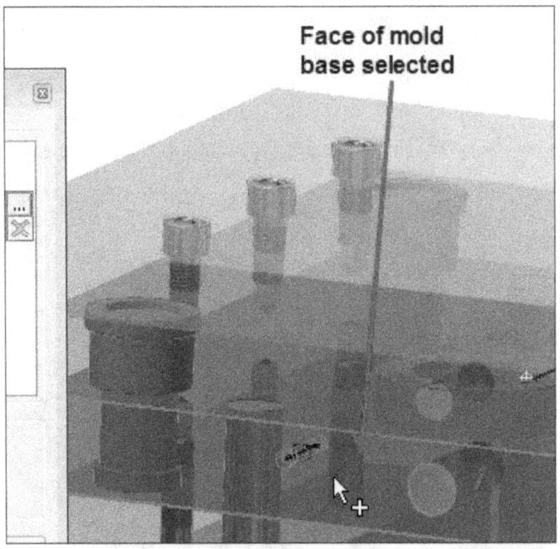

Figure-111. Face selected for cooling channel line

- Select the first reference edge and then second reference edge to place the cooling line fully constrained; refer to Figure-112.

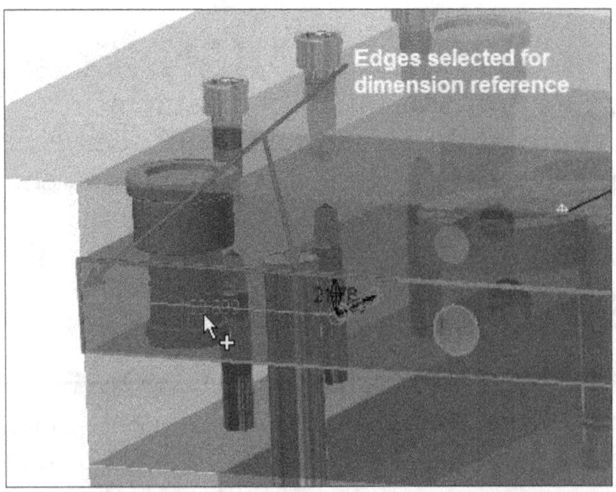

Figure-112. Edges selected for placement of cooling line

- Set the dimensions as required by clicking on them in the preview.

- If you want the cooling line to be passing through all the objects in the mold assembly then select the **Through All** option from the drop-down in the **Extents** area of the dialog box.
- Select desired components of the cooling line using the buttons given in the center of the dialog box. You can change the parameters of the selected components by clicking on the ellipse button for that component; refer to Figure-113.
- Click on the **OK** button from the dialog box to create the cooling line.
- Repeat the procedure to create other lines of cooling channel.

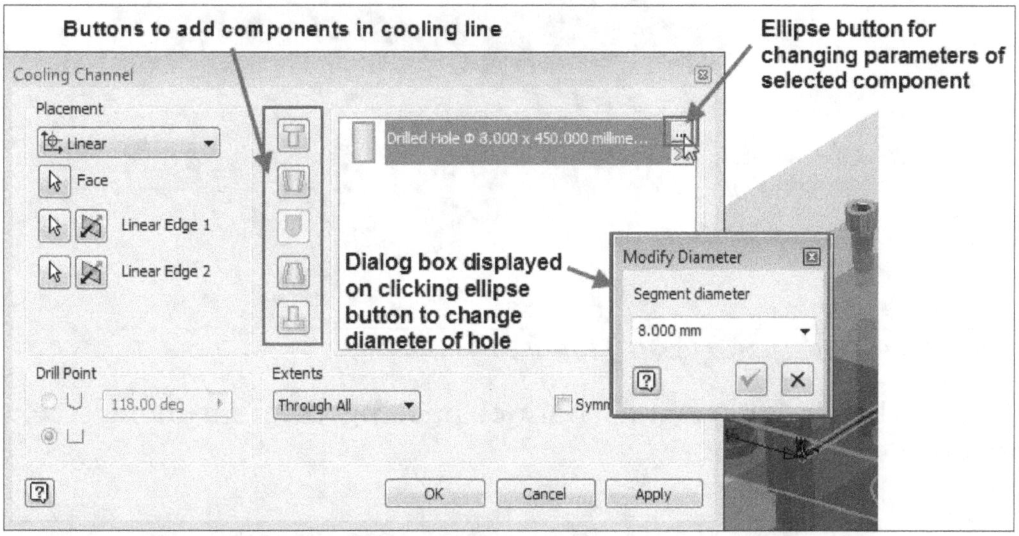

Figure-113. Adding and changing components for cooling line

Sketch Method for Cooling Channel Creation

In this method, we will first create sketched lines for cooling channel. Based on these sketch lines we will create the cooling channel. The procedure is discussed next.

- Create a workplace using the **Plane** tools at the location suitable for cooling channels.
- Click on the **Manual Sketch** button from the **Runner** drop-down in the **Runners and Channels** panel of the **Mold Layout** tab in the **Ribbon**. The **Manual Sketch** dialog box will be displayed as discussed earlier.
- Select the **Cooling Sketch** radio button from the dialog box. You will be asked to select a plane for creating sketch.
- Select the work plane you have created for cooling sketch; refer to Figure-114. Click on the **OK** button from the dialog box. The sketching environment will be activated.

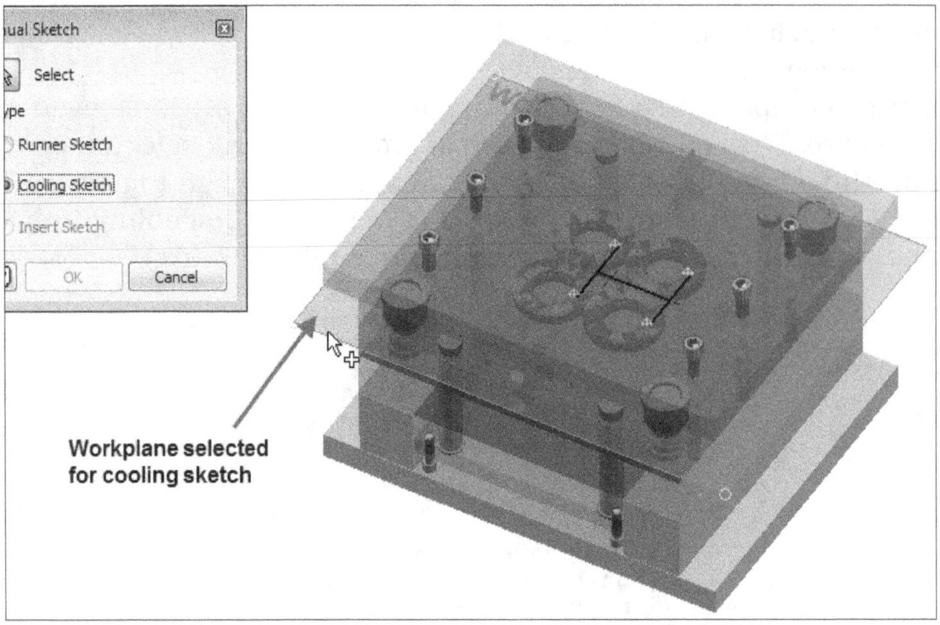

Figure-114. Selecting workplane for cooling sketch

- Create the sketch for cooling channel passing through mold steel; refer to Figure-115.

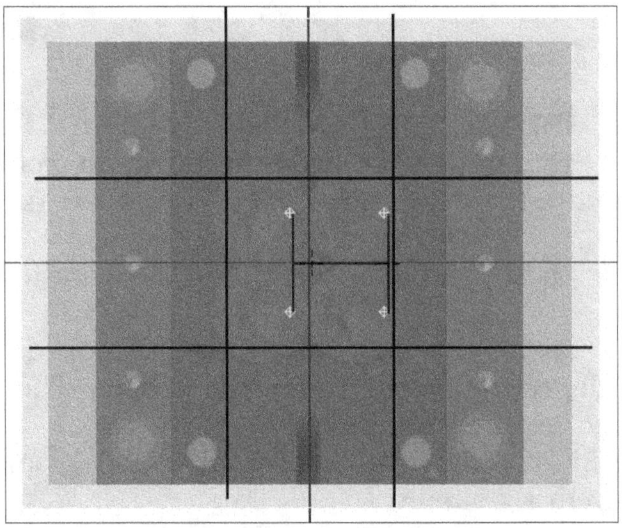

Figure-115. Sketch lines created for cooling channel

- Click on the **Finish Sketch** button from the **Finish** drop-down in the **Exit** panel of the **Ribbon** and then click on the **Return** button from the **Return** panel in the **Ribbon**.
- Click on the **Cooling Channel** tool from the **Runners and Channels** panel in the **Mold Layout** tab of the **Ribbon**. The **Cooling Channel** dialog box will be displayed as discussed earlier.
- Select the **From Sketch** option from the **Placement** drop-down in the dialog box. You will be asked to select the reference line.
- Select a line of the sketch and add/modify the cooling channel components as discussed earlier.
- Click on the **Apply** button and then select the next line of cooling channel. Repeat the procedure till you have created all the lines of cooling channel.
- Click on the **Done** button to exit the dialog box.

Guidelines for Cooling Channel Design

In thermoplastic molding, the mold performs three basic functions: forming molten material into the product shape, removing heat for solidification, and ejecting the solid part. Of the three, heat removal usually takes the longest time and has the greatest direct effect on cycle time. Despite this, mold cooling-channel design often occurs as an afterthought in the mold-design process. Consequently, many cooling designs must accommodate available space and machining convenience rather than the thermodynamic needs of the product and mold. This section discusses mold cooling, a topic to consider early in the mold-design process.

Mold-surface temperature can affect the surface appearance of many parts. Hotter mold-surface temperatures lower the viscosity of the outer resin layer and enhance replication of the fine micro texture on the molding surface. This can lead to reduced gloss at higher mold-surface temperatures. In glass-fiber-reinforced materials, higher mold-surface temperatures encourage formation of a resin-rich surface skin. This skin covers the fibers, reducing their silvery appearance on the part surface. Uneven cooling causes variations in mold-surface temperature that can lead to non-uniform part-surface appearance.

Before, heat from the melt can be removed from the mold, it must first conduct through the layers of plastic thickness to reach the mold surface. Material thermal conductivity and part wall thickness determine the rate of heat transfer. Generally, good thermal insulators, plastics conduct heat much more slowly than typical mold materials. Cooling time increases as a function of part thickness squared; doubling wall thickness quadruples cooling time.

Below are some points to be taken care of while designing cooling channel:

- Core out thick sections or provide extra cooling in thick areas to minimize the effect on cycle time.
- Avoid low-conductivity mold materials, such as stainless steel, when fast cycles and efficient cooling are important.
- Place cooling-channel center lines approximately 2.5 cooling-channel diameters away from the mold cavity surface.
- As a general rule of thumb, use center-to-center spacing of no more than three cooling-channel diameters.
- Consider using baffles and bubblers to remove heat from deep cores.
- Adjust the bubbler tube or baffle length for optimum cooling. If they are too long, flow can become restricted. If too short, coolant flow may stagnate at the ends of the hole.
- Consider using spiral channels cut into inserts for large cores.

CREATING COLD WELL

The cold well is created in runner line to hold the plastic which is cold compared to the melt in the runner line. The procedure to create cold well is discussed next.

- Click on the **Cold Well** tool from the **Runners and Channels** panel in the **Mold Layout** tab of the **Ribbon**. The **Cold Well** dialog box will be displayed; refer to Figure-116.

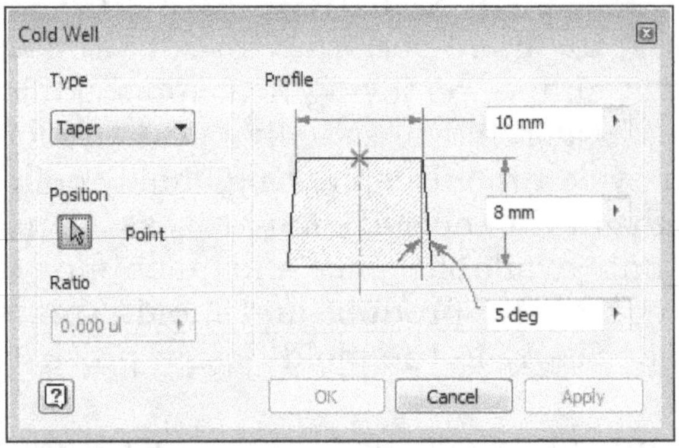

Figure-116. Cold Well dialog box

- Click in the **Type** drop-down and select desired type of cold well. You will be asked to select a point on the runner line.
- Click on the runner line at desired location to place the cold well. Preview of the cold well will be displayed; refer to Figure-117.

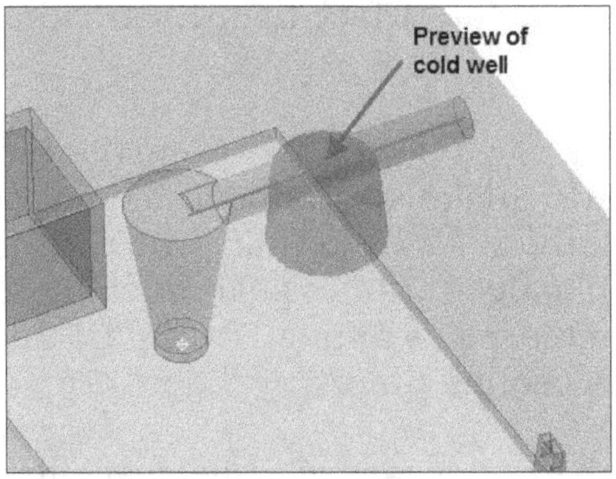

Figure-117. Preview of cold well

- Set the ratio value in **Ratio** edit box to position the cold well on the runner line.
- Set the parameters of cold well as required in the dialog box and click on the **OK** button to create the cold well.

MOLD SHRINKAGE

The **Mold Shrinkage** tool is used to modify the dimensions of all parts in the model to compensate for polymer shrinkage. The procedure is same as discussed earlier for **Part Shrinkage** tool in this chapter.

EXPORT

The **Export** tool is used to current mold assembly SAT format for use in other analysis software. The procedure to use this tool is discussed next.

- Click on the **Export** tool from the **Tools** panel in **Mold Layout** tab of the **Ribbon**. The **Export** dialog box will be displayed; refer to Figure-118.

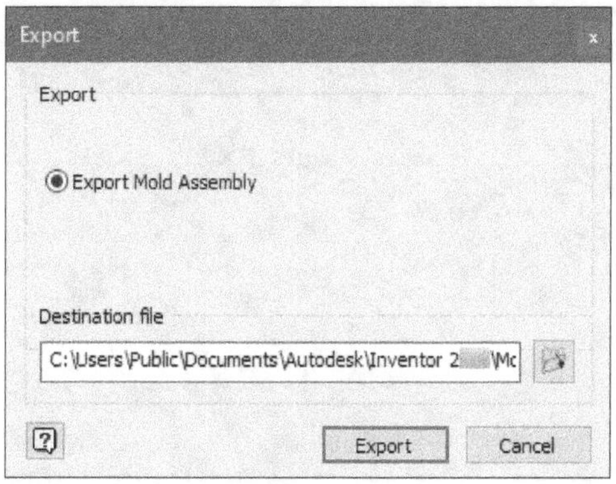

Figure-118. Export dialog box

- Click on the Browse button in **Destination file** area of dialog box to define name and directory for exported file. The **Export** dialog box will be displayed; refer to Figure-119.

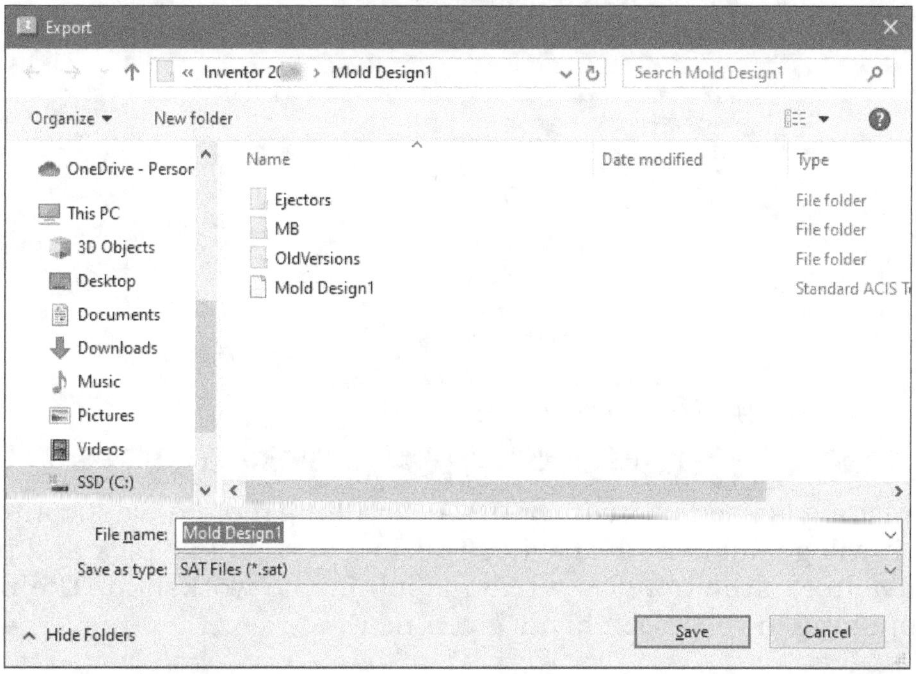

Figure-119. Export dialog box

- Specify desired name and location of file in the dialog box and click on the **Save** button.
- Click on the **Export** button to export the file. The **Export Options** dialog box will be displayed; refer to Figure-120. The **Mold Blocks** tab display the objects to be exported and the **Cooling System** tab display the cooling channel to be exported; refer to Figure-121.
- Select check boxes for the components to be exported in the sat file and click on the **OK** button from the dialog box. The model will be exported.

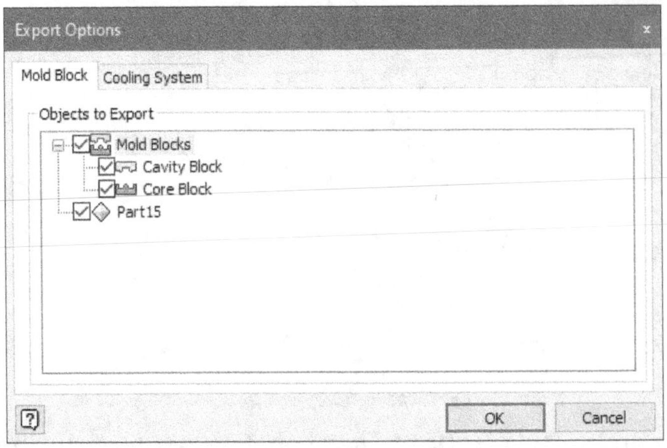

Figure-120. Export options dialog box

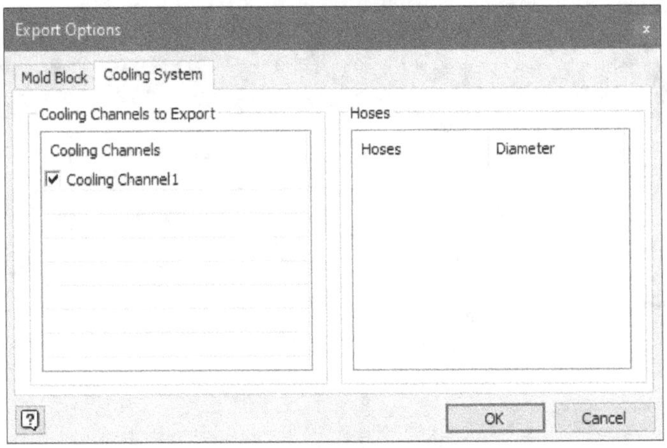

Figure-121. Cooling system tab

ADDING SPRUE BUSHING

The sprue bushing is used to create pathway for filling molten plastic into the runner from where it will get filled in the cavity. This is a very simple pick and place step in Autodesk Inventor, although it is a tedious job in the workshop. The procedure to add sprue bushing in the assembly is given next.

- Click on the **Sprue Bushing** tool from the **Mold Assembly** panel in the **Mold Assembly** tab of the **Ribbon**. The **Sprue Bushing** dialog box will be displayed; refer to Figure-122.

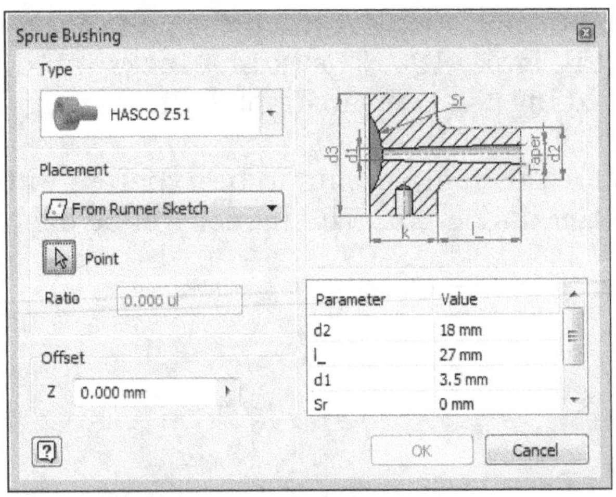

Figure-122. Sprue Bushing dialog box

- Select desired bushing type from the **Type** selection box in the dialog box.
- Select the **From Runner Sketch** option from the **Placement** drop-down to select a point on the runner sketch or select the **Linear** option from the drop-down to select two references to place the sprue. Since, the **From Runner Sketch** option is more widely used by mold makers so we will select this option.
- On selecting the **From Runner Sketch** option, you will be asked to select a point on the runner sketch. Select a point on the runner sketch, preview of the sprue bushing will be displayed; refer to Figure-123.

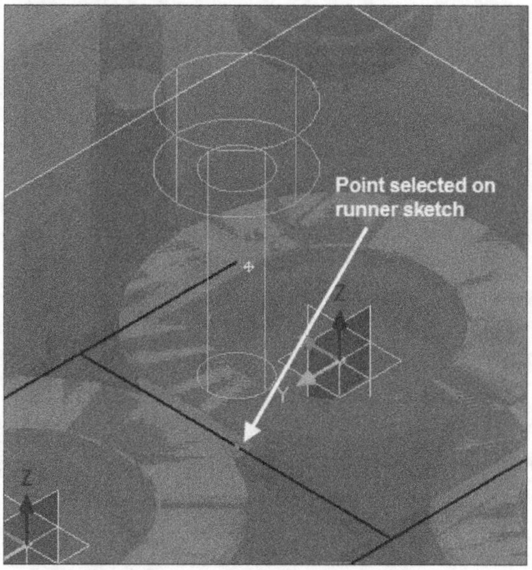

Figure-123. Point selected for sprue bushing

- Set the parameters of sprue bushing as required by using the options in the table.
- Click on the **OK** button to create the sprue bushing.

Now, you can run the mold fill analysis on the assembly of runner, gate, and cavities by using the **Mold Fill Analysis** tool in the **Mold Simulation** panel of **Mold Layout** tab in the **Ribbon** (if Autodesk Moldflow Adviser app is installed).

PLACING LOCATING RING

Locating Ring is an important part of mold base. This ring helps to align the mold with the plastic injection machine. It is also used to align and fasten the sprue bushing. The procedure to place locating ring in mold base is given next.

- Click on the **Locating Ring** tool from the **Mold Assembly** panel in the **Mold Assembly** tab of the **Ribbon**. The **Locating Ring** dialog box will be displayed and preview of locating ring will be displayed automatically aligned to the sprue bushing; refer to Figure-124.

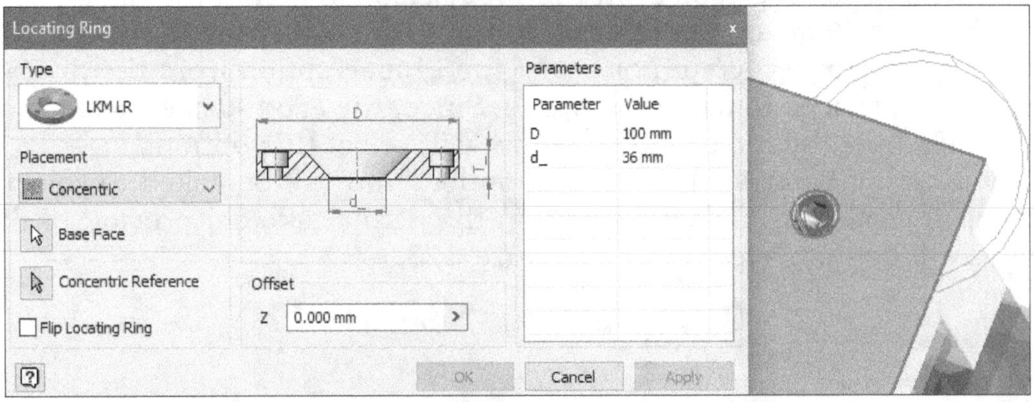

Figure-124. Locating Ring dialog box and preview

- Set the parameters of ring as required and then click on the **OK** button to create the locating ring.

COOLING COMPONENTS

The **Cooling Component** tool is used to create a cooling component that enable coolant to flow through the cooling channel. The procedure to use this tool is given next.

- Click on the **Cooling Component** tool from the **Mold Assembly** panel in the **Mold Assembly** tab of the **Ribbon**. The **Cooling Component** dialog box will be displayed; refer to Figure-125.

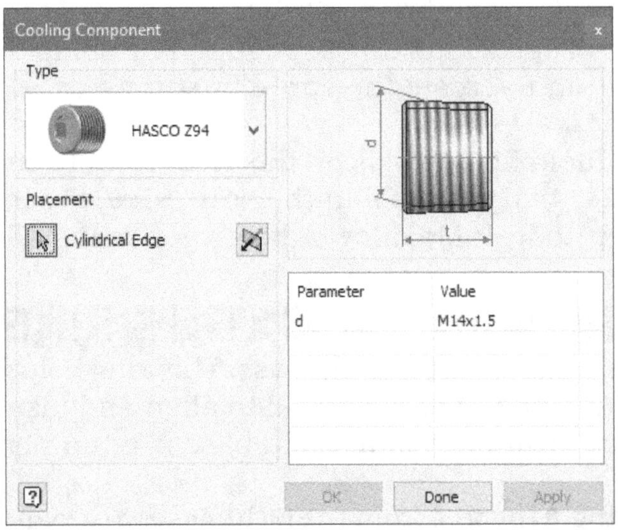

Figure-125. Cooling Component dialog box

- Click in the **Type** box of the dialog box. The list of cooling components available in library will be displayed in the selection box for selected category; refer to Figure-126.

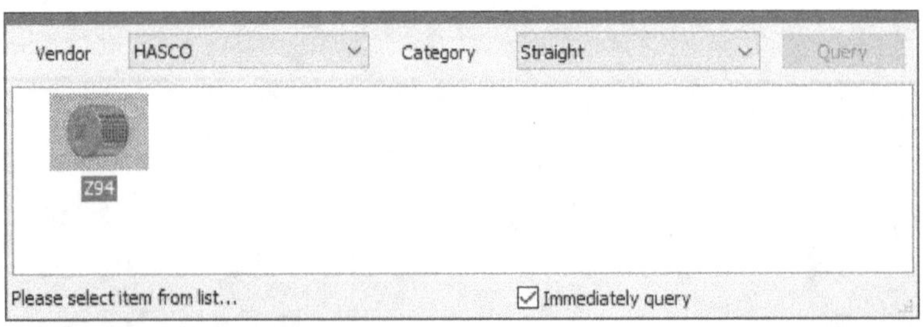

Figure-126. list of cooling component

- Select desired component from the dialog box and then select related reference geometry from the model for placement.
- Set the parameters of cooling as required and then click on the **OK** button to create the cooling component; refer to Figure-127.

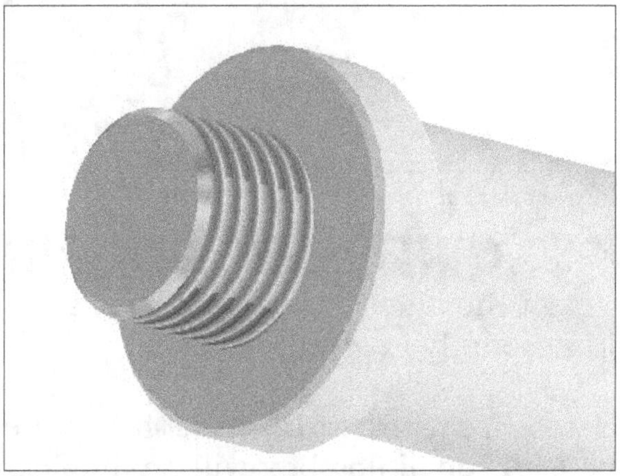

Figure-127. Cooling component created

LOCK SET

The **Lock Set** tool is used to add a side lock or interlock feature to the mold assembly. This feature is generally added to the mold when fluid pressure is high and there is a chance of molten material leakage. The procedure to use this tool is discussed next.

- Click on the **Lock Set** tool from the **Mold Assembly** panel in the **Mold Assembly** tab of the **Ribbon**. The **Lock Set** dialog box will be displayed; refer to Figure-128.

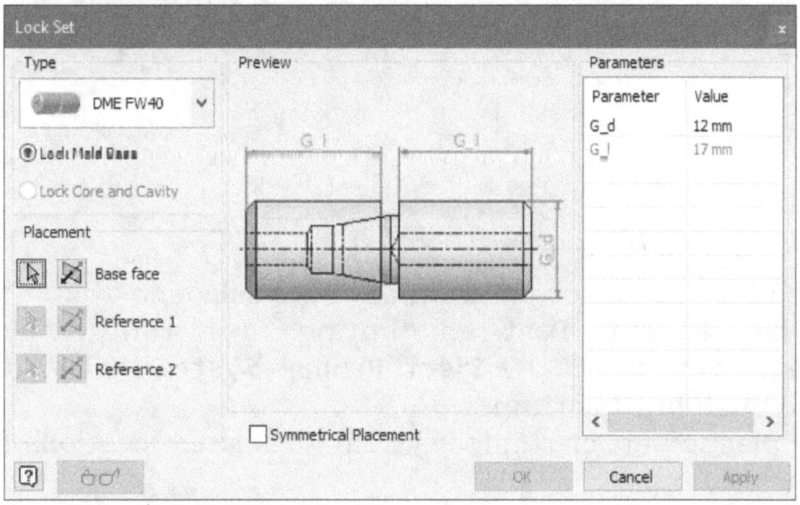

Figure-128. Lock set dialog box

- Select **Lock Model Base** radio button to position lock sets that secure the mold base.
- Select **Lock Core and Cavity** radio button to insert an interlock that secures the core and cavity together.
- Select **Symmetrical Placement** check box to generate a second lock set positioned symmetrically to the first one.
- Select the face dividing two interlocking mold components as Base face.
- Select reference geometries for **Reference 1** and **Reference 2** to define placement location for the lock set. Double-click on displayed dimensions to modify them.
- Click on the **OK** button to create the lock set; refer to Figure-129.

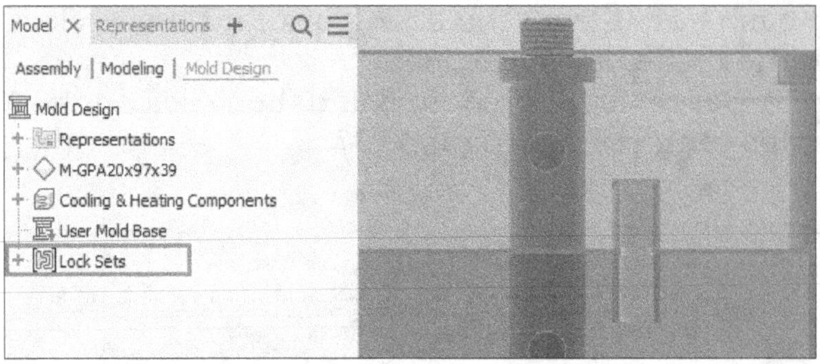

Figure-129. Lock set created

PLACING EJECTOR PIN

Ejector pins are used to eject the plastic part from the cavity steel. The procedure to place ejector pin in mold assembly is given next.

- Click on the **Ejector** tool from the **Mold Assembly** panel in the **Mold Assembly** tab of the **Ribbon**. The **Ejector** dialog box will be displayed with plastic part and runoff surface in drawing area; refer to Figure-130.

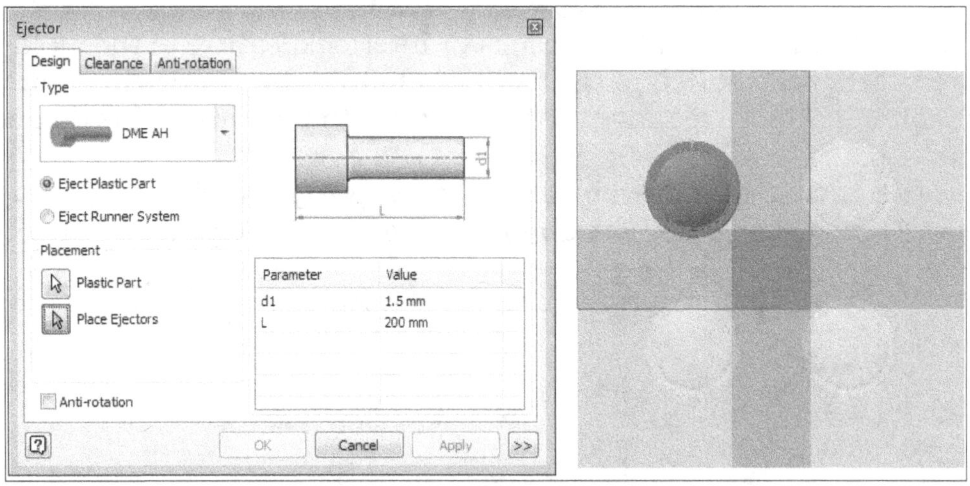

Figure-130. Ejector dialog box with plastic model

- Select desired type of ejector pin from the **Type** selection box.
- Select the **Eject Plastic Part** radio button if you want the ejector pins to be used on plastic part. Select the **Eject Runner System** radio button if you want the ejector to push out the runner.
- Click on the plastic part or runner system at desired locations to create ejector pins at those locations.
- Set the parameters of pins as required.
- Click on the **OK** button from the dialog box to create the ejector pins.

ADDING SLIDER TO MOLD ASSEMBLY

Slider is used to create undercuts by pushing in the insert in the mold. On the designers part, it is advisable to avoid undercuts in the plastic part because it can raise the cost of production in handsome amount. But if there is no escape from undercuts then use the slider insert assembly to create them in mold; refer to Figure-131. Make sure you have created inserts for undercuts before using this procedure. The procedure to add slider is given next.

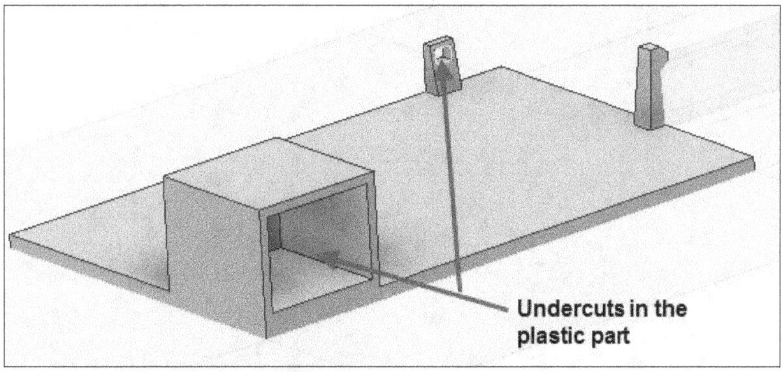

Figure-131. Undercut in plastic part

- Click on the **Slider** tool from the **Mold Assembly** panel in the **Mold Assembly** tab of the **Ribbon**. The **Slider** dialog box will be displayed; refer to Figure-132.

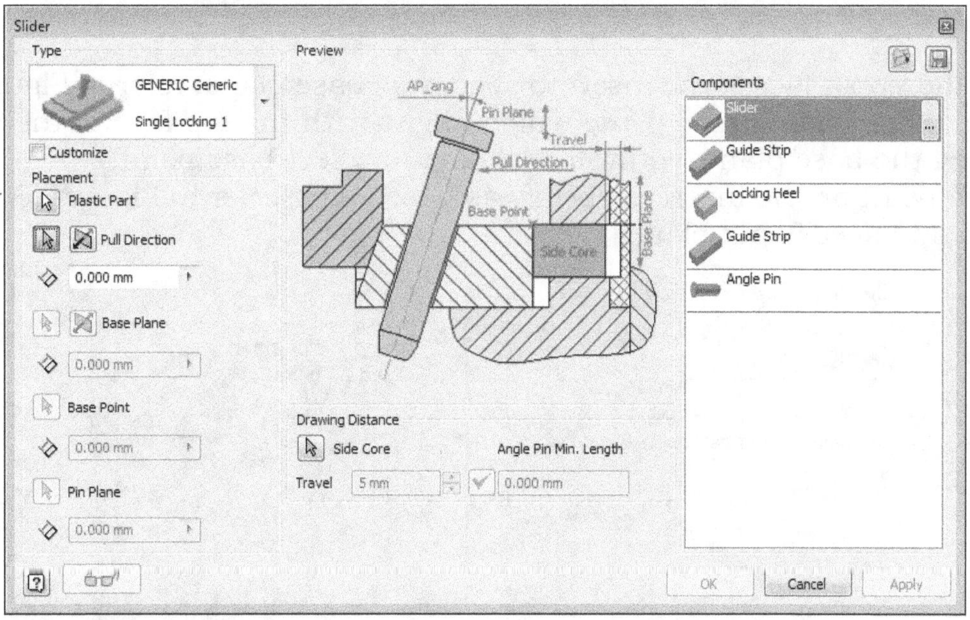

Figure-132. Slider dialog box

- Select desired type of slider from the **Type** selection box in the dialog box. You will be asked to select plane for pull direction.
- Select a face on the insert to specify pull direction. Note that pull direction is the direction opposite to the insert insertion; refer to Figure-133. On selecting the face, you will be asked to select base plane.

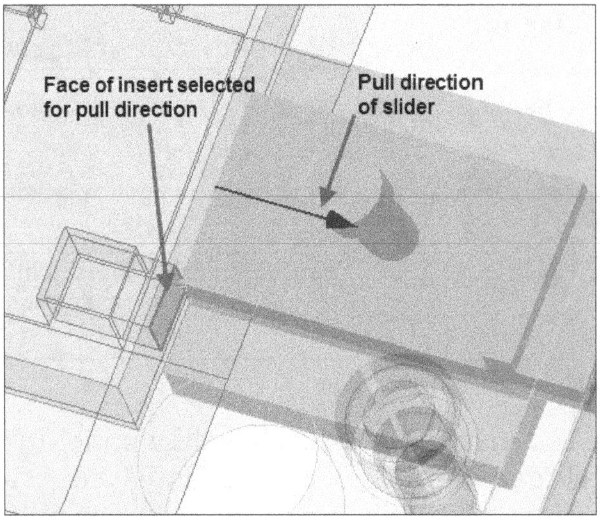

Figure-133. Selecting face for pull direction

- Select the upper face of the insert to specify as base plane; refer to Figure-134. In general, base plane is the plane which aligns with the top face of the slider. On selecting the base plane, you will be asked to select base point.
- Select a point on the insert to specify as base point; refer to Figure-135. You will be asked to specify pin plane.

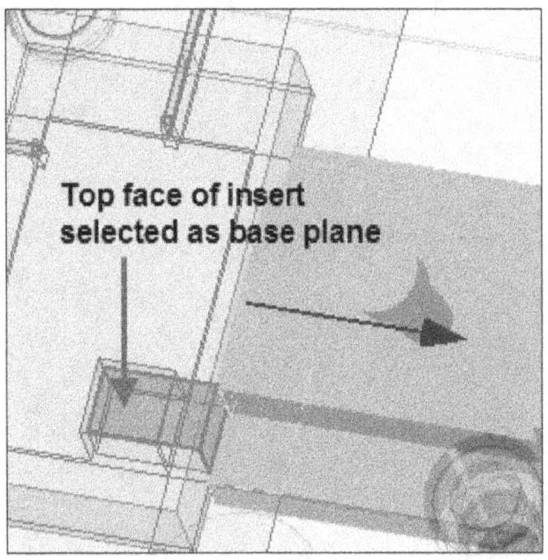

Figure-134. Face selected for base plane

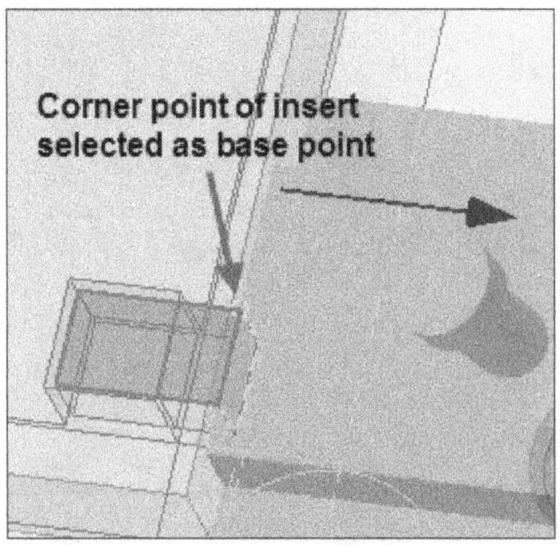

Figure-135. Selecting base point of slider

- Select a plane/face at which you want the pin to be when mold assembly is closed; refer to Figure-136.

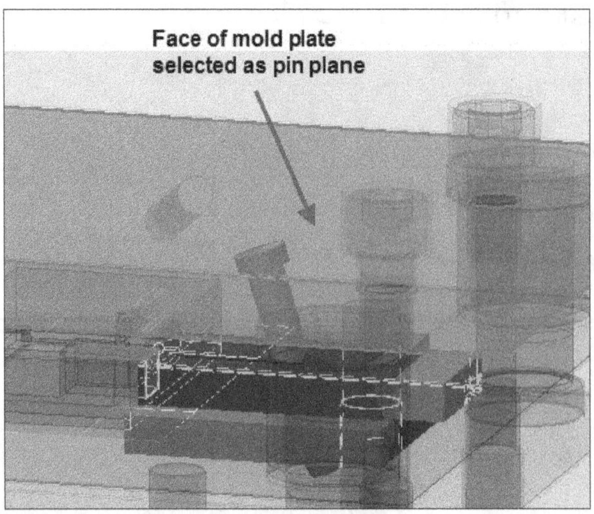

Figure-136. Face selected as pin plane

- Click on the **Side core** selection button from the **Drawing Distance** area of the dialog box. You will be asked to select the insert.
- Select the insert created earlier for slider; refer to Figure-137.

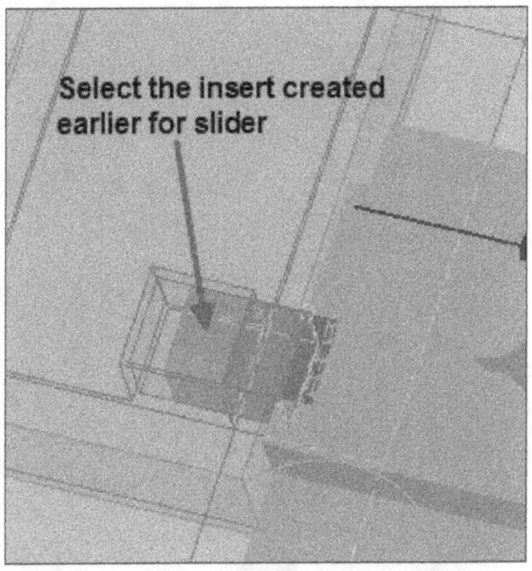

Figure-137. Selecting insert for slider

- Specify the total travel of slider along with insert when the mold is open in the **Travel** edit box in the **Drawing Distance** area of the dialog box. This should be enough travel so that the insert is completely out of core/cavity block; refer to Figure-138.

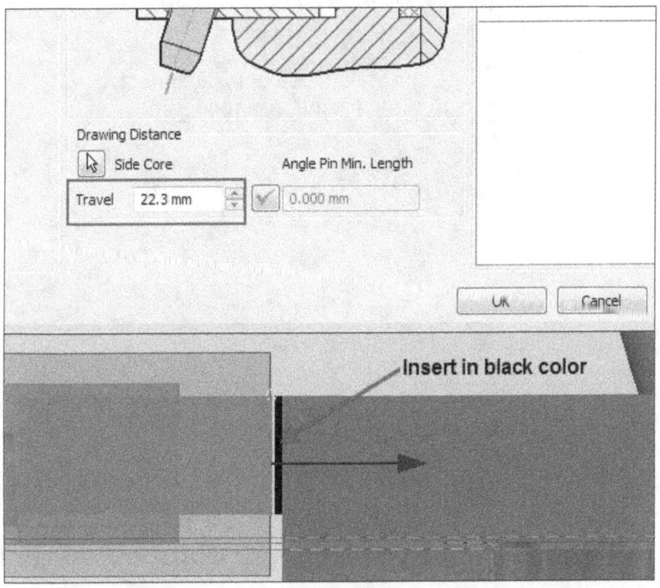

Figure-138. Travel of slider specified

- Now, you may find that slider components are bigger or smaller than what is required. So, edit the components of slider as we did for cooling channel components.
- Click on the **OK** button to create the slider.

ADDING LIFTER TO MOLD ASSEMBLY

Lifter is used to create the small undercut features. Like snap fits on the plastic part. The procedure to add lifter is given next.

- Click on the **Lifter** tool from the **Mold Assembly** panel in the **Mold Assembly** tab of the **Ribbon**. The **Lifter** dialog box will be displayed as shown in Figure-139. Also, you will be asked to select a face for pull direction.

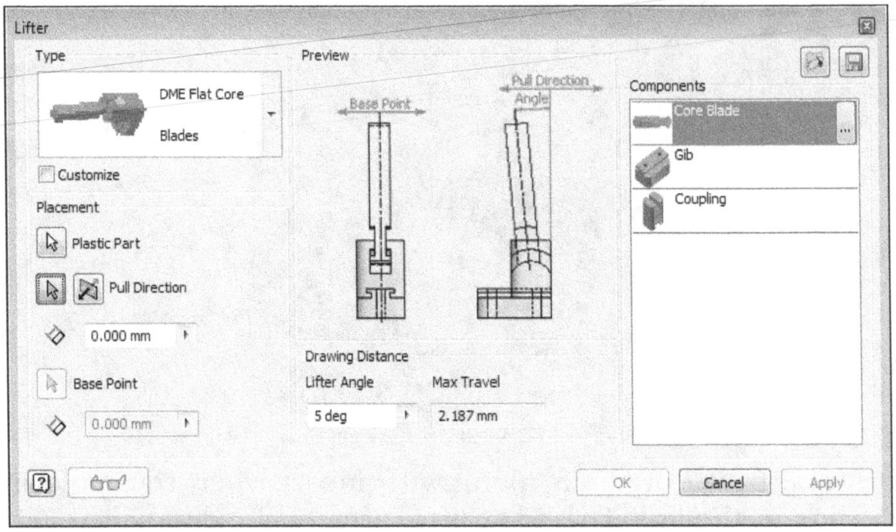

Figure-139. Lifter dialog box

- Select the flat face of insert created for lifter to specify pull direction; refer to Figure-140. You will be asked to select the base point.

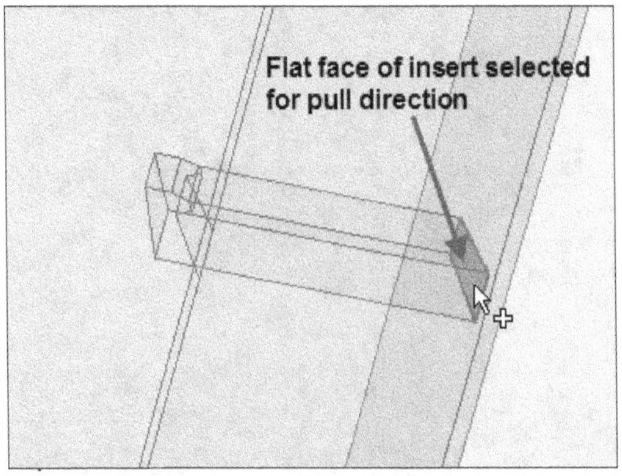

Figure-140. Face selected for pull direction

- Click at a point on lifter insert. Note that the selected point will align to the mid plane of the lifter assembly.
- Set the pull direction offset distance and base point offset distance in their related edit boxes.
- Specify the lifter angle in the **Lifter Angle** edit box and click on the **OK** button to create the lifter assembly. The lifter assembly will be added to the mold assembly; refer to Figure-141.

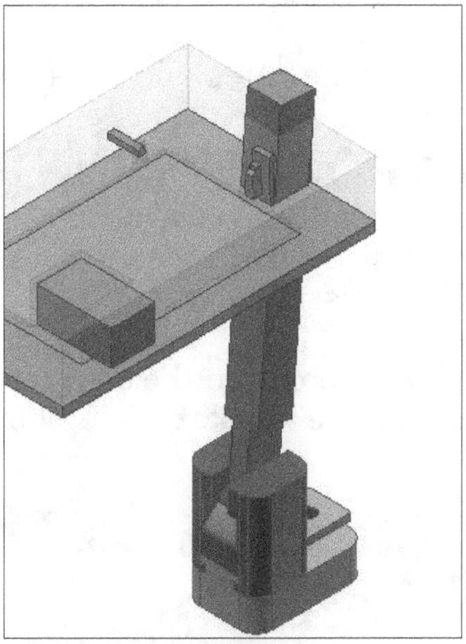

Figure-141. Lifter assembly created

COMBINING CORES AND CAVITIES

The **Combine Cores and Cavities** tool is used to combine the selected cores and cavities in one set of core and cavity plates. The procedure to use this tool is given next.

- Click on the **Combine Cores and Cavities** tool from the **Boolean** panel in the **Mold Assembly** tab of the **Ribbon**. The **Combine Cores/Cavities** dialog box will be displayed along with the cores and cavities in the assembly; refer to Figure-142.

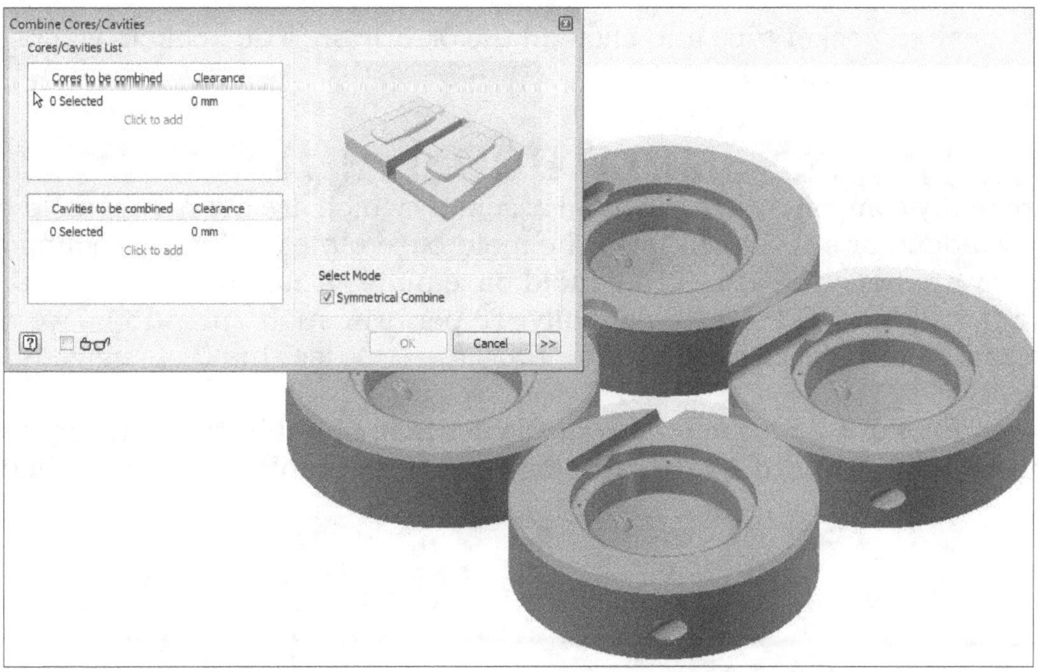

Figure-142. Combine Cores/Cavities dialog box

- One by one select the models displayed in the drawing area.
- Select the **Symmetrical Combine** check box if you want to combine the core-cavities in symmetry.

- Click on the more button to expand the dialog box and set desired corner conditions.
- Click on the **OK** button to combine cores and cavities.

CREATING POCKET IN WORKPIECE

In Autodesk Inventor, pockets for core and cavity are not created automatically in the mold plates. So, this work need to be performed manually. The procedure to create the pockets in mold plates is discussed next.

- Click on the **Workpiece Pocket** tool from the **Boolean** panel in the **Mold Assembly** tab of the **Ribbon**. The **Workpiece Pocket** dialog box will be displayed; refer to Figure-143.

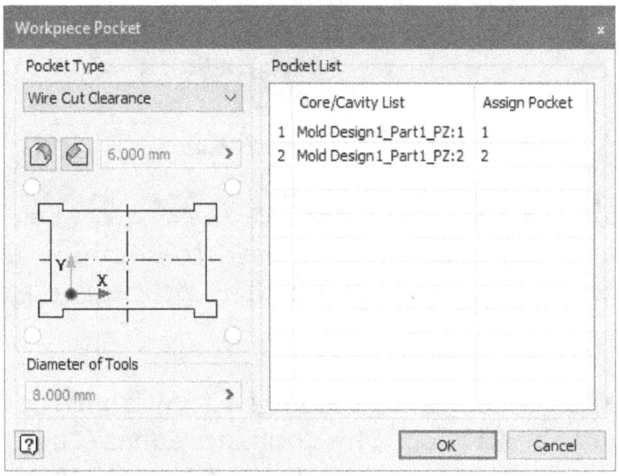

Figure-143. Workpiece Pocket dialog box

- Select desired pocket type and click on the **OK** button. The pockets will be created in the workpiece accordingly.

MOLD BOOLEAN

There are many components in the mold assembly which are not part of mold base but need to be added or subtracted from the mold base plates. Like the cooling channel and runner are not subtracted from mold base plates automatically, inserts are not added to the slider or lifter automatically. To perform such operations, we use **Mold Boolean** tool in Autodesk Inventor. The procedure to use this tool is given next.

- Click on the **Mold Boolean** tool from the **Boolean** panel in the **Mold Assembly** tab of the **Ribbon**. The **Mold Boolean** dialog box will be displayed; refer to Figure-144.

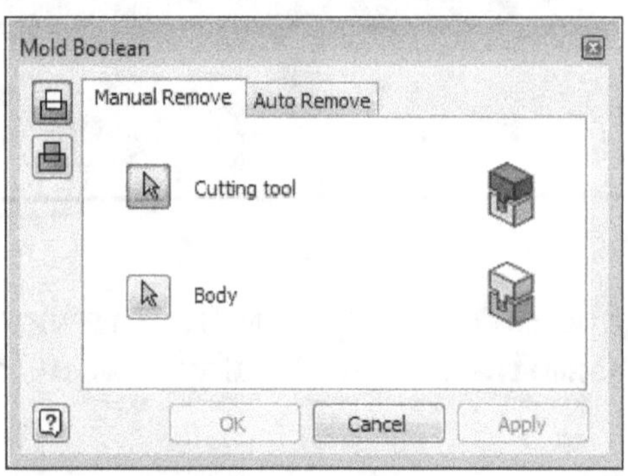

Figure-144. Mold Boolean dialog box

Removing Material

- Make sure the **Remove** button is selected at the left in the dialog box. Select the cutting tool like cooling channel tube, runner, etc. from the mold assembly. You will be asked to select the body from which material is to be cut.
- Select the plate of mold from which you want to cut the tube, runner, etc.
- Click on the **OK** button to cut the material. Click on the **Apply** button if you want to perform more material removal operations.

You can find the interfering parts and speed up the process of removing material from the mold plates by using the **Auto Remove** tab in the dialog box. The method is discussed next.

- Click on the **Auto Remove** tab in the dialog box. The **Mold Boolean** dialog box will be displayed as shown in Figure-145.

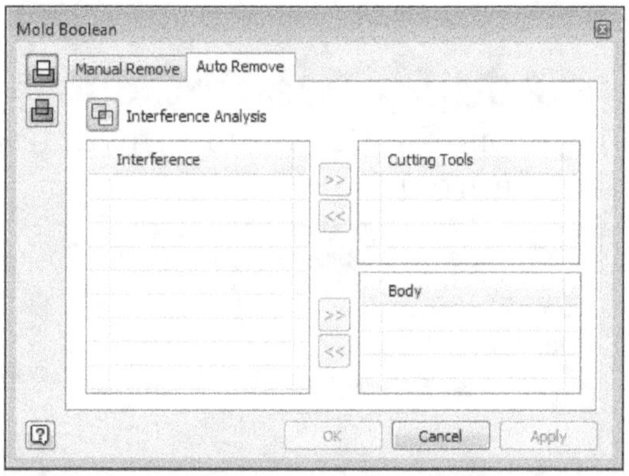

Figure-145. Auto Remove tab in Mold Boolean dialog box

- Click on the **Interference Analysis** button from the dialog box. The list of interfering components will be displayed.
- Select the component from the list and click on the **>>** button of **Cutting Tools** or **Body** list as required; refer to Figure-146.

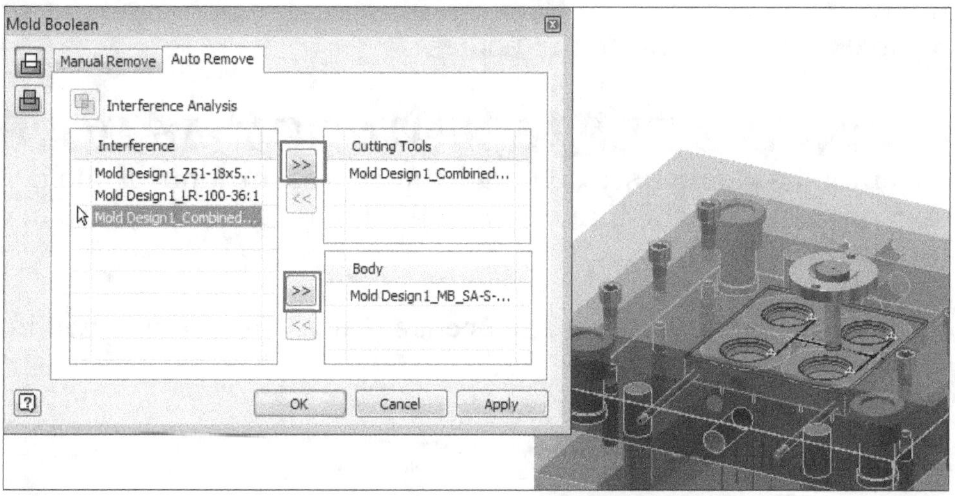

Figure-146. Categorizing interfering components for material removal

- Click on the **OK** or **Apply** button to perform the material removal operation; refer to Figure-147.

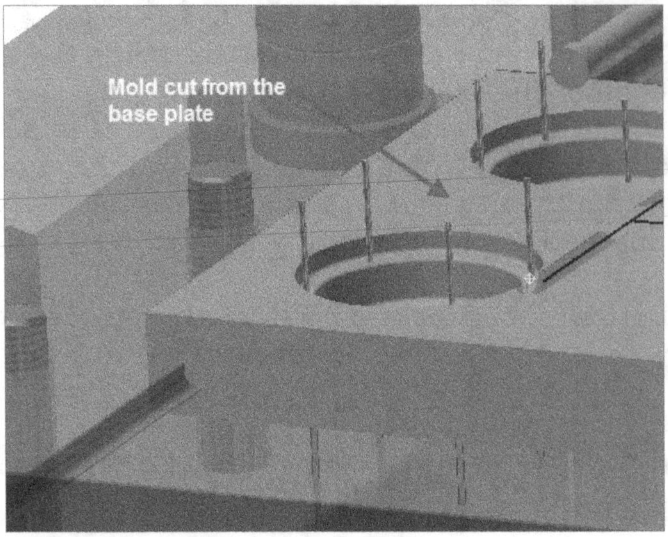

Figure-147. Mold cut from the base plate

Adding Two Bodies

- Click on the **Add** button from the left area in the dialog box. The dialog box will be displayed as shown in Figure-148.

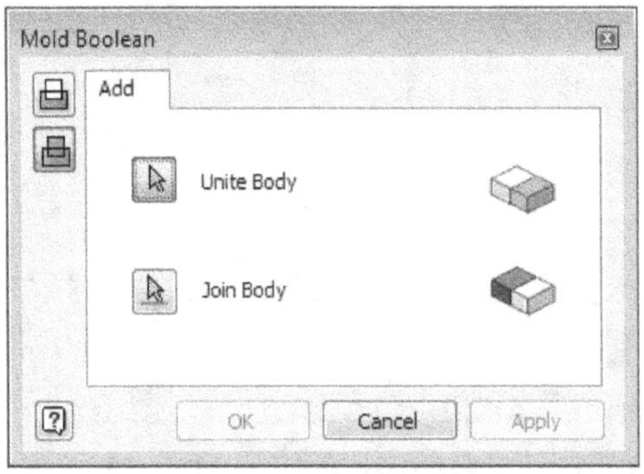

Figure-148. Add tab in Mold Boolean dialog box

- Select the first body (insert) to be united and then the second body (slider or lifter) to be united.
- Click on the **OK** button to unite the bodies.

CHANGING REPRESENTATION OF MOLD

Autodesk Inventor has options to change the representation of mold as open or closed so that you can view the inner area of the mold. The procedure to change the representation is discussed next.

- Click on the **Show tabs** option in the **Browse Bar**. A drop-down will be displayed with options as shown in Figure-149.

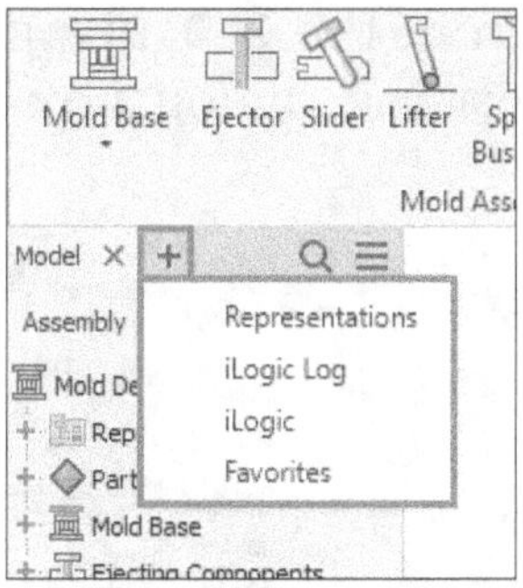

Figure-149. Options on clicking Show tabs

- Click on the **Representations** option from the drop-down. The **Representations Browse Bar** will be displayed; refer to Figure-150.

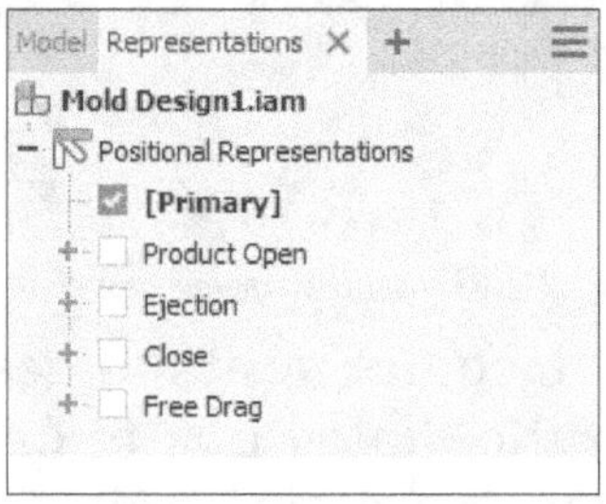

Figure-150. Representations Browse Bar

- Expand the **Positional Representations** node and double-click on the representation that you want to check; refer to Figure-151 which shows open position of mold.

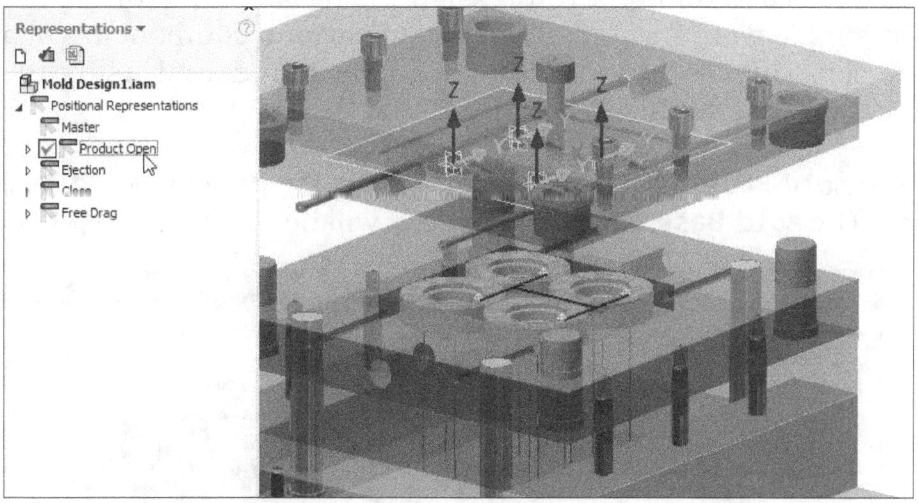

Figure-151. Product Open position of mold

- Remember that if you want to perform any change in the mold assembly then you need to double-click on the **Master** positional representation to return back to original form.
- To return back to **Mold Design Browse Bar**, click on the **Model** tab in the **Browse Bar**.

CREATING 2D DRAWINGS OF MOLD

Creation of 2D drawings is very crucial step for all the manufacturing work. In Autodesk Inventor, there is a direct tool to create 2D drawings for mold assembly. The procedure to create the 2D drawings is given next.

- Click on the **2-D Drawing** tool from the **2-D Drawing** panel in the **Mold Assembly** tab of the **Ribbon**. The **2-D Drawing** dialog box will be displayed as shown in Figure-152.

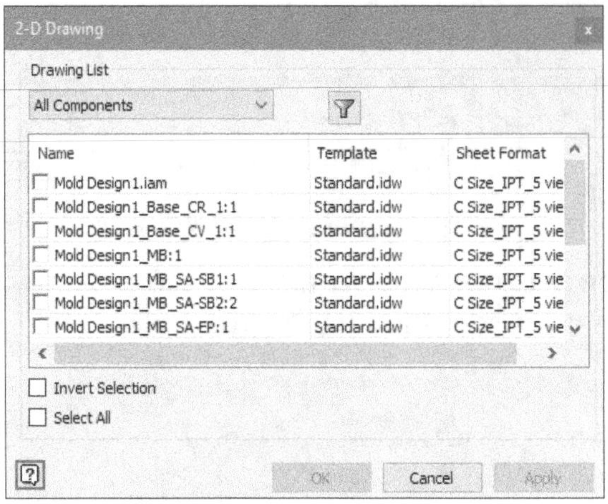

Figure-152. 2-D Drawing dialog box

- Select the check boxes for the components to generate drawings for them.
- Click on the **OK** button from the dialog box to create the selected drawings. The drawing environment will become active and drawings recently created will be displayed.

MOLD BASE AUTHOR

The **Mold Base Author** tool is used to assign mold base attribute to a user defined mold base. In simple words, you can designate various components of an assembly as mold base components so that later they can be inserted using the **Mold Base** tool. The procedure to use this tool is discussed next.

- Click on the **Mold Base Author** tool from the **Author** panel in **Mold Assembly** tab of the **Ribbon**. The **Mold Base Author** dialog box will be displayed; refer to Figure-153.

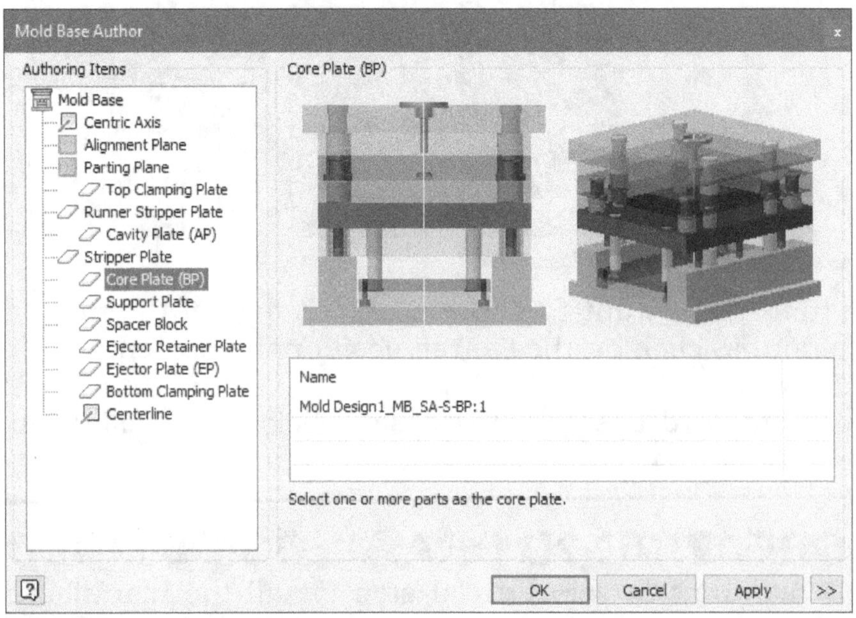

Figure-153. Mold base author dialog box

- Select desired items to defined mold base in the dialog box and click on the **OK** button. The **Assemble** contextual tab will be displayed. You can use the assembly tools as discussed in previous chapters to modify the mold base assembly.
- Click on the **Return** button to exit the tool.

SELF ASSESSMENT

Q1. Which of the following statements is correct about designing wall thickness in mold design?

a) The critical thickness increases with lowering temperature and molecular weight.
b) The critical thickness increases with increasing temperature and molecular weight.
c) The critical thickness reduces with lowering temperature and molecular weight.
d) The critical thickness reduces with increasing temperature and molecular weight.

Q2. Which of the following issues should be considered when properly designing the ribs?

a) Mold-ability
b) Thickness
c) Location
d) All of the Above

Q3. Which of the following resins is not used in designing undercuts in mold design?

a) Polycarbonate
b) Unfilled Polyamide 6
c) Thermoplastic polyurethane elastomer
d) Polymethylene

Q4. Which of the following options shows the correct workflow of mold design assembly?

a) Insert Plastic Part --> Specifying Material --> Generating Core-Cavity --> Generating 2D drawings and CAM data

b) Insert Plastic Part --> Generating Core Cavity --> Specifying Material --> Generating 2D drawings and CAM data

c) Generating Core-Cavity --> Specifying Material --> Insert Plastic Part --> Generating 2D drawings and CAM data

d) Specifying Material --> Insert Plastic Part --> Generating Core-Cavity --> Generating 2D drawings and CAM data

Q5. In which of the following Gate Designs in preparing core and cavity, the Ejector Pins are necessary for automatic trimming of the gate?

a) Edge Gate
b) Sub Gate

c) Hot Tip Gate
d) Direct or Sprue Gate

Q6. Which of the following Gates is used in two plate mold construction for creating gate in core and cavity?

a) Submarine Gate
b) Fan Gate
c) Edge Gate
d) Pin Gate

Q7. Which of the following issues can cause problems with Pressure and Temperature parameters in creating mold?

a) Excessive Injection Fill Speed
b) Low Injection Pressure
c) Low Mold Temperature
d) All of the Above

Q8. Which of the following cross-sectional shape of the runner is not used in a mould when creating core and cavity?

a) Fully round
b) U-Shaped
c) Hexagonal
d) Pentagonal

Q9. The **Define Workpiece Setting** tool is used to create a block of steel from which the core and cavity is to be join. (True/False)

Q10. The higher the hydraulic diameter of runner used in mold, the lower the flow resistance. (True/False)

Q11. .... are rib-like features that add support to structures such as bosses, ribs, and walls.

Q12. As the molten plastic cools down in mold, it gets shrunk by certain amount called ....

Q13. Which tab do you use to set the thickness and height of the grill boundary?

A. Island
B. Boundary
C. Draft
D. More

Q14. What is the purpose of the Boss tool?

A. To create grills
B. To create fillets
C. To create boss features at specified locations
D. To adjust mold shrinkage

Q15. In the Boss tool, what feature is created when you select the “Thread” button?

A. Female part of the boss fastener
B. Male part of the boss fastener
C. Snap fit hook
D. Lip-groove joint

Q16. What is the function of the Rest tool?

A. To create grills
B. To create a flat landing area
C. To create snap fits
D. To place core and cavity

Q17. In the Rest tool, what option can you select to limit the landing surface?

A. Landing Distance
B. To Surface
C. Clearance Taper
D. Thickness

Q18. What is the Snap Fit tool primarily used for?

A. To create grills
B. To create snap fits joining two components without screws
C. To create boss features
D. To adjust mold dimensions

Q19. Which button is used to set the direction of the hook in the Snap Fit tool?

A. Cantilever Snap Fit Hook
B. Hook Direction
C. Beam
D. Catch

Q20. What does the Rule Fillet tool do?

A. Creates snap fit hooks
B. Creates a flat surface
C. Fillets edges based on specified rules
D. Creates boss features

Q21. Which Rule Fillet option fillets only the edges formed by faces of the selected feature?

A. Against Part
B. Against Features
C. Free Edges
D. All Edges

Q22. What is the Lip tool used to create?

A. Fillets between faces
B. A lip-groove joint between two plastic parts
C. A snap fit hook
D. A rib structure

Q23. In the Lip tool, what is selected first to define the path of the lip/groove?

A. Face
B. Sketch
C. Edge
D. Point

Q24. What is the first step in mold designing in Autodesk Inventor?

A. Placing core and cavity
B. Inserting a plastic part
C. Adjusting orientation
D. Creating mold layout

Q25. After inserting the plastic part, where is it placed automatically?

A. At the origin
B. At a selected point
C. At the coordinate system
D. On a predefined plane

Q26. What does the Place Core and Cavity tool define?

A. Insert plastic parts
B. Core and cavity components positioning
C. Plastic part layout
D. Fillet application

Q27. Which checkbox allows immediate editing of assembly after importing core and cavity?

A. Enable Assembly Edit
B. Activate Assembly Edit immediately
C. Import Assembly
D. Activate Core

Q28. What does adjusting the orientation of the part decide in mold design?

A. Draft angle
B. Opening direction
C. Surface finish
D. Shrinkage factor

Q29. In the Adjust Orientation tool, which face should be selected?

A. Flat face perpendicular to opening direction
B. Flat face parallel to parting line
C. Curved face parallel to the mold axis
D. Any random face

Q30. Which tool allows free positioning of the part along X, Y, and Z directions?

A. Align with Axis
B. Free Transform
C. Align Center
D. Adjust Orientation

Q31. Which tool is selected from the Adjust Orientation drop-down to position the part?
A. Adjust Position
B. Flip moldable part
C. Free Transform
D. Core Position

Q32. Which tab becomes available after selecting the Core/Cavity tool from the Mold Layout panel?

A. Mold Design
B. Mold Layout
C. Core/Cavity
D. Plastic Part

Q33. What is the main purpose of the Part Shrinkage tool?

A. To create gates for filling
B. To provide shrinkage allowance
C. To create surface patches
D. To define workpiece settings

Q34. When using the Part Shrinkage tool, which checkbox should be selected if shrinkage is equal in all directions?

A. Directional
B. Anisotropic
C. Isotropic
D. Symmetric
Q35. Which tool is used to specify the location of orifice for filling molten plastic into the mold?

A. Gate Design
B. Gate Creation
C. Gate Location
D. Insert Creation

Q36. Which gate design is best suited for flat parts and leaves a scar at the parting line?

A. Sub Gate
B. Edge Gate
C. Hot Tip Gate
D. Direct Gate

Q37. Which gate design is automatically trimmed and leaves a pin-sized scar?

A. Sub Gate
B. Edge Gate
C. Hot Tip Gate
D. Direct Gate

Q38. What problem can occur if two gates are used and the weld line falls on a highly stressed area?

A. Increased strength
B. Product failure
C. Better surface finish
D. Faster filling

Q39. If a part is round and needs to be absolutely round, where should the gate be placed?

A. At the edge
B. At the end
C. In the center
D. Anywhere

Q40. Which problem arises if the injection fill speed is too fast?

A. Blushing
B. Voiding
C. Welding
D. Bubbling

Q41. What is the solution if the melt temperature is too high or too low causing surface defects?

A. Increase mold size
B. Adjust fill speed
C. Adjust melt temperature
D. Increase injection pressure

Q42. Low injection pressure can cause what type of visual defect?

A. Brightness
B. Dullness

C. Blistering
D. Cracking

Q43. Which tool is used to create a block of steel from which the core and cavity are cut?

A. Define Workpiece Setting
B. Create Insert
C. Part Shrinkage
D. Create Patching Surface

Q44. Which tool is used to patch the cuts and holes in a model?

A. Create Runoff Surface
B. Create Patching Surface
C. Use Existing Surface
D. Create Insert

Q45. What does the Use Existing Surface tool allow you to do?

A. Patch and runoff surfaces
B. Create new surfaces only
C. Fill cavities
D. Create inserts

Q46. Which tool allows you to manually create a surface patch by selecting edges?

A. Define Workpiece Setting
B. Create Planar Patch
C. Create Runoff Surface
D. Extrude Runoff Surface

Q47. What does the Create Runoff Surface tool use to split the core and cavity?

A. Inner boundaries
B. Outer boundary edges
C. Mold centerline
D. Plastic shrinkage

Q48. The Extrude Runoff Surface tool creates a runoff surface by doing what?

A. Rotating a curve
B. Extruding a curve/edge
C. Cutting a surface
D. Filling a patch

Q49. The Bounded Runoff Surface tool creates a runoff surface based on what?

A. Freehand sketches
B. Circular paths
C. Selected curves
D. Mold walls

Q50. Radiate Runoff Surface tool is used to create which type of surfaces?

A. Planar surfaces
B. Cylindrical surfaces
C. Non-planar surfaces
D. Flat patches

Q51. What is the purpose of the Extend Runoff Surface tool?

A. Extend mold cavity
B. Extend an edge of selected face
C. Stretch the gate
D. Expand cooling channels

Q52. Which tool activates the moldable part file for editing?

A. Edit Core
B. Edit Moldable Part
C. Mold Layout
D. Insert Creation

Q53. What is the main function of the Create Insert tool?

A. Create shrinkage
B. Create slider inserts
C. Patch cavities
D. Design gates

Q54. In Create Insert tool, which option under Termination is used to end the insert at a specific face?

A. Distance
B. Mold
C. Profile
D. Clearance

Q55. In Create Insert tool, what is the purpose of specifying a clearance value?

A. Increase gate size
B. Ensure easy extraction
C. Reduce shrinkage
D. Enhance surface texture

Chapter 15

Surface Design and Freeform Creation

Topics Covered

The major topics covered in this chapter are:

- ***Introduction to Surface Design***
- ***Surfacing Tools***
- ***Freeform Designing Tools***
- ***Practical and Practice on Surface Design***

INTRODUCTION TO SURFACE DESIGN

Surface design is a very important aspect of CAD software. Surface designing gives the power to design any shape of object which is possible in real-world. There can be many modeling problems which can not be solved by solid modeling. In such situations, the surface modeling comes for rescue. Check the model shown in Figure-1 and ask yourself how much effort will it take to create in solid modeling.

In this chapter, we will learn about the tools related to surface design and Freeform modeling. **The tools for surface design and freeform modeling are available in the Part environment so you need to start a new part file now.**

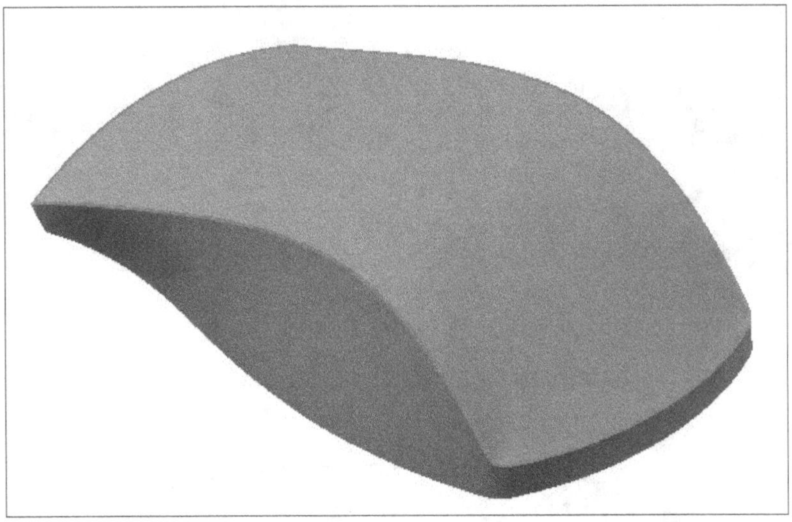

Figure-1. Model of a mouse

Some of the tools discussed in solid modeling can also be used for surface designing. So, we will start discussing these tools and then we will discuss the tools in **Surface** panel.

EXTRUDED SURFACE

An extruded surface can be created by using the same **Extrude** tool that we have discussed for solid modeling. The procedure to do so is given next.

- Click on the **Extrude** tool from the **Create** panel in the **3D Model** tab of the **Ribbon**. If there is no sketch in the drawing area then you will be asked to select a sketching plane to create the sketch.
- Select the sketching plane and create an open or close loop sketch.
- Click on the **Finish Sketch** button from the **Finish** drop-down in the **Exit** panel of the **Sketch** tab in the **Ribbon**. The **Extrude** dialog box will be displayed along with the sketch extruded as solid model; refer to Figure-2.
- Click on the button in the upper right side of the dialog box to toggle for surface mode; refer to Figure-3.
- Set the other parameters as required and then click on the **OK** button.

In the same way, you can use the **Revolve**, **Sweep**, **Loft**, and **Coil** tools to create surfaces.

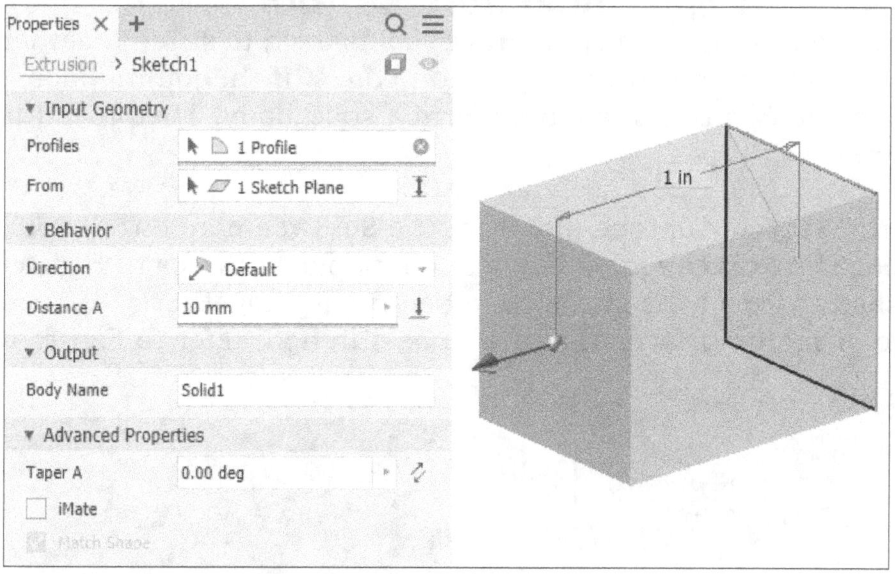

Figure-2. Extrude dialog box in solid mode

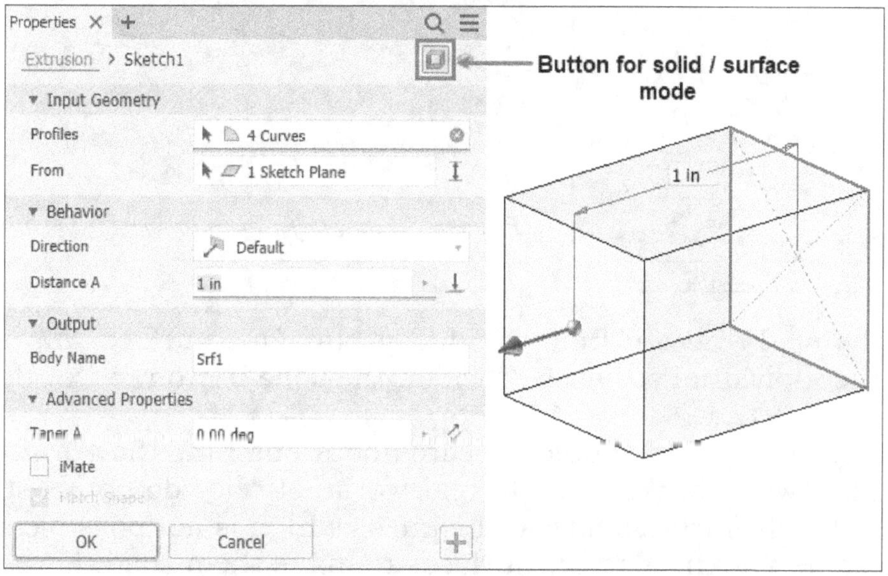

Figure-3. Extrude dialog box in surface mode

SURFACING TOOLS

The tools to perform surfacing operations are available in the **Surface** panel in the **3D Model** tab of the **Ribbon**; refer to Figure-4.

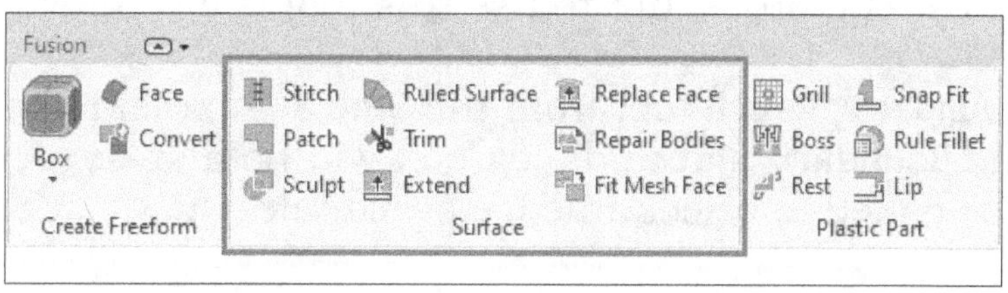

Figure-4. Surface panel

The applications of these tools are discussed next.

Stitch Surface Tool

As the name suggests, the **Stitch Surface** tool is used to stitch together (or say join) the surfaces, which are meeting at common edges. If the joining faces form a close boundary then you can use this tool to form a solid body. The procedure to use this tool is given next.

- Click on the **Stitch Surface** tool from the **Surface** panel in the **3D Model** tab of the **Ribbon**. The **Stitch** dialog box will be displayed; refer to Figure-5. Also, you will be asked to select the surfaces to be stitched together.
- Select two or more surfaces that are to be stitched; refer to Figure-6.

Figure-5. Stitch dialog box

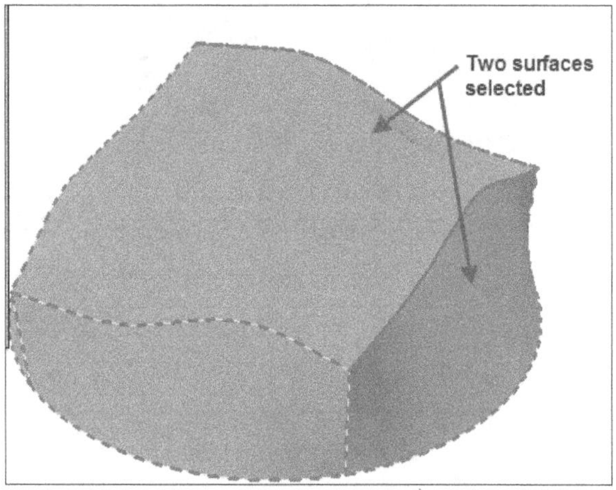

Figure-6. Selecting surfaces for stitching

- Click on the **Apply** button from the dialog box. One surface will be created by stitching the individual surfaces. Click on the **Done** button to exit the dialog box.

A question arises here, Why should we care about stitching the surface? Answer of this question lies with **Thicken** tool. In real-world, surface do not exist as an entity because theoretically surfaces have 0 thickness which is not possible in real world. So, we apply some thickness to the surfaces to make them solid. If we do not stitch the surfaces before applying **Thicken** tool then there will be gap between individual surfaces which makes the manufacturing impossible.

Boundary Patch Tool

The **Boundary Patch** is used to create planar or 3D surface patch based on the selected edges and guidelines. The procedure to use this tool is given next.

- Click on the **Boundary Patch** tool from the **Surface** panel in the **3D Model** tab of the **Ribbon**. The **Boundary Patch** dialog box will be displayed; refer to Figure-7. Also, you will be asked to select an edge or sketch curve.

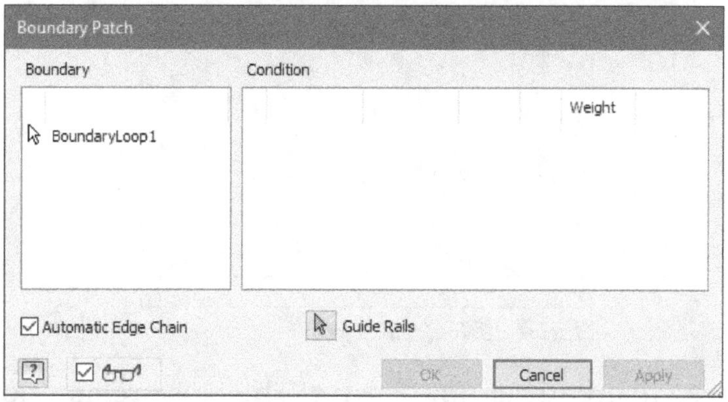

Figure-7. Boundary Patch dialog box

- Select the edges to form a closed loop to create patch. Preview of the boundary patch will be displayed; refer to Figure-8.

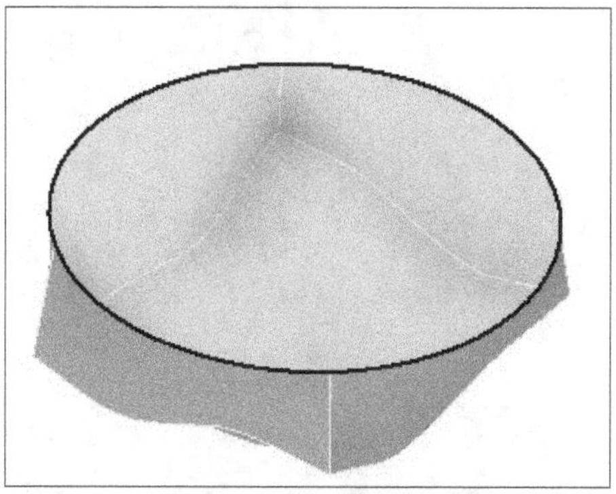

Figure-8. Preview of boundary patch

- Select the **Automatic Edge Chain** check box if you want to select the connecting edges along with the selected edge to form a closed loop.
- Click on the **Guide Rails** selection button to select the guide rail for boundary patch; refer to Figure-9.

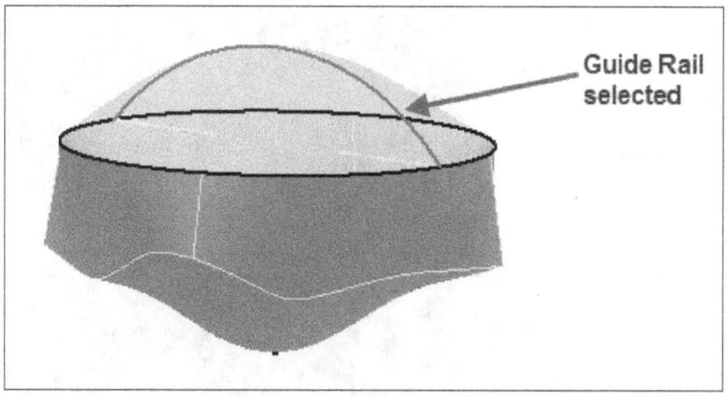

Figure-9. Boundary Patch surface with guide rail

- Click on the **OK** button to create the patch.

Sculpt Tool

The **Sculpt** tool is used to create a solid region bounded by selected surfaces. The procedure to use this tool is given next.

- Click on the **Sculpt** tool from the **Surface** panel in the **3D Model** tab of the **Ribbon**. The **Sculpt** dialog box will be displayed; refer to Figure-10.

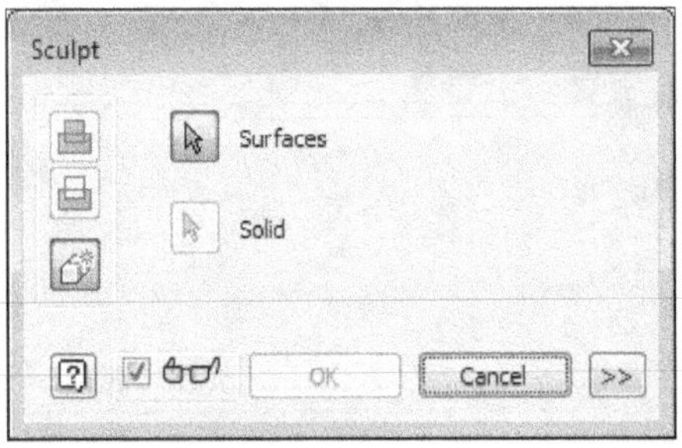

Figure-10. Sculpt dialog box

- Select the surfaces to create sculpt feature. The close region bounded by surfaces will be displayed as preview of sculpt feature; refer to Figure-11.

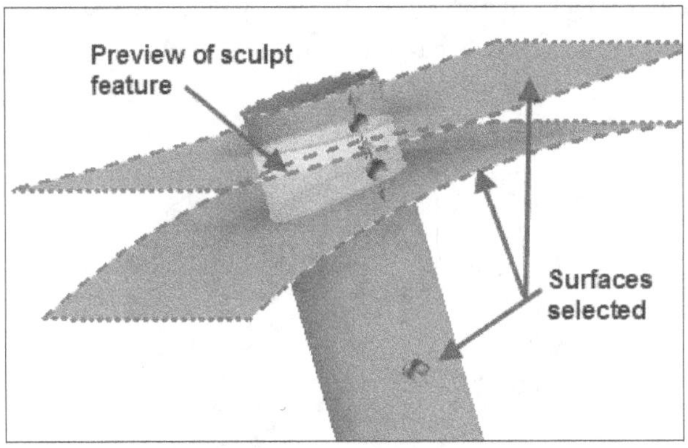

Figure-11. Preview of sculpt feature

- If there is any solid feature passing through the sculpt feature then you can add or subtract the sculpt feature from the solid feature by using the **Add** or **Remove** button from the dialog box; refer to Figure-12.

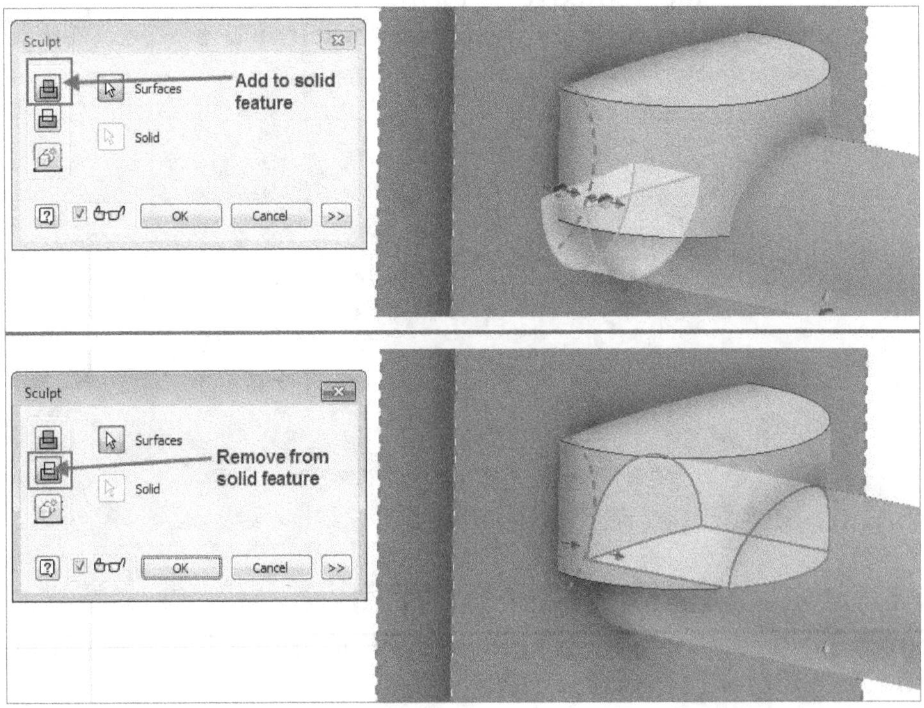

Figure-12. Add or remove sculpt feature

- Click on the **OK** button from the dialog box to create the feature.

Ruled Surface Tool

The **Ruled Surface** tool is used to create surface(s) normal or tangent to the faces of selected edges. The procedure to use this tool is given next.

- Click on the **Ruled Surface** tool from the **Surface** panel in the **3D Model** tab of the **Ribbon**. The **Ruled Surface** dialog box will be displayed as shown in Figure-13.

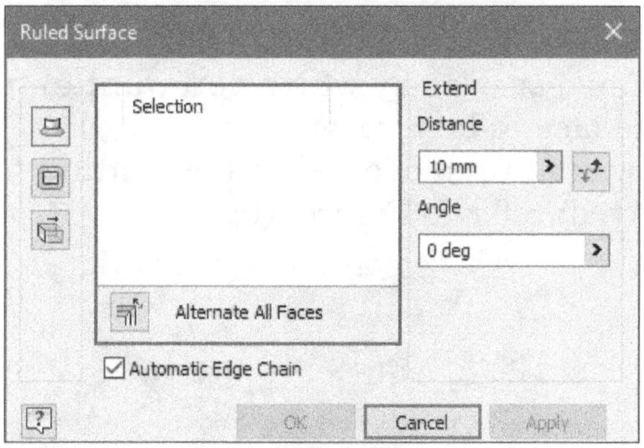

Figure-13. Ruled Surface dialog box

- Select the edge(s) for which you want to create the ruled surface. Preview of the ruled surface will be displayed; refer to Figure-14.

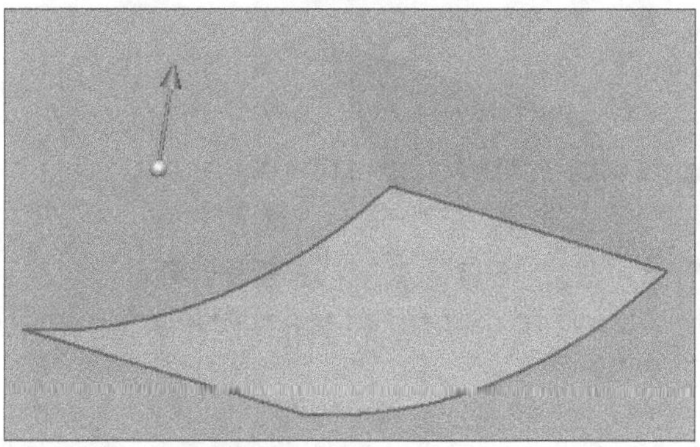

Figure-14. Preview of ruled surface

- Set desired angle in the **Angle** edit box of the dialog box.
- Note that by default, the **Normal** button is selected in the right side of the dialog box and hence the surfaces are created perpendicular to the selected edges. Select the **Tangent** button if you want to create the tangent surfaces. Select the **Vector** button and select desired direction reference to create surfaces in that direction.
- Click on the **OK** button to create the surface.

Trim Surface Tool

As the name suggests, the **Trim Surface** tool is used to trim the surfaces using the other surface, work plane, or sketch. The procedure to use this tool is given next.

- Click on the **Trim Surface** tool from the **Surface** panel in the **3D Model** tab of the **Ribbon**. The **Trim Surface** dialog box will be displayed; refer to Figure-15.

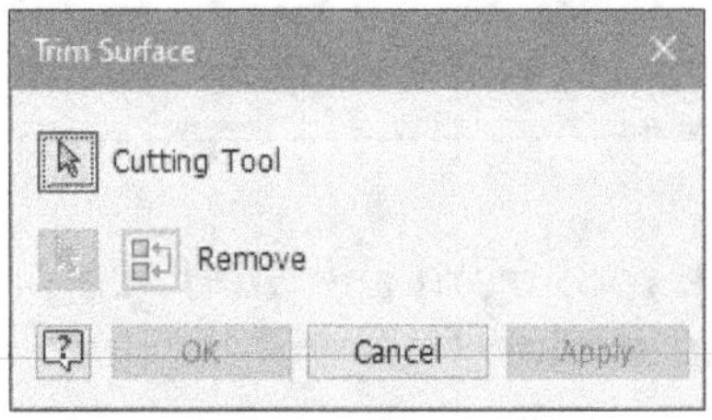

Figure-15. Trim Surface dialog box

- Select the surface, plane, or edge by which you want to trim the surface. You will be asked to select the face to be removed.
- Select the face you want to remove using the cutting tool. Preview of the trim feature will be displayed; refer to Figure-16.

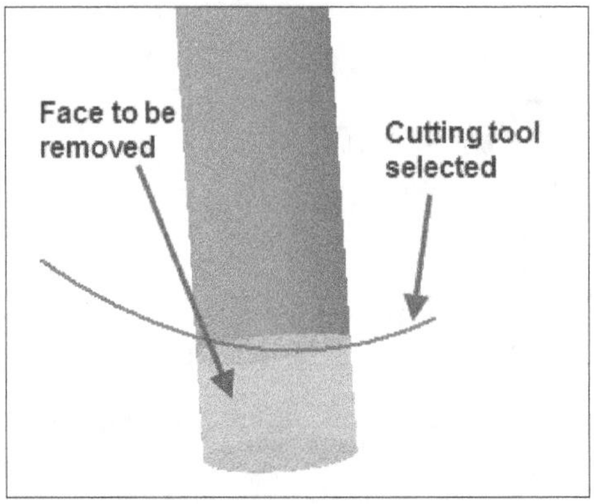

Figure-16. Preview of trim feature

- Click on the **OK** or **Apply** button to create the feature.

Extend Surface Tool

The **Extend Surface** tool is used to extend faces using edges of the faces. The procedure to use this tool is given next.

- Click on the **Extend Surface** tool from the **Surface** panel in the **3D Model** tab of the **Ribbon**. The **Extend Surface** dialog box will be displayed; refer to Figure-17.

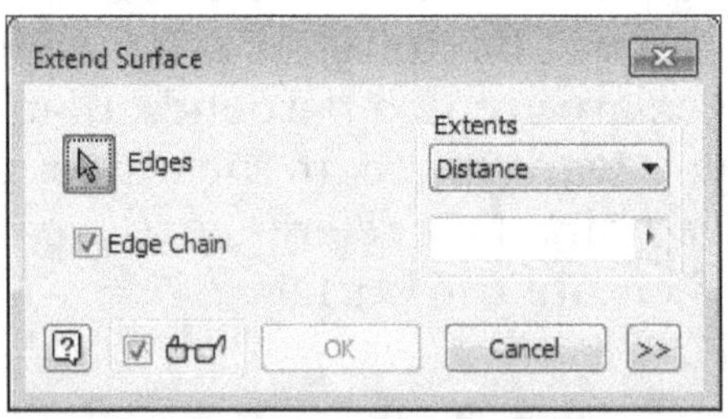

Figure-17. Extend Surface dialog box

- Select the edge(s) that you want to use for extending the corresponding face. Preview of the extended surface will be displayed; refer to Figure-18.

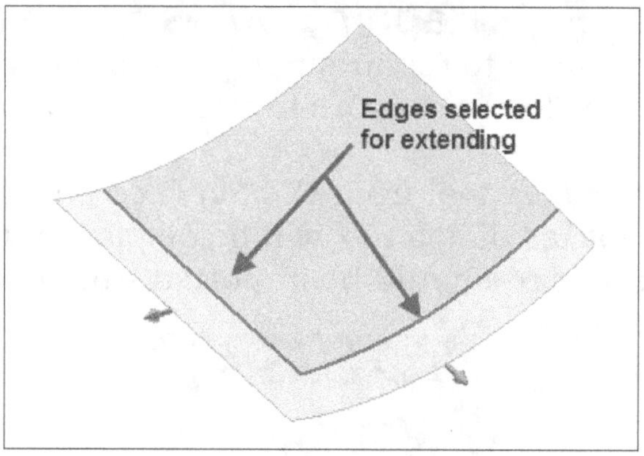

Figure-18. Preview of extend surface

- Set desired distance value in the **Extents** edit box or select the **To** option from the drop-down and select the reference for extension.
- Click on the **OK** button to create the extension surface.

Replace Face Tool

The **Replace Face** tool is used to replace the face of a solid by selecting surface/face. The procedure to use this tool is given next.

- Click on the **Replace Face** tool from the **Surface** panel in the **3D Model** tab of the **Ribbon**. The **Replace Face** dialog box will be displayed; refer to Figure-19.

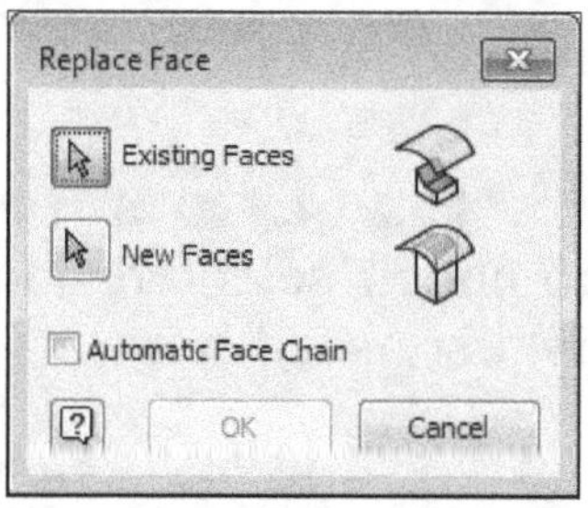

Figure-19. Replace Face dialog box

- Select the face(s) of solid which you want to replaced.
- Click on the **New Faces** selection button from the dialog box and select the face/surface by which you want the face(s) to be replaced; refer to Figure-20.

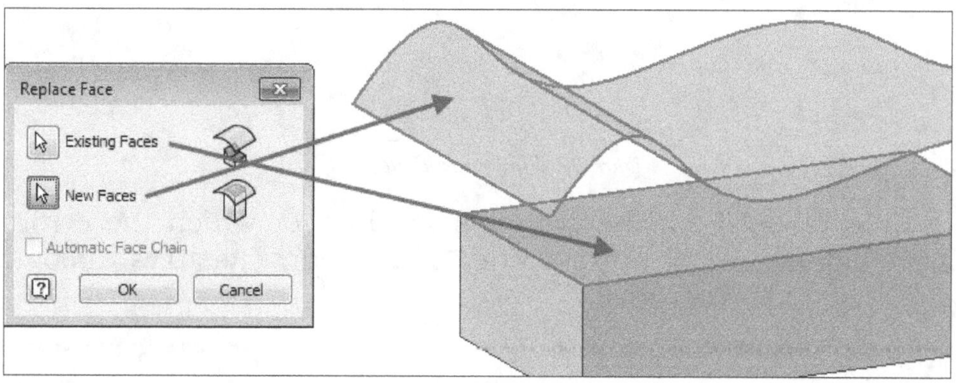

Figure-20. Faces selected for replacement

- Click on the **OK** button from the dialog box to create the feature.

Repair Bodies

The **Repair Bodies** tool is used to repair small gaps and distortions in the imported body using surfacing tools. The procedure to use this tool is discussed next.

- Click on the **Repair Bodies** tool from the **Surface** panel in **3D Model** tab of the **Ribbon**. The **Repair Bodies** dialog box will be displayed; refer to Figure-21. (Note that the body to be repaired should be imported from the non-native software.)

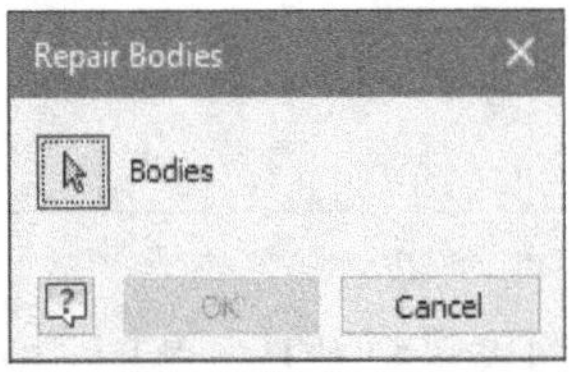

Figure-21. Repair bodies dialog box

- Select desired body from the graphics window to be repaired and click on the **OK** button. The **Repair** contextual tab will be displayed; refer to Figure-22.

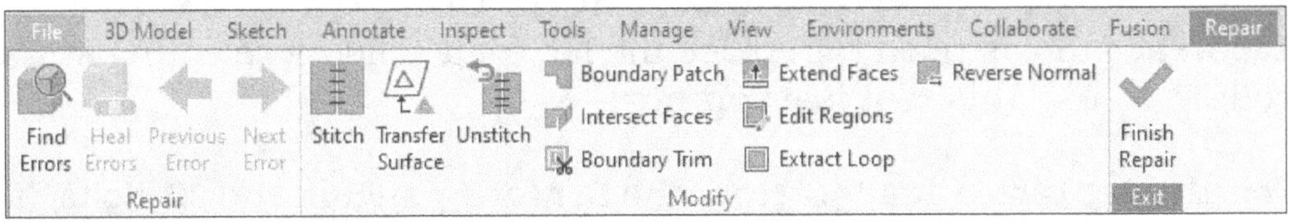

Figure-22. Repair contextual tab

- Now repair the body using desired tools.

Find Errors

The **Find Errors** tool is used to check selected bodies for quality and find errors. The procedure to use this tool is discussed next.

- Click on the **Find Errors** tool from the **Repair** panel in **Repair** contextual tab of the **Ribbon**. The **Find Errors** dialog box will be displayed; refer to Figure-23.

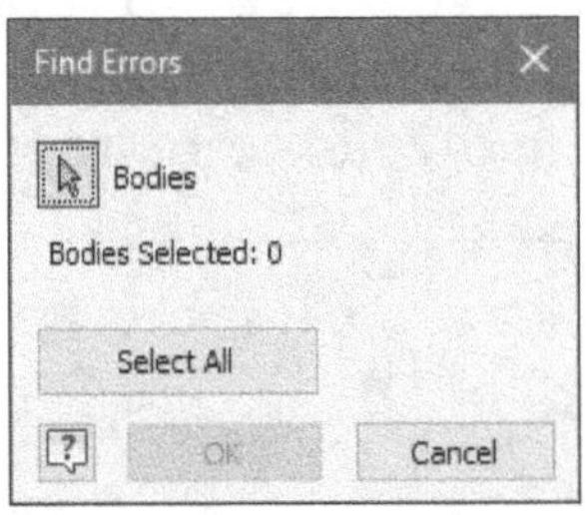

Figure-23. Find errors dialog box

- Select desired model from the graphics window for which the errors are to be found and click on the **OK** button. The **Find Errors Results** dialog box will be displayed; refer to Figure-24.

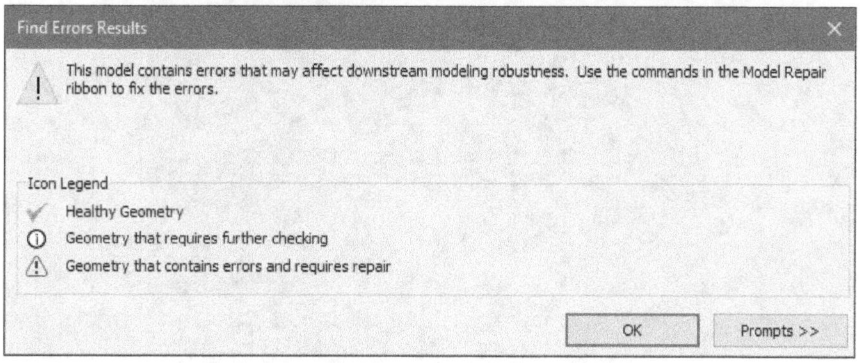

Figure-24. Find errors results dialog box

- After checking the errors, click on the **OK** button from the dialog box.

Heal Errors

The **Heal Errors** tool is used to heal selected model bodies which have gaps or distortions within specified tolerance range. The procedure to use this tool is discussed next.

- Click on the **Heal Errors** tool from **Repair** panel in the **Repair** tab of the **Ribbon**. The **Heal Errors** dialog box will be displayed; refer to Figure-25.

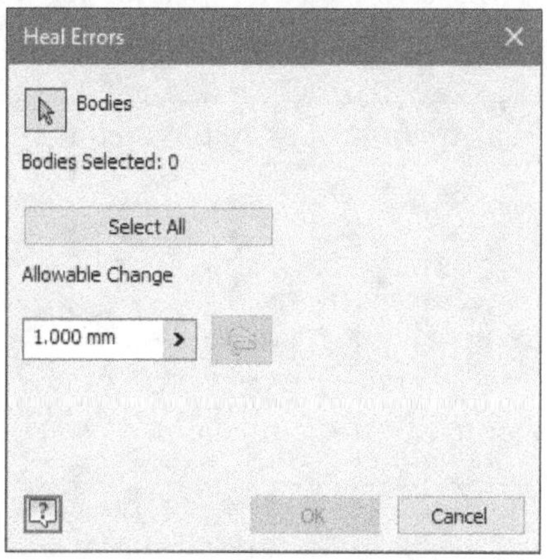

Figure-25. Heal errors dialog box

- Select desired body from the graphics window for which the errors are to be healed.
- Click on the **Select All** button to select all the bodies present in the graphics window.
- Specify desired allowable tolerance between the free edges in the **Allowable Change** edit box.
- Select **Analyze Selected Bodies** button to obtain a report of how many errors are fixed at this tolerance.
- After specifying desired parameters, click on the **OK** button from the dialog box.

Previous Errors

The **Previous Errors** tool is used to display the previous model error that were repaired. The procedure to use this tool is discussed next.

- Click on the **Previous Errors** tool from the **Repair** panel in **Repair** tab of the **Ribbon**. The model will be shown as Figure-26.

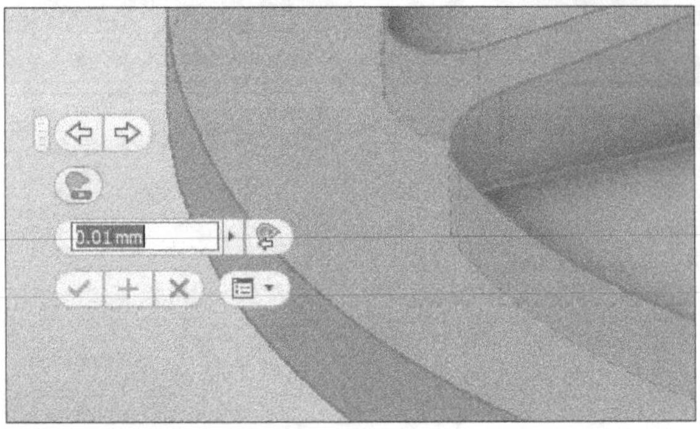

Figure-26. Previous error toolbar

- Specify desired parameters and click on the **OK** button.

Next Errors

The **Next Errors** tool is used to display the next model errors.

Stitch

The **Stitch** tool is used to join surface together to form a quilt or solid. The procedure to use this tool is discussed next.

- Click on the **Stitch** tool from the **Modify** panel in **Repair** tab of the **Ribbon**. The **Stitch** dialog box will be displayed; refer to Figure-27.

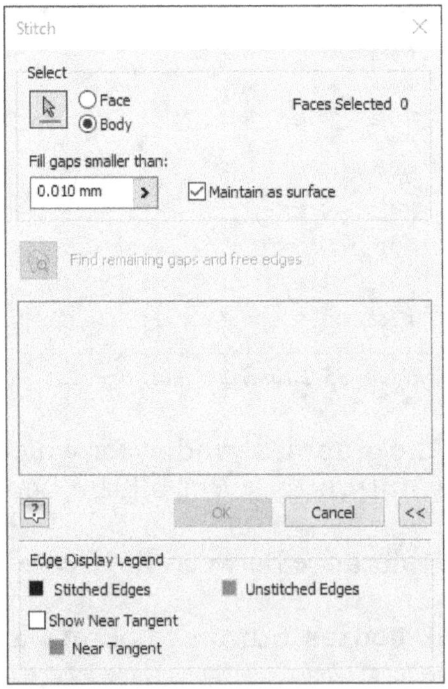

Figure-27. Stitch dialog box

- Select the Face radio button to select individual surfaces to be stitched. Select the Body radio button from dialog box to select surface bodies to be stitched together.
- Select desired surface/body in the graphics window to be stitched.
- Click in the **Fill gaps smaller than** edit box and specify desired size of gaps at the connection zone of two surfaces/bodies that will be automatically filled when stitching the gaps.
- Select the **Maintain as surface** check box to maintain a closed volume as a surface instead of default solid conversion.

- Select the **Find remaining gaps and free edges** button to check preview before stitching.
- After specify desired parameters, click on the **OK** button from the dialog box. The stitch will be created; refer to Figure-28.

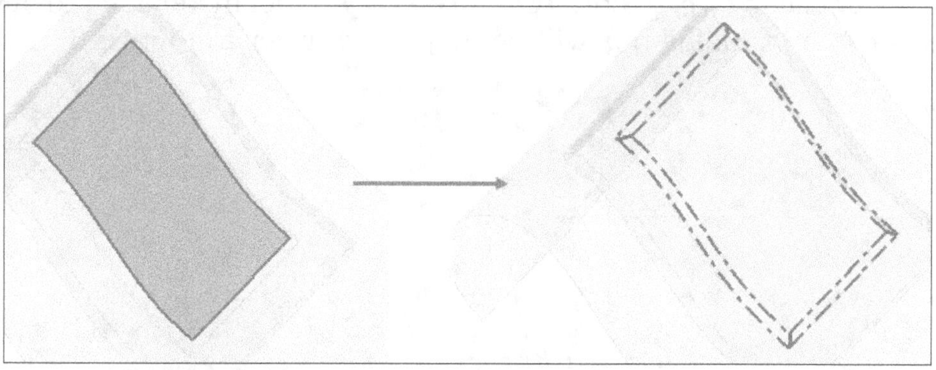

Figure-28. Stitch created

Unstitch

The **Unstitch** tool is used to separate selected face from composite solid or quilts. The procedure to use this tool is discussed next.

- Click on the **Unstitch** tool from the **Modify** panel in **Repair** tab of the **Ribbon**. The **Unstitch** dialog box will be displayed; refer to Figure-29.

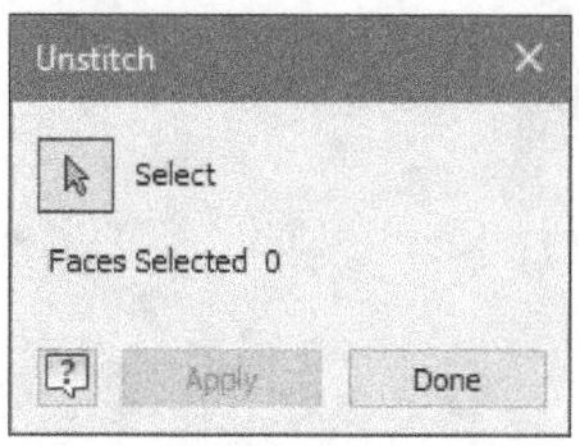

Figure-29. Unstitch dialog box

- Select desired face(s) from the graphics window to be unstitched.
- Click on the **Apply** button from the dialog box. The unstitched surfaces will be displayed; refer to Figure-30.

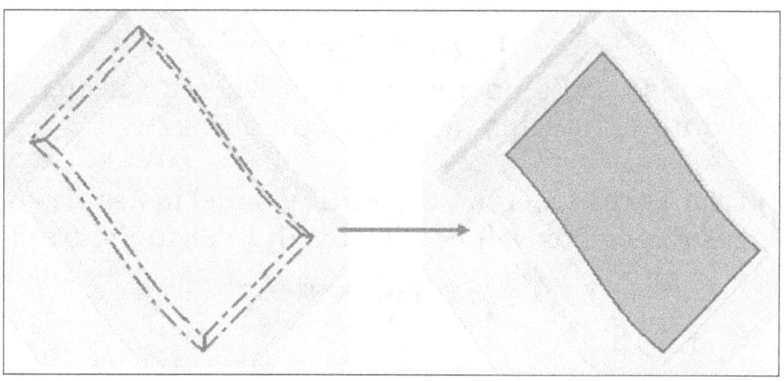

Figure-30. Unstiched created

Boundary Patch

The **Boundary Patch** is used to create planar or 3D surface patch based on selected edges and guidelines. The procedure to use this tool has been discussed earlier.

Boundary Trim

The **Boundary Trim** tool is used to remove the area of the surface defined by the selected boundary curves. The procedure to use this tool is discussed next.

- Click on the **Boundary Trim** tool from the **Modify** panel in **Repair** tab of the **Ribbon**. The **Boundary Trim** dialog box will be displayed; refer to Figure-31.

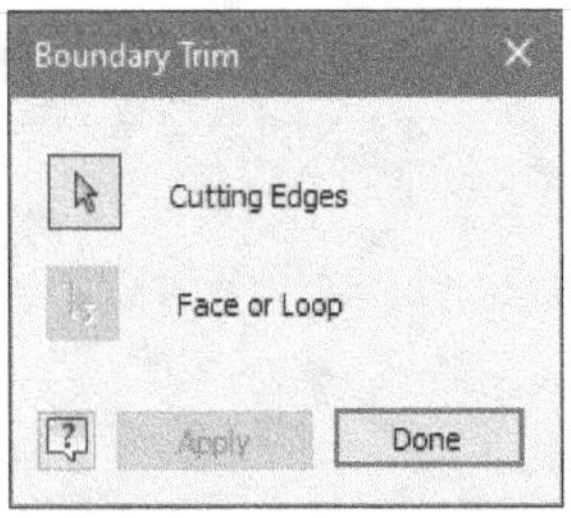

Figure-31. Boundary trim dialog box

- Select desired cutting edges of the model that you want to trim and then select desired face for loop.
- After specifying desired parameters, click on the **Apply** button from the dialog box. The model will be created; refer to Figure-32.

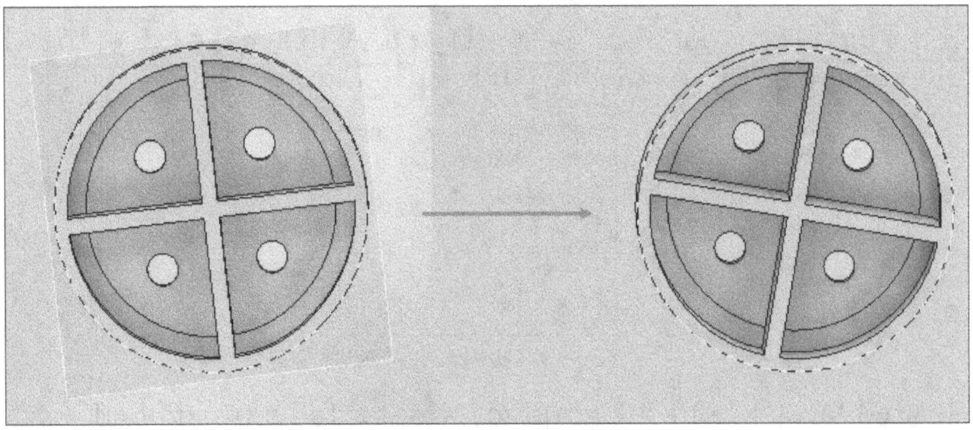

Figure-32. Boundary trim created

- Press **ESC** to exit the tool.

Extend Faces

The **Extend Faces** tool is used to increase size of face at selected edge by specified distance. The procedure to use this tool is discussed next.

- Click on the **Extend Faces** tool from the **Modify** panel in **Repair** tab of the **Ribbbon**. The **Extend Faces** dialog box will be displayed; refer to Figure-33.

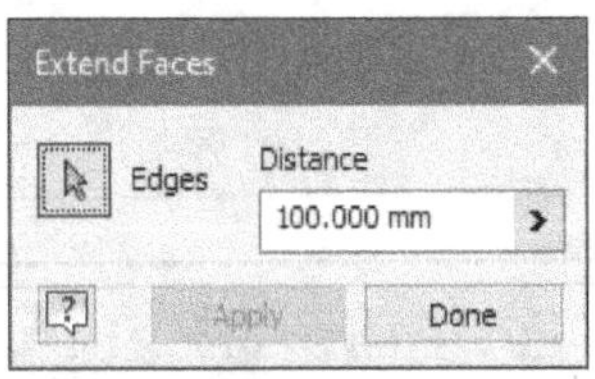

Figure-33. Extend Faces dialog box

- Select desired edge of the model to be extended. Preview of extension will be displayed; refer to Figure-34.

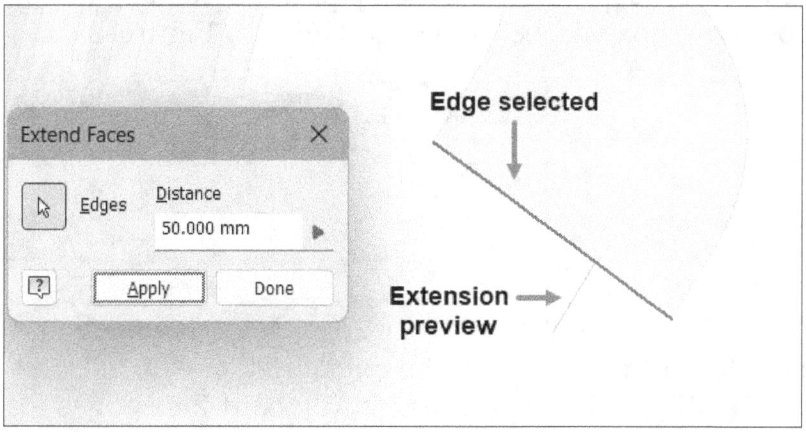

Figure-34. Selecting the Edge for extension

- Click in the **Distance** edit box and specify desired value of the dialog box.
- After specifying desired parameters, click on the **Apply** button from the dialog box. The face will be extend.
- Press **ESC** to exit the tool.

Edit Regions

The **Edit Regions** tool is used to reverse the trimming side of surface when boundary trim was applied earlier on it and it can remove inner surface loop. The procedure to use this tool is discussed next.

- Click on the **Edit Regions** tool from the **Modify** panel in **Repair** tab of the **Ribbon**, The **Edit Regions** dialog box will be displayed; refer to Figure-35.

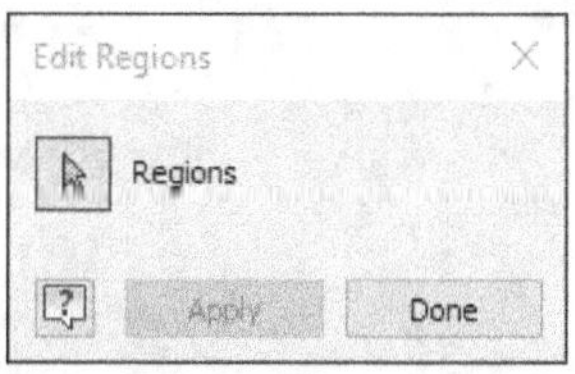

Figure-35. Edit Regions dialog box

- Select desired boundary of the model and click on the **Apply** button from the dialog box; refer to Figure-36.

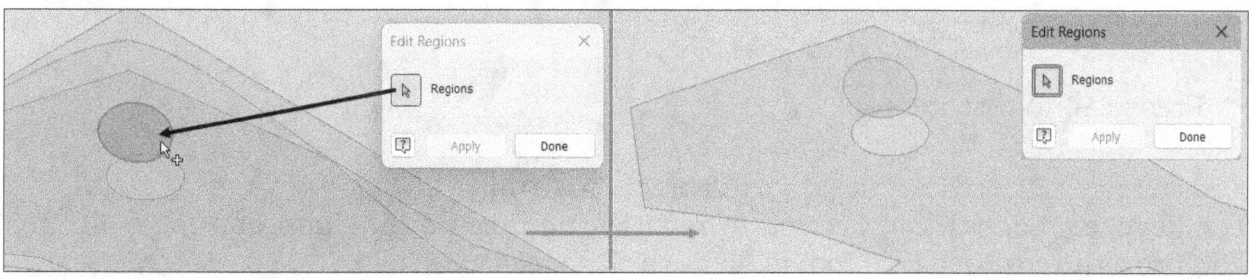

Figure-36. Edit region created

- Press **ESC** to exit the tool.

Extract Loop

The **Extract Loop** tool is used to generate copy of the edges of a trimmed surface to a locked 3D sketch. The procedure to use this tool is discussed next.

- Click on the **Extract Loop** from the **Modify** panel in **Repair** tab of the **Ribbon**. The **Extract Loop** dialog box will be displayed; refer to Figure-37.

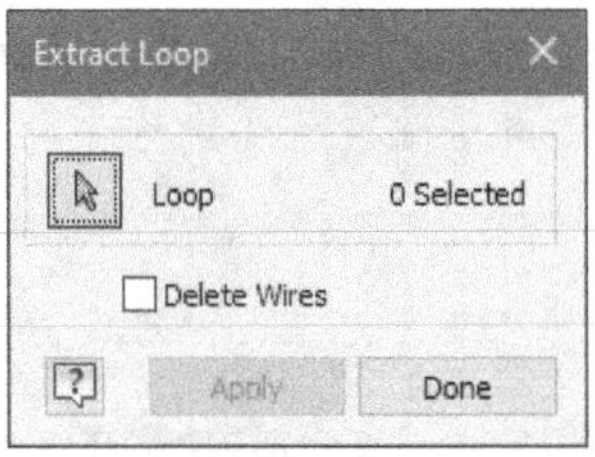

Figure-37. Extract loop dialog box

- Select desired edges of the model to be extracted.
- Select the **Delete Wires** check box to use adjacent face edges for trimming. This will remove all the inner loops.
- After specifying desired parameters, click on the **Apply** button from the dialog box; refer to Figure-38.

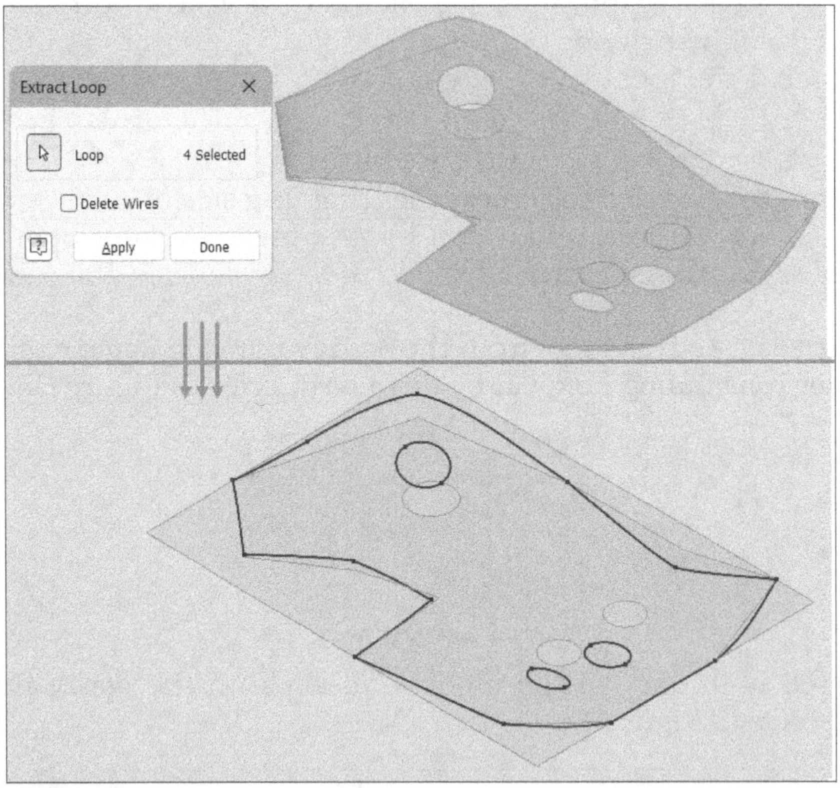

Figure-38. Extract loop created

- Press **ESC** to exit the tool.

Reverse Normal

The **Reveres Normal** tool is used to reverse the normal direction of a face/surface. The procedure to use this tool is discussed next.

- Click on the **Reverse Normal** button from the **Modify** panel in **Repair** tab of the **Ribbon**. The **Reverse Normal** dialog box will be displayed; refer to Figure-39.

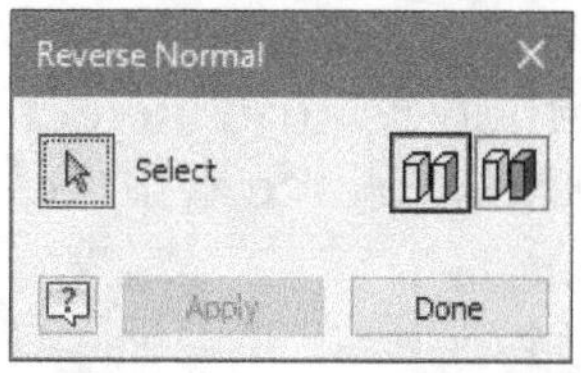

Figure-39. Reverse normal dialog box

- Select the **Individual Face** button to reverse normal for the selected face of the body.
- Select the **Lump** button to reverse all face of the body; refer to Figure-40.

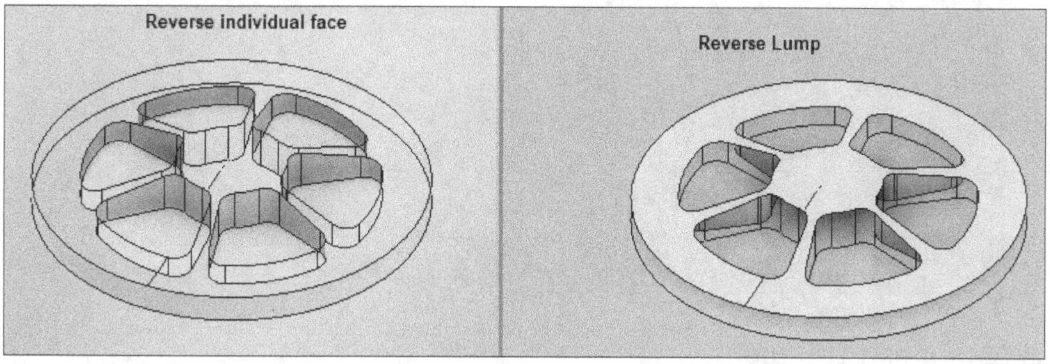

Figure-40. Selecting the model for reverse normal

- After specifying desired parameters, click on the **Apply** button from the dialog box.
- Press **ESC** to exit the tool.

After performing desired repair operations, click on the **Finish Repair** button.

Fit Mesh Face

The **Fit Mesh Face** tool is used to create part face using mesh facets as input. This tool is specially useful when you have imported a triangulated mesh file like STL and want to reverse engineer it. Make sure you have imported an STL model or other mesh model before using this tool. The procedure to use this tool is discussed next.

- Click on the **Fit Mesh Face** button from the **Surface** panel in **3D Model** tab of the **Ribbon**. The **Fit Mesh Face** dialog box will be displayed; refer to Figure-41.

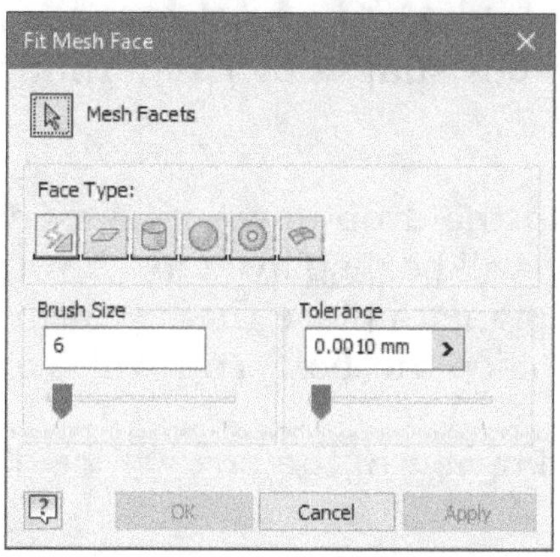

Figure-41. Fit mesh face dialog box

- Select desired face type filter from the **Face Type** section to select mesh with respective shape.

- Click in the **Brush Size** edit box to define size of selection brush.
- After specifying desired parameters and selecting mesh facets, click on the **OK** button from the dialog box. The surface will be generated; refer to Figure-42.

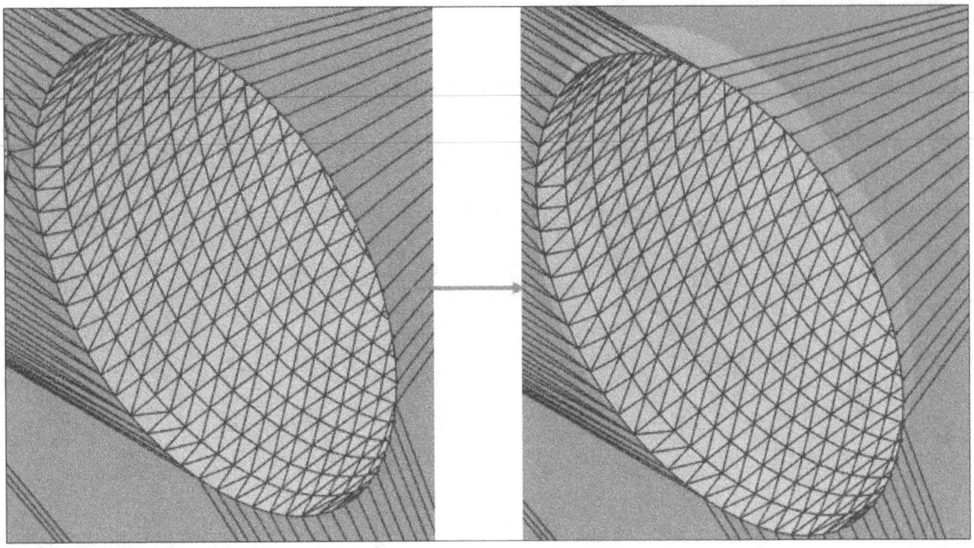

Figure-42. Fit mesh face created

- Press **ESC** to exit the tool.

FREEFORM DESIGNING

Freeform designing has many applications in CAD and CAE. Whenever you need an unconventional shape of the object, you can always use the freeform modeling techniques. The tools to perform freeform modeling are available in the **Create Freeform** panel in the **3D Model** tab of the **Ribbon**; refer to Figure-43. Various tools in this panel are discussed next.

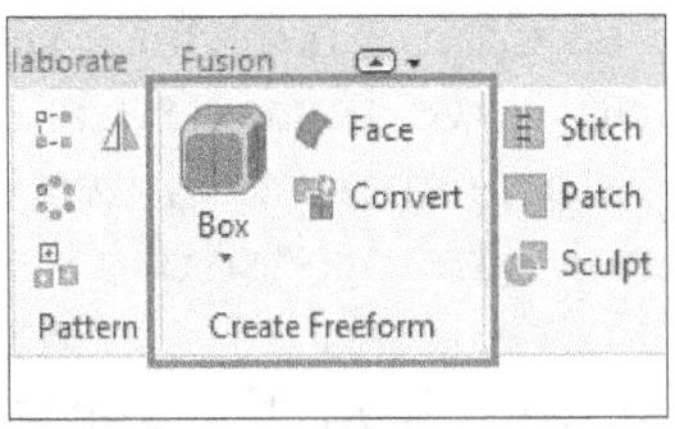

Figure-43. Create Freeform panel

BOX TOOL

The **Box** tool is used to create box shapes by free forming. The procedure to use this tool is given next.

- Click on the **Box** tool from the drop-down in the **Create Freeform** panel of the **Ribbon**. The **Box** dialog box will be displayed as shown in Figure-44. Also, you will be asked to select a face/plane to place the freeform box.
- Select the face/plane to place the box. You will be asked to specify the center point of the box.
- Click at desired location. Preview of the box will be displayed; refer to Figure-45.

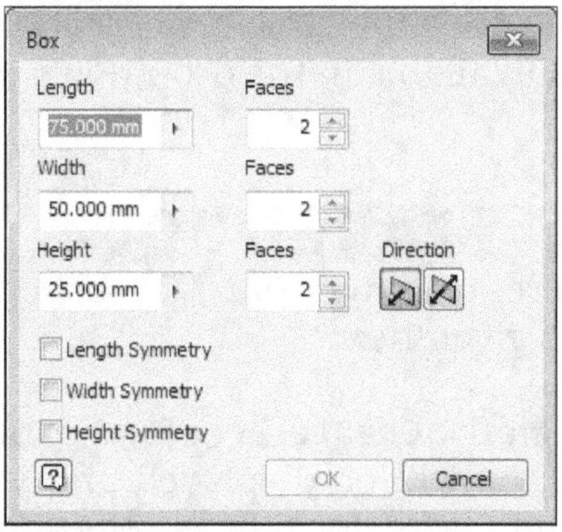

Figure-44. Box dialog box

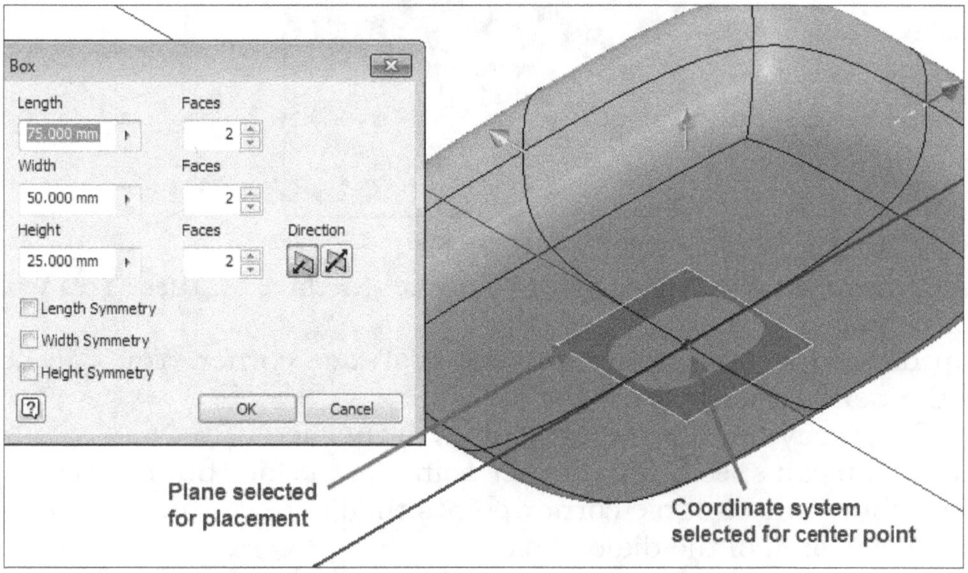

Figure-45. Preview of the freeform box

- Specify the length, width, and height of the box in the respective edit boxes of the dialog box or drag the arrows in preview.
- Select the **Length Symmetry**, **Width Symmetry**, and **Height Symmetry** check boxes to make the box symmetric in length, width, and height with respect to corresponding center planes.
- Set the number of faces on each side of the box by using the **Faces** spinners.
- Click on the **OK** button to activate the **Freeform** contextual tab in the **Ribbon**; refer to Figure-46.

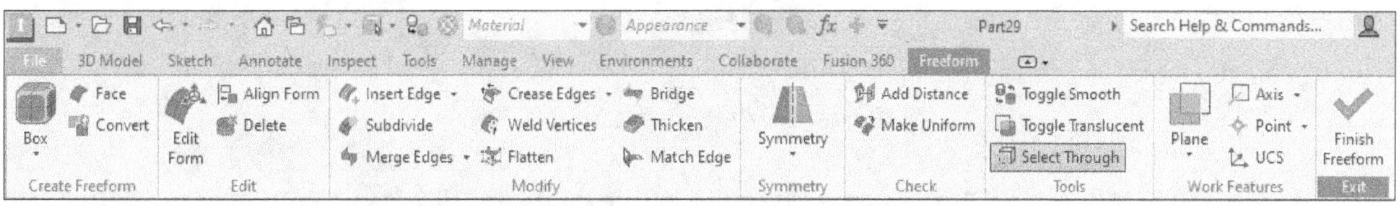

Figure-46. Freeform contextual tab

- The tools in this tab are used to modify the shape of box and other freeform objects. We will discuss the tools of this tab later in this chapter.
- After modifications, click on the **Finish Freeform** button in the **Exit** panel of the **Freeform** contextual tab in the **Ribbon**.

In the same way, you can use the other freeform creation tools like **Plane**, **Cylinder**, **Sphere**, **Torus**, and **Quadball** available in the drop-down in the **Create Freeform** panel of the **Ribbon**.

FACE TOOL

The **Face** tool is used to create individual face based on selected vertices. The procedure to use this tool is given next.

- Click on the **Face** tool from the **Create Freeform** panel in the **3D Model** tab of the **Ribbon**. The **Face** dialog box will be displayed and you will be asked to select a plane or face for placement of freeform face; refer to Figure-47.

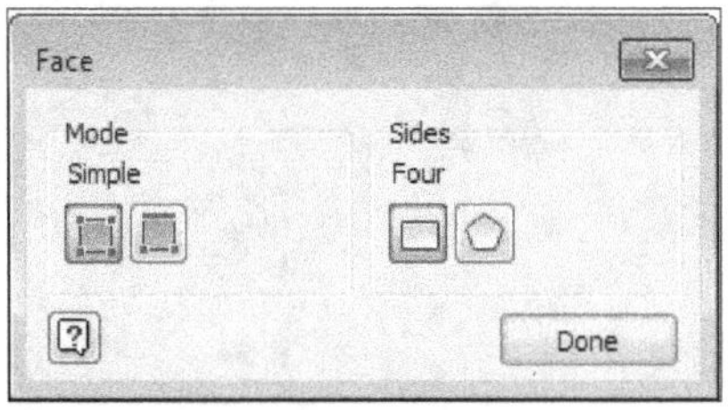

Figure-47. Face dialog box

- Select the plane on which you want to create the face feature. You will be asked to specify the face corner.
- Click on desired location to specify the first face corner. You will be asked to specify the next corner point of the face.
- One by one specify the next corner points of the face.
- By default, you can specify four corner points of the face but if you want to create a freeform face with multiple corner points then click on the **Multiple** button from the **Sides** area of the dialog box.
- After specifying desired points for multiple corner face, press **ENTER** from the keyboard. The freeform face will be created; refer to Figure-48. Perform the freeform operations and click on the **Finish Freeform** button from the **Exit** panel in the contextual tab of the **Ribbon**.

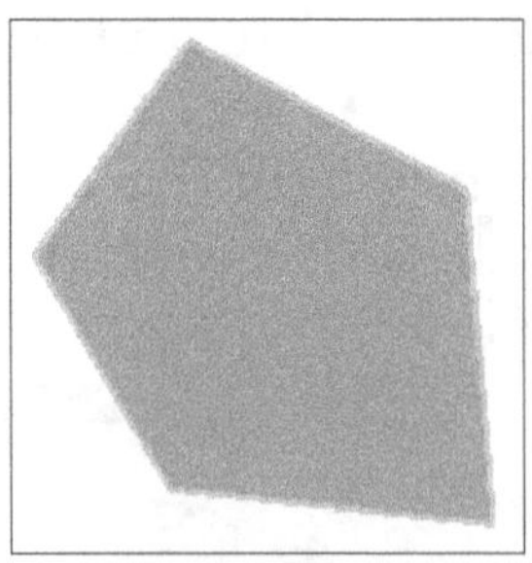

Figure-48. Freeform face created

CONVERT TOOL

The **Convert** tool is used to convert the selected solid face or surface to freeform face. The procedure to use this tool is given next.

- Click on the **Convert** tool from the **Create Freeform** panel in the **3D Model** tab of the **Ribbon**. The **Convert to Freeform** dialog box will be displayed; refer to Figure-49.

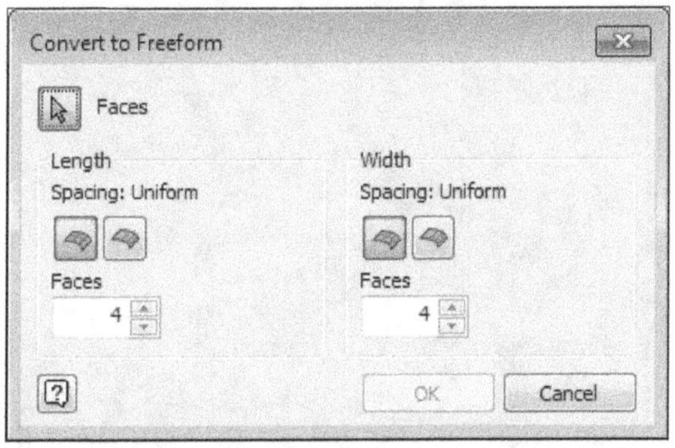

Figure-49. Convert to Freeform dialog box

- Select the face that you want to be converted to freeform face. Preview of the freeform face will be displayed; refer to Figure-50.

Figure-50. Preview of freeform face

- Set the number of faces across length and width in the respective edit boxes in the dialog box.
- Click on the **OK** button. The **Freeform** contextual tab will be displayed.
- Perform the modifications on face and click on the **Finish Freeform** tool from the **Exit** panel.

FREEFORM CONTEXTUAL TAB

The tools in the **Freeform** contextual tab are used to modify the shape of selected freeform object. Various tools in this tab are discussed next.

Edit Form Tool

The **Edit Form** tool is used to edit the shape of freeform object. The procedure to use this tool is given next.

- Click on the **Edit Form** tool from the **Edit** panel in the **Freeform** contextual tab of the **Ribbon**. The **Edit Form** dialog box will be displayed; refer to Figure-51.

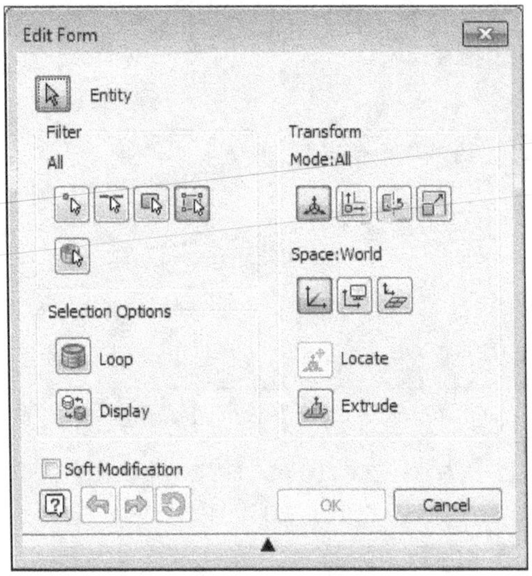

Figure-51. Edit Form dialog box

- Make sure **All** buttons are selected in the **Filter** and **Transform** area of the dialog box so that you can edit every type of geometry of freeform object.
- Select desired coordinate system for modification in the **Space** area.
- Click on the edge/vertex/face of the object to modify it. The transformation handles will be displayed on the selected entity; refer to Figure-52.

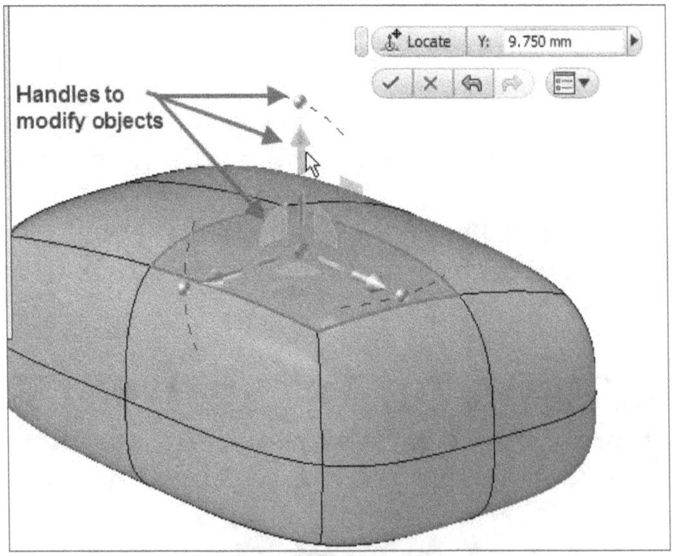

Figure-52. Handles to modify freeform object

- If you do not want the other entities of the freeform to be affected by modification then select the **Extrude** button from the dialog box and then perform the modifications.
- You can use the **Undo**, **Redo**, and **Reset** buttons in the dialog box to undo, redo, and reset the model, respectively.
- Click on the **OK** button from the dialog box, once you have performed the modifications.

Align Form Tool

The **Align Form** tool is used to align the vertex of freeform object to the selected plane. The procedure to use this tool is given next.

- Click on the **Align Form** tool from the **Edit** panel in the **Freeform** contextual tab of the **Ribbon**. The **Align Form** dialog box will be displayed; refer to Figure-53.

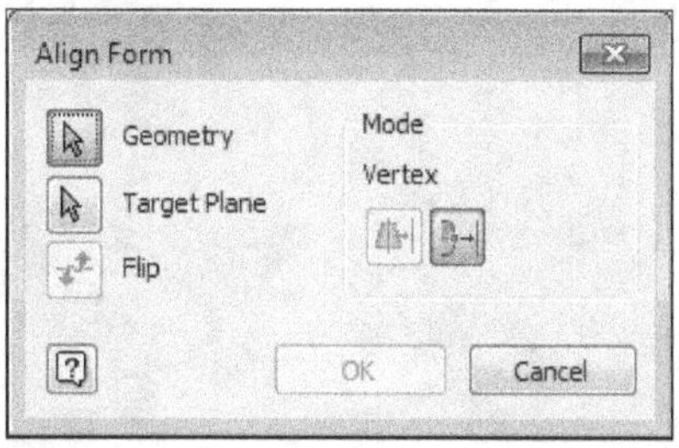

Figure-53. Align Form dialog box

- Select the vertex of object that you want to be aligned. You will be asked to select the plane to which you want to align the vertex.
- Select desired plane or planar face. The object will be aligned at the selected plane/ face through the vertex; refer to Figure-54.

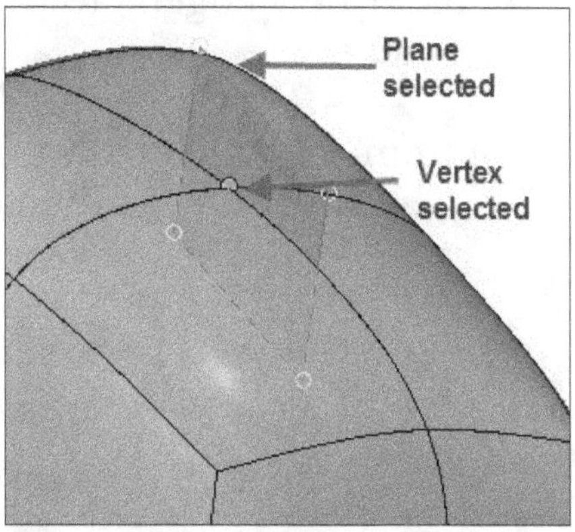

Figure-54. Aligning object

- Click on the **OK** button from the dialog box.

Delete Tool

The **Delete** tool is used to delete the selected entity of the freeform object. The procedure to use this tool is given next.

- Click on the **Delete** tool from the **Edit** panel in the **Freeform** contextual tab of the **Ribbon**. The **Delete** dialog box will be displayed as shown in Figure-55.

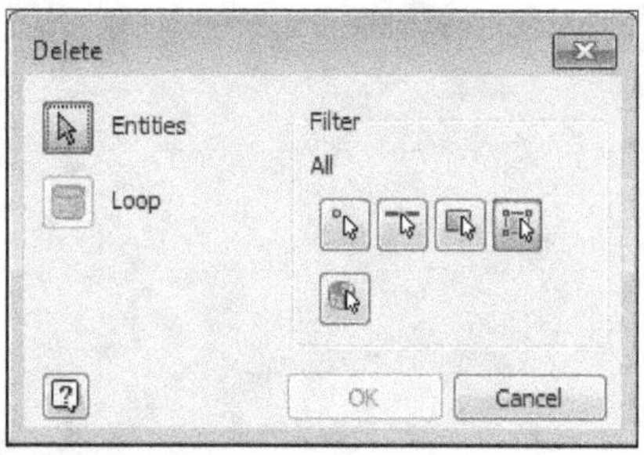

Figure-55. Delete dialog box

- Select the entity that you want to delete and click on the **OK** button. The model after deleting the selected entity will be displayed; refer to Figure-56.

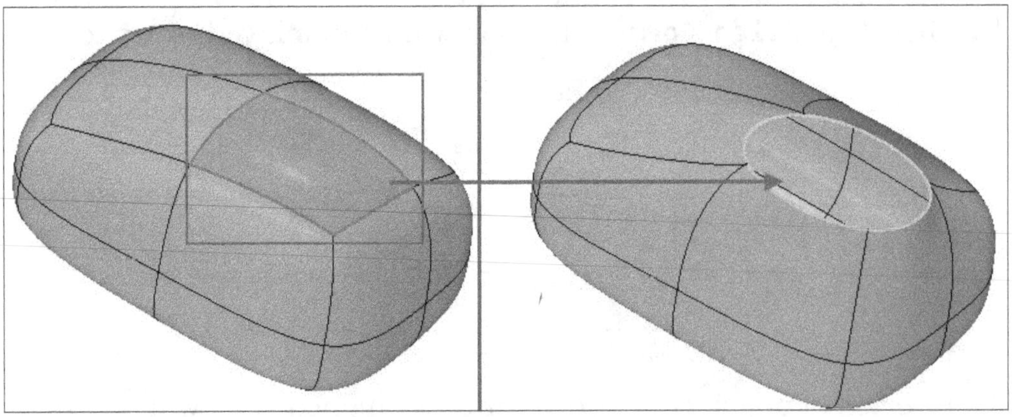

Figure-56. Deleting face of freeform object

Insert Edge Tool

The **Insert Edge** tool is used to insert new edge(s) to the sides of selected edge. The procedure to use this tool is given next.

- Click on the **Insert Edge** tool from the **Insert** drop-down in the **Modify** panel of the **Ribbon**; refer to Figure-57. The **Insert Edge** dialog box will be displayed; refer to Figure-58.z

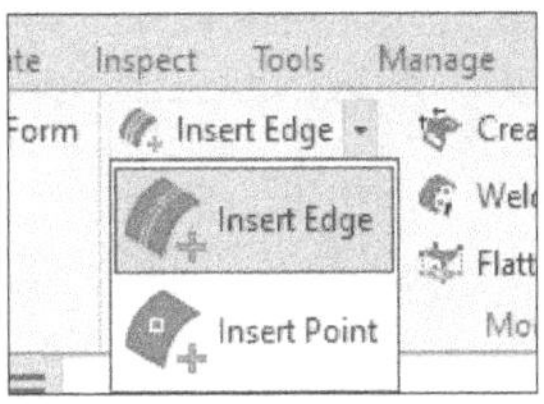

Figure-57. Insert Edge tool

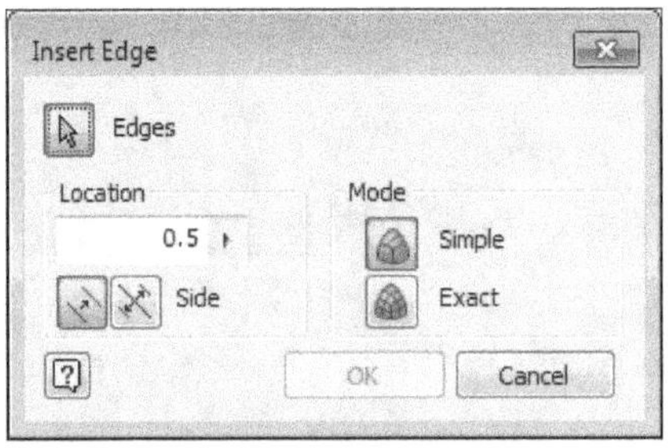

Figure-58. Insert Edge dialog box

- Select the reference edge on sides of which you want to create the new edges. Preview of the edges will be displayed; refer to Figure-59.

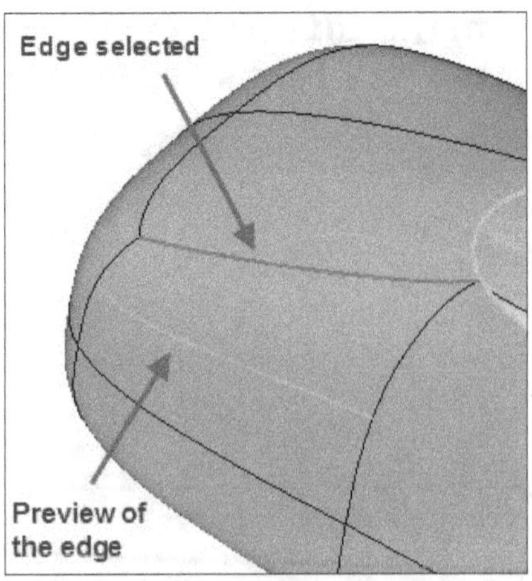

Figure-59. Preview of inserted edge

- Select the **Both** button to create edge on both the sides of the selected edge.
- Select the location ratio in the **Location** edit box and click on the **OK** button to create the edges.

Insert Point Tool

The **Insert Point** tool is used to insert a new point on the selected edge of the freeform object. The procedure to use this tool is given next.

- Click on the **Insert Point** tool from the **Insert** drop-down in the **Modify** panel of the **Freeform** tab in the **Ribbon**. The **Insert Point** dialog box will be displayed; refer to Figure-60.

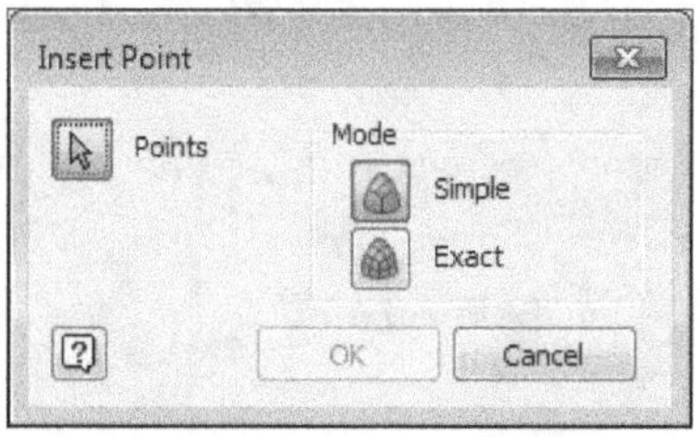

Figure-60. Insert Point dialog box

- Select points on edges of the freeform object and click on the **OK** button to create the points.

Subdivide Tool

The **Subdivide** tool is used to divide the selected face into sub-divisions. The procedure to use this tool is given next.

- Click on the **Subdivide** tool from the **Modify** panel in the **Freeform** contextual tab of the **Ribbon**. The **Subdivide** dialog box will be displayed; refer to Figure-61.

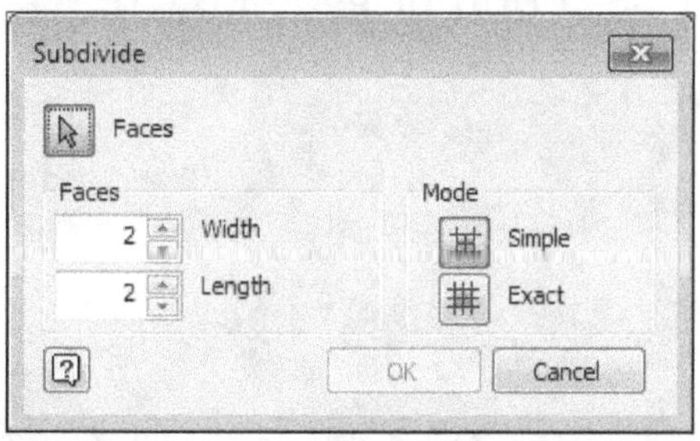

Figure-61. Subdivide dialog box

- Set the number of faces along width and length in the respective spinners in the dialog box.
- Select desired mode of division and click on the face of freeform object. Preview of the sub-division will be displayed; refer to Figure-62.

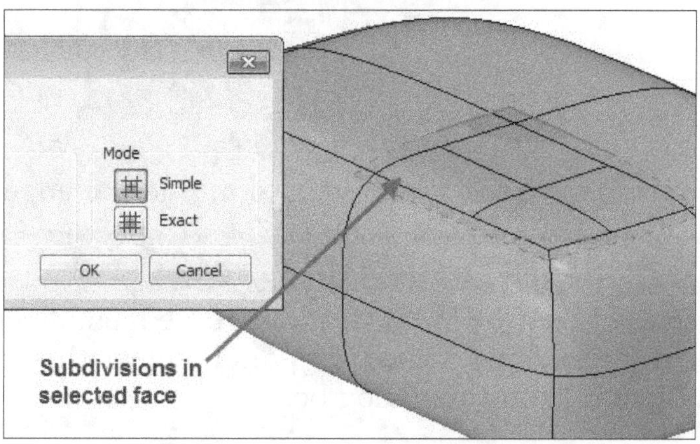

Figure-62. Preview of subdivisions

- Click on the **OK** button to create the sub-division faces.

Merge Edges Tool

The **Merge Edges** tool is used to merge open edges of the two freeform bodies. The procedure to use this tool is given next.

- Click on the **Merge Edges** tool from the **Edges** drop-down in the **Modify** panel of the **Freeform** contextual tab in **Ribbon**. The **Merge Edge** dialog box will be displayed; refer to Figure-63.

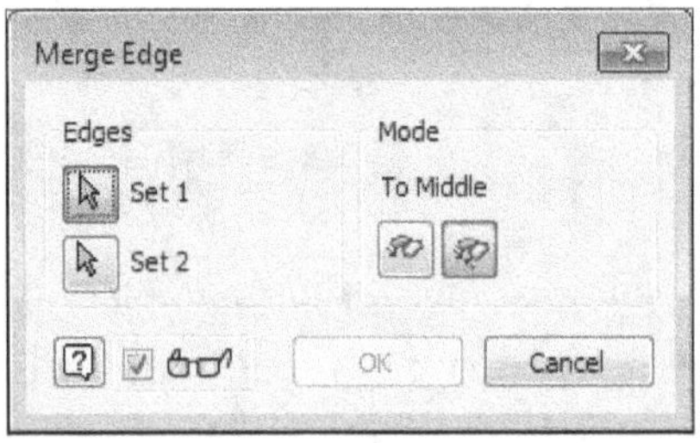

Figure-63. Merge Edges dialog box

- Select the open edges of first freeform object. Note that you can select only adjacent edges of the first selected edge.
- Click on the **Set 2** selection button from the **Edges** area of the dialog box and select the open edges of the second freeform object; refer to Figure-64. Preview of the edge merge will be displayed if possible. The **Preview** check box is selected in the dialog box and still preview is not displayed on your selection then you need to change your selection or geometry of edges selected.

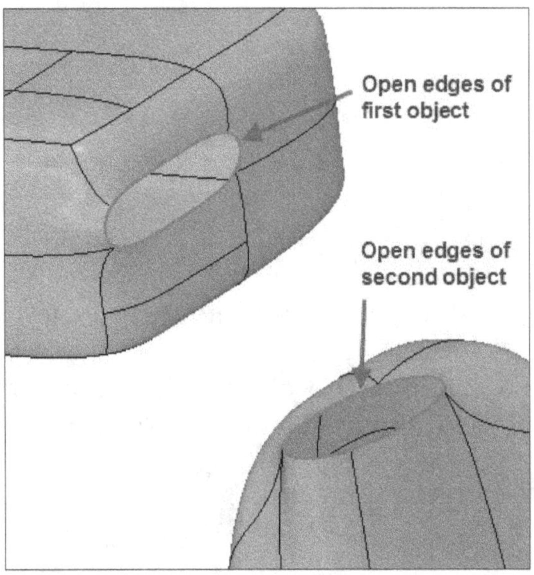

Figure-64. Edges selection for merging

- Click on the **OK** button from the dialog box to merge the edges.

Unweld Edges Tool

The **Unweld Edges** tool is used to break the merged edges. After selecting this tool from the **Merge Edges** drop-down in **Modify** panel, select the edges earlier merged and click on the **OK** button from the dialog box.

Crease Edges Tool

The **Crease Edges** tool is used to straighten the curve of selected edges of the freeform object. The procedure to use this tool is given next.

- Click on the **Crease Edges** tool from the **Edges** drop-down in the **Modify** panel in the **Freeform** contextual tab of the **Ribbon**. The **Crease** dialog box will be displayed; refer to Figure-65.

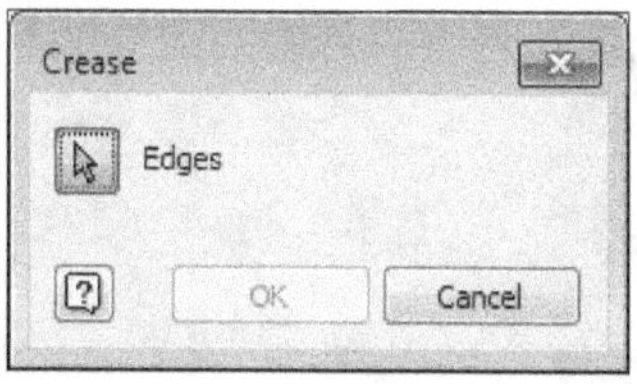

Figure-65. Crease dialog box

- Select the edges to which you want to apply the crease. Preview of the crease feature will be displayed; refer to Figure-66. Click on the **OK** button from the dialog box to create the feature.

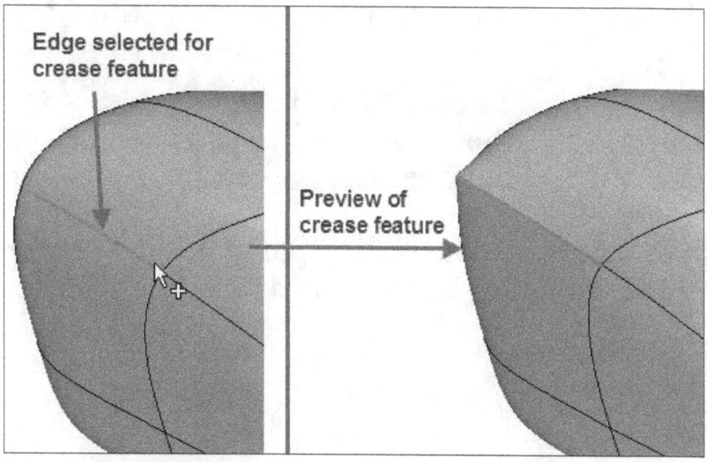

Figure-66. Preview of crease feature

Uncrease Edges Tool

The **Uncrease Edges** tool is used to undo the crease created by **Crease Edges** tool. The procedure of using this tool is similar to **Crease Edges** tool.

Weld Vertices Tool

The **Weld Vertices** tool is used to join two vertices of a freeform object. The procedure to use this tool is given next.

- Click on the **Weld Vertices** tool from the **Modify** panel in the **Freeform** contextual tab of the **Ribbon**. The **Weld Vertices** dialog box will be displayed; refer to Figure-67.

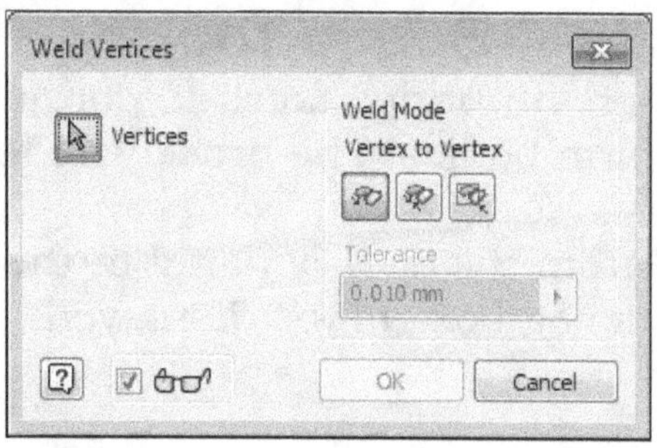

Figure-67. Weld Vertices dialog box

- Select desired button to set mode of joining vertices from the **Weld Mode** area of the dialog box.
- Select the two vertices that you want to be joined. Preview of the welded vertices will be displayed; refer to Figure-68.

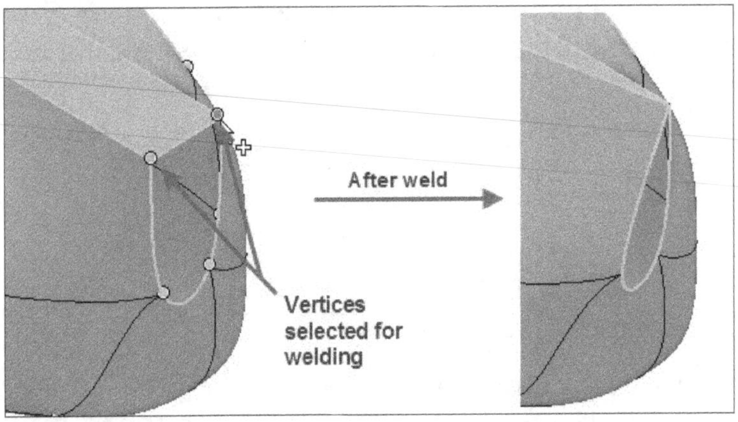

Figure-68. Vertices weld feature

- Click on the **OK** button from the dialog box to create the feature.

Flatten Tool

The **Flatten** tool is used to fit the selected vertices to the selected plane or in best position based on curvature of surface. The procedure to use this tool is given next.

- Click on the **Flatten** tool from the **Modify** panel in the **Freeform** contextual tab of the **Ribbon**. The **Flatten** dialog box will be displayed; refer to Figure-69.

Figure-69. Flatten dialog box

- Select the vertices to be flatten. Preview of flatten feature will be displayed.
- Select the **Plane** or **Parallel Plane** button from the **Direction** area of the dialog box to flatten the vertices on selected plane or parallel to selected plane.
- After selecting the required geometries, click on the **OK** button to flatten the vertices.

Bridge Tool

The **Bridge** tool is used to create bridge faces to connect two faces/open-edges of same body or different freeform bodies. The procedure to use this tool is given next.

- Click on the **Bridge** tool from the **Modify** panel in the **Freeform** contextual tab of the **Ribbon**. The **Bridge** dialog box will be displayed; refer to Figure-70.

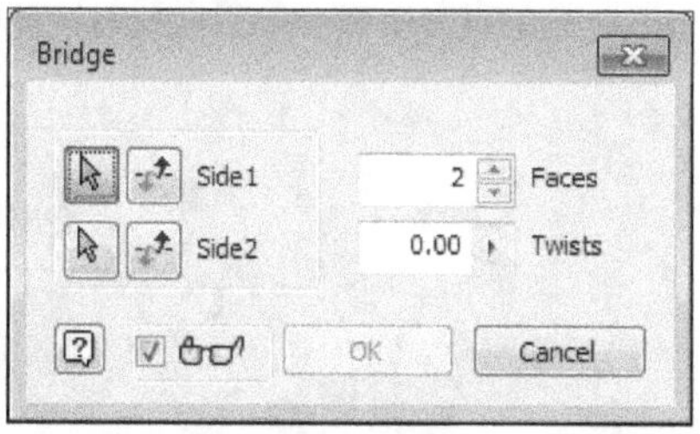

Figure-70. Bridge dialog box

- Select the face or open edge of first side. You will be asked to select the face/edge on the other side.
- Select the edge/face on the other side. Preview of the bridge surface will be displayed; refer to Figure-71.

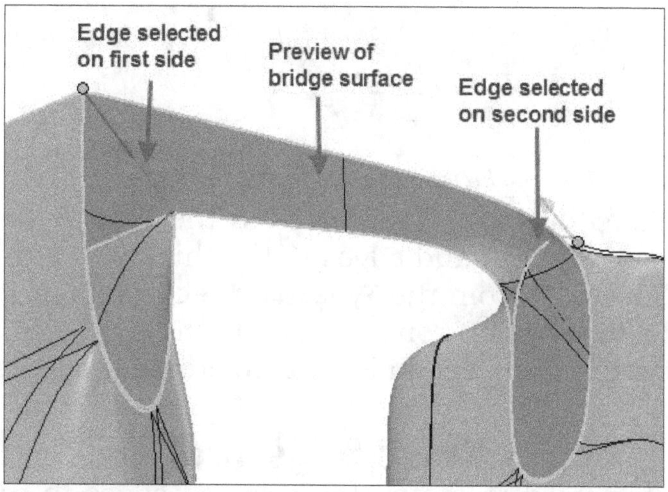

Figure-71. Preview of bridge surface

- You can keep on selecting the edges/faces from side 1 and side 2 to form more surfaces.
- Click on the **OK** button to create the bridge surfaces.

Thicken Tool

The **Thicken** tool is used to thicken the surfaces or offset the faces of solid bodies. The procedure to use this tool is given next.

- Click on the **Thicken** tool from the **Modify** panel in the **Freeform** contextual tab of the **Ribbon**. The **Thicken** dialog box will be displayed; refer to Figure-72.

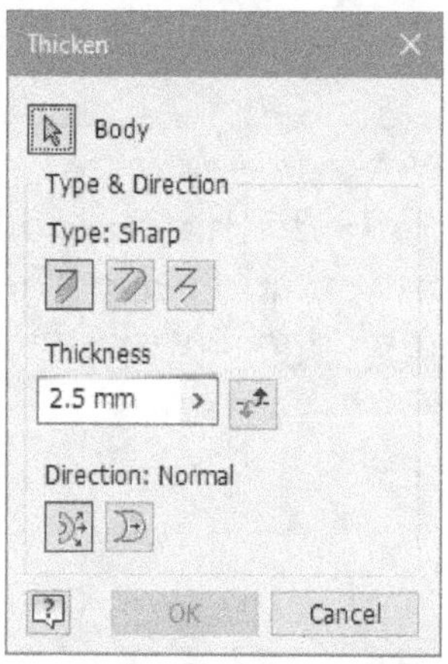

Figure-72. Thicken dialog box

- Select the body to be thicken. Preview of the thicken feature will be displayed; refer to Figure-73.

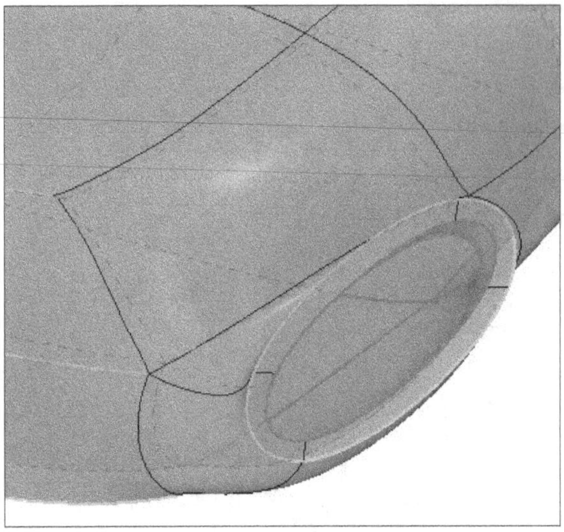

Figure-73. Preview of thicken feature

- By default, the **Sharp** button is selected in the **Type & Direction** area of the dialog box. Hence, the joints and edges in the thicken feature are sharp.
- Select the **Soft** button from the **Type & Direction** area to soften the thicken feature. Select the **No Edge** button to create the surface offset.
- Click on the **OK** button from the dialog box to create the feature.

Match Edge Tool

The **Match Edge** tool is used to match the selected edges to the sketch section or curve. The procedure to use this tool is given next.

- Click on the **Match Edge** tool from the **Modify** panel in the **Freeform** contextual tab of the **Ribbon**. The **Match Edge** dialog box will be displayed; refer to Figure-74.

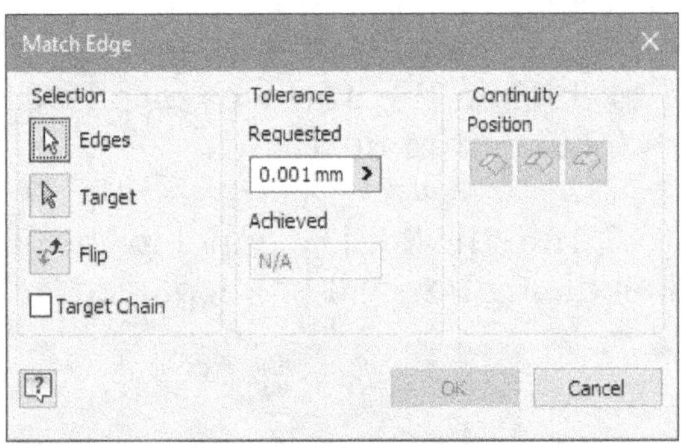

Figure-74. Match Edge dialog box

- Select the edges of the freeform body that are to be matched with sketch section.
- Click on the **Target** selection button and select the sketch curve to be matched with selected edges. Preview of match edge feature will be displayed; refer to Figure-75.

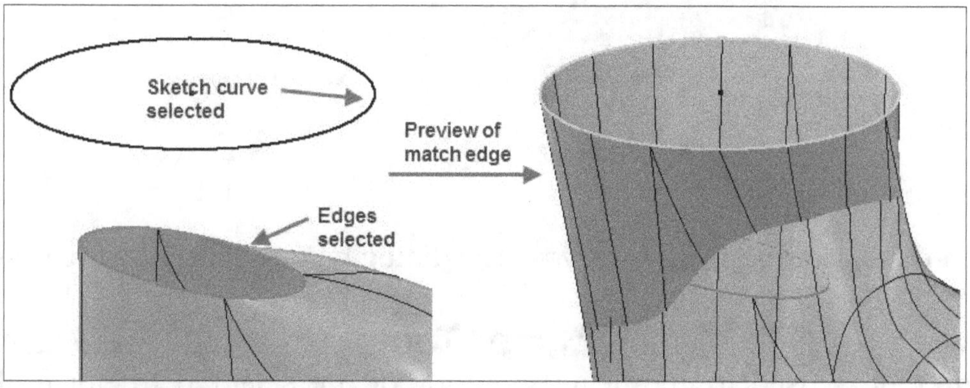

Figure-75. Preview of match edge feature

- Set desired tolerance value in the edit box of **Tolerance** area in the dialog box.
- If the edges are matched opposite to what you need then click on the **Flip** button from the dialog box.
- Click on the **OK** button from the dialog box to create the feature.

Symmetry Tool

The **Symmetry** tool is used to make two faces of the freeform bodies symmetric. Once the faces are symmetric then any change made in one face will also be reflected in other symmetric face. The procedure to use this tool is given next.

- Click on the **Symmetry** tool from the **Symmetry** drop-down in the **Symmetry** panel of the **Ribbon**. The **Symmetry** dialog box will be displayed; refer to Figure-76.

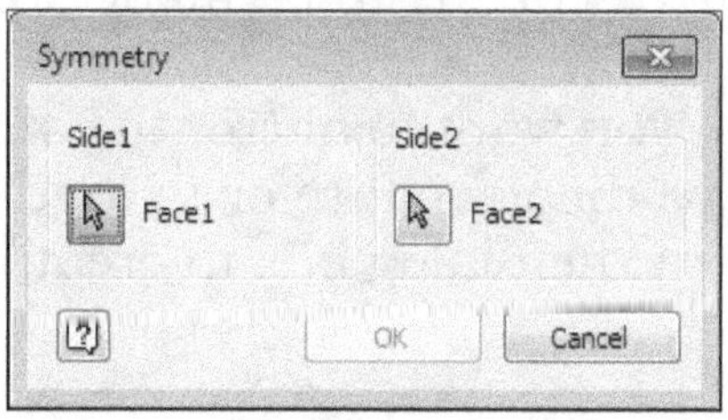

Figure-76. Symmetry dialog box

- Select the face on first side and then a face on other side to make the two faces symmetric. If there is possibility of symmetry in two faces then the **OK** button will become active in dialog box; refer to Figure-77. Otherwise, a warning message will be displayed; refer to Figure-78.

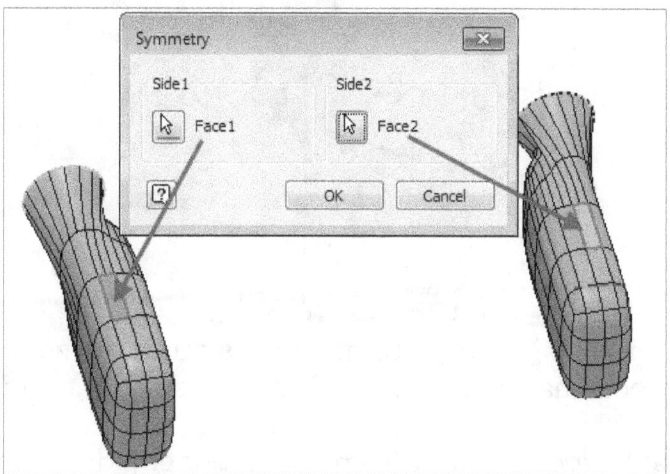

Figure-77. Faces selected for symmetry

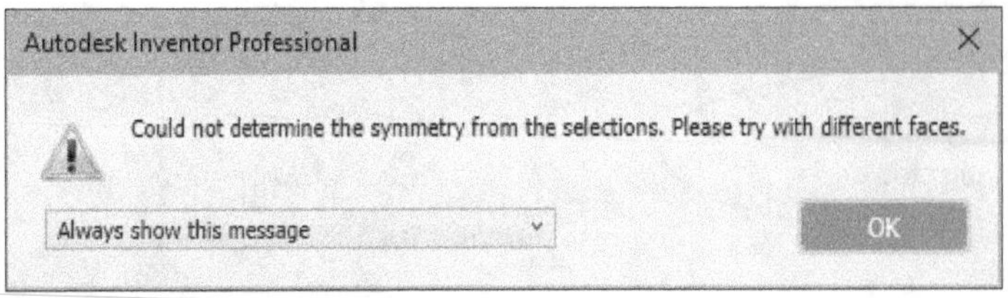

Figure-78. Warning message

- Click on the **OK** button from the **Symmetry** dialog box to make the faces symmetric.

Mirror Tool

The **Mirror** tool is used to create mirror copy of the selected freeform object. The procedure to use this tool is given next.

- Click on the **Mirror** tool from the **Symmetry** drop-down in the **Symmetry** panel of the **Ribbon**. The **Mirror** dialog box will be displayed; refer to Figure-79.

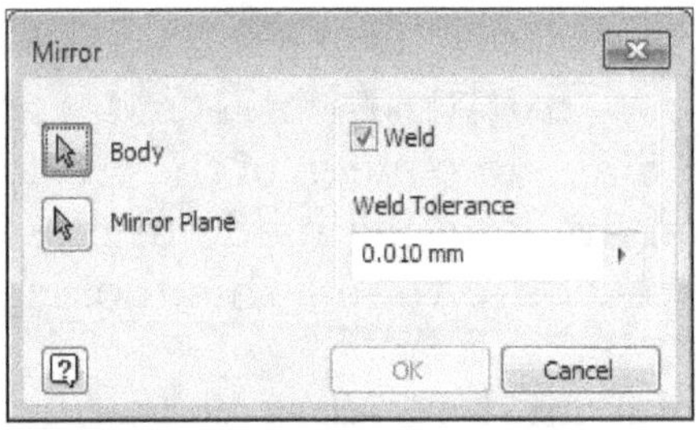

Figure-79. Mirror dialog box

- Select the body whose mirror copy is to be made. You will be asked to select the mirror plane.
- Select a plane about which you want to mirror the selected freeform body. Preview of the mirror feature will be displayed; refer to Figure-80.
- Click on the **OK** button from the dialog box to create the feature.

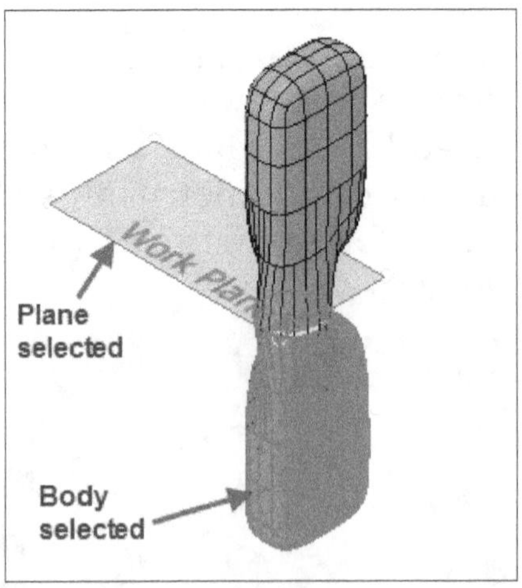

Figure-80. Preview of mirror feature

Clear Symmetry

The **Clear Symmetry** tool is used to remove all symmetry zones that were created using the Symmetry command. The procedure to use this tool is discussed next.

- Click on the **Clear Symmetry** tool from the **Symmetry** drop-down in the **Symmetry** panel of the **Ribbon**.

- Select desired face from the graphics window to be clear; refer to Figure-81. Now modifying this face will not affect the other face which was earlier bound by symmetry.

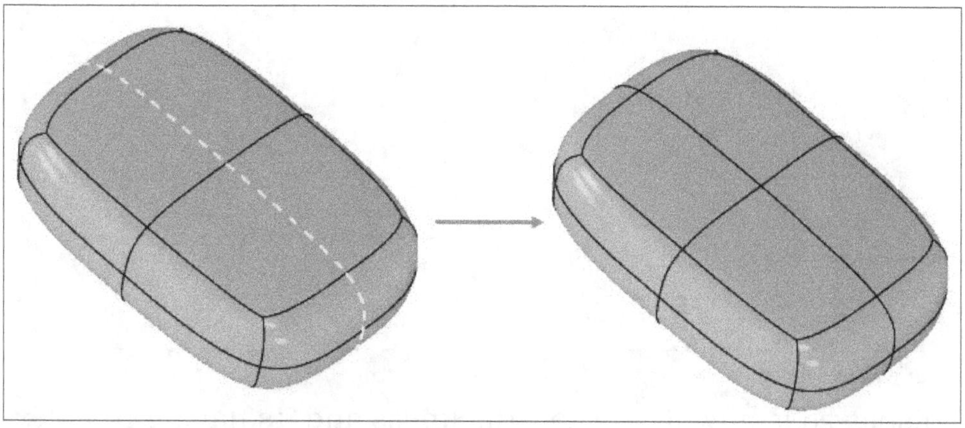

Figure-81. Clear symmetry created

In the same way, you can use the other tools in the **Freeform** contextual tab to modify the freeform bodies.

Once you have performed all the modifications, click on the **Finish Freeform** tool from the **Exit** panel in the **Freeform** contextual tab of the **Ribbon** to return to modeling environment.

If you have created a closed freeform body then you will get a solid freeform object as output on clicking the **Finish Freeform** tool otherwise, you will get a surface body.

PRACTICAL

Create the model of helmet glass as shown in Figure-82. The dimensions of the model are given in Figure-83.

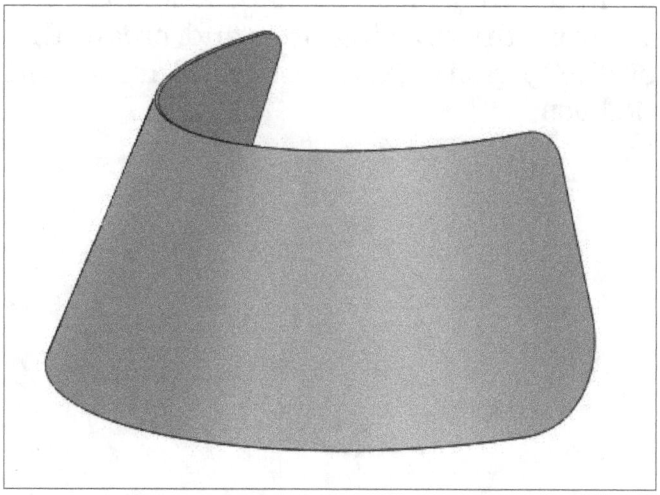

Figure-82. Practical model 1

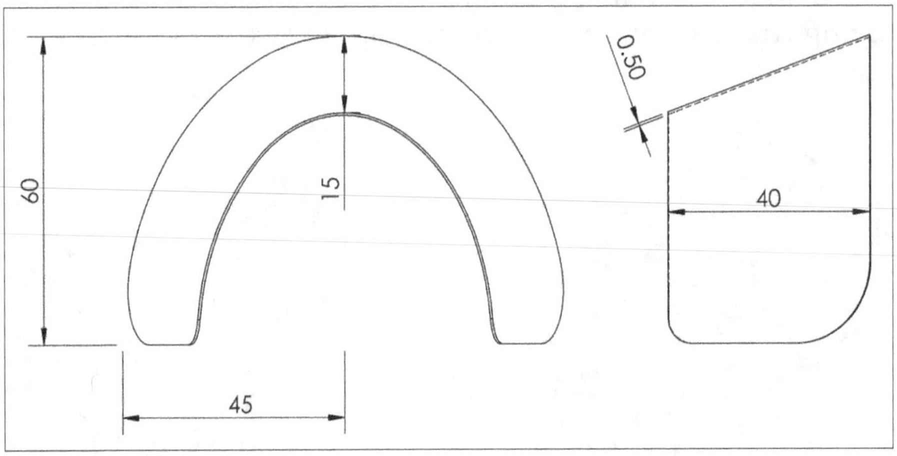

Figure-83. Practical drawing

The model displayed is having very low thickness and its having complex 3D shape. So, it is a good idea to use surfacing in this case.

We can create this model by loft surface easily. For using the **Loft** tool, we need two sketches.

Starting Part file

- Start Autodesk Inventor, if not started yet. Click on the **New** button from **New** cascading menu in the **File** menu of the **Ribbon**. The **Create New File** dialog box will be displayed.
- Double-click on the **Standard(mm).ipt** part file template from the **Metric** templates in the dialog box. The part modeling environment will be displayed.

Creating Sketches

- Click on the **Start 2D Sketch** tool from the **Sketch** drop-down in the **Sketch** panel of the **3D Model** tab in the **Ribbon**. You will be asked to select a sketching plane.
- Select the **XZ** Plane from the drawing area and create the sketch as shown in Figure-84. Click on the **Finish Sketch** button from the **Finish** drop-down in the **Exit** panel of the **Ribbon**.

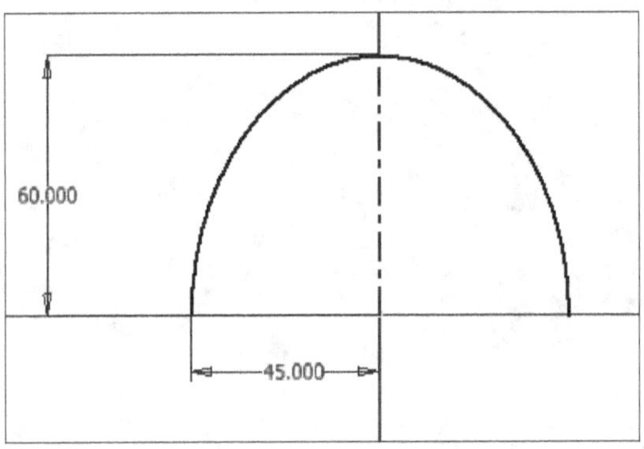

Figure-84. Semi ellipse created as sketch

- Create a plane at an offset distance of **40** above the **XZ** plane; refer to Figure-85.
- Click on the **Start 2D Sketch** tool again and select the newly created plane as sketching plane.

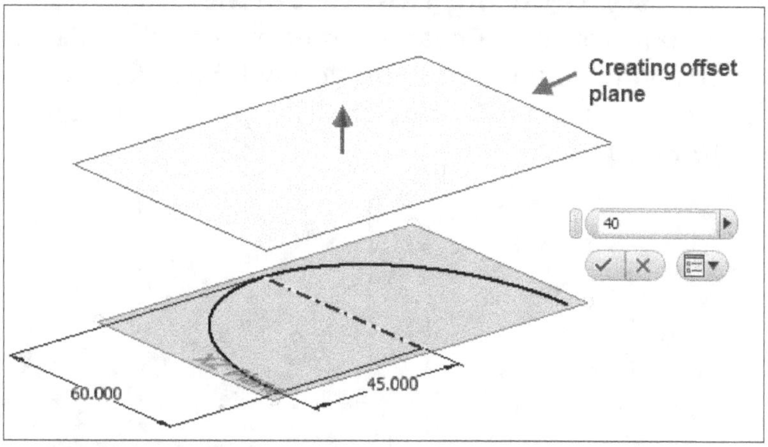

Figure-85. Offset plane to be created

- Click on the **Project Geometry** tool from the **Create** panel in the **Sketch** contextual tab and select the sketch earlier created. A yellow curve will be created coinciding with the sketch; refer to Figure-86.

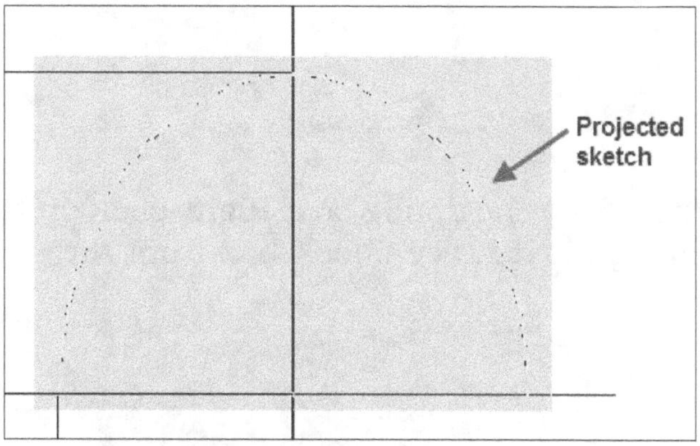

Figure-86. Projected sketch curve

- Click on the **Offset** tool from the **Modify** panel in the **Sketch** contextual tab and select the projected sketch curve. You will be asked to specify the offset distance.
- Move the cursor inside the curve and enter the value as **15** in the edit box displayed attached to cursor. The offset feature will be created; refer to Figure-87.

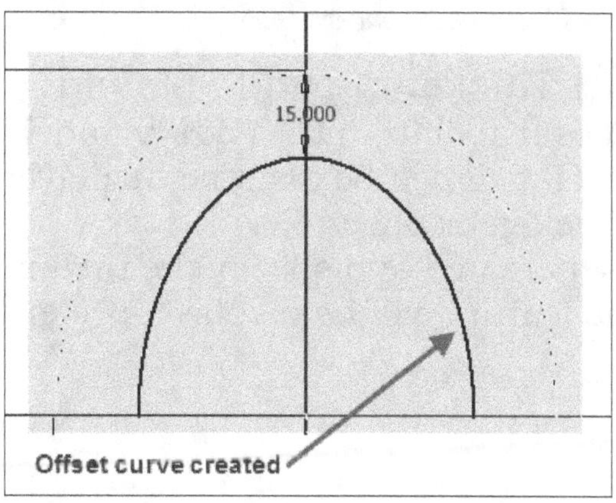

Figure-87. Offset curve created

- Click on the **Finish Sketch** button from the **Finish** drop-down in the **Exit** panel of the **Ribbon**.

Creating Lofted Surface

- Click on the **Loft** tool from the **Create** panel in the **3D Model** tab of the **Ribbon**. The **Loft** dialog box will be displayed and you will be asked to select the sketches.
- Select the sketch curves created earlier. The preview of lofted surface will be displayed; refer to Figure-88.

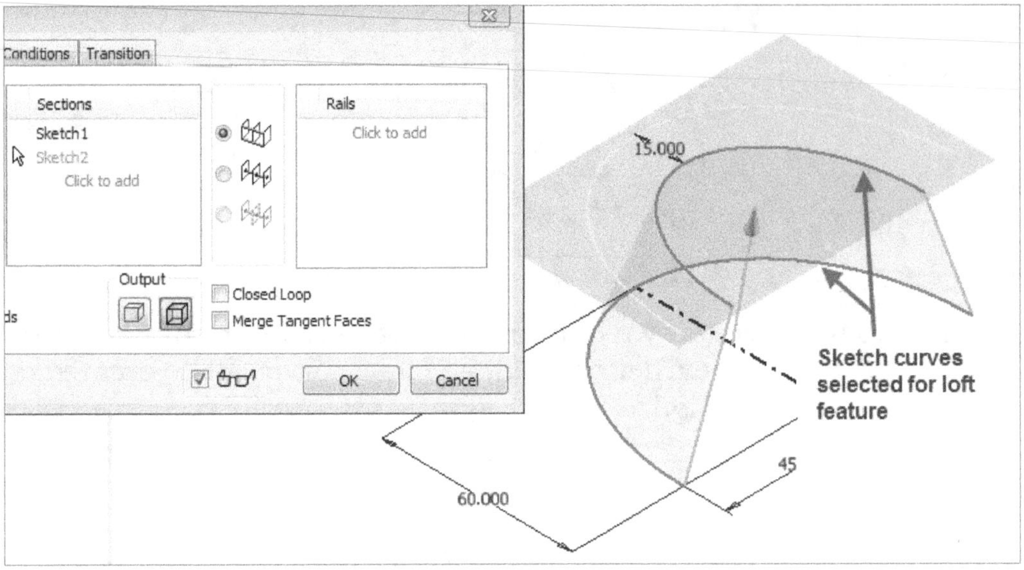

Figure-88. Preview of lofted surface

- Click on the **OK** button from the dialog box. Right-click on the work plane created and hide it by clearing **Visibility** check box from the shortcut menu; refer to Figure-89.

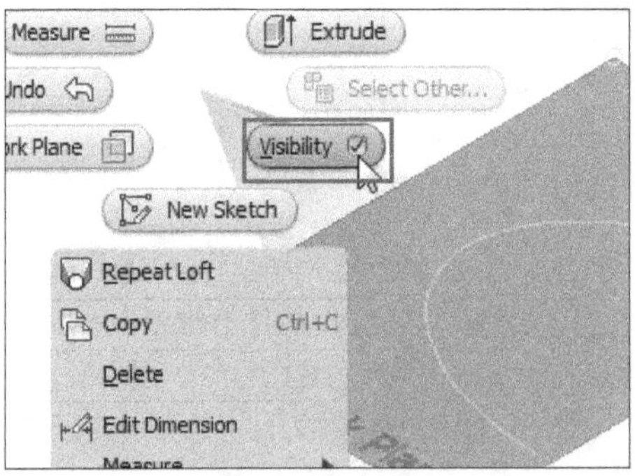

Figure-89. Hiding workplane

Thickening and Filleting

- Click on the **Thicken/Offset** tool from the **Modify** panel in the **3D Model** tab of the **Ribbon**. The **Thicken/Offset** dialog box will be displayed. Also, you will be asked to select the faces to thicken or offset.
- Select the surface earlier created and specify the thickness as **0.5** in the **Distance** edit box. Preview of the feature will be displayed; refer to Figure-90.

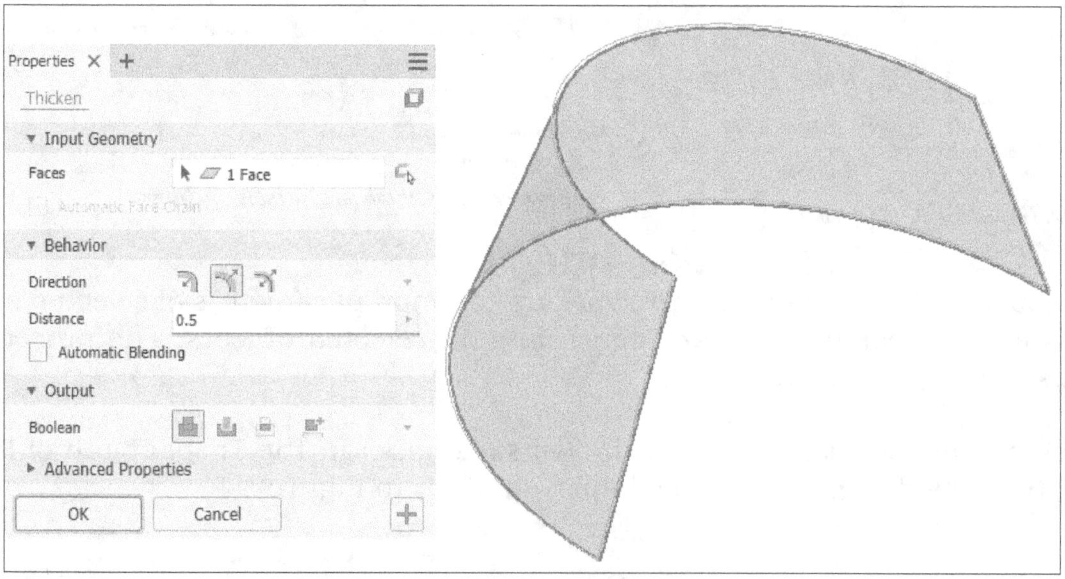

Figure-90. Preview of thicken feature

- Click on the **OK** button from the dialog box. Hide the surface earlier created by using the right-click shortcut menu.
- Click on the **Fillet** tool from the **Modify** panel in the **3D Model** tab of the **Ribbon**. The **Fillet** dialog box will be displayed.
- Select the corner edges of the thicken feature and specify suitable value of radius in the edit box. Preview of fillet will be displayed; refer to Figure-91.

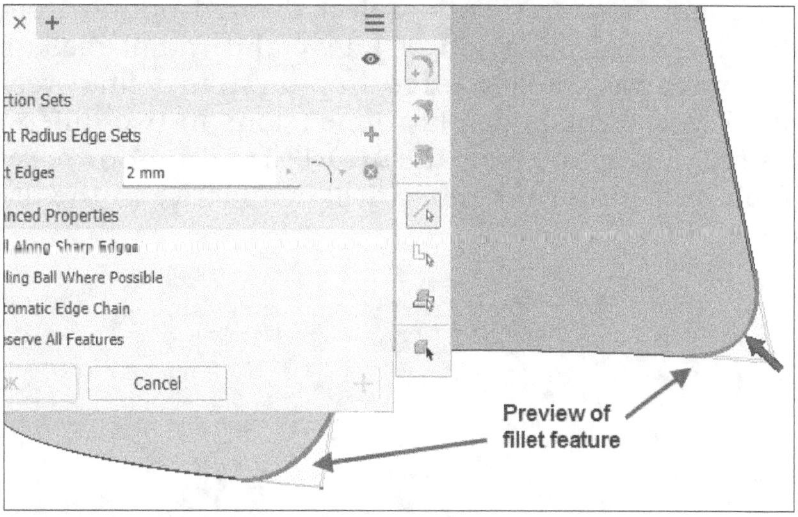

Figure-91. Preview of fillet feature

- Click on the **OK** button from the dialog box to create the feature.

MEASUREMENT TOOLS

When you are working with surfaces, there are various aspects of surface which can not be measured by using standard dimensioning tools. For example, if there are two surfaces joined together at a curve then how will we measured the smoothness of that joint. There are also conditions in mold design that require measurement of taper angle to confirm that the component can be ejected from mold safely. These type of measurements are performed by using the tools available in **Inspect** tab of the **Ribbon**; refer to Figure-92 and Figure-93. We will first discuss the measurement tools for part design and then we will discuss the tools for assembly design.

Figure-92. Inspect tab for Part modeling

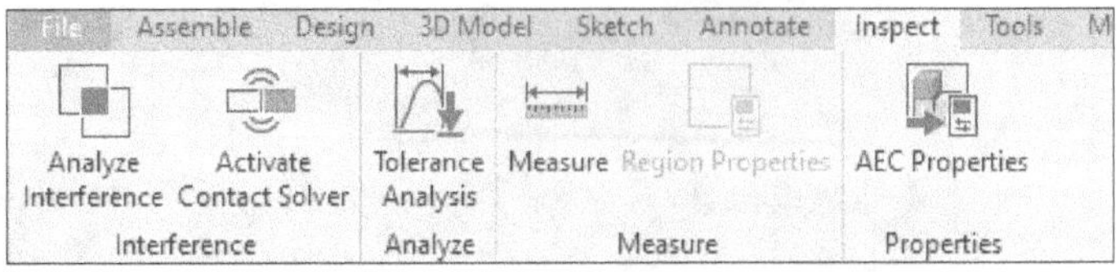

Figure-93. Inspect tab for Assembly modeling

Measuring Entities

The **Measure** tool is used to measure various common parameters of selected entities. The results of measure tool vary depending on selected objects. The procedure to use this tool is given next.

- Click on the **Measure** tool from the **Measure** panel in the **Inspect** tab of **Ribbon**. The **Measure** dialog box will be displayed; refer to Figure-94.

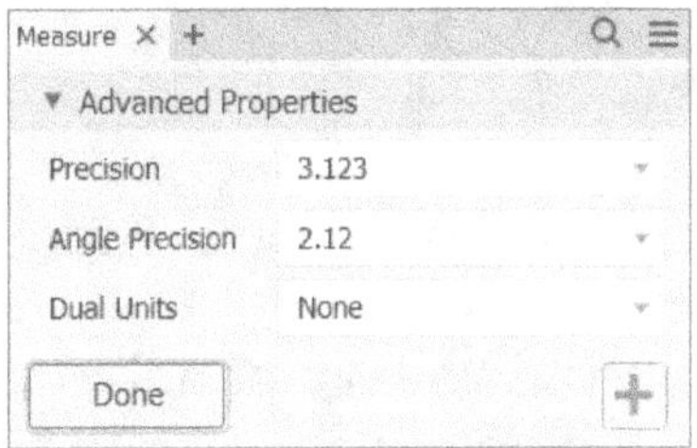

Figure-94. Measure dialog box

- Expand the **Advanced Properties** node from the dialog box to set precision for general and angular measurements. Select desired option from the **Precision** drop-down to set general precision of linear and radial measurements. Select desired option from the **Angle Precision** drop-down to define precision for angular measurements. If you want to display dimensions in two different unit systems then select desired unit option from the **Dial Units** drop-down; refer to Figure-95. Note that default unit set for the model will be inactive in the drop-down as it is already selected.

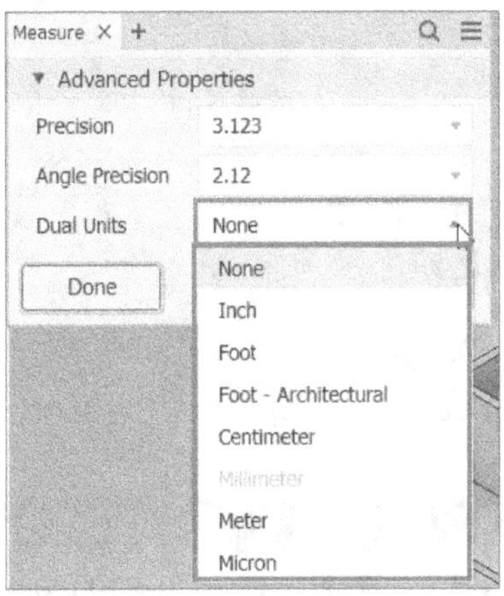

Figure-95. Dual Units drop-down

Based on selected entities, you will get different measurement results which are discussed next.

Measuring Points

- Select desired point from the model to find out its location with respect to origin.

- Select two points from the model to check their location as well as distance between the two; refer to Figure-96. Click on the **Restart Measure** button at the bottom in the dialog box to select next set of entities.

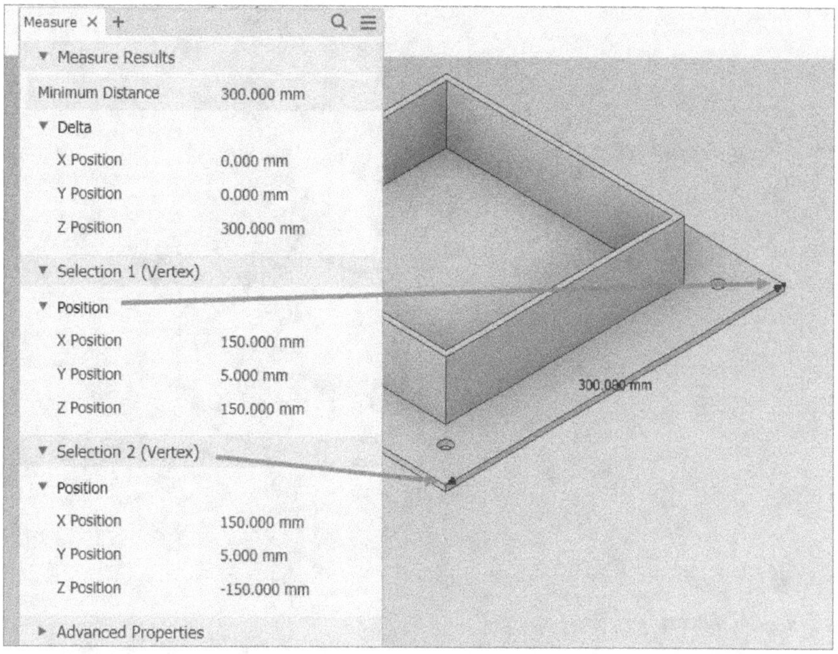

Figure-96. Measuring points

Measuring Lines

- Select a line or edge from the model to check its length. Select another line/edge if you want to check distance between the two lines as well as angle between them; refer to Figure-97.

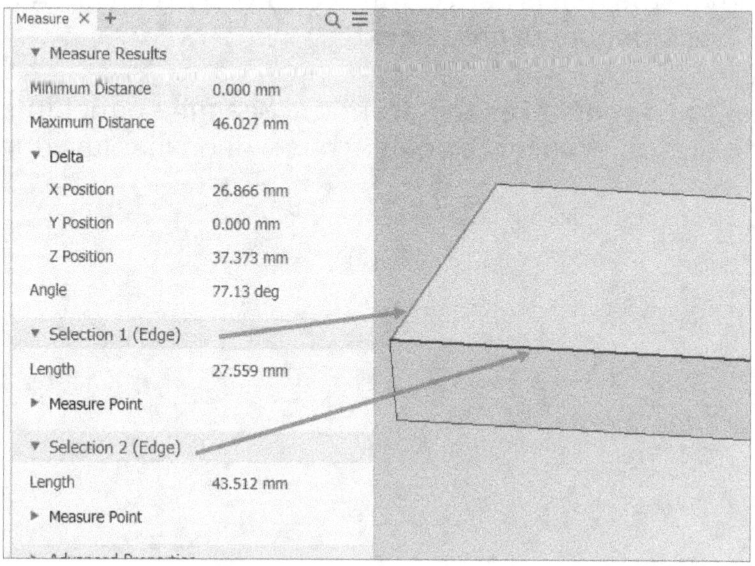

Figure-97. Measuring lines/edges

Measuring Circle/Arc

- Select a circle or arc curve/edge from the model to check diameter, radius, length, and swap angle of selected curves. If two circular curves/edges are selected then distance between center of two curves/edges will be displayed; refer to Figure-98.

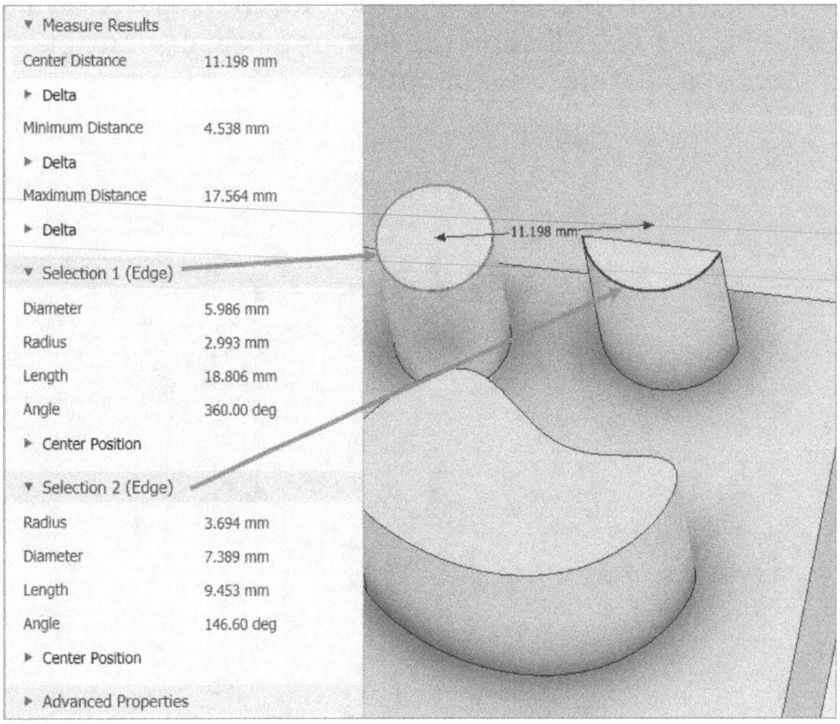

Figure-98. Measuring circle and arc

Similarly, you can measure length of the spline by selecting it. If you select a face then its perimeter, total loop length, and area will be displayed. If two faces selected then distance between the faces will be displayed as well.

Inspecting Region Properties

The **Region Properties** tool is used to check region properties of selected closed sketch loop. Note that this tool is active only when you are in sketching environment. The procedure to use this tool is given next.

- Click on the **Region Properties** tool from the **Measure** panel in the **Inspect** tab of the **Ribbon**. The **Region Properties** dialog box will be displayed; refer to Figure-99.

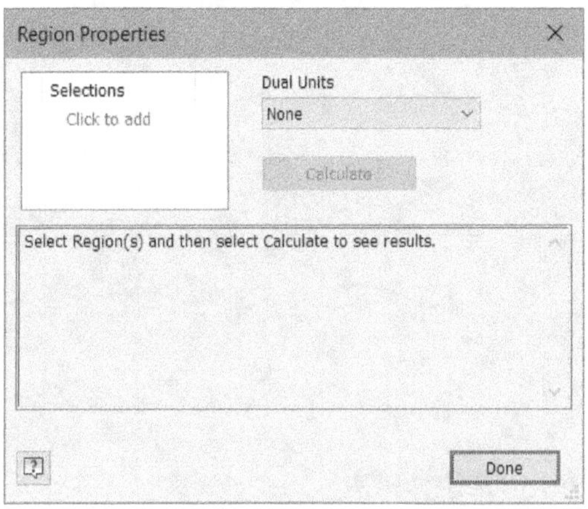

Figure-99. Region Properties dialog box

- Click inside the closed region of desired sketch loop to check its properties and click on the **Calculate** button. The properties of region will be displayed; refer to Figure-100.

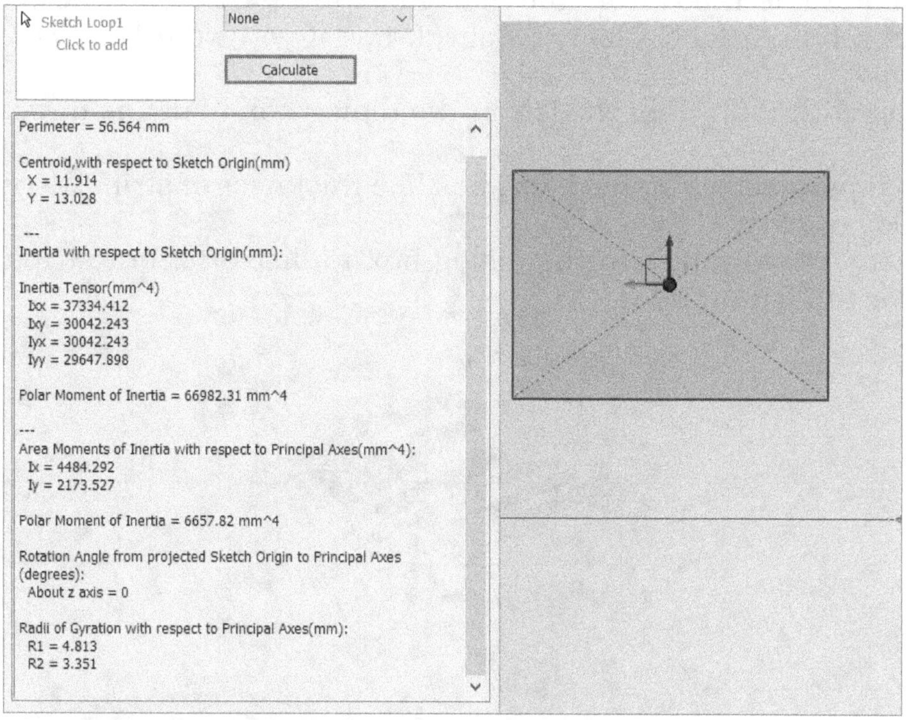

Figure-100. Region properties

- Click on the **Done** button after checking result to exit the dialog box.

Analyzing Surface Continuity using Zebra Pattern

The **Zebra** tool is used to display zebra strips on selected surfaces to check continuity in the surfaces. The procedure to use this tool is given next.

- Click on the **Zebra** tool from the **Analyze** panel in the **Inspect** tab of the **Ribbon**. The **Zebra Analysis** dialog box will be displayed; refer to Figure-101.

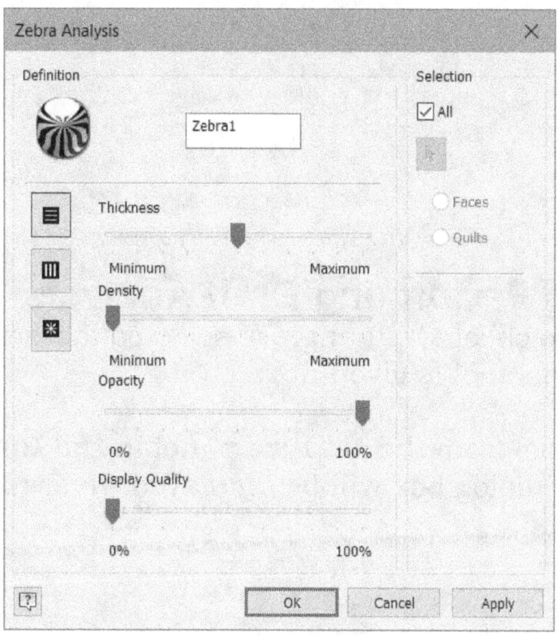

Figure-101. Zebra Analysis dialog box

- Select the **All** check box from the dialog box to select all the faces of the model to display zebra surface. Clear the check box if you want to select faces/quilts individually.
- Select desired button from the left in the dialog box to define direction of zebra strips.
- Set desired parameters in the dialog box like thickness of strips, density, opacity, and display quality.
- Click on the **OK** button from the dialog box to display zebra strips on selected faces; refer to Figure-102.

Figure-102. Zebra strips placed on faces

- To hide the result of analysis, right-click on the **Analysis: Zebra** folder from the **Model Browser** and clear the **Analysis Visibility** option; refer to Figure-103. Expand the **Analysis: Zebra** folder and delete the zebra by pressing **DELETE** key.

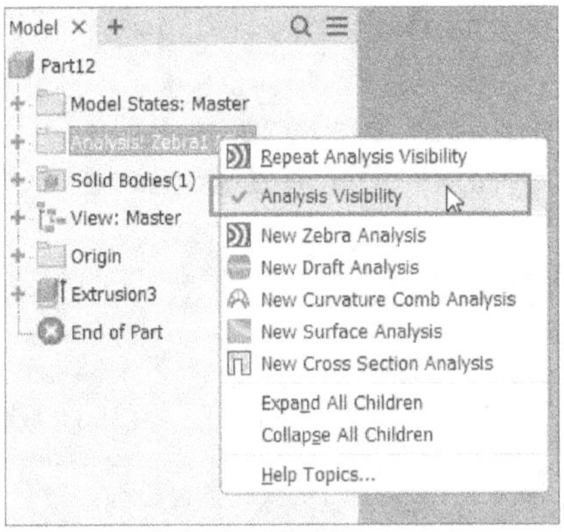

Figure-103. Analysis Visibility option

Performing Draft Analysis

The **Draft** tool is used to check draft angle of selected faces with respect to pull face. The procedure to use this tool is given next.

- Click on the **Draft** tool from the **Analyze** panel in the **Inspect** tab of the **Ribbon**. The **Draft Analysis** dialog box will be displayed; refer to Figure-104.

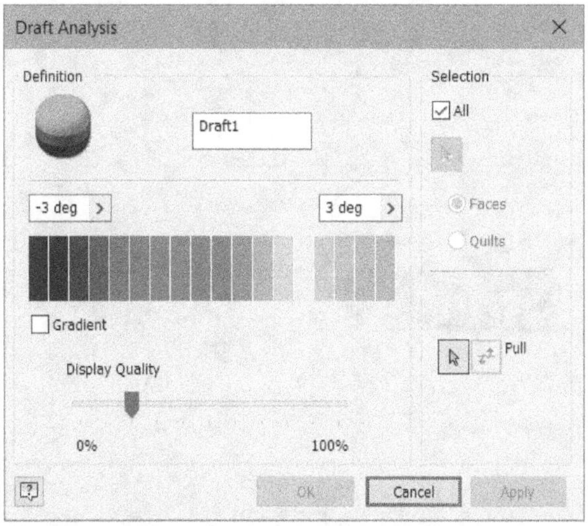

Figure-104. Draft Analysis dialog box

- Set desired values in the **Draft start angle** and **Draft end angle** edit boxes to define angle range for performing draft analysis.
- If **All** check box is selected then all the faces of model will be selected for draft analysis. Clear the check box and select desired faces for performing analysis.
- Click on the **Pull** selection button and select the face to be used as reference face for checking face angles; refer to Figure-105.

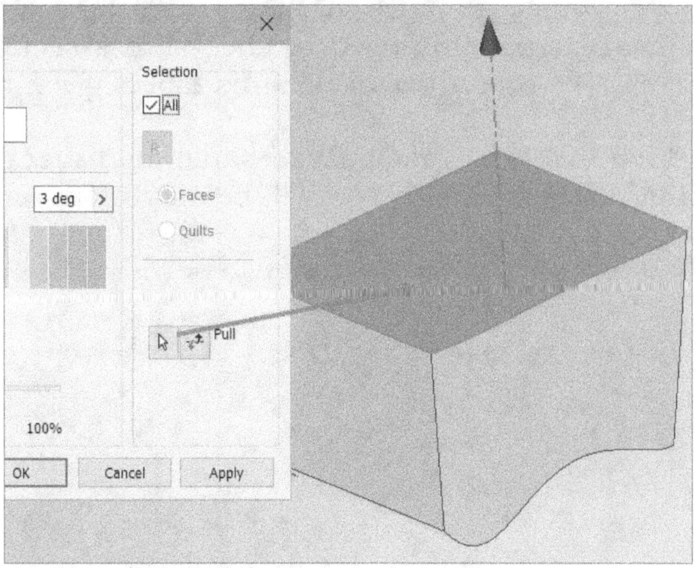

Figure-105. Pull direction face

- Click on the **OK** button from the dialog box to check results of analysis.

Surface Analysis

The **Surface** tool in **Analyze** panel is used to check curvature of surface using color gradient. The procedure to use this tool is given next.

- Click on the **Surface** tool from the **Analyze** panel in the **Inspect** tab of the **Ribbon**. The **Surface Analysis** dialog box will be displayed; refer to Figure-106.

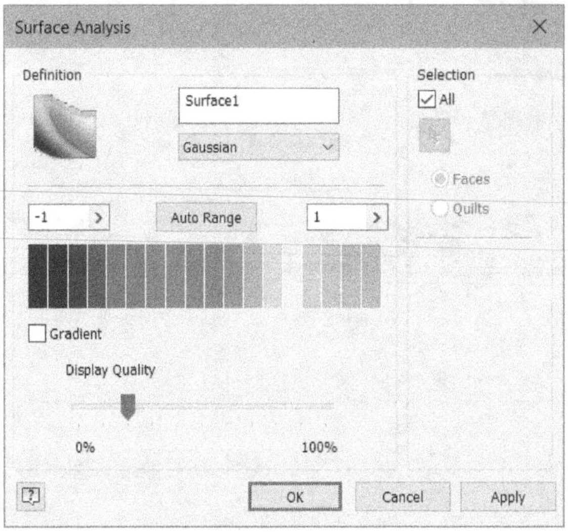

Figure-106. Surface Analysis dialog box

- Select desired method for surface curvature analysis from the **Definition** drop-down.
- Set the other parameters as discussed earlier and click on the **OK** button. The result of surface analysis will be displayed on the model.

Sections

The **Section** tool of **Analyze** panel is used to check cross-section of the model by cutting it using a plane. The procedure to use this tool is given next.

- Click on the **Section** tool from the **Analyze** panel in **Inspect** tab of the **Ribbon**. The **Cross Section Analysis** dialog box will be displayed; refer to Figure-107.

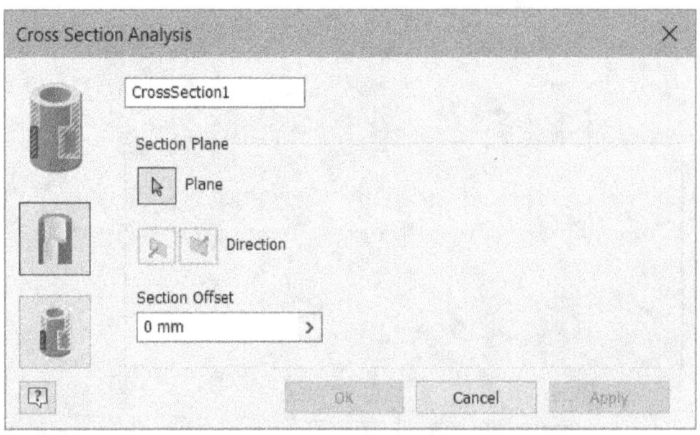

Figure-107. Cross Section Analysis dialog box

- Select desired face/plane to be used as section plane for cutting the model. The **Direction** buttons will become active.
- Select desired direction button to define direction in which section will be performed. The direction of section should be towards the model.
- Set desired value in the **Section offset** edit box to move the section plane in earlier specified direction. You can also use the arrow handle to move section plane; refer to Figure-108.

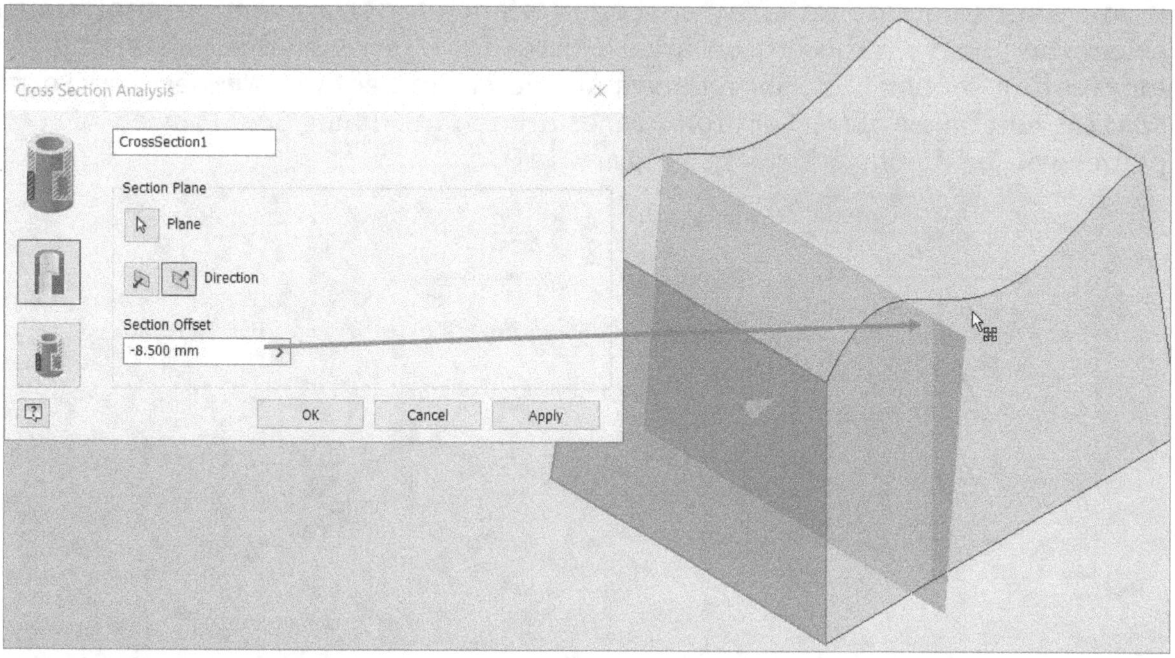

Figure-108. Moving section plane

- Click on the **Apply** button to create section.

Applying Advanced Sections

The options in the **Advanced Cross Section Analysis** dialog box are used to create multiple sections in the model. Click on the **Advanced** button from the left side in the dialog box. The options in the dialog box will be displayed as shown in Figure-109.

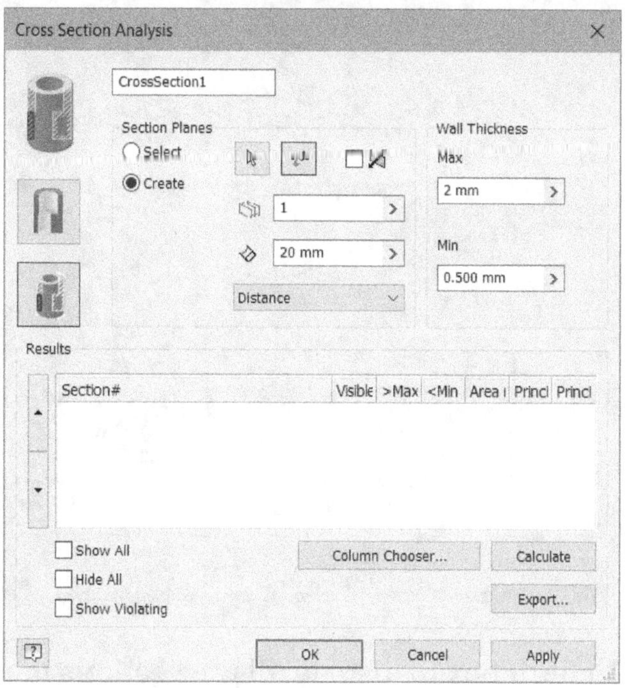

Figure-109. Advanced options

- Select the **Select** radio button from the **Section Planes** area of dialog box and select desired planes from the drawing area to be defined as section planes.

- If you want to create an array of section planes for cross section analysis then select the **Create** radio button and select a face/plane to define starting plane for creating section. Specify related parameters in **Section Number** and **Section Spacing** edit boxes of the **Section Planes** area in the dialog box. Preview of section planes will be displayed; refer to Figure-110.

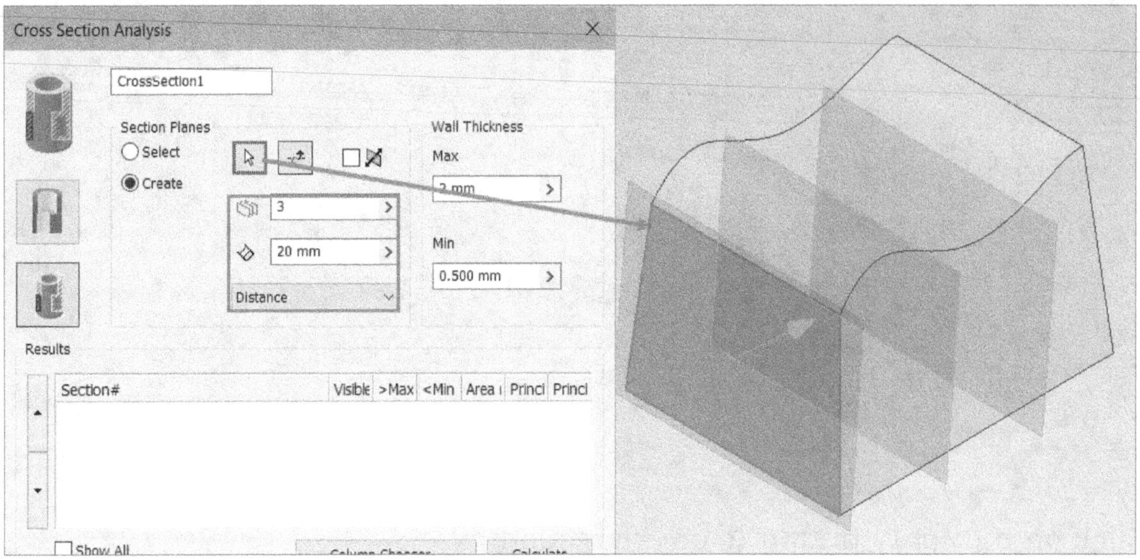

Figure-110. Section planes created

- Set desired parameters in **Wall Thickness** area as discussed earlier.
- After setting desired parameters, click on the **Calculate** button from the dialog box. The sections will be created and their results will be displayed in Results area; refer to Figure-111.

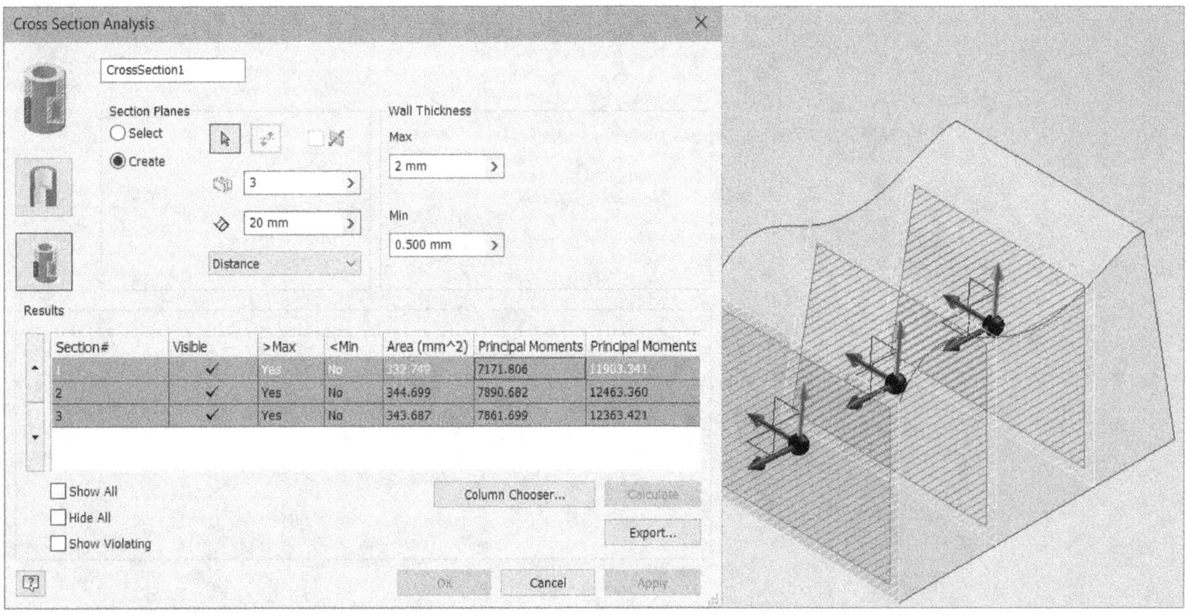

Figure-111. Multiple sections created

- Select the **Show All** check box to display all the sections in model. Select the **Hide All** check box to hide all the sections from model. Select the **Show Violating** check box to display only those sections which exceed the minimum and maximum wall thickness range.
- Click on the **Column Chooser** button if you want to add more result parameters in the table. The **Customization** dialog box will be displayed with list of available parameters.

- Drag desired parameter from the **Customization** dialog box to columns in the table; refer to Figure-112.

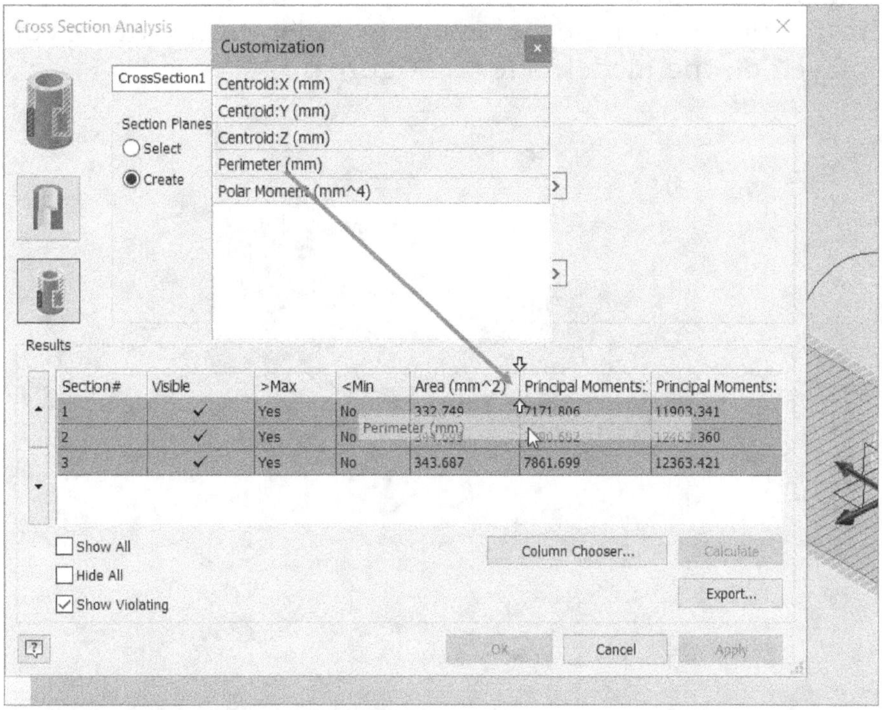

Figure-112. Adding parameters in columns of table

- Close the **Customization** dialog box after performing desired changes.
- Click on the **Export** button to save the data as text file.
- Close the **Cross Section Analysis** dialog box after setting desired parameters. You can delete or hide the cross section analysis results as discussed earlier for other analyses.

Curvature Comb Analysis

The **Curvature** tool in **Analyze** panel is used to determine smoothness and curvature of a surface. The procedure to use this tool is given next.

- Click on the **Curvature** tool from the **Analyze** panel in **Inspect** tab of the **Ribbon**. The **Curvature Analysis** dialog box will be displayed; refer to Figure-113.

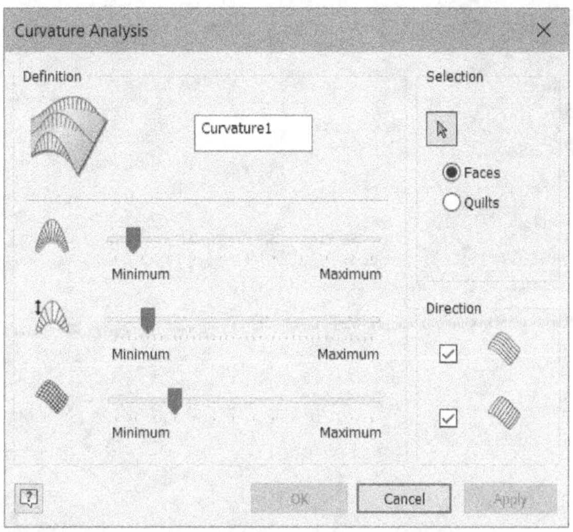

Figure-113. Curvature Analysis dialog box

- Select the face(s) of model on which you want to display curvature comb.
- Set the other parameters like direction, comb scale, comb density, and surface density as discussed earlier.
- Click on the **OK** button from the dialog box to generate curvature comb. The comb will be displayed on the model; refer to Figure-114.

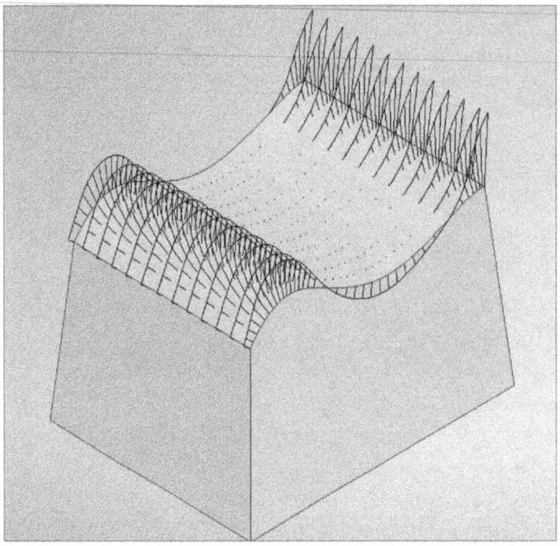

Figure-114. Curvature comb

PRACTICE 1

Create the model of flower vase as shown in Figure-115. The dimensions of the model are given in Figure-116.

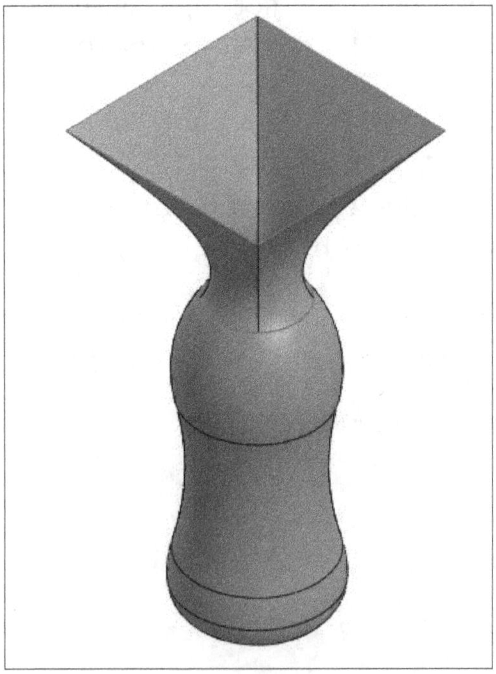

Figure-115. Flower vase model

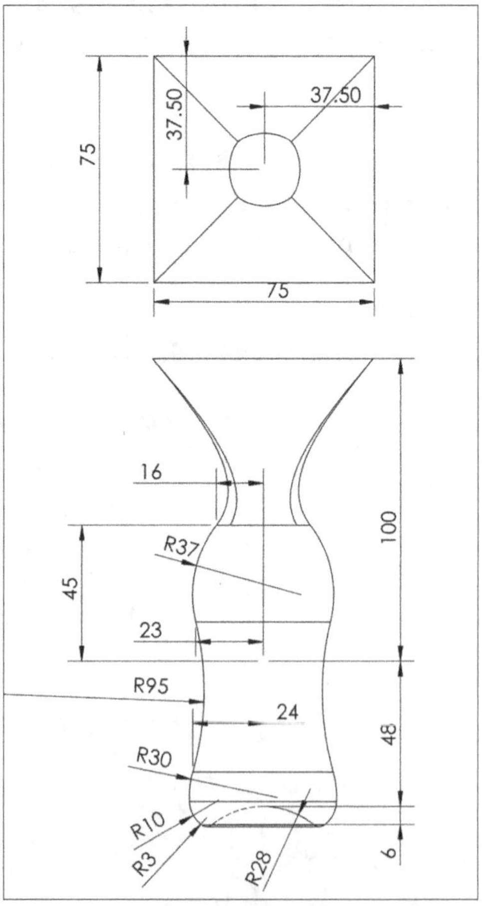

Figure-116. Practice 1 Drawing

PRACTICE 2

Create the surface model of tank as shown in Figure-117. The dimensions of the model are given in Figure-118.

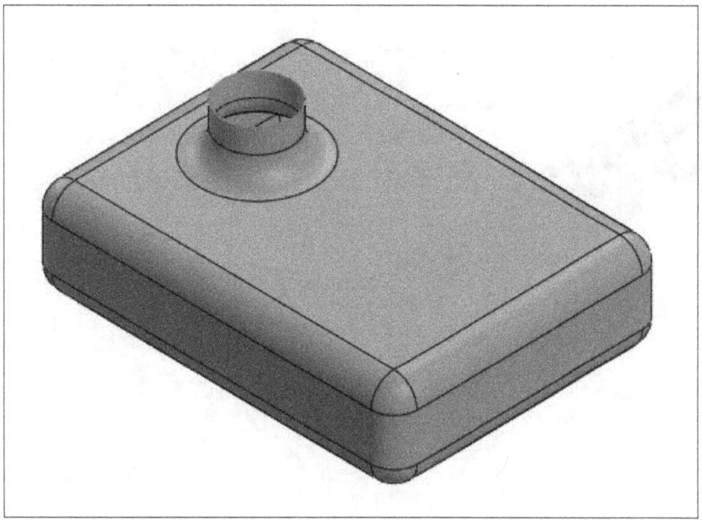

Figure-117. Practice 2 model

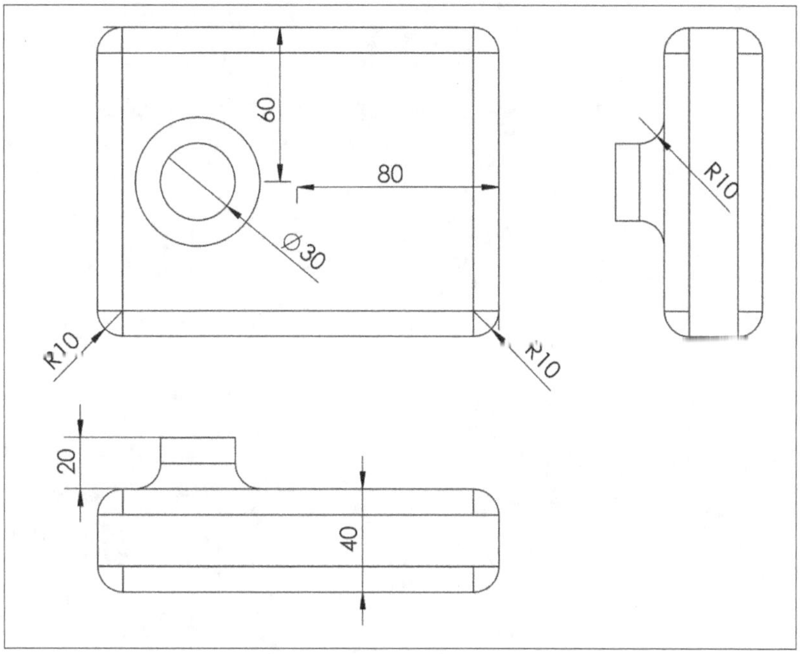

Figure-118. Practice 2 Drawing

PRACTICE 3

Create the surface model of car bumper as shown in Figure-119. The dimensions of the model are given in Figure-120. **Assume the missing dimensions**.

Figure-119. Practice 3 model

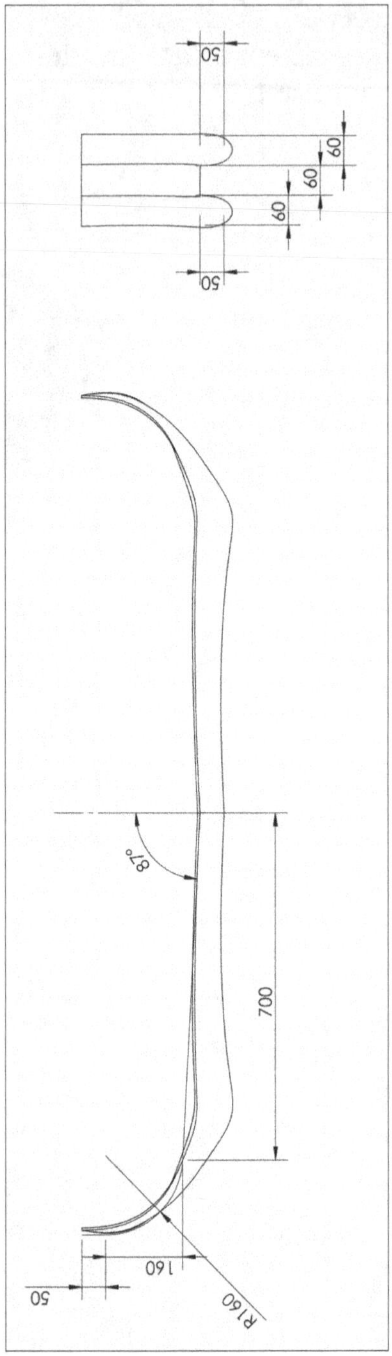

Figure-120. Car bumper

SELF ASSESSMENT

Q1. Which of the following tools is used to join the surfaces, meeting at common edges to form a solid body?

a) Extend Surface
b) Ruled Surface
c) Sculpt
d) None of the Above

Q2. Which of the following tools is the Freeform modeling tool?

a) Box
b) Sculpt
c) Boundary Patch
d) All of the Above

Q3. Which of the following categories consists of tools like Sphere, Torus, Quadball, etc.?

a) Freeform Designing
b) Surface Designing
c) Pattern Designing
d) None of the Above

Q4. Which of the following tools is used to break the merged edges in modifying the freeform objects?

a) Delete
b) Subdivide
c) Unweld Edges
d) Crease Edges

Q5. Which of the following tools is applied to the faces of freeform bodies so that any change made in one face will also be reflected in other face?

a) Mirror
b) Symmetry
c) Bridge
d) Both a and b

Q6. The **Thicken** tool is used to thicken the surfaces. (True/False)

Q7. The **Flatten** tool is used to fit selected vertices to the selected plane. (True/False)

Q8. The two vertices of a freeform object can be breaked by **Weld Vertices** tool. (True/False)

Q9. The **Merge Edges** tool is used to merge .... of the two freeform bodies.

Q10. Whenever you need an unconventional shape of the object, you can always use the .... modeling techniques.

Q11. The .... tool is used to create bridge faces to connect two faces/ open-edges of same body or different freeform bodies.

Q12. The **Crease Edges** tool is used to .... the curve of selected edges of the freeform object.

Q13. Which tool is used to create an extruded surface from a sketch?

A. Revolve tool
B. Extrude tool
C. Loft tool
D. Sweep tool

Q14. Which button must be clicked to toggle the Extrude dialog box into surface mode?

A. Middle button
B. Lower left button
C. Upper right button
D. Bottom right button

Q15. What is the function of the Stitch Surface tool?

A. To extend surfaces
B. To join surfaces at common edges
C. To delete surfaces
D. To replace faces

Q16. Before applying the Thicken tool effectively, what must be done to surfaces?

A. Trimmed
B. Mirrored
C. Stitched
D. Extended

Q17. What tool is used to create a patch based on selected edges and guidelines?

A. Stitch Surface
B. Boundary Patch
C. Sculpt
D. Trim Surface

Q18. Which tool allows you to create a solid region bounded by selected surfaces?

A. Boundary Patch
B. Sculpt
C. Extend Surface
D. Ruled Surface

Q19. The Ruled Surface tool creates surfaces that are by default:

A. Parallel to edges
B. Tangent to faces
C. Normal to edges
D. Perpendicular to guide rails

Q20. Which tool trims surfaces using another surface, plane, or sketch?

A. Trim Surface
B. Extend Surface
C. Replace Face
D. Sculpt

Q21. What is used to extend faces using the edges of the faces?

A. Sculpt tool
B. Replace Face tool
C. Extend Surface tool
D. Fit Mesh Face tool

Q22. What does the Replace Face tool do?

A. Stitches faces together
B. Extends faces along an edge
C. Replaces solid faces with selected surfaces
D. Trims faces using a plane

Q23. In freeform designing, what is created using the Box tool?
A. Plane surface
B. Cylindrical surface
C. Box-shaped freeform object
D. Sphere-shaped object

Q24. Which tool is used to create an individual freeform face based on selected vertices?

A. Face tool
B. Convert tool
C. Align Form tool
D. Edit Form tool

Q25. What does the Convert tool do in freeform modeling?

A. Create a new sketch
B. Convert a solid face to a freeform face
C. Trim surfaces
D. Create a boundary patch

Q26. What is the purpose of the Edit Form tool in freeform design?

A. Trim a face
B. Edit the shape of a freeform object
C. Extend a face
D. Replace an object

Q27. The Align Form tool aligns a vertex of a freeform object to:
A. An edge
B. A solid body
C. A selected plane or planar face
D. A sculpted region

Q28. What is the function of the Insert Edge tool?

A. To insert new points on an edge
B. To divide faces into sub-divisions
C. To insert new edges on sides of a selected edge
D. To merge two vertices together

Q29. Which button should you select in Insert Edge to create edges on both sides?

A. Single
B. Both
C. Double
D. Mirror

Q30. The Insert Point tool is primarily used for:

A. Creating new faces
B. Subdividing faces
C. Inserting a new point on a selected edge
D. Merging edges

Q31. What does the Subdivide tool do?

A. Merge vertices
B. Insert edges
C. Divide a face into sub-divisions
D. Thicken the surface

Q32. To merge open edges of two freeform bodies, which tool should you use?

A. Weld Vertices
B. Merge Edges
C. Flatten
D. Mirror

Q33. If you want to break merged edges, which tool will you use?

A. Crease Edges
B. Uncrease Edges
C. Unweld Edges
D. Subdivide

Q34. The Crease Edges tool is used to:

A. Smoothen the curve of edges
B. Break edges
C. Straighten the curve of selected edges
D. Offset surfaces

Q35. What is the purpose of the Uncrease Edges tool?

A. Straighten curves
B. Undo crease created by Crease Edges tool
C. Create sub-divisions
D. Weld vertices

Q36. The Weld Vertices tool joins:

A. Two faces
B. Two edges
C. Two vertices
D. Two surfaces

Q37. The Flatten tool is used to:

A. Merge two freeform bodies
B. Divide faces
C. Fit selected vertices to a plane
D. Insert points on edges

Q38. Which tool is used to connect two faces or open edges with a bridge surface?

A. Match Edge
B. Bridge
C. Mirror
D. Insert Edge

Q39. What does the Thicken tool help you achieve?

A. Sharpen edges
B. Thicken surfaces or offset faces
C. Divide faces into parts
D. Break merged edges

Q40. Which tool matches selected edges to a sketch curve?

A. Flatten
B. Insert Point
C. Match Edge
D. Weld Vertices

For Student Notes

Chapter 16

Analyses and Simulation

Topics Covered

The major topics covered in this chapter are:

- ***Introduction to Stress Analysis***
- ***Benefits of Stress Analysis***
- ***Starting Analysis in Autodesk Inventor***
- ***Performing Static Analysis***
- ***Performing Modal Analysis***
- ***Performing Shape Generator Study***
- ***Performing Frame Analysis***
- ***Report generation***

INTRODUCTION TO STRESS ANALYSIS

Stress analysis is used to find out the stress induced in the selected part under specified loading and contact conditions. In Autodesk Inventor, FEA (Finite Element Analysis) is used to solve the equations for stress analysis. Before we start using Stress Analysis which is based on FEA, we should understand the basics of FEA and its limits.

Basics of FEA

In engineering problems, there are some basic unknowns. If they are found, the behavior of the entire structure can be predicted. The basic unknowns or the Field variables which are encountered in the engineering problems are displacements in solid mechanics, velocities in fluid mechanics, electric and magnetic potentials in electrical engineering, and temperatures in heat flow problems.

In a continuum, these unknowns are infinite. The finite element procedure reduces such unknowns to a finite number by dividing the solution region into small parts called elements and by expressing the unknown field variables in terms of assumed approximating functions (Interpolating functions/Shape functions) within each element. The approximating functions are defined in terms of field variables of specified points called nodes or nodal points. Thus in the finite element analysis, the unknowns are the field variables of the nodal points. Once these are found, the field variables at any point can be found by using interpolation functions.

After selecting elements and nodal unknowns, next step in finite element analysis is to assemble element properties for each element. For example, in solid mechanics, we have to find the force-displacement i.e. stiffness characteristics of each individual element. Mathematically, this relationship is in the form

$$[k]_e \{\delta\}_e = \{F\}_e$$

where $[k]_e$ is element stiffness matrix, $\{\delta\}_e$ is nodal displacement vector of the element, and $\{F\}_e$ is nodal force vector. The element of stiffness matrix k_{ij} represent the force in coordinate direction 'i' due to a unit displacement in coordinate direction 'j'. Four methods are available for formulating these element properties viz. direct approach, variational approach, weighted residual approach, and energy balance approach. Any one of these methods can be used for assembling element properties. In solid mechanics, variational approach is commonly employed to assemble stiffness matrix and nodal force vector (consistent loads).

Element properties are used to assemble global properties/structure properties to get system equations $[k]\{\delta\} = \{F\}$. Then the boundary conditions are imposed. The solution of these simultaneous equations give the nodal unknowns. Using these nodal values, additional calculations are made to get the required values e.g. stresses, strains, moments, etc. in solid mechanics problems.

Thus the various steps involved in the finite element analysis are:

(i) Select suitable field variables and the elements.

(ii) Discretize the continua.

(iii) Select interpolation functions.
(iv) Find the element properties.
(v) Assemble element properties to get global properties.
(vi) Impose the boundary conditions.
(vii) Solve the system equations to get the nodal unknowns.
(viii) Make the additional calculations to get the required values.

Assumptions for using FEA

Some assumptions are made in this type of analysis, like:

1. The loads applied does not vary with time.
2. All loads are applied slowly and gradually until they reach to the full magnitude and after reaching the full magnitude, the loads remain constant. Thereby, neglecting impact, inertial, and damping forces.
3. The materials applied to the components satisfy the Hooke's law.
4. The change in stiffness due to loading is neglected.
5. Boundary conditions do not vary during the application of loads. Loads must be constant in magnitude, direction, and distribution.

Geometry Assumptions

1. The part model must represent the required CAD geometry.
2. Only the internal fillets in the area of interest will be included in the study.
3. Shells are created when thickness of the part is small in comparison to its width and length.
4. Thickness of the shell is assumed to be constant.
5. If the dimensions of a particular part are not critical and do not affect the analysis results, some approximations can be made in modeling the particular part.
6. Primary members of structure are long and thin like a beam then idealization is required.
7. Local behavior at the joints of beams or other discontinuities are not of primary interest, so no special modeling of these area is required.
8. Decorative or external features will be assumed insignificant to the stiffness and the performance of the part and will be omitted from the model.

Material Assumptions

1. Material remain in the linear regime. It is understood that either stress levels exceeding yield or excessive displacements will constitute a component failure. That is non linear behavior cannot be accepted.
2. Nominal material properties adequately represent the physical system.
3. Material properties are not affected by load rate.
4. Material properties can be assumed isotropic (Orthotropic) and homogeneous.
5. Part is free of voids or surface imperfections that can produce stress risers and skew local results.
6. Actual non linear behavior of the system can be extrapolated from the linear material results.
7. Weld material and the heat affected zone will be assumed to have same material properties as the base material.
8. Temperature variations may have a significant impact on the properties of the materials used. Change in material properties is neglected.

Boundary Conditions Assumptions

1. Choosing proper BC's require experience.
2. Using BC's to represent parts and effects that are not or cannot be modeled leads to the assumption that the effects of these un-modeled entities can truly be simulated or has no effect on the model being analyzed.
3. For a given situation, there would be many ways of applying boundary conditions. But these various alternatives can be wrong if the user does not understand the assumptions they represent.
4. Symmetry/ anti-symmetry/ reflective symmetry/ cyclic symmetry conditions if exists can be used to minimize the model size and complexity.
5. Displacements may be lower than they would be if the boundary conditions being more appropriate. Stress magnitudes may be higher or lower depending on the constraint used.

Fasteners Assumptions

1. Residual stress due to fabrication, pre-loading of bolts, welding and/or other manufacturing, or assembly processes are neglected.
2. Bolt loading is primarily axial in nature.
3. Bolt head or washer surface torque loading is primarily axial in nature.
4. Surface torque loading due to friction will produce only local effects.
5. Bolts, spot welds, welds, rivets, and/or fasteners which connect two components are considered perfect and acts as rigid joint.
6. Stress relaxation of fasteners or other assembly components will not be considered. Load on threaded portion of the part is evenly distributed on engaged threads.
7. Failure of fasteners will not be reflected in the analysis.

General Assumptions

1. If the results in the particular area are of interest then mesh convergence will be limited to this area.
2. No slippage between interfacing components will be assumed.
3. Any sliding contact interfaces will be assumed frictionless.
4. System damping will be normally small and assumed constant across all frequencies of interest unless otherwise available from published literature or actual tests.
5. Stiffness of bearings in radial or axial directions will be considered infinite.
6. Elements with poor or less than optimal geometry are only allowed in areas that are not of concern and do not affect the overall performance of the model.

Now, we will not go deeper in theoretical area of FEA. We will now start stress analysis in Autodesk Inventor.

STARTING STRESS ANALYSIS

- Open the part file or assembly file on which you want to perform stress analysis in Autodesk Inventor. (C'mon you know it how to open file)
- Click on the **Stress Analysis** tool from the **Begin** panel in the **Environments** tab of the **Ribbon**; refer to Figure-1. The **Analysis** contextual tab will be added in the **Ribbon**; refer to Figure-2.

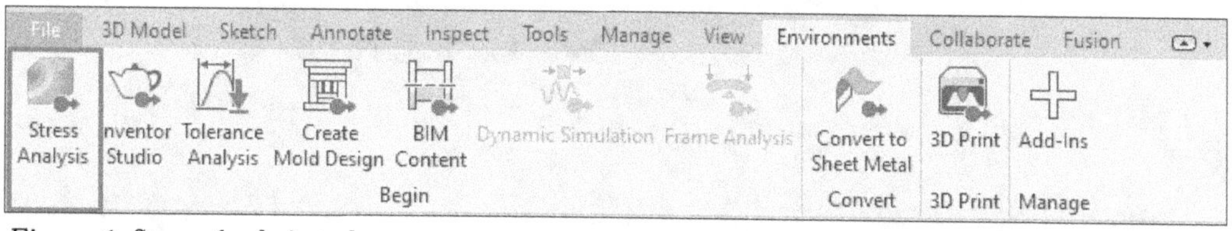

Figure-1. Stress Analysis tool

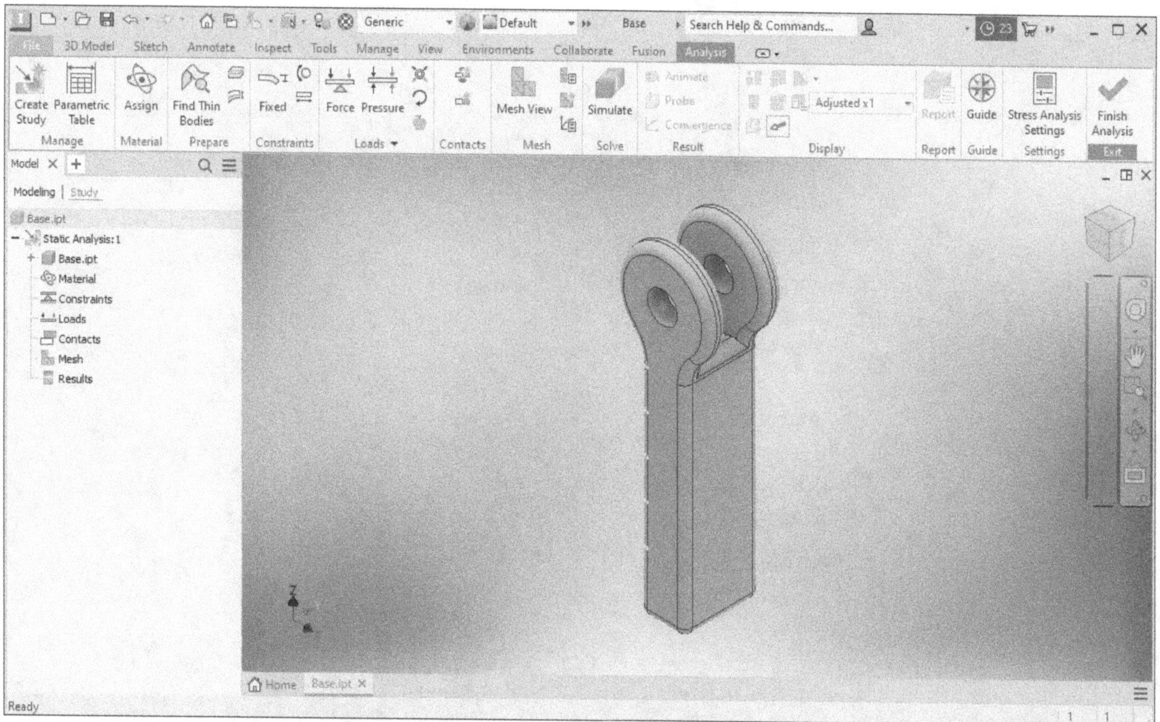

Figure-2. Tools in Analysis contextual tab

Note that only **Create Study** tool is active in the contextual at beginning which means you need to create a simulation study first to use the other tools in tab.

CREATING STUDY

This is the first and very important step in performing stress analysis in Autodesk Inventor. All the results of analysis are directly linked with the options specified here. The procedure to create simulation study is given next.

- Click on the **Create Study** tool from the **Manage** panel in the **Analysis** contextual tab of the **Ribbon**. The **Create New Study** dialog box will be displayed; refer to Figure-3.

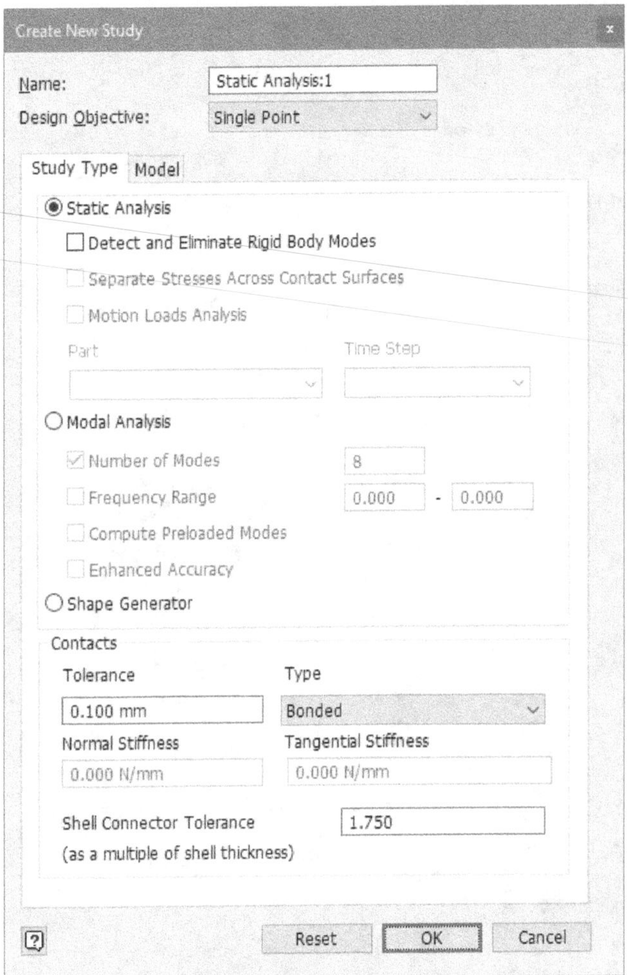

Figure-3. Create New Study dialog box

- Select the type of analysis from the **Study Type** tab of the dialog box. There are three radio buttons to select study type; **Static Analysis**, **Modal Analysis**, and **Shape Generator**. Select the **Static Analysis** radio button if you want to check the stresses induced in part due to applied loads. Select the **Modal Analysis** radio button if you want to find out the natural frequencies and mode shapes along with effect of applied loads on the part. Select the **Shape Generator** radio button if you want to reduce the weight of part for specified loading conditions. This option is available for parts only. Note that **Shape Generator** option will give you the shape mathematically satisfying the weight and loading conditions but it is your duty to find the practicality of shape on our planet!!
- Specify the name of analysis in the **Name** edit box of dialog box.
- Select **Single Point** or **Parametric Dimension** option from the **Design Objective** drop-down. If selected **Single Point** option then analysis result deformation will occur on structure of part. If **Parametric Dimension** option is selected then deformation will obey dimensional stability.

Static Analysis Options

- Select the **Detect and Eliminate Rigid Body Modes** check box if you want to eliminate rigid body modes which are not restricted by providing constraints. In general words, rigid body mode is translational and rotational degree of freedom of complete part. In rigid body, particles of part do not change their position on applying load which means shape of part is constant.

- Select the **Separate Stresses Across Contact Surfaces** check box if you want to discontinue the stress representations of the model at contact surfaces. In simple words, the stress representations at the contact surfaces will be according to their parts rather than mixing of stress shades in results. This option is active for assemblies only.
- Select the **Motion Loads Analysis** check box if you want to run the motion loads analysis on the part. You can run the motion load analysis using the **Dynamic Simulation** tool in the **Environments** tab of **Ribbon** in assembly environment.

Modal Analysis Options

- Select the **Number of Modes** check box and specify the number of modes in the adjacent check box. Number of modes means number of natural frequency for which you want to check the deformation of the part.
- Select the **Frequency Range** check box to define the range of frequency in which natural frequencies should be checked. On selecting this check box, the frequency range edit boxes will become active. Specify desired values in the edit boxes.
- Select the **Compute Preloaded Modes** check box if you want to run a stress analysis first and then run the Modal analysis. In this case, the natural frequencies will be calculated using the pre-stressed model.
- Select the **Enhanced Accuracy** check box if you want to find out natural frequencies up to the order of **10**.

Shape Generator

The **Shape Generator** radio button is used to run analysis to find out the best possible shape of part to survive the applied loads and reduce the mass of part as much as possible. This option is available for parts only.

Contact Options

The options in the **Contacts** area of dialog box are used to specify the parameters related to contacts in analysis. Contact is relation between material structures of two parts in contact. There are various contact type like bonded, spring, and so on. The options in the **Contacts** area of the dialog box are discussed next.

- Select the contact type from the **Type** drop-down in the **Contacts** area of the dialog box which will be automatically applied while working with assemblies in analysis.
- Specify the value of maximum distance/gap in the **Tolerance** edit box up to which the automatic contacts will be created.
- If you have selected the **Spring** option as automatic contact from the **Type** drop-down then you can specify the tangential stiffness and normal stiffness in their respective edit boxes in **Contacts** area of the dialog box.
- Set the representation of assembly in the **Model** tab of the dialog box.
- After specifying all the options as required in the dialog box, click on the **OK** button to create the study.

ASSIGNING MATERIAL

Once you have started an analysis, the very next step is to assign material to the part(s) if not applied earlier. There are various properties that are taken into account while performing analysis like ultimate strength, young's modulus, Poisson's ratio, etc. The procedure to apply material is given next.

- Click on the **Assign** tool from the **Material** panel in the **Analysis** contextual tab of the **Ribbon**. The **Assign Materials** dialog box will be displayed; refer to Figure-4.

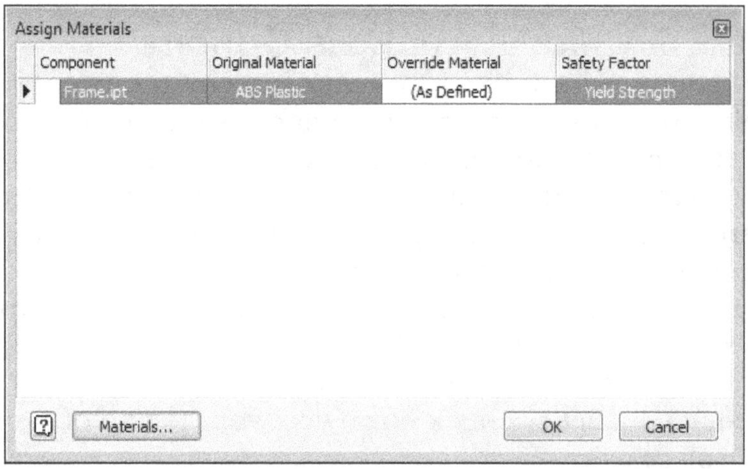

Figure-4. Assign Materials dialog box

- If you have applied any material earlier then it will be displayed for the part under **Original Material** column. Click in the field under **Override Material** column in the table. A drop-down will become active.
- Select desired material from the drop-down.
- Click on the **OK** button from the dialog box to apply the material. Note that we have discussed about creating custom materials earlier in the book. So, you can create and use the custom materials in the same way.

APPLYING CONSTRAINTS

Constraints means restriction to motion. There are three tools to apply constraints in Stress Analysis environment of Autodesk Inventor. These tools are discussed next.

Fixed Tool

The **Fixed** tool in the **Constraints** panel is used to create fixed constraint. Using this constraint, you can fix the selected portion of part/assembly so that it cannot move in any direction even under the maximum loading conditions. The procedure to use **Fixed** tool is given next.

- Click on the **Fixed** tool from the **Constraints** panel in the **Analysis** contextual tab of the **Ribbon**. The **Fixed Constraint** dialog box will be displayed; refer to Figure-5. Also, you will be asked to select the entities to be fixed.

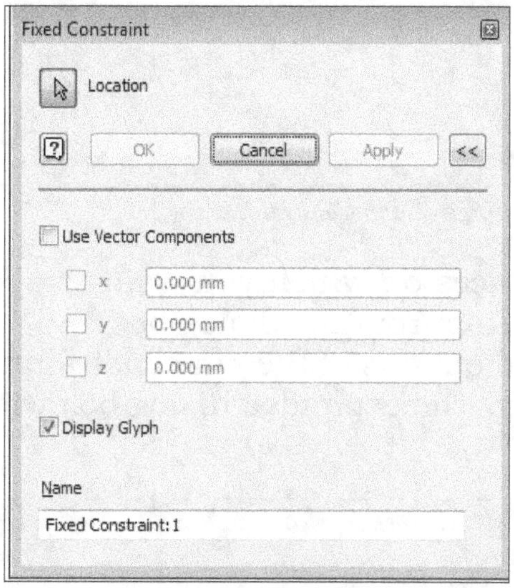

Figure-5. Fixed Constraint dialog box

- Select the entity/entities to be fixed and click on the **OK** button. The selected entities will be fixed for analysis; refer to Figure-6.

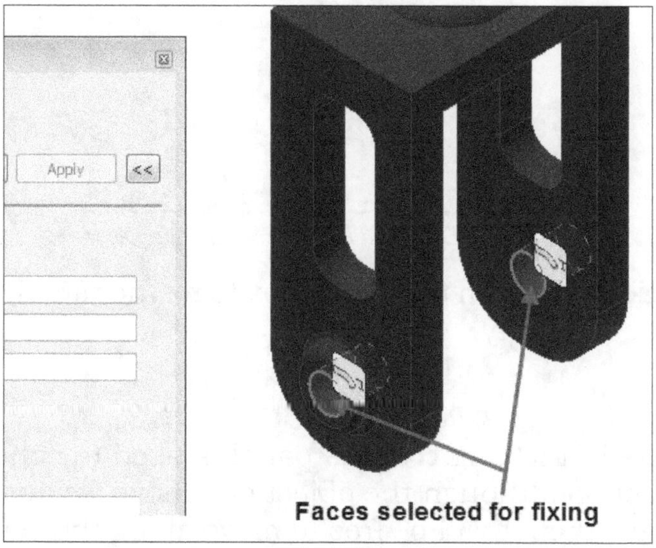

Figure-6. Faces selected for fixing

Pin Tool

The **Pin** tool in the **Constraints** panel is used to constraint selected entities in such a way that the object is free to rotate but cannot translate in any direction. Note that the constraint represents an imaginary pin at the faces selected. This constraint should be applied to shafts or holes for shafts. The procedure to use **Pin** tool is given next.

- Click on the **Pin** tool from the **Constraints** panel in the **Analysis** contextual tab of the **Ribbon**. The **Pin Constraint** dialog box will be displayed; refer to Figure-7. Also, you will be asked to select the entity/entities on which you want to apply the pin constraint.

Figure-7. Pin Constraint dialog box

- Select the round face/faces on which you want to apply the pin constraint and then click on the **OK** button from the dialog box.
- To change the advanced options of the pin constraint, click on the **More Options** button in the dialog box. The expanded dialog box will be displayed as shown in Figure-8.

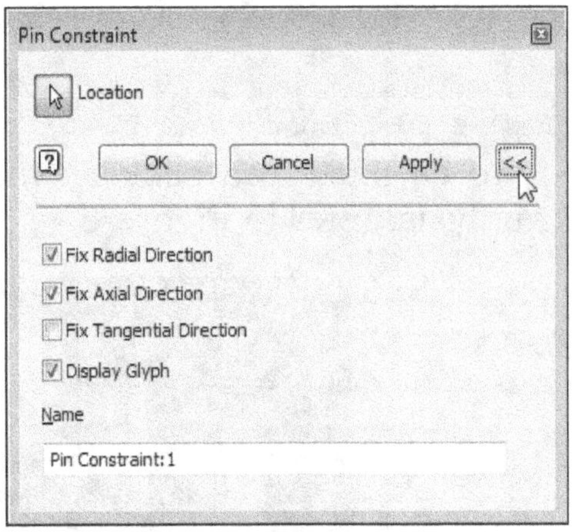

Figure-8. Expanded Pin Constraint dialog box

- Select the fix check boxes from the dialog box to fix the radial, axial, and tangential motion of the selected entity.

Frictionless Tool

The **Frictionless** tool in the **Constraints** panel is used to constraint the motion of object in normal direction although the object can move freely in same plane. If you select a cylindrical face then it will be free to move along the center axis but can not move perpendicular to axis. The procedure to use the tool is given next.

- Click on the **Frictionless** tool from the **Constraints** panel in the **Analysis** tab of the **Ribbon**. The **Frictionless Constraint** dialog box will be displayed; refer to Figure-9. Also, you will be asked to select entities.

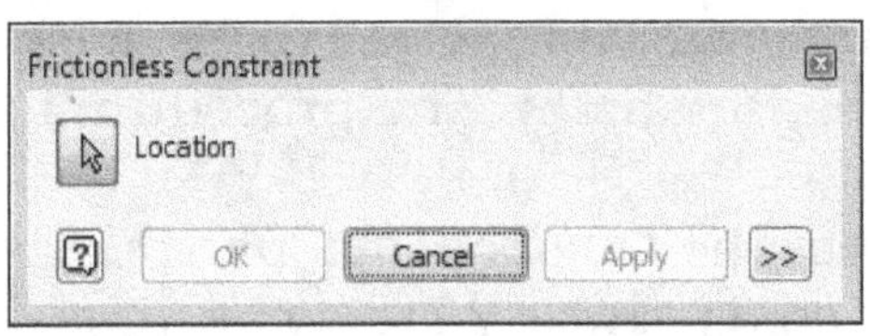

Figure-9. Frictionless Constraint dialog box

- Select the face/faces to which frictionless constraint is to be applied and click on the **OK** button. The constraint will be applied.

APPLYING LOADS

The loads in Analysis environment of Autodesk Inventor represent forces acting on the part/assembly during its practical application. There are seven tools available to apply different type of loads in the **Loads** panel of the **Analysis** contextual tab of **Ribbon**. These tools are discussed next.

Force Tool

The **Force** tool is used to apply force at the selected entity at desired direction. The procedure to use this tool is given next.

- Click on the **Force** tool from the **Loads** panel in the **Analysis** contextual tab of the **Ribbon**. The **Force** dialog box will be displayed; refer to Figure-10.

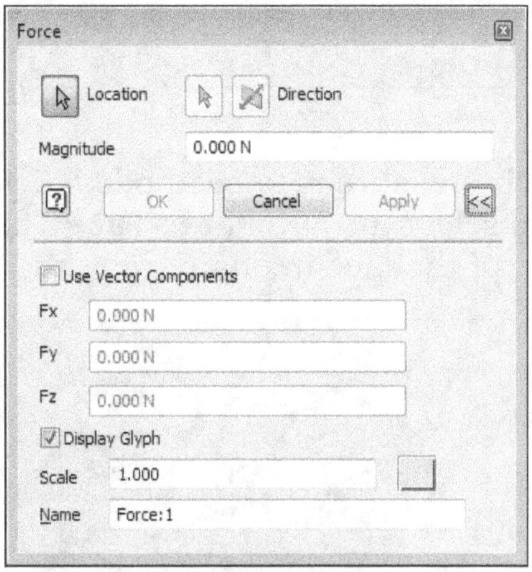

Figure-10. Force dialog box

- Select the face/edge/vertex on which you want to apply force. Arrow for force direction will be displayed on the selected face/edge/vertex; refer to Figure-11.

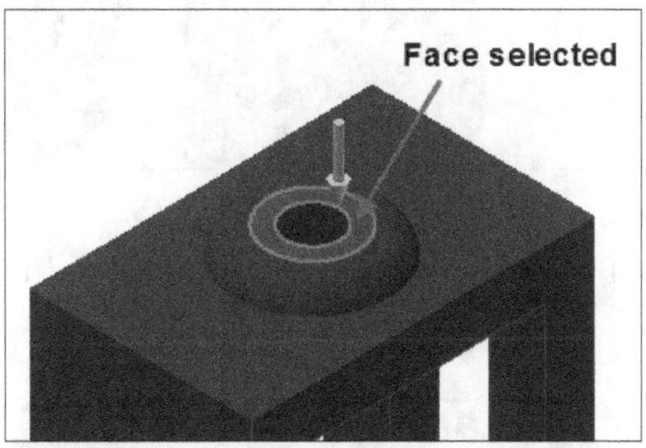

Figure-11. Face selected for applying force

- Specify desired value of force in the **Magnitude** edit box of the dialog box.
- By default, force is applied normal to the selected entity. If you want to explicitly specify the force direction then click on the selection button for **Direction** and select the reference for direction of force. Flip the direction if required by using the **Flip** button for **Direction** in the dialog box.
- If you want to specify the X, Y, and Z component of force vector then select the **Use Vector Components** check box in the expanded dialog box and specify desired values in the edit boxes below it.

Pressure Tool

The force applied per unit area is called pressure. Generally, pressure is used to represent the force applied by fluids on the enclosures. The **Pressure** tool is used to apply pressure on the workpiece in Autodesk Inventor Analysis environment. The procedure to use this tool is given next.

- Click on the **Pressure** tool from the **Loads** panel in the **Analysis** contextual tab of the **Ribbon**. The **Pressure** dialog box will be displayed; refer to Figure-12. Also, you will be asked to select the faces on which pressure is to be applied.

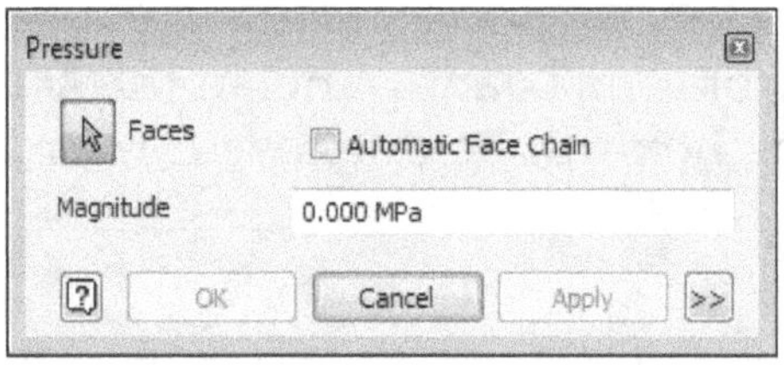

Figure-12. Pressure dialog box

- Select the faces on which pressure is to be applied. If you want to select the faces connected in chain then select the **Automatic Face Chain** check box in the dialog box and then select one of the face in chain; refer to Figure-13.

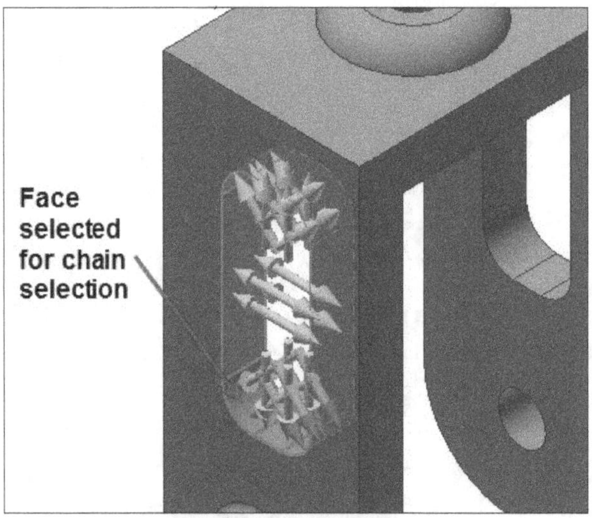

Figure-13. Face selected for applying pressure

- Specify desired value of pressure in the **Magnitude** edit box of the dialog box and click on the **OK** button.

Bearing Load Tool

The **Bearing Load** tool is used to apply the load on part which is sustained by bearing in the actual assembly. The procedure to use **Bearing Load** tool is given next.

- Click on the **Bearing Load** tool from the **Loads** panel in the **Analysis** contextual tab of the **Ribbon**. The **Bearing Load** dialog box will be displayed; refer to Figure-14.

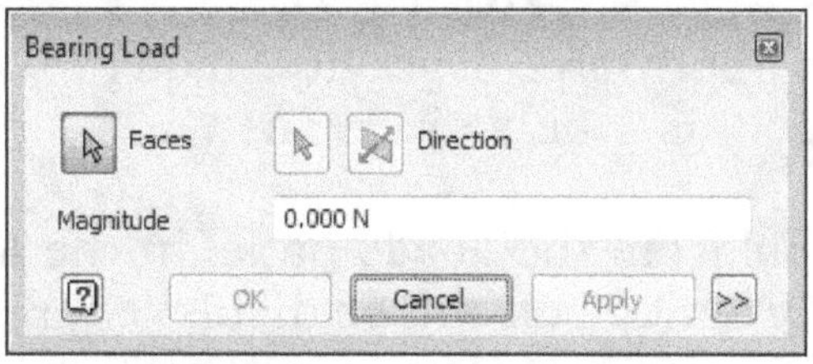

Figure-14. Bearing Load dialog box

- Select the round face on which you want to apply bearing load and specify the value of load in the **Magnitude** edit box.
- Using the options in the expanded dialog box, you can specify the component of the bearing load vector.
- Click on the **OK** button to apply the load.

Moment Tool

The **Moment** tool is used to apply general moment on the selected face. The procedure to use this tool is given next.

- Click on the **Moment** tool from the **Loads** panel in the **Analysis** contextual tab of the **Ribbon**. The **Moment** dialog box will be displayed; refer to Figure-15. Also, you will be asked to select faces.

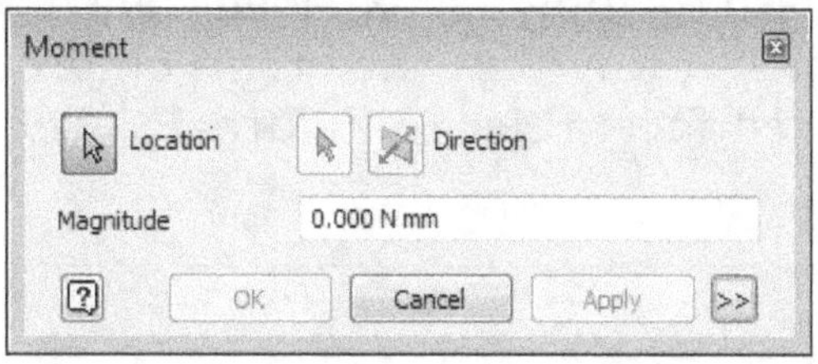

Figure-15. Moment dialog box

- Select the round face on which you want to apply moment and specify desired value in the **Magnitude** edit box of the dialog box; refer to Figure-16.

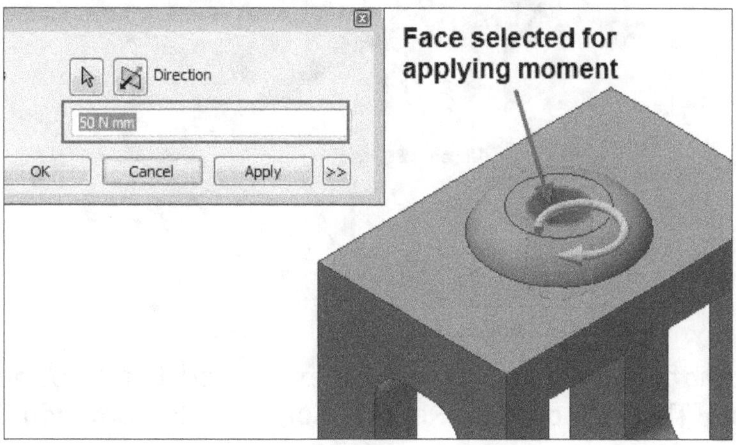

Figure-16. Applying moment

- Click on the **OK** button to apply moment.

Gravity Tool

The **Gravity** tool is used to apply force of gravity on all the components in the drawing area. The procedure to use this tool is given next.

- Click on the **Gravity** tool from the **Loads** panel in the **Analysis** contextual tab of the **Ribbon**. The **Gravity** dialog box will be displayed; refer to Figure-17. Also, you will be asked to select a reference to specify direction of gravity.

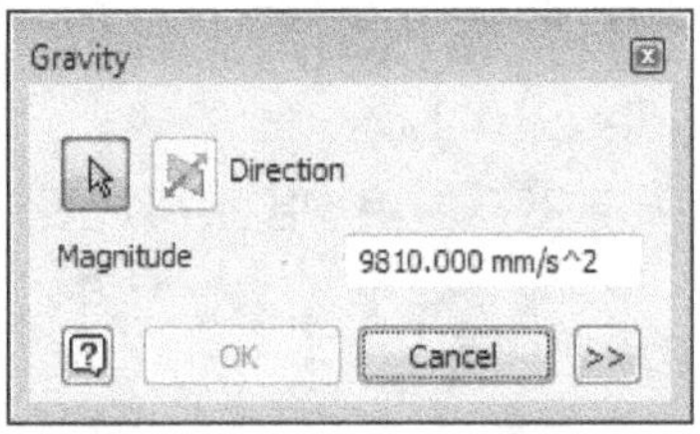

Figure-17. Gravity dialog box

- Select a flat face/edge/axis to specify the direction.
- Specify the magnitude of gravity in the **Magnitude** edit box of the dialog box.
- Use the options in the expanded dialog box to specify components of gravity force.
- Click on the **OK** button to apply the force.

Remote Force Tool

The **Remote Force** tool is used to apply remote load/mass. Remote load/mass is force applied on an object in such a way that the origin of force is somewhere else but it is also affecting the selected face; refer to Figure-18. The procedure to use **Remote Force** tool is given next.

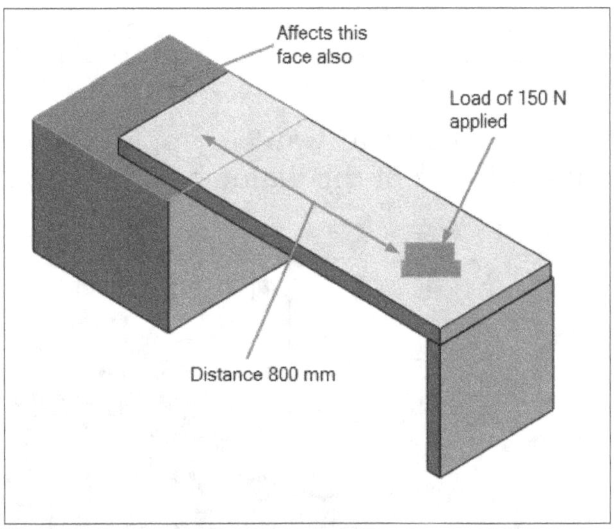

Figure-18. Remote load example

- Click on the **Remote Force** tool from the expanded **Loads** panel in the **Analysis** contextual tab of the **Ribbon**. The **Remote Force** dialog box will be displayed; refer to Figure-19.

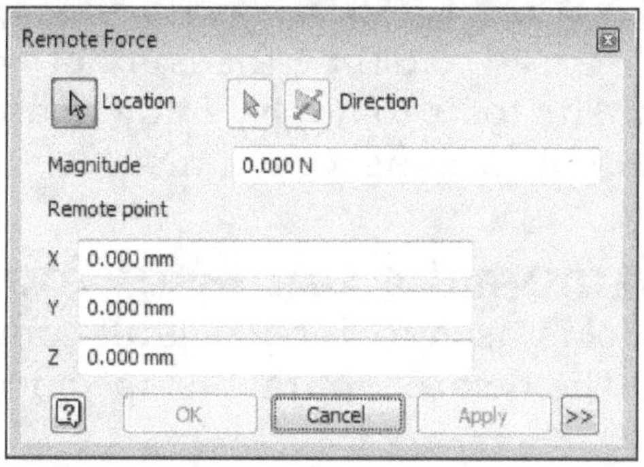

Figure-19. Remote Force dialog box

- Select the face on which you want to apply remote force.
- Click in the **Magnitude** edit box and specify desired value of force.
- Specify the location of remote point in the edit boxes **X**, **Y**, and **Z** given for **Remote point** in the dialog box.
- Click on the **OK** button to create the force.

Body Loads Tool

The **Body Load** tool is used to apply loads causing motion in the body. These loads imitate the effect of forces like centrifugal force, centripetal force, etc. The procedure to apply the body loads is given next.

- Click on the **Body Load** tool from the expanded **Loads** panel in the **Analysis** contextual tab of the **Ribbon**. The **Body Loads** dialog box will be displayed; refer to Figure-20.

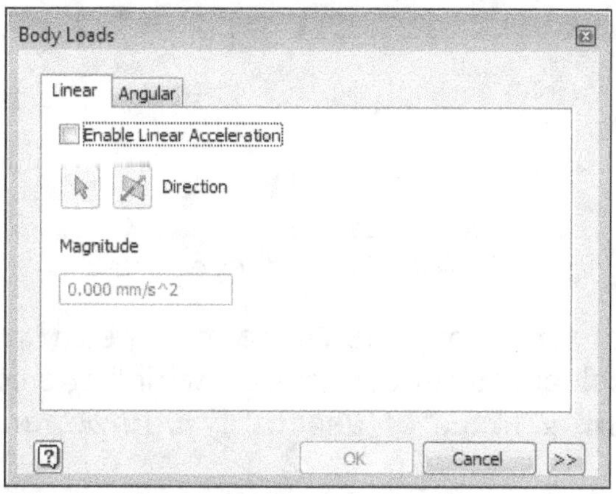

Figure-20. Body Loads dialog box

- Select the **Enable Linear Acceleration** check box from the **Linear** tab if you want to apply linear acceleration. Select the **Enable Angular Velocity and Acceleration** check box from the **Angular** tab if you want to apply angular velocity and acceleration. You can select both check boxes to apply both motions to the selected body.
- Specify the value of velocity and acceleration in their respective **Magnitude** edit boxes in the dialog box.
- Click on the selection button and select the references for body loads.
- Click on the **OK** button to apply the loads.

APPLYING CONTACTS

The contacts in analysis are used to define the contact between two components of assembly at selected faces. The tools to apply contacts are available in the **Contacts** panel in the **Ribbon**. These tools are discussed next.

Automatic Contacts Tool

The **Automatic Contacts** tool is used to apply default contact type to all the possible locations in the assembly. The default contact is specified in the **Create New Study** dialog box discussed earlier.

- Click on the **Automatic Contacts** tool from the **Contacts** panel in the **Analysis** contextual tab of the **Ribbon**. The **Detecting Automatic Contacts** information box will be displayed for a moment and then the default contacts will be applied automatically.

Manual Contact Tool

The **Manual Contact** tool is used to manually apply contacts in the assembly. The procedure to use this tool is given next.

- Click on the **Manual Contact** tool from the **Contacts** panel in the **Analysis** contextual tab of the **Ribbon**. The **Manual Contact** dialog box will be displayed; refer to Figure-21.

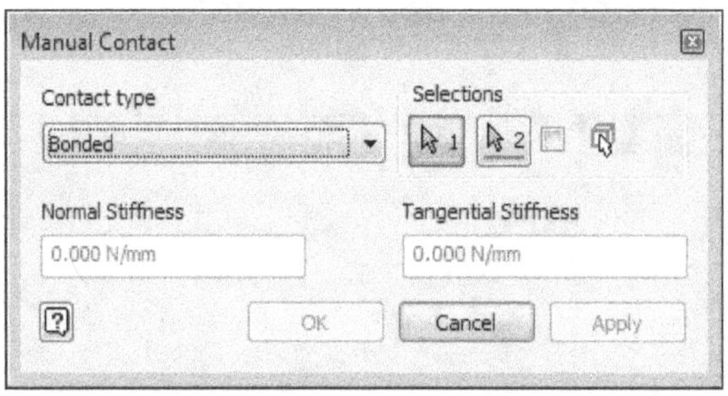

Figure-21. Manual Contact dialog box

- Select desired contact type from the **Contact Type** drop-down in the dialog box. You will be asked to select reference faces on which the contacts are to be applied.
- Select the two touching faces of assembly components one by one; refer to Figure-22.

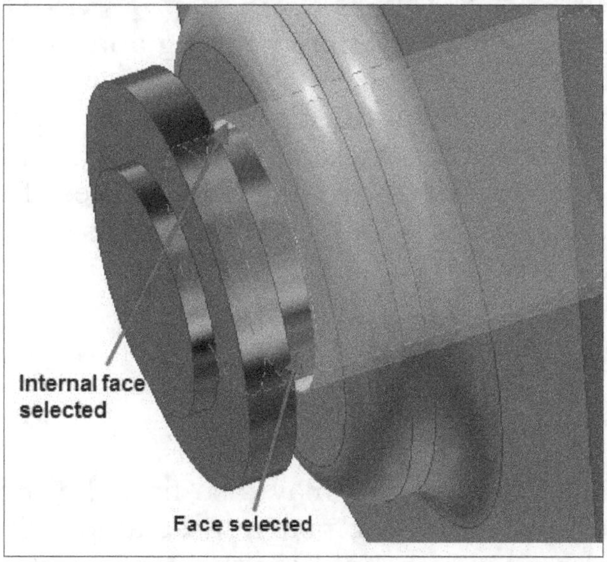

Figure-22. Faces selected for contact

- If you have selected the **Spring** option from the **Contact type** drop-down then specify the stiffness of spring in normal and tangential direction.
- Click on the **Apply** button to apply the contact and start with other faces or click on the **OK** button from the dialog box to apply the contact and exit.

The description of different type of contacts is given next.

Bonded

This creates a rigid bond between selected faces.

Separation

This partially or fully separates selected faces while sliding.

Sliding/No Separation

This creates a normal-to-face direction bond between selected faces while sliding under deformation.

Separation/No Sliding

This partially or fully separates selected faces without them sliding against one another.

Shrink Fit/Sliding

This creates conditions similar to **Separation** but with a negative distance between contact faces, resulting in overlapping parts at the start.

Shrink Fit/No Sliding

This creates conditions of **Separation/No Sliding** but with a negative distance between contact faces, resulting in overlapping parts at the start.

Spring

This creates equivalent springs between the two faces. The **Normal Stiffness** and **Tangential Stiffness** options are available for the **Spring** contact only.

PREPARATION OF PART

It is very important to prepare part before running analysis as there may be many features of part which are not useful in analysis but slow the processing time. There are thousands of iterations that run during analysis, so we should always keep the part model as simple as possible while not destroying the meaning of analysis. In part preparation step, we suppress the non-acting features of part and make sure the part has comparable thickness at all areas. The features that we generally suppress before running analysis are:

- Fillets and rounds
- Cosmetic features like threads, taps, etc.
- Chamfers at edges and so on.

Apart from suppressing features, you may also find the models which have very irregular thickness like sheetmetal component assembled with solid parts or plastic parts. In such models, components that have thin walls compared to the overall size of the model cause problem in stress calculation. We need the tools in **Prepare** panel of the **Analysis** contextual tab to convert such parts to surface bodies to speed up the stress calculations. The tools in the **Prepare** panel are discussed next.

Finding Thin Bodies

In Autodesk Inventor, Shell bodies are considered as Thin bodies. The procedure to find thin bodies and create mid surface is given next.

- After starting the analysis, click on the **Find Thin Bodies** tool from the **Prepare** panel in the **Analysis** tab of the **Ribbon**. If there are bodies which have high length to thickness radio then a message box will be displayed telling you that thin bodies have found in your model, if you want to generate mid-surfaces then click on the **OK** button.
- Click on the **OK** button from the dialog box. The **Midsurface** dialog box will be displayed; refer to Figure-23 and the faces of solids to be converted into midsurface will get selected.

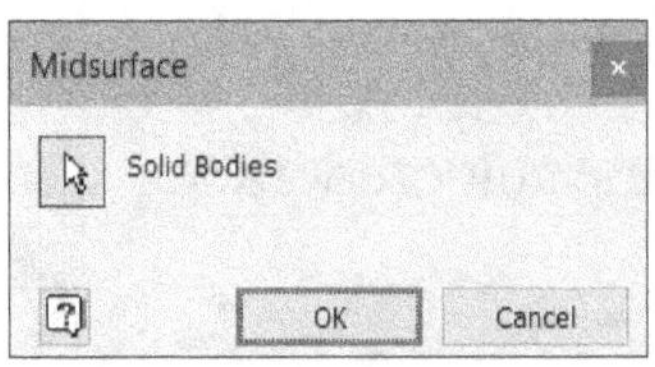

Figure-23. Midsurface dialog box

- Click on the **OK** button from the dialog box. The mid-surfaces will get created; refer to Figure-24.

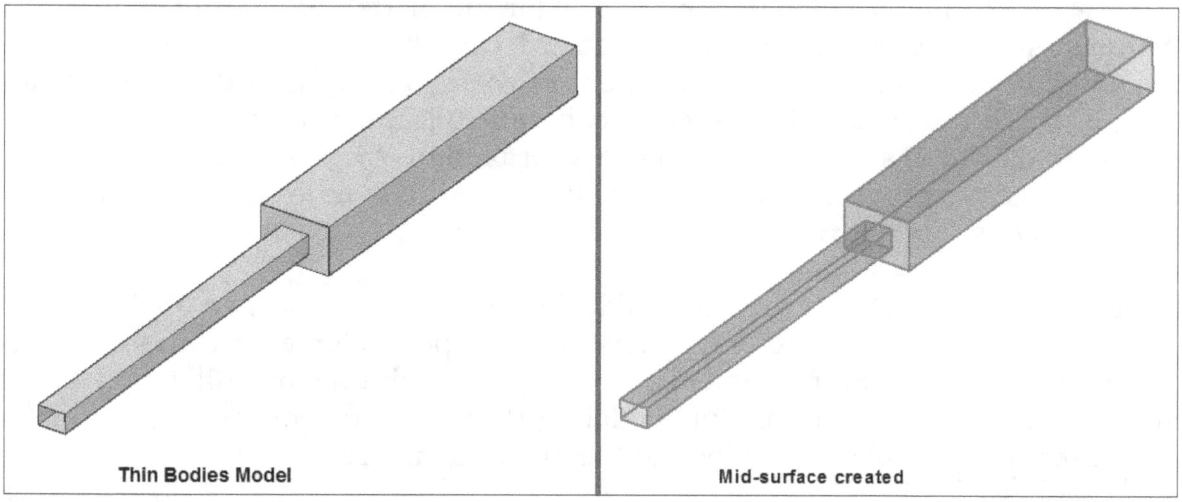

Figure-24. Midsurface created automatically

Similarly, you can use the **Midsurface** tool in the **Prepare** panel to create shell bodies.

Offset

The **Offset** tool in **Prepare** panel is used to create surfaces by offsetting selected faces of the model. The procedure to use this tool is given next.

- Click on the **Offset** tool from the **Prepare** panel in the **Analysis** tab of the **Ribbon**. The **Offset** dialog box will be displayed; refer to Figure-25. Also, you will be asked to select the faces of the model.

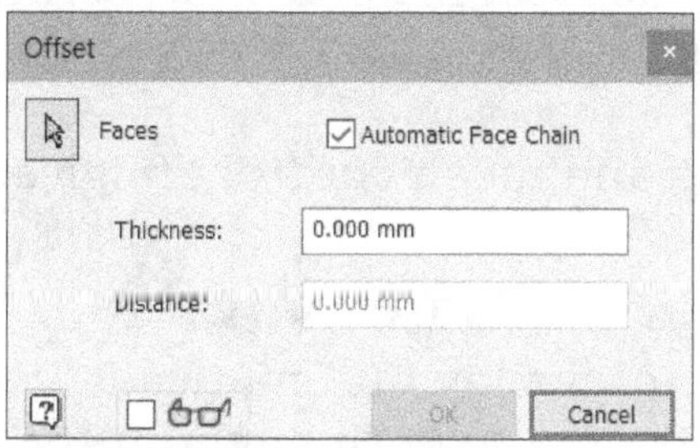

Figure-25. Offset dialog box

- Select the faces of the model to offset and specify desired thickness in the **Thickness** edit box of the dialog box. The distance value will be half of the thickness specified.
- Click on the **OK** button to create the surfaces.

MESHING

Meshing of Autodesk Inventor is not advanced so there is a limit on accuracy of analysis to be performed by Autodesk Inventor but still it is useful for less accurate products and educational purposes. Meshing is the base of FEM. Meshing divides the solid/shell models into elements of finite size and shape. These elements are joined at some common points called nodes. These nodes define the load transfer from one element to other element. Meshing is a very crucial step in design analysis. The automatic mesher in the software generates a mesh based on a global element size, tolerance, and local mesh control specifications. Mesh control lets you specify different sizes of elements for components, faces, edges, and vertices.

The software estimates a global element size for the model taking into consideration its volume, surface area, and other geometric details. The size of the generated mesh (number of nodes and elements) depends on the geometry and dimensions of the model, element size, mesh tolerance, mesh control, and contact specifications. In the early stages of design analysis where approximate results may suffice, you can specify a larger element size for a faster solution. For a more accurate solution, a smaller element size may be required.

Meshing generates 3D tetrahedral solid elements, 2D triangular shell elements, and 1D beam elements. A mesh consists of one type of elements unless the mixed mesh type is specified. Solid elements are naturally suitable for bulky models. Shell elements are naturally suitable for modeling thin parts (sheet metals), and beams and trusses are suitable for modeling structural members.

Before you run a simulation, ensure that the mesh is current, and view it in relation to the geometric features of the model. Integrity errors such as small gaps, overlaps, overhangs that are sometimes overlooked in models can cause trouble for mesh creation. In that case, recreate or modify the problematic geometric features. Some spring models mesh when the long helical face is split by a cutting plane containing the axis. If the model is too complex and has geometric singularity, divide it into less complex parts that you can mesh independently. Use a bonded contact between them to make these components behave as a single part.

Use a finer mesh in troublesome areas that you cannot simplify. Decreasing the global mesh size, as well as the local mesh size on certain faces and edges, can help to create a successful mesh.

The tools related to meshing and mesh control are given next.

Mesh View

The **Mesh View** tool is used to display automatically generated mesh of the model. Click on the **Mesh View** tool from the **Mesh** panel in the **Analysis** tab of the **Ribbon**. The mesh model will be displayed; refer to Figure-26.

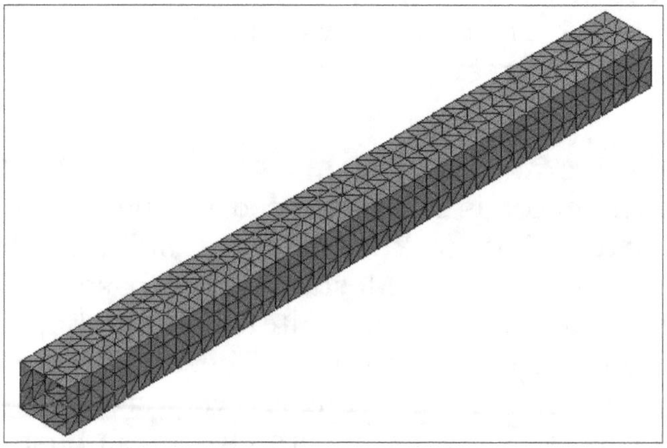

Figure-26. Mesh model

Mesh Settings

The **Mesh Settings** tool is used to change the element size and other parameters for the mesh. The procedure to change mesh settings is given next.

- Click on the **Mesh Settings** tool from the **Mesh** panel in the **Analysis** tab of the **Ribbon**. The **Mesh Settings** dialog box will be displayed; refer to Figure-27.

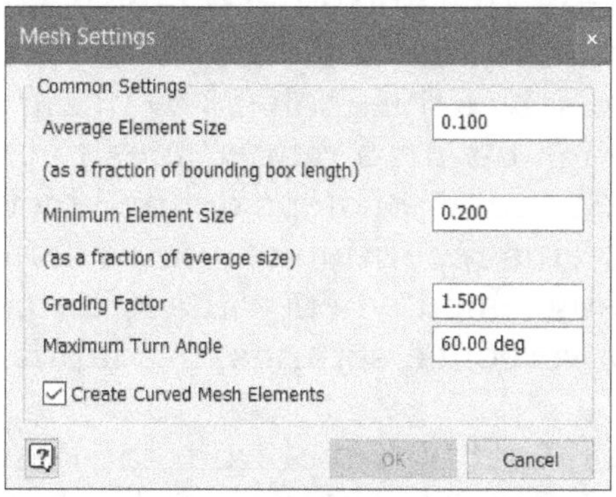

Figure-27. Mesh Settings dialog box

- Specify desired average size and minimum size of elements in the respective edit boxes.
- Specify desired grading factor in the **Grading Factor** edit box. Grading factor is the multiply factor for edge length by which an edge can be bigger than the adjacent edge in case of combination of fine and coarse mesh.
- Set desired maximum turn angle value in the **Maximum Turn Angle** edit box to specify size of element at curves.
- Select the **Create Curved Mesh Elements** check box if you want to create curved elements. Note that it takes more CPU power to generate curved elements. You can use a finer mesh in the stress concentration area around a concave fillet or round to compensate for the lack of curvature if this check box is cleared.
- After specifying desired parameters, click on the **OK** button.

Local Mesh Control

The **Local Mesh Control** tool is used to increase or decrease the density of elements at a specified region. The procedure to use this tool is given next.

- Click on the **Local Mesh Control** tool from the **Mesh** panel in the **Analysis** tab of the **Ribbon**. The **Local Mesh Control** dialog box will be displayed; refer to Figure-28 and you will be asked to select edges/faces to apply local mesh control.

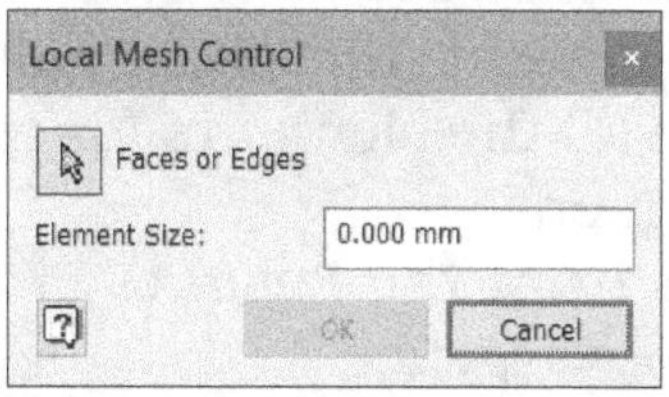

Figure-28. Local Mesh Control dialog box

- Select the faces/edges on which you want to apply local mesh control and specify desired element size in the edit box of the dialog box.
- Click on the **OK** button to apply local mesh control.

Convergence Settings

The **Convergence Settings** tool is used to specify the conditions for refinement of analysis results at stress areas. In some other analysis software, we call this adaptive meshing. In Autodesk Inventor, this tool allows to define h-adaptive meshing. In h-adaptive meshing, system solves the analysis by using standard meshing and then system solves the analysis again with a refined mesh at the locations of strain. This process continues up to the number of steps defined by us or till desired accuracy is achieved from the analysis. This repetition of analysis increases the processing time so this type of meshing is suggested when you are concerned about high accuracy. The procedure to define convergence settings/h-adaptive meshing is given next.

- Click on the **Convergence Settings** tool from the **Mesh** panel in the **Analysis** tab of the **Ribbon**. The **Convergence Settings** dialog box will be displayed; refer to Figure-29.

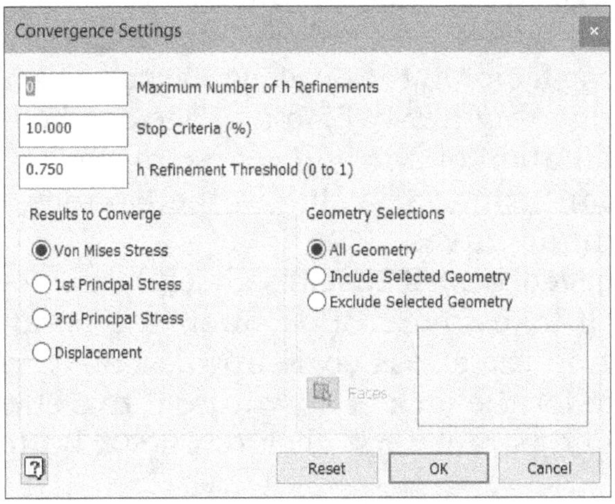

Figure-29. Convergence Settings dialog box

- Specify the number of h-refinements you want to perform in the **Maximum Number of h Refinements** edit box. If you specify value higher than 2 then system will warn you that performance of your system may decrease with such refinements.
- In the **Stop Criteria** edit box, specify the value in percentage to cease refinement. If there is a difference of less than specified value for last two results after refinement then system will cease refinement. For example, if before refinement the stress value was **10.0** and now it becomes **9.0** then system will not refine meshing further.
- Specify desired value in **h Refinement Threshold** edit box. The value can be specified from **0** to **1**. **0** means include all the elements for refinement and **1** means exclude all the elements from refinement.
- Select desired radio button from the **Results to Converge** area to specify the parameter being used for convergence.
- Specify the other parameters as required and click on the **OK** button.

RUNNING STUDY

- After setting all the parameters (applying loads, constraints, and contacts), click on the **Simulate** button from the **Solve** panel in the **Analysis** tab of the **Ribbon**. The **Simulate** dialog box will be displayed; refer to Figure-30.

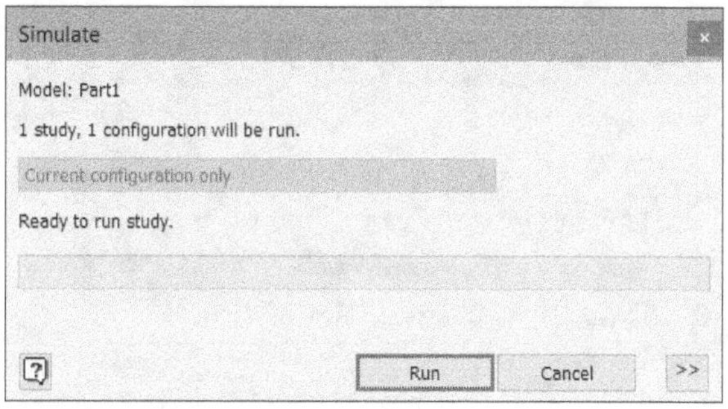

Figure-30. Simulate dialog box

- Click on the **Run** button from the dialog box. The results of analysis will be displayed in the graphics area; refer to Figure-31.

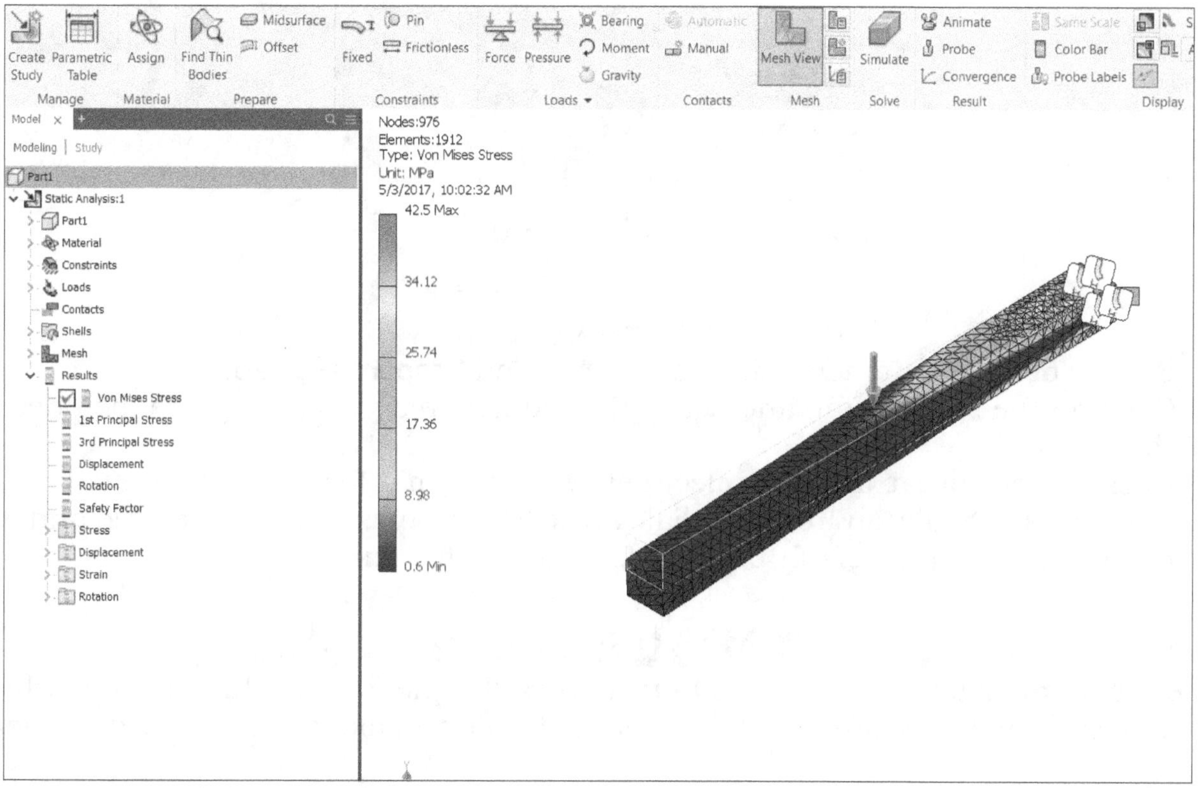

Figure-31. Result of stress analysis

Check the factor of safety and other results to evaluate the feasibility of your component. Generally, the factor of safety should be **3** or higher.

GENERATING REPORTS

After performing the analysis, it is important to properly document the results of analysis. The **Report** tool is used to generate the analysis reports. The procedure to use this tool is given next.

- Click on the **Report** tool from the **Report** panel in the **Analysis** tab of the **Ribbon** after performing the analysis. The **Report** dialog box will be displayed; refer to Figure-32.

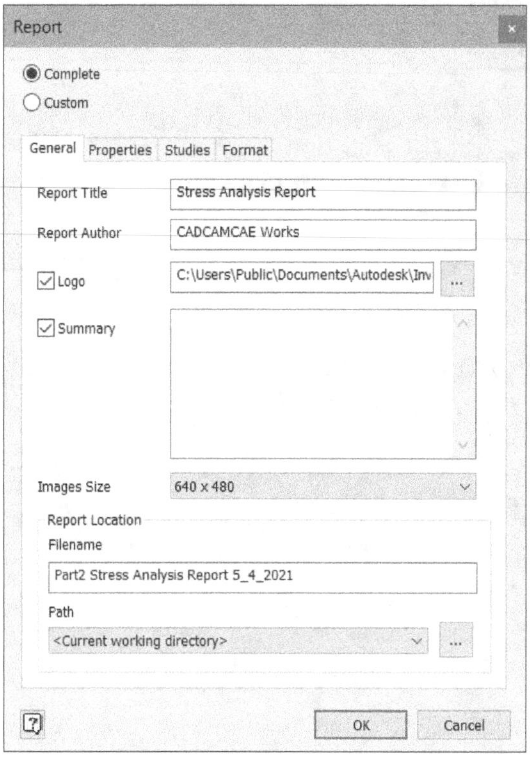

Figure-32. Report dialog box

- Specify desired parameters in the **General** and **Properties** tab.
- Click on the **Studies** tab and select the studies that you want to be included in the report.
- Click on the **Format** tab and select desired file format for report generated.
- Click on the **OK** button from the dialog box. The reports will be generated and will be displayed in the default browser for selected file format.

MODAL ANALYSIS

The Modal analysis is used to find out natural frequencies of the model at which component can deform largely. The procedure to perform modal analysis is given next.

- Click on the **Create Study** tool from the **Manage** panel in the **Analysis** tab of the **Ribbon**. The **Create New Study** dialog box will be displayed as discussed earlier.
- Click on the **Modal Analysis** radio button. The options for the modal analysis will become active.
- Select the **Number of Modes** check box and specify the maximum number of natural frequencies you want to find out.
- Select the **Frequency Range** check box and specify the range in which you are concerned about natural frequencies.
- Set the other parameters as required and click on the **OK** button from the dialog box. The tools to perform modal analysis will become active in the **Analysis** tab.
- Apply constraints and contacts to limit the motion of part. Apply the loads if required.
- Click on the **Simulate** button and then **Run** button from the dialog box displayed. Result of modal analysis will be displayed; refer to Figure-33.

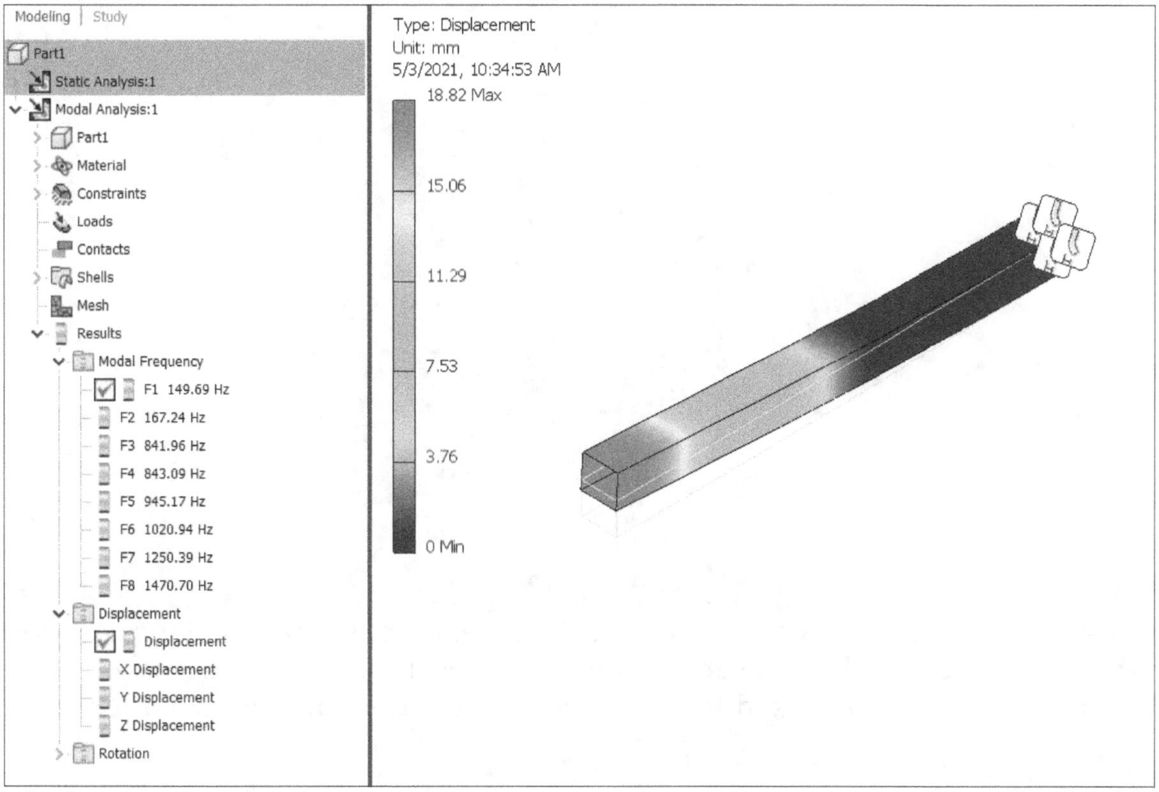

Figure-33. Result of modal analysis

Note that our motive to perform this analysis is to find out the natural frequencies and add/remove material from the part to make sure, the natural frequency do not match with the frequency generated in assembly due to shocks and other working conditions.

SHAPE GENERATOR

The **Shape Generator** tool is used to generate a light weight component based on the load conditions and parameters specified by you. Note that the shape generator analysis can be performed only on parts. You can not perform shape generator study on assembly or surfaces. The procedure to use this tool is given next.

- Click on the **Create Study** tool from the **Manage** panel in the **Analysis** tab of the **Ribbon**. The **Create New Study** dialog box will be displayed as discussed earlier.
- Select the **Shape Generator** radio button from the dialog box and click on the **OK** button. The **Shape Generator** dialog box will be displayed describing the function of tool.
- Click on the **OK** button from the dialog box. The tools related to shape generation will be displayed; refer to Figure-34.

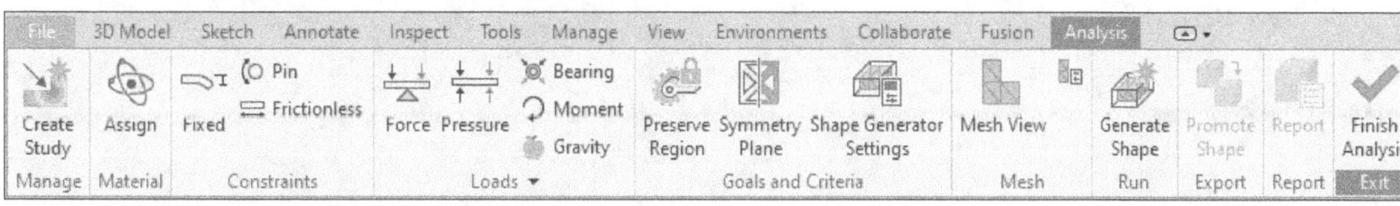

Figure-34. Tools in Analysis tab for shape generation study

- Assign the material, constraints, and load conditions as required; refer to Figure-35.

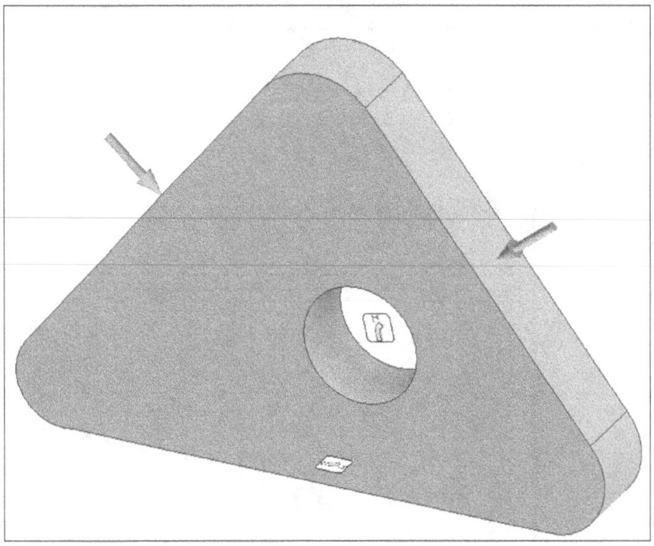

Figure-35. Load and constraint applied to model

Preserve Region

- Click on the **Preserve Region** tool from **Goals and Criteria** panel in the **Analysis** tab of the **Ribbon**; the **Preserve Region** dialog box will be displayed; refer to Figure-36. You will be asked to select the regions to be unchanged after analysis.

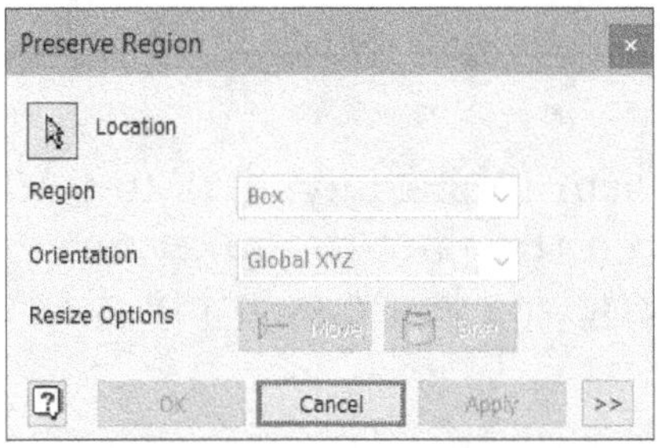

Figure-36. Preserve Region dialog box

- Select the regions like holes, slots, and grooves that you want to be unchanged after shape generation.
- Click on the **Apply** button after selecting one region to select another region or click on the **OK** button if you want to preserve only one region.

Symmetry Plane

The **Symmetry Plane** tool is used to reduce the calculation time of analysis. If your part is symmetric about any plane then system will calculate for half of the part and result will be distributed over the full part. The procedure to use this tool is given next.

- Click on the **Symmetry Plane** tool from the **Goals and Criteria** panel in the **Analysis** tab of the **Ribbon**. The **Symmetry Plane** dialog box will be displayed; refer to Figure-37.

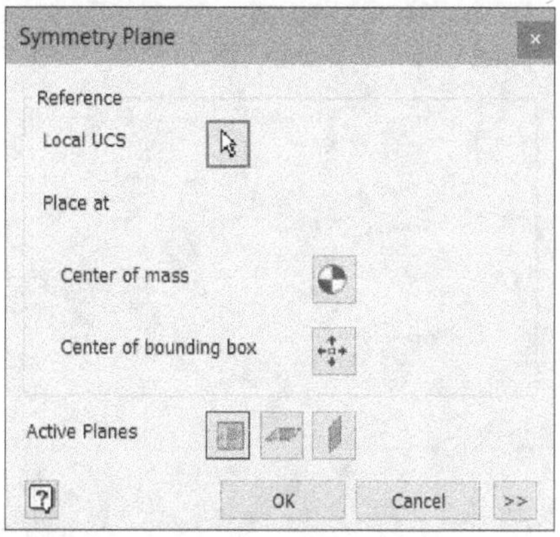

Figure-37. Symmetry Plane dialog box

- Select desired button(s) from the **Active Planes** buttons to use respective planes as symmetry plane; refer to Figure-38.

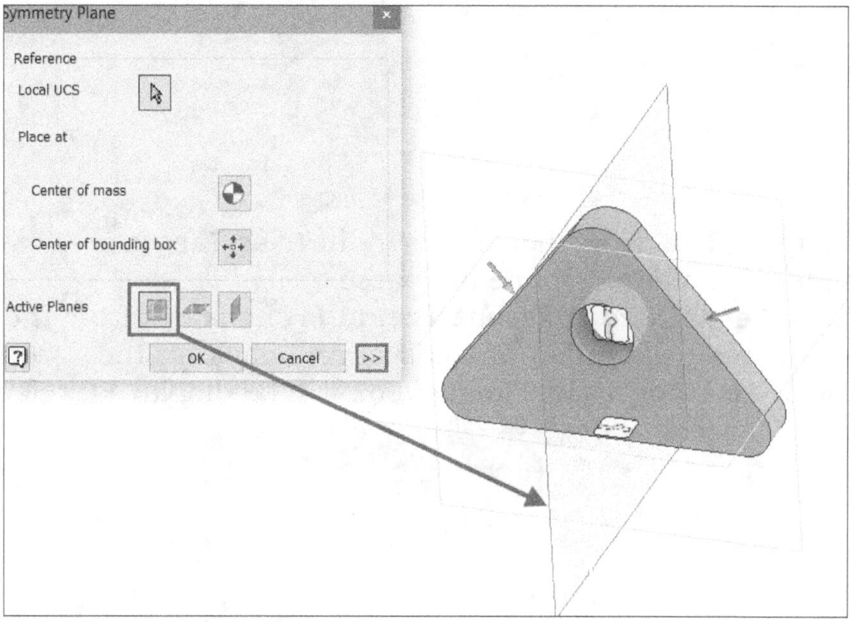

Figure-38. Symmetry plane selected

- Click on the **OK** button from the dialog box.

Shape Generator Settings

The **Shape Generator Settings** tool is used to specify the objectives for shape generation like the percentage of mass to be reduced or the target mass goal. The procedure to use this tool is given next.

- Click on the **Shape Generator Settings** tool from the **Goals and Criteria** panel in the **Analysis** tab of the **Ribbon**. The **Shape Generator Settings** dialog box will be displayed; refer to Figure-39.

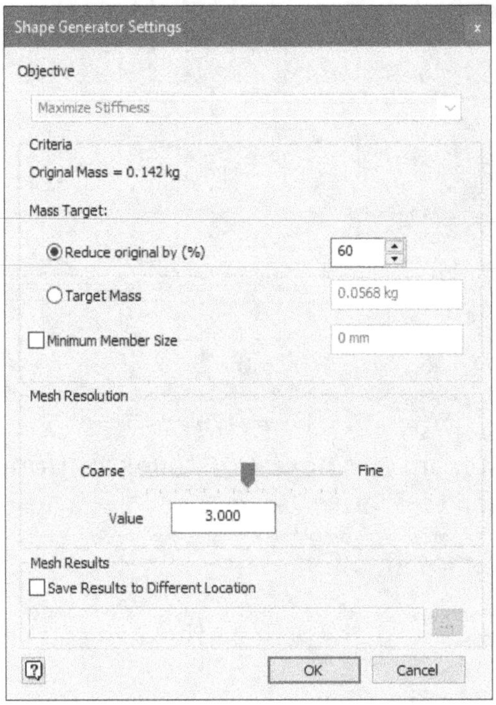

Figure-39. Shape Generator Settings dialog box

- Specify the target mass using the options in the **Mass Target** area of the dialog box.
- Move the slider to make mesh fine or coarse.
- Select the **Save Results to Different Location** check box from the **Mesh Results** area to save the result in different location and click on the ... button to define location. The **Browse For Folder** dialog box will be displayed; refer to Figure-40.

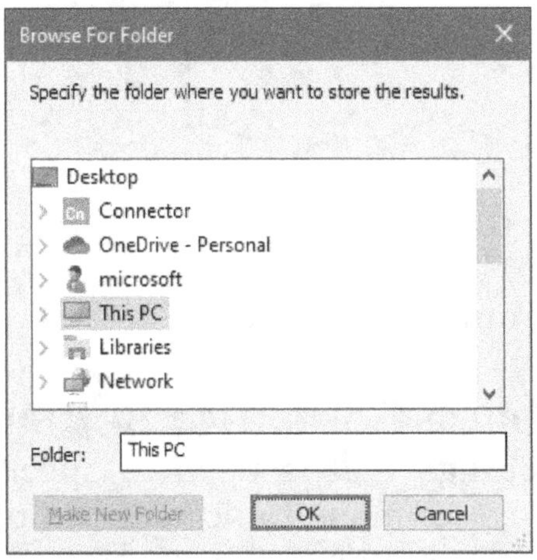

Figure-40. Browse for folder dialog box

- Select desired folder in the dialog box where you want to store the results.
- Click on the **OK** button to apply settings.

Performing Shape Generation

- Click on the **Generate Shape** button from the **Run** panel in the **Analysis** tab of the **Ribbon**. The **Generate Shape** dialog box will be displayed similar to **Simulate** dialog box discussed earlier.
- Click on the **Run** button from the dialog box. Depending on computing power of your system, the results will be displayed in a few moments.
- Click on the **Finish Analysis** button to exit the analysis environment.

FRAME ANALYSIS

The Frame analysis is performed to check the ability of assembly frame for sustaining the specified load conditions. As discussed in Chapter 11 of this book, structural frame members are used to create skeleton structure of various appliances and machines like table, car, ship, aeroplanes, and so on. Figure-41 shows a frame assembly which we will use as an example to perform load testing. It is a frame made using 60x40x2 rectangular tubes.

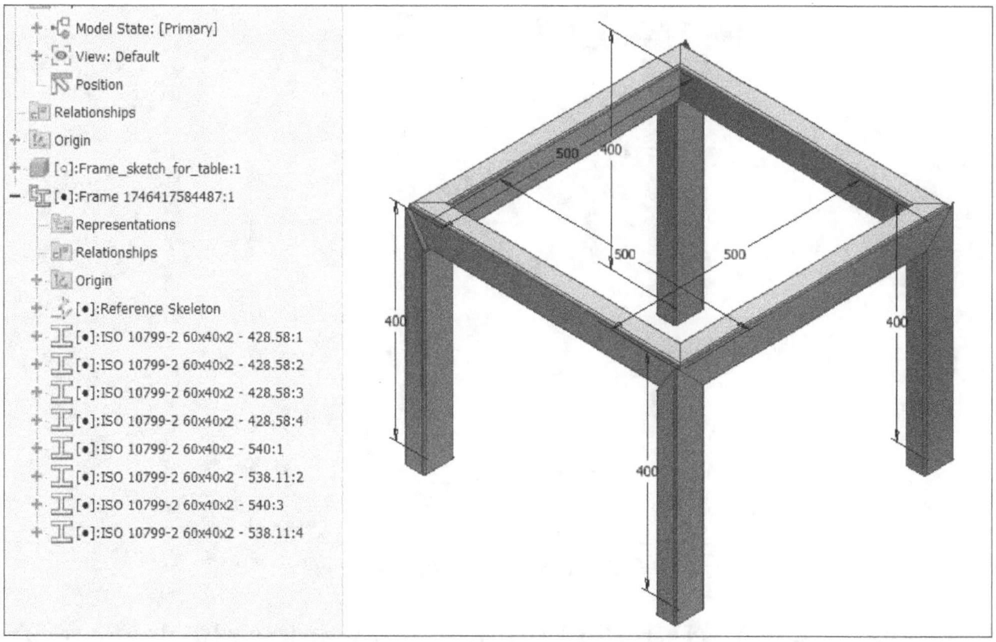

Figure-41. Frame table for analysis

Starting Frame Analysis

The **Frame Analysis** tool is used to activate tools related to frame analysis. This tool is available in **Frame** panel of **Design** tab in **Ribbon** as well as **Begin** panel of **Environments** tab in **Ribbon** when working in Assembly environment; refer to Figure-42. The procedure to start a frame analysis is given next.

- Click on the **Frame Analysis** tool after opening or creating the frame assembly. The **Frame Analysis** contextual tab will be displayed; refer to Figure-43.

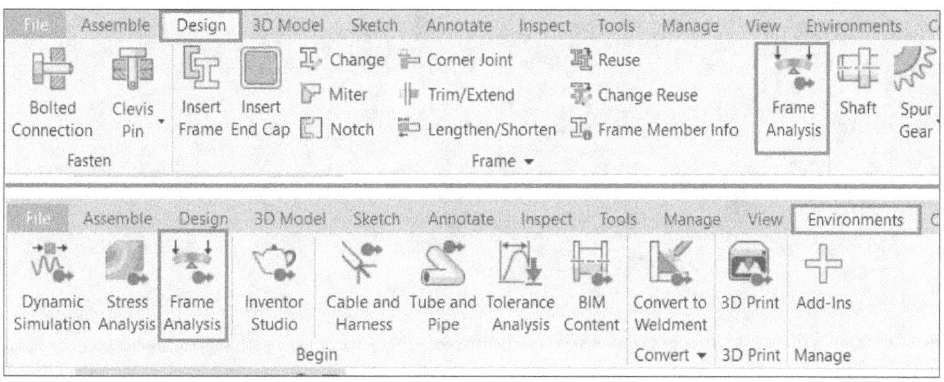

Figure-42. Frame Analysis tool

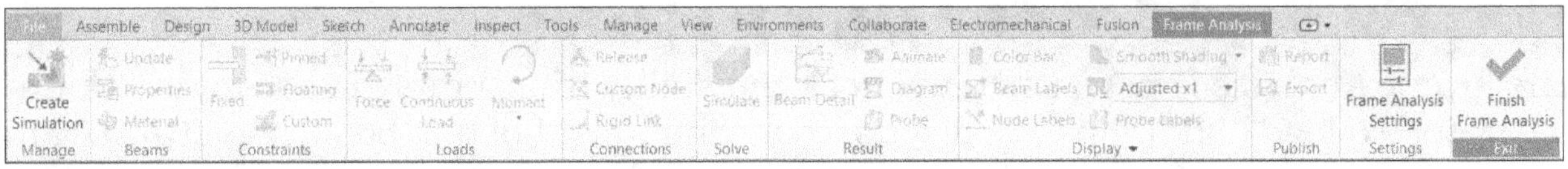

Figure-43. Frame Analysis contextual tab

- Click on the **Create Simulation** tool from the **Frame Analysis** contextual tab in the **Ribbon**. The **Create New Simulation** dialog box will be displayed; refer to Figure-44.

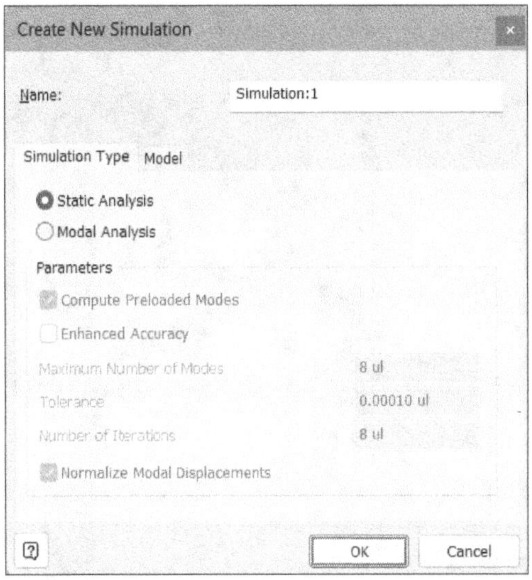

Figure-44. Create New Simulation dialog box

- Select the **Static Analysis** radio button if you want to check effect of fixed load on the design. Select the **Modal Analysis** radio button if you want to find out natural frequencies (Resonance frequencies) of the design.
- Select desired state of model from the Model tab in the dialog box if your design is created in multiple design states.
- After selecting desired radio button (We are using **Static Analysis** in our case to explain tools), click on the **OK** button. The tools to perform analysis will become active in the contextual tab; refer to Figure-45.

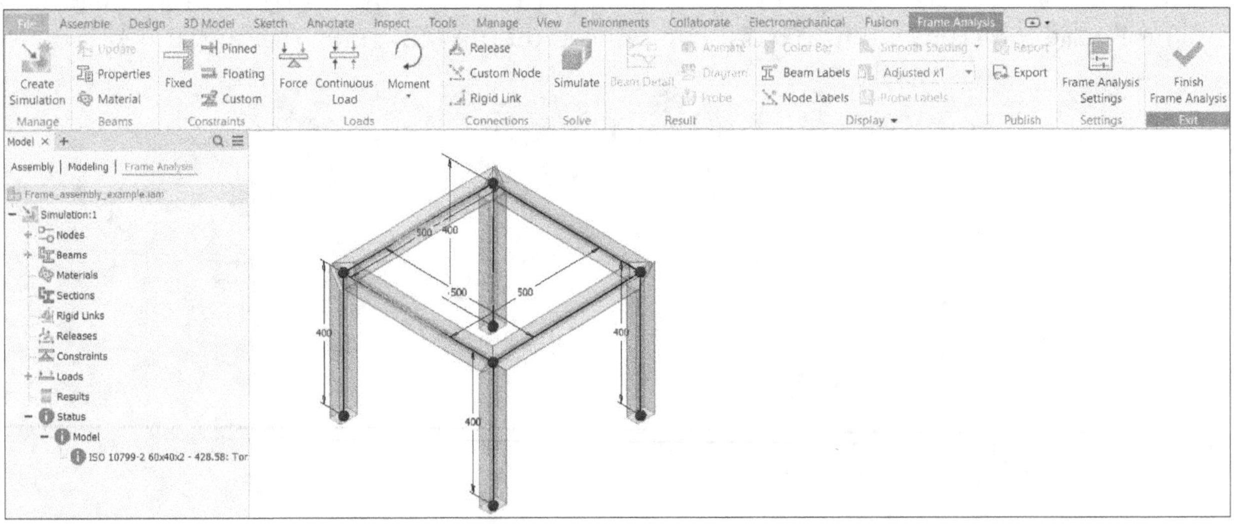

Figure-45. Frame analysis tools for static simulation

Defining Frame Analysis Settings

The **Frame Analysis Settings** tool is used to define parameters related to colors, scale of frame elements (node,load, and constraint), beam models, solvers, load diagrams. After starting a new analysis, you should always check these settings. The procedure to use this tool is given next.

- Click on the **Frame Analysis Settings** tool from the **Settings** panel in the **Frame Analysis** contextual tab of the **Ribbon**. The **Frame Analysis Settings** dialog box will be displayed; refer to Figure-46.

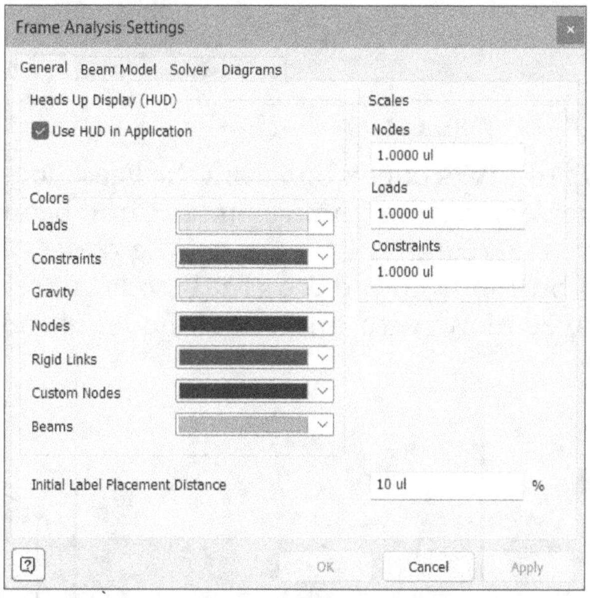

Figure-46. Frame Analysis Settings dialog box

General Settings

- Set desired colors for loads, constraints, gravity, nodes, and other graphical elements of analysis setup using the drop-downs in the **Colors** area of the dialog box.
- In the **Scales** area, you can specify scale factor value in the **Nodes**, **Loads**, and **Constraints** edit boxes to increase/decrease the size of graphical representations of nodes, loads, and constraints respectively.
- Specify desired value in the **Initial Label Placement Distance** edit box to define the distance from frame structures at which labels will be placed. The value is specified in percentage of diagonal of bounding box for current model.

Beam Model

Select the **Beam Model** tab in the dialog box to define parameters related to conversion of structural members into beam model. The options will be displayed as shown in Figure-47.

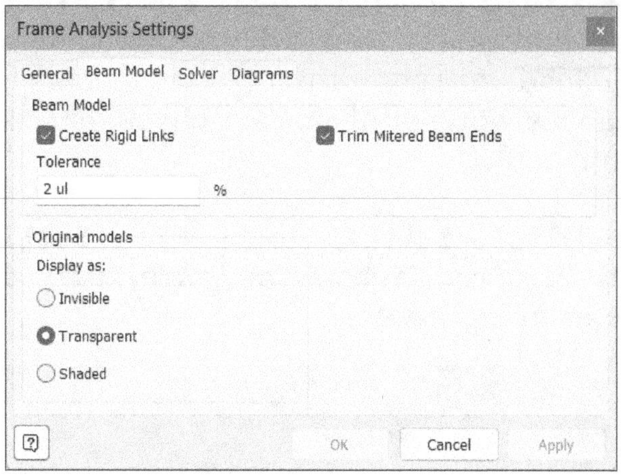

Figure-47. Beam Model tab

- Select the **Create Rigid Links** check box from the **Beam Model** area to automatically create rigid links when converting frame elements into beam elements for analysis. For example in our case, rectangular tube will be converted to a rigid beam.
- Select desired radio button from the **Original models** area to define how original model will be displayed along with analytical model of frame; refer to Figure-48.

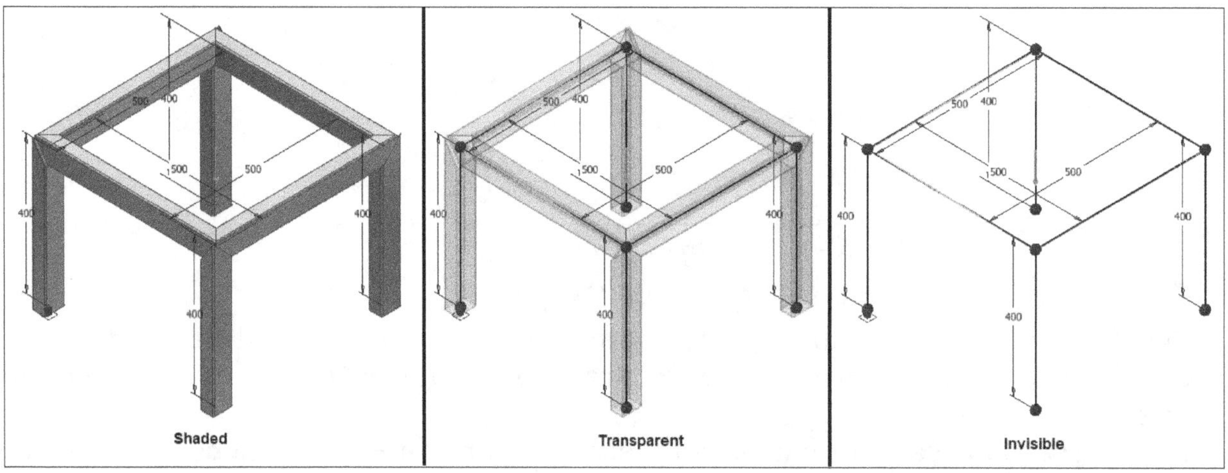

Figure-48. Original model display state

- Select the **Trim Mitered Beam Ends** check box to automatically trim overlapping and extending portions of structural elements when converting them to analytical model.

Solver Settings

Select the **Solver** tab from the dialog box to define parameters related to analysis solver. The options in the dialog box will be displayed as shown in Figure-49.

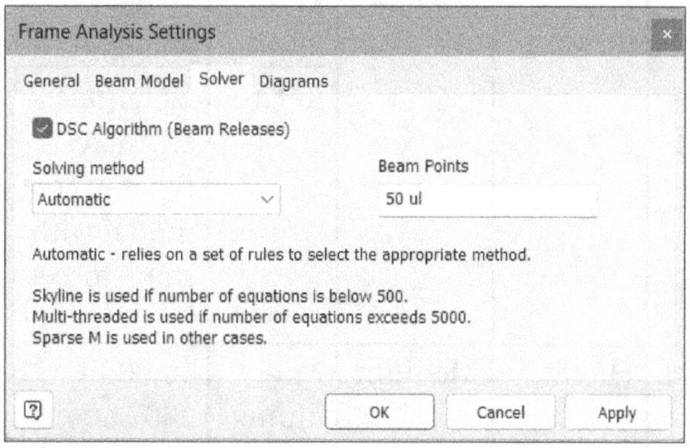

Figure-49. Solver tab

- By default, the **DSC Algorithm (Beam Releases)** check box is selected which allows discontinuity of beams elements during calculation where release conditions are specified for the nodes. This happens when load applied on model is capable of large deformation in structure. Clear this check box if you want to stop calculation at discontinuity.
- Select desired option from the **Solving method** drop-down to define method for calculating solution of analysis. Select the **Frontal** option from the drop-down to use Gauss elimination method, select the **Skyline** option from the drop-down to use Cholesky LDLt factorization method, select the **Sparse** option from the drop-down to use Nested Disection Method (NDM), select the **Sparse M** option to use Minimal Degrees Algorithm (MDA) method, and select the **Multi-threaded** option to use PARDISO solver. If you have selected Automatic option then Skyline method will be used when equations are below 500, Multi-threaded method will be used when equations are more than 5000, and Sparse M will be used for other cases. Below is a table which defines cases for using different solvers:

Solver	Method Used	Memory Use	Disk Use	Speed	Application Scope	Additional Notes
Frontal	Gauss elimina-tion	Low	High	Slow	Up to 50,000 equations; linear & non-linear statics, harmonic analysis	Helps identify calculation issues in statics (e.g., improp-erly constrained structures); shows number of nodes and DOFs during problems.
Skyline	Cho-lesky LDL t factor-ization	Low	High	Slow	Up to 50,000 equations; all types of analysis	Similar to Frontal: identifies node and DOF issues; useful for structure-related calculation prob-lems.

Sparse	Nested Dissection Method (NDM)	High	Medium	Medium to Fast	10,000–200,000 equations; all analysis types except modal with static forces	Best for large 3D FE models (e.g., buildings, shells); detects ill-conditioned structures but does not show node/DOF counts; good when iterative solvers fail.
Sparse M	Minimal Degree Algorithm (MDA)	High	Medium	Medium to Fast	10,000–200,000 equations; all analysis types except modal with static forces	Same benefits and limitations as Sparse; uses a different re-ordering algorithm (MDA) for efficiency in large, complex FE models.
Multi-threaded	PARDISO (Intel® MKL solver)	Optimized	Optimized	Very Fast	Large-scale structural models	Multi-core support for speed; uses optimal renumbering and memory management for efficient solving of very large systems.

- Specify desired value in the Beam Points edit box to define number of points to be created on each beam for calculating results. High number of points means more solving time and computation power required.

Diagrams Setting

Select the **Diagrams** tab in the dialog box to define parameters related to various result diagrams generated after performing analysis; refer to Figure-50.

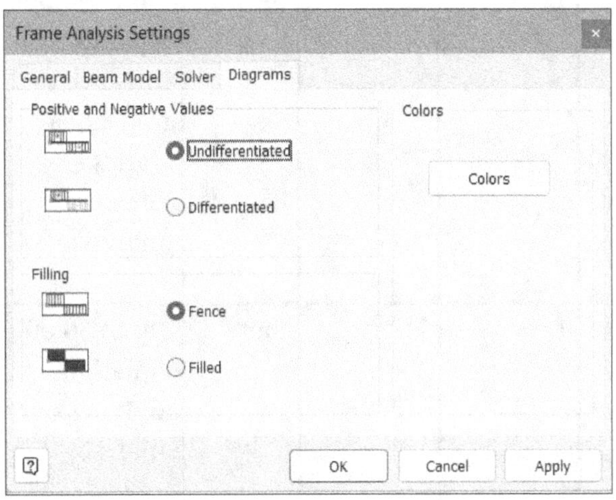

Figure-50. Diagrams tab

- Select the **Undifferentiated** radio button if you want to keep same color for positive and negative values in the diagram. Select the **Differentiated** radio button to do vice-versa.

- Select the **Fence** or **Filled** radio button from the **Filling** area in the dialog box to define whether you want to graph displayed in fence format or completely solid filled under the curve, respectively.
- Click on the **Colors** button and set desired colors for various result parameters.
- After setting desired parameters, click on the **OK** button from the **Frame Analysis Settings** dialog box to apply the changes.

Updating Beam Data

The **Update** tool in **Beams** panel of contextual tab is used to update the analytical model based on changes in the 3D assembly of frame.

Checking Beam Properties

The **Properties** tool is used to check and modify physical properties of various beam elements in the analytical model. The procedure to use this tool is given next.

- Click on the **Properties** tool after loading the analytical model. The **Beam Properties** dialog box will be displayed; refer to Figure-51.

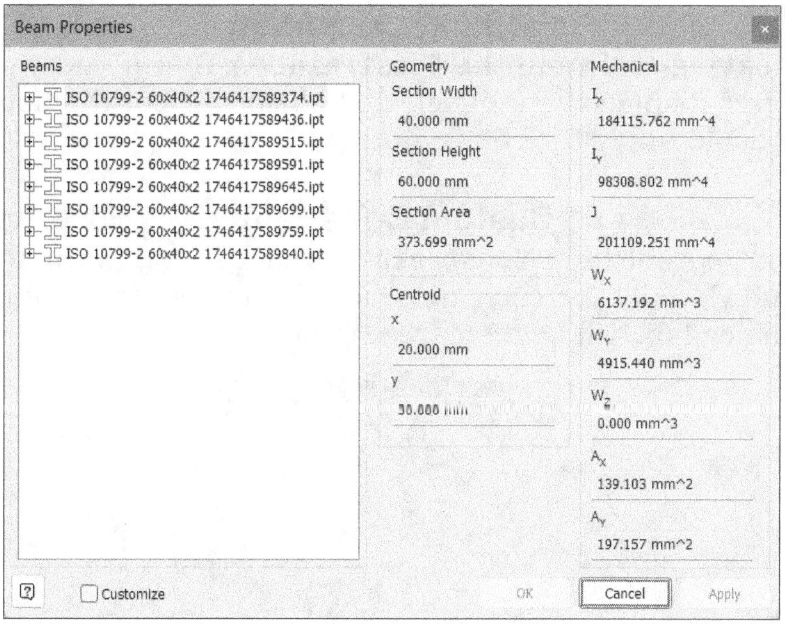

Figure-51. Beam Properties dialog box

- Select the **Customize** check box if you want to modify the physical parameters of frame elements like width, height, and so on.
- Click on the **OK** button from the dialog box to apply changes. These changes will be reflected in Bill Of Materials (BOM) and other tables.

Checking Material Properties

The **Material** tool in **Beams** panel is used to check and customize material properties of the frame elements. The procedure is same as discussed for **Properties** tool earlier.

Applying Constraints

The tools in **Constraints** panel (refer to Figure-52) are used to apply various constraints (restrictions) to the model so that reaction of applied loads can be studied.

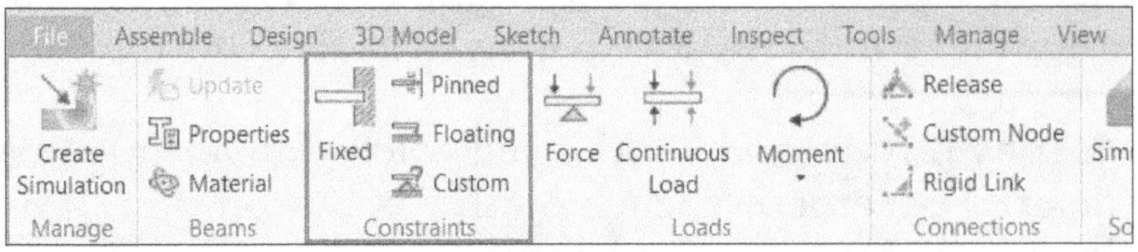

Figure-52. Constraints panel

Fixed Constraint

- Select the **Fixed** tool from the **Constraints** panel if you want to restrict all linear and rotational motions of selected object. Select the node/element from analytical model to apply the constraint.

Pinned Constraint

- Select the **Pinned** tool from the **Constraints** panel if you want to allow rotational movement of selected object but do not want it to move in any linear direction like a pin in hinge of door. Select the node/element from analytical model to apply the constraint.

Floating Constraint

- Select the **Floating** tool from the **Constraints** panel if you want to allow free rotation and free displacement of selected object. Select the node/element from analytical model to apply the constraint.

Custom Constraint

- Select the **Custom** tool from **Constraints** panel if you want to define degrees of freedom individually for each direction for the selected object. The **Custom Constraint** dialog box will be displayed; refer to Figure-53.

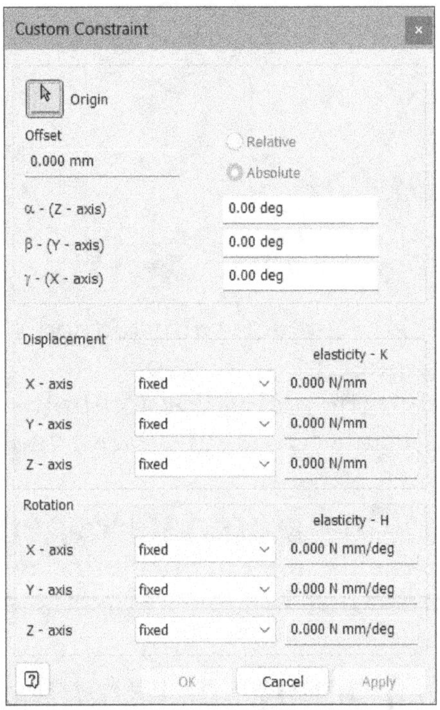

Figure-53. Custom Constraint dialog box

- Select desired node or object to which you want to apply the custom constraint from graphics area.
- Set desired values in the **α**, **β**, and **γ** edit boxes to define angle of rotation for constraints with respect to Z axis, Y axis, and X axis; respectively.
- Select desired options for **X-axis**, **Y-axis**, and **Z-axis** drop-downs in the **Displacement** area to define linear displacement degree of freedom for the constraint. Select the **fixed** option if you do not want the node to move in linear direction. Select the **uplift none** option from the drop-down if you want to allow displacement in both positive and negative direction with little resistance define by elasticity coefficient of material. Select the **uplift +** option from the drop-down to allow displacement along positive direction of axis. Similarly, select the **uplift -** option to allow negative direction displacement for axis. Note that elastic coefficient will define the restriction against this displacement.
- Similarly, specify rotational degree of freedom for each axis using the options in the **Rotation** area of the dialog box.
- After specifying the parameters, click on the **OK** button from the dialog box to apply the constraint.

Applying Loads

The tools in the **Loads** panel of the **Ribbon** are used to apply various forces and loads to represent real-world loading conditions for the model. Various tools of this panel are discussed next.

Applying Force

The **Force** tool is used to apply specified value of force on a node or a beam. The procedure to use this tool is given next.

- Click on the **Force** tool from the **Loads** panel in the **Frame Analysis** contextual tab of the **Ribbon**. You will be asked to select the node/beam to which you want to apply the force.
- Select desired node/beam; refer to Figure-54. If you have selected beam element then you will be asked to specify offset distance from end point of beam to define position of force on the beam. Enter desired value to place the force load. If you have selected node element then you will be asked to specify value of force in the input box. Enter desired value to apply force.

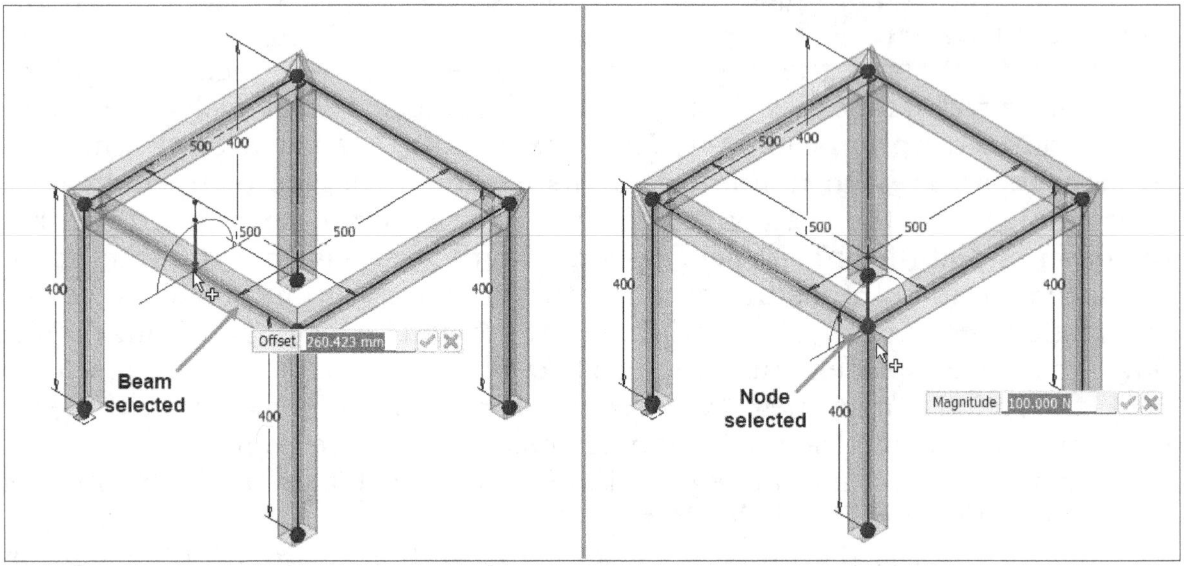

Figure-54. Selection for force

- If you want to change the value of force after placing on beam then right-click on **Force** option in the **Loads** category of **Frame Analysis Model Tree** and select the **Edit** option from the shortcut menu displayed; refer to Figure-55. The **Force** dialog box will be displayed as shown in Figure-56.
- By default, the force is applied normal to beam plane. If you want to change the direction of force, then click on the **Define Direction** selection button from the dialog box and select desired reference geometry (face/edge/plane/axis) to define load direction.
- Set the values of force magnitude, offset distance, angle of force direction and so on in respective edit boxes.
- Click on the **>>** button to expand the dialog box and select the Vector components check box to define components of force along X, Y, and Z axes at the application point.
- Set desired parameters in the dialog box and click on the **OK** button from the dialog box.

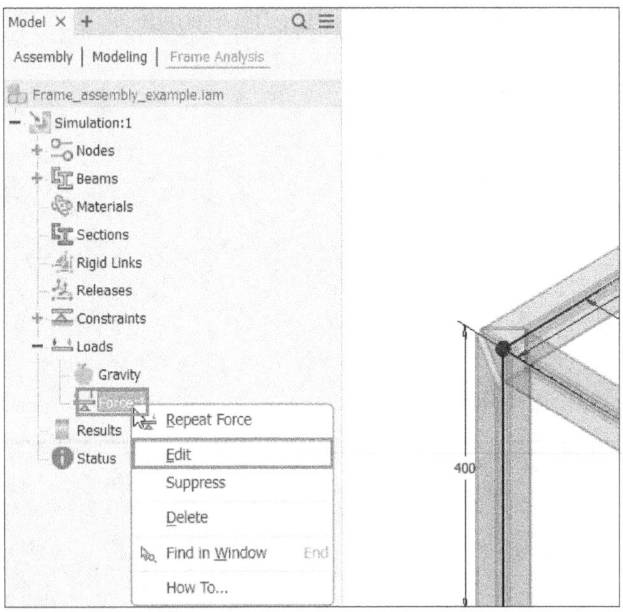

Figure-55. Edit option

Figure-56. Force dialog box

Similarly, you can apply other loads using the tools in **Loads** panel of the **Ribbon**.

Assigning Release

The **Release** tool is used to allow some degree of freedom at the start and end points of beams so that they can more realistically represent connections of beam elements in the analysis. Generally, when load is applied to beams and other structural members connected using pins, hinges, and other elements; the load is not fully transferred between elements. There is some deflection and even unscrewing of elements like hinges. When we apply release at such locations then we are representing this real world condition. The procedure to apply release is given next.

- Click on the **Release** tool from the **Connections** panel in the **Frame Analysis** contextual tab of **Ribbon**. The **Release** dialog box will be displayed; refer to Figure-57.

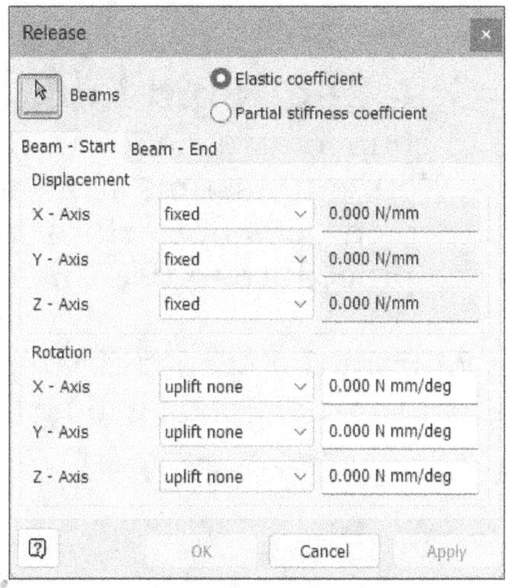

Figure-57. Release dialog box

- Select the beam to which you want to apply release condition.
- Select the **Elastic coefficient** radio button if you want to keep the beam attached (not released) till load applied upto full value of elastic coefficient. Select the **Partial stiffness coefficient** radio button if you want to define release condition in multiple factor of stiffness coefficient.
- Set the other parameters as discussed earlier for beam start and beam end points using respective tabs in the dialog box and click on the **OK** button from the dialog box to apply release.

Creating Custom Node

By default, end points of beams are generated as nodes for performing frame analysis. If you want to apply loads or constraint conditions on non-standard points on the beams then you can use the **Custom Node** tool to create such nodes. The procedure to use this tool is given next.

- Click on the **Custom Node** tool from the **Connections** panel in the **Frame Analysis** contextual tab of the **Ribbon**. You will be asked to select a location on the beam where you want to place the custom node.

- Click at desired location on the beam and set the offset value in input box to fine tune the position of node on beam; refer to Figure-58. Click on the OK button from the input box to create the node.

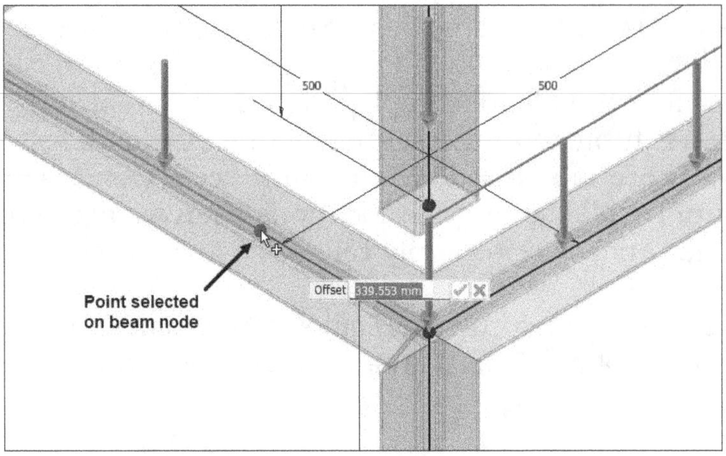

Figure-58. Point selected for node

Creating Rigid Link

The **Rigid Link** tool is used to connect two nodes in the analytical model for rigid load transfer during analysis. You can assume it as perfectly welding two points in the model with a metal rod which does not deform underload and transfers full reaction load to other node. The procedure to use this tool is given next.

- Click on the **Rigid Link** tool from the **Connections** panel in the **Frame Analysis** tab of the **Ribbon**. The **Rigid Link** dialog box will be displayed; refer to Figure-59.

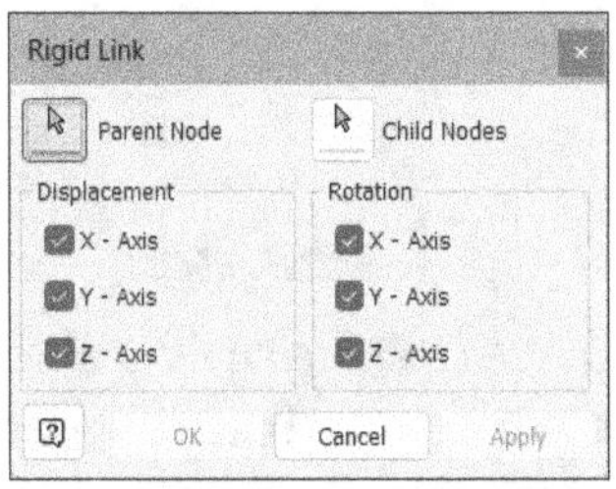

Figure-59. Rigid Link dialog box

- Select the primary node from graphics area which can be joined to multiple child nodes using rigid link. You will be asked to select child nodes.
- Select desired nodes from the model. The rigid link will be created.

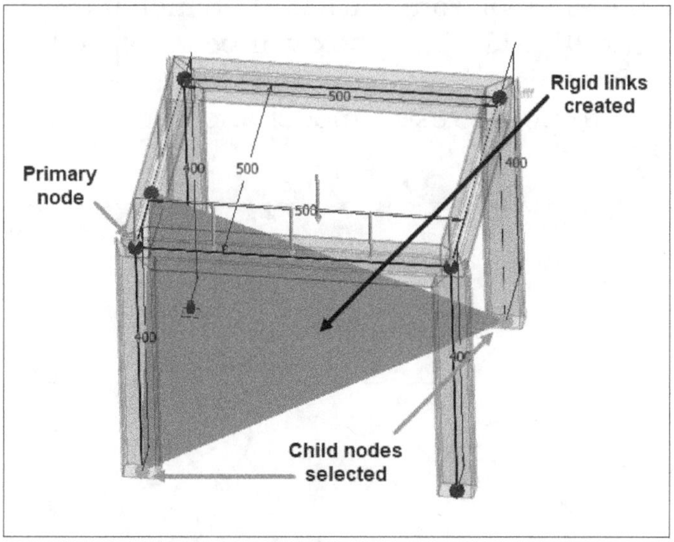

Figure-60. Rigid link created

- Click on the **OK** button from the dialog box to create the link.

Performing Simulation

The **Simulate** tool is used to run the analysis based on specified parameters. Once you have setup all the analysis parameters like material, load, constraint etc. then click on the **Simulate** tool from the **Solve** panel in the **Frame Analysis** tab of the **Ribbon**. The system will start solving the analysis. Once the process is complete, result of analysis will be displayed; refer to Figure-61.

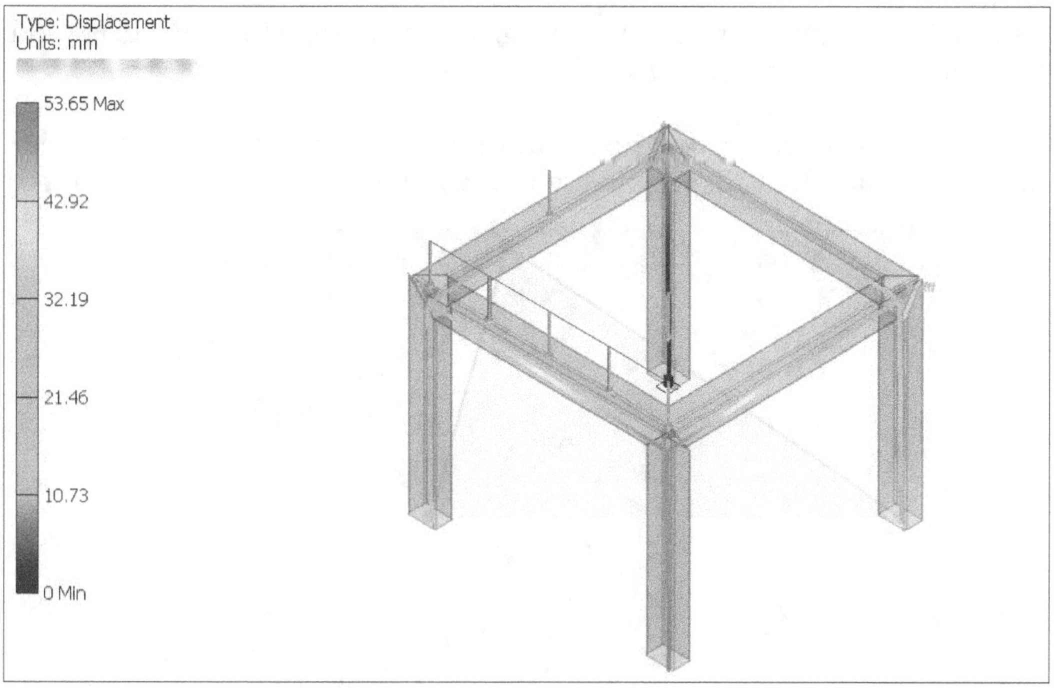

Figure-61. Result of frame analysis

Checking Beam Details

The **Beam Detail** tool is used to check diagrams and tables of selected beam under specified loads. This tool is active after generating simulation results. The procedure to use this tool is given next.

- Click on the **Beam Detail** tool from the **Result** panel in the **Frame Analysis** tab of the **Ribbon**. The **Beam Detail** dialog box will be displayed and you will be asked to select the beam for which details are to be displayed.
- Select desired beam from the result model and check the results in dialog box; refer to Figure-62.

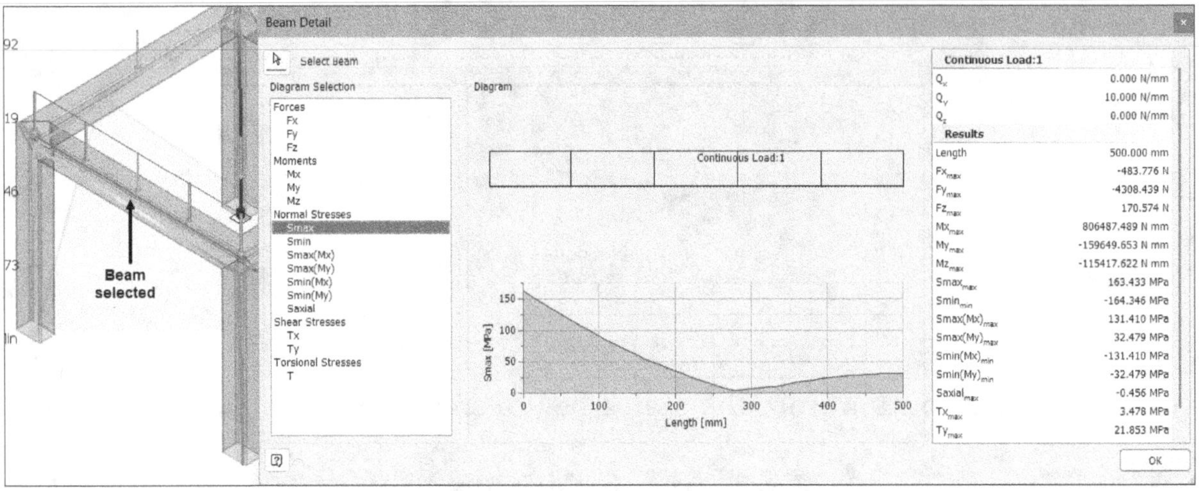

Figure-62. Beam Detail dialog box

- Click on the **OK** button from the dialog box to exit the dialog box after checking the result.

Checking Diagrams

The **Diagram** tool is used to check the result parameters by maximum value and distribution diagram on beam element in graphics area. The procedure to use this tool is given next.

- Click on the **Diagram** tool from the **Result** panel in the **Frame Analysis** contextual tab of the **Ribbon**. The **Diagram** dialog box will be displayed; refer to Figure-63.

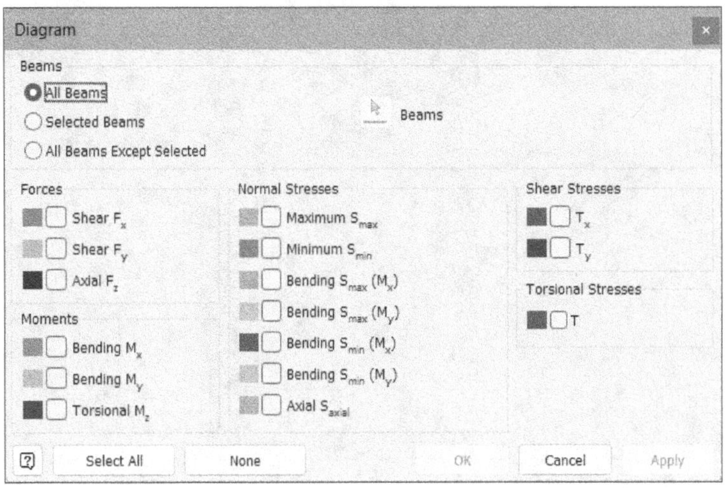

Figure-63. Diagram dialog box

- Select desired radio button from the **Beams** area of the dialog box to define scope of beams for which results will be displayed in the graphics area. Select **All Beams** radio button to display results on all the beams. Select the **Select Beams** radio button if you want to display results only on selected beam elements. Select the **All Beams Except Selected** radio button to exclude selected beams and show results on all the other beams.
- Select check boxes from the dialog box to display respective results on the model in the form of values and diagrams; refer to Figure-64.

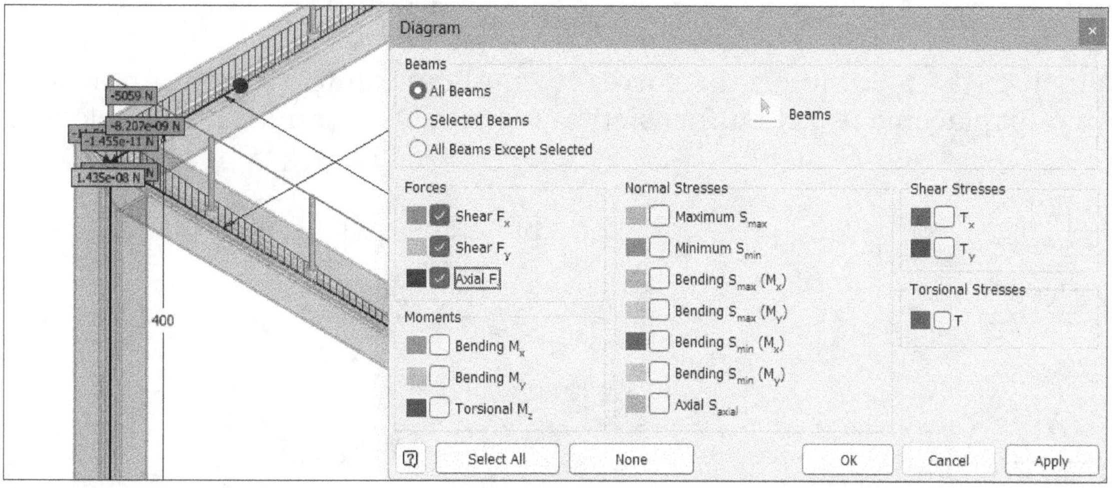

Figure-64. Results for diagram

- Click on the **OK** button from the dialog box to exit.

Similarly, use other tools to check results and then click on the **Finish Frame Analysis** tool from the contextual tab to exit the environment.

PRACTICE

Run a static analysis on the model as shown in Figure-65. Find out the factor of safety. Model is available in resources of this book.

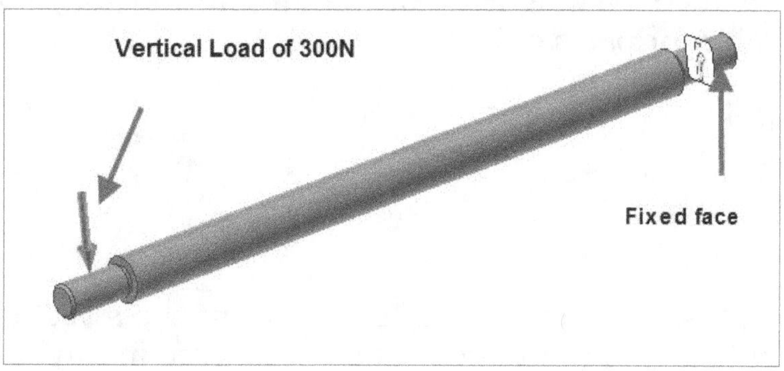

Figure-65. Practice 1

SELF ASSESSMENT

Q1. In Autodesk Inventor, FEA is used to solve the equations for stress analysis? What is the full form of FEA?

a) Fixture Element Analysis
b) Fixture Extract Analysis
c) Finite Element Analysis
d) Finite Extract Analysis

Q2. Which of the following is the correct formula in Finite Element Analysis to find the force-displacement, i.e, stiffness characteristics of each individual element?

a) $\frac{[k]_e}{\{F\}_e} = \{\delta\}_e$

b) $[k]_e \{\delta\}_e = \{F\}_e$

b) $\frac{\{\delta\}_e}{\{F\}_e} = [k]_e$

d) None of the Above

Q3. Which of the following assumptions is not made using Finite Element Analysis?

a) The loads applied does not vary with time.
b) The change in stiffness due to loading is neglected.
c) The materials applied to the components satisfy the Stefan's Law.
d) Loads must be constant in magnitude, direction, and distribution.

Q4. Which of the following study types is used in **Create New Study** dialog box in Stress Analysis to reduce the weight of part for specified loading conditions and this study type is available for parts only?

a) Shape Generator
b) Modal Analysis
c) Static Analysis
d) All of the Above

Q5. Which of the following tools is used to constraint the selected entity in such a way that the object is free to rotate but cannot translate in any direction?

a) Fixed
b) Pin
c) Frictionless
d) Both b and c

Q6. Which of the following loads is applied on an object when the origin of force is somewhere else but it is affecting the selected face?

a) Body Loads
b) Remote Force
c) Bearing Load
d) Pressure

Q7. Which of the following tools is used to increase or decrease the density of elements at a specified region in meshing of models in Autodesk Inventor?

a) Offset
b) Mesh Settings
c) Local Mesh Control
d) Convergence Settings

Q8. The **Modal Analysis** tool is used to find the natural frequencies of the model at which component can deform largely. (True/False)

Q9. In Autodesk Inventor, Shell bodies are considered as thick bodies. (True/False)

Q10. The Force applied per unit area is called ....

Q11. Once you have started an analysis, the very next step is to assign .... to the part.

Q12. The .... tool is used to reduce the calculation time of analysis.

Q13. What is the first step after opening a part or assembly file for stress analysis in Autodesk Inventor?

A. Apply loads
B. Create a study
C. Assign materials
D. Apply constraints

Q14. Which tool is initially active in the Analysis contextual tab?

A. Assign Material
B. Create Study
C. Apply Loads
D. Automatic Contacts

Q15. What does the Static Analysis study type allow you to find?

A. Natural frequencies
B. Weight reduction
C. Stresses induced due to applied loads
D. Deformation modes

Q16. Which option should you select if you want to find natural frequencies and mode shapes?

A. Static Analysis
B. Shape Generator
C. Modal Analysis
D. Contact Options

Q17. What is the purpose of the Shape Generator?

A. Find the weight of the part
B. Create rigid contacts
C. Find the best possible shape reducing mass
D. Detect stress zones

Q18. If you select "Single Point" in Design Objective, what will happen?

A. Deformation obeys dimensional stability
B. Deformation will occur in the structure of the part
C. No deformation
D. Only rotation allowed

Q19. What does selecting "Detect and Eliminate Rigid Body Modes" do?

A. Remove face contacts
B. Eliminate unrestricted movement
C. Add extra constraints
D. Create automatic bonds

Q20. Which option helps in discontinuing stress representations across different parts in assemblies?

A. Detect Rigid Body Modes
B. Separate Stresses Across Contact Surfaces
C. Shape Generator
D. Assign Material

Q21. In Modal Analysis, what does selecting "Compute Preloaded Modes" mean?

A. Ignore stress effects
B. Run Modal Analysis on a pre-stressed model
C. Increase load magnitude
D. Apply extra constraints

Q22. Which study option finds natural frequencies up to order of 10?

A. Static Analysis
B. Enhanced Accuracy
C. Separate Stress
D. Motion Loads

Q23. In Contact Options, what type of contact joins two faces rigidly?

A. Sliding/No Separation
B. Separation
C. Bonded
D. Spring

Q24. What does the Assign Material tool affect in stress analysis?

A. Color of model
B. Surface finish
C. Mechanical properties like strength and modulus
D. Boundary conditions

Q25. Which constraint completely restricts all motion of selected entities?

A. Pin
B. Frictionless
C. Fixed
D. Spring

Q26. What does the Pin constraint allow the part to do?

A. Free translation
B. Fixed at all points
C. Free rotation but no translation
D. Free translation and rotation

Q27. Which constraint allows movement in-plane but restricts motion normal to the face?

A. Fixed
B. Pin
C. Frictionless
D. Bonded

Q28. Which tool applies a direct force to a selected face/edge/vertex?

A. Pressure
B. Force
C. Moment
D. Gravity

Q29. In Autodesk Inventor, which load represents force per unit area?

A. Bearing Load
B. Remote Force
C. Pressure
D. Body Load

Q30. The Bearing Load tool is specifically used for which type of faces?

A. Flat faces
B. Sharp edges
C. Round faces
D. Freeform surfaces

Q31. Which load applies a general rotational force on selected entities?

A. Force
B. Gravity
C. Moment
D. Pressure

Q32. What does the Gravity tool apply on all components?

A. Pressure
B. Centrifugal force
C. Force of gravity
D. Magnetic force

Q33. Which load acts at a distance from the selected face but affects the face?

A. Body Load
B. Remote Force
C. Bearing Load
D. Pressure

Q34. The Body Loads tool is used to simulate:

A. Static pressure
B. Centrifugal and centripetal forces
C. Surface tension
D. Thermal expansion

Q35. Which tool automatically detects and applies contacts between parts?

A. Manual Contact
B. Automatic Contacts
C. Spring Contact
D. Remote Contact

Q36. In Manual Contact, selecting "Spring" contact allows you to specify:

A. Bond stiffness
B. Normal and tangential stiffness
C. Separation speed
D. Shrink distance

Q37. Which contact type allows faces to separate while sliding?

A. Bonded
B. Shrink Fit/No Sliding
C. Sliding/No Separation
D. Separation

Q38. Shrink Fit/Sliding contact assumes parts are initially:

A. Perfectly bonded
B. Slightly overlapped
C. Completely separated
D. Loosely fixed

Q39. Which tool is used to manually define contact between selected faces?

A. Assign
B. Manual Contact
C. Apply Force
D. Create Study

Q40. What is the main purpose of performing a frame analysis?
A. To create a detailed CAD model
B. To analyze motion in a mechanism
C. To check the ability of a frame to sustain load conditions
D. To apply paint on the frame

Q41. Where can the Frame Analysis tool be found in the software interface?
A. Inspect tab only
B. Render tab only
C. Frame panel of Design tab and Begin panel of Environments tab
D. Export tab of File menu

Q42. Which option must be selected in the Create New Simulation dialog box to analyze natural frequencies of a design?
A. Static Analysis
B. Frequency Analysis
C. Modal Analysis
D. Linear Buckling Analysis

Q43. What does the Frame Analysis Settings tool allow you to customize?
A. Model material properties only
B. Beam colors, scales, solvers, and diagrams
C. Export formats
D. Lighting and shadows

Q44. Which solver method uses the Gauss elimination technique?
A. Sparse M
B. Frontal
C. Skyline
D. Multi-threaded

Q45. Which solver is used automatically for equations more than 5000?
A. Skyline
B. Frontal
C. Sparse M
D. Multi-threaded

Q46. What does the 'Create Rigid Links' checkbox do in Beam Model settings?
A. Adds elasticity to beams
B. Removes overlapping beams
C. Automatically connects frame elements with rigid links
D. Prevents trimming of beam ends

Q47. What is the function of the 'Pinned Constraint'?
A. Restricts all motion
B. Allows rotational but no linear motion
C. Allows all types of motion
D. Restricts rotational but allows linear motion

Q48. Which constraint allows defining freedom degrees separately for each axis?
A. Fixed Constraint
B. Floating Constraint
C. Custom Constraint
D. Pinned Constraint

Q49. Which axis setting in Custom Constraint allows displacement in both directions with resistance?
A. Fixed
B. Uplift +
C. Uplift none
D. Uplift -

Q50. What is the default direction of applied force when using the Force tool?
A. Along beam length
B. Opposite to gravity
C. Normal to beam plane
D. Random user-defined direction

Q51. How can you define force direction explicitly in the Force dialog box?
A. Use the Define Direction button
B. Use the Load Curve tool
C. Type direction in comment box
D. Set it from Solver tab

Q52. What does the Release tool simulate in a frame analysis?
A. Rigid joints
B. Beam breaks
C. Realistic joint flexibility and partial load transfer
D. Material hardening

Q53. Which tool allows adding nodes at non-standard positions on a beam?
A. Fixed Constraint
B. Beam Properties
C. Custom Node
D. Rigid Link

Q54. What is the purpose of the Rigid Link tool?
A. To remove flexibility in beam joints
B. To merge materials
C. To connect nodes for full load transfer
D. To create beam curvature

Q55. Which tool starts the solving process for frame analysis?
A. Load Tool
B. Properties
C. Simulate
D. Rigid Link

Q56. How can you check details of a beam after simulation?
A. Using Force Tool
B. Using Beam Detail Tool
C. Using Solver Settings
D. Using Constraints Panel

Q57. What does the Diagram tool in result tab help visualize?
A. Beam physical dimensions
B. Load direction
C. Value distribution and maximum value diagrams
D. Custom material settings

Q58. What happens when you click Finish Frame Analysis?
A. All constraints are deleted
B. The assembly model is removed
C. You exit the Frame Analysis environment
D. Simulation results are lost

FOR STUDENTS NOTES

Chapter 17

Model Based Annotations

Topics Covered

The major topics covered in this chapter are:

- ***Introduction to Model Based Annotation***
- ***Applying Dimensional Annotations to 3D Model***
- ***Creating Tolerance Feature***
- ***Applying Hole/Thread Notes***
- ***Applying Surface Finish Symbol***
- ***Creating Leader Note***
- ***Creating General Note***
- ***Sectioning Model***

INTRODUCTION

In earlier chapters, you have learned to generate drawings after creating solid part or assembly. You have then applied annotations in the drawing to represent the intent of model. In Autodesk Inventor, you can apply the annotations directly to the model in Part or Assembly environment. You can use electronic gadgets at the shop floor to let the machinist find dimensions of his/her interest directly from 3D model, hence saving lot of time which gets wasted in generating 2D drawings (layouts). The scheme by which we apply annotations to 3D model is called **Model Based Annotation**. The tools to apply model based annotations are available in the **Annotate** tab of the **Ribbon**; refer to Figure-1.

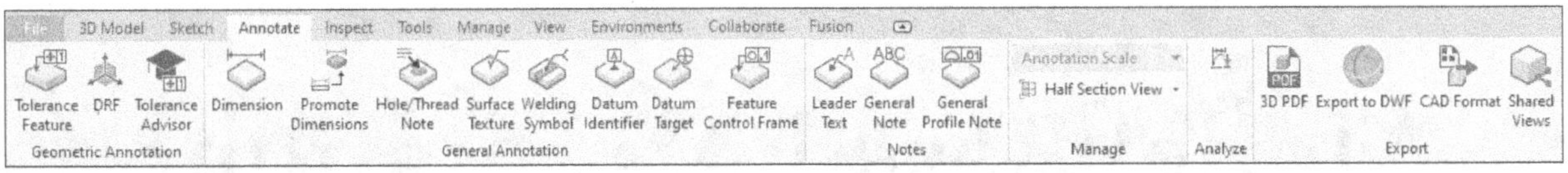

Figure-1. Annotate tab in Ribbon

WORKFLOW FOR MODEL BASED ANNOTATIONS

While performing model based annotations, you can use the tools randomly wherever they are required but if you follow the standard workflow then it can greatly reduce the pain of annotating complex products. Figure-2 shown the workflow for model based annotations. We will discuss the tools of the **Annotate** tab in the same sequence as they are in workflow.

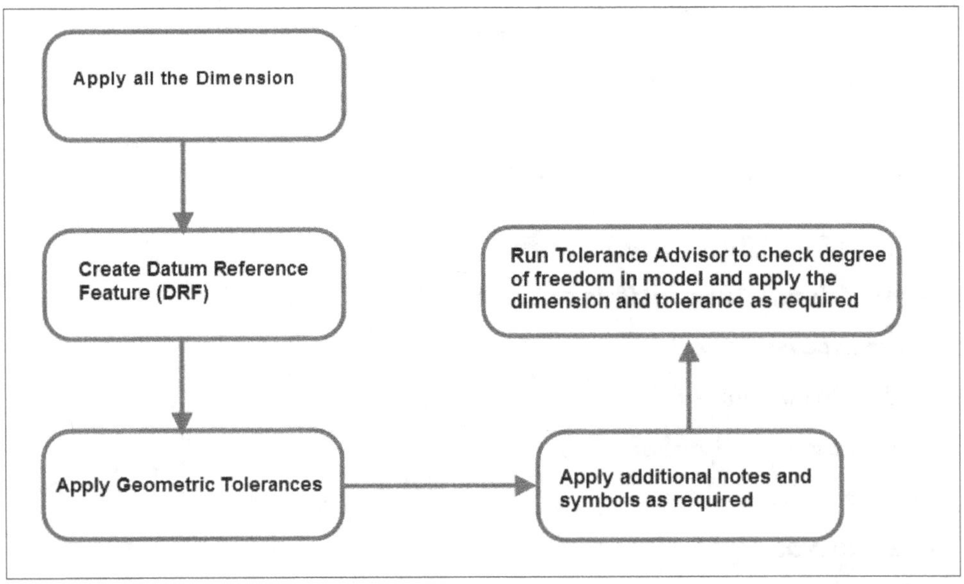

Figure-2. Workflow for Model based annotations

APPLYING DIMENSIONS TO 3D MODEL

The **Dimension** tool in the **Annotate** tab of **Ribbon** in Part/Assembly environment is used to apply dimensions to the 3D model. The procedure to use this tool is given next.

- Click on the **Dimension** tool from the **General Annotation** panel in the **Annotate** tab of the **Ribbon**. The **Standard** dialog box will be displayed; refer to Figure-3 if this is first time you are using this tool.

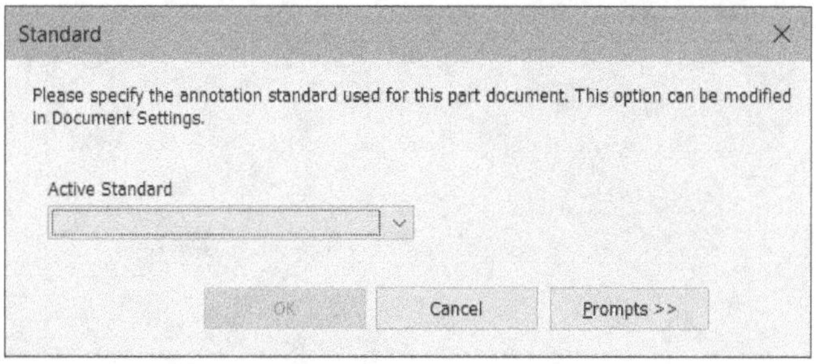

Figure-3. Standard dialog box

- Select desired standard from the **Active Standard** drop-down and click on the **OK** button. You will be asked to select the geometry to be dimensioned.
- Apply the dimensions by selecting the geometries. Like, to create diameter dimension - select the round face of model, to create distance dimension - select the two parallel faces, to apply angle dimension - select the two non-planar faces. Figure-4 shows different type of dimensions applied to the model. Note that you need to click on the **Apply** button from pop-up toolbar after placing each dimension.

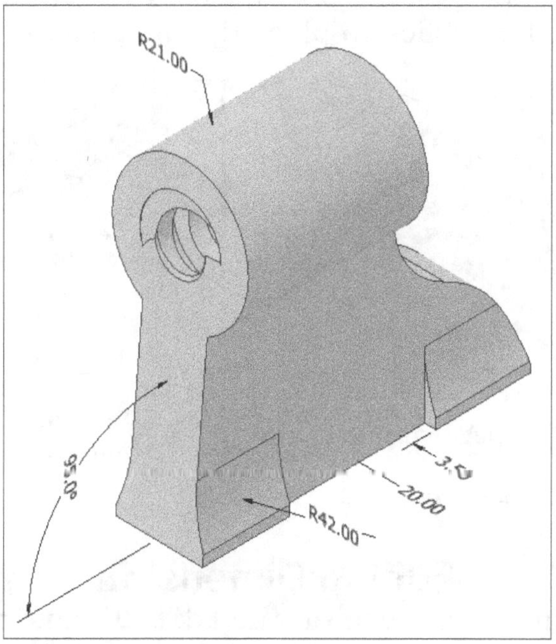

Figure-4. Dimensions applied to model

Changing Annotation Plane

While applying the annotations to 3D model, many times you will feel the need of changing plane for annotations. The procedure to change annotation plane is given next.

- Click on the **Dimension** tool from the **General Annotation** panel in the **Annotate** tab of the **Ribbon**. You will be asked to select geometry to be dimensioned.
- Select the face/edge to apply dimension. The dimension will get attached to cursor. Right-click after moving the dimension away from model. The right-click shortcut menu will be displayed; refer to Figure-5.

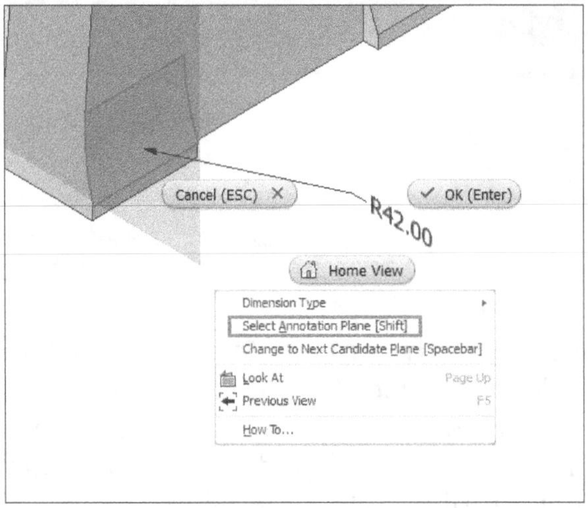

Figure-5. Right-click shortcut menu for annotation

- Click on the **Select Annotation Plane [Shift]** option from the menu. You will be asked to select the face/plane to be used as annotation plane.
- Select desired plane/face. Click to place the dimension; refer to Figure-6.

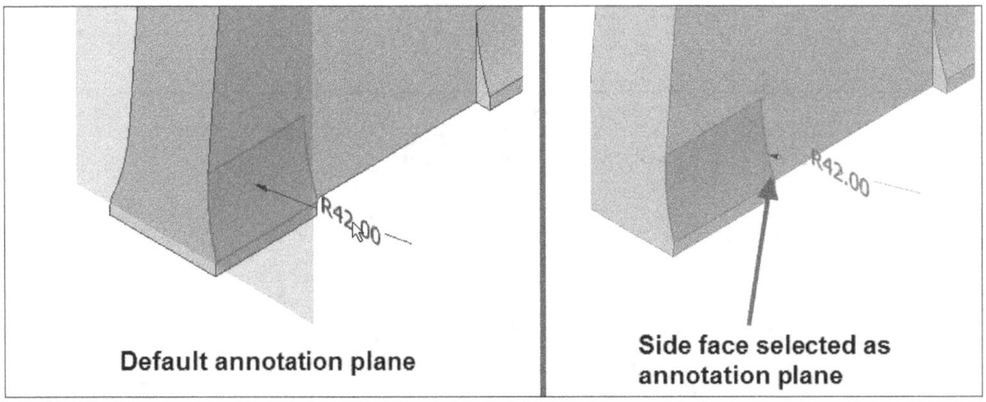

Figure-6. Annotation plane selected

Editing Dimension

- After placing the dimension, click on the **Edit Dimension** tool from the pop-up toolbar; refer to Figure-7. The **Edit Dimension** dialog box will be displayed; refer to Figure-8.

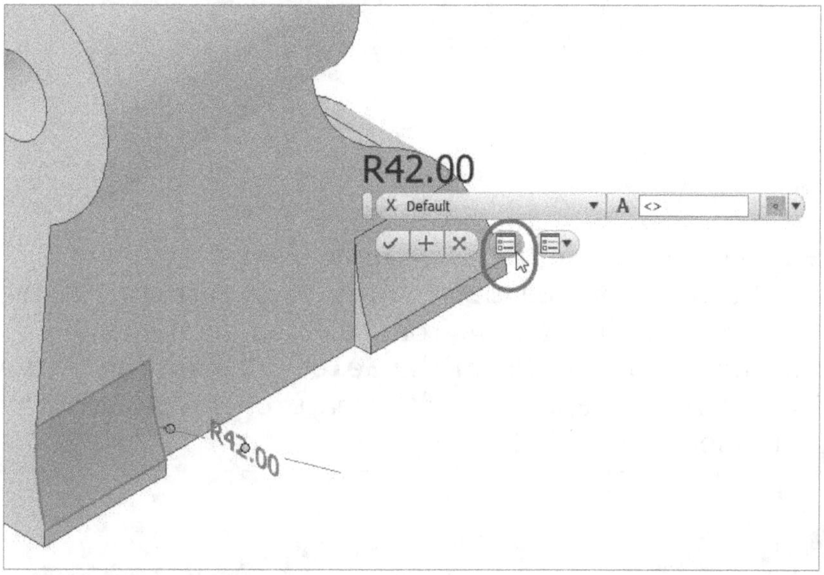

Figure-7. Edit Dimension tool

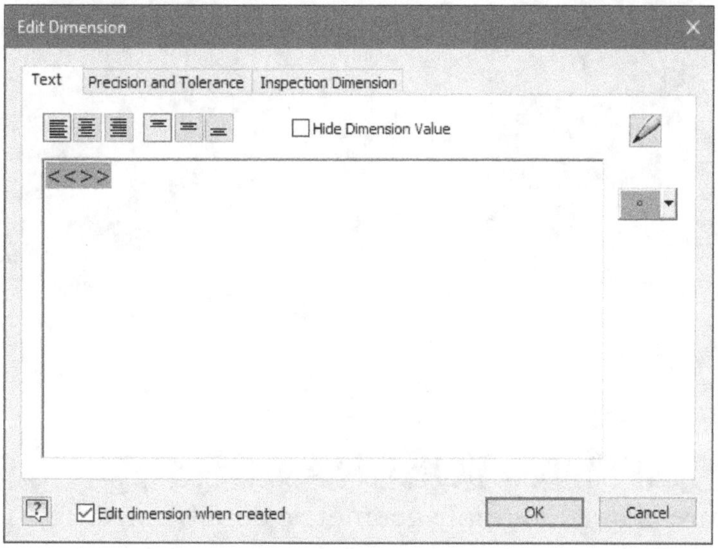

Figure-8. Edit Dimension dialog box

- The options of this dialog box has been discussed in **Chapter 14: Drawing Creation**. After setting desired dimension, click on the **OK** button from the dialog box to apply settings. The pop-up toolbar will be displayed again. Click on the **OK** button to exit the pop-up toolbar.

PROMOTE DIMENSION

The **Promote Dimension** tool is used to create 3D annotation dimensions from selected sketch or feature dimensions. The procedure to use this tool is discussed next.

- Click on the **Promote Dimension** tool from **General Annotation** panel in the **Annotate** tab of the **Ribbon**. The dialog box will be displayed as shown in Figure-9. You will be asked to select the geometry.

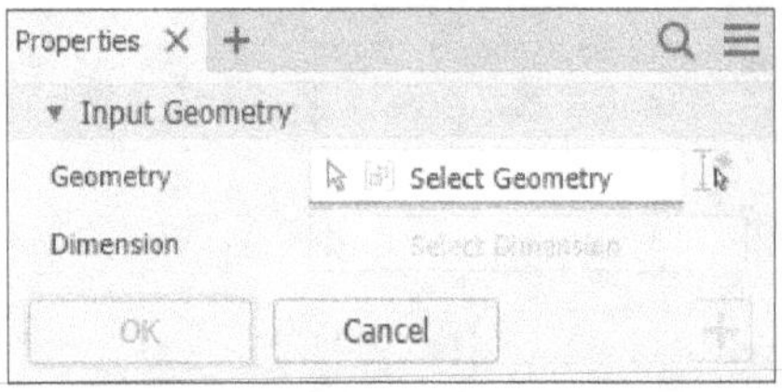

Figure-9. Dialog box for Promote Dimension tool

- Select desired features or sketches to enable their dimensions.
- Toggle the button from **Geometry** area of the **Input Geometry** rollout to automatically select all dimensions from selected geometries.
- After selecting the feature, click on the **Select Dimension** button of **Dimension** area and select desired dimension(s) of the feature. The 3D annotation dimensions will be created; refer to Figure-10.

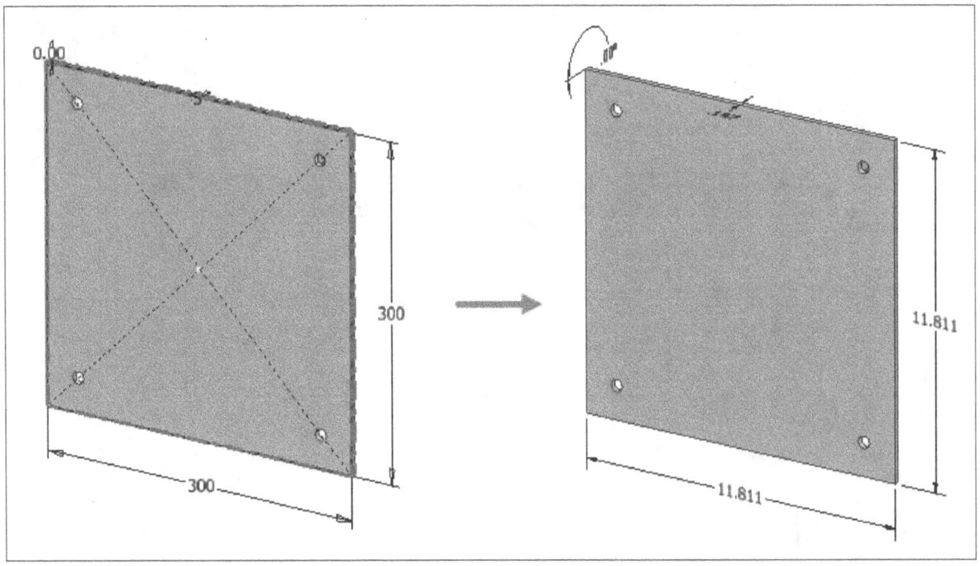

Figure-10. 3D annotation dimensions created

CREATING TOLERANCE FEATURE

The tolerance feature is used to apply geometric constraints. The procedure to create tolerance feature is given next.

- Click on the **Tolerance Feature** tool from the **Geometric Annotation** panel in the **Annotate** tab of the **Ribbon**. You will be asked to select a face.
- Select the face to which you want to apply geometric tolerance and datum feature and click on the **OK** button from the pop-up toolbar. The tolerance feature will get attached to the cursor. Press **TAB** to change the orientation of tolerance feature.
- Click at desired location to place the feature. The pop-up toolbar will be displayed; refer to Figure-11.

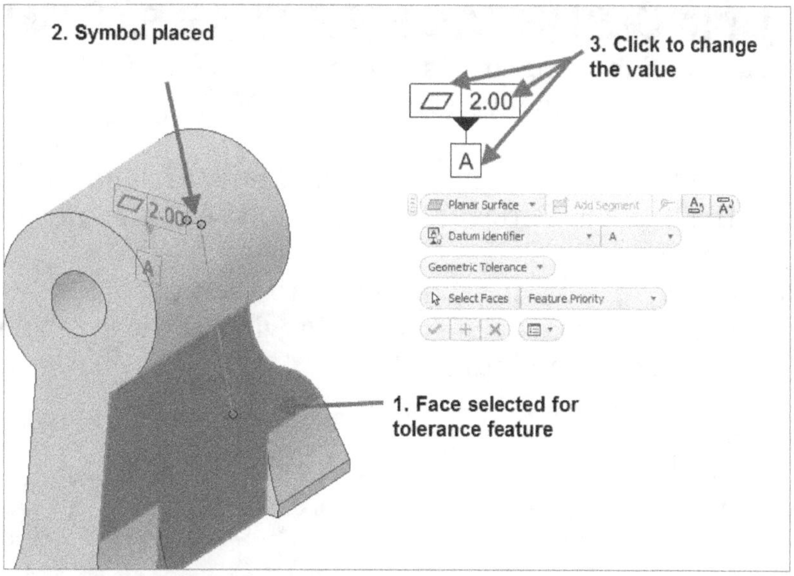

Figure-11. Placing Tolerance feature

- Click on the boxes of tolerance feature to change the values.
- To hide/show the datum feature, click on the **Toggle Datum Feature** button from the pop-up toolbar.
- If you want to add a note then click on the **Add Comment Above** or **Add Comment Below** button from the pop-up toolbar.
- After creating the tolerance feature, click on the **Apply** button to create next geometric tolerance.
- After creating all desired geometric tolerances, click on the **OK** button from the popup toolbar to exit the tool.

HOLE/THREAD NOTES

The **Hole/Thread Note** tool is used to annotate hole or threads in the model. The procedure to use this tool is given next.

- Click on the **Hole/Thread Notes** tool from the **General Annotation** panel in the **Annotate** tab of the **Ribbon**. You will be asked to select the geometry to be annotated.
- Select the thread or hole to annotate. The dimension will get attached to cursor; refer to Figure-12.

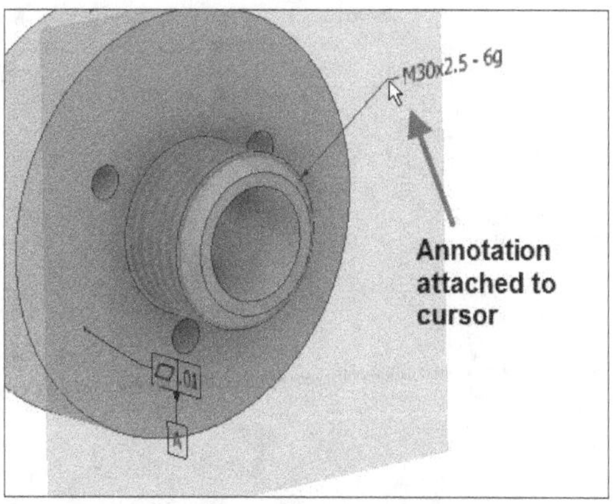

Figure-12. Thread annotation

- Click at desired location to place the dimension.

APPLYING SURFACE TEXTURE SYMBOL

The **Surface Texture** tool is used to add symbol of surface texture to the 3D model. The procedure to use this tool is given next.

- Click on the **Surface Texture** tool from the **General Annotation** panel in the **Annotate** tab of the **Ribbon**. You will be asked to select the face on which surface texture is to be applied.
- Select desired face. Symbol will get attached to the cursor.
- Click at desired location to place the symbol. Preview of the symbol will be displayed with pop-up toolbar; refer to Figure-13.

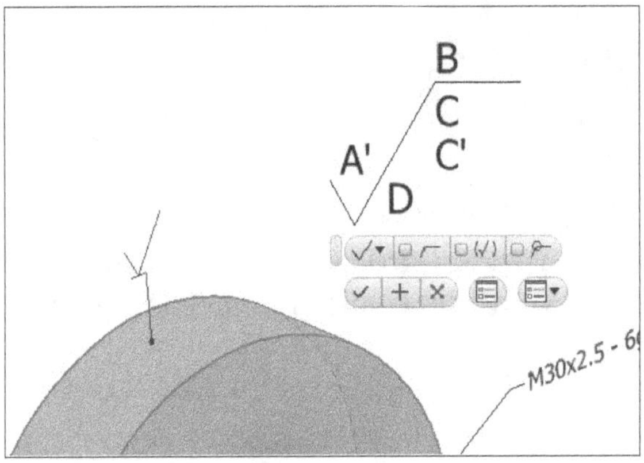

Figure-13. Preview of surface finish symbol

- Select the alphabet to specify surface finish value.
- Use the options in the pop-up toolbar to modify the symbol as required.
- Click on the **Apply** button to apply other surface finish symbols or click on the **OK** button to exit.

APPLYING DATUM TARGET

The **Datum Target** tool is used to add geometric control datum to a plane, axis, or point. The datum provides control for flatness, straightness, cylindricity, and circularity. The procedure to use this tool is given next.

- Create the sketch points and position them at desired places in the model; refer to Figure-14.

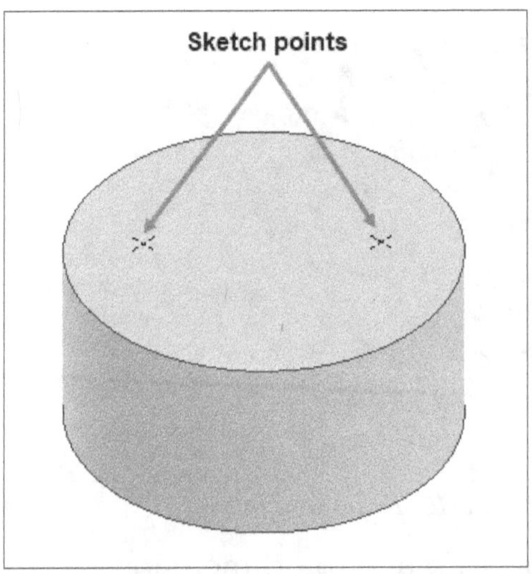

Figure-14. Sketch points created

- Click on the **Datum Target** tool from the **General Annotation** panel in the **Annotate** tab of the **Ribbon**. The **Datum Target** dialog box will be displayed along with the datum targets attached to the points; refer to Figure-15.

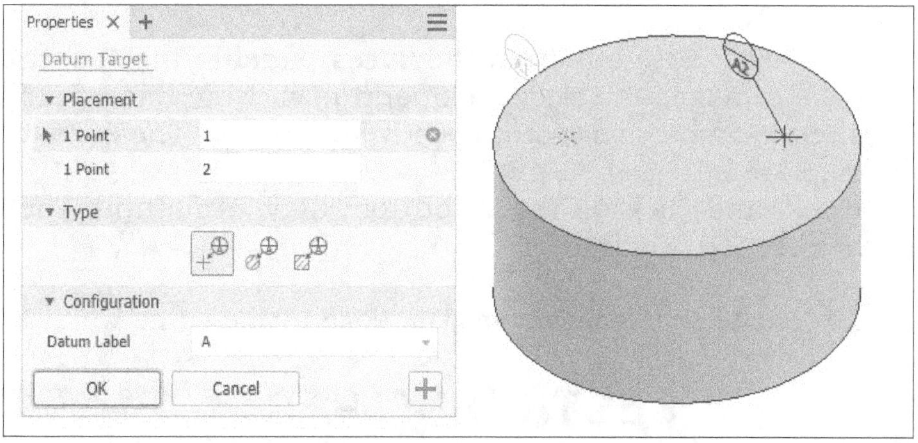

Figure-15. Datum Target dialog box along with datum targets attached to points

- Select **Point** button from **Type** rollout to use point locations to define the datum target zone. Select **Circle** button to create a circular datum target zone. Select **Rectangle** button to create a rectangular datum target zone.
- Select desired datum label from **Datum Label** drop-down in the **Configuration** rollout.
- After specifying desired parameters, click on the **OK** button from the dialog box. The datum targets will be attached.

CREATING LEADER TEXT

Leader text is used to insert text annotation with leader attached to the 3D model. The procedure to create leader text is given next.

- Click on the **Leader Text** tool from the **Notes** panel in the **Annotate** tab of the **Ribbon**. You will be asked to select the geometry to which leader will be attached.
- Select the face, edge, axis, point, or other geometric entity. End point of the leader will get attached to cursor.
- Click at desired location to place the note text. The **Format Text** dialog box will be displayed as discussed in previous chapters.
- Type desired text and set the parameters as required and then click on the **OK** button from the dialog box. The text will be created with leader; refer to Figure-16.

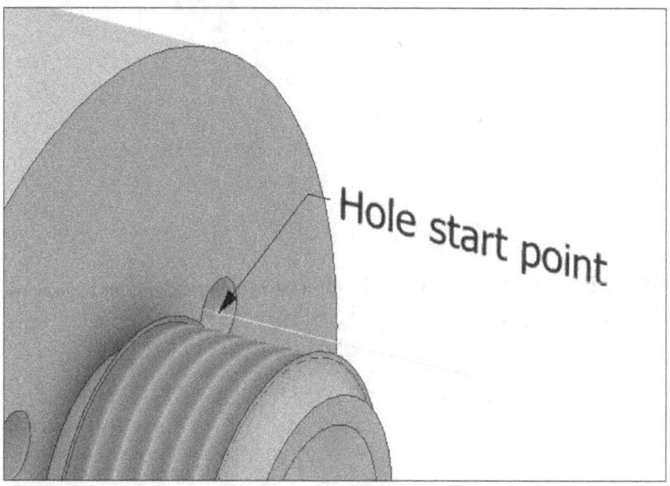

Figure-16. Leader text created

CREATING GENERAL NOTE

The **General Note** tool is used to create notes applicable to the whole part/assembly. The procedure to use this tool is given next.

- Click on the **General Note** tool from the **Notes** panel in the **Annotate** tab of the **Ribbon**. You will be asked to select the quadrant in which note is to be placed.
- Click on desired location to select respective quadrant. The **Format Text** dialog box will be displayed.
- Type desired text and click on the **OK** button after formatting. The note will be created in the selected quadrant.

Note that you can create the **General Profile Note** in the same way.

SECTIONING PART

The tools to perform sectioning of 3D model are available in the **Section View** drop-down from the **Manage** panel in the **Annotate** tab of the **Ribbon**. The procedure to use **Quarter Section View** option is discussed next. You can apply the same procedure to other section options.

- Click on the **Quarter Section View** option from the **Section View** drop-down in the **Manage** panel of the **Annotate** tab in the **Ribbon**. You will be asked to select work plane for sectioning.
- Select the plane from graphics area or from the **Model browser** in the left of the application window. Preview of section by first work plane will be displayed; refer to Figure-17.

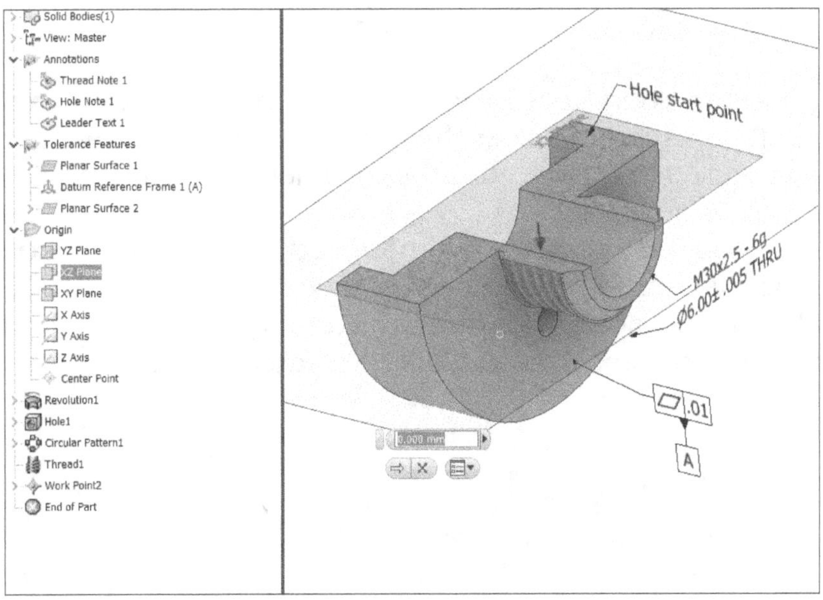

Figure-17. Preview section by first plane

- Specify desired offset value in the edit box of pop-up toolbar and click on the **Continue** button from the pop-up toolbar. You will be asked to select the next sectioning plane.
- Select the next plane. Preview of quarter section will be displayed; refer to Figure-18.

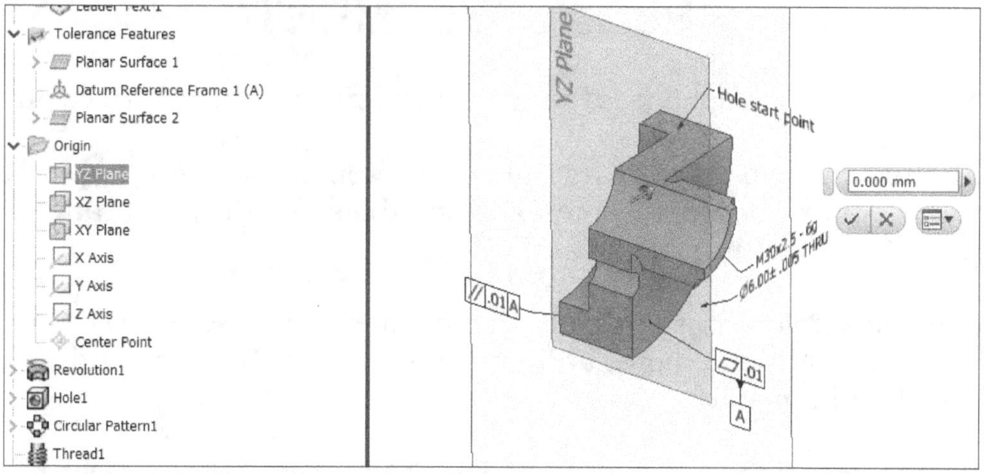

Figure-18. Preview of quarter section

- Set desired parameters and click on the **OK** button from the pop-up toolbar.

The methods for creating 3D PDF and exporting file to other formats have already been discussed in previous chapters.

PRACTICE

Create the model and apply the model based annotations as shown in Figure-19.

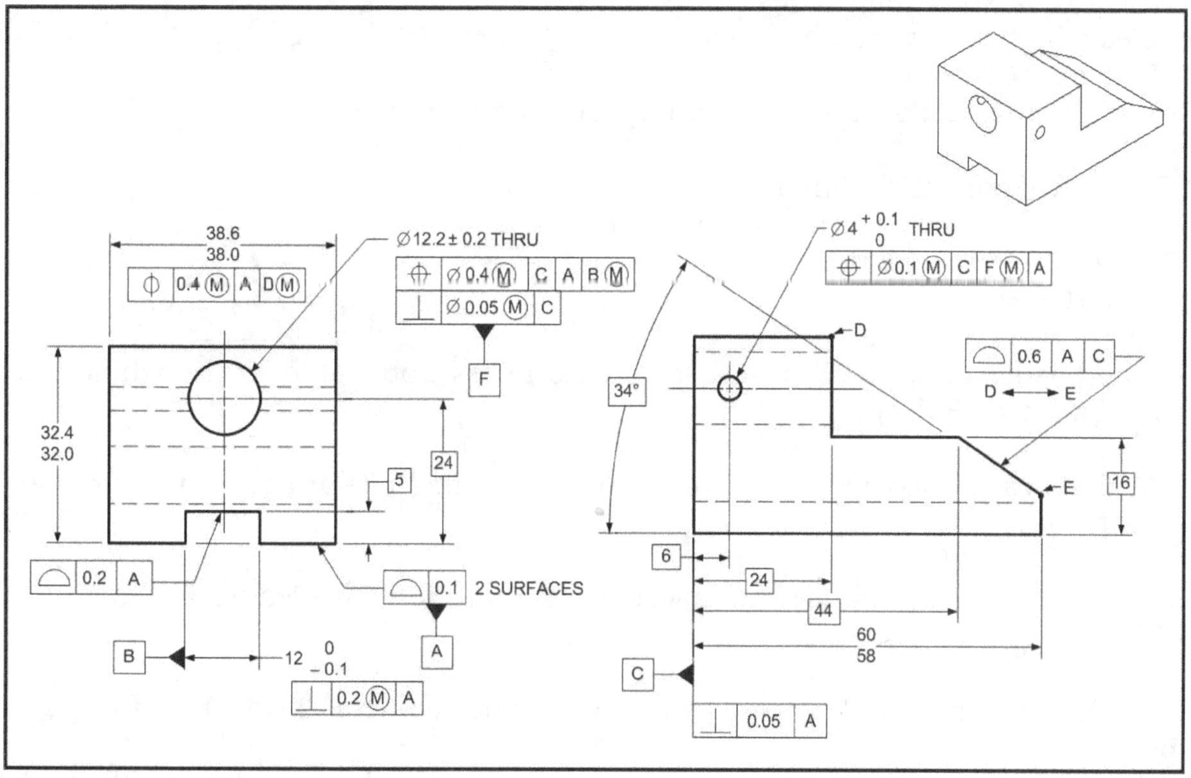

Figure-19. Practice

SELF ASSESSMENT

Q1. Which of the following options is the correct workflow for model based annotations?

a) Apply all the dimension --> Create Datum Reference Feature --> Apply Geometric Tolerances --> Apply additional notes and symbols --> Run Tolerance Advisor to check degree of freedom in model

b) Apply Geometric Tolerances --> Apply all the dimension --> Create Datum Reference Feature --> Apply additional notes and symbols --> Run Tolerance Advisor to check degree of freedom in model

c) Apply all the dimension --> Apply Geometric Tolerances --> Create Datum Reference Feature --> Run Tolerance Advisor to check degree of freedom in model --> Apply additional notes and symbols

d) None of the Above

Q2. Which of the following geometries is to be selected to create distance dimension?

a) Select the round face of model
b) Select the two parallel faces
c) Select the two non-planar faces
d) None of the Above

Q3. Which of the following statement specify the use of Tolerance Feature?

a) To apply Geometric Constraint
b) To change plane for annotations
c) To edit the dimension
d) All of the Above

Q4. The **Leader Text** tool is used to create notes applicable to the whole parts/ assembly. (True/False)

Q5. The **Surface Texture** tool is used to add symbol of surface texture to the 3D model. (True/False)

Q6. .... is used to insert text annotation with leader attached to the 3D Model.

Q7. The .... tool is used to add geometric control datum to a plane, axis, or point.

Q8. Which tool from the Annotate tab is used to apply dimensions to a 3D model?

A. Surface Texture
B. Dimension
C. Tolerance Feature
D. Promote Dimension

Q9. What should you select to create a diameter dimension on a 3D model?

A. Two parallel faces
B. Two non-planar faces
C. Round face of the model
D. Plane surface

Q10. How can you change the annotation plane while applying dimensions?

A. By pressing TAB key
B. By selecting Select Annotation Plane [Shift] from right-click menu
C. By dragging the dimension line
D. By double-clicking the dimension

Q11. After placing a dimension, which tool allows you to modify its value?

A. General Note
B. Edit Dimension
C. Hole/Thread Note
D. Leader Text

Q12. What is the function of the Promote Dimension tool?

A. Hide dimensions
B. Create annotations from sketch or feature dimensions
C. Edit dimension values
D. Create sectional views

Q13. Which tool is used to apply geometric constraints to a 3D model?

A. Dimension
B. Surface Texture
C. Tolerance Feature
D. General Note

Q14. How can you hide or show the datum feature while creating tolerance features?

A. Right-click and select Toggle Datum Feature
B. Press Enter
C. Click on Toggle Datum Feature button in the pop-up toolbar
D. Click outside the model area

Q15. The Hole/Thread Note tool is specifically used for:
A. Editing general notes
B. Annotating holes or threads
C. Creating section views
D. Changing planes

Q16. What must you select to place a Surface Texture symbol on the model?

A. Axis
B. Sketch
C. Face
D. Point

Q17. Which tool is used to add a datum target to a model?

A. Dimension
B. Datum Target
C. Leader Text
D. Surface Texture

Q18. When defining a datum target zone, which shape option is not available?

A. Point
B. Circle
C. Rectangle
D. Triangle

Q19. Leader Text is primarily used to:

A. Attach text with a leader to geometry
B. Create surface finish symbols
C. Create sectional views
D. Promote dimensions

Q20. General Note tool allows you to:

A. Add text linked to specific geometry
B. Add general notes applicable to the whole part/assembly
C. Create sketches
D. Apply section views

Q21. Which operation would you perform using the Quarter Section View tool?

A. Create 3D sketches
B. Apply surface finish
C. Perform a section view of the 3D model
D. Promote dimension

Q22. Which panel contains the Dimension tool in the Annotate tab?

A. Notes Panel
B. Manage Panel
C. General Annotation Panel
D. Geometric Annotation Panel

Q23. After selecting the geometry for dimensioning, what must you click to confirm placing the dimension?

A. OK button
B. Apply button from the pop-up toolbar
C. Right-click menu
D. Shift key

Q24. To change the orientation of a Tolerance Feature, you should press:

A. Shift
B. TAB
C. Ctrl
D. Alt

Q25. In the Promote Dimension tool, which area allows automatic selection of all dimensions from selected geometries?

A. Input Geometry rollout
B. Configuration rollout
C. Dimension area
D. Geometry Settings panel

Q26. What happens when you toggle the Geometry button in Promote Dimension tool?

A. It hides selected dimensions
B. It automatically selects all dimensions from selected geometries
C. It deletes all dimensions
D. It creates a quarter section

Q27. Which of the following symbols is associated with the Surface Texture tool?

A. Tolerance feature symbol
B. Surface finish symbol
C. Hole annotation symbol
D. Leader text symbol

Q28. Which button is clicked to add a note above a Tolerance Feature?

A. Toggle Datum Feature
B. Apply
C. Add Comment Above
D. Format Text

Q29. What is the primary use of the Datum Target tool?

A. Create general notes
B. Add geometric control to planes, axes, or points
C. Insert dimensions automatically
D. Create holes and threads

Q30. Which shapes can be used for a Datum Target zone?

A. Point, Circle, Rectangle
B. Circle, Triangle, Square
C. Point, Oval, Circle
D. Rectangle, Line, Circle

Q31. When creating Leader Text, after selecting the face or edge, what appears for formatting text?

A. Format Text dialog box
B. General Note box
C. Edit Dimension box
D. Section View settings

Q32. Which panel in Annotate tab contains the General Note tool?

A. General Annotation
B. Manage Panel
C. Notes Panel
D. Geometric Annotation

Q33. While sectioning a 3D model, where can you find the Quarter Section View option?

A. General Annotation panel
B. Section View drop-down in Manage panel
C. Notes panel
D. Format Text dialog

Q34. What is the first step after clicking Quarter Section View tool?

A. Select section planes
B. Specify offset value
C. Click Apply button
D. Select work plane for sectioning

Q35. After previewing the first work plane section, what is the next step?

A. Select the second plane
B. Click the OK button
C. Hide the first section
D. Edit dimensions

Index

F

G

H

I

K

L

M

N

O

Ethics of an Engineer

- Engineers shall hold paramount the safety, health and welfare of the public and shall strive to comply with the principles of sustainable development in the performance of their professional duties.
- Engineers shall perform services only in areas of their competence.
- Engineers shall issue public statements only in an objective and truthful manner.
- Engineers shall act in professional manners for each employer or client as faithful agents or trustees, and shall avoid conflicts of interest.
- Engineers shall build their professional reputation on the merit of their services and shall not compete unfairly with others.
- Engineers shall act in such a manner as to uphold and enhance the honor, integrity, and dignity of the engineering profession and shall act with zero-tolerance for bribery, fraud, and corruption.
- Engineers shall continue their professional development throughout their careers, and shall provide opportunities for the professional development of those engineers under their supervision.

www.ingramcontent.com/pod-product-compliance
Lightning Source LLC
LaVergne TN
LVHW080009210926
848481LV00011B/2977
9781774592168